Lecture Notes in Artificial Intelligence 10331

Subseries of Lecture Notes in Computer Science

More information about this series at http://www.springer.com/series/1244

Elisabeth André · Ryan Baker
Xiangen Hu · Ma. Mercedes T. Rodrigo
Benedict du Boulay (Eds.)

Artificial Intelligence in Education

18th International Conference, AIED 2017
Wuhan, China, June 28 – July 1, 2017
Proceedings

 Springer

Editors
Elisabeth André ⓘ
Human-Centered Multimedia
University of Augsburg
Augsburg
Germany

Ryan Baker ⓘ
University of Pennsylvania
Philadelphia, PA
USA

Xiangen Hu
Department of Psychology
University of Memphis
Memphis, TN
USA

Ma. Mercedes T. Rodrigo
Ateneo de Manila University
Quezon City
Philippines

Benedict du Boulay
University of Sussex
Brighton
UK

ISSN 0302-9743   ISSN 1611-3349 (electronic)
Lecture Notes in Artificial Intelligence
ISBN 978-3-319-61424-3   ISBN 978-3-319-61425-0   (eBook)
DOI 10.1007/978-3-319-61425-0

Library of Congress Control Number: 2017944320

LNCS Sublibrary: SL7 – Artificial Intelligence

Preface

The 18th International Conference on Artificial Intelligence in Education (AIED 2017) was held from June 28 to July 1, 2017, in Wuhan, China. AIED 2017 was the latest in a longstanding series of biennial international conferences for high-quality research in intelligent systems and cognitive science for educational computing applications. The conference provides opportunities for the cross-fertilization of approaches, techniques, and ideas from the many fields that comprise AIED, including computer science, cognitive and learning sciences, education, game design, psychology, sociology, linguistics, as well as many domain-specific areas. Since the first AIED meeting over 30 years ago, both the breadth of the research and the reach of the technologies have expanded in dramatic ways.

There were 121 submissions as full papers to AIED 2017, of which 36 were accepted as long papers (12 pages) with oral presentation at the conference (for an acceptance rate of 30%), and 37 were accepted for poster presentation with four pages in the proceedings. Of the 17 papers directly submitted as poster papers, seven were accepted. Apart from a few exceptions, each submission was reviewed by four Program Committee (PC) members including one senior PC member serving as a meta-reviewer. In addition, submissions underwent a discussion period to ensure that all reviewers' opinions would be considered and leveraged to generate a group recommendation to the program chairs.

Four distinguished speakers gave plenary invited talks illustrating prospective directions for the field: Ronghuai Huang (Beijing Normal University, China), Sanya Liu (Central China Normal University, China), Antonija "Tanja" Mitrovic (University of Canterbury), and Riichiro Mizoguchi (Japan Advanced Institute of Science and Technology, Japan). The conference also included:

- A Doctoral Consortium that provided doctoral students with the opportunity to present their ongoing doctoral research at the conference and receive invaluable feedback from the research community.
- An Interactive Events session during which AIED attendees could experience first-hand new and emerging intelligent learning environments via interactive demonstrations.
- An Industry and Innovation Track intended to support connections between industry (both for-profit and non-profit) and the research community. The participating companies presented the need of and involvement with educational technologies with five (out of nine accepted) industry papers and engaged with AIED researchers to learn about the most promising new developments in the field and connect with academic partners.

AIED 2017 hosted four workshops focused on providing in-depth discussion of current and emerging topics of interest to the AIED 2017 community, including:

- Second International Workshop on Intelligent Mentoring Systems: Linking Learning in Real and Virtual Environments
- Workshop: Sharing and Reusing Data and Analytic Methods with LearnSphere
- Workshop: How Do We Unleash AIEd at Scale to Benefit all Teachers and Learners?
- Workshop: Turn Theories into Products: Implementation of Artificial Intelligence in Education

In parallel with the workshops, two tutorials presented advanced topics and current developments that have a level of maturity in AIED research.

The conference was co-located with EDM 2017, the 10th International Conference on Educational Data Mining, and shared some workshops with it.

We offer our most heartfelt thanks to our colleagues at Central China Normal University for hosting AIED 2017. We also wish to acknowledge the considerable effort by our colleagues at the Ateneo de Manila University in making this conference possible. We would also like to thank Marija Filimonovic from Augsburg University for providing excellent support when editing the proceedings. Special thanks goes to Springer for sponsoring the AIED 2017 Best Paper Award and the AIED 2017 Best Student Paper Award.

We also want to acknowledge the amazing work of the AIED 2017 Organizing Committee, the senior PC members, the PC members, and the reviewers (listed herein), who with their enthusiastic contributions gave us invaluable support in putting this conference together.

April 2017

Elisabeth André
Ryan Baker
Xiangen Hu
Ma. Mercedes T. Rodrigo
Benedict du Boulay

Organization

General Chairs

Benedict du Boulay   University of Sussex, UK

Program Chairs

Ryan Baker   University of Pennsylvania, USA
Elisabeth André   Universität Augsburg, Germany

Local Arrangements Chairs

Xiangen Hu   Central China Normal University,
      China and University of Memphis, USA
Ma. Mercedes T. Rodrigo   Ateneo de Manila University, Philippines

Workshop and Tutorial Chairs

Bert Bredeweg   University of Amsterdam, The Netherlands
Michael Yudelson   Carnegie Mellon University, USA

Industry Track Chairs

Shirin Mojarad   McGraw-Hill Education, USA
Guojie Song   Peking University, China
Jie Tang   Tsinghua University, China

Doctoral Consortium Chairs

Tak-Wai Chan   National Central University, China
Erin Walker   Arizona State University

Poster Chairs

Tsukasa Hirashima   Hiroshima University, Japan
Paul Inventado   Carnegie Mellon University, USA

Interactive Event Chairs

Benjamin Goldberg   US Army Research Laboratory, USA
Amali Weerasinghe   University of Adelaide, Australia

Panel Chair

Michael Timms   Australian Council For Educational Research, Australia

Publicity Chair

Sharon Hsiao   Arizona State University, USA

Sponsorship Chair

Moffat Mathews   University of Canterbury, New Zealand

Web Master

Alexandra Andres   Ateneo de Manila University, Philippines
Yun Tang   Central China Normal University, China

Senior Program Committee

Vincent Aleven   Carnegie Mellon University, USA
Ivon Arroyo   Worcester Polytechnic Institute, USA
Kevin Ashley   University of Pittsburgh, USA
Gautam Biswas   Vanderbilt University, USA
Jesus G. Boticario   UNED, Spain
Bert Bredeweg   University of Amsterdam, The Netherlands
Tak-Wai Chan   National Central University, Taiwan
Cristina Conati   University of British Columbia, Canada
Scotty Craig   Arizona State University, Polytechnic, USA
Vania Dimitrova   University of Leeds, UK
Judy Kay   University of Sydney, Australia
Kenneth Koedinger   Carnegie Mellon University, USA
H. Chad Lane   University of Illinois, Urbana-Champaign, USA
James Lester   NC State University, USA
Chee-Kit Looi   National Institute of Education, Singapore
Rose Luckin   The London Knowledge Lab, UK
Manolis Mavrikis   UCL Knowledge Lab, UK
Gordon McCalla   University of Saskatchewan, Canada
Bruce M. McLaren   Carnegie Mellon University, USA
Tanja Mitrovic   University of Canterbury, New Zealand
Riichiro Mizoguchi   JAIST, Japan
Helen Pain   HCRC/Informatics, University of Edinburgh, UK
Ana Paiva   INESC, Portugal
Niels Pinkwart   Humboldt-Universität zu Berlin, Germany
Kaska Porayska-Pomsta   UCL Knowledge Lab, UK
Ido Roll   University of British Columbia, Canada
Carolyn Rose   Carnegie Mellon University, USA

Olga C. Santos	aDeNu Research Group (UNED), Spain
Robert Sottilare	US Army Research Laboratory, USA
John Stamper	Carnegie Mellon University, USA
Pierre Tchounikine	University of Grenoble, France
Kurt VanLehn	Arizona State University, USA
Julita Vassileva	University of Saskatchewan, Canada
Felisa Verdejo	UNED, Spain
Beverly Woolf	University of Massachusetts Amherst, USA
Kalina Yacef	The University of Sydney, Australia

Program Committee

Ani Aghababyan	McGraw-Hill Education, USA
Lalitha Agnihotri	McGraw Hill Education, USA
Nilufar Baghaei	UNITEC, New Zealand
Ryan Baker	University of Pennsylvania, USA
Nigel Bosch	University of Illinois Urbana-Champaign, USA
Jacqueline Bourdeau	TELUQ, Canada
Kristy Elizabeth Boyer	University of Florida, USA
Paul Brna	University of Leeds, UK
Maiga Chang	Athabasca University, Canada
Min Chi	BeiKaZhouLi, USA
Albert Corbett	Carnegie Mellon University, USA
Mark G. Core	University of Southern California, USA
Alexandra Cristea	University of Warwick, USA
Scott Crossley	Georgia State University, USA
Darina Dicheva	Winston-Salem State University, USA
Peter Dolog	Aalborg University, Denmark
Stephen Fancsali	Carnegie Learning, Inc., USA
Mingyu Feng	SRI International, USA
Carol Forsyth	Educational Testing Service, USA
Davide Fossati	Emory University, USA
Reva Freedman	Northern Illinois University, USA
Elena Gaudioso	UNED, Spain
Ashok Goel	Georgia Institute of Technology, USA
Ilya Goldin	2U, Inc., USA
José González-Brenes	Chegg Inc., USA
Joseph Grafsgaard	North Carolina State University, USA
Monique Grandbastien	LORIA, Universitè de Lorraine, France
Agneta Gulz	Lund University Cognitive Science, Sweden
Jason Harley	University of Alberta, Canada
Peter Hastings	DePaul University, USA
Pentti Hietala	University of Tampere, Finland
Tsukasa Hirashima	Hiroshima University, Japan
Ulrich Hoppe	University of Duisburg-Essen, Germany
Sharon Hsiao	Arizona State University, USA

Paul Salvador Inventado   Carnegie Mellon University, USA
Sridhar Iyer   IIT Bombay, India
G. Tanner Jackson   Educational Testing Service, USA
Pamela Jordan   University of Pittsburgh, USA
Tanja-Christina Käser   Stanford University, USA
Sandra Katz   University of Pittsburgh, USA
Fazel Keshtkar   St. John's University, USA
Amruth Kumar   Ramapo College of New Jersey, USA
Jean-Marc Labat   Université Paris 6, France
Sébastien Lallé   University of British Columbia, Canada
Blair Lehman   Educational Testing Service, USA
Nicholas Lewkow   McGraw-Hill Education, USA
Manli Li   Tsinghua University
Vanda Luengo   Université Pierre et Marie Curie, France
Collin Lynch   North Carolina State University, USA
Noboru Matsuda   Texas A&M University, USA
Alain Mille   Universitè de Lyon, France
Marcelo Milrad   Linnaeus University, Sweden
Kazuhisa Miwa   Nagoya University, Japan
Shirin Mojarad   McGraw Hill Education, USA
Kasia Muldner   Carleton University, USA
Kiyoshi Nakabayashi   Chiba Institute of Technology, Japan
Roger Nkambou   Université du Québec à Montréal, Canada
Amy Ogan   Carnegie Mellon University, USA
Andrew Olney   University of Memphis, USA
Luc Paquette   University of Illinois at Urbana-Champaign, USA
Zach Pardos   UC Berkeley, USA
Philip I. Pavlik Jr.   University of Memphis, USA
Radek Pelánek   Masaryk University Brno, Czech Republic
Anna Rafferty   Carleton College, USA
Martina Rau   University of Wisconsin-Madison, USA
Ma. Mercedes T. Rodrigo   Ateneo de Manila University, Philippines
Jonathan Rowe   North Carolina State University, USA
Vasile Rus   The University of Memphis, USA
Demetrios Sampson   Curtin University, Australia
Maria Ofelia San Pedro   Teachers College, Columbia University, USA
Valerie Shute   FSU, USA
Erica Snow   Arizona State University, USA
Michael Timms   ACER, Australia
Maomi Ueno   University of Electro-Communications, Japan
Erin Walker   Arizona State University, USA
Candace Walkington   Southern Methodist University, USA
Joseph Jay Williams   Harvard University, USA
Michael Yudelson   Carnegie Mellon University, USA
Diego Zapata-Rivera   Educational Testing Service, USA

Additional Reviewers

Oluwabunmi Adewoyin	University of Saskatchewan, Canada
Laura Allen	Arizona State University, USA
Kavya Alse	IIT Bombay, India
Mohammed Alzaid	Arizona State University, USA
Juan Miguel Andres	University of Pennsylvania
Fabrísia Araújo	Federal University of Campina Grande, Brazil
Brenna Beirne	2U, Inc., USA
Ig Ibert Bittencourt	Federal University of Alagoas, Brazil
Mary Jean Blink	TutorGen Inc., USA
Anthony F. Botelho	Worcester Polytechnic Institute, USA
Irina Borisova	Chegg Inc., USA
François Bouchet	Université Paris 6, France
Thibault Carron	Université Paris 6, France
Paulo Carvalho	Carnegie Mellon University, USA
Cheng Yu Chung	Arizona State University, USA
Evandro Costa	Universidade Federal de Alagoas, Brazil
Veronica Cucuait	University College London, UK
Steven Dang	Carnegie Mellon University, USA
Daniel Davis	Delft University of Technology, The Netherlands
Anurag Deep	IIT Bombay, India
Jose Delgado	Georgia Institute of Technology, USA
Nicholas Diana	Carnegie Mellon University, USA
Rick Doherty	Shrewsbury Highschool, UK
Monika Domanska	Humboldt-Universität zu Berlin, Germany
Yi Dong	Vanderbilt University, USA
Bobbie Eicher	Georgia Institute of Technology, USA
Geela Fabic	University of Canterbury, New Zealand
Marissa Gonzales	Georgia Institute of Technology, USA
Julio Guerra	Universidad Austral de Chile, Chile
Beate Grawemeyer	Birkbeck, University of London, UK
Md Asif Hasan	Vanderbilt University, USA
Yugo Hayashi	Ritsumeikan University, Japan
Yusuke Hayashi	Hiroshima University, Japan
Tobias Hecking	University of Duisburg-Essen, Germany
Tomoya Horiguchi	Kobe University, Japan
Xueyan Hu	Texas A&M University, USA
Stephen Hutt	University of Notre Dame, USA
Shiming Kai	Columbia University, USA
Sokratis Karkalas	UCL Knowledge Lab, UK
Madiha Khan	University College London, UK
Joshua Killingsworth	Georgia Institute of Technology, USA
Yoon Jeon Kim	MIT, USA

International Artificial Intelligence in Education Society

Management Board

President-Elect
Bruce McLaren   Carnegie Mellon University, USA

President
Benedict du Boulay   University of Sussex, UK
  (Emeritus)

Secretary/Treasurer
Tanja Mitrovic   University of Canterbury, New Zealand

Journal Editors
Vincent Aleve   Carnegie Mellon University, USA
Judy Kay   University of Sydney, Australia

Executive Committee

Ryan S.J.d. Baker   Worcester Polytechnic Institute, USA
Tiffany Barnes   North Carolina State University, USA
Gautam Biswas   Vanderbilt University, USA
Susan Bull   University of Birmingham, UK
Cristina Conati   University of British Columbia, Canada
Ricardo Conejo   University of Malaga, Spain
Vania Dimitrova   University of Leeds, UK
Sidney DMello   University of Notre Dame, USA
Benedict du Boulay   University of Sussex, UK
  (Emeritus)
Art Graesser   University of Memphis, USA
Neil Heffernan   Worcester Polytechnic Institute, USA
Rose Luckin   University College London, UK
Noboru Matsuda   Texas A&M University, USA
Bruce McLaren   Carnegie Mellon University, USA
Riichiro Mizoguchi   Osaka University, Japan
Amy Ogan   Carnegie Mellon University, USA
Zachary Pardos   University of California at Berkeley, USA
Ido Roll   University of British Columbia, Canada
Carolyn Penstein Rose   Carnegie Mellon University, USA
Julita Vassileva   University of Saskatchewan, Canada
Erin Walker   Arizona State University, USA
Kalina Yacef   University of Sydney, Australia

Keynotes

A Conceptual Framework
for Smart Learning Engine

Ronghuai Huang

Smart Learning Institute, Beijing Normal University, Beijing, China
huangrh@bnu.edu.cn

Abstract. In a life-long learning society, learning scenarios can be categorized into five types, which are "classroom learning", "self-learning", "inquiry learning", "learning in doing" and "learning in working". From a life-wide learning perspective, all these scenarios play vital roles for personal development. How to recognize these learning scenarios (including learning time, learning place, learning peers, learning activities, etc.) and provide the matched learning ways (including learning path, resources, peers, teachers, etc.) are the basis for smart learning environments, however few research could be found to address this problem.

In order to solve this problem, we propose a conceptual framework of smart learning engine that is the core of integrated, interactive and intelligent (i^3) learning environments. The smart learning engine consists of three main functions.

The first function is to identify data from student, teacher, subject area, and the environment using wireless sensors, the established learning resources and scenarios, and a learner modeling technology. The acquired data includes prior knowledge, theme-based context, leaner/teacher profile, physical environments, etc.

The second function is to compute the best ways of learning based on the learning scenario and learning preference. In detail, this function includes modeling learner's affective data, building knowledge structure, optimizing knowledge module, and connecting learners.

The third function is to deploy personalized and adaptive strategy, resources and tools for students and teachers based on the computed results in the second function. Deploy interactive strategies, learning paces, learning resources, and delivery approaches are the core elements for this function.

Quantified Learning

Liu Sannyuya

Central China Normal University, Wuhan, China

Abstract. Emerging technologies, including internet of things and big data, are leading to educational revolutions in learning environment, learning applications, and learning approaches. Recent advancement in data collection and data analysis offers opportunities in accurate description and quantification of learning activities. Quantified Learning refers to the process of utilizing appropriate approaches and methods to gain insights from students' explicit and implicit behavioral features, and offering analysis and intervention services to accommodate students' personalized learning needs. With "learner-centered" philosophy, Quantified Learning will develop data-oriented perception and effectively facilitate knowledge construction and personal development. With data, learners, shakeholders, and connected learning services, Quantified Learning is a closed-loop with adaptive feedbacks. The four stages of quantified learning, including quantification, data collection, integration and analysis, and intelligent services will enhance research and practices of teaching and learning with more accuracy and intelligence.

From Databases to Prospective Memory: The Saga of CBM Continued

Antonija Mitrovic

Intelligent Computer Tutoring Group, Department of Computer Science and Software Engineering, University of Canterbury, Christchurch, New Zealand
tanja.mitrovic@canterbury.ac.nz

Abstract. Twelve years ago, I presented an invited talk at AIED 2005, which focused on the early days of the Intelligent Computer Tutoring Group[1]. (ICTG), and the tutors we developed. Our early work focused on teaching design tasks, such as database querying and design. Since then, we have employed CBM successfully in many other domains. Some of those tutors also taught design tasks, such as Java programs and UML design, while other were procedural in nature. We also developed ASPIRE, an authoring system and deployment environment for constraint-based tutors. ASPIRE has served as the foundation for developing new tutors, ranging from teaching how to solve thermodynamics problems, manage oil palm plantations, diagnosing problems with X ray images. ASPIRE allowed embedding constraint-based tutors into other software packages, such as accounting software and management information systems. It also allowed having sophisticated interfaces, such as the Augmented Reality interface of MAT. During these 12 years, we were successful in developing a constraint-based model of collaborative skills, modeling meta-cognitive skills and affect of our students. We also investigated feedback strategies, especially the effect of how feedback is phrased on learning, and the effect of positive feedback. The most recent studies focused on multiple teaching strategies: comparing learning from problem-solving, worked examples, and erroneous examples. And then we investigated whether we can model prospective memory using constraints; in a recently completed project, the prospective memory functioning of 15 stroke survivors increased significantly after 10 sessions of computer-based training on how to memorize prospective tasks, and practising in a Virtual Reality environment. In this talk, I will present highlights of our recent projects.

---

[1] www.ictg.canterbury.ac.nz.

An AI Methodology and a New Learning Paradigm

Riichiro Mizoguchi

Japan Advanced Institute of Science and Technology (JAIST),
Nomi, Ishikawa, Japan
mizo@jaist.ac.jp

Abstract. My talk consists of two topics: One is how ontology engineering as an AI methodology helps you modeling of AIED matters and the other is Negotiation-Driven Learning: NDL as a new learning paradigm. After reviewing several AI methodologies, I discuss ontology engineering to explain that it is a promising methodology and it contributes to modeling rather than to metadata. I will try convince you that it provides a powerful conceptual tool to tackle and handle complex objects/concepts /theories/systems/etc. It also enables you to design systems with clear separation between domain-dependent and domain-independent parts, which is exploited in the research on NDL. NDL is a new learning paradigm in OLM, in which I have been intensively involved with my former PhD student, Raja Suleman recently. It is a framework built by integrating dialog-based tutoring, interest-based negotiation and affective computing in the negotiation process of OLM. I will discuss its role in AIED in terms of learning paradigm and methodology of system design.

Keywords: Modeling · Ontology engineering · Negotiation-driven learning

Contents

Full Papers

An Adaptive Coach for Invention Activities 3
  Vincent Aleven, Helena Connolly, Octav Popescu, Jenna Marks,
  Marianna Lamnina, and Catherine Chase

Evaluating the Effect of Uncertainty Visualisation in Open Learner
Models on Students' Metacognitive Skills 15
  Lamiya Al-Shanfari, Carrie Demmans Epp, and Chris Baber

Collaboration Improves Student Interest in Online Tutoring 28
  Ivon Arroyo, Naomi Wixon, Danielle Allessio, Beverly Woolf,
  Kasia Muldner, and Winslow Burleson

Improving Sensor-Free Affect Detection Using Deep Learning 40
  Anthony F. Botelho, Ryan S. Baker, and Neil T. Heffernan

ReaderBench Learns Dutch: Building a Comprehensive Automated
Essay Scoring System for Dutch Language. 52
  Mihai Dascalu, Wim Westera, Stefan Ruseti, Stefan Trausan-Matu,
  and Hub Kurvers

Keeping the Teacher in the Loop: Technologies for Monitoring Group
Learning in Real-Time. 64
  Avi Segal, Shaked Hindi, Naomi Prusak, Osama Swidan, Adva Livni,
  Alik Palatnic, Baruch Schwarz, and Ya'akov (Kobi) Gal

An Extensible Domain-Specific Language for Describing
Problem-Solving Procedures. 77
  Bastiaan Heeren and Johan Jeuring

Effects of Error-Based Simulation as a Counterexample
for Correcting MIF Misconception 90
  Tsukasa Hirashima, Tomoya Shinohara, Atsushi Yamada,
  Yusuke Hayashi, and Tomoya Horiguchi

Algorithm for Uniform Test Assembly Using a Maximum Clique
Problem and Integer Programming 102
  Takatoshi Ishii and Maomi Ueno

Personalized Tag-Based Knowledge Diagnosis to Predict the Quality
of Answers in a Community of Learners 113
  Oluwabukola Mayowa Ishola and Gordon McCalla

iSTART-ALL: Confronting Adult Low Literacy with Intelligent Tutoring
for Reading Comprehension   125
    Amy M. Johnson, Tricia A. Guerrero, Elizabeth L. Tighe,
    and Danielle S. McNamara

Adapting Step Granularity in Tutorial Dialogue Based on Pretest Scores   137
    Pamela Jordan, Patricia Albacete, and Sandra Katz

The Impact of Student Individual Differences and Visual Attention
to Pedagogical Agents During Learning with MetaTutor   149
    Sébastien Lallé, Michelle Taub, Nicholas V. Mudrick,
    Cristina Conati, and Roger Azevedo

Automatic Extraction of AST Patterns for Debugging Student Programs   162
    Timotej Lazar, Martin Možina, and Ivan Bratko

Dusting Off the Messy Middle: Assessing Students' Inquiry Skills
Through Doing and Writing   175
    Haiying Li, Janice Gobert, and Rachel Dickler

Impact of Pedagogical Agents' Conversational Formality on Learning
and Engagement   188
    Haiying Li and Art Graesser

iSTART Therefore I Understand: But Metacognitive Supports Did
not Enhance Comprehension Gains   201
    Kathryn S. McCarthy, Matthew E. Jacovina, Erica L. Snow,
    Tricia A. Guerrero, and Danielle S. McNamara

Inducing Stealth Assessors from Game Interaction Data.   212
    Wookhee Min, Megan H. Frankosky, Bradford W. Mott, Eric N. Wiebe,
    Kristy Elizabeth Boyer, and James C. Lester

Supporting Constructive Video-Based Learning: Requirements Elicitation
from Exploratory Studies   224
    Antonija Mitrovic, Vania Dimitrova, Lydia Lau, Amali Weerasinghe,
    and Moffat Mathews

Affect Dynamics in Military Trainees Using vMedic: From Engaged
Concentration to Boredom to Confusion   238
    Jaclyn Ocumpaugh, Juan Miguel Andres, Ryan Baker, Jeanine DeFalco,
    Luc Paquette, Jonathan Rowe, Bradford Mott, James Lester,
    Vasiliki Georgoulas, Keith Brawner, and Robert Sottilare

Behavioral Engagement Detection of Students in the Wild   250
    Eda Okur, Nese Alyuz, Sinem Aslan, Utku Genc, Cagri Tanriover,
    and Asli Arslan Esme

Improving Reading Comprehension with Automatically Generated
Cloze Item Practice.................................... 262
    Andrew M. Olney, Philip I. Pavlik Jr., and Jaclyn K. Maass

Variations of Gaming Behaviors Across Populations of Students
and Across Learning Environments.......................... 274
    Luc Paquette and Ryan S. Baker

Identifying Productive Inquiry in Virtual Labs Using Sequence Mining..... 287
    Sarah Perez, Jonathan Massey-Allard, Deborah Butler, Joss Ives,
    Doug Bonn, Nikki Yee, and Ido Roll

"Thanks Alisha, Keep in Touch": Gender Effects and Engagement
with Virtual Learning Companions 299
    Lydia G. Pezzullo, Joseph B. Wiggins, Megan H. Frankosky,
    Wookhee Min, Kristy Elizabeth Boyer, Bradford W. Mott, Eric N. Wiebe,
    and James C. Lester

Hint Generation Under Uncertainty: The Effect of Hint Quality
on Help-Seeking Behavior 311
    Thomas W. Price, Rui Zhi, and Tiffany Barnes

Balancing Learning and Engagement in Game-Based Learning
Environments with Multi-objective Reinforcement Learning............ 323
    Robert Sawyer, Jonathan Rowe, and James Lester

Is More Agency Better? The Impact of Student Agency
on Game-Based Learning................................ 335
    Robert Sawyer, Andy Smith, Jonathan Rowe, Roger Azevedo,
    and James Lester

Can a Teachable Agent Influence How Students Respond to Competition
in an Educational Game?................................ 347
    Björn Sjödén, Mats Lind, and Annika Silvervarg

Face Forward: Detecting Mind Wandering from Video During Narrative
Film Comprehension................................... 359
    Angela Stewart, Nigel Bosch, Huili Chen, Patrick Donnelly,
    and Sidney D'Mello

Modeling the Incubation Effect Among Students Playing
an Educational Game for Physics 371
    May Marie P. Talandron, Ma. Mercedes T. Rodrigo, and Joseph E. Beck

Predicting Learner's Deductive Reasoning Skills
Using a Bayesian Network................................ 381
    Ange Tato, Roger Nkambou, Janie Brisson, and Serge Robert

Group Optimization to Maximize Peer Assessment Accuracy
Using Item Response Theory   393
  Masaki Uto, Nguyen Duc Thien, and Maomi Ueno

What Matters in Concept Mapping? Maps Learners Create
or How They Create Them.   406
  Shang Wang, Erin Walker, and Ruth Wylie

Reliability Investigation of Automatic Assessment of Learner-Build
Concept Map with Kit-Build Method by Comparing
with Manual Methods   418
  Warunya Wunnasri, Jaruwat Pailai, Yusuke Hayashi,
  and Tsukasa Hirashima

Characterizing Students' Learning Behaviors Using Unsupervised
Learning Methods   430
  Ningyu Zhang, Gautam Biswas, and Yi Dong

Poster Papers

Student Preferences for Visualising Uncertainty in Open Learner Models. . . .   445
  Lamiya Al-Shanfari, Chris Baber, and Carrie Demmans Epp

Intelligent Augmented Reality Tutoring for Physical Tasks
with Medical Professionals.   450
  Mohammed A. Almiyad, Luke Oakden-Rayner, Amali Weerasinghe,
  and Mark Billinghurst

Synthesis of Problems for Shaded Area Geometry Reasoning   455
  Chris Alvin, Sumit Gulwani, Rupak Majumdar,
  and Supratik Mukhopadhyay

Communication Strategies and Affective Backchannels for Conversational
Agents to Enhance Learners' Willingness to Communicate
in a Second Language   459
  Emmanuel Ayedoun, Yuki Hayashi, and Kazuhisa Seta

A Multi-layered Architecture for Analysis of Non-technical-Skills
in Critical Situations   463
  Yannick Bourrier, Francis Jambon, Catherine Garbay,
  and Vanda Luengo

Conceptual Framework for Collaborative Educational Resources
Adaptation in Virtual Learning Environments   467
  Vitor Bremgartner, José de Magalhães Netto, and Crediné Menezes

Minimal Meaningful Propositions Alignment in Student
Response Comparisons 472
    Florin Bulgarov and Rodney Nielsen

Does Adaptive Provision of Learning Activities Improve Learning
in SQL-Tutor? 476
    Xingliang Chen, Antonija Mitrovic, and Moffat Mathews

Constraint-Based Modelling as a Tutoring Framework
for Japanese Honorifics 480
    Zachary T. Chung, Takehito Utsuro, and Ma. Mercedes Rodrigo

Teaching iSTART to Understand Spanish 485
    *Mihai Dascalu, Matthew E. Jacovina, Christian M. Soto, Laura K. Allen,
    Jianmin Dai, Tricia A. Guerrero, and Danielle S. McNamara*

Data-Driven Generation of Rubric Parameters from an Educational
Programming Environment....................................... 490
    *Nicholas Diana, Michael Eagle, John Stamper, Shuchi Grover,
    Marie Bienkowski, and Satabdi Basu*

Exploring Learner Model Differences Between Students 494
    *Michael Eagle, Albert Corbett, John Stamper, Bruce M. McLaren,
    Ryan Baker, Angela Wagner, Benjamin MacLaren, and Aaron Mitchell*

Investigating the Effectiveness of Menu-Based Self-explanation Prompts
in a Mobile Python Tutor...................................... 498
    Geela Venise Firmalo Fabic, Antonija Mitrovic, and Kourosh Neshatian

Striking a Balance: User-Experience and Performance in Computerized
Game-Based Assessment 502
    *Carol M. Forsyth, Tanner Jackson, Del Hebert, Blair Lehman,
    Pat Inglese, and Lindsay Grace*

Interactive Score Reporting: An AutoTutor-Based System for Teachers 506
    *Carol M. Forsyth, Stephanie Peters, Diego Zapata-Rivera,
    Jennifer Lentini, Art Graesser, and Zhiqiang Cai*

Transforming Foreign Language Narratives into Interactive Reading
Applications Designed for Comprehensibility and Interest 510
    Pedro Furtado, Tsukasa Hirashima, and Yusuke Hayashi

Exploring Students' Affective States During Learning
with External Representations.................................. 514
    *Beate Grawemeyer, Manolis Mavrikis, Claudia Mazziotti, Alice Hansen,
    Anouschka van Leeuwen, and Nikol Rummel*

Enhancing an Intelligent Tutoring System to Support Student
Collaboration: Effects on Learning and Behavior.   519
   Rachel Harsley, Barbara Di Eugenio, Nick Green, and Davide Fossati

Assessing Question Quality Using NLP   523
   Kristopher J. Kopp, Amy M. Johnson, Scott A. Crossley,
   and Danielle S. McNamara

The Effect of Providing Motivational Support in Parsons Puzzle Tutors   528
   Amruth N. Kumar

Assessing Student Answers to Balanced Tree Problems   532
   Chun W. Liew, Huy Nguyen, and Darren J. Norton

A Comparisons of BKT, RNN and LSTM for Learning Gain Prediction   536
   Chen Lin and Min Chi

Uncovering Gender and Problem Difficulty Effects in Learning
with an Educational Game   540
   Bruce McLaren, Rosta Farzan, Deanne Adams, Richard Mayer,
   and Jodi Forlizzi

Analyzing Learner Affect in a Scenario-Based Intelligent
Tutoring System   544
   Benjamin Nye, Shamya Karumbaiah, S. Tugba Tokel, Mark G. Core,
   Giota Stratou, Daniel Auerbach, and Kallirroi Georgila

Proficiency and Preference Using Local Language
with a Teachable Agent   548
   Amy Ogan, Evelyn Yarzebinski, Roberto De Roock,
   Cristina Dumdumaya, Michelle Banawan, and Ma. Mercedes Rodrigo

LiftUpp: Support to Develop Learner Performance   553
   Frans A. Oliehoek, Rahul Savani, Elliot Adderton, Xia Cui,
   David Jackson, Phil Jimmieson, John Christopher Jones,
   Keith Kennedy, Ben Mason, Adam Plumbley, and Luke Dawson

StairStepper: An Adaptive Remedial iSTART Module   557
   Cecile A. Perret, Amy M. Johnson, Kathryn S. McCarthy,
   Tricia A. Guerrero, Jianmin Dai, and Danielle S. McNamara

AttentiveLearner[2]: A Multimodal Approach for Improving
MOOC Learning on Mobile Devices   561
   Phuong Pham and Jingtao Wang

Automated Analysis of Lecture Video Engagement Using Student Posts   565
   Nicholas R. Stepanek and Brian Dorn

A Study of Learners' Behaviors in Hands-On Learning Situations
and Their Correlation with Academic Performance   570
    Rémi Venant, Kshitij Sharma, Pierre Dillenbourg, Philippe Vidal,
    and Julien Broisin

Assessing the Collaboration Quality in the Pair Program Tracing
and Debugging Eye-Tracking Experiment   574
    Maureen Villamor, Yancy Vance Paredes, Japheth Duane Samaco,
    Joanna Feliz Cortez, Joshua Martinez, and Ma. Mercedes Rodrigo

EMBRACE: Applying Cognitive Tutor Principles
to Reading Comprehension.   578
    Erin Walker, Audrey Wong, Sarah Fialko, M. Adelaida Restrepo,
    and Arthur M. Glenberg

Effects of a Dashboard for an Intelligent Tutoring System
on Teacher Knowledge, Lesson Plans and Class Sessions.   582
    Françeska Xhakaj, Vincent Aleven, and Bruce M. McLaren

Dynamics of Affective States During MOOC Learning   586
    Xiang Xiao, Phuong Pham, and Jingtao Wang

Learning from Errors: Identifying Strategies in a Math Tutoring System   590
    Jun Xie, Keith Shubeck, Scotty D. Craig, and Xiangen Hu

Can Short Answers to Open Response Questions Be Auto-Graded
Without a Grading Rubric?   594
    Xi Yang, Lishan Zhang, and Shengquan Yu

Regional Cultural Differences in How Students Customize
Their Avatars in Technology-Enhanced Learning   598
    Evelyn Yarzebinski, Cristina Dumdumaya, Ma. Mercedes T. Rodrigo,
    Noboru Matsuda, and Amy Ogan

Doctoral Consortium Papers

Teaching Informal Logical Fallacy Identification with a Cognitive Tutor   605
    Nicholas Diana, Michael Eagle, John Stamper,
    and Kenneth R. Koedinger

Digital Learning Projection: Learning Performance Estimation
from Multimodal Learning Experiences.   609
    Daniele Di Mitri

Learning with Engaging Activities via a Mobile Python Tutor   613
    Geela Venise Firmalo Fabic, Antonija Mitrovic, and Kourosh Neshatian

Math Reading Comprehension: Comparing Effectiveness of Various
Conversation Frameworks in an ITS   617
   Keith T. Shubeck, Ying Fang, and Xiangen Hu

Industry Papers

4C: Continuous Cognitive Career Companions   623
   *Bhavna Agrawal, Rong Liu, Ravi Kokku, Yi-Min Chee,
Ashish Jagmohan, Satya Nitta, Michael Tan, and Sherry Sin*

Wizard's Apprentice: Cognitive Suggestion Support for Wizard-of-Oz
Question Answering   630
   *Jae-wook Ahn, Patrick Watson, Maria Chang, Sharad Sundararajan,
Tengfei Ma, Nirmal Mukhi, and Srijith Prabhu*

Interaction Analysis in Online Maths Human Tutoring:
The Case of Third Space Learning   636
   *Mutlu Cukurova, Manolis Mavrikis, Rose Luckin, James Clark,
and Candida Crawford*

Using a Model for Learning and Memory to Simulate Learner Response
in Spaced Practice.   644
   *Mark A. Riedesel, Neil Zimmerman, Ryan Baker, Tom Titchener,
and James Cooper*

Bridging the Gap Between High and Low Performing Pupils Through
Performance Learning Online Analysis and Curricula   650
   Tej Samani, Kaśka Porayska-Pomsta, and Rose Luckin

Erratum to: Dusting Off the Messy Middle: Assessing Students' Inquiry
Skills Through Doing and Writing E1
   Haiying Li, Janice Gobert, and Rachel Dickler

Tutorials and Workshops

2nd International Workshop on Intelligent Mentoring Systems (IMS2017) . . .   659
   *Vania Dimitrova, Art Graesser, Andrew J. Hampton, Lydia Lau,
Antonija Mitrovic, David Williamson Shaffer, and Amali Weerasinghe*

Workshop: Sharing and Reusing Data and Analytic Methods
with LearnSphere   662
   Kenneth Koedinger, John Stamper, Phil Pavlik, and Ran Liu

How Do We Unleash AIEd at Scale to Benefit All Teachers and Learners?   665
   *Rose Luckin, Manolis Mavrikis, Mutlu Cukurova, Kaska
Porayska-Pomsta, Wayne Holmes, Bart Rienties, Daniel Spikol,
Vincent Aleven, and Laurie Forcier*

Turn Theories into Products: Implementation of Artificial Intelligence
in Education. 668
    Ryan Baker, Xiangen Hu, Jeff Wang, and Will Ma

AutoTutor Tutorial: Authoring Conversational Intelligent Systems. 669
    *Zhiqiang Cai, Xiangen Hu, Keith Shubeck, Kai-Chih Bai, Art Graesser,
    Bor-Chen Kuo, and Chen-Huei Liao*

Propensity Score Analysis: Hands-on Approach to Measuring
and Modeling Educational Data (Tutorial) 671
    Vivekanandan Kumar, David Boulanger, and Shawn N. Fraser

Author Index 675

Full Papers

An Adaptive Coach for Invention Activities

Vincent Aleven[1](✉), Helena Connolly[2], Octav Popescu[1],
Jenna Marks[2], Marianna Lamnina[2], and Catherine Chase[2]

[1] Human Computer Interaction Institute,
Carnegie Mellon University, Pittsburgh, PA, USA
aleven@cs.cmu.edu, octav@cmu.edu
[2] Teachers College, Columbia University, New York, NY, USA
{hc2808,ml3648,chase}@tc.columbia.edu,
marksjennan@gmail.com

Abstract. A focus in recent AIED research is to create adaptive support for learners in inquiry learning environments. However, only few examples of such support have been demonstrated. Our work focuses on Invention activities, inquiry activities in which students generate representations that explain data presented as contrasting cases. To help teachers implement these activities in their classrooms, we have created and pilot-tested a dedicated adaptive computer coach (the Invention Coach) and are currently evaluating it in a classroom study. The Coach's pedagogical strategy balances structuring and problematizing, unlike many ITSs, which favor structuring. The Coach is implemented in CTAT as a model-tracing tutor, with a rule-based model that captures its pedagogical coaching strategy, designed in part based on data from human tutors. We describe the Invention Coach and its pedagogical model. We present evidence from our pilot tests that illustrate the tutor's versatility and provide preliminary evidence of its effectiveness. The contributions of the work are: identifying an adaptive coaching strategy for Invention tasks that balances structuring and problematizing, and an automated coach for a successful instructional method (Invention) for which few tutors have been built.

Keywords: Invention · Adaptive coach · Intelligent tutoring system · STEM education · Productive failure · Inquiry learning

1 Introduction

Although the field of AIED has devoted much time and energy to systems that support tutored problem solving [3, 22, 36], the field has always been interested in supporting other pedagogical approaches as well, including inquiry learning [8, 10, 11, 25, 33]. Our work focuses on Invention activities [34], a form of inquiry in which students invent equations to describe data presented in contrasting cases. Many studies have found evidence that Invention activities, combined with subsequent expository instruction, are very effective in fostering a deep understanding of scientific and mathematical concepts and transfer of those ideas to novel contexts [32, 35]. In spite of these results, however, Invention activities are not widely used in educational practice.

© Springer International Publishing AG 2017
E. André et al. (Eds.): AIED 2017, LNAI 10331, pp. 3–14, 2017.
DOI: 10.1007/978-3-319-61425-0_1

A major impediment to going to scale is that students need extensive help to work through Invention tasks productively, as one of us has observed in 10 years of experience running classroom studies with Invention activities. Students have difficulty understanding the goal of the task, creating a general solution that works for all cases, evaluating their solutions, and generating new ideas when old ideas fail. A typical study of Invention activities involves up to five research assistants and one classroom teacher to guide one class of thirty students. Obviously, this high level of assistance poses a problem for scaling up.

Our project aims to make it easier for students to conduct Invention activities in classrooms, by creating a dedicated adaptive web-based computer coach for Invention tasks, called the Invention Coach. The current implementation of the Invention Coach handles ratio problems applied to science contexts (e.g. density, velocity) [5, 20]. It is implemented in the CTAT/Tutorshop infrastructure for tutor development [1, 2], although it is different from the typical tutor built in this infrastructure in that it supports Invention, not problem-solving practice, and has a rule-based model that captures pedagogical strategy, rather than problem-solving knowledge (but see [12]).

The design of the Coach provides one answer to an important question in the learning sciences and science education: How should educational technology scaffold inquiry processes? [9, 24, 26, 28] Many approaches have been tried [27, 31, 37], including some that involve adaptive coaching [11, 30, 33]. A key open issue in devising support for inquiry is finding a good balance between giving and withholding assistance [16], or in the words of Reiser [28], between structuring and problematizing. Whereas structuring scaffolds reduce task complexity, problematizing scaffolds increase complexity by challenging learners' current understanding. Problematizing scaffolds encourage learners to articulate their ideas, express their understanding in disciplinary terms, and surface knowledge gaps [28]. However, opinions differ as to where a good balance might be. Some argue for greater structure because learners cannot handle the high cognitive load of problematizing [15, 21]. Others argue for a high degree of problematizing by eliciting construction, articulation, and argumentation [17, 23]. We believe, based in part on our prior empirical studies of teachers supporting students one-on-one in Invention tasks [6], that both are necessary to support learning in exploratory learning paradigms like Invention [13]. The Invention Coach therefore balances structuring and problematizing, which sets it apart not just from standard ITSs, but also from other systems that have been built to support Invention activities [30], which have a fixed subgoal structure. It is important to ask, however, how well the Coach's strategy works in helping students engage with the Invention process in a way that prepares them to learn from later instruction on the same topic, as is Invention's key strength and purpose.

In this paper, we present the Invention Coach, detail its adaptive coaching strategy, and explain how it balances structuring and problematizing. We present preliminary evidence from our pilot studies and on-going classroom study of its effectiveness in helping students work through Invention tasks and acquire a deep understanding of the modeled physics phenomena.

2 The Invention Coach

The Invention Coach supports students in constructing mathematical expressions for scientific phenomena, based on their analysis of carefully designed sets of contrasting cases that are provided with the task. Figure 1A shows the Coach, with an Invention activity that has been used in studies prior to the Invention Coach [35]. The student's goal in this task is to create a numerical index of "clown crowdedness" that accounts for the crowdedness in the contrasting cases (buses with clowns), while observing basic task constraints, for instance, that the index numbers should be based on a (to-be-invented) mathematical method, applied consistently to all cases.

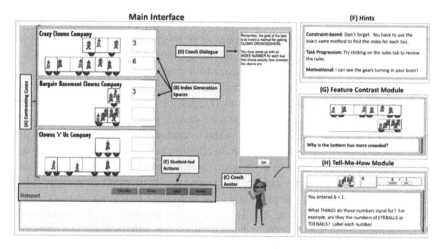

Fig. 1. Invention coach. Labels in bold are annotations, not part of the actual interface, except for the names of the bus companies.

Although they do not know it, in this task students are inventing the formula for density (mass/volume), where density is conceived as a number of objects packed into a space. Many students do not generate the correct equation (clowns/bus compartments), but attempting to do so helps them notice deep domain features and explore how they may be related in a mathematical structure. Invention activities create a "time for telling" [4]; they are followed by expository instruction. The combination of these learning activities has been shown to be highly effective [32, 35].

We designed the Invention Coach's coaching strategy based on learning mechanisms underlying learning with Invention [18], our empirical studies of human teachers guiding students through Invention activities [6], our Wizard-of-Oz study with a prior, partially automated version of the Invention Coach, and, finally, the desire to balance structuring and problematizing scaffolds, as discussed above [28]. Specifically, in our studies of human coaching of Invention, we found that explicit explanations by the coach were associated with lower rates of transfer, suggesting that too much structure may hinder learning from Invention tasks [6]. On the other hand, we noticed in our many user-testing sessions with early versions of the Coach that too much problematizing can lead to high levels of frustration and unproductive behaviors like guessing or reverse-engineering solutions. A productive balance is necessary. Thus, we adopted a fundamental "ask more, tell less" pedagogical philosophy, with the goal to get students to self-diagnose their misunderstandings without telling them their invention is right or wrong and without providing lengthy explanations. Further, we wanted to support opportunistic Invention processes, so students could follow individual solution paths rather than follow a fixed subgoal sequence. Thus, the Coach's main interface provides only limited structure: It presents a statement of general task constraints, available at any time as one of the student resources (Fig. 1E), contrasting cases, and prompts to enter index values for the cases. It does not lay out problem-solving steps, as many ITSs do. Therefore, the Coach problematizes to a substantial degree: It is left up to the student to figure out how to define an index and how to test whether it is correct. We developed three adaptive scaffolds that aim to help students to engage in the core learning processes of Invention, The Coach also provides adaptive feedback messages. Both the scaffolding strategies (dubbed "modules") and feedback add structure but also problematize to a considerable degree.

Specifically, as students enter indices that capture their notion of crowdedness (Fig. 1B), the Invention Coach provides short feedback messages that remind students of constraints, encourage task progression, or motivate continued effort (Fig. 1F). The messages never point out specific strengths and weaknesses of student Inventions, in an attempt to both structure and problematize. In addition to providing feedback messages, the Coach can launch students into longer, interactive modules, which too balance structuring and problematizing. They provide structure by focusing on a single subgoal or task constraint, breaking the reasoning into steps, and providing correctness feedback. But they also problematize, by (1) contradicting students' current understanding and (2) leaving it up to the students to diagnose the error in their inventions and to infer how to fix them. For example, the Feature Contrast module (Fig. 1G) makes use of the contrasting cases to help students notice key features of the domain, a key learning mechanism behind Invention [4, 18, 19, 29, 30, 35]. In the example in Fig. 1G, the coach highlights two of the given cases and asks the student which is more crowded and why. The comparison is designed to confront learners with the often-overlooked feature of bus size: across these two cases, the number of clowns is constant but bus size differs. While this module structures how learners process the cases, it also problematizes by showing learners that their invention is inadequate, and by leaving it up to the students to figure out how to fix their indices.

Similarly, the Ranking module (not depicted), balances structuring and problematizing: It asks learners to order the companies from most to least crowded. Ranking is designed to elicit learners' intuitive prior knowledge, another core learning process of Invention [14, 18]. This module structures by providing a clear subgoal (to rank) and correctness feedback. However, it also problematizes the learner's current solution (since this module is only given when the learner's solution contradicts the rank order of the cases), and in true problematizing fashion, the Coach leaves it up to the student to notice whether her indices are consistent with the ranking, and, if not, what to do about it. Finally, the Tell-Me-How (TMH) module (Fig. 1H) encourages learners to articulate and explain how they generated their index numbers. Students describe their solution method in an open text box before selecting from a set of explicit strategy types ("I counted", "I estimated", or "I calculated"). Then they are pushed to describe their answers in disciplinary terms, such as mathematical expressions and units (shown in Fig. 1H). Getting learners to self-explain and elaborate on their answers is one way to surface gaps in their knowledge, a key learning process in Invention [7, 19, 29, 30] and an important problematizing mechanism [28].

3   Adaptive Coaching Strategy

The Coach's adaptive strategy consists of two levels of decision-making. First, it has a *global strategy* that classifies students' Inventions and decides at a high level how to respond, by providing a feedback message or by launching a module. Second, it has a specific control strategy for each of its *modules*. The global strategy supports an opportunistic, free-flowing approach to Invention, whereas modules tend to be more structured, even though they also problematize, as noted.

The Coach's *global strategy* works as follows: When students submit their Invention or ask for help (and have entered at least 4 indices), the Coach attempts to classify the student's solution strategy based on the indices the student has provided and (if available) the student's formula entered in self-explanation boxes during Tell-Me-How. The student's Invention is evaluated against 5 broad classes of solutions approaches (no strategy, estimating, counting, math, ratio), with 20 subclasses, identified in our previous Wizard-of-Oz studies. The categories represent increasing levels of sophistication in the student's Invention. For example, if there is no discernible logic behind the student's Invention, it will be classified as "no strategy." If the students' indices rank the cases correctly (and assign the same index to the two cases in each case pair – e.g., the two buses of a bus company), the Coach classifies this strategy as "estimating."Alternatively, if the student seems to have focused on a single feature (e.g., entered the number of clowns in each bus as their index, ignoring bus size), the Coach would classify the solution as "counting." Inventions that show evidence of considering two features, but not in a ratio relation, are classified as "math." Inventions that correctly capture a ratio are classified as "ratio." There are a number of more nuanced classifications as well. The Coach classifies the student's Invention under one of its solution strategies if more than half of the indices (i.e., at least 4) or more than half of the TMH boxes (at least 2) are consistent with that strategy.

Once a strategy has been identified, the Coach chooses an appropriate response, contingent on the strategy. In pilot testing, we discovered that the student's solution strategy often reveals one or more misconceptions. Thus, the Coach responds to a student solution by selecting from a set of hints and modules that address the student's most critical knowledge gap, problematizing the student's solution. As long as students maintain a strategy in the same category, he/she will receive alternating hint messages and modules first targeting the most critical knowledge gap revealed by their strategy, and then secondary (less important) knowledge gaps. Within any given category, the Coach has multiple options for hint messages and modules. The hint messages identify a constraint that the student's Invention violates. The modules for any given classification are a subset of Ranking, Feature Contrast, and some variation of TMH. Although these modules have broad applicability and can be used in many situations, they are geared toward different kinds of knowledge gaps. For example, in response to the "counting" strategy described above, the Coach may launch into the Feature Contrast module, selecting an appropriate pair of cases to contrast that highlight the importance of bus size (i.e., two buses with the same number of clowns but evidently different density). As a second example, if there is evidence of attending to the right features but of incorrect math (category "math"), the Coach might prompt for self-explanation through a TMH module. The Coach keeps track of which feedback messages and modules have been tried, and will cycle through them as long as the student uses the given strategy, to avoid repetition. In addition, the Coach complains if the student is inactive for a certain amount of time.

When the student has succeeded in providing a set of 6 correct indices, the Coach goes to a final stage, where it asks students to "show their work" by entering math calculations for at least 3 indices in the TMH module. The purpose of this is to encourage learners to mathematize their answers, pushing them beyond intuitive answers (e.g., seeing 3 clowns per car) to calculating with mathematical operations (e.g., clowns divided by bus compartments). The Coach ends with a pair of free-text boxes where the student must describe their invention method and write a general formula for it. The Coach does not interpret these free-form descriptions.

The Invention Coach is implemented as a model-tracing tutor within the CTAT/Tutorshop infrastructure [1, 2], as in [30]. As a measure of its complexity, it is implemented as 140 production rules and 150 functions, divided into 6 modules. The Coach's global strategy and modules have been fully implemented and tested, and in our ongoing study, have proven to be robust for classroom use. The Coach currently implements two different Invention tasks, both with a ratio structure.

4 Preliminary Evidence of Effectiveness

The Invention Coach has undergone three cycles of iterative development, including a Wizard-of-Oz study and piloting in after-school programs, which provide preliminary evidence of its effectiveness with students from an urban, racially, and socioeconomically diverse public school. In addition, it is currently undergoing a much more extensive evaluation in a school. In an experimental study with an earlier version of the Invention Coach, 47 seventh and eighth grade students worked with the software in Wizard-of-Oz (WOz) mode. All guidance was built into the system, but an experimenter or "Wizard" on a paired computer adaptively selected appropriate guidance (i.e., made high-level coaching decisions, like the Coach's global strategy). Students demonstrated sizeable gains from pre- to posttest in both conceptual learning ($d = .5$) and transfer ($d = .6$) after only 30 min of instruction. Process data showed that, even in these brief sessions, learners engaged in productive exploration by generating a variety of solutions (2.5 on average), noticing the deep features of the domain (76% of students), attempting to relate these features mathematically (59% of students), and some even generating a correct ratio-based index (35% of students). While 35% may seem like a low number, the goal of Invention is not for learners to produce the correct solution. Attempting to generate their own solutions can lead to productive failures [14], which prepare students to learn from later expository instruction. In addition to these formal studies, we have informally tested the fully adaptive Invention Coach with 30 seventh and eighth-grade students. The Coach's adaptive guidance appeared to be effective in addressing each student's misunderstandings. Students frequently responded to the Coach by re-working their solutions. As a result, they often attempted 2–4 different solutions (a good thing!). Over one-third of students began with a single-feature solution, but most recognized both critical features by the end of the task. Experimenter observations suggest that the majority of students were highly engaged, and almost all persisted to the end of a 30-minute session.

5   Case Studies

To illustrate how the Invention Coach, with its balance of structuring and problematizing, helps students make progress in Invention tasks, we present two case studies from our on-going classroom study of 200+ middle school students using the Coach.

5.1   Case Study 1

Clowns 'r' Us Company

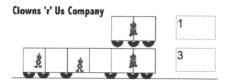

Fig. 2. Counting solution

Adrian's first strategy is to count clowns in each bus (Fig. 2). In response, the Invention Coach gives a hint that problematizes Adrian's solution, reminding him of the basic task constraint that buses from the same company should have the same index (but without explaining specifically which indices violate the constraint or how to fix the problem). When Adrian submits the same answer again, he receives a Feature Contrast Module, in which the Coach focuses him on two of the cases to help him notice the second, less salient feature: size of the bus. After completing the module, Adrian writes: "A place can be called crowded based on the size of the place and the amount of people in that place." Although he now notices both key features, he still has trouble generating a two-feature mathematical solution. After several "counting" and "no strategy" solutions, he attempts an "estimating" solution, in which the indices are in the correct rank order, but are not correctly calculated. The Invention Coach then gives Adrian a Tell-Me-How-Calculate module, He leaves the module without completing it but immediately after, uses the calculator in the Coach's interface to divide numbers, then inputs four correct indices. He receives motivational feedback about his progress and a Tell-Me-How module for a *correct* index. He correctly explains his method, but does not change the incorrect indices. Then the Invention Coach gives Adrian a Tell-Me-How-Calculate module for one of the *incorrect* indices of 2, pushing him to notice his own error. When asked to show his calculation, he inputs 2/1, which is the inverse of the correct solution, a common shortcoming in student Inventions (Fig. 3). The Coach reminds Adrian that he needs to use the same method for all cases, another basic task constraint. However, time is up.

Clowns 'r' Us Company

Fig. 3. Incorrect index calculated by inverting critical features

When asked to write a formula for lown crowdedness at the end of the activity, Adrian correctly writes: "crowdness = number of clowns divided by number of square boxes that make up the square."

Thus, Adrian made significant progress in the task, more so than most students, advancing to a correct ratio solution for four out of six cases, together with a correct explanation for how to calculate the indices. Although his progress is not always linear, his actions and explanations seem responsive to the Coach's hints and modules. The Feature Contrast module helps him notice the less salient feature (bus size). At multiple points, the Tell-Me-How module helps Adrian articulate his approach, which at times prompts immediate changes to his method. It also spurs Adrian on towards a math solution, leading to correct indices for two-thirds of the cases.

5.2 Case Study 2

Ella's experience illustrates that Adrian's marked progress is not shared by all students. She starts by submitting several estimating solutions (i.e., solutions that rank the cases correctly but without an apparent mathematical basis). The Coach presents a problematizing hint reminding her that an index should be an *exact* measure of crowdedness, but this hint does not appear to help her. When given a Tell-Me-How module asking her to articulate her method for the index of 5 (see Fig. 4), she claims to be counting clowns, but there are 6 clowns in the bus, not 5. The next time Ella enters an

Fig. 4. Ella's counting solution

estimating index, she receives additional problematizing feedback: "Here's a hint: Try calculating your index." When this hint does not have the intended effect (she enters more estimating solutions) the Coach responds with a Tell-Me-How module, prompting Ella to enter a calculation and explain it. She writes that she "estimated from how many clowns [there are] in the bus." Thus, although Ella's estimating strategy might implicitly consider two features, she only articulates one, namely, the number of clowns. Prompted by the Coach, she then uses the calculator to *multiply* the total number of clowns in the bus company by the total number of boxes in the company (see Fig. 5). This is the first evidence of her using math to create an index, though with the right features combined in an incorrect way. Ella updates the indices for the Bargain Basement Clowns Company, but does not apply the same strategy to the other companies. Given that this solution was only applied to one bus company, the Invention Coach continues to classify it as estimating, not as math. As a result, Ella receives the Feature Contrast module to help her explicitly articulate both features. This move is successful, because at the end of the module, Ella writes: "the size of the space matters so does the number of people in that space." She does not succeed in correctly combining the features, mathematically, but continues to submit various types of estimating solutions until time runs out. However, when asked to write a formula for

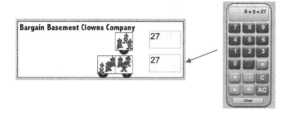

Fig. 5. Ella's explanation does not match her index

clown crowdedness at the end of the activity, she writes the inverse of the correct formula: "C = space/clowns."

Although Ella has trouble consistently using math to incorporate both features, she shows signs of progress during the task. Her initial estimating strategies suggest she might have been intuitively considering both features (clowns and bus size). Receiving the Feature Contrast module helped her explicitly articulate the importance of both features. Although the best she did in generating indices was to multiply the two features, she wrote a ratio formula at the end of the activity (albeit an incorrect one). The disconnect between her ability to state this formula and her generated indices (which show no evidence of applying a ratio formula) shows that she lacked the clarity to apply a ratio solution to the cases.

5.3   Analysis

The two case studies illustrate the challenging nature of the Invention task and the non-linear progressions students often follow. Ella's final formula and explanation constitute cumulative progress, but each iteration of her indices does not demonstrate this progress in her thinking. Adrian follows a more systematic progression, following a path of increasingly more sophisticated strategies, but he too does not always respond to feedback immediately and often needs multiple reminders to respond to a hint. Neither student fully succeeds in generating the ratio formula and consistently applying it, although Adrian came very close. It is however quite typical in Invention tasks that students do not succeed in generating the correct indices and formula. The task may nonetheless have prepared Adrian and Ella to learn from the ensuing expository instruction about ratios in physics, as has been shown in many prior studies on Invention [32, 35]. Our on-going classroom study tests whether the Invention Coach indeed prepares students to learn deeper from future expository instruction.

What makes the students' task challenging is that the Coach is not designed to help them succeed efficiently at generating a correct Invention. Rather, it is designed to help students think through the problem, typically through problematizing – contradicting incorrect solutions and encouraging students to uncover their own knowledge gaps through self-explanation – not direct feedback. These approaches seem to help students reflect on their own understandings and make progress in the task. The case studies also illustrate how our modules both structure and problematize a student's solution. For example, the Feature Contrast module uncovered a problem with students' solutions – that they were focusing on a single feature (e.g. clowns only). However, the Feature Contrast module also structures how students compare the cases, which led both students to articulate both critical features when prompted at the end of the module, ultimately steering them towards a two-feature solution. However, when asked to describe her strategy during a Tell-Me-How module, Ella's declared strategy was inconsistent with her index, exposing a gap in her thinking. This problematized Ella's solution, providing an opportunity for her to reassess her approach.

6 Discussion

We found some preliminary evidence that the Invention Coach helps students make progress through Invention tasks, even if it is definitely a challenging process for them. This gradual improvement is what one hopes to get from Invention activities. The data from our earlier Wizard-of-Oz and pilot studies suggests that this challenging work prepares students well for subsequent learning from expository instruction. Our on-going classroom study will provide further data on this question.

A practical contribution of the current work is a software coach that guides students during Invention activities. The Coach might take some of the burden off teachers as they have their students do Invention activities. Our hope is that eventually, through further perfecting and generalization, the Invention Coach will help spread and scale the proven instructional method of Invention. We will make the web-based Invention Coach easily available for free to whoever wants to use it.

A limitation of the current Coach is that it deals only with Invention problems that have a ratio structure (e.g., density, velocity) but not with other types of Invention tasks. Past research shows that Invention can be effective with a wide range of tasks. One of our future research goals is to generalize to Coach to guide students as they invent other sorts of equations (e.g. multiplicative, exponential, and so on).

Despite the lack of generalization, the current prototype Coach demonstrates a novel adaptive coaching strategy for Invention activities, based in part on theory, in part on empirical work with human tutors. In the design of the Coach, we apply the problematizing/structuring framework [28] to the design of an open-ended learning platform. In a manner quite different from other computer-based learning environments for Invention [30],the Coach balances structuring and problematizing. Generally, the level of problematizing is high, in the sense that it is left up to the students to make sense of the information they gather in the environment. However, the Coach adds some structure (while maintaining a high level of problematizing) by invoking modules that poke holes in learners' solutions, and by providing feedback without providing a specific error diagnosis. For the future, it may be interesting to compare against design alternatives that lean further towards structuring or further towards problematizing, or that balance in a more adaptive, dynamic way. The Invention Coach adds to the range of learning environments that have been built for open-ended, exploratory tasks, a key concern in the field of AIED.

Acknowledgments. The research is supported by NSF grant 1361062.

References

1. Aleven, V.: Rule-based cognitive modeling for intelligent tutoring systems. In: Nkambou, R., Bourdeau, J., Mizoguchi, R. (eds.) Advances in Intelligent Tutoring Systems, pp. 33–62. Springer, Berlin, Heidelberg (2010)
2. Aleven, V., McLaren, B.M., Sewall, J., van Velsen, M., et al.: Example-tracing tutors: intelligent tutor development for non-programmers. Int. J. Artif. Intell. Educ. **26**, 224–269 (2016)
3. Anderson, J.R., Corbett, A.T., Koedinger, K.R., Pelletier, R.: Cognitive tutors: lessons learned. J. Learn. Sci. **4**, 167–207 (1995)
4. Bransford, J.D., Franks, J.J., Vye, N.J., Sherwood, R.D.: New approaches to instruction: because wisdom can't be told. In: Vosniadou, S., Ortony, A. (eds.) Similarity and Analogical Reasoning, pp. 470–497. Cambridge University Press, New York (1989)
5. Chase, C., Marks, J., Bernett, D., Aleven, V.: The design of an exploratory learning environment to support invention. In: Proceedings, Workshop on Intelligent Support in Exploratory and Open-Ended Learning Environments, held during AIED 2015 (2015)
6. Chase, C.C., Marks, J., Bernett, D., Bradley, M., Aleven, V.: Towards the development of the invention coach: a naturalistic study of teacher guidance for an exploratory learning task. In: Conati, C., Heffernan, N., Mitrovic, A., Verdejo, M. (eds.) AIED 2015. LNCS (LNAI), vol. 9112, pp. 558–561. Springer, Cham (2015). doi:10.1007/978-3-319-19773-9_61
7. Chi, M.T.H., de Leeuw, N., Chiu, M., LaVancher, C.: Eliciting self-explanations improves understanding. Cognit. Sci. **18**, 439–477 (1994)
8. de Jong, T., van Joolingen, W.R.: Scientific discovery learning with computer simulations of conceptual domains. Rev. Educ. Res. **68**, 179–201 (1998)
9. Donnelly, D.F., Linn, M.C., Ludvigsen, S.: Impacts and characteristics of computer-based science inquiry learning environments for precollege students. Rev. Educ. Res. **84**, 572–608 (2014)
10. Dragon, T., Arroyo, I., Woolf, B.P., Burleson, W., Kaliouby, R., Eydgahi, H.: Viewing student affect and learning through classroom observation and physical sensors. In: Woolf, B.P., Aïmeur, E., Nkambou, R., Lajoie, S. (eds.) ITS 2008. LNCS, vol. 5091, pp. 29–39. Springer, Heidelberg (2008). doi:10.1007/978-3-540-69132-7_8
11. Gobert, J.D., Sao Pedro, M., Raziuddin, J., Baker, R.S.: From log files to assessment metrics: measuring students' science inquiry skills using educational data mining. J. Learn. Sci. **22**, 521–563 (2013)
12. Heffernan, N.T., Koedinger, K.R., Razzaq, L.: Expanding the model-tracing architecture: a 3rd generation intelligent tutor for Algebra symbolization. Int. J. Artif. Intell. Educ. **18**, 153–178 (2008)
13. Hmelo-Silver, C.E., Duncan, R.G., Chinn, C.A.: Scaffolding and achievement in problem-based and inquiry learning: a response to Kirschner, Sweller, and Clark (2006). Educ. Psychol. **42**, 99–107 (2007)
14. Kapur, M., Bielaczyc, K.: Designing for productive failure. J. Learn. Sci. **21**, 45–83 (2012)
15. Kirschner, P.A., Sweller, J., Clark, R.E.: Why minimal guidance during instruction does not work: an analysis of the failure of constructivist, discovery, problem-based, experiential, and inquiry-based teaching. Educ. Psychol. **41**, 75–86 (2006)
16. Koedinger, K.R., Aleven, V.: Exploring the assistance dilemma in experiments with cognitive tutors. Educ. Psychol. Rev. **19**, 239–264 (2007)
17. Kuhn, D., Crowell, A.: Dialogic argumentation as a vehicle for developing young adolescents' thinking. Psychol. Sci. **22**, 545–552 (2011)

18. Loibl, K., Roll, I., Rummel, N.: Towards a theory of when and how problem solving followed by instruction supports learning. Educ. Psychol. Rev., 1–23 (2016). https://link.springer.com/article/10.1007/s10648-016-9379-x
19. Loibl, K., Rummel, N.: Knowing what you don't know makes failure productive. Learn. Instruct. **34**, 74–85 (2014)
20. Marks, J., Bernett, D., Chase, C.C.: The invention coach: integrating data and theory in the design of an exploratory learning environment. Int. J. Des. Learn. **7**, 74–92 (2016)
21. Mayer, R.E.: Should there be a three-strikes rule against pure discovery learning? Am. Psychol. **59**, 14–19 (2004)
22. Mitrovic, A.: Fifteen years of constraint-based tutors: what we have achieved and where we are going. User Model. User Adapt. Interact. **22**, 39–72 (2011)
23. Papert S.: Mindstorms: Children, Computers, and Powerful Ideas. Basic Books, Inc., New York (1980)
24. Pea, R.D.: The social and technological dimensions of scaffolding and related theoretical concepts for learning, education, and human activity. J. Learn. Sci. **13**, 423–451 (2004)
25. Poitras, E.G., Lajoie, S.P.: Developing an agent-based adaptive system for scaffolding self-regulated inquiry learning in history education. Educ. Technol. Res. Dev. **62**, 335–366 (2014)
26. Puntambekar, S., Hubscher, R.: Tools for scaffolding students in a complex learning environment: what have we gained and what have we missed? Educ. Psychol. **40**, 1–12 (2005)
27. Quintana, C., Reiser, B.J., Davis, E.A., Krajcik, J., et al.: A scaffolding design framework for software to support science inquiry. J. Learn. Sci. **13**, 337–386 (2004)
28. Reiser, B.J.: Scaffolding complex learning: the mechanisms of structuring and problematizing student work. J. Learn. Sci. **13**(3), 273–304 (2004)
29. Roll, I., Aleven, V., Koedinger, K.R.: Helping students know 'further'—increasing the flexibility of students' knowledge using symbolic invention tasks. In: Taatgen, N.A., van Rijn H. (eds.), Proceedings (CogSci 2009), pp. 1169–1174. Cognitive Science Society, Austin (2009)
30. Roll, I., Aleven, V., Koedinger, K.R.: The invention lab: using a hybrid of model tracing and constraint-based modeling to offer intelligent support in inquiry environments. In: Aleven, V., Kay, J., Mostow, J. (eds.) ITS 2010. LNCS, vol. 6094, pp. 115–124. Springer, Heidelberg (2010). doi:10.1007/978-3-642-13388-6_16
31. Roll, I., Holmes, N.G., Day, J., Bonn, D.: Evaluating metacognitive scaffolding in guided invention activities. Instruct. Sci. **40**, 1–20 (2012)
32. Shemwell, J.T., Chase, C.C., Schwartz, D.L.: Seeking the general explanation: a test of inductive activities for learning and transfer. J. Res. Sci. Teach. **52**, 58–83 (2015)
33. Shute, V.J., Glaser, R.: A large-scale evaluation of an intelligent discovery world: smithtown. Interact. Learn. Environ. **1**, 51–77 (1990)
34. Schwartz, D.L., Martin, T.: Inventing to prepare for future learning: the hidden efficiency of encouraging original student production in statistics instruction. Cognit. Instruct. **22**, 129–184 (2004)
35. Schwartz, D.L., Chase, C.C., Oppezzo, M.A., Chin, D.B.: Practicing versus inventing with contrasting cases: the effects of telling first on learning and transfer. J. Educ. Psychol. **103**, 759–775 (2011)
36. VanLehn, K., Lynch, C., Schulze, K., Shapiro, J.A., et al.: The Andes physics tutoring system: lessons learned. Int. J. Artif. Intell. Educ. **15**, 147–204 (2005)
37. Xun, G.E., Land, S.M.: A conceptual framework for scaffolding Ill-structured problem-solving processes using question prompts and peer interactions. Educ. Technol. Res. Dev. **52**, 5–22 (2004)

Evaluating the Effect of Uncertainty Visualisation in Open Learner Models on Students' Metacognitive Skills

Lamiya Al-Shanfari[1(✉)], Carrie Demmans Epp[2(✉)], and Chris Baber[1(✉)]

[1] School of Engineering, University of Birmingham, Birmingham, UK
{lsa339, c.baber}@bham.ac.uk
[2] Learning Research and Development Center,
University of Pittsburgh, Pittsburgh, USA
cdemmans@pitt.edu

Abstract. Self-assessment is widely used in open learner models (OLMs) as a metacognitive process to enhance students' self-regulated learning. Yet little research has investigated the impact of the visualisation when the OLM shows the conflict (i.e., uncertainty) between the system's beliefs about student knowledge and students' confidence in the correctness of their answers. We deployed such an OLM and studied its use. The impact of the uncertainty visualisation on student learning, confidence gains and actions was determined by comparing these measures across two treatment conditions and a control condition. Those who accessed the OLM performed significantly better on the post-test, and those in the treatment group who could see both sets of beliefs separately showed greater confidence gains and used the system more.

Keywords: Open learner models · Uncertainty · Self-confidence · Visualisation · Metacognitive skills · Learning dashboards

1 Introduction

Lifelong learning requires improved knowledge monitoring skills [1] that allow students to accurately evaluate their own knowledge. These monitoring skills are a prerequisite metacognitive process that is essential to self-regulated learning. Studies have shown the importance of metacognitive confidence and its relation to decision making and academic achievement [2]. It has been claimed that giving students feedback that contains the relationship of their performance to the students' estimate of achievement may be more effective than providing only outcome information [3]. It is argued that the greater the discrepancy between students' confidence about the correctness of the answer and their response, the more motivated the student is to reveal this discrepancy and more time is spent processing the feedback [4].

Research into student metacognitive skills within intelligent tutoring systems (ITS) has explored varied aspects of metacognition which include student reflection, help-seeking, self-awareness and self-assessment [5]. This, however, is not the main

© Springer International Publishing AG 2017
E. André et al. (Eds.): AIED 2017, LNAI 10331, pp. 15–27, 2017.
DOI: 10.1007/978-3-319-61425-0_2

goal of ITSs. Rather, they aim to provide effective personalised learning experiences that fit the needs of the individual learner and thus improve learning [6]. ITSs provide personalisation using a learner model that represents student's knowledge, interests, affect, or other cognitive dimensions [6]. The contents of the learner model are inferred based on the learner's interactions with the system. The evidence used to infer student knowledge may come from consistently demonstrated skills or a lucky guess. This variability poses challenges to model accuracy and is one of the many forms of uncertainty within the modelling process [7, 8]. Other forms include imprecise assessment of learner knowledge and a lack of information. Uncertainty related to students' diagnoses within the learner model has been managed using different methods such as Bayesian networks [9], fuzzy logic [10] or verification procedures [11]. However, learners are not usually made aware of the uncertainty in the model [7].

The visual representation of these learner models are called open learner models (OLMs). Students can be given access to system information about their knowledge through OLMs to help improve their metacognitive skills [12]. Open learner models support improved student self-assessment accuracy [13, 14] and student learning [13, 15, 16]. Some OLMs also show the discrepancy between students' confidence about the correctness of the system's automated assessment and their level of knowledge which provides an opportunity to increase the accuracy of the learner model [9, 14, 17]. These systems present the learner model as two separate visualisations which can allow learners to compare directly between their self-perceptions and the system's beliefs of their knowledge. However, these studies did not use an experimental control condition in order to test the impact of the OLM visualisation method on students' self-assessment accuracy or interactions with the system.

In this work, we focus on visualising model uncertainty within OLMs in terms of the conflict between the model developed by the system (how well students perform on the system's automated assessments) and student confidence about the correctness of their answers. The visualisation of the learner model used a skill meter that indicated the conflict of the two beliefs by manipulating the opacity of the skill meters' fill colour and including an option to expand the model to view two separate skill meters. Opacity is rarely used within OLM, but it has been commonly used to indicate uncertainty in non-educational fields [18], where opacity has been shown to effectively communicate data limitations [7]. This augmented visualisation of the learner model may motivate students to reconcile any conflict shown in their OLM and thus, promote metacognitive awareness. We conducted an experiment in a real class setting to test our hypothesis that uncertainty visualisation in OLMs will impact students' learning, their confidence judgments and behaviour in using the system, such as the number of times the OLM was viewed and the number of questions answered.

2 Methods

To understand better how students respond to being shown the inconsistencies between their confidence in their abilities and their actual answers during learning, we have extended the OLMlets OLM to include the visualisations we previously proposed [19]. This extension uses three versions of the learner model: skill meters that hide learner model uncertainty, a combined model and a version that has the same features of the combined model with the option to expand the model to show two separate models – the expandable model.

2.1   The OLMlets OLM

OLMlets is a tutoring system that provides an open learner model to help students become independent learners. OLMlets identifies students' weaknesses, strengths or misconceptions. The learner model in OLMlets [20] is constructed based on students' responses to multiple-choice questions using the last five questions attempted. Student knowledge can change over time due to learning a new concept, revising previously learnt concepts or simply forgetting an old concept. To manage this temporal uncertainty, the model in OLMlets relies on an algorithm that weighs student responses based on when a question was answered rather than the question's difficulty since questions are expected to have similar difficulty levels within a topic. Thus, it helps to keep the learner model recent. The total weight (t) is calculated iteratively for all questions (q) within a 5-question window, see formula (1). The initial weight (w) of the first question attempted is calculated by applying formula (2). The learner model assigns higher weights to recent responses and lower weights to earlier responses.

$$t = t + (1.3)^q, 0 < q \le 5 \tag{1}$$

$$weight = \frac{q}{5} * \frac{(1.3)^{q-1}}{t}, 0 < q \le 5, \tag{2}$$

OLMlets offers a skill meter visualisation that uses different colors to indicate the students' weaknesses (grey), misconceptions (red) or strengths (green) - see Fig. 1. A fully green skill meter shows the student has answered the last five questions correctly. A skill meter that is half green and half grey shows that the student performed some correct answers and the remaining half of the skill meter comprises incorrect answers. Incorrect answers show the learner has some weakness in the topic and needs to invest effort into his or her learning. The skill meter contains a red colour when misconceptions have been detected. A misconception is an answer that shows the student misunderstands a concept. The misconception library used in OLMlets is determined by the teacher. When a misconception has been identified, a link can be clicked to see a description of the misconception.

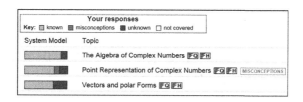

Fig. 1. The standard (skill meter) OLM visualisation within OLMlets. (Color figure online)

To collect the information needed to build the learner model, the answer given to each question is marked as correct, incorrect or a misconception. Also, to collect information to build a model of the students' confidence in their knowledge, students assess their confidence in their responses to multiple choice questions. They are asked "How confident are you that your answer is correct?" and can choose between 'very unsure', 'unsure', 'sure', and 'very sure'. This strategy has been shown to encourage reflection in action, which enhances students' metacognitive awareness by answering questions and thinking about their confidence in their answers at the same time [21].

Uncertainty in the underlying learner model arises when the system's model of student knowledge conflicts with the student-confidence model. For example, when a student selects "very sure" but the answer is incorrect, this shows disagreement between the student's and the system's beliefs. This disagreement is reflected in the model that has been augmented with a specific measure of model uncertainty. In this case, the uncertainty value will be decreased by the weight of the attempted question. The lower the uncertainty value, the higher the uncertainty in the learner model. If the uncertainty value lies between 0.0 and 0.3, the model is considered to be highly uncertain (i.e., Low agreement status). Values between 0.3 and 0.7 are considered to have a medium level of uncertainty, and low uncertainty is defined as values between 0.7 and 1.0. The opacity of the skill meter varies from one uncertainty level to another: high transparency indicates high uncertainty and full opacity indicates certainty or agreement. To study how visualising this uncertainty influences student learning, self-assessment accuracy and actions, three versions of the system were deployed: baseline, combined, and expandable. The two treatment groups (combined model and expandable model) show different amounts of information about model uncertainty.

Baseline (Control Group, Condition 1). The baseline condition used the original visualisation of the OLMlets OLM, where model uncertainty is hidden (Fig. 1).

The Combined Model (Treatment Group A, Condition 2). The combined model shows the levels of agreement between students' answers and their confidence by increasing or decreasing the opacity of the skill meter's colour. The skill meter's fill colour becomes increasingly transparent as the level of agreement decreases (Low agreement). In Fig. 2, topic 1 and topic 3 show high agreement (are fully opaque), whereas topic 2 (Point Representation of Complex Numbers) shows low agreement (the green is less opaque), which indicates that the uncertainty value for the known concept was decreased to a value less than 0.3. The unknown (grey colour) in topic 1 and topic 2 is more transparent indicating the student was confident that the answer was correct when answering the question incorrectly. The opaque grey shown in topic 3

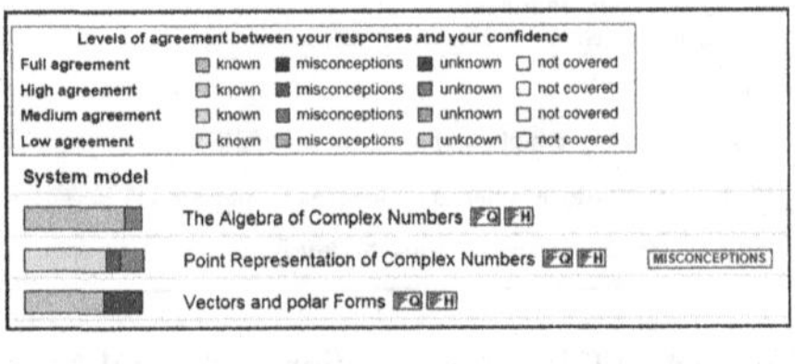

Fig. 2. An example of the OLM for the combined model group. (Color figure online)

(Vectors and Polar Forms) indicates the student fully agrees with the system that his answer was incorrect. The misconception (red) in topic 2 shows that the student may not have the misconception the system has diagnosed because he lacked confidence in his answer, which means he may have guessed incorrectly.

The Expandable Model (Treatment Group B, Condition 3). The base visualisation presented in this condition is the same as that of the combined model. This OLM differs in that students can see more information about model uncertainty by expanding the OLM to view the two models separately (system, student confidence). This expansion allows the learner to compare directly between the two models. The student can expand the model by clicking on "show models" (Fig. 3a). After selecting this option, the model is expanded (Fig. 3b).

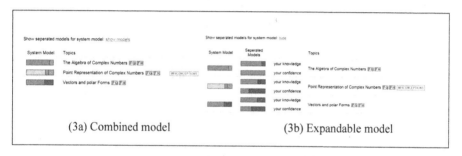

(3a) Combined model   (3b) Expandable model

Fig. 3. An example of the OLM visualisation for the expandable model group.

2.2   Experimental Design, Participants, Instruments and Analysis

To study the influence that the system has on learners in real settings, OLMlets was integrated into an undergraduate mathematics course. Questions related to three topics from the existing curriculum were added to OLMlets. Approximately 25 multiple choice questions were added for each topic. A pre-questionnaire was distributed at the start of the study to explore students' metacognitive skills before using the system. A post-questionnaire was used to explore their perceptions and metacognitive skills following OLMlets use. In addition to students' perceptions, paper based pre- and post-tests were used to measure students' knowledge and the accuracy of their self-confidence in their knowledge. The post-test and the post-questionnaire were conducted at the end of the third week of the study. Students were given OLMlets user accounts and were introduced to OLMlets by the researcher. A user manual was also given to all students. The system was accessible online at all times. Students were randomly divided into three groups. The control group used the original skill meter (Fig. 1). The second group used the combined model (Fig. 2) and the third group used the expandable model (Fig. 3).

Instruments. The pre-questionnaire had two sections. The first section focused on how students plan and monitor their learning and the second section related to students' confidence level while learning. The pre-test used the same self-assessment procedure as that used in OLMlets. The post-questionnaire had four sections. The first two sections (planning and monitoring learning, and student's confidence) were the same for all groups. The third section contained statements about the open learner model visualisation: only students from the combined and expandable models groups answered these questions. The fourth section was given only to the expandable model group; questions related to how seeing the different levels of agreement in a separated model view influenced their behaviour and their self-assessment skills.

Analysis. To calculate student scores for the pre- and post-test, a skipped question was considered an incorrect answer as this method is followed in class settings. Kruskal-Wallis tests were conducted on questionnaire data to identify any significant differences among the groups. After conducting the post-test, student Confidence Gain from the pre- to post-test was calculated to investigate the impact of the OLM on students and the impact of the different versions of the visualisation on its users. Pearson's correlations were used to identify the relationships between students' system usage (numbers of questions answered, number of times the model was viewed) and their pre- and post-confidence.

Participants. Undergraduate students ($N = 110$) from Sultan Qaboos University in Oman were enrolled in a mathematics course called Introduction to Complex Variables, where OLMlets was used to complement their course activities. That is, using the system was voluntary. Of those 110, 79 (36 females, 43 males) agreed to participate. These students were randomly divided into three groups: baseline group (n = 27), treatment group A (combined model, n = 27), and treatment group B (expandable model, n = 25). The pre- and post-tests were completed by 54 students, but only 38 logged on to OLMlets. Those who logged on but did not view the OLM (n = 13) were excluded. This meant that 25 students had used the OLM and 29 students had not used the OLM. Of the OLM users, 9 students remained in the baseline group, 9 students in the combined group and 7 in the expandable model group.

3 Results

We investigated the impact of the OLM on student learning and confidence judgment by comparing students who did not use the OLM to those who used it. We also explored how the OLM visualisations impacted student learning for OLM users (baseline group and the two treatment groups) to see the influence of uncertainty visualisation on student learning, confidence-judgment and actions. We divided the results into five sub-sections: student perceptions from the pre- and post-questionnaire, student knowledge on the pre- and post-test, student confidence on the pre- and post-test, system use and the relationship between system use and confidence.

3.1 Student Perceptions: Pre/Post-questionnaire

Students from all three groups showed similar views about their planning for their learning except for two questionnaire items where there were significant differences between the groups (shown in Fig. 4a). Students expressed different opinions ($\chi^2(2) = 8.39, p = .015$) when answering "Taking tests helps me to identify gaps in my knowledge", with mean rank ratings of 23.78 for the baseline group, 16.38 for the combined model group, and 29.33 for the expandable model group. Student opinions also differed ($\chi^2(2) = 6.37$, $p = .041$) for "Taking tests helps me to identify my misconceptions", with a mean rank of 23.44 for the baseline group, 16.04 for the combined model group and 27.10 for the expandable model group. We can see that the combined model group had more students who felt that tests did not help them identify their gaps or misconceptions, whereas students in the other groups tended to feel that tests helped them with those tasks. In relation to students' confidence, a group-level difference was found ("I try to increase my knowledge when my confidence is high"), $\chi^2(2) = 7.57$, $p = .023$, shows similar differences between the groups, with a mean rank of 22.85, 16.19 and 29.07 for the baseline group, combined model group and the expandable model group respectively: those in the expandable group claim to always try to learn when they are confident (shown in Fig. 4b).

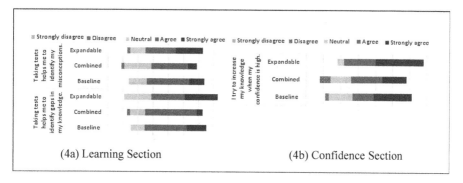

(4a) Learning Section   (4b) Confidence Section

Fig. 4. Pre-questionnaire items where differences were found

Figure 5a, OLM Learning Section, shows the distribution of responses to post-questionnaire items where a significant difference was found between groups. "OLMlets encouraged me to answer more questions" differed significantly ($\chi^2(2) = 7.19$, $p = .027$). The mean rank for the baseline group was 7.39, which indicates that the standard skill meter is less effective at encouraging students to complete more work than the augmented OLMs that were shown to the combined model (mean rank = 14.64) and expandable model (mean rank = 14.00) groups.

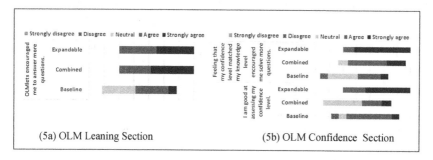

(5a) OLM Leaning Section   (5b) OLM Confidence Section

Fig. 5. Post-questionnaire items where differences were found after OLM use.

Group-level differences were also found in two items related to confidence (shown in Fig. 5b), "I am good at assessing my confidence level", $(\chi^2(2) = 6.80, p = .033)$ with a mean rank 10.39 for the baseline group, 8.36 for the combined models group and 16.83 for the expandable model group. The second item with differences $(\chi^2(2) = 9.06, p = .011)$ was "Feeling that my confidence level matches my knowledge level encourages me to answer more questions" which also had the higher mean rank for the expandable model group (mean rank = 17.17) in contrast to the combined model group (mean rank = 11.86) and the baseline group (mean rank = 7.44). Students from the treatment groups (combined and expandable models) seemed to have comparable abilities for interpreting the visualisation: significant differences were not found in the third section of the post-questionnaire that related to OLM uncertainty visualisation. Figure 6 shows students' perceptions from the expandable model group about the ability to expand the models. Students believed that seeing the two models separated is useful and helped them to be more accurate in assessing their confidence.

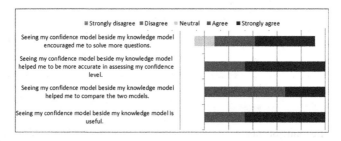

Fig. 6. Students' perceptions of the option to see the two models separated.

3.2   Student Knowledge on Paper Pre/Post-tests

To analyse the effect of the OLM on student knowledge using their pre-and post-test, we compared students who used the OLM with students who did not use the OLM. There was no significant difference between the two groups on the pre-test using an independent t-test $(t(50.92) = 1.62, p = .112, d = .04)$. The pre-test performance of OLM users was also analysed across the three groups: no significant differences were found $(\chi^2(2) = 1.59, p = .452, \eta^2 = .07)$ with a mean rank of 15, 13 and 10.43 for the baseline, combined model and expandable model groups respectively. Table 1 shows student scores on the knowledge portion of the pre-test and post-test for no-OLM users, OLM-users and the three sub-groups of OLM users. Students' post-test scores were lower than the pre-test, which indicates that the post-test was more difficult than the pre-test. However, our focus is to compare group scores on each test rather than the amount of learning from the pre- to post-test. The OLM users significantly outperformed the no-OLM users on the post-test, $(t(51.69) = 2.06, p = .045, d = .56)$ equal variance is not assumed, implying that students benefited from using OLMlets. However, there were no significant differences between OLM user sub-groups on the post-test $(\chi^2(2) = .36, p = .833, \eta^2 = .02)$ with a mean rank 12 for the baseline group, 14.06 for the combined model group and 12.93 for the expandable model group.

Table 1. Descriptive statistics for pre- and post-test of knowledge for those who did not use the OLM (no-OLM) and those who did (OLM, including experimental groups).

Groups		Pre-knowledge		Post-knowledge	
	n	M (SD)	95% CI	M (SD)	95% CI
no-OLM	29	6.21 (2.53)	[5.25, 7.17]	5.52 (1.99)	[4.76, 6.28]
OLM	25	7.32 (2.51)	[6.28, 8.36]	6.52 (1.58)	[5.87, 7.17]
Baseline	9	8.25 (1.75)	[6.78, 9.72]	6.63 (1.06)	[5.74, 7.51]
Combined model	9	7.5 (2.20)	[5.66, 9.34]	6.5 (1.31)	[5.41, 7.59]
Expandable model	7	6.12 (3.87)	[2.11,10.23]	6.5 (2.07)	[4.32, 8.68]

3.3   Student Confidence on Paper Pre/Post Tests

Students' self-assessed confidence in their mathematical knowledge on the pre-test was reliable ($\alpha = .88$). There was a strong positive relationship between students' confidence on the pre-test and students' pre-test score ($r = .80$, $p < 0.001$). Table 2 shows students' pre- and post-confidence scores. A difference in student confidence on the pre-test was observed between the no-OLM group and OLM users ($U = 230$, $p = .021$, $r = .31$). There was also a significant difference between the no-OLM and OLM users' confidence on the post-test ($U = 176$, $p = .001$, $r = .44$), with a mean rank of 21.07 for no-OLM users and 34.96 for OLM users. The post-test effect was stronger than the pre-test one, which reflects that using OLMlets influenced student confidence: those who used OLMlets experienced a small confidence gain ($M = 0.25$, $SD = 0.78$, 95% CI = [−0.07, 0.57]) in contrast to the no-OLM users who experienced almost no confidence gain ($M = 0.06$, $SD = 0.76$, 95% CI = [−0.23, 0.35]).

Table 2. Descriptive statistics for pre- and post-test of confidence for those who did not use the OLM (no-OLM) and those who did (OLM, including experimental groups).

Groups		Pre-confidence		Post-confidence	
	n	M (SD)	95% CI	M (SD)	95% CI
No-OLM	29	2.76 (0.64)	[2.52, 3.00]	2.82 (0.68)	[2.56, 3.08]
OLM	25	3.15 (0.65)	[2.89, 3.42]	3.40 (0.42)	[3.23, 3.58]
Baseline	9	3.41 (0.37)	[3.12, 3.69]	3.20 (0.45)	[2.85, 3.55]
Combined model	9	3.24 (0.47)	[2.88, 3.60]	3.38 (0.34)	[3.12, 3.65]
Expandable model	7	2.71 (0.94)	[1.85, 3.58]	3.69 (0.33)	[3.38, 4.00]

Analysing the three sub-groups of OLM users, no significant differences were found in student confidence on the pre-test ($\chi^2(2) = 2.94, p = .230, \eta^2 = .12$ with a mean rank of 15.78 for the baseline group, 13.00 for the combined group and 9.43 for the expandable model group. There was also no significant difference in their confidence on the post-test $\chi^2(2) = 5.28, p = .068, \eta^2 = .22$ with a mean rank of 9.44 for the baseline group, 12.67 for the combined model group and 18 for the expandable model group. However, there was a significant difference in their confidence gain from the pre- to post-test $\chi^2(2) = 7.58, p = .023, \eta^2 = .32$ with a mean rank of 8.39 for the baseline group, 13.28 for the combined model group and 18.57 for the expandable model group. Both the combined model group ($M = 0.14$, $SD = 0.42$, 95% CI = [−0.18, 0.46]) and the expandable model group ($M = 0.98$, $SD = 0.98$, 95% CI = [0.07, 1.9]) experienced gains. In contrast, students in the baseline group had a small loss in confidence as shown through their negative gain score ($M = −0.21$, $SD = 0.46$, 95% CI = [−0.56, 0.14]), indicating the standard skill meters did not enhance student confidence in comparison to both treatment conditions. There was no correlation between student confidence in their pre-test and their confidence in the post-test for sub-groups of OLM users ($r = −.01$, $p = .948$) or between students' pre-test score and their post-test score ($r = .01$, $p = .967$), but there was a correlation between students' confidence in the post test and their post-test score ($r = .61$, $p = .001$).

3.4 System Use

Using the log data, we investigated the impact of the visualisation on the behavior of each group in terms of number of questions answered and number of times they viewed the model. Table 3 shows the descriptive statistics for the number of questions answered and the number of times the model was viewed between the groups.

Table 3. Descriptive statistics for number of questions answered (No. Q. Answered) and number of times the model was viewed (No. Model Views) by OLM condition.

Groups		No. Q. Answered		No. Model Views	
	n	M (SD)	95% CI	M (SD)	95% CI
Baseline	9	23.00 (6.20)	[18.23, 27.70]	3.11 (5.25)	[−0.93, 7.15]
Combined model	9	37.56 (25.26)	[18.14, 56.98]	3.78 (5.09)	[−0.14, 7.69]
Expandable model	7	59.29 (23.75)	[37.32, 81.25]	8.86 (10.33)	[−0.70, 18.42]

We found a significant difference between groups for the number of questions answered, $\chi^2(2) = 7.62$, $p = .022$, $\eta^2 = .32$, with a mean rank of 8.44, 13.28 and 18.50 for the baseline group, combined group and expandable model group respectively. This shows that adding information about the level of agreement between their confidence and their knowledge encouraged additional learning activity. We also found a significant effect on the number of times students viewed the model $\chi^2(2) = 8.74$, $p = .013$, $\eta^2 = .36$, with a mean rank of 9.11 for the baseline group, 11.89 for the combined model group and 19.43 for the expandable model group. This shows that students who had the option to expand the model were more motivated to know how close their level of knowledge was to their confidence. The log data shows that students from this group expanded the model an average of 4.86 times ($SD = 5.79$) while viewing their OLM.

3.5 Relationship of System Use to Confidence

To determine whether students' willingness to use OLMlets may have been linked to their confidence, we tested for relationships between students' activities within

OLMlets and their pre-test confidence. No relationship was found between their confidence at the beginning of the study and the number of questions that they answered within OLMlets ($r = -.16$, $p = .437$). Similarly, no relationship was found between their score on the pre-test and their OLMlets usage ($r = -.21$, $p = .303$). In contrast, a moderate relationship ($r = .51$, $p = .009$) was found between their post-test confidence and the number of questions answered in OLMlets suggesting that their OLMlets use positively influenced their confidence.

4 Discussion and Conclusion

Our evaluation showed OLMlets use had a moderate effect ($d = .56$) on student knowledge as measured by their post-test performance. While prior findings show that less able students benefit from OLM use [13, 15], few empirical studies show all OLM users benefit when compared against a non-OLM control group [16]. Our findings contribute to the literature by showing how those who used the OLM learned, regardless of prior knowledge. Although, we did not find a significant difference among the sub-groups for students' knowledge, the large effect of the OLM visualisation ($\eta^2 = .32$) was visible in student confidence gains, with those who used the expandable model benefitting the most. A moderate positive relationship between students' confidence and students' knowledge in the pre- and post-test was observed, confirming previous findings [2] within a new instructional domain. This shows that the group who was able to see the expandable models benefited the most. The expandable (separated) model view has been shown in previous studies to allow students to compare directly between the two beliefs (system, student) which can promote their metacognitive skills through negotiation [14, 17].

Our findings imply showing model uncertainty that is due to a conflict between the system and student's beliefs had an impact on students' confidence which in turn impacted their interaction with the system. It has been claimed that showing students information about their confidence in their correctness of answers with their actual answers influences students to try to align their confidence with their knowledge when inconsistencies are present [3]. This supports our finding that both treatment groups answered significantly more questions than the control group. Also, the expandable model treatment group, who could view the model separately or combined, was more motivated to view the OLM than the other groups. This suggests that students benefited from the two ways of viewing the model (combined and expanded). In conclusion, our study supports the claim of the benefit of OLMs on students' learning activities. Also, measures of their confidence and system-logged activities show that adding additional information in the OLM visualisation can impact student confidence and behavior within an ITS. We are completing studies that explore the impact of uncertainty visualisation on metacognitive skills (comparing visualisation against textual description). Future studies could explore the role that negotiation (between learner and system) could play in the interactive maintenance of learner models.

References

1. Boud, D.: The role of self-assessment in student grading. Assess. Eval. High. Educ. **14**(1), 20–30 (1989)
2. Jackson, S.A., Kleitman, S.: Metacognit. Learn. **9**(1), 25–49 (2014). Springer
3. Butler, D.L., Winne, P.H.: Feedback and self-regulated learning: a theoretical synthesis. Rev. Educ. Res. **65**(3), 245–281 (1995)
4. Kulhavy, R.W., Stock, W.A.: Feedback in written instruction: the place of response certitude. Educ. Psychol. Rev. **1**(4), 279–308 (1989)
5. Bull, S., Kay, J.: Open learner models as drivers for metacognitive processes. In: Azevedo, R., Aleven, V. (eds.) International Handbook of Metacognition and Learning Technologies. SIHE, vol. 28, pp. 349–365. Springer, New York (2013). doi:10.1007/978-1-4419-5546-3_23
6. Woolf, B.: Building Intelligent Interactive Tutors: Student-Centered Strategies for Revolutionizing E-learning, pp. 49–94. Morgan Kaufmann, Burlington (2009)
7. Demmans Epp, C., Bull, S.: Uncertainty representation in visualizations of learning analytics for learners: current approaches and opportunities. IEEE Trans. Learn. Technol. **8**(3), 242–260 (2015)
8. Zwick, R., Zapata-Rivera, D., Hegarty, M.: Comparing graphical and verbal representations of measurement error in test score reports. Educ. Assess. **19**(2), 116–138 (2014). Routledge
9. Zapata-Rivera, J.D., Greer, J.E.: Interacting with inspectable bayesian models. Int. J. Artif. Intell. Educ. **14**, 127–163 (2004)
10. Mohanarajah, S., Kemp, R.H., Kemp, E.: Opening a fuzzy learner model. In: Proceedings of Workshop on Learner Modelling for Reflection, International Conference on Artificial Intelligence in Education, pp. 62–71 (2005)
11. Aleven, V., Popescu, O., Ogan, A., Koedinger, K.R.: A formative classroom evaluation of a tutorial dialogue system that supports self-explanation. In: Aleven, V., Hoppe, U., Kay, J., Mizoguchi, R., Pain, H., Verdejo, F., Yacef, K. (eds.) Supplemental Proceedings of the 11th International Conference on Artificial Intelligence in Education, AIED 2003, vol. VI, pp. 345–355. School of Information Technologies, University of Sydney (2003)
12. Bull, S., Kay, J.: SMILI☺: a framework for interfaces to learning data in open learner models, learning analytics and related fields. Int. J. Artif. Intell. Educ. **26**(1), 293–331 (2016)
13. Mitrovic, A., Martin, B.: Evaluating the effect of open student models on self-assessment. Int. J. Artif. Intell. Educ. **17**(2), 121–144 (2007)
14. Kerly, A., Bull, S.: Children's interactions with inspectable and negotiated learner models. In: Woolf, Beverley P., Aïmeur, E., Nkambou, R., Lajoie, S. (eds.) ITS 2008. LNCS, vol. 5091, pp. 132–141. Springer, Heidelberg (2008). doi:10.1007/978-3-540-69132-7_18
15. Brusilovsky, P., Somyürek, S., Guerra, J., Hosseini, R., Zadorozhny, V.: The value of social: comparing open student modeling and open social student modeling. In: Ricci, F., Bontcheva, K., Conlan, O., Lawless, S. (eds.) UMAP 2015. LNCS, vol. 9146, pp. 44–55. Springer, Cham (2015). doi:10.1007/978-3-319-20267-9_4
16. Long, Y., Aleven, V.: Supporting students' self-regulated learning with an open learner model in a linear equation tutor. In: Lane, H.C., Yacef, K., Mostow, J., Pavlik, P. (eds.) AIED 2013. LNCS, vol. 7926, pp. 219–228. Springer, Heidelberg (2013). doi:10.1007/978-3-642-39112-5_23
17. Bull, S., Pain, H.: "Did i say what i think i said, and do you agree with me?" Inspecting and questioning the student model. In: Greer, J. (ed.) Proceedings of World Conference on Artificial Intelligence and Education. Association for the Advancement of Computing in Education, VA, USA, pp. 501–508 (1995)

18. Kinkeldey, C., MacEachren, A.M., Schiewe, J.: How to assess visual communication of uncertainty? A systematic review of geospatial uncertainty visualisation user studies. Cartographic J. **51**(4), 372–386 (2014). Taylor & Francis
19. Al-Shanfari, L., Demmans Epp, C., Bull, S.: Uncertainty in open learner models: visualising inconsistencies in the underlying data. In: Bull, S., Ginon, B., Kickmeier-Rust, M., Kay, J., Johnson, M.D. (eds.) Workshop on Learning Analytics for Learners (LAK 2016), CEUR, pp. 23–30 (2016)
20. Bull, S., Jackson, T., Lancaster, M.: Students' interest in their misconceptions in first year electrical circuits and mathematics courses. Int. J. Electr. Eng. Educ. **47**(3), 307–318 (2010)
21. Schön, D.A.: Educating the Reflective Practitioner. Jossey-Bass Publishers, San Francisco (1987)

Collaboration Improves Student Interest
in Online Tutoring

Ivon Arroyo[1]([⊠]), Naomi Wixon[1], Danielle Allessio[2], Beverly Woolf[2],
Kasia Muldner[3], and Winslow Burleson[4]

[1] Worcester Polytechnic University, Worcester, MA, USA
{iarroyo,nwixon}@wpi.edu
[2] University of Massachusetts, Amherst, MA, USA
allessio@educ.umass.edu, bev@cs.umass.edu
[3] Carleton University, Ottawa, Canada
kmuldner@gmail.com
[4] New York University, New York City, NY, USA
wb50@nyu.edu

Abstract. Prior research indicates that students often experience negative emotions while using online learning environments, and that most of these negative emotions can have a detrimental impact on their behavior and learning outcomes. We investigate the impact of a particular intervention, namely face-to-face collaboration with a neighboring student, on student boredom and frustration. The data comes from a study with 106 middle school students interacting with a mathematics tutor that provided varying levels of collaboration. Students were randomly assigned to a collaboration or no-collaboration condition. Collaboration was associated with reduced boredom: Students who collaborated more frequently reported increased interest.

Keywords: Affective states · Negative/positive emotion · Collaborative learning · Intelligent tutoring system · Boredom · Frustration

1 Introduction

Key factors that influence students' academic success include their emotions and affective experiences while learning. For instance, student interest has a facilitative effect on cognitive functioning in general [10], and a myriad of positive emotions have an impact on academic performance [19]. Even some emotions traditionally viewed as negative can be beneficial, e.g., confusion is associated with learning under certain conditions [10]. In contrast, the negative affective state of boredom reduces task performance [20] and increases ineffective behaviors within tutoring systems, such as 'gaming the system' [7, 8]. Given increasing recognition of the pivotal role that affective states and predispositions play in learning, developing educational technologies that recognize and respond to student affect is clearly important. To date, however, the emphasis has been on data mining and user-modeling techniques to improve detection of student affect (e.g., [6, 10]). In contrast, less work has focused on assessing and evaluating the impact of interventions to respond to student emotion.

© Springer International Publishing AG 2017
E. André et al. (Eds.): AIED 2017, LNAI 10331, pp. 28–39, 2017.
DOI: 10.1007/978-3-319-61425-0_3

In our research, we have investigated a variety of ways to improve student affect as students work in tutoring systems. In the present paper, we focus on one pedagogical intervention designed to (1) to reduce frustration and (2) promote interest by reducing boredom (which is inversely related to interest [3, 8] and has been shown to be especially detrimental to student learning [5]).

The underlying theoretical framework for our research is based on the Control-Value Theory of Achievement emotions, which states that students' appraisals of control and value are determinants of the emotions that they experience. For instance, boredom is due to a lack of value perceived in relation to the learning activity. There are many ways to increase students' perception of "value" – with the present intervention, we aim to increase "social value", by inviting students to collaborate during their interaction with an intelligent tutor called MathSpring^{TM} (see Fig. 1). Unlike other collaborative approaches with learning technologies that involve collaborating via screen time with remote partners, collaboration in the present study is face-to-face, under the hypothesis that a variety of social cues in the interaction might help students to engage with each other and increase their interest in problem solving.

The target domain is middle school mathematics, a challenging topic for many students. By the time students reach high school, they report boredom and lack of excitement in mathematics at an alarming rate [1]. Thus, there is an important need to address these emotions earlier, e.g., during middle school.

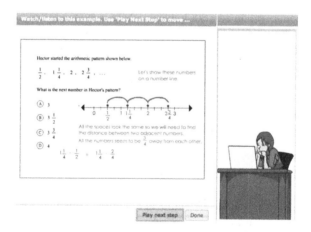

Fig. 1. MathSpring provides math problems aligned to the Common Core Standards in the USA. Scaffolds are provided, such as companions who reflect the student's emotion (bottom, right), hints, animated problems, audio help, worked-out examples, and video tutorials to aid students.

2   Collaboration as a Way to Add Social Value

In traditional classrooms, students often passively absorb topics from teachers, worksheets, and books. Such teaching approaches are marginally effective and produce inert knowledge [29]. Collaboration-based instruction, which is student-centered, differs from traditional teacher-centered approaches because it provides students the opportunity to be active participants in their learning, by explaining to their peers, posing questions, and interacting with one another.

Collaborative learning activities within classrooms have been successful for teaching mathematics [12], both in terms of cognitive and affective outcomes. On the cognitive side, collaboration has been shown to increase achievement in standardized test scores as compared to control groups, with large effect sizes [13, 24]. Moreover, the literature suggests that collaboration can produce in novel ideas and learning gains over and beyond the ability of the best individuals in the group – in other words, collaboration can produce knowledge that none of its members would have produced on their own [14]. Peer-to-peer interactions are vital aspects of collaboration [24, 25], giving students opportunities to question processes, make mistakes, and monitor each other's reasoning.

For the present study, we were especially interested in the affective impact of collaborative learning. Past studies in classroom contexts have shown that collaborative learning has improved student attitudes, such as more altruism and positive attitudes toward classroom life. Collaboration also increases self-esteem, social acceptance, and peer ratings, particularly for students with disabilities [21, 22]. While there is less research exploring the potential of collaboration in online tutoring environments, there are notable exceptions (e.g., [26, 28]) – however, to date research in this area has focused on the cognitive dimension (e.g., learning gains) and not on the impact and effectiveness of collaboration on students' affective states.

Outside the collaboration context, however, there is evidence that tutor features can improve student affect [15]. For example, in our prior work [17], we investigated the impact of providing students access to a dashboard that graphically and textually summarized student performance, e.g., number of problems solved, utility of strategies used, and knowledge gained. While this research did not find an overall impact of this intervention on student excitement, there were indications that the intervention reduced boredom. In particular, the dashboard's utility depended on the way its use was encouraged (either prompted or not prompted).

3   Experiment and Results

The present research was conducted within an established intelligent mathematics tutor called MathSpring^{TM} (see Figs. 1 and 2) [4]. The tutoring system includes a student model that assesses individual student knowledge and effort exerted and adapts the difficulty of mathematics problems accordingly [2]; it also provides hints, tutorial videos and animated worked-out examples with sound played aloud.

For the present research, we extended MathSpring to encourage students to engage in face-to-face collaboration with a neighbor (see Fig. 2). Specifically, MathSpring recorded which student sat next to which student (at login time, students identify neighbors) and subsequently invited students to work together at various times during their interaction with MathSpring – this invitation was provided every eight problems solved or every five minutes, whichever came first. The first student in the pair was free to accept or reject the invitation to collaborate. To increase the likelihood that pairs would work well together, the teacher encouraged pairs who apparently got along well,

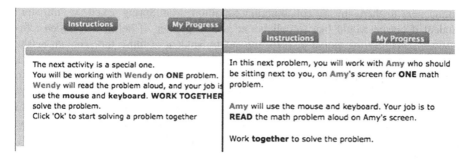

Fig. 2. Collaboration feature in MathSpring invites students to collaborate in problem solving with a peer sitting next to them (a classmate sitting to the left or right). The left screen invites Amy to work with Wendy. Amy might have to wait for a short time untilWendy completes the math problem she is working on ("Waiting for a partner..."). Special roles are assigned to each student to make the collaboration more productive. After students solve the problem together on Amy's screen, they are led back to work on their own computers.

such as friends, to sit next to each other in the classroom, since this can be beneficial for collaboration [18, 23].

3.1   Method

To evaluate the relationship between collaboration and student affect, we conducted a study with students in three 8th grade math classes in a school district in Southern California in the Spring of 2016 ($N = 106$). Students used MathSpring over three consecutive class sessions. Students solved math problems in the following topics: exponents and square roots, expressions, univariate equations, linear functions, angles, triangles, pythagorean theorem and special triangles. On part of the first and last day, students completed pre- and post-affective surveys, which included questions related to affect, including interest and frustration towards mathematics on the pre-survey that provided baseline data on affect. As part of the posttest, questions asked students about their preference towards the collaboration component, if received. Students also filled in pre and post domain questionnaires.

To obtain additional information on affect as students solved problems, MathSpring prompted students to self-report their interest or frustration every five minutes, or after every eight problems, whichever came first, but only after a problem was completed to avoid interruption. The prompts were shown on a separate window and invited students to report on their emotion (interest or frustration). Students could choose to skip self-reporting on their emotion if they wished. Emotion was recorded via a 1–5 point Likert scale (e.g., *"How interested are you feeling right now?" Not at all interested (1) somewhat interested (3) extremely interested (5)).* The software cycled through the two emotions and students typically self-reported several times for each emotion.

The experiment used a between-subjects design with two conditions: (1) *no-collaboration* ($N = 57$), where students worked individually, or (2) *collaboration* ($N = 52$), where students were invited by MathSpring to collaborate with a student sitting next to them. In the collaboration condition, MathSpring asked an "initiator" student if he/she would like to collaborate with a partner. If he/she responded affirmatively, MathSpring would wait for the nearby student to finish the problem he/she was working on and then would invite that student to join the "initiator" to work on a new mathematics problem together. Special roles were assigned to each student, to encourage both students to participate at solving the problem. For example, the first student was asked to use the mouse and keyboard and the second student was asked to read the problem aloud on the first student's computer - both students then solved the problem together on the first student's screen (see Fig. 1).

Teachers running the study ensured that students assigned to the collaboration condition generally sat on one side the room, so that students in the control condition were not distracted by their collaborations. Students were randomly assigned to conditions, with the exception of attempting to place students that got along close to each other within the collaboration condition.

Table 1. Pretest measures of math skills, interest, and frustration in math.

	Collaboration N	Collaboration Mean (SD)	Individual N	Individual Mean (SD)
Mathematics Pretest	42	0.09 (0.15)	38	0.11 (0.16)
Interest Pretest	51	2.61 (1.19)	41	2.76 (1.18)
Frustration Pretest	51	3.15 (1.13)	41	2.93 (1.22)

3.2   Results

We first confirmed that the students' baseline affective survey scores and pretest math scores in the experimental and control conditions were not significantly different (see Table 1). Unfortunately, due to a miscommunication in how the pre and posttest should be administered a large amount of data was lost[1]- we ended up with pretest data for $N = 89$ students and posttest data for only $N = 47$ students. In addition, some students simply decided not to answer the math questions in the surveys, leaving blank answers. This lack of posttest data in particular led us to focus on the data within the tutor ($N = 106$ students), and to use pre to posttest changes as a form of 'extra data' to triangulate the findings. In general, differences in pretest results between students in the experimental and control groups were small (ns), see Table 1.

Relationship Between Collaborative Learning, Affect and Engagement. We examined the relationship between collaboration and three high-level constructs: learning, affect, and engagement: (1) Learning was assessed through students' gain from pre to posttest on the domain questions; (2) The affective constructs of frustration and interest were measured both through self-reports and pre and post surveys; (3) Engagement was defined as a student's "affective and cognitive state during task

---

[1] This experiment was run from the other end of the country, which meant we were not able to personally monitor the administration of the tests.

performance as well as performance" [16], obtained from analyzing students' interaction with MathSpring data.

How Are Collaboration and Student Affect Related? To determine the relationship between collaboration and student affect, we obtained a mean value of self-reported *interest* and *frustration* for each student and condition, see Table 2. We measured both of these affective constructs before/after students used the tutor (*pre and post surveys*) and while they worked with the MathSpring tutor (*within tutor*). The sample size in each condition varied somewhat, due to the fact that some students chose not to self-report their affective state. Students reported both less *interest* and less *frustration* within the tutoring environment than they did during pretest questionnaires regarding their overall interest and frustration with math. This is consistent with the findings of Bieg et al. [9] who found that students tended to report less intense affect within a learning environment than they did upon reflection outside of the learning environment.

All students in the control condition had zero collaborations. Students in the

Table 2. Mean affective differences between students in the experimental (Collaboration) and control (Individual) conditions. Measures are *before* use of the tutor (Pretest) and *while* working in the tutor (Within Tutor).

	Collaboration N	Collaboration Mean (SD)	Individual N	Individual Mean (SD)
Pretest **Interest**	47	2.70 (1.16)	45	2.64 (1.21)
Mean **Interest** within tutor	50	2.36 (1.17)	55	2.36 (1.03)
Interest Change from pretest to tutor	45	−0.40 (1.16)	44	−0.38 (1.45)
Pretest **Frustration**	47	3.17 (1.11)	45	2.92 (1.22)
Mean **Frustration** within tutor	48	2.55 (1.18)	53	3.17 (1.11)
Frustration Change from pretest to tutor	44	−0.53 (1.04)	42	−0.47 (1.15)

experimental condition experienced a range of collaboration activities: students were invited to collaborate from zero to 17 times and students completed collaborations from zero to 14 times ($M = 3.8$, $SD = 3.3$). Some students collaborated only 1–2 times and so were closer to the control condition in terms of their collaborative experience. It became clear that given the present data, a conventional Analysis of Variance (ANOVA) would not be applicable. Thus, our main analysis consisted instead of partial correlations between total amount of collaboration activities and a variety of outcomes of interest, after controlling for time spent working with MathSpring.

In our analysis, we accounted for several types of collaboration in order to better understand how students interacted in the collaboration condition (summarized in Table 3). Since the first student in a pair might have to wait for a partner to be ready, MathSpring asked the first student every few minutes if he/she still wanted to wait to begin the collaboration. Table 3 accounts for events in which a student was invited to collaborate (*Invitation*) and completed the collaboration, as well as a split between whether the student was the *First student* or *Partner* for a given completed collaboration. We also tracked the number of times a student waited and the times he/she declined a collaboration.

Table 3 also shows the correlations between student affective and cognitive factors (rows) and collaboration factors (columns) – note that this analysis includes students in the control condition, all of whom had zero collaborations. For example, Row 1 shows a partial correlation between *completed collaborations* and a change in mathematics interest (from pretest to mean self-reported interest while within the tutor), accounting for time spent in the tutor. This suggests that students who collaborated more frequently had a more positive increase in mathematics interest from pre test time ($p < 0.06$). While this is a positive result, a preference for collaboration may be driving the result – students who preferred to collaborate may have accepted more collaboration invitations, and in turn have been more interested than the rest of the students. However, students did not have a choice for collaborations initiated by a neighboring student, and still there is a significant positive correlation between collaborations occurring in the partner's screen and students' boost in interest since the pretest. Thus, we discard that possibility, and conclude that collaboration is positively associated with student interest.

Engagement. Engagement was established based on output from rules embedded in Mathspring to measure that construct. For example, students could elect to "skip" any problem in MathSpring and be given a new problem instead. A student's work on a problem was classified by MathSpring as *disengagement* if the student either immediately skipped the problem to try a new one, or made an attempt in under 4 s after seeing the problem (we considered 4 s as being not enough time to even read the problem, much less to think about how to solve it). Two measures of *engagement* were collected: if a student solved a problem correctly on the first attempt or solved a problem correctly after asking for a few hints.

The significant negative correlation shown in Row 7 of Table 3 suggests that students who received more invitations to collaborate tended to be less *disengaged*. However, because students with high engagement also declined more offers to collaborate, the relationship between collaboration and engagement is not as clear cut.

Students who tended to solve problems correctly on their first attempt (see Row 5) were less likely to be invited to initiate (i.e., host) a collaboration; therefore, unsurprisingly, they were less likely to work on collaborative problems on their own computers (see Column 3). We suspect that these students were going slower and thinking through problems carefully to avoid making mistakes, and thus received fewer opportunities between problems in which they were invited to collaborate. On the other hand, as shown in Row 6, students who tended to solve problems using hints were more likely to receive invitations to collaborate, Column 1 and to work on these problems on their own computers (see Column 3).

Table 3. Partial correlation R values and significance, after controlling for time spent in tutor.

	Invitations to collaborate	Collaborations completed	Collaborations on my screen	Collaborations on second student's screen	'Continue to wait' for a partner	Declines to collaborate per invitation
1. **Interest Change** from Pretest to Inside Tutor ($N = 86$)	0.04	**0.20**[+]	**0.18**[+]	**0.21**[*]	−0.74	**−0.29**[+]
2. Raw Post-Pre **Interest** ($N = 37$)	0.18	0.18	0.23	0.08	0.26	−0.17
3. **Frustration Change** from Pretest to Inside Tutor ($N = 83$)	−0.06	−0.06	−0.05	−0.07	**−0.27**[+]	0.06
4. Raw **Math Improvement** Post-Pre ($N = 27$)	−0.12	0.14	0.15	0.11	−0.43	−0.34
5. **Total Problems Solved** Correctly on First Attempt ($N = 106$)	**−0.19**[*]	−0.16	**−0.17**[+]	−0.11	−0.1	−0.05
6. Total **Problems solved** where **Hints** were requested ($N = 106$)	**0.18**[+]	0.14	**0.17**[+]	0.07	−0.2	0.16
7. **Disengagement Behaviors** – Not reading, or skipping ($N = 106$)	**−0.17**[+]	0.03	0.03	0.02	0.01	**−0.55**[**]
8. Mean Time to **First Action** (Attempt or Hint) ($N = 106$)	−0.08	**−0.17**[+]	**−0.17**[+]	**−0.16**[+]	0.02	0.2

[+]Marginally Significant $p < 0.1$, [*]Significant $p < 0.05$, [**]Significant $p < 0.01$

Further analyses showed a significant correlation between baseline interest in mathematics problem solving and the number of completed collaborations ($N = 42$, $r = -0.33$, $p < .05$), which indicates that students with lower a priori interest in math problem solving completed more problems in collaborative mode. This helps to explain why students who solved more problems correctly on first attempt also received fewer invitations to collaborate in shared problem solving.

Another result was that students with lower math ability as estimated by Math-Spring using within tutor variables accepted more invitations to collaborate ($N = 52$, $r = -.28$, $p < .05$). This confirms our results from [4] that students who are lower achieving prefer additional support (cognitive, meta-cognitive and affective) – in our prior work, provided by interventions such as animated agents, hints, and worked out examples. Thus students who struggled in mathematics accepted more collaboration invitations, which might help explain why students who requested more hints also received more invitations to collaborate.

Student Perceptions About Collaboration. Results from the open questions in the posttest described students' perceptions about the collaboration. There were 26 responses from students in the collaboration condition to the question "*If you worked with a partner, did you like collaborating with your neighbor? Why or why not?*". Seventeen students (65%) reported that they liked collaborating and nine students (35%) reported that they did not.

The qualitative data was examined based on grounded theory methods. First open coding was preformed on the student open-ended responses wherein the coder parsed and reflected on the data with the goal of naming and categorizing phenomena that occur within. A set of four categories was developed that encompassed approximately 80% of the responses. Then the key properties and dimensions of the categories were identified. Next, during axial coding, the coder examined the relationships between the categories, looking to see how they related. Finally, selected coding was preformed, relating the categories and explicating the storyline.

The themes that came up for those who liked the collaboration, regarded **the partner as a helper**, ("*if it is hard math, the other person can help me because they may know something I don't*"); **shared knowledge** ("*It is like there are two different ideas put together to make a big idea*"); **mutual support** ("*they can tell me if they need help or I can ask them for help*"); and **ease** ("*it makes the work easier and faster to finish*").

Additional qualitative research not reported here but carried out in parallel provided further details on the impact of this collaboration on students' enjoyment and learning [27]. Specifically analysis of videos and surveys suggest that collaboration encouraged students to work together and to enjoy the experience, even though students might not necessarily have followed the prompt scripts to play the roles they were assigned.

3.3   Discussion and Future Work

The present research evaluated the relationship between collaboration and students' emotion and demonstrated that collaboration can counter boredom. Specifically, the more collaborations students completed in the tutoring session, the higher their interest in solving math problems, after accounting for baseline interest before tutoring. The following factors were significant predictors of student improvement in interest: number of collaborations completed, number of collaborations originated on the partner's screen, and number of collaborations originated on the individual's screen (marginal). Students who started off with low interest worked collaboratively more often; in the end, students who needed to boost their interest more also benefited most from the collaboration. Students' reported less frustration within the tutoring environment than they did during pretest questionnaires, but we did not find a clear relationship between collaboration per se and frustration. Results from open-ended survey questions after the tutoring session was completed revealed that students' perceptions about collaborative problem solving activities indicate added social value.

Two measures of engagement were collected: solving a problem correctly on the first attempt or solving a problem correctly after asking for hints. Students who tended to be more disengaged also received more invitations to collaborate, as they were going faster, and more collaboration invitations were accrued in between math problems, every 5 min or 8 problems. In addition, these students declined significantly fewer offers to collaborate. Additionally, students who solved problems on their first attempt were less likely to receive invitations to collaborate, which likely led them to originate and decline fewer collaborations.

According to the Control-Value Theory of emotion [19, 20], boredom is an emotion originated in low value appraisals of the learning task, while frustration is related to low perceived control over the learning task. We hypothesized that inviting students to engage in face-to-face collaboration would provide added *social value* to solving math problems; we did not hypothesize that collaboration might be a tool to place a student in greater control over the learning task. We did expect that collaboration would be associated with increased student interest but not necessarily reduced student frustration. According to the control-value theory, frustration should be resolved by increased control, and not necessarily by adding social value. Our results are in line with these predictions: we found no evidence that collaboration reduced student frustration, and we did find that student interest increased with increased collaboration. The qualitative data helped to support the claim that the reason for the boost in student interest was due to the added value associated with socially sharing knowledge and support.

In terms of future work, we intend to investigate whether our measures of student behavior occur within collaboration problems or as a result of more collaborations taking place. In other words, collaboration may impact student behaviors *during* collaboration vs. *after* collaboration. Distinguishing among these possible scenarios requires further analysis, focusing on finer grain interactions in which data has not been aggregated across all students. Particularly, there are two conflicting causal hypotheses for the results. First, students who solve problems quickly may have more opportunities to collaborate, because collaborations do not interrupt students as they work on a problem and occur only after a math problem is completed. Conversely, when students do collaborate on a problem they may spend time conferring with their partner rather than seeking help from MathSpring; they may be more cautious and methodical in their attempts as well given that they must now reach consensus. These two possible explanations may be at odds: working faster makes collaboration more likely and collaboration itself may slow students down. Distinguishing among behaviors within collaborative problem solving against individual problem solving, for students in the collaboration condition, may help clarify this.

In addition, we acknowledge that various factors may impact the success of collaboration (e.g., preference for collaboration, placing two bored students together might not work, etc.). In future work we will explore these factors and fine-tune when and how students should be invited to collaborate. We also plan to investigate student affect using a finer granularity, to shed light on how students transitioned among affective states (e.g., can collaboration help students become "unstuck" from a state of disinterest/boredom). Addressing this question requires information on student affect more frequently than is provided by the self-reports. One solution to this involves could the construction of student models that can provide frequent predictions of student affect (e.g., interest). These various avenues await future research.

References

1. Arroyo, I., Burleson, W., Tai, M., Muldner, K., Woolf, B.: Gender differences in the use and benefit of advanced learning technologies for mathematics. J. Educ. Psychol. **105**(4), 957 (2013)
2. Arroyo, I., Mehranian, H., Woolf, B.: Effort-based tutoring: an empirical approach to intelligent tutoring. In: Proceedings of Educational Data Mining, pp. 1–10 (2010)
3. Arroyo, I., Shanabrook, D., Woolf, B.P., Burleson, W.: Analyzing affective constructs: emotions, motivation and attitudes. In: International Conference on Intelligent Tutoring Systems (2012)
4. Arroyo, I., Woolf, B.P., Burleson, W., Muldner, K., Rai, D., Tai, M.: A multimedia adaptive tutoring system for mathematics that addresses cognition, metacognition and affect. Int. J. Artif. Intell. Educ. **24**(4), 387–426 (2014). Special Issue on Landmark AIED Systems for STEM Learning
5. Baker, R.S.J.d., D'Mello, S.K., Rodrigo, M.M.T., Graesser, A.C.: Better to be frustrated than bored: the incidence, persistence, and impact of learners' cognitive-affective states during interactions with three different computer-based learning environments. Int. J. Hum. Comput. Stud. **68**(4), 223–241 (2010)
6. Baker, R.S.J.d., Gowda, S.M., Wixon, M., Kalka, J., Wagner, A.Z., Salvi, A., Aleven, V., Kusbit, G., Ocumpaugh, J., Rossi, L.: Sensor-free automated detection of affect in a cognitive tutor for Algebra. In: Proceedings of EDM, pp. 126–133 (2012)
7. Baker, R.S.J.d, Corbett, A.T., Koedinger, K.R., Evenson, S., Roll, I., Wagner, A.Z., Naim, M., Raspat, J., Baker, D.J., Beck, J.E.: Adapting to when students game an intelligent tutoring system. In: Ikeda, M., Ashley, K.D., Chan, T.-W. (eds.) ITS 2006. LNCS, vol. 4053, pp. 392–401. Springer, Heidelberg (2006). doi:10.1007/11774303_39
8. Baker, R., Walonoski, J., Heffernan, N., Roll, I., Corbett, A., Koedinger, K.: Why students engage in "gaming the system" behavior in interactive learning environments. J. Interact. Learn. Res. **19**(2), 185 (2008)
9. Bieg, M., Goetz, T., Lipnevich, A.A.: What students think they feel differs from what they really feel-academic self-concept moderates the discrepancy between students' trait and state emotional self-reports. PLoS ONE **9**(3), e92563 (2014)
10. D'Mello, S.K., Lehman, B., Pekrun, R., Graesser, A.: Confusion can be beneficial for learning. Learn. Instruct. **29**(1), 153–170 (2014)

11. Hidi, S.: Interest and its contribution as a mental resource for learning. Rev. Educ. Res. **60** (4), 549–571 (1990)
12. Jeong, H., Chi, M.T.: Knowledge convergence and collaborative learning. Instruct. Sci. **35**(4), 287–315 (2007)
13. Johnson, D.W., Johnson, R.T.: Cooperation and Competition: Theory and Research. Interaction Book Company, Edina (1989)
14. Johnson, D.W., Johnson, R.T.: New developments in social interdependence theory. Genet. Soc. General Psychol. Monographs **131**(4), 285–358 (2005)
15. Long, Y., Aleven, V.: Supporting students' self-regulated learning with an open learner model in a linear equation tutor. In: Lane, H.C., Yacef, K., Mostow, J., Pavlik, P. (eds.) AIED 2013. LNCS (LNAI), vol. 7926, pp. 219–228. Springer, Heidelberg (2013). doi:10. 1007/978-3-642-39112-5_23
16. McGregor, H.A., Elliot, A.J.: Achievement goals as predictors of achievement-relevant processes prior to task engagement. J. Educ. Psychol. **94**(2), 381 (2002)
17. Muldner, K., Wixon, M., Rai, D., Burleson, W., Woolf, B., Arroyo, I.: Exploring the impact of a learning dashboard on student affect. In: Conati, C., Heffernan, N., Mitrovic, A., Verdejo, M. Felisa (eds.) AIED 2015. LNCS, vol. 9112, pp. 307–317. Springer, Cham (2015). doi:10.1007/978-3-319-19773-9_31
18. Ogan, A., Finkelstein, S., Walker, E., Carlson, R., Cassell, J.: Rudeness and rapport: insults and learning gains in peer tutoring. In: Cerri, S.A., Clancey, W.J., Papadourakis, G., Panourgia, K. (eds.) ITS 2012. LNCS, vol. 7315, pp. 11–21. Springer, Heidelberg (2012). doi:10.1007/978-3-642-30950-2_2
19. Pekrun, R., Elliot, A.J., Maier, M.A.: Achievement goals and achievement emotions: testing a model of their joint relations with academic performance. J. Educ. Psychol. **101**(1), 115–135 (2009)
20. Pekrun, R., Goetz, T., Daniels, L., Stupinsky, R., Perry, R.: Boredom in achievement settings: exploring control-value antecedents and performance outcomes of a neglected emotion. J. Educ. Psychol. **102**(3), 531–549 (2010)
21. Putnam, J., Markovchick, K., Johnson, D.W., Johnson, R.T.: Cooperative learning and peer acceptance of students with learning disabilities. J. Soc. Psychol. **136**, 741–752 (1996)
22. Ryan, R., Deci, E.: Self-determination theory and the facilitation of intrinsic motivation, social development, and well-being. Am. Psychol. **55**, 68 (2000)
23. Santos, J.L., Verbert, K., Govaerts, S., Duval, E.: Addressing learner issues with StepUp! An evaluation. In: Proceedings of Learning Analytics and Knowledge, pp. 14–22 (2013)
24. Slavin, R.: Cooperative learning: Theory, Research, & Practice. Englewood Cliffs, Prentice-Hall, Boston (1990)
25. Slavin, R., Lake, C., Groff, C.: Effective programs in middle and high school mathematics: a best-evidence synthesis. Rev. Educ. Res. **79**(2), 839–911 (2009)
26. Stahl, G.: Sustaining group cognition in a math chat environment. Res. Pract. Technol. Enhanced Learn. (RPTEL) **1**(2), 85–113 (2006)
27. Tai, M., Allessio, D., Arroyo, I., Woolf, B.: Understanding student collaboration in an intelligent tutoring system (in preparation)
28. Walker, E., Rummel, N., Koedinger, K.R.: Designing automated adaptive support to improve student-helping behaviors in a peer tutoring activity. Int. J. Comput. Supp. Collaborative Learn. **6**(2), 279–306 (2011)
29. Waterman, M.A., Matlin, K.S., D'Amore, P.A.: Using Cases for Teaching and Learning in the Life Sciences: An Example from Cell Biology. Coalition for Education in the Life Sciences, Woods Hole (1993)

Improving Sensor-Free Affect Detection Using Deep Learning

Anthony F. Botelho[1]([⊠]), Ryan S. Baker[2], and Neil T. Heffernan[1]

[1] Worcester Polytechnic Institute, Worcester, MA, USA
{abotelho,nth}@wpi.edu
[2] Teachers College, Columbia University, New York, NY, USA
ryanshaunbaker@gmail.com

Abstract. Affect detection has become a prominent area in student modeling in the last decade and considerable progress has been made in developing effective models. Many of the most successful models have leveraged physical and physiological sensors to accomplish this. While successful, such systems are difficult to deploy at scale due to economic and political constraints, limiting the utility of their application. Examples of "sensor-free" affect detectors that assess students based solely using data on the interaction between students and computer-based learning platforms exist, but these detectors generally have not reached high enough levels of quality to justify their use in real-time interventions. However, the classification algorithms used in these previous sensor-free detectors have not taken full advantage of the newest methods emerging in the field. The use of deep learning algorithms, such as recurrent neural networks (RNNs), have been applied to a range of other domains including pattern recognition and natural language processing with success, but have only recently been attempted in educational contexts. In this work, we construct new "deep" sensor-free affect detectors and report significant improvements over previously reported models.

Keywords: Deep learning · Affect · Sensor-free · Recurrent neural networks · Educational data mining

1 Introduction

While intelligent tutors have a long history of development and use, the most widely-used systems remain less sophisticated than initial visions for how they would operate. The systems now used at scale are often cost-effective and have been shown in large-scale randomized controlled trials to lead to better learning outcomes (e.g. [1,2]), but do not reach the full level of interactivity of which human tutors are capable. For example, one positive aspect of human tutors is the ability to observe student affective state and adjust teaching strategies if students are exhibiting disengaged behavior [3]. Student emotion and affective state have been found to correlate with academic performance [4,5] and can even be used to predict which students will attend college [6].

© Springer International Publishing AG 2017
E. André et al. (Eds.): AIED 2017, LNAI 10331, pp. 40–51, 2017.
DOI: 10.1007/978-3-319-61425-0_4

With increasing evidence supporting the benefits of utilizing student affective state to drive tutoring strategies [7], it is important to develop accurate means of detecting these states from students working in these systems. While strides have been made to build accurate detectors, many successful approaches include the use of physical and physiological sensors [7–9]. However, it can be impractical to deploy such sensors to classrooms at scale, both for political and financial reasons. Detecting affect solely from the interaction between the student and learning system, sometimes referred to as sensor-free affect detection, may be more feasible to deploy at scale. However, while these models' predictions have been usable in aggregate for scientific discovery, the goodness of these approaches has often been insufficient for use in real-world intervention.

Sensor-free affect detectors have existed for several years and have been used to assess student affective states using low-level student data as students interact with a mouse and keyboard [10], but also using features extracted from a range of learning platforms including Cognitive Tutor [11], AutoTutor [12], Crystal Island [13], and ASSISTments [14,15]. While these detectors have been better than chance, their goodness has fallen short of detectors of disengaged behavior, for example (cf. [5]). Increasing the accuracy of sensor-free affect detectors would lead to higher confidence in their use to drive intervention.

In this paper, we attempt to enhance sensor-free affect detection through the use of "deep learning," or specifically, recurrent neural networks (RNNs) [16]. Previous affect detectors have utilized a range of algorithms to detect student affective state; we study whether deep learning can produce better predictive accuracy than those prior algorithms. We study this possibility within a previously published data set to facilitate comparison with and understanding of the benefit derived from using this algorithm. Recurrent neural networks are a type of deep learning neural network that incorporates at least one hidden layer, but also provides an internal hidden node structure that captures recurrent information in time series data.

RNNs are most appropriately applied to time series data, where the output of the current time step is believed to be influenced or impacted by previous time steps. In this way, it is believed that affect detection could benefit from a model that observes the temporal structure of input data. Several internal node structures have been proposed, yielding variants of traditional RNNs such as Long-Short Term Memory networks (LSTMs) [17] and more recently Gated Recurrent Unit networks (GRUs) [18]. Applications of these deep learning algorithms have been used in other domains for pattern recognition [19] and improving natural language processing [20]. Performance in these domains certainly suggest large benefits in using deep learning on temporal or time series information.

Deep learning prediction models have not yet been used extensively in educational domains, but have been studied as a potential method to improve the decisions of virtual agents in game-based learning environments [21] and also to improve the prediction of student correctness on the next problem [22]. However, the results of the "Deep Knowledge Tracing" (DKT) model presented in [22] are as yet uncertain; initial reports suggested profoundly better performance than previous approaches, but later investigation by other researchers indicated that the same data points were being replicated and used to predict themselves, artificially inflating goodness [23]. When this error was corrected, performance seemed to be equivalent to previous approaches [24]. Nonetheless, recurrent neural networks may be highly effective for problems with the complexity and the quantity of data available to fully leverage their benefits.

As such, this work seeks to apply deep learning to utilize student information to better detect students' affective states without the use of sensors. We explore the application of recurrent neural networks for the task of detecting affective states using data collected in the context of the ASSISTments online learning platform.

2   Dataset

The dataset[1] used to evaluate our proposed deep learning approach to detecting affective state is drawn from the ASSISTments learning platform [25]. ASSISTments is a free web-based platform that is centered around providing immediate feedback to the many students who use it in the classroom and for homework daily. ASSISTments also provides on-demand hints and sequences of scaffolding support when students make errors. The system was used by over 40,000 students across nearly 1,400 teachers during the 2015–2016 school year, and has been found to be effective in a large-scale randomized controlled trial [2].

2.1   Data Collection and Feature Distillation

The ground truth labels used in this dataset come from in-class human observations conducted using the Baker-Rodrigo Ocumpaugh Monitoring Protocol (BROMP) [26]. These quantitative field observations (QFOs) were made by trained human coders who observed students using the ASSISTments learning platform in a classroom environment. The coders observed students and labeled their affect as bored, frustrated, confused, engaged concentration, or other/impossible to code. They collected affect observations over 20-second intervals in a round-robin fashion, cycling through the entire class between observations of a specific student. Unlike approaches using video coding or retrospective emote-aloud (e.g. [27]), this approach inherently leads to missing labels between observations of the same student. These missing intervals for each student are known, as timestamps are recorded for each observation, and will be taken into account when formatting the data for input into the recurrent neural network; this process is described in more detail in a later section.

A total of 7,663 field observations were obtained from 646 students in six schools in urban, suburban, and rural settings. In prior work [15], a set of 51 action-level features was developed using an extensive feature engineering process; these features consist of within- and across-problem behaviors including response behavior, time working within the system, hint and scaffold usage

---

[1] Our dataset is made available at http://tiny.cc/affectdata.

within the system, and other such features attempting to capture various low-level student interactions with the system. As the observation intervals, or clips, often contain more than one student action within the learning system, the features were aggregated within each clip by taking the average, min, max, and sum of each feature. The end result was 204 features per clip.

In this paper we will compare our deep learning-based detectors of student affect to two earlier sensor-free models of student affect within ASSISTments (e.g. [14,15]). In doing so, we will use the exact same training labels and features as in [15], in order to focus our comparison solely on the use of deep learning.

3   Methodology

We input these labels and features into three deep learning models representing three common variants of recurrent networks including a traditional recurrent neural network (RNN), a Gated Recurrent Unit (GRU) neural network, and a Long-Short Term Memory network (LSTM). The GRU variant was chosen when exploring network structures and hyperparameters for training for both its faster training times in comparison to the LSTM variant and also for its increased ability to avoid problems such as vanishing gradients to which traditional RNNs are more susceptible. The models explored in this work were built in python using the Theano [28] and Lasagne [29] libraries.

3.1   Network Structure

Our implementations each use the same three layer design, with an input layer feeding into a hidden recurrent layer of 200 nodes, progressing to an output layer of four nodes corresponding to each of four classes of affective state. The input layer accepts a student-feature vector of 204 generated covariates per time step normalized using the mean and standard deviation of the training set, and each network ultimately outputs 4 values representing the network's confidence that the input matches each of the four labels of engaged concentration, boredom, confusion, and frustration. A rectified nonlinear activation function is used on the output of the hidden layer, while a softmax activation function is used for the final model output.

Due to the large number of parameters present in deep learning networks, it is common to implement techniques to avoid overfitting. We adopt the common practice of incorporating dropout [30] into our model, which, in a general sense, sets some network weights to 0 with a given probability during each training step. This creates a changing network structure in terms of its interconnectivity during training to help prevent the model from relying on just a small number of input values. In our three layer model, dropout can be applied before and/or after the recurrent layer, and this is explored to determine which location of placement produces superior performance. We incorporate 30% dropout, such that each weight in the network, in the location dropout is applied, has a 30% chance of being dropped for a single training step; many implementations instead describe dropout in terms of a "keep" probability, but is described here as a "drop" probability to remain consistent with the library used to build the models. As is standard practice, dropout is not used when applying the model to the test set.

3.2 Handling Time Series Data and Labels

The dataset used for the previous detectors in ASSISTments, and again in this work, consists of 20 s interval clips to which an affect label has been applied. The recurrent network takes as input a sequence of these clips to make use of the recurrent information within the sequence. The labeled clips, however, are not consecutive due to the design of the field observations, leading to gaps in student observations; during a gap in one student's sequence, the human coders present in the classroom were observing other students. It is possible to represent the non-consecutive clips as a full sequence, however, treating clips that are distant in time as consecutive may confuse the network and reduce performance. For this reason, we treat clips as consecutive only if they occur within 5 min of the previous labeled clip. Clips that occur beyond this threshold form a new sequence sample, resulting in a larger number of samples consisting of shorter sequences.

Another issue presented by the classification task is the non-uniformity of the distribution of the labels. The vast majority, approximately 80% of the clips, are labeled as engaged concentration, followed by 12% labeled as boredom, and only 4% each of confusion and frustration. While it is perhaps encouraging to know that students are mostly concentrating when working within ASSISTments, a model trained with labels in such non-uniformity may bias in favor of the more frequent labels. While it is often beneficial for the model to understand this distribution to some extent, it is better for the model to learn the trends in the data that correspond to each label rather than simply learn the overall distribution.

The original, non-recurrent affect detectors corrected for this issue by resampling each of the labels [5], but this cannot be directly reproduced here due to the time-series input into the recurrent network. In that previous work, the training data was sampled with replacement proportional to the distribution such that the resulting dataset is balanced across the distribution of labels and then evaluating on a non-resampled test set [31]. Rather than representing each sample as independent as in previous detectors, the recurrent network observes a sequence of observations within a single training sample. As such, we resample entire sequences including rarer affective states. Resampling in this way is likely to also resample the other labels as well, particularly when resampling the more scarce labels of frustration and confusion. While it is difficult to achieve perfect uniformity, sampling with replacement is performed using a threshold to balance the labels to a feasible degree. In this way, each sample of the training set is selected at least once, duplicating only those sequences containing at least 20% of one of the less common labels. From the resulting resampled data, we randomly downsample to the size of the original non-resampled training set for faster training times; training on the full resampled dataset did not produce substantial gains in model goodness over using the downsampled training set.

In an effort to further account for the non-uniformity of the distribution of labels, a final normalization is applied to the output of the network. The training data is used to determine the minimum and maximum prediction values for each label that is then used to scale the resulting predictions during model evaluation to span the entire 0 to 1 range (any prediction values in the test set outside of this range are truncated). This rescaling helps to deter the model from making overly conservative estimates of the less frequent labels. The output normalization is found to be necessary in this regard as estimates for the scarce labels rarely surpassed a 0.5 rounding threshold after the softmax activation of the output.

3.3   Model Training

All models are evaluated using 5-fold cross validation, split at the student level to evaluate how the model performs for unseen students. It is often common, in working with neural networks, to train using mini-batches of samples, updating model weights based on the outputs over several training steps. In the case of recurrent neural networks, the data contains multiple time steps that the model treats as a batch and updates the network weights at the end of the sequence. We update the model after each sample sequence using an adaptive gradient descent calculation [32], and categorical cross-entropy is used as the cost function for model training due to its ability to handle multi-label classification; each sample contains a varying number of individual time steps, over which the network makes a single update from the aggregated cost.

Each model is trained over a multitude of epochs, or full cycles through the training set. Training over too many epochs or too few can reduce performance through overfitting and underfitting respectively. The appropriate number of epochs will also differ when applying models of different complexities, as is being done in this work. For this reason, we hold out 20% of each training set as a validation set and incorporate an "early stop" criterion for model training. After each epoch the model evaluates its performance on the unseen validation set to determine the point in training where there is little or no improvement.

A moving average of the model's error on the validation set, expressed as average cross-entropy (ACE) for training, is calculated over the most recent 10 epochs (starting with the 11th epoch). The model stops training when it finds that moving average value at a particular epoch is larger than or equal to the previously calculated average (lower values indicate superior ACE values). Using this criterion allows for a more fair comparison of the performance of each model. Although a maximum number of 100 epochs was allowed, no models in this paper reached that maximum threshold.

4   Measures

We will evaluate the results of each of our model evaluations through three statistics, AUC ROC/A', Cohen's kappa, and Fleiss' kappa. Each kappa uses a 0.5 rounding threshold. This is a multi-label classification task such that each sample has one of four possible labels of confusion, concentration, boredom, or confusion. For this reason, the metrics of AUC and Cohen's kappa are first calculated for each of the four labels independently, and the final result is an average across the four labels [33]. It is not common to report average Cohen's kappa for multi-label classification; we include this metric for comparison to previous results reporting this metric. We also report Fleiss' kappa, which is better suited for multi-label classification, taking all label comparisons into account in a single metric. Both kappa metrics are reported as secondary measures, as AUC is unaffected by scaling and rounding threshold-setting procedures. In all cases, we report performance on the test data, averaged across each fold of a 5-fold cross validation.

5   Results

5.1   Adjusting the Dropout Context

Our initial analysis pertains to the degree of impact the context of dropout has on model goodness. We investigate this question in the context of the GRU model and the resampled training dataset, looking at whether dropout occurs before the recurrent layer, after the recurrent layer, or both. In all cases, a 30% hyperparameter is used for the dropout percentage. Table 1 shows that when dropout occurs has little impact on performance. When dropout is applied to both areas of the model, however, there is a mild reduction in both metrics, suggesting that applying dropout in both locations impedes model training to a noticeable degree. For this reason, all further models reported used dropout applied after the recurrent layer. This placement is chosen as there is a very slight increase in both Cohen's and Fleiss' kappa; additionally, it is more common for researchers and practitioners to apply dropout after the recurrent layer.

Table 1. Comparing locations of dropout within the GRU model.

Model	AUC	Cohen's Kappa	Fleiss' Kappa
30% dropout before recurrent layer	0.74	0.12	0.22
30% dropout after recurrent layer	0.74	0.13	0.23
30% dropout before & after recurrent layer	0.73	0.11	0.21

5.2   Comparing RNN Variants

We next compare a traditional recurrent neural network (RNN), a Gated Recurrent Unit (GRU) network, and a Long-Short Term Memory network (LSTM), which vary in their complexity, and as such in their number of parameters and flexibility of fit. These models are compared using the same training and test data sets and differ only in the internal node structure used for the network.

Table 2. Three recurrent model variants, trained on both the resampled and non-resampled datasets, are compared to the previous highest reported results on the ASSISTments dataset.

Model	AUC	Cohen's Kappa	Fleiss' Kappa
RNN with resampling	0.73	0.14	0.22
GRU with resampling	0.74	0.13	0.23
LSTM with resampling	0.73	0.11	0.22
RNN without resampling	**0.78**	0.19	0.24
GRU without resampling	0.77	0.19	0.24
LSTM without resampling	0.77	**0.21**	**0.27**
Wang et al. [15]	0.66	0.25	–
Ocumpaugh et al. [14]	0.65	0.24	–

In parallel, we examine the effects of adjusting the training data (but not the test data) using resampling, by comparing each model variant trained on the resampled dataset to that model variant trained on a data set without resampling.

The performance of each model is compared in Table 2. In all three model variants, training on the non-resampled data produced superior performance in all metrics over training with the resampled data, contrary to our initial hypothesis. Also contrary to our initial hypothesis, the GRU models did not produce the best outcomes; instead, the simplest model, the traditional RNN, was found to have superior AUC performance to the other models, albeit only by a small margin. This may be because it had the fewest parameters; the RNN trains approximately 82,000 parameters as compared to the over 244,000 parameters in the GRU model and nearly 326,000 parameters in the LSTM model. This smaller number of parameters also leads to the RNN being the fastest model to train. The LSTM model, however, had higher kappa values than the other network variants, and as such, could also be argued to be the best model as it exhibits comparably high AUC values and also would be able to handle longer sequences than a traditional RNN if used in real-time applications. All three deep learning models achieve substantially better AUC than the best models produced through prior work using more traditional machine learning algorithms (e.g. [14,15]). Cohen's kappa, however, is found to be slightly worse than in the prior efforts.

Performance was generally good for AUC across all affective states, as shown in Table 3. It becomes apparent, however, that performance is not well-balanced across the labels. The difference between AUC and kappa values suggests that the model for confusion, for example, is generally able to distinguish between confused and non-confused students, but is poor at selecting a single threshold for this differentiation. The difference between affective states is likely associated with their relative frequency; the best-detected affective states (concentrating and boredom) were also the most common ones. While resampling was chosen

Table 3. LSTM model performance for each individual affect label.

	Resampled		Non-resampled	
	AUC	Cohen's Kappa	AUC	Cohen's Kappa
Confused	0.67	−0.01	0.72	0.09
Concentrating	0.78	0.24	0.80	0.34
Bored	0.76	0.18	0.80	0.28
Frustrated	0.68	0.01	0.76	0.15
Average	0.73	0.11	0.77	0.21

to address this problem, Table 3 also shows that this technique, as implemented, did not lead to better performance.

6   Discussion and Future Work

Despite their broad application in other domains, deep learning models have been relatively under-utilized in education? and their application often has not led to better results than other common algorithms [24]. In this paper, we attempt to apply deep learning to the problem of sensor-free affect detection, using a data set previously studied using more traditional machine learning algorithms. Three deep learning models (RNN, GRU, and LSTM) were compared to previously published work. All three deep learning models explored here obtained substantially better AUC than past results reported using the same dataset, although they did not lead to better values of Kappa. This difference between metrics is not surprising, given that the cost function implemented in the deep learning models does not round each prediction before evaluating each class label, but instead evaluates the degree of error across all classes each training step. Nonetheless, the substantially higher AUC values argue that deep learning models may prove a very useful tool for research and practice in sensor-free affect detection, eventually leading to models that can be more effectively used both to promote basic discovery and to drive affect-sensitive intervention.

There are several aspects of the deep learning models that may have contributed to the improved AUC over the previous machine learning approach to constructing affect detectors for this dataset. In previous detectors, four separate models were built, trained, and evaluated independently while the deep learning model allows all four affective states to be evaluated and updated together with each training sample; such a process likely helps the model determine aspects of the data that help to make more accurate distinctions between each affective state in a temporal sense. Another aspect is in the flexibility of fit supplied by the neural network, allowing the model to capture the high complexity in student affect. This flexibility, however, also exhibits a drawback in terms of lacking interpretability; the large number of parameters and complexity of each model used in this work make it infeasible to study and understand how the model makes its predictions from the features it has available, particularly as it learns from previous time steps. At best, we can understand that the model is relatively better at predicting the more common categories (boredom and concentration) than the more scarce classes (frustration and confusion).

It is desirable to achieve excellent predictive accuracy for the more scarce, yet very important, affective states, in addition to the more common labels. It is possible that a different resampling approach could be more productive, although any resampling approach will be limited by the inter-connection of the observations, leading to non-uniformity across the labels; it is likely that in duplicating sequences containing the scarce labels numerous times, the model overfit to these sequences, which led to poorer extrapolation to unseen data. A possible alternate approach for the iterative refinement of these models would be to send field coders to classrooms working through material that is known to be more confusing and frustrating (e.g. [34]).

One further aspect not addressed by this work is differences introduced by student geographical factors. Earlier affect detectors in ASSISTments were found to perform relatively poorly on rural students when trained on urban and suburban populations [14]. Analyzing how robust deep learning models of affect are to population differences will help us to understand the degree to which these models generalize.

Acknowledgments. We thank multiple current NSF grants (IIS-1636782, ACI-1440753, DRL-1252297, DRL-1109483, DRL-1316736, DGE-1535428 & DRL-1031398), the US Dept. of Ed (IES R305A120125 & R305C100024 and GAANN), and the ONR.

References

1. Pane, J.F., Griffin, B.A., McCaffrey, D.F., Karam, R.: Effectiveness of cognitive tutor algebra I at scale. Educ. Eval. Policy Anal. (2013). doi:10.3102/0162373713507480
2. Roschelle, J., Feng, M., Murphy, R.F., Mason, C.A.: Online mathematics homework increases student achievement. AERA Open **2**(4) (2016). doi:10.1177/2332858416673968
3. Lehman, B., Matthews, M., D'Mello, S., Person, N.: What are you feeling? Investigating student affective states during expert human tutoring sessions. In: Woolf, B.P., Aïmeur, E., Nkambou, R., Lajoie, S. (eds.) ITS 2008. LNCS, vol. 5091, pp. 50–59. Springer, Heidelberg (2008). doi:10.1007/978-3-540-69132-7_10
4. Craig, S.D., Graesser, A., Sullins, J., Gholson, B.: Affect and learning: an exploratory look into the role of affect in learning with AutoTutor. J. Educ. Media **29**(3), 241–250 (2004)
5. Pardos, Z.A., Baker, R.S., San Pedro, M.O., Gowda, S.M.: Affective states and state tests: investigating how affect and engagement during the school year predict end-of-year learning outcomes. J. Learn. Anal. **1**(1), 107–128 (2014)
6. Pedro, M.O., Baker, R., Bowers, A., Heffernan, N.: Predicting college enrollment from student interaction with an intelligent tutoring system in middle school. In: Proceedings of the 6th International Conference on Educational Data Mining (2013)

7. D'Mello, S.: A time for emoting: when affect-sensitivity is and isn't effective at promoting deep learning. In: Aleven, V., Kay, J., Mostow, J. (eds.) ITS 2010. LNCS, vol. 6094, pp. 245–254. Springer, Heidelberg (2010). doi:10.1007/978-3-642-13388-6_29

8. Arroyo, I., Cooper, D.G., Burleson, W., Woolf, B.P., Muldner, K., Christopherson, R.: Emotion sensors go to school. AIED **200**, 17–24 (2009)

9. Paquette, L., Rowe, J., Baker, R., Mott, B., Lester, J., DeFalco, J., Brawner, K., Sottilare, R., Georgoulas, V.: Sensor-free or sensor-full: a comparison of data modalities in multi-channel affect detection. International Educational Data Mining Society (2016)

10. Salmeron-Majadas, S., Santos, O.C., Boticario, J.G.: An evaluation of mouse and keyboard interaction indicators towards non-intrusive and low cost affective modeling in an educational context. Procedia Comput. Sci. **35**, 691–700 (2014)

11. Baker, R.S.J.d., Gowda, S.M., Wixon, M., Kalka, J., Wagner, A.Z., Salvi, A., Aleven, V., Kusbit, G., Ocumpaugh, J., Rossi, L.: Towards sensor-free affect detection in cognitive tutor algebra. In: Proceedings of the 5th International Conference on Educational Data Mining, pp. 126–133 (2012)

12. D'Mello, S., Craig, S.D., Witherspoon, A., Mcdaniel, B., Graesser, A.: Automatic detection of learner's affect from conversational cues. User Modeling User Adapt. Interact. **18**(1–2), 45–80 (2008)

13. Sabourin, J., Mott, B., Lester, J.C.: Modeling learner affect with theoretically grounded dynamic bayesian networks. In: D'Mello, S., Graesser, A., Schuller, B., Martin, J.-C. (eds.) ACII 2011. LNCS, vol. 6974, pp. 286–295. Springer, Heidelberg (2011). doi:10.1007/978-3-642-24600-5_32

14. Ocumpaugh, J., Baker, R., Gowda, S., Heffernan, N., Heffernan, C.: Population validity for educational data mining models: a case study in affect detection. Br. J. Educ. Technol. **45**(3), 487–501 (2014)

15. Wang, Y., Heffernan, N.T., Heffernan, C.: Towards better affect detectors: effect of missing skills, class features and common wrong answers. In: Proceedings of the Fifth International Conference on Learning Analytics and Knowledge, pp. 31–35. ACM (2015)

16. Williams, R.J., Zipser, D.: A learning algorithm for continually running fully recurrent neural networks. Neural Comput. **1**(2), 270–280 (1989)

17. Hochreiter, S., Schmidhuber, J.: Long short-term memory. Neural Comput. **9**(8), 1735–1780 (1997)

18. Cho, K., Van Merrinboer, B., Bahdanau, D., Bengio, Y.: On the properties of neural machine translation: encoder-decoder approaches. In: Eighth Workshop on Syntax, Semantics and Structure in Statistical Translation (2014)

19. Chung, J., Gulcehre, C., Cho, K., Bengio, Y.: Empirical evaluation of gated recurrent neural networks on sequence modeling. arXiv preprint (2014). arXiv:1412.3555

20. Socher, R., Lin, C.C., Manning, C., Ng, A.Y.: Parsing natural scenes and natural language with recursive neural networks. In: Proceedings of the 28th International Conference on Machine Learning (ICML 2011), pp. 129–136 (2011)

21. Min, W., Vail, A.K., Frankosky, M.H., Wiggins, J.B., Boyer, K.E., Wiebe, E.N., et al.: Predicting dialogue acts for intelligent virtual agents with multimodal student interaction data. In: 9th International Conference on Educational Data Mining (2016)

22. Piech, C., Bassen, J., Huang, J., Ganguli, S., Sahami, M., Guibas, L.J., Sohl-Dickstein, J.: Deep knowledge tracing. In: Advances in Neural Information Processing Systems, pp. 505–513 (2015)

23. Xiong, X., Zhao, S., Van Inwegen, E.G., Beck, J.E.: Going deeper with deep knowledge tracing. In: 9th International Conference on Educational Data Mining, pp. 545–550 (2016)

24. Khajah, M., Lindsey, R.V., Mozer, M.C.: How deep is knowledge tracing? In: Proceedings of the 9th International Conference on Educational Data Mining (2016)

25. Heffernan, N.T., Heffernan, C.L.: The ASSISTments ecosystem: building a platform that brings scientists and teachers together for minimally invasive research on human learning and teaching. Int. J. Artif. Intell. Educ. **24**(4), 470–497 (2014)

26. Ocumpaugh, J., Baker, R., Rodrigo, M.M.T.: Baker rodrigo ocumpaugh monitoring protocol (BROMP) 2.0 technical and training manual. Technical report, Teachers College, New York, NY, Columbia University. Ateneo Laboratory for the Learning Sciences, Manila, Philippines (2015)

27. Craig, S.D., D'Mello, S., Witherspoon, A., Graesser, A.: Emote aloud during learning with autotutor: applying the facial action coding system to cognitive-affective states during learning. Cognit. Emotion **22**(5), 777–788 (2008)

28. Theano Development Team: Theano: a Python framework for fast computation of mathematical expressions (2016). http://arxiv.org/abs/1605.02688

29. Dieleman, S., Schlüter, J., Raffel, C., Olson, E., et al.: Lasagne: first release. (2015). doi:10.5281/zenodo.27878

30. Srivastava, N., Hinton, G.E., Krizhevsky, A., Sutskever, I., Salakhutdinov, R.: Dropout: a simple way to prevent neural networks from overfitting. J. Mach. Learn. Res. **15**(1), 1929–1958 (2014)

31. Estabrooks, A., Jo, T., Japkowicz, N.: A multiple resampling method for learning from imbalanced data sets. Comput. Intell. **20**(1), 18–36 (2004)

32. Duchi, J., Hazan, E., Singer, Y.: Adaptive subgradient methods for online learning and stochastic optimization. J. Mach. Learn. Res. **12**, 2121–2159 (2011)

33. Hand, D.J., Till, R.J.: A simple generalisation of the area under the ROC curve for multiple class classification problems. Mach. Learn. **45**(2), 171–186 (2001)

34. Slater, S., Ocumpaugh, J., Baker, R., Scupelli, P., Inventado, P.S., Heffernan, N.: Semantic features of math problems: relationships to student learning and engagement. In: Proceedings of the 9th International Conference on Educational Data Mining, pp. 223–230 (2016)

ReaderBench Learns Dutch: Building a Comprehensive Automated Essay Scoring System for Dutch Language

Mihai Dascalu[1,2(✉)], Wim Westera[3], Stefan Ruseti[1],
Stefan Trausan-Matu[1,2], and Hub Kurvers[3]

[1] Faculty of Automatic Control and Computers,
University "Politehnica" of Bucharest,
313 Splaiul Independenţei, 60042 Bucharest, Romania
{mihai.dascalu,stefan.ruseti,
stefan.trausan}@cs.pub.ro
[2] Academy of Romanian Scientists,
Splaiul Independenţei 54, 050094 Bucharest, Romania
[3] Open University of the Netherlands, Heerlen, The Netherlands
{wim.westera,hub.kurvers}@ou.nl

Abstract. Automated Essay Scoring has gained a wider applicability and usage with the integration of advanced Natural Language Processing techniques which enabled in-depth analyses of discourse in order capture the specificities of written texts. In this paper, we introduce a novel Automatic Essay Scoring method for Dutch language, built within the *Readerbench* framework, which encompasses a wide range of textual complexity indices, as well as an automated segmentation approach. Our method was evaluated on a corpus of 173 technical reports automatically split into sections and subsections, thus forming a hierarchical structure on which textual complexity indices were subsequently applied. The stepwise regression model explained 30.5% of the variance in students' scores, while a Discriminant Function Analysis predicted with substantial accuracy (75.1%) whether they are high or low performance students.

Keywords: Automated Essay Scoring · Textual complexity assessment · Academic performance · *ReaderBench* framework · Dutch semantic models

1 Introduction

Automated Essay Scoring (AES) is one of the important benefits of Natural Language Processing (NLP) in assisting teachers. AES may analyze the degree to which a student covers in the written text the concepts acquired within the learning process. In addition, it should analyze also the quality of the text, that means its coherence and complexity. Latent Semantic Analysis (LSA) [1, 2] was one of the first methods to introduce the possibility of measuring the semantic similarity when comparing a text written by a student to the corresponding learning base. Later on, Latent Dirichlet Allocation (LDA) [3] was introduced as a topic modeling technique that overcomes some problems

© Springer International Publishing AG 2017
E. André et al. (Eds.): AIED 2017, LNAI 10331, pp. 52–63, 2017.
DOI: 10.1007/978-3-319-61425-0_5

of LSA. Even if LSA and LDA are powerful techniques, due to their inherited bag of words approach, they cannot be used alone for evaluating the complexity and quality of a written text.

Our aim is to build a comprehensive Automated Essay Scoring model for Dutch language. However, text complexity is a hard to define concept and, therefore, it cannot be measured with only a few metrics. Moreover, the complexity of a text is directly related to its ease of reading and to comprehension, which means it also involves human reader particularities, for example, age, level of knowledge, socio-cultural features, and even skill and motivation. *Coherence*, the main feature of a good discourse, of a good quality text, a premise of reducing complexity, is also related to human's perception and it is very hard to measure [4]. *Cohesion* is a simpler to handle and operationalize concept that is tightly connected to semantic similarity.

Many metrics and qualitative criteria for analyzing complexity have been proposed, as it will be discussed in the next section, and various computer systems for computing such metrics have become available [5]. In the research presented in this paper, we used the *ReaderBench* NLP framework [6, 7], which integrates a wide range of metrics and techniques, covering both the cognitive and socio-cultural paradigms. *ReaderBench* makes extensive usage of Cohesion Network Analysis (CNA) [8, 9] in order to represent discourse in terms of semantic links; this enables the computation of various local and global cohesion measures described later on. In addition, *ReaderBench* is grounded in Bakhtin's dialogism [10], which provides a unified framing for both individual and collaborative learning [9, 11].

An important parameter that should be considered for AES is the specific language. First, LSA, LDA and any statistical approaches for analyzing essays require text corpora written in the language of the essays. Second, there may be significant differences among languages with respect to the average length of sentences and even words, size of vocabulary, discourse structuring, etc. Dutch language, in contrast to English, contains a high number of compound words (which inherently decreases the number of tokens per phase); moreover, besides compound words, general words tend to be longer [12]. In this idea, this paper presents the stages required for porting the *ReaderBench* framework, which was developed mainly for English, to Dutch language.

The paper continues with a state of the art section, followed by an in-depth presentation of the undergone steps required to build our comprehensive Dutch assessment model. Our evaluation is based on a corpus of student reports in the domain of environmental sciences. While engaging in a serious game, students adopt the role of principal researcher for investigating a multifaceted environmental problem and, on various occasions throughout the game. they are required to report about their findings. After discussing the results, the fifth section presents the conclusions, as well as further enhancements to be integrated within our approach.

2 State of the Art

The idea of quantifying textual complexity or difficulty has been studied intensively over the years, having in mind two major goals: presenting readers with materials aligned with their level of comprehension, and evaluating learners' abilities and knowledge levels from their writing traces. In our current research, we are focusing on the latter goal, evaluating students' writing capabilities in order to discover significant correlations to their knowledge level.

From a global perspective, textual complexity is relative to the student's knowledge of the domain, language familiarity, interest and personal motivation [6]. In addition, the reader's education, cognitive capabilities and prior experiences influence readability and comprehension [6]. In accordance to the Common Core State Standards Initiative [13], textual complexity can be evaluated from three different perspectives: *quantitative* (e.g., word frequency, word/phrase length), *qualitative* (e.g., clarity, structure, language familiarity) and from the *reader and task orientation* (e.g., motivation, prior knowledge or interest). In practice, these dimensions of textual complexity can be used to determine if a student is prepared for college or for a career. The scope of the standard is to reduce and eliminate knowledge gaps by offering students a coherent flow of materials that have a slightly higher textual complexity in order to challenge the reader.

A significant effort has been put into developing automated tools of textual complexity assessment as part of the linguistic research domain. *E-Rater* [14] is one of the first automated systems to evaluate text difficulty based on three general classes of essay features: structure (e.g., sentence syntax, proportion of spelling, grammar, usage or mechanics errors), organization based on various discourse features, and content based on prompt-specific vocabulary. Several other tools for automated essay grading or for assessing the textual complexity of a given text have been developed and employed in various educational programs [5, 15]: *Lexile* (MetaMetrics), *ATOS* (Renaissance Learning), *Degrees of Reading Power: DRP Analyzer* (Questar Assessment, Inc.), *REAP* (Carnegie Mellon University), *SourceRater* (Educational Testing Service), *Coh-Metrix* (University of Memphis), Markit (Curtin University of Technology) [16], IntelliMetric [17] or *Writing Pal* (Arizona State University) [18, 19].

In terms of Dutch language, there are only a few systems that perform automated essay scoring by integrating multiple textual complexity indices. T-Scan (http://languagelink.let.uu.nl/tscan) is one of the most elaborated solutions as it considers multiple features, including [20]: lexical and sentence complexity, referential cohesion and lexical diversity, relational coherence, concreteness, personal style, verbs and time, verbs and time, as well as probability features, all derived from Coh-Metrix [21–23]. Besides T-Scan, various Dutch surface tools have been reported that provide lexical indices for text difficulty, as well as recommendations to reorganize the text: e.g., Texamen, Klinkende Taal and Accessibility Leesniveau Tool [24].

3 Building the Dutch Complexity Model

3.1 The NLP Processing Pipeline for Dutch Language

Before establishing a comprehensive list of textual complexity indices that can be used to predict a learner's understanding level, we first need to build a Natural Language Processing (NLP) pipeline for Dutch language. This processing pipeline integrates key techniques that are later on used also within the scoring algorithm. Multiple challenges were encountered besides mere translation issues while adapting our *ReaderBench* framework from English to Dutch language; thus, we see fit to provide prescriptive information regarding our NLP specific processes.

First, a new thorough dictionary was required to perform a comprehensive cleaning of the input text, by filtering and selecting only dictionary words. Elimination of noise within the unsupervised training process of semantic models, as well as facile identification of typos are important elements while building our textual complexity model. Moreover, as the essays used were academic reports we were also constrained to include low-frequency, scientific words, in order to be capable to grasp the specificity of our texts. E-Lex (formerly named TST-lexicon) [25] is a lexical database of Dutch language consisting of both one-word and multi-word lexicons, and it represented the best starting point after manually reviewing multiple dictionaries. Besides providing a comprehensive list of words, E-Lex was also used to build a static lemmatizer that reduces each inflected word form to its corresponding lemma, therefore normalizing the input.

Second, similar to the requirement of a new dictionary, a new stop words list (i.e. words having limited or no content information) was required in order to disregard certain words for scoring purposes. Again, upon manual review, we opted for http://snowball.tartarus.org/algorithms/dutch/stop.txt which was expanded with numbers, interjections, as well frequent words with low semantic meaning. These words induced noise within the emerging topics from Latent Dirichlet Allocation (LDA) [3] by having a high occurrence rate, as well as a high probability, in multiple topics.

Third, new semantic models, namely vector space models based on Latent Semantic Analysis [1] and Latent Dirichlet Allocation topic distributions [3] needed to be trained. The Corpus of Contemporary Dutch (Hedendaags Nederlands; 1.35 billion words; http://corpushedendaagsnederlands.inl.nl) represented the best alternative in terms of dimension, breadth of topics, as well as novelty of comprised documents. After preprocessing, the corpus was reduced to around 500 million content words from approximately 11.5 million paragraphs, each surpassing the minimum imposed threshold of at least 20 content words. The LSA space was built using the stochastic SVD decomposition from Apache Mahout [26] which was applied on the term-document matrix weighted with log-entropy, across 300 dimensions. LDA made use of parallel Gibbs sampling implemented in Mallet [27] and the model was created with 100 topics, as suggested by Blei [28]. A manual inspection of top 100 words from each LDA topic suggested that the space was adequately constructed due to the fact that the most representative words from each topic were semantically related one to another.

Fourth, complementary to our LSA and LDA models, the Open Dutch WordNet, the most complete Dutch lexical semantic database up-to-date with more than 115,000 synsets, was also integrated, enabling the following: (a) the identification of lexical chains and word sense disambiguation [29], as well as (b) the computation of various semantic distances in ontologies, namely Wu-Palmer, Leacock-Chodorow and path length distances [30].

3.2   Textual Complexity Indices

Starting from the wide range of textual complexity indices available within the *ReaderBench* framework [6, 7] for English language, and based on the previously described NLP processing pipeline, we present the multitude of textual complexity indices that we have made available into Dutch language.

In contrast to the systems mentioned within the state of the art section and besides covering multiple layers of the analysis ranging from surface indices, syntax to semantics, *ReaderBench* focuses on text cohesion and discourse connectivity. The framework provides a more in-depth perspective of discourse structure based on Cohesion Network Analysis [8, 9], a multi-layered cohesion graph [31] that considers semantic links between different text constituents. We further describe the indices integrated in our framework and used for this study, categorized by their textual analysis scope.

Surface, lexicon and syntax analyses. The first approaches to text complexity were developed by Page [32] in his search to develop an automatic grading system for students' essays. Page discovered a strong correlation between human intrinsic variables (trins) and proxes (i.e., computer approximations or textual complexity indices), thus proving that statistical analyses can provide reliable textual automated estimations. Our model integrates the most representative and predictive proxes from Page's initial study, corroborated with other surface measures frequently used in other automated essay grading systems (e.g., average word/phrase/paragraph length, average unique/ content words per paragraph, average commas per sentence/paragraph). Entropy at word level, derived from Shannon's Information Theory [33], is a relevant metric for quantifying textual complexity based on the hypothesis that a more complex text contains more information, more diverse concepts and requires more working memory. In contrast, character entropy is a language specific characteristic [34] and does not exhibit a significant variance in texts written in English. Moreover, of particular interest at this level due to the inherit implications in co-reference resolution, are the different categories of pronouns (i.e., first, second and third person, interrogative, and indefinite pronouns), implemented as predefined words lists and considered within our model. Coverage statistics with regards to specific pronouns usage were computed at sentence, paragraph, and document levels.

Semantic analysis and discourse structure. In order to comprehend a text, the reader must create a coherent and well connected representation of the information, commonly referred to as the situation model [35]. According to McNamara et al. [15], textual complexity is linked with cohesion in terms of comprehension, as the lack of cohesion can artificially increase the perceived difficulty of a text. Thus, our model uses a local and global evaluation of cohesion within the CNA graph, computed as the average value of the semantic similarities of all linksat intra- and inter-paragraph levels [31, 36]. Cohesion is estimated as the average value of [6]: (a) Wu-Palmer semantic distances applied on the WordNet lexicalized ontology, (b) cosine similarity in Latent Semantic Analysis (LSA) vector space models, and (c) the inverse of the Jensen Shannon dissimilarity (JSD) between Latent Dirichlet Allocation (LDA) topic distributions [37].

Besides semantic models, lexical chains provide a strong basis for assessing text cohesion and several indices have been also introduced: (a) the average and the maximum span of lexical chains (the distance in words between the first and the last occurrence of words pertaining to the same chain), (b) the average number of lexical chains per paragraph, as well as (c) the percentage of words that are included in lexical chains (i.e., words that are not isolated within the discourse, but inter-linked with other concepts from the same chain).

In addition, starting from the Referentiebestand Nederlands (RBN) [38], several discourse connectors identifiable via cue phrases have been added to our complexity model in order to provide a fine-grained view over the discourse with regards to the following relevant relationships: cause, circumstance, comparison, concession, condition, conjunctive, contrast, degree, disjunctive, effect, exception, nonrestrictive, other, purpose, restriction, time, and interrogative.

Word complexity represents a mixture of different layers of discourse analysis covering a wide set of estimators for each word's difficulty: (a) syllable count, (b) distance in characters between the inflected form, lemma and word stem (adding multiple prefixes or suffixes increases the difficulty of using a certain word), (c) specificity reflected in the inverse document frequency from LSA/LDA training corpus, (d) the average and the maximum path distance in the hypernym tree based on all word senses and (e) the word polysemy count from WordNet [39]. In order to reflect individual scores at sentence and paragraph level, all these indices were averaged, taking into consideration only lemmatized content words generated after applying the NLP processing pipeline. Moreover, normalized occurrences at both paragraph and sentence levels of all major word categories from the Dutch LIWC dictionary [40] have been considered, providing additional insights in terms of underlying concept categories.

3.3   Automated Text Segmentation

The previously introduced textual complexity indices become less relevant when facing longer documents comprising of thousands or tens of thousands of words. Besides the computational power required for building a complete CNA graph that captures all potential cohesive links, different sections might exhibit different traits which can be easily disregarded at document level. A commonly encountered approach is to automatically split longer texts using an imposed fixed window of words. The most frequently used threshold value is of 1,000 words [5]. However, this method fails to consider the natural discourse structure of the text, its hierarchical decomposition, as most documents contain sections, subsections and so forth, constituent elements that emerge as a more viable manner of splitting the text. Therefore, the headings from the initial document produce a hierarchical structure in which each section contains its own text and list of subsections that can be possibly empty.

Thus, we developed a new segmentation method applicable for Microsoft Word documents, assuming that sections are correctly annotated with the appropriate heading styles reflecting its hierarchical structure (e.g., Heading 1 is automatically considered as a section, Heading 2 a subsection, Heading 3 a subsubsection, etc.). From a technical perspective, due to the constraint that the entire framework is written entirely in Java, we have opted to rely on the Apache POI library (https://poi.apache.org) for parsing the *.docx* documents. The newly generated meta-document contains multiple layers of well-defined and self-contained document segments on which we can apply the previously introduced textual complexity indices. The results for each textual complexity index and for each extracted section are averaged in order to obtain the scores for the entire meta-document.

4   Results

4.1   Corpus

The corpus used for performing a preliminary validation of our model consisted of 173 technical reports in Dutch written by master degree students from the Open University of the Netherlands and Utrecht University. The students play an online game in the domain of environmental policy, which confronts them multidimensional environmental problems. During the game, they are required to upload technical reports about their findings, in subsequent stages (i.e., analysis, 2 design tasks, 2 evaluation tasks and a final evaluation) [41]. As these reports need to be evaluated manually by teachers in very short time spans, the need for Automated Essay Scoring arose. All essays are scored by human tutors on the bases of an assessment framework and scores express a linear variable ranging from 1 (utterly weak) to 10 (excellent). The reports used for this experiment address only the first stage (i.e., analysis) and contained an average of 1832 words (SD = 790), ranging from a minimum of 243 words to a maximum of 6186 words. All reports were manually corrected in terms of formatting in order to ensure an appropriate usage of heading styles, a process that afterwards facilitates their automated assessment.

Because of the limited number of students whose scores span multiple levels, we applied a binary split of student scores into two distinct classes: high performance students with scores ≥ 7, while the rest were catalogued as low performance students. Moreover, for the scope of these preliminary experiments, we opted to rely only on the LDA topic model besides WordNet, instead of both LSA and LDA. This was due to the fact that only the LDA space was inspected by native speakers with regards to comprising relevantword associations within corresponding topics.

4.2   Statistical Analyses

The Dutch indices from *ReaderBench* that lacked normal distributions were discarded (e.g., average number of sentences, words and content words, average number of commas at paragraphs and sentence levels, word polysemy counts, different connectors and word lists at paragraph and sentence level). Correlations between the selected indices and the dependent variable (the students' score for their technical report) were then calculated for the remaining indices to determine whether there was a statistically significant relation ($p < .05$). Indices that were highly collinear ($r \geq .9$) were flagged, and the index with the strongest correlation with the assigned score corresponding to each report was retained, while the other indices were removed. The remaining indices were included as predictor variables in a stepwise regression to explain the variance in the students' scores, as well as predictors in a Discriminant Function Analysis [42] used to classify students based on their performance.

4.3   Relationship Between *ReaderBench* and Students' Final Scores

To address our research question of automatically scoring students' reports, we conducted correlations between the *ReaderBench* indices that were normally distributed and were not multicollinear and their final scores. As shown in Table 1, medium to weak effects were found for *ReaderBench* indices related to the number of words, paragraphs, unique words per sentence, lexical chains, lower local cohesion induced by a more varied vocabulary (higher word entropy), different types of discourse connectors at both sentence and paragraph levels (concession, condition, circumstance), as well as pronouns (both third person and indefinite).

Table 1. Correlations between *ReaderBench* indices and report score.

Index	r	p
Logarithmic number of words	.461	<.001
Average number of lexical chains per paragraph	.338	<.001
Average sentence-paragraph cohesion (Wu-Palmer semantic distance in WordNet)	-.284	<.001
Average number of concession connectors per paragraph	.269	<.001
Average number of condition connectors per paragraph	.260	.001
Word entropy	.258	.001
Average number of circumstance connectors per paragraph	.254	.001
Percentage of words that are included in lexical chains	.250	.001
Average number of indefinite pronouns per sentence	.237	.002
Average sentence length (number of characters)	.193	.011
Average number of third person pronouns per sentence	.187	.014
Average number of circumstance connectors per sentence	.187	.014
Average number of unique content words per sentence	.184	.015
Number of paragraphs	.160	.035
Average number of condition connectors per sentence	.154	.044

The correlations indicate that students who received higher scores had longer reports in terms of words and paragraphs, greater word entropy, used more discourse connectors and pronouns, and produced more unique words. Moreover, students who received higher scores had lower inner cohesion per paragraph, indicating more elaborated paragraphs that reflect a mixture of diverse ideas.

4.4   Regression Analysis and Discriminant Function Analysis

To analyze which *ReaderBench* features best predicted the students' score, we conducted a stepwise regression analysis using the 15 significant indices as the independent variables. This yielded a significant model, $F(3, 169) = 24.676$, $p < .001$, $r = .552$, $R^2 = .305$. Three variables were significant and positive predictors of report scores: logarithmic number of words, average number of pronouns per sentence (indefinite), percentage of words that are included in lexical chains. These variables explained 30.5% of the variance in the students' report scores.

The stepwise Discriminant Function Analysis (DFA) retained three different variables as significant predictors (i.e., 1. logarithmic number of words, 2. average number of indefinite pronouns per sentence, and 3. average sentence-paragraph cohesion using Wu-Palmer semantic distance), and removed the remaining variables as non-significant predictors.

Table 2. Confusion matrix for DFA classifying students based on performance

		Predicted performance membership		Total
		Low	High	
Whole set	Low	54	21	75
	High	20	78	98
Cross-validated	Low	53	22	71
	High	21	77	98

The results prove that the DFA using these three indices correctly allocated 132 of the 173 students from our dataset, $\chi^2(df = 3, n = 173) = 40.948$, $p < .001$, for an accuracy of 76.3% (the chance level for this analysis is 50%). For the leave-one-out cross-validation (LOOCV), the discriminant analysis allocated 130 of the 173 students for an accuracy of 75.1% (see the confusion matrix reported in Table 2 for results). The measure of agreement between the actual student performance and that assigned by our model produced a weighted Cohen's Kappa of .517, demonstrating moderate agreement.

5   Conclusions

The *ReaderBench* NLP framework was extended to support automatic scoring of students' technical reports written in Dutch language. Existing textual complexity indices and methods had to be adapted from English language, and specifically tweaked for Dutch language, thus introducing one of the most comprehensive models available for Dutch to our knowing. Moreover, we have also introduced an automatic segmentation method that creates a hierarchical structure based on document sections and headings.

Initial results indicate that our model, which goes beyond the replication of the English version of *ReaderBench* due to the performed customizations, has a high accuracy and is suitable for automatically scoring Dutch technical reports. In addition, the performance of our model is comparable to systems available in English language. Our framework integrates the widest range of textual complexity indices available for Dutch language, emphasizing the semantic dimension of the analysis instead of frequently used surface measures. Nevertheless, we must point out that the variance explained by the regression model, as well as the weighted Cohen's Kappa, are rather low in contrast to the accuracy of the DFA model which only assumes a binary classification. Only the index with the highest correlation (i.e., logarithmic number of words) was retained in both the linear regression and in the DFA model. The remaining indices are specific for each model that is fundamentally different – the regression model predicts a linear score, while the DFA performs a classification into two performance categories.

As limitations, we must also point out the discrepancies in the evaluation of the technical reports as the automatic evaluation is mostly focused on students' writing style, while the tutors evaluate the technical quality of the report. Moreover, the population for our study consists of master degree students who have, in general, relatively high writing skills; in return, this may reduce the variance in complexity among the essays. Therefore, new metrics should be introduced in order to address the technical soundness of a document in relation to a given theme or an imposed set of topics of interest. Moreover, the Dutch language imposes additional challenges, like the high number of compound words. While relating to the process of building semantic models, these words could be more relevant if taken separately. Thus, automated splitting rules should be enforced upon compound words in order to provide a clearer contextualization of the input text.

Acknowledgments. This work was partially funded by the 644187 EC H2020 *Realising an Applied Gaming Eco-system* (RAGE) project, by the FP7 208-212578 LTfLL project, as well as by University Politehnica of Bucharest through the "Excellence Research Grants" Program UPB–GEX 12/26.09.2016.

References

1. Landauer, T.K., Dumais, S.T.: A solution to Plato's problem: the Latent Semantic Analysis theory of acquisition, induction and representation of knowledge. Psychol. Rev. **104**(2), 211–240 (1997)
2. Miller, T.: Essay assessment with Latent Semantic Analysis. J. Educ. Comput. Res. **29**(4), 495–512 (2003)
3. Blei, D.M., Ng, A.Y., Jordan, M.I.: Latent Dirichlet Allocation. J. Mach. Learn. Res. **3**(4–5), 993–1022 (2003)
4. Crossley, S.A., McNamara, D.S.: Text coherence and judgments of essay quality: models of quality and coherence. In: 33rd Annual Conference of the Cognitive Science Society, pp. 1236–1231. Cognitive Science Society, Boston (2011)

5. Nelson, J., Perfetti, C., Liben, D., Liben, M.: Measures of Text Difficulty: Testing their Predictive Value for Grade Levels and Student Performance. Council of Chief State School Officers, Washington, DC (2012)

6. Dascalu, M.: Analyzing Discourse and text complexity for learning and collaborating, Studies in Computational Intelligence, vol. 534. Springer, Cham (2014)

7. Dascalu, M., Dessus, P., Bianco, M., Trausan-Matu, S., Nardy, A.: Mining texts, learner productions and strategies with *ReaderBench*. In: Peña-Ayala, A. (ed.) Educational Data Mining. SCI, vol. 524, pp. 345–377. Springer, Cham (2014). doi:10.1007/978-3-319-02738-8_13

8. Dascalu, M., McNamara, D.S., Trausan-Matu, S., Stavarache, L.L., Allen, L.K.: Cohesion network analysis of CSCL participation. Behavior Research Methods, PP. 1–16 (2017)

9. Dascalu, M., Trausan-Matu, S., McNamara, D.S., Dessus, P.: ReaderBench – automated evaluation of collaboration based on cohesion and dialogism. Int. J. Comput. Support. Collaborative Learn. **10**(4), 395–423 (2015)

10. Bakhtin, M.M.: The dialogic imagination: four essays. The University of Texas Press, Austin (1981)

11. Dascalu, M., Allen, K.A., McNamara, D.S., Trausan-Matu, S., Crossley, S.A.: Modeling comprehension processes via automated analyses of dialogism. In: 39th Annual Meeting of the Cognitive Science Society (CogSci 2017). Cognitive Science Society, London (2017, in Press)

12. Duyck, W., Desmet, T., Verbeke, L.P., Brysbaert, M.: WordGen: A tool for word selection and nonword generation in Dutch, English, German, and French. Behav. Res. Methods **36**(3), 488–499 (2004)

13. National Governors Association Center for Best Practices & Council of Chief State School Officers: Common Core State Standards. Authors, Washington D.C. (2010)

14. Powers, D.E., Burstein, J., Chodorow, M., Fowles, M.E., Kukich, K.: Stumping e-rater®: Challenging the Validity of Automated Essay Scoring. Educational Testing Service, Princeton (2001)

15. McNamara, D.S., Graesser, A.C., Louwerse, M.M.: Sources of text difficulty: Across the ages and genres. In: Sabatini, J.P., Albro, E., O'Reilly, T. (eds.) Measuring up: Advances in How we Assess Reading Ability, pp. 89–116. R&L Education, Lanham (2012)

16. Williams, R., Dreher, H.: Automatically grading essays with Markit©. J. Issues Informing Sci. Inform. Technol. **1**, 693–700 (2004)

17. Elliot, S.: IntelliMetric: from here to validity. In: Shermis, M.D., Burstein, J.C. (eds.) Automated Essay Scoring: A Cross Disciplinary Approach, pp. 71–86. Lawrence Erlbaum Associates, Mahwah (2003)

18. Crossley, S.A., Allen, L.K., McNamara, D.S.: The Writing Pal: a writing strategy tutor. In: Crossley, S.A., McNamara, D.S. (eds.) Handbook on Educational Technologies for Literacy. Taylor & Francis, Routledge, New York (in press)

19. McNamara, D.S., Crossley, S.A., Roscoe, R., Allen, L.K., Dai, J.: A hierarchical classification approach to automated essay scoring. Assessing Writ. **23**, 35–59 (2015)

20. Pander Maat, H.L.W., Kraf, R.L., van den Bosch, A., van Gompel, M., Kleijn, S., Sanders, T.J.M., van der Sloot, K.: T-Scan: a new tool for analyzing Dutch text. Comput. Linguist. Neth. J. **4**, 53–74 (2014)

21. Graesser, A.C., McNamara, D.S., Louwerse, M.M., Cai, Z.: Coh-Metrix: Analysis of text on cohesion and language. Behav. Res. Methods Instrum. Comput. **36**(2), 193–202 (2004)

22. Graesser, A.C., McNamara, D.S., Kulikowich, J.M.: Coh-Metrix: Providing multilevel analyses of text characteristics. Educ. Res. **40**(5), 223–234 (2011)

23. McNamara, D.S., Graesser, A.C., McCarthy, P., Cai, Z.: Automated Evaluation of Text and Discourse with Coh-Metrix. Cambridge University Press, Cambridge (2014)

24. Kraf, R., Lentz, L., Pander Maat, H.: Drie Nederlandse instrumenten voor het automatisch voorspellen van begrijpelijkheid. Een klein consumentenonderzoek. Tijdschift voor Taalbeheersing **33**(3), 249–265 (2011)
25. CGN Consortium: e-Lex, lexicale databank (lexical database). Instituut voor Nederlandse Taal, Leiden, the Netherlands (2017)
26. Owen, S., Anil, R., Dunning, T., Friedman, E.: Mahout in Action. Manning Publications Co., Greenwich (2011)
27. McCallum, A.K.: MALLET: A Machine Learning for Language Toolkit (2002). http://mallet.cs.umass.edu/
28. Blei, D.M.: Probabilistic topic models. Commun. ACM **55**(4), 77–84 (2012)
29. Galley, M., McKeown, K.: Improving word sense disambiguation in lexical chaining. In: 18th International Joint Conference on Artificial Intelligence (IJCAI 2003), pp. 1486–1488. Morgan Kaufmann Publishers, Inc., Acapulco (2003)
30. Budanitsky, A., Hirst, G.: Evaluating WordNet-based measures of lexical semantic relatedness. Comput. Linguist. **32**(1), 13–47 (2006)
31. Trausan-Matu, S., Dascalu, M., Dessus, P.: Textual complexity and discourse structure in computer-supported collaborative learning. In: Cerri, Stefano A., Clancey, William J., Papadourakis, G., Panourgia, K. (eds.) ITS 2012. LNCS, vol. 7315, pp. 352–357. Springer, Heidelberg (2012). doi:10.1007/978-3-642-30950-2_46
32. Wresch, W.: The imminence of grading essays by computer—25 years later. Comput. Compos. **10**(2), 45–58 (1993)
33. Shannon, C.E.: Prediction and entropy of printed English. Bell Syst. Tech. J. **30**, 50–64 (1951)
34. Gervasi, V., Ambriola, V.: Quantitative assessment of textual complexity. In: Barbaresi, M.L. (ed.) Complexity in Language and Text, pp. 197–228. Plus, Pisa, Italy (2002)
35. van Dijk, T.A., Kintsch, W.: Strategies of Discourse Comprehension. Academic Press, New York (1983)
36. Dascalu, M., Dessus, P., Trausan-Matu, Ş., Bianco, M., Nardy, A.: *ReaderBench*, an environment for analyzing text complexity and reading strategies. In: Lane, H.Chad, Yacef, K., Mostow, J., Pavlik, P. (eds.) AIED 2013. LNCS, vol. 7926, pp. 379–388. Springer, Heidelberg (2013). doi:10.1007/978-3-642-39112-5_39
37. Manning, C.D., Schütze, H.: Foundations of statistical Natural Language Processing. MIT Press, Cambridge (1999)
38. van der Vliet, H.: The Referentiebestand Nederlands as a multi-purpose lexical database. Int. J. Lexicogr. **20**(3), 239–257 (2007)
39. Miller, G.A.: WordNet: a lexical database for English. Commun. ACM **38**(11), 39–41 (1995)
40. Zijlstra, H., van Meerveld, T., van Middendorp, H., Pennebaker, J.W., Geenen, R.: De Nederlandse versie van de Linguistic Inquiry and Word Count (LIWC), een gecomputeriseerd tekstanalyseprogramma [Dutch version of the Linguistic Inquiry and Word Count (LIWC), a computerized text analysis program]. Gedrag & Gezondheid **32**, 273–283 (2004)
41. Westera, W., Nadolski, N., Hummel, H.: Serious gaming analytics: what students' log files tell us about gaming and learning. Int. J. Serious Games **1**(2), 35–50 (2014)
42. Klecka, W.R.: Discriminant Analysis. Quantitative Applications in the Social Sciences Series, vol. 19. Sage Publications, Thousand Oaks (1980)

Keeping the Teacher in the Loop: Technologies for Monitoring Group Learning in Real-Time

Avi Segal[1], Shaked Hindi[1], Naomi Prusak[2], Osama Swidan[2], Adva Livni[2], Alik Palatnic[2], Baruch Schwarz[2], and Ya'akov (Kobi) Gal[1(✉)]

[1] Ben-Gurion University of the Negev, Beersheba, Israel
kobig@bgu.ac.il
[2] Hebrew University of Jerusalem, Jerusalem, Israel

Abstract. Learning in groups allows students to develop academic and social competencies but requires the presence of a human teacher that is actively guiding the group. In this paper we combine data-mining and visualization tools to support teachers' understanding of learners' activities in an inquiry based learning environment. We use supervised learning to recognize salient states of activity in the group's work, such as reaching a solution to a problem, exhibiting idleness, or experiencing technical challenges. These "critical" moments are visualized to teachers in real time, allowing them to monitor several groups in parallel and to intervene when necessary to guide the group. We embedded this technology in a new system, called SAGLET, which augments existing collaborative educational software and was evaluated empirically in real classrooms. We show that the recognition capabilities of SAGLET are compatible with that of a human domain expert. Teachers were able to use the system successfully to make intervention decisions in groups when deemed necessary, without overwhelming them with information. Our results demonstrate how AI can be used to augment existing educational environments to support the "teacher in the group", and to scale up the benefits of group learning to the actual classroom.

1 Introduction

Group learning has been shown to develop academic and social competencies and to foster knowledge creation and idea development [22,27]. A chief example of activities where group learning has been shown to be preferable includes inquiry based learning in mathematics and in science [16,28]. Other examples include educational domains requiring critical dialogues such as history or civic education [15].

As students increasingly communicate using technology, this creates new opportunities for realizing the benefits of group learning in distance learning and on line settings. However, the benefits of group learning (whether face-to-face or mediated by a computer) rarely materialize without a human teacher that is actively monitoring and guiding the group [14]. When several groups work in parallel, as in a classroom or on-line setting, the burden of moderating

© Springer International Publishing AG 2017
E. André et al. (Eds.): AIED 2017, LNAI 10331, pp. 64–76, 2017.
DOI: 10.1007/978-3-319-61425-0_6

these groups can become overwhelming, and teachers are not able to provide or do not have enough information to propose proper support for each student [25].

This paper addresses this gap by combining machine learning and visualization methods to improve teacher's ability to monitor and support group learning in the classroom. It describes the SAGLET system (System for Advancing Group Learning in Educational Technologies) which allows teachers to monitor and moderate student groups working together in a shared space. SAGLET augments existing collaborative educational environments to include technological tools with the capabilities for (1) recognizing critical moments of emergent learning in groups, and (2) providing automatic feedback to teachers in the form of alerts that they may use in order to track multiple groups engaging in parallel on a learning task and intervene when deemed necessary.

Students used an inquiry based geometry setting that supports a shared interaction space as well as the ability to converse with each other in free text [25]. We collected 37 sessions of groups of two or three students solving different inquiry-based Geometry problems requiring the testing of hypotheses and manipulating geometrical objects [7].

SAGLET provides a set of alerts for teachers that recognize whether a group has reached consensus about a (possibly incorrect) solution to the problem, whether students in the group are experiencing technical difficulties, or engaging in off-task behavior. These "critical moments" are examples of actions that lead to particular development in the group's interaction [4] and thus convey important information to teachers. The critical moments are built on computational models that classify the utterances making up students' conversations using shallow NLP techniques that rely on a set of dictionaries that can be easily configured for different languages.[1] The system was evaluated in two classroom settings using both grade 9 and college students and two different teachers. These settings varied the number of groups working in parallel and the geometry tasks solved by the students. We evaluated the performance of the different modules in several ways: the degree to which the inferred utterance types agreed with a post-hoc analysis by a domain expert, and teachers' perception of whether the critical moments provided useful information, and increased their ability to track of the different groups using the visualization tools. In both studies the recognition capabilities of SAGLET were compatible with that of a human expert, and teachers used the system successfully to identify critical moments and make intervention decisions in real time.

Our results have important insight to educational designers, showing that AI techniques allow to scale up the benefits of group learning from the lab to real classroom settings, despite the inherent difficulties involved with data collection and evaluation of the models. This can lead to making group learning more prevalent in the classroom context and improve educational outcomes for students.

---

[1] The original language of operation for SAGLET was Hebrew, and all of the examples shown in this paper are translations.

2   The SAGLET System

SAGLET is composed of two main components: The first component (recognition module) identifies utterances of individual students that convey information to the other group members. The second component (alert module) uses the outcome of the recognition module to define "critical moments" [14] which provides teachers with information about the progression of the group, and may require them to intervene and help guide the group. We provided teachers with automatic feedback about several types of critical moments, which indicate group consensus about the solution to a problem, as well as idleness and off-task behavior that is exhibited by a subset of the group members. The alerts are visualized to teachers in a way that provides them with a bird's eye view of the different rooms and allows them to monitor several groups simultaneously. Teachers may also zoom in on a specific room to get additional information, investigate critical moments and intervene accordingly. The SAGLET architecture is shown in Fig. 1.

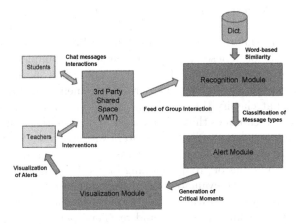

Fig. 1. Architecture of SAGLET system

We integrated SAGLET with the Virtual Math Teams (VMT) software [25]. VMT includes two components: Fig. 3 shows a Geogebra applet (https://www. geogebra.org/) that is an inquiry space in which small groups of students can share their mathematical explorations and co-construct geometric figures online. When one of the participant drags or constructs a geometrical figure, all the others can see the changes of the figure. The second component of VMT is a chat window, in which students can write their ideas and share them with their peers. Students can scroll up and down to return to previous conversations. There is no face-to-face communication between students.

For the purpose of this study, a sequence of inquiry based tasks in geometry were designed that encourage the students to use the VMT platform to draw assumptions, to check their hypotheses and to prove them. The students were instructed to discuss among themselves and to argue for or against the hypotheses laid out by the group members. At the end of this process, the group was required to form a joint claim, write it in the chat room, and explain why it is correct. An example of one of the tasks in our study, with the goal to study the inclusion relation of quadrilaterals, is shown in Fig. 2.

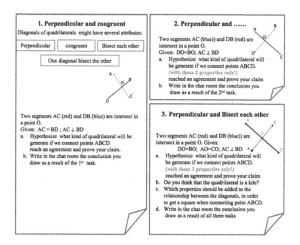

Fig. 2. Inquiry based task given to students

SAGLET allows teachers to observe on line the work of groups of students engaged in learning tasks in different rooms and to intervene as needed via the chat interface. As learners progress in their group work, SAGLET alerts the teacher about critical moments. Figure 4 shows a "bird eye's view" of several groups that are interacting simultaneously. An alert that is generated for a room is easily visible as a colored frame that surrounds the room. In this case, the teacher was alerted about off-task behavior in room 785 (blue frame) and about a technical problem in room 782 (orange frame). The teacher can decide to enter and actively moderate any room she wishes based on this alert. Once a teacher presses a room icon in the alerts view, she zooms into an extended room view, which includes an "Alerts Dashboard" showing a scrolled list of all of the alerts that were generated for this room. A "Last Tagged Messages" panel displays the utterance types on the right of the screen. In this example, the off-task alert in room 785 of Fig. 4 was generated on account of a series of consecutive utterances reflecting off-task behavior (e.g., "Hi Naomi, we are all good" by the student Bingo). The rules governing the alerts are explained in Sect. 4.

3   Inferring Utterance Types

The recognizer module identifies, in real time, which messages in the group's conversation convey informative data, and relays them to the alert module, which

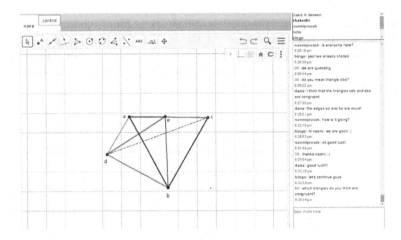

Fig. 3. VMT shared inquiry space (left panel) and chat screen (right panel)

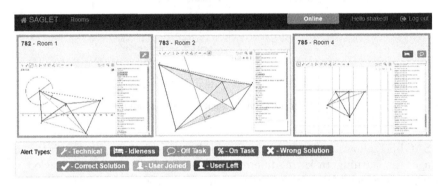

Fig. 4. Teacher's bird eye's view: rooms and alerts (Color figure online)

uses these messages to generate feedback to teachers. It classifies each utterance in the group's discussion to one of three types: utterances indicating engagement with the task [6], off-task statements that relate to group maintenance and cohesion [2,23], and utterances expressing technical challenges with the collaborative shared space. The first two categories were inspired by studies that have documented teacher's need to understand group progression [26], and the detrimental effect of lack of engagement on the learning task at stake [6]. The technical challenge category was necessary to identify issues relating to the use of the VMT shared work space, which commonly occur in the real classroom. Table 1 shows examples of each of these message types that were generated in our studies.

Table 1. Examples of communication message categories

On-task	"Do we all agree that the answer is a parallelogram?",
	"We also have to justify the answer",
	"You are correct, I did not pay attention to the third item in the question."
Technical	"Please release the control",
	"Where is the diagram?",
	"The Drawing Tool is not operating"
Off-task	"How are you?",
	"I am finding it hard to focus",
	"I have to leave"

3.1 Feature Selection

To identify the utterance types, we created a set of features that were based on the lexical similarities between the messages and a set of dictionaries containing between 30–100 words and phrases relating to geometry, software usage, etc. These were extracted from four logs of student group interactions that were collected separately.

SAGLET uses shallow NLP techniques to avoid relying on language-dependent approaches. The first type of features (term frequency) counted the occurrence of unigram tokens from students' utterances in the dictionaries.

The second type of features (similarity-based) computed the similarity between students' utterances and the dictionaries. Let a represent an utterance and b represent a phrase in the dictionary. We computed separate features for the following similarity measures for each utterance type l.

- The *cosine similarity* between utterance a and the closest phrase in dictionary d_l ($cos(a, d_l) = \arg\min_{b \in d_l} cos(a, b)$), where the cosine similarity $cos(a, b)$ computes the angle between utterance a and phrase b using a word vector representation.
- The *bi-gram similarity* between utterance a and the closest phrase in dictionary d_l ($bi(a, d_l) = \arg\min_{b \in d_l} bi(a, b)$). Here, $bi(a, d_l)$ measure the ratio of normalized token pairs that are common to both a and d_l. We also included features for trigram similarities, measuring the ratio of common triples between the utterance and the dictionaries.
- The *TF-IDF similarity* of utterance a that appears in all the dictionaries. $w_l = \sum_{a_i \in D_l} TI(a_i, R)$ where R is the combined set of dictionaries and $TI(a_i, R)$ is the TF-IDF similarity between each token a_i and the dictionaries. This term is the product between the term frequency of utterance a and the ratio of the documents in R that contain a: $TI(a, R) = tf(a, R) \cdot idf(a, R)$. Where $idf(a, R) = log \frac{N}{|\{r \in R | a \in r\}|}$

To capture context, we included similarity and term-count features for the previous communication message. By reasoning about prior messages, we begin to capture the discourse structure that is inherent in the conversation. We show later in this section how reasoning about context improves performance for the classification models. Lastly, we also included the following features for capturing summary information: the label with the highest number of frequency counts ($\arg\max_l tf(a, d_l)$), the label with the highest number of bi- and tri-gram similarities ($\arg\max_l bi(a, d_l)$, $\arg\max_l tri(a, d_l)$), the label with the highest TF-IDF weights ($\arg\max_l w_l$).

3.2 Classification Models

To classify utterance types, we employed a random forest model which uses an ensemble of learner models for classification.[2] Each learner model is a classification tree in which leaves represent class labels and branches represent conjunctions of features that lead to the class labels. The ensemble consisted of a few hundred classification trees with varying depth. The predicted class of an input sample is a vote by the trees in the forest, weighted by their probability estimates. To avoid overfitting, we require that splitting on a new node distinguish at least 50 instances in the data set. The depth of the trees varied between 5 and nine decision nodes.

We collected data from 37 group sessions in which 90 students solved Geometry problems using the VMT shared workspace. The sessions varied in the number of students in the groups (pairs or triads), the geometry tasks given to students, and the length of the session. The mean session length was 45 min, with 150 utterances. We employed two domain experts (education researchers with expertise in collaborative learning) to annotate the communication messages from each session. For sessions annotated individually, the domain experts exhibited an inter-reliability measure of over 90%. In other sessions the domain experts worked together as a group, and had to reach agreement about tagging each utterance. The distribution over utterance types in the data set were as follows: 2,340 on-task type messages, 431 off-task type messages, and 242 technical type messages.

We divided the data into a training and test sets containing 70% and 30% of the training data, respectively. The instances in the test set followed those in the training set in chronological order, preserving temporal consistency. We compared the performance of the random forest model to that of a hand-designed model that was designed by the two domain experts, using the same set of features. The hand-designed model classified the utterance type according to the label achieving the highest degree of similarity when combining the different features. Figure 5 shows the F1-score of both of these models. As shown by the figure, both models achieved the best performance on recognizing on-task message types, followed by technical challenge and off-task message types. We can see that the lowest performance was attributed to recognizing off-task type utterances, which comprise a significantly richer space than the other types.

---

[2] Random forest achieved superior results to two alternative models, a Multi-Layer Perceptron, and a Gaussian Naive Bayes model.

However, this did not impede the performance of the system in the classroom, as shown in the next section.

Lastly, we note that reasoning about contextual information significantly improved performance for the random forest model by an average of 7%. To illustrate this benefit, we present the following example from the test-set, which contains the message "Great, thanks!". Without reasoning about context, this message was classified to belong to the off-task category. However, the previous message "Please fix the angle of your drawing..." conveys that the intention of the current message was to confirm a request for action in the shared work space. When adding contextual features, this sentence was correctly classified to belong to the on-task message category.

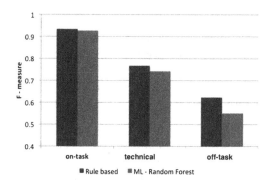

Fig. 5. Performance comparison (F-measure) between random forest and rule-based models

4   Deployment and Evaluation in the Classroom

In this section we describe experiments aimed at evaluating the ability of SAGLET to aid teachers in the orchestration of multiple groups of students working simultaneously. Although alerts intuitively seem helpful tools for improving teaching (and learning) processes, they may divert the attention of teachers in their guidance of multiple groups of learners. This can happen, for example, when a teacher tracks the progression of one group at a micro level, and is informed at the same time about a critical moment in another group. In addition, informing a teacher about a critical moment does not mean that the teacher will necessarily decide to intervene. She may decide to refrain from intervening, after gaining better understanding on the progression of the group up to this point. To study these tradeoffs, we used experts in education research in Geogebra to design several alerts that signal critical moments in the group's progression that are of value to the instructor. The alerts directly build on the inferred utterance types provided by the recognition module, as well as the students' interaction with the shared work space.

- A *Non-Mathematical Discourse* (NMD) alert was generated when at least one of the following holds: (1) The group produced ten consecutive (and exclusive) off-task utterances; (2) The group produced at least ten utterances in a 3-minute time window, of which at least 70% were off-task utterances; (3) One of the group members generated at least six consecutive off-task utterances. To illustrate, suppose that within a 3 min window, two group members produced five off-task messages each, and two other group members produced two on-task messages each. In this case, condition (2) raised an NMD alert, despite the fact that no individual student satisfied condition (3).
- An *idleness* alert was generated when one of the following conditions was met: (1) the group did not generate any communication, and did not interact with the shared work space for three minutes; (2) one student generated 10% or less communication messages within a 5 min window with at least 10 communication messages that were generated by other group members.
- A *Technical Challenge* alert was generated when (1) the group generated four consecutive technical type utterances; (2) one student in the group generated three consecutive technical type utterances.
- A *Final Answer* alert was generated when the group declared having reached consensus on the problem solution (e.g., "We think the solution is a parallelogram").

In all cases, for the purposes of avoiding of overwhelming the teacher, once an alert of any type is generated, new alerts are withheld for at least three minutes. In addition, no alerts are generated in the first five minutes of interaction, when students are introducing themselves and preambling the task.

We evaluated SAGLET configured with the above alerts in two settings. The first setting included 17 K9 students as part of their math curriculum. For this setting, the recognition module of SAGLET used the hand-designed model. The second setting included 15 college students majoring in education studies. For this setting, the recognition module of SAGLET used the random forest model. In both settings, the students were distributed to groups of pairs and triplets. Teachers used SAGLET to monitor up to five rooms simultaneously after receiving basic training about the system. We used the same domain experts to evaluate the recognition module in both cases.

Table 2 shows the F-measure performance of the recognition module for the machine learning (ML) setting, and the rule based (RB) setting. The performance of the recognition module using machine learning was generally higher than that of the rule based approach (the difference for Technical and Off-Task types was statistically significant in the $p < 0.05$ range). Second, the performance of the ML recognition module was higher than its performance of the ML module for the test sessions in the data collection phase. This can be attributed to the fact that there were significantly more on-task utterance types (87% when teacher moderated using SAGLET, compared to 76% without SAGLET moderation). A possible reason for this is that students were more engaged due to good moderation decisions of the teacher. For example, we observed at least two cases in which the teacher actively intervened in a group's interaction following a final solution alert. In one case, the teacher requested additional clarifications about the final answer ("You have to prove your answer"). In the other case, the teacher complemented the group on its answer and instructed them to move on to the next question ("Your answer is correct! You may move on to the next question.").

Table 2. F-measure of recognition module results for classroom setting

	ML	RB
On-task	0.967	0.947
Technical	0.750	0.647
Off-Task	0.660	0.547

We describe the teachers' subjective experiences from using SAGLET. We surveyed both teachers following the study, asking them the following questions: Whether and how they felt that SAGLET improved their ability to moderate the groups in the classroom; describe a moderation decision that followed a SAGLET alert; compare their ability to support groups in the classroom with and without SAGLET. Both teacher's perspective was highly positive. Both claimed that SAGLET allowed them to keep track of all groups' progression.

One teacher added that without SAGLET, she would not be able to "visit" a group more than once per class. She found that the SAGLET dashboard provided her with a useful tool for keeping track of five rooms simultaneously, without burdening her with information. Interestingly, she described a situation where SAGLET alerted her to an idle group (no communication messages), however she chose not to intervene, because the group was interacting together on the shared space. This is an example of the ways in which the "teacher in the loop" can complement the imperfections of the existing alert module. Another teacher claimed that without SAGLET, she was not able to provide the right kind of support for all groups in the class. She struggled to remember the state of each group, and would lose track of one group once she was providing support to another. Both teachers were unequivocal in their wish to use SAGLET in their classroom.

5 Related Work

The field of computer supported collaborative learning has a rich history of building and supporting collaborative learning environments in different domains [11,18,19,21]. Soller [24] used temporal models to train a system to recognize students' difficulties when collaborating using a controlled interface, but these were not conveyed to a teacher. Other works embed collaborative scripts as a tool to guide students' behavior in collaborative educational settings [1,5,17]. Israel and Aiken have used dialogue features to build collaborative agents that detect points of impasse and confusion and generate instructional interventions to guide the group [8].

There are several works on using dashboards and other visualization techniques to support teachers' guiding collaborative learning in groups [9,12,13]. Martinez et al. [12] presented an interactive dashboard for a multi-tabletop learning environment consisting of a set of visual real-time indicators of the groups' activity. The notifications were generated by assessing, in real-time, qualitative aspects of students' work and comparing to expert knowledge. McLaren et al. [14] identified contributions and patterns in students' interaction using visual argumentation tools. Similar to our work, they used these insights to construct critical moments that were conveyed to teachers for the purpose of guiding the students' toward fruitful discussion and collaboration. We extend their work to showing how the alerts can assist teachers in the real classroom, when students use open ended collaborative environments. Existing automated support for teachers towards facilitating group learning is limited to specific contexts or to small-scale studies in which the group interaction is heavily controlled [3,20].

6   Conclusion

In this paper, we investigated the use of AI technology to provide tools for teachers to simultaneously monitor and understand the progression of student groups. We presented the SAGLET system, which augments existing technological tools that support students' learning in groups to combine "the teacher in the loop" and to support long term and large scale collaborative learning situations. This diversity in the kinds of possible settings in classrooms currently puts a considerable burden on the teacher whose role becomes more flexible and multifaceted. We conjectured that informing teachers in real time about critical moments might help them in understanding the progression of the groups. Such critical moments offer opportunities for teachers to intervene and guide the group as they see fit. SAGLET was designed to be used by teachers in a real classroom, alerting teachers to critical moments in the group's interaction whose occurrence may affect further trajectories of participation and that may require teachers to intervene [10]. We evaluated the performance of SAGLET in two classroom settings, demonstrating the system's ability to perform basic discourse analysis on the logs generated by the group, as well as teachers' subjective experience when using the system in a real classroom. Our results highlight the benefits of combining AI technologies with "the teacher in the loop", providing useful and unobtrusive feedback to teachers. Our next steps is to extend the SAGLET system to other domains, such as argumentation and genetics, and to conduct a quantitative user study with teachers.

Acknowledgements. Thanks very much to the Math Forum for making it possible for us to use the development version of the VMT software. Thanks to Roy Fairstein for developing the NLP and visualization interfaces to SAGLET. This work was funded in part thanks to the Kamin fund by the Israeli Ministry of Trade and Industry.

References

1. Adamson, D., Dyke, G., Jang, H., Rosé, C.P.: Towards an agile approach to adapting dynamic collaboration support to student needs. Int. J. Artif. Intell. Educ. **24**(1), 92–124 (2014)
2. Asterhan, S.C., Schwarz, B.B.: Argumentation and explanation in conceptual change: indications from protocol analyses of peer-to-peer dialog. Cognit. Sci. **33**(3), 374–400 (2009)
3. Chen, W.: Supporting teachers' intervention in collaborative knowledge building. J. Netw. Comput. Appl. **29**(2), 200–215 (2006)
4. Damşa, C.I., Ludvigsen, S.: Learning through interaction and co-construction of knowledge objects in teacher education. Learn. Cult. Soc. Interact. **11**, 1–18 (2016)
5. Diziol, D., Walker, E., Rummel, N., Koedinger, K.R.: Using intelligent tutor technology to implement adaptive support for student collaboration. Educ. Psychol. Rev. **22**(1), 89–102 (2010)
6. Engle, R.A., Conant, F.R.: Guiding principles for fostering productive disciplinary engagement: explaining an emergent argument in a community of learners classroom. Cognit. Instr. **20**(4), 399–483 (2002)
7. Fujita, T., Jones, K.: Learners understanding of the definitions and hierarchical classification of quadrilaterals: towards a theoretical framing. Res. Math. Educ. **9**(1), 3–20 (2007)
8. Israel, J., Aiken, R.: Supporting collaborative learning with an intelligent web-based system. Int. J. Artif. Intell. Educ. **17**(1), 3–40 (2007)
9. Kazemitabar, M.A., et al.: Creating instructor dashboards to foster collaborative learning in on-line medical problem-based learning situations. In: Zaphiris, P., Ioannou, A. (eds.) LCT 2016. LNCS, vol. 9753, pp. 36–47. Springer, Cham (2016). doi:10.1007/978-3-319-39483-1_4
10. Ludvigsen, S.: Sociogenesis and cognition. In: Transformation of Knowledge Through Classroom Interaction, p. 302 (2009)
11. Magnisalis, I., Demetriadis, S., Karakostas, A.: Adaptive and intelligent systems for collaborative learning support: a review of the field. IEEE Trans. Learn. Technol. **4**(1), 5–20 (2011)
12. Martinez-Maldonado, R., Clayphan, A., Yacef, K., Kay, J.: MTFeedback: providing notifications to enhance teacher awareness of small group work in the classroom. IEEE Trans. Learn. Technol. **8**(2), 187–200 (2015)
13. Martinez Maldonado, R., Kay, J., Yacef, K., Schwendimann, B.: An interactive teacher's dashboard for monitoring groups in a multi-tabletop learning environment. In: Cerri, S.A., Clancey, W.J., Papadourakis, G., Panourgia, K. (eds.) ITS 2012. LNCS, vol. 7315, pp. 482–492. Springer, Heidelberg (2012). doi:10.1007/978-3-642-30950-2_62
14. McLaren, B.M., Scheuer, O., Mikšátko, J.: Supporting collaborative learning and e-discussions using artificial intelligence techniques. Int. J. Artif. Intell. Educ. **20**(1), 1–46 (2010)
15. Michaels, S., O'Connor, C., Resnick, L.B.: Deliberative discourse idealized and realized: accountable talk in the classroom and in civic life. Stud. Philos. Educ. **27**(4), 283–297 (2008)
16. Mullins, D., Rummel, N., Spada, H.: Are two heads always better than one? Differential effects of collaboration on students' computer-supported learning in mathematics. Int. J. Comput. Supp. Collaborative Learn. **6**(3), 421–443 (2011)

17. Olsen, J.K., Belenky, D.M., Aleven, V., Rummel, N.: Using an intelligent tutoring system to support collaborative as well as individual learning. In: Trausan-Matu, S., Boyer, K.E., Crosby, M., Panourgia, K. (eds.) ITS 2014. LNCS, vol. 8474, pp. 134–143. Springer, Cham (2014). doi:10.1007/978-3-319-07221-0_16

18. Reimann, P., Frerejean, J., Thompson, K.: Using process mining to identify models of group decision making in chat data. In: Proceedings of the 9th International Conference on Computer Supported Collaborative Learning (CSCL 2009), vol. 1, pp. 98–107. International Society of the Learning Sciences (2009)

19. Rosé, C., Wang, Y.-C., Cui, Y., Arguello, J., Stegmann, K., Weinberger, A., Fischer, F.: Analyzing collaborative learning processes automatically: exploiting the advances of computational linguistics in computer-supported collaborative learning. Int. J. Comput. Supp. Collaborative Learn. 3(3), 237–271 (2008)

20. Scardamalia, M., Bereiter, C.: Knowledge building: theory, pedagogy, and technology. In: Sawyer, K. (ed.) Handbook of the Learning Sciences, pp. 97–118. Cambridge University Press, Cambridge (2006)

21. Scheuer, O., Loll, F., Pinkwart, N., McLaren, B.M.: Computer-supported argumentation: a review of the state of the art. Int. J. Comput. Supp. Collaborative Learn. 5(1), 43–102 (2010)

22. Schwarz, B.B.: Argumentation and learning. In: Mirza, N.M., Perret-Clermont, A.-N. (eds.) Argumentation and Education: Theoretical Foundations and Practices, pp. 91–126. Springer, Heidelberg (2009)

23. Soller, A.: Supporting social interaction in an intelligent collaborative learning system. Int. J. Artif. Intell. Educ. (IJAIED) 12, 40–62 (2001)

24. Soller, A.: Computational modeling and analysis of knowledge sharing in collaborative distance learning. User Model. User Adapt. Interact. 14(4), 351–381 (2004)

25. Stahl, G.: Studying Virtual Math Teams, vol. 11. Springer, Heidelberg (2009)

26. Webb, N.M.: The teacher's role in promoting collaborative dialogue in the classroom. Br. J. Educ. Psychol. 79(1), 1–28 (2009)

27. Weinberger, A., Stegmann, K., Fischer, F.: Knowledge convergence in collaborative learning: concepts and assessment. Learn. Instr. 17(4), 416–426 (2007)

28. White, B.Y., Frederiksen, J.R.: Technological tools and instructional approaches for making scientific inquiry accessible to all. In: Innovations in Science and Mathematics Education: Advanced Designs for Technologies of Learning, pp. 321–359 (2000)

An Extensible Domain-Specific Language for Describing Problem-Solving Procedures

Bastiaan Heeren[1]([✉]) and Johan Jeuring[1,2]

[1] Faculty of Management, Science & Technology,
Open University of the Netherlands, P.O.Box 2960,
6401 DL Heerlen, The Netherlands
Bastiaan.Heeren@ou.nl
[2] Department of Information and Computing Sciences,
Universiteit Utrecht, Utrecht, The Netherlands
J.T.Jeuring@uu.nl

Abstract. An intelligent tutoring system (ITS) is often described as having an inner loop for supporting solving tasks step by step, and an outer loop for selecting tasks. Many task domains have problem-solving procedures that express how tasks can be solved by applying steps or rules in a controlled way. In this paper we collect established ITS design principles, and use the principles to compare and evaluate existing ITS paradigms with respect to the way problem-solving procedures are specified. We argue that problem-solving procedures need an explicit representation, which is missing in most ITSs. We present an extensible domain-specific language (DSL) that provides a rich vocabulary for accurately describing procedures. We give three examples of tutors from different task domains that illustrate our DSL approach and highlight important qualities such as modularity, extensibility, and reusability.

1 Introduction

Intelligent tutoring systems (ITSs) are large and complex software systems that typically take many years to build and improve. Full-blown ITSs offer a range of functionality, including components for providing hints and feedback, modeling student skills, tutoring strategies, course administration, tools for authoring content, etc. Developing an ITS and its instructional content requires many areas of expertise, such as skills in educational design, software engineering, user experience, AI techniques, cognitive psychology, the task domain, and more. Software architecture and solid design principles help us to deal with this complexity.

In this paper we look at the step-based inner loop of an ITS [25] that is responsible for giving feedback and providing hints. An ITS with an inner loop, such as Andes [27] or PAT [13], lets a user enter steps that she would take when solving problems normally, without using a digital tutor. Such systems are almost as effective as human tutors [26]. For many task domains, a problem-solving procedure can be specified to provide hints and feedback for the inner loop. An example of such a procedure is adding two fractions [17], which consists of the

© Springer International Publishing AG 2017
E. André et al. (Eds.): AIED 2017, LNAI 10331, pp. 77–89, 2017.
DOI: 10.1007/978-3-319-61425-0_7

following steps: (1) find the lowest common denominator (LCD), (2) convert fractions to LCD as denominator, (3) add the resulting fractions, and (4) simplify the final result. A more detailed analysis of these steps reveals that adding two fractions that already have the same denominator is a special case (the first two steps can be skipped), other multiples of the denominators also work (although this is not preferred), step 2 consists of two smaller conversions, and the simplification (step 4) is not always needed. How is this procedure encoded in software? Can we access the high-level structure of the procedure, e.g. for presenting an outline of the problem-solving procedure? This paper addresses these questions by analyzing the relevant literature, and proposing an alternative.

The services that are offered by different ITSs to support the inner loop are very similar [25], but their internal structures and representations (i.e., *how* they provide these services) are not. Non-functional requirements, also called quality attributes, are concerned with how a system provides its functionality [8], and they become increasingly important for larger systems. ITSs are no exception: the internal structures and models for representing knowledge determine important non-functional qualities such as reusability, modularity, and maintainability.

Various approaches and paradigms for intelligent tutoring exist. In particular, there are model-tracing tutors [2], example-tracing tutors [1], constraint-based tutors [16], and data-driven tutors [14]. A significant difference between the paradigms lies in the way the expert knowledge necessary for following the steps of a student, is specified. Authoring tools built on top of these paradigms simplify the construction of an ITS: they hide the underlying software layer from the developer of an ITS, sometimes completely removing the need for programming skills [19]. Using such a tool, the developer focuses on the tutoring interface and the expert knowledge necessary for the tutor. Murray [19] clearly describes the design space for authoring tools, and identifies design trade-offs. For example, the advantage of an easy-to-use authoring environment often comes together with reduced expressiveness, since the programming layer is hidden for the developer.

According to Nkambou et al. [20] there is a large biodiversity or even a Tower of Babel in the field of authoring ITSs. As a result, after thirty years, existing solutions are still not widely shared in the field, making it difficult to find adequate building blocks and guidance to build an ITS. The first contribution of this paper is a critical evaluation of how problem-solving procedures are specified in various ITS paradigms and authoring tools, based on reported design principles. More specifically, we argue that it is important to have an explicit knowledge representation for problem-solving procedures, which is absent in most ITSs. We present an extensible domain-specific language (DSL) that provides a rich vocabulary for accurately describing procedures and demonstrate how this has been used to develop several tutoring systems, which is our second contribution.

This paper is organized as follows. Based on the scientific literature on tutoring systems and on software quality, Sect. 2 introduces a number of design principles and best-practices for developing ITSs and authoring tools. Section 3 describes the most common ITS paradigms and evaluates how they follow the principles. In Sect. 4 we propose to define explicit knowledge models for representing problem-solving procedures in an extensible DSL. We present three examples of task domains (Sect. 5) for which explicit problem-solving procedures have been constructed successfully. Finally, Sect. 6 concludes this paper.

2   Design Principles for the Inner Loop

The inner loop of an ITS is about the steps within a task and the services that are available for tutoring [25]. As VanLehn points out, the behavior of systems with an inner loop is surprisingly similar, but their internal structures can be very different. We first collect design principles from successful ITSs and authoring tools that provide insight into how to construct software that supports an inner loop. We have found five papers [1, 3, 4, 18, 19] that explicitly describe such design principles. We only include principles that are particularly relevant for the inner loop. Quite a few more papers discuss authoring tools for ITSs (e.g. [7, 17, 20]), but the former set specifically gives design principles for specifying the inner loop. The set of selected design principles is listed in Table 1.

The internal structure of an ITS is often described in terms of four components [21]: the expert knowledge, a student model, tutoring or instructional strategies, and the user interface. This decomposition into four parts is a separation of concerns. In particular, instructional content and instructional strategies

Table 1. Design principles for the inner loop

Anderson et al. (cognitive tutors) [3]
- Represent student competence as a production set   (a)
- Communicate the goal structure underlying the problem solving   (b)
- Promote an abstract understanding of the problem-solving knowledge   (c)
- Adjust the grain size of instruction with learning   (d)

Beeson (algebra and calculus tutor) [4]
- Cognitive fidelity   (e)
- Glass box computation   (f)
- Customize step size to individual user   (g)

Murray (Eon authoring tools) [18]
- Represent instructional content and instructional strategies separately (h)
- Modularize the instructional content for multiple use and reuse   (i)
- Explicitly represent abstract pedagogical entities (such as topics)   (j)

Murray (analysis of authoring tools) [19]
- Instructional content should be modular and reusable   (k)
- Authoring tools should provide customization, extensibility, and scriptability (l)
- Include customizable representational formalisms   (m)

Aleven et al. (example-tracing tutors) [1]
- Support authoring of effective, intelligent computer-based tutors   (n)
- Facilitate the development of tutors across a range of applications domains (o)
- Support cost-effective tutor development   (p)
- Create tutors that are easy to maintain   (q)

are separated (h). The principles *glass box computation* (f: the student can see how the system solves the problem step by step) and *cognitive fidelity* (e: the system solves the problem in the same way as the student) are clear guidelines for how to support the inner loop.

An accurate model of the target skill is needed [3], and this model should be *abstract* (a) and *explicit* (j). Preferably, such a model is also *modular* and *reusable* (i, k). Modular content can be used for multiple instructional purposes [19], and thus promotes reuse. Repetitive and template-like content should be avoided: an *expressive* representation helps to concisely describe content. Having modular procedures with an explicit representation simplifies decomposing a problem into a set of goals and subgoals (b), and may help to promote an abstract understanding of the procedure (c).

The *generality* of a tool or technique is one dimension in the design space [19] that determines how many application domains can be supported (o). However, a tool cannot anticipate everything an author will want, and this is even more problematic for general tools. Authoring tools should therefore be *customizable*, *extensible*, and *scriptable* (l, m), just as all modern design and authoring software. Important for the inner loop is the ability to customize the step size (from many small rules to a few powerful rules) and the grain size of instruction (d, g). Such customizations can be steered by authors, students, the student model, or a combination.

The ultimate goal is to develop ITSs that support effective tutoring (n), which requires a *flexible* inner loop that can deal with multiple solution paths [1, 27]. Aleven et al. [1] explain that flexibility and avoiding repetitive authoring tasks make ITS maintenance easier (q). A final consideration is that ITS development should be cost-effective (p), especially because estimations of 200–300 development hours per hour of instruction are not uncommon [19]. Proven tactics to reduce the development time are authoring tools that simplify content creation, and reuse (e.g. by better interoperability between systems). Reusability is the key to improving productivity and quality [8].

3   ITS Paradigms

In this section we present approaches for developing an ITS and we discuss how problem-solving procedures can be defined or authored. All of these approaches have been successfully used to develop systems that have been tested and used in practice. We evaluate the approaches using the design principles from the previous section, and highlight their limitations.

Cognitive tutors (based on production rules). Many cognitive tutors have been developed that are based on the ACT-R theory for simulating and understanding human cognition [2, 3]. In this theory, declarative knowledge (facts) and procedural knowledge (problem-solving behavior) are distinguished. An ACT-R tutor uses an ideal student model to trace the steps of a student. This process is called model tracing. The ideal student model is defined as a set of production rules in the form of if-then statements. There are no further facilities for structuring the production rules. The ACT-R software framework is developed in the Lisp programming language, which can be used to introduce more structure.

The set of production rules describing the ideal student model in an ACT-R tutor contains an implicit description of the problem-solving procedure. It is in general very hard to extract an *explicit* description of the procedure from this model. When a large number of rules are involved, understanding the interactions between multiple rules affected by the same facts can become very difficult [24]. Subprocedures that are encoded as sets of production rules cannot be combined without carefully considering the possible interactions. We conclude that (sets of) production rules are not *modular* and not straightforward to *reuse*.

Model-tracing tutors (based on procedures). The Extensible Problem Specific Tutor (xPST) system [7] is an authoring environment that enables non-programmers to create an ITS on top of an existing software application by providing instruction inside this application. 'Extensible' in the system's name refers to the plug-in architecture for connecting to different software applications. An ITS is specified in an xPST instruction file, which contains a sequence section (among other sections) for specifying the problem-solving procedure. Four types of operators are available for the developer: THEN, OR, AND, and UNTIL. Similarly, ASTUS [22] represents hierarchical procedure knowledge as a graph.

In both systems, procedures are specified *explicitly* and they are *modular*. Unfortunately, the set of operators is not *expressive* enough for describing procedures in more complex domains without repetition, and there is no way to easily *extend* this set with more operators or traversals.

Constraint-based tutors. The constraint-based tutoring paradigm [16,17,23] simplifies ITS development by focusing on conditions that should hold for correct solutions, rather than defining how to reach such a solution. In this paradigm, constraints have three parts: a relevance condition (when is it applicable), a satisfaction condition (what should hold), and a feedback message that is reported if the constraint is violated. The constraint-based approach can be very effective, especially for domains in which there is no clear path to reach a correct solution. Although a constraint-based tutor can evaluate solutions, it is not capable of actually solving the given problem itself. Hence, the *cognitive fidelity* (e) and *glass box computation* (f) design principles are violated by this paradigm.

Example-tracing tutors. The Cognitive Tutor Authoring Tools (CTAT) [1] can be used to create cognitive tutors without programming. The main idea behind these tutors is that worked-out examples are used for tracing student steps. Example-tracing tutors target particular tasks (e.g. solve $3x - 6 = 8 + x$) instead of a class of similar tasks (e.g. linear equations) and thus prefer usability and a low entry level over productivity for trained users. The worked-out examples are recorded in a behavior graph that contains sequences of steps. These graphs can be generalized to increase the *flexibility* and recognize more solution paths, for instance by making steps optional or unordered.

Behavior graphs make the problem-solving steps *explicit*, but there is no general problem-solving procedure. The facilities for generalizing behavior graphs are key in making the approach viable [1], but are provided on an ad-hoc basis and are limited in *expressiveness*. The generalization step complicates creating a tutor (for CTAT's intended users), which once again demonstrates the inherent design trade-off between flexibility and usability [19].

Data-driven tutors. An approach that is recently gaining more and more attention is to use historical student data for developing an ITS [14]. Successful solutions from the past can be used to provide feedback and hints for students in the present, which circumvents the need to create an expert model. A data-driven tutoring system can be bootstrapped by experts providing missing data. The data-driven approach has proven to work well in combination with AI and machine-learning techniques for learning an expert model by demonstration.

Data-driven ITSs have no *explicit* expert model, which makes it hard for instructors to *customize* a tutor. Instructors cannot express preferences, such as shorter solution paths that are not found by the average student.

4   Problem-Solving Procedures

We now present a different approach to developing tutoring systems, which is based on having an *explicit* representation (model) for problem-solving procedures. This representation is based on operators that allows simple procedures to be combined into more complex, composite procedures (in the spirit of the composite design pattern). For instance, sequence ('first do A, then B', denoted $A \; ; B$) and choice ('do A or B', denoted $A \mid B$) are operators that can be used to create composite procedures. The primitive procedures (i.e., the leaf nodes in the tree structure) are the steps or production rules that may or may not apply in a particular situation. A fixed point construct is used for expressing recursive procedures. Because of the operators, the models for describing problem-solving procedures are *modular*, and therefore also *reusable* instructional content.

An advantage of having an explicit model is that it can be used for multiple purposes and interpreted in different ways: the model can be executed step by step, used to generate a student model, visualized (e.g. to increase the understanding), sent to another tool, etc. For an ITS, the stepwise execution of a procedure is a particularly important interpretation of the model since this is needed for generating next-step hints and worked-out solutions, and for tracing student steps (services of the inner loop [25]). Figure 1 presents trace-based semantics $\mathcal{T}$ for core procedures. Each trace represents a sequence of steps, where symbol $\checkmark$ denotes successful termination of the procedure. From these traces, alternative next steps can be calculated, and worked-out solutions can be constructed. The technical details can be found elsewhere [9,10].

We argue that this approach is *extensible*: new composition operators can be added easily by defining their stepwise execution $\mathcal{T}$, or by expressing the operator in terms of existing operators. For example, performing a procedure s zero or

$$\mathcal{T}(s\,;t) \quad = \{x \mid x \in \mathcal{T}(s), \checkmark \notin x\} \cup \{xy \mid x\checkmark \in \mathcal{T}(s), y \in \mathcal{T}(t)\} \quad \text{(sequence)}$$
$$\mathcal{T}(s \mid t) \quad = \mathcal{T}(s) \cup \mathcal{T}(t) \hspace{6.5cm} \text{(choice)}$$
$$\mathcal{T}(\mu x.f(x)) = \mathcal{T}(f(\mu x.f(x))) \hspace{4.3cm} \text{(fixed point)}$$
$$\mathcal{T}(r) \quad\quad = \{\epsilon, r, r\checkmark\} \hspace{5.6cm} \text{(rule)}$$
$$\mathcal{T}(succeed) = \{\epsilon, \checkmark\} \hspace{5.7cm} \text{(success)}$$
$$\mathcal{T}(fail) \quad\; = \{\epsilon\} \hspace{6.4cm} \text{(failure)}$$

Fig. 1. Trace-based semantics for problem-solving procedures

Table 2. Selection of composition operators

operator	description	operator	description
$s\,;t$	first s, then t	$not\ s$	succeeds if procedure s is not
$s \mid t$	either s or t		applicable
$succeed$	ever succeeding procedure	$repeat\ s$	apply s as long as possible
$fail$	ever failing procedure	$repeat1\ s$	as $repeat$, but at least once
$\mu x.f(x)$	fixed point combinator	$try\ s$	apply s once if possible
$label\ \ell\ s$	attach label ℓ to s	$s \triangleright t$	apply s, or else t
$many\ s$	apply s zero or more times	$somewhere\ s$	apply s at some location
$many1\ s$	apply s one or more times	$bottomup\ s$	search location bottom-up
$option\ s$	either apply s or not	$topdown\ s$	search location top-down

more times (the Kleene star) can be defined by $many\ s = \mu x.(s\,;x) \mid succeed$. We have defined many more useful operators (see Table 2), such as for interleaving procedures, for making some part optional, and for various kinds of generic traversals (for domains that have a notion of subterms). Such extensibility is essential for supporting a diversity of task domains.

The composition operators can be considered a simple domain-specific language (DSL) [5] for expressing problem-solving procedures. The DSL captures common patterns that are found in procedures and provides a vocabulary for these patterns. The rich vocabulary combined with the possibility to add more operators make the language *expressive*. The DSL helps authors to articulate problem-solving processes in their task domain.

For example, consider the procedure for adding two fractions from the introduction, which uses four rules and can be expressed in the DSL as:

FindLCD ; *many* (*somewhere* Convert) ; Add ; *try* Simplify

This procedure produces the following stepwise solution for $\frac{1}{2} + \frac{4}{5}$:

$$\frac{1}{2} + \frac{4}{5} \xrightarrow{\text{FindLCD}} \frac{1}{2} + \frac{4}{5} \xrightarrow{\text{Convert}} \frac{5}{10} + \frac{4}{5} \xrightarrow{\text{Convert}} \frac{5}{10} + \frac{8}{10} \xrightarrow{\text{Add}} \frac{13}{10} \xrightarrow{\text{Simplify}} 1\frac{3}{10}$$

The step for finding the LCD calculates the value used by Convert, and this step may or may not show up in a learning environment, depending on step size and the exact user interface. Similarly, sub-procedure *many* (*somewhere* Convert) can be collapsed into a single step, which shows how the step size can be adjusted.

Our DSL for problem-solving procedures is very similar to other formalisms for describing sequences. The DSL was mainly inspired by context-free grammars and Hoare's communicating sequential processes (CSP) [11]. Because of the similarity with these formalisms, we can reuse techniques and definitions from these formalisms, such as parsing and interleaving, and apply these in the context of an ITS. Similar languages have been used in different application domains for describing workflows, term rewriting, and proof tactics.

5   Examples of Problem-Solving Procedures in ITSs

We illustrate how we have used the DSL for problem-solving procedures in a number of tutoring systems that have been used in a classroom setting. These systems cover three completely different domains: math, introductory programming, and practicing communication skills. For each system, we describe how the procedures are developed, and we discuss what the advantages are of having explicit procedures. Where applicable, we discuss non-functional qualities of the system such as reusability, interoperability, and customizability.

5.1   Math Tutor

We have constructed an expert knowledge module for (high school) mathematics that covers many topics, such as solving equations, calculations, and linear algebra. The problem-solving procedures are defined in an embedded domain-specific language that offers the operators in Table 2 (and many more), and also provides access to the underlying programming language. The math domain allows for a lot of reuse: for example, the procedure for solving a linear equation is part of the procedure for quadratic equations. Many tasks have alternative methods for solving, resulting in different configurations that can be used. Such variation is easy to deal with in the DSL.

The expert knowledge module for math is used by at least three external learning environments, which provides some evidence for the interoperability of our approach. The module provides a number of request-response feedback services [9] that are derived from the problem-solving procedures. These services are used by the learning environments in different ways and with different choices in how and when feedback and hints are offered. For example, one environment uses the hierarchical structure of a problem-solving procedure to automatically decompose a problem into a group of subproblems when a student is not able to solve the complete task. The Digital Mathematics Environment[1] has an authoring tool that allows content developers to tailor the feedback and hints that are calculated by our expert knowledge module. For example, feedback messages can be customized and certain inner loop services can be enabled or disabled.

5.2   Functional Programming Tutor

Programs are written step by step: starting with an empty (or skeleton) program, the program gradually becomes more defined. The Ask-Elle programming

---

[1] https://www.dwo.nl/site/index_en.html.

tutor [6] for Haskell was developed to help students with writing typical beginner's programs by giving feedback and hints (see Fig. 2). Students can use holes (?) in their functions for parts that are not yet defined. The steps towards a full solution are refinement rules that replace a hole by some expression that may contain new holes.

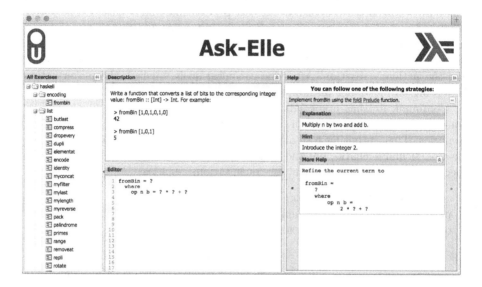

Fig. 2. The Ask-Elle programming tutor for learning Haskell

Teachers can specify new programming tasks by providing one or more model solutions for the task: these solutions follow good programming practice and are written in the target language. Writing model solutions does not require any knowledge about the structure or inner workings of the tutoring system. Model solutions can be annotated by the teacher to customize and further specialize the tutoring, for instance, to attach specific feedback messages to parts in the solution, or to indicate that a certain language construct must be used.

For each model solution, a problem-solving procedure is generated in the DSL, and these procedures are combined as choices. The final procedure can be used to provide hints or to trace student steps, automatically disambiguating between the different model solutions. Tracing student programs in a programming tutor is difficult because there are many ways and variations to define something. This variation is partly dealt with during generation: alternative solutions are generated for standard functions and for some language constructs. The remaining variation is tackled by aggressively normalizing the student program.

When a student takes off-path steps, the tutor can no longer guarantee that these steps can lead to a correct solution. In such cases, the tutor uses testing to decide about the correctness of the solution. This illustrates that a constraint-based (testing) approach can complement the problem-solving procedures.

5.3   Serious Game for Communication Skills

The serious game Communicate! [12] was developed for practicing interpersonal communication skills between a healthcare professional and a patient. The player is offered a list of alternative sentences during a consultation with a virtual patient. These sentences are the steps in the inner loop. During the consultation, the player receives feedback by means of emotions shown by the virtual patient and the patient's reaction. After the consultation is finished, the player gets a final score and feedback on how appropriate each step was.

Communicate! has a specialized scenario editor (see Fig. 3), which enables non-technical communication trainers to develop and test their communication scenarios. This authoring tool allows trainers to develop a graph-like structure for a particular scenario, but the tool also offers scenario authors some domain-specific features that are typical for consultations, such as:

- conditions under which certain options are offered or not;
- parts of consultations that may be interleaved in any order;
- or that (part of) a consultation may be stopped at any point.

These scenarios are translated to stepwise procedures that control the sequencing. These procedures in the DSL give us very fine control over the structure of consultation compared to dialog trees and avoid repeating subtrees.

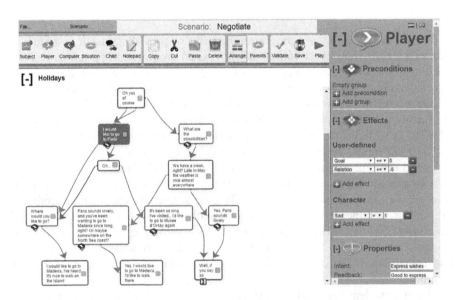

Fig. 3. The Communicate! authoring tool for developing communication scenarios

6 Conclusions and Future Work

We have proposed to use a domain-specific language to describe problem-solving procedures for an ITS. This language is extensible, and enables content authors to articulate procedures in a modular and reusable way. We have exemplified the DSL approach and its feasibility by describing three tutors for different task domains that are based on this language. Other domains for which the DSL was used are proposition logic, logical equivalence, axiomatic proofs [15], evaluating expressions, and microcontroller programming. The DSL provides an explicit representation for problem-solving procedures, which is missing in other ITS paradigms. The need for an explicit, modular, and expressive representation is supported by several design principles that are reported in the literature.

The DSL is general and independent of the task domain: it works best for domains in which the order of steps must be controlled, with various degrees of freedom in how strict the order must be. The procedures capture deep domain knowledge that makes further reasoning steps possible. With respect to Murray's design space [19], our approach is positioned more towards productivity and expressiveness than learnability. However, the specialized scenario editor for the communication skills serious game, which is targeted at scenario authors without technical skills, shows that the DSL can also be used as an intermediate layer between a graphical editor and a tutoring system.

In the future, we want to simplify the authoring of procedures and provide more guidance to authors. We want to approach this problem from several angles (e.g. with graphical editors) because there is no 'one size fits all' solution. Ideally we can use ITS techniques to generate feedback for content authors. We are also interested in interpreting problem-solving procedures in new ways, for example, to present procedures visually, to transform procedures into simpler or more efficient procedures (using algebraic laws for the composition operators), and to calculate the coverage of procedures given a set of stepwise solutions.

We conclude the paper with observing that there is a trend away from having problem-solving procedures in an ITS. The procedures are either absent (in constraint-based and data-driven tutors), or very restricted (in authoring tools): the motivation is mostly to make ITS development more cost-effective. We claim that investing in techniques that improve interoperability between systems and large-scale reuse is a good alternative strategy that deserves more attention. The DSL we presented is a small step in that direction.

References

1. Aleven, V., McLaren, B.M., Sewall, J., Koedinger, K.R.: A new paradigm for intelligent tutoring systems: example-tracing tutors. J. AIED **19**(2), 105–154 (2009)
2. Anderson, J.R., Boyle, C.F., Corbett, A.T., Lewis, M.W.: Cognitive modeling and intelligent tutoring. Artif. Intell. **42**(1), 7–49 (1990)
3. Anderson, J.R., Corbett, A.T., Koedinger, K.R., Pelletier, R.: Cognitive tutors: lessons learned. J. Learn. Sci. **4**(2), 167–207 (1995)

4. Beeson, M.J.: Design principles of MathPert: software to support education in algebra and calculus. In: Kajler, N. (ed.) Computer-Human Interaction in Symbolic Computation, pp. 89–115. Springer, Vienna (1998)
5. van Deursen, A., Klint, P., Visser, J.: Domain-specific languages: an annotated bibliography. SIGPLAN Not. **35**(6), 26–36 (2000)
6. Gerdes, A., Heeren, B., Jeuring, J., van Binsbergen, L.T.: Ask-Elle: an adaptable programming tutor for Haskell giving automated feedback. J. AIED **27**(1), 65–100 (2017). doi:10.1007/s40593-015-0080-x
7. Gilbert, S.B., Blessing, S.B., Guo, E.: Authoring effective embedded tutors: An overview of the extensible problem specific tutor (xPST) system. J. AIED **25**(3), 428–454 (2015)
8. Gorton, I.: Essential Software Architecture. Springer, Heidelberg (2006)
9. Heeren, B., Jeuring, J.: Feedback services for stepwise exercises. Sci. Comput. Program. **88**, 110–129 (2014)
10. Heeren, B., Jeuring, J., Gerdes, A.: Specifying rewrite strategies for interactive exercises. Math. Comput. Sci. **3**(3), 349–370 (2010)
11. Hoare, C.A.R.: Communicating Sequential Processes. Prentice-Hall Inc., Englewood Cliffs (1985)
12. Jeuring, J., et al.: Communicate! — a serious game for communication skills. In: Conole, G., Klobučar, T., Rensing, C., Konert, J., Lavoué, É. (eds.) EC-TEL 2015. LNCS, vol. 9307, pp. 513–517. Springer, Cham (2015). doi:10.1007/978-3-319-24258-3_49
13. Koedinger, K.R., Anderson, J.R., Hadley, W.H., Mark, M.A.: Intelligent tutoring goes to school in the big city. J. AIED **8**, 30–43 (1997)
14. Koedinger, K.R., Brunskill, E., Baker, R.S.J.D., McLaughlin, E.A., Stamper, J.: New potentials for data-driven intelligent tutoring system development and optimization. AI Magazine **34**(3), 27–41 (2013)
15. Lodder, J., Heeren, B., Jeuring, J.: Generating hints and feedback for Hilbert-style axiomatic proofs. SIGCSE **2017**, 387–392 (2017)
16. Mitrovic, A., Martin, B., Suraweera, P.: Intelligent tutors for all: the constraint-based approach. IEEE Intell. Syst. **22**(4), 38–45 (2007)
17. Mitrovic, A., Martin, B., Suraweera, P., Zakharov, K., Milik, N., Holland, J., McGuigan, N.: ASPIRE: an authoring system and deployment environment for constraint-based tutors. J. AIED **19**(2), 155–188 (2009)
18. Murray, T.: Authoring knowledge-based tutors: tools for content, instructional strategy, student model, and interface design. J. Learn. Sci. **7**(1), 5–64 (1998)
19. Murray, T.: An overview of intelligent tutoring system authoring tools: updated analysis of the state of the art. In: Murray, T., Blessing, S.B., Ainsworth, S. (eds.) Authoring Tools for Advanced Technology Learning Environments, pp. 491–544. Springer, The Netherlands (2003)
20. Nkambou, R., Bourdeau, J., Psyché, V.: Building intelligent tutoring systems: an overview. In: Nkambou, R., et al. (eds.) Advances in Intelligent Tutoring Systems. SCI, vol. 308, pp. 361–375. Springer, Heidelberg (2010). doi:10.1007/978-3-642-14363-2_18
21. Nwana, H.S.: Intelligent tutoring systems: an overview. AI Rev. **4**(4), 251–277 (1990)
22. Paquette, L., Lebeau, J.-F., Beaulieu, G., Mayers, A.: Designing a knowledge representation approach for the generation of pedagogical interventions by MTTs. J. AIED **25**(1), 118–156 (2015)

23. Sottilare, R., Graesser, A., Hu, X., Brawner, K. (eds.): Design Recommendations for Intelligent Tutoring Systems. Volume 3: Authoring Tools and Expert Modeling Techniques. Adaptive Tutoring Series (2015)
24. Taylor, R.N., Medvidovic, N., Dashofy, E.M., Architecture, S.: Foundations, Theory, and Practice. Wiley Publishing (2009)
25. VanLehn, K.: The behavior of tutoring systems. J. AIED **16**(3), 227–265 (2006)
26. VanLehn, K.: The relative effectiveness of human tutoring, intelligent tutoring systems, and other tutoring systems. Educ. Psychol. **46**(4), 197–221 (2011)
27. VanLehn, K., Lynch, C., Schulze, K., Shapiro, J.A., Shelby, R., Taylor, L., Treacy, D., Weinstein, A., Wintersgill, M.: The Andes physics tutoring system: lessons learned. J. AIED **15**(3), 147–204 (2005)

Effects of Error-Based Simulation as a Counterexample for Correcting MIF Misconception

Tsukasa Hirashima[1(✉)], Tomoya Shinohara[1], Atsushi Yamada[1],
Yusuke Hayashi[1], and Tomoya Horiguchi[2(✉)]

[1] Graduate School of Engineering, Hiroshima University,
1-4-1, Kagamiyama, Higashihiroshima, Hiroshima, Japan
{tsukasa,sinohara,yamada,
hayashi}@lel.hiroshima-u.ac.jp
[2] Graduate School of Maritime Sciences, Kobe University,
5-1-1, Fukaeminami, Higashinada, Kobe, Hyogo, Japan
horiguti@maritime.kobe-u.ac.jp

Abstract. MIF (Motion Implies a Force) misconception is commonly observed in elementary mechanics learning where students think some force is applied to moving objects. This paper reports a practical use of Error-based Simulation (EBS) for correcting students' MIF misconceptions in a junior high school and a technical college. EBS is a method to generate a phenomenon by using students' erroneous idea (e.g., if a student thinks forward force applied to a skater traveling straight on ice at a constant velocity, EBS shows the skater accelerates). Such a phenomenon is supposed to work as a counterexample to students' misconception. In the practice, students first worked on pre-test of five problems (called 'learning task'), in each of which they drew all the forces applied to objects in a mechanical situation. They then worked on the same problems on system where EBSs were shown based on their answer. They last worked on post-test of the previous plus four new problems (called 'transfer task'). As a result, in both schools, the numbers of MIF-answers (the erroneous answers supposed due to MIF misconception) in learning task decreased significantly between pre-test and post-test. Effect sizes of the decrease of MIF-answers were larger than that of other erroneous answers. Additionally, the percentages of MIF-answers to the whole erroneous answers in transfer task were much lower than those in learning task. These results suggest learning with EBS not only has the effect on the resolution of MIF misconception, but also promoted the correction of errors in conceptual level.

Keywords: Mechanics · MIF misconception · Error-based simulation · Counterexample · Practical use

1 Introduction

One of the most important purposes of elementary science education is to enable students to explain and predict natural phenomena with scientific concepts. However, students often comprehend natural phenomena with scientifically inappropriate

© Springer International Publishing AG 2017
E. André et al. (Eds.): AIED 2017, LNAI 10331, pp. 90–101, 2017.
DOI: 10.1007/978-3-319-61425-0_8

concepts that are called misconceptions. Especially in physics, misconceptions often occur and remain even after students are taught scientific concepts [3, 5, 18, 21]. Such misconceptions are usually very hard to overcome because they are deeply rooted in students' daily experiences [1, 3, 19]. This paper describes a method to generate counterexamples to students' misconceptions that help students overcome the misconceptions, and presents experimental results.

Scientific experiment is a popular teaching method to make students comprehend phenomena with scientific concepts. In the teaching, first, a phenomenon is shown to students, and then, it is explained with scientific concepts that are the targets of teaching. Simulation-based learning environments (SLE) have been investigated to assist such learning from experiments and have been confirmed that they are useful for introduction or acquisition of scientific concepts [22, 23]. However, showing the correct phenomenon and explaining it with scientific concepts isn't always useful. Especially when students have wrong concepts for explaining correct phenomena, the misconceptions often recur [1, 3, 19]. For example, in elementary mechanics, students often answer that gravity is the only force acting on the block on a table even after a teacher explained the concept of normal force. Most students are satisfied with the explanation that the table 'supports' the block's weight. That is, if misconceptions somehow 'explain' experiences and no shortcoming is revealed, students don't need scientific concepts that is less familiar to them. Therefore, in order to overcome misconceptions, it is important to show students a concrete fact that reveals the shortcoming of their misconceptions and has more impact than their daily experiences. Such a fact is usually called 'counterexample.'

Error-based simulation (EBS), which is a method to generate a phenomenon by using students' erroneous idea, is a promising method to make such counterexample. EBS helps students be aware of errors especially when they know the correct phenomenon but comprehend it with wrong concepts [11]. For the above example, EBS generates an unnatural phenomenon where the block sinks into the table because the gravity is the only force applied to the block. The important role of EBS is to show counterexamples to students' misconceptions or erroneous answers. To show counterexamples makes students think why their idea is inappropriate and integrate the idea rooted in daily life to scientific concepts. In our previous work, we practically used EBS in junior high schools for teaching 'normal reaction' in static situations like the above example [12, 13]. The results strongly suggested that students who learned with EBS acquired deeper conceptual understanding compared to students who learned in the usual way.

In this paper, we describe a practical use and evaluation of EBS for correcting students' 'MIF (Motion Implies a Force) misconception' in dynamic situations. The practice was made in a junior high school and a technical college. MIF misconception is very commonly observed in elementary mechanics learning where students think some force is applied to moving objects. In the practice, students learned what forces were/weren't applying to moving objects in dynamical situations with EBS. For example, if students thought some force was applying to a skater traveling straight on ice at a constant velocity, the EBS was shown where the skater was accelerated. We investigated the effect of EBS by comparing the scores of pre-test (before the learning with EBS) with post-test (after the learning with EBS). In both schools, the average number of erroneous answers in post-test significantly decreased compared to that in pre-test, and the decrease of erroneous answers caused by MIF misconception was more dominant than that of other erroneous answers. This effect was observed not only in the problems students learned with EBS but also in the problems they saw for the first time in post-test. These results suggest that EBS contributed to correct students' MIF misconception at conceptual level.

In this paper, in Sect. 1, the framework of EBS is introduced and its feature is discussed compered with related work. The purpose of this practical use and the procedure of the experiments are described in Sect. 2. In Sect. 3, we show the results of the practice and discuss them.

2   Error-Based Simulation: A Method to Make Counterexample to Students' Misconceptions

In this section, we first introduce the framework of EBS, and then point out its feature compared to other teaching methods to correct students' misconception.

2.1   Framework of EBS

Figure 1 shows the framework of EBS. EBS is generated by mapping errors in symbolic expression to erroneous behavior. The difference in behavior expression is better to make students be aware of the errors and motivate them to correct the errors. If students have some misconception expressed in their wrong answer, the erroneous behavior they didn't predict works as a counterexample to their misconception. We have developed the simulators that generate EBS in elementary mechanics and other domains, and also developed the learning environments in which EBSs are managed from several educational viewpoints [11, 14–17].

We introduce an example of EBS by using mechanics problems shown in Fig. 2 used in this practice. A student is shown a mechanical situation and is required to draw all the forces acting on the objects in the situation. The students may make an erroneous drawing because of some misconceptions, which are regarded as the externalization of their erroneous idea. Based on the drawing, the acceleration of each object is calculated

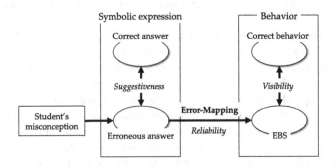

Fig. 1. Framework of Error-based Simulation

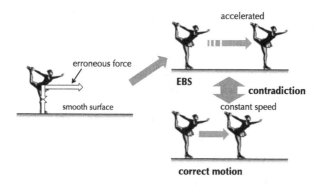

Fig. 2. An example of EBS

and the motion of them is simulated. In the problem of Fig. 2 (a skater traveling straight on (frictionless) ice at a constant velocity), for example, students often draw the force in the direction of travel. In EBS, the skater accelerates in the direction. It is expected that such unnatural phenomenon is useful as a counterexample to students' erroneous ideas and it contributes to correction of the errors with high and intrinsic motivation.

2.2   Related Work

For changing students' strong misconceptions, several teaching methods have been proposed. For example, Clement proposed using 'bridging analogies' [4] in which the gap between students' correct belief and their misconception is bridged by some intermediate analogous situations. That is, suppose students misunderstand the situation of a book on a table, which is called the 'target.' First, a situation is introduced in which a hand is pushing down a spring on a table. Most students understand the spring pushes back up against the hand. This is called the 'anchor.' Then, another situation is introduced in which a book is on a flexible board on a table. Students can understand the board pushes up the book because this situation is similar to that of the anchor. Additionally, this situation is similar to that of the target. Therefore, students can connect the anchor to the target, to understand that a 'normal force' is applied to the book from the table. It was reported that using bridging analogies in class effectively activated students' discussion and scientific thinking, through which they understand the concept normal force [4].

For another example, Elby designed 'epistemology-focused instruction' [6] in which students' conceptual development is integrated with their epistemological development. That is, suppose students misunderstand the situation of a running car at a constant velocity. Most students first think the force applied to the car in the direction of motion is greater than that by air resistance in the reverse direction. Then the teacher assists students to think about the acceleration of the car, and to connect their idea to Newton's second law. If students' first idea was correct, the car would have positive net-force, therefore it couldn't run at a constant velocity because its acceleration must be positive according to the formula 'F = ma.' In this case, students' intuition contradicts scientific concepts. After that, the teacher introduces another situation of a shoved dolly on a floor that starts to move. In this case, most students think the dolly gets accelerated because the shoving force is greater than the friction from the floor, and their intuition doesn't contradicts Newton's second law. Through such instruction, students reflected when their intuition was correct/wrong and consistent/inconsistent with scientific concepts, and could integrate the intuition with scientific concepts [6].

The common point between these teaching methods is to integrate students' intuition based on their daily life with scientific concepts, not to merely deny the misconception. Especially, making counterexample to the misconceptions plays an important role.

Making counterexample, which is to show students the fact that can't be explained based on their idea, is known as a useful method to correct misconceptions. It can be a trigger of 'cognitive conflict' which often cause students' conceptual change [7, 9, 10, 20, 21]. Additionally, less students who learned with counterexamples recur misconceptions than those who learned with the explanation of correct concepts [1].

However, counterexamples should be carefully made and shown because students often ignore them or need help to comprehend them to reach correct understanding [2, 8, 20]. That is, counterexamples should be accepted by students as something important, and some help should be given to lead them to correct understanding [8, 20]. Though the teaching methods described above appropriately utilize counterexamples in view of these points, they have a common problem. That is, in these methods, a set of situations must be prepared beforehand in each of which students' idea goes well or doesn't go well. For example, in using bridging analogies, an appropriate situation should be found that is similar to both the target and the anchor. In epistemology-focused instruction, such situations should be carefully designed and sequenced based on the scenario of instruction. This is a very difficult task even for human teachers.

The advantage of EBS compared with these methods is that no other situation is necessary to make counterexamples. If students have a wrong idea, EBS is directly generated based on their answer. (Note that students' answer should be the expression of the wrong idea and include sufficient information to generate simulation.) Additionally, even when students predict the correct phenomenon but explain it with wrong concepts, EBS can be a useful counterexample. (When students think no force except gravity, a book sinks into a table. When they think a car's net-force is positive, it accelerates instead of keeping a constant velocity) Furthermore, since the simulator for EBS (called 'robust simulator') explicitly handles the constraints of the model for generating simulation, it understands what constraint is violated [14, 15]. (The constraints 'two solid objects never overlap' and 'the car keeps a constant velocity' are violated in the above examples, respectively.) Therefore, it becomes possible to define the criteria for estimating the 'surprisingness' of EBSs as counterexamples.

3   Experiment

3.1   Purpose

In this research, we investigated the usefulness of EBS to correct students' MIF misconception. MIF (Motion Implies a Force) misconception is very commonly observed in elementary mechanics class where students think some force is applying to moving objects. According to [3], we classified MIF misconception as follows. MIF-(1): Force in the direction of motion is necessary to cause and keep objects' motion even when they move at a constant velocity, MIF-(2): Especially when there is explicit resistance against motion, force that is greater than the resistance is necessary to keep the motion, and MIF-(3): The force in the direction of motion increases/decreases according to the velocity of the motion. When students' wrong answer can be explained based on these misconceptions, we call it 'MIF-answer.' If the number of students' MIF-answers decreases after the learning, it is supposed that their MIF-misconception was resolved through the learning.

3.2   Instruments

Learning Environment. In this research, an EBS-based learning environment (hereafter, called 'the system') was implemented as an Android tablet-PC application, in which students worked on a set of problems in mechanics. Figure 3 is a snapshot of the system. In each problem, students were given a figure of mechanical situation and required to draw all the forces acting on the objects in the situation as arrows (After choosing the magnitude and direction of force from a menu, students tapped 'create' button to make such an arrow appear on the screen. They then dragged it onto an object to apply.). As for each object, the net-force was calculated based on the drawing, then the motion was simulated by using Newton's second law. When the drawing included errors, the motion of objects often became unnatural against students' prediction. Such simulation was expected to work as a counterexample to students' solution, therefore students would get aware of the errors and correct them.

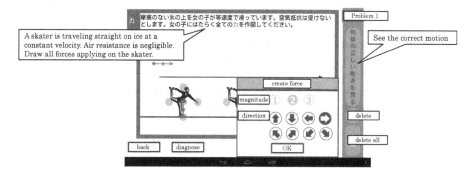

Fig. 3. A snapshot of the system

Tests. In the experiment, the MIF misconceptions (1), (2) and (3) described in the previous section were targeted. If students' idea reflected these misconceptions before using EBS and didn't after using EBS, their MIF misconceptions were supposed to be resolved. We implemented the following five problems on the system:

Problem-(a): A skater traveling straight on (frictionless) ice at a constant velocity (in which MIF-(1) is predicted. Students are likely to draw the force in the direction of travel. In EBS, the skater accelerates in the direction.)
Problem-(b): A man who is descending in the air with a parachute at a constant velocity (in which MIF-(2) is predicted. Students are likely to draw the downward and upward forces the former of which is greater than the latter. In EBS, the man accelerates downward (in the direction of motion).)
Problem-(c): A thrown ball rising vertically upward. (in which, MIF-(3) is predicted. Students are likely to draw the upward force which decreases as the ball ascends. In EBS, the ball accelerates upward (in the direction of motion).)
Problem-(d): An object on a floor shoved horizontally with friction at a constant velocity (in which MIF-(2) is predicted)
Problem-(e): A thrown ball rising in an oblique direction against the horizon (in which MIF-(3) is predicted)

These five problems were called the 'learning task.' Problem-(a), (b) and (c) were used as the 'basic problems.' Problem-(d) and (e) were used as the advanced problems of problem-(b) and (c) respectively. Additionally, we predicted MIF-(1) could appear in all the problems. For example, in problem-(b), students could draw only the downward force. In such a case, it was counted as MIF-(1).

In the pre-test, students solved the five problems of learning task (which they would learn on the system) as a written test. In the post-test, in addition to the five problems, they solved the following four problems of 'transfer task' as a written test.

Problem-(f): A dolly first descends a slope and then comes to a horizontal floor. There is no friction throughout the motion.
Problem-(g): A sled is accelerating on (frictionless) ice with continuous horizontally force.
Problem-(h): A box is decelerating on a horizontal floor with friction.
Problem-(i): An elevator is being lifted up at a constant velocity.

Subjects and Procedure. We practically used our system for teaching mechanics in a junior high school and a technical college. In a junior high school, thirty-five third grade students participated in the class. In a technical college, thirty-two third grade students participated in the class. In both schools, subjects first worked on the pre-test, then worked on the learning task with the system. After that, they worked on the post-test.

4   Results and Discussion

We scored the answers of the subjects in pre-test and post-test as follows. If there was an erroneous arrow that was supposed due to MIF misconception in a drawing, the answer was classified as 'MIF-answer.' If there was erroneous arrows but none of them was supposed due to MIF misconception, the answer was classified as 'other erroneous answer.'

4.1   Result in a Junior High School

Figure 4 shows the result of learning task in pre-test and post-test. As for the learning task (five problems), the average number of erroneously answered problems was 4.6 in the pre-test, while it significantly decreased to 1.3 in the post-test (Wilcoxon signed-rank test, $p = 0.418 \times 10E-6$; effect size, $r = 0.673$). The average number of MIF-answered problems was 2.9 in the pre-test, while it significantly decreased to 0.4 in the post-test (Wilcoxon signed-rank test, $p = 0.116 \times 10E-5$; effect size, $r = 0.640$). The average number of other erroneously answered problems was 1.7 in the pre-test, while it significantly decreased to 0.9 in the post-test (Wilcoxon signed-rank test, $p = p = 0.783 \times 10E-3$; effect size, $r = 0.499$). This result reveals MIF-answered problems decreased more dominantly than other erroneously answered problems. Additionally, the rate of MIF-answered problems to the whole erroneously answered problems was 63% in the pre-test, while it was 33% in the post-test.

Figure 6 shows the result of transfer task in post-test. As for the transfer task (four problems), the average number of MIF-answered problems was 1.2, while the average number of other erroneously answered problems was 1.6. The rate of MIF-answered problems to the whole erroneously answered problems was 42%.

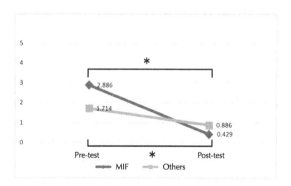

Fig. 4. Learning task in junior high school

4.2   Result in a Technical College

Figure 5 shows the result of learning task in pre-test and post-test. As for the learning task (five problems), the average number of erroneously answered problems was 4.3 in

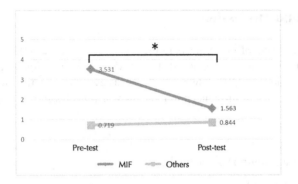

Fig. 5. Learning task in technical college

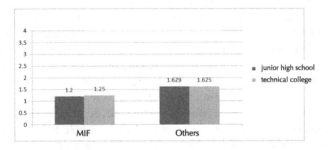

Fig. 6. Transfer task

the pre-test, while it significantly decreased to 2.4 in the post-test (Wilcoxon signed-rank test, p = 0.343 × 10E-4; effect size, r = 0.597). The average number of MIF-answered problems was 3.5 in the pre-test, while it significantly decreased to 1.6 in the post-test (Wilcoxon signed-rank test, p = 0.880 × 10E-5; effect size, r = 0.624). The average number of other erroneously answered problems was 0.7 in the pre-test, while it was 0.8 in the post-test (there was no significant difference between them). Additionally, the rate of MIF-answered problems to the whole erroneously answered problems was 83% in the pre-test, while it was 65% in the post-test.

Figure 6 shows the result of transfer task in post-test. As for the transfer task (four problems), the average number of MIF-answered problems was 1.3, while the average number of other erroneously answered problems was 1.6. The rate of MIF-answered problems to the whole erroneously answered problems was 43%.

4.3   Implication

As for the learning task, in both schools, the average numbers of MIF-answered problems decreased significantly between pre-test and post-test. Therefore, this result suggests learning with EBS has the effect on the resolution of MIF misconceptions, while our previous research only showed using EBS decreased the number of students' erroneous answers.

Additionally, in both schools, the effect size of decrease of MIF-answers was large ($r = 0.640$ in junior high school; $r = 0.624$ in technical college). Though the numbers of other erroneous answers in junior high school also decreased significantly, the effect size of decrease of them was medium ($r = 0.499$). In technical college, the decrease of the numbers of other erroneous answers wasn't significant.

Though the problems of learning task were the same as those subjects learned with the system, this result indicates certain effect of EBS. That is, if subjects had answered in the post-test merely based on the memorized correct answers they met during learning with the system, both types of erroneous answers would decrease to the same degree, but actually there was the difference between them. This fact suggests learning with EBS triggered the correction of errors in conceptual level.

As for transfer task, on the other hand, the rate of MIF-answers to the whole erroneous answers was 42% in junior high school and 43% in technical college respectively. These percentages are much lower than those in pre-test (63% in junior high school; 83% in technical college; note that these data are of learning task). This fact suggests students who learned with EBS make less MIF-answers even in problems they first met, which means the possibility of the correction of errors in conceptual level.

The effect on the decrease of MIF-answers was observed in both junior high school and technical college students. We then consider the difference between them. Junior high school students had learned the relation between force and motion with qualitative explanation but hadn't with mathematical formalism (i.e., equations) yet. On the other hand, technical college students had already learned mechanics with mathematical formalism. The fact that technical college student made a lot of MIF-answers confirms the finding of preceding literature that learning mechanics with mathematical formalism is inefficient for resolving MIF misconception. On the other hand, the fact that technical college students made less other erroneous answers than junior high school students suggests that technical college students better understands mechanics except MIF misconception. Additionally, the decrease of MIF-answers was observed more clearly in junior high school students than technical college students. This fact suggests the possibility that learning with equations promotes the correction of non-MIF misconceptions but doesn't (or rather obstructs) the resolution of MIF misconceptions. Though the number of subjects in this experiment was not enough to derive general conclusion, we think our method is promising for clarify the relation between learning with mathematical formalism and MIF and other misconception, and the effect of EBS on them.

5 Conclusion

In this paper, we reported a practical use of Error-based Simulation (EBS) for correcting students' MIF misconceptions in a junior high school and a technical college. As a result, in both schools, it was suggested that EBS not only had the effect on the resolution of MIF misconception, but also promoted the correction of errors in conceptual level. The number of problems used in the experiment wasn't so large, but they covered most typical situations of MIF misconceptions, the resolution of which is a central issue in learning elementary mechanics. Therefore, we think this result has a certain amount of generality and usefulness.

Our future work is, first, to confirm the result with larger number of subjects. Additionally, as described above, we should investigate the effect of EBS before and after learning mechanics with mathematical formalism. It is also important to clarify how to combine EBS with other teaching methods and embed EBS in lessons in pedagogically effective way.

References

1. Bransford, J.D., Brown, A.L., Cocking, RR. (eds.) How People Learn: Brain, Mind, Experience, and School (Expanded Edition). National Academy Press (2000)
2. Chinn, C.A., Brewer, W.F.: Factors that influence how people respond to anomalous data. In: the Cognitive Science Society (ed.) Proceedings of the 15th Annual Conference of the Cognitive Science Society, pp. 318–323. Lawrence Erlbaum Associates, Hillsdale (1993)
3. Clement, J.: Students' preconceptions in introductory mechanics. Am. J. Phys. **50**, 66–71 (1982)
4. Clement, J.: Using bridging analogies and anchoring intuitions to deal with students' preconceptions in physics. J. Res. Sci. Teach. **30**(10), 1241–1257 (1993)
5. Driver, R., Guesne, E., Tiberghien, A. (eds.): Children's Ideas in Science. Open University Press, London (1985)
6. Elby, A.: Helping physics students learn how to learn. Am. J. Phys. **69**, 54–64 (2001)
7. Fujii, T.: Mathematical learning and cognitive conflict. In: Japan Society of Mathematical Education (ed.) Rethinking Lesson Organization in School Mathematics, Sangyotosho, Tokyo (1997) (in Japanese)
8. Fukuoka, T., Suzuki, K.: A case study on lower secondary school pupils' conceptual changes through demonstration of counterexamples: the concept of dynamics in the case of roller coaster models. Bull. Soc. Japan Sci. Teach. **35**(2), 21–32 (1994). (in Japanese)
9. Gagne, E.D.: The Cognitive Psychology of School Learning. Little Brown and Company, Boston (1985)
10. Glynn, S.M., Yeany, R.H., Britton B.K.: The Psychology of Learning Science. Lawrence Erlbaum Associates, New Jersey (1991)
11. Hirashima, T., Horiguchi, T., Kashihara, A., Toyoda, J.: Error-based simulation for error-visualization and its management. Int. J. Artif. Intell. Educ. **9**(1-2), 17–31 (1998)
12. Hirashima, T., Imai, I., Horiguchi, T., Toumoto, T.: Error-based simulation to promote awareness of errors in elementary mechanics and its evaluation. In: Proceedings of AIED 2009, pp. 409–416 (2009)
13. Horiguchi, T., Imai, I., Toumoto, T., Hirashima, T.: Error-based simulation for error-awareness in learning mechanics: an evaluation. J. Educ. Technol. Soc. **17**(3), 1–13 (2014)
14. Horiguchi, T., Hirashima, T.: Robust simulator: a method of simulating learners' erroneous equations for making error-based simulation. In: Ikeda, M., Ashley, Kevin D., Chan, T.-W. (eds.) ITS 2006. LNCS, vol. 4053, pp. 655–665. Springer, Heidelberg (2006). doi:10.1007/11774303_65
15. Horiguchi, T., Hirashima, T., Forbus, K.D.: A model-building learning environment with error-based simulation. Paper presented at the 26th International Workshop on Qualitative Reasoning (QR12), Playa Vista, CA (2012)

16. Kunichika, H., Hirashima, T. and Takeuchi, A.: Visualizing errors for self- correcting discrepancy between thinking and writing. In: Proceedings of ICCE 2006, pp. 483–490 (2006)
17. Matsuda, N., Takagi, S., Soga, M., Hirashima, T., Horiguchi, T., Taki, H., Shima, T., Yoshimoto, F.: Tutoring system for pencil drawing discipline. In: Proceedings of ICCE 2003, pp. 1163–1170 (2003)
18. McCloskey, M.: Naive theories of motion. In: Gentner, D., Stevens, A.L. (eds.) Mental Models, pp. 299–324. Lawrence Erlbaum Associates (1994)
19. Mestre, J.P.: Cognitive aspects of learning and teaching science In: Fitzsimmons, S.J., Kerplelman, L.C. (eds.) Teacher Enhancement for Elementary and Secondary Science and Mathematics: Status, Issues, and Problems, pp. 31–53. National Science Foundation (NSF 94-80), Washington, D.C. (1994)
20. Nakajima, N.: The Role of Counterevidence in Rule Revision: The effects of instructing metaknowledge concerning non adhocness of theory. Japanese J. Educ. Psychol. **45**, 263–273 (1997). (in Japanese)
21. Osborne, R., Freyberg, P. (eds.): Learning in Science -The Implications of Children's Science-, Heinemann (1985)
22. Towne, D.M., de Jong, T., Spada, H. (eds.): Simulation-Based Experiential Learning. Springer, Heidelberg (1993)
23. Wenger, E.: Artificial Intelligence and Tutoring Systems: Computational and Cognitive Approaches to the Communication of Knowledge. Morgan Kaufmann, San Francisco (1987)

Algorithm for Uniform Test Assembly Using a Maximum Clique Problem and Integer Programming

Takatoshi Ishii[1(✉)] and Maomi Ueno[2]

[1] Tokyo University of Science, Tokyo, Japan
t.ishii@rs.tus.ac.jp
[2] University of Electro-Communications, Tokyo, Japan
ueno@ai.is.uec.ac.jp

Abstract. Educational assessments occasionally require "uniform test forms" for which each test form consists of a different set of items, but the forms meet equivalent test specifications (i.e., qualities indicated by test information functions based on item response theory). For uniform test assembly, one of most important issues is to increase the number of assembled tests. This study proposes a new algorithm, RIPMCP, to improve the number of assembled tests. RIPMCP applies a maximum clique algorithm and integer programming for assembling uniform tests. RIPMCP requires less computational space resources, thus, the proposal can assemble a greater number of tests than the previous methods on the same computational environment. Finally, we demonstrate the advantage of the proposal using simulated and actual data.

Keywords: Uniform test assembly · Maximum clique problem · Integer programming

1 Introduction

ISO/IEC 23988:2007 [6] is a global standard on the use of IT to deliver assessments to the examinees, and it recommends the use of *uniform test forms*, which are also called *parallel test forms* to secure the test reliability. Uniform test forms are the set of test forms for which each form comprises a different set of items but which must have equivalent specifications such as equivalent amounts of test information based on the item response theory [1,8], equivalent question area, equivalent average test score, and equivalent time limits. By providing different forms for each examinee, the e-testing systems employing uniform tests protect the security of tests and test items. Thus, the number of tests should be larger than the number of examinees, and one of most important issues in uniform test assembly is to increase the number of assembled tests.

To increase the number of assembled tests, Ishii and Ueno proposed a maximum clique problem (MCP) for test assemblies [4,5]. MCP is a combinational optimization in a graph. They proposed a graph in which the vertices

© Springer International Publishing AG 2017
E. André et al. (Eds.): AIED 2017, LNAI 10331, pp. 102–112, 2017.
DOI: 10.1007/978-3-319-61425-0_9

are described as the generated tests and the edges are the satisfaction of the testsf constraints. In this graph, the maximum clique indicates the uniform tests with the maximum number of tests. From extracting the maximum clique, these methods assemble a greater number of uniform tests than any other traditional method [9–11]. However, these methods have a major computational space cost. Thus, there the number of assembled tests is restricted by the calculation cost.

In this paper, we propose a new algorithm, RIPMCP, to reduce the computational space cost and to increase the number of assembled tests. RIPMCP is a similar algorithm to the previous algorithm [4,5]. The major difference between RIPMCP and the previous algorithm is that RIPMCP generates graph structures for maximum clique searching by solving the integer programming. From this graph generation, RIPMCP can assemble tests with lower computational space cost than the previous method [4,5]. Thus, RIPMCP can assemble a greater number of assembled tests than the previous methods using the same computational environment. Therefore, the proposed algorithm can utilize the item pool more efficiently than traditional methods. Finally, we demonstrate the effectiveness of the proposed methods using simulated and actual data.

2   Item Response Theory

Many previous studies (such as [4,5,9–11]) use item response theory (IRT) [1,8] to measure the quality of tests for uniform test assembly. This section provides IRT equations to prepare the later description.

IRT, which describes the relation between item characteristics and examinee abilities, can measure examinee abilities on the same scale even when the examinees are taking different tests. For IRT, u_{ij} denotes the response of item $i\ (= 1, \ldots, n)$ on examinee $j\ (= 1, \ldots, m)$ as

$$u_{ij} = \begin{cases} 1 \text{ If the } j\text{th examinee answers} \\ \quad i\text{th item correctly,} \\ 0 \text{ Otherwise.} \end{cases}$$

In the two-parameter logistic model which is one of the most popular IRT models, the probability of a correct answer to item i by examinee j with ability $\theta_j \in (-\infty, \infty)$ is assumed as

$$p_i(\theta_j) \equiv p(u_{ij} = 1 | \theta_j) = \frac{1}{1 + \exp(-1.7a_i(\theta_j - b_i))},$$

where $a_i \in [0, \infty)$ is the ith item's discrimination parameter, and $b_i \in (-\infty, \infty)$ is the ith item's difficulty parameter. This probability is called the item characteristic curve (ICC).

Using this probability, we can define the item reliability that measures how accurately the item can estimate the examinee's ability levels θ. The ith item reliability $I_i(\theta_j)$ based on the two-parameter logistic model is defined as

$$I_i(\theta) = a_i^2 p_i(\theta)(1 - p_i(\theta)).$$

This function is a Fisher information metric calculated from the ICC. Furthermore, on the condition called the local independence, the probability of one item being used is not related to any other item(s) being used and that response to an item is each and every examinees' independent decision, the test reliability of tests is described as the sum of the information functions of the items in the test form. The test information function $I_{Test}(\theta)$ of a test $Test$ is defined as

$$I_{Test}(\theta_j) = \sum_{i \in Test} I_i(\theta_j).$$

By using this measure, a test administrator can estimate how accurate a test form is. In traditional uniform test assembly methods (e.g. [9,11]), the test information function is treated discretely: the test information function has been compared on some points $\Theta = \{\theta_1, \ldots, \theta_k, \ldots, \theta_K\}$ in ability level θ. In this paper, we treat the test information function in the same way.

3   Maximum Clique Algorithm for Uniform Test Assembly

Ishii and Ueno proposed the MCP for uniform test assembly [4,5]. The clique problem is a combinational optimization in graph theory [2,7]. A graph is represented as a pair $G = \{V, E\}$, where V denotes a set of vertices, and E denotes a set of edges. The clique problem seeks a special structure called the *clique* from a given graph. A clique is a set of vertices for which each pair of vertices is connected. The MCP searches for the clique which has the maximum number of vertices in the given graph. Letting $G = \{V, E\}$ be a finite graph and letting $C \subseteq V$ be the clique, then the MCP is formally defined as follows:

maximize $|C|$
subject to
$$\forall v, w \in C, \ \{v, w\} \in E \tag{1}$$
(clique constraint).

In this study [5], they employed the MCP to search for the maximum number of uniform tests. In general, uniform tests are defined as a set of tests that has following specifications:

1. any test satisfies all test constraints;
2. any two tests satisfy the overlapping constraint. (i.e. any two test forms have fewer overlapping items than the allowed number in the overlapping constraint).

Accordingly, the assembling of the maximum number of uniform test forms can be described as the maximum clique extraction from the following *corresponding graph*:

$$V = \left\{ \begin{array}{l} s : s \in S, \text{ Feasible test } s \text{ satisfies all test constraints} \\ \quad \text{except for the overlapping constraint from a given item pool} \end{array} \right\}$$

$$E = \left\{ \{s, s'\} : \text{The pair of } s \text{ and } s' \text{ satisfies the overlapping constraint} \right\}.$$

Here, the test constraints include a constraint for the number of items and a test information function. Letting L_{θ_k} be a lower bound and letting U_{θ_k} be a upper bound for test information function on $I_{Test}(\theta_k)$, a constraint for the test information function is written as the following equation:

$$L_{\theta_k} \leq I_{Test}(\theta_k) \leq U_{\theta_k}. \tag{2}$$

In addition, if we let O be the allowed number in the overlapping constraint and both s and s' be tests which are the sets of items, the overlapping constraint is defined as follows:

$$\forall s, \forall s' \in V, \tag{3}$$
$$|s \cap s'| \leq O. \tag{4}$$

The proposed MCP seeks the maximum set of feasible test forms in which any two test forms satisfy the overlapping constraint. Therefore, this set of tests is the maximum number of uniform tests from a given item pool.

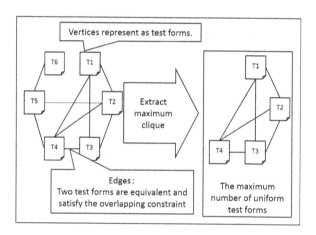

Fig. 1. Maximum clique algorithm for uniform test assembly.

Figure 1 presents an example of uniform test form assembly using the MCP. The graph G has six feasible test forms T1–T6 with nine satisfactions of the overlapping constraint and the maximum uniform tests $C_{max} = \{T1, T2, T3, T4\}$, that is the maximum number of tests in which any pair of tests satisfies the given overlapping constraint.

Unfortunately, this problem for assembling uniform tests cannot be solved exactly because it has heavy computational time and space costs. To solve the problem, in previous work [5] an approximate algorithm called RndMCP was proposed.

This algorithm has the following three parameters for computational costs:

C_1 is the number of feasible tests assembled in Step 1;
C_2 is the time limit of Step 3;
C_3 is the total time limit of the test assembly.

This algorithm contains the following four stpdf.

Step 1: This step assembles C_1 feasible tests, and stores those tests.
Step 2: This step builds graph structures by checking the number of overlapping items between any two stored tests. If the number of overlapping items between two vertices (tests) is less than a given O, those vertices are connected.
Step 3: This step extracts the maximum clique from the structure built by **Step 2**. **Step 3** is aborted by the calculation time C_2. By comparing the size of the extracted clique and current maximum clique, this step stores the larger clique as the current maximum clique.
Step 4: If the calculation time is less than C_3, go to **Step 1**; otherwise return the current maximum clique.

RndMCP repeatedly extracts the maximum number of uniform tests from a subgraph of the global corresponding graph. Therefore, in the case where C_1 is larger than the size of the maximum clique in the global corresponding graph, RndMCP asymptotically extracts the maximum clique as the maximum number of uniform test forms from the global corresponding graph.

The computational time cost of RndMCP is C_3 and the space cost is $O(C_1{}^2)$. Therefore, it is possible to extract uniform tests in a limited computing environment by controlling computational time and space costs.

However, when this algorithm assembles $|C|$ uniform tests, this algorithm requires at least $O(|C|^2)$, because the extracted uniform tests are a subset of the C_1 tests assembled by **Step 1**. Therefore, this algorithm has a problem of requiring a calculation cost proportional to the square of the number of configuration tests.

4   Uniform Test Assembly Using the Maximum Clique Algorithm and Integer Programming

To reduce the computational space cost and to increase the number of assembled tests, we propose a new algorithm: RIPMCP. By employing integer programming to generate a subgraph, the proposal divides the extraction of the maximum clique from the global graph into repeated extractions from subgraphs.

In the corresponding graph, the edges describe the satisfactions of the overlapping constraint which implies that there are fewer overlap items between two connected vertices. Therefore, the searching of a vertex connected with a certain vertex becomes an optimization problem with a constraint for the connection.

RIPMCP has the same constraint parameters for computational costs as Ishii and Ueno's method [4,5], and contains the following five stpdf.

Step 1: This step sets the current searching clique Q as empty, and the current maximum clique Q_{max} as empty.

maximize

$$\sum_{i=1}^{n} \lambda_i x_i \qquad (5)$$

where

$$x_i = \begin{cases} 1 \text{ If the } i\text{th item is selected in the feasible test,} \\ 0 \text{ Otherwise.} \end{cases}$$

subject to

$$\sum_{i=1}^{n} x_i = M \qquad (6)$$

$$L_{\theta_k} \leq \sum_{i=1}^{n} I_i(\theta_k) x_i \leq U_{\theta_k}, (k = 1 \dots K) \qquad (7)$$

$$\sum_{i=1}^{n} x_{i,r} x_i \leq O, (r = 1 \dots |Q|) \qquad (8)$$

In this problem, t_i is the average response time of item i,

$$x_{i,r} = \begin{cases} 1 \text{ If the } i\text{th item is selected in the } r\text{th test} \\ \quad \text{ in the current searching clique } Q, \\ 0 \text{ Otherwise.} \end{cases}$$

Therein, coordinates $\lambda_1, \lambda_2, \dots, \lambda_n$ denote random variables distributed uniformly on $[0, 1]$. Here $\lambda_i (0 \leq i \leq n)$ are re-sampled after each problem is solved.

Fig. 2. Integer programming problem for assembling the feasible test.

Step 2: This step assembles C_1 tests by solving the integer programming problem. Figure 2 shows the integer programming problem. This problem contains the test constraints and overlapping constraints. The solution vertex (test) is feasible and has fewer overlapping items between each test in the current searching clique. Then, this step stores those tests.

Step 3: This step builds graph structures by checking the number of overlapping items between any two stored tests. If the number of overlapping items between two vertices (tests) is lower than a given O, those vertices are connected.

Step 4: This step extracts the maximum clique from the structure built by **Step 3**. **Step 4** is aborted by the calculation time C_2. Then, this step adds the maximum clique solution to the current searching clique Q. By comparing the size of the current searching clique Q and the current maximum clique Q_{max}, this step stores the larger clique as the current maximum clique Q_{max}.

Step 5: If the calculation time is less than C_3, go to **Step 2**; otherwise output the current maximum clique Q_{max}. If the integer programming is in **Step 2**, go to **Step 1**.

RIPMCP is similar to the RndMCP algorithm. RndMCP randomly assembles feasible tests as vertices and searches for the maximum clique from those vertices. The proposal randomly assembles feasible tests but those tests are connected to all vertices in the current searching clique Q. Thus, $Q \cup$ the clique in those feasible tests is also the clique in the global corresponding graph. Then, the

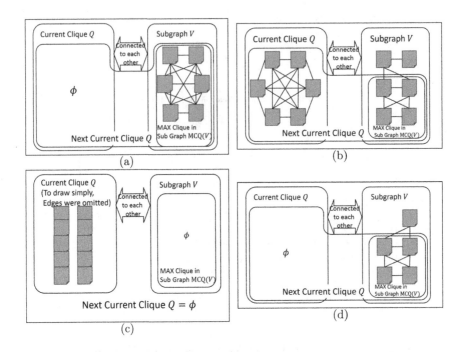

Fig. 3. Searching image of the proposed method.

proposal searches for the maximum clique from those vertices, and adds that maximum clique to the current searching clique Q.

Figure 3 presents a searching image of the proposal. In Fig. 3, the search will be conducted in the order (a)→(b)→(c)→(d). First, the proposed method sets $Q := \phi$ and randomly assembles the $\mathbf{C_1}$ tests V that satisfy the given test constraint by solving the integer programming problem. Then, the method constructs the corresponding graph G by checking the overlap constraint among assembled tests in V. In Fig. 3(a), the proposal searches for the maximum clique in the random tests V. The proposal adds the found clique to the current clique Q. For the first time, this step is the same as the first step of the RndMCP method.

Next, the proposal assembles the $\mathbf{C_1}$ tests V that satisfy the test constraint and the overlap constraint between all tests in the current clique Q by solving the integer programming problem. Then, the proposal constructs the graph structure and extracts the maximum clique in the graph. In case (b), a vertex in the found clique $\mathrm{MCQ}(V)$ has edges to all vertices in the current clique Q. Therefore, $Q \cup \mathrm{MCQ}(V)$ is a clique in the global corresponding graph. Thus, the method sets $Q \cup \mathrm{MCQ}(V)$ as the next current clique Q.

Third, the proposed method tries to assemble the $\mathbf{C_1}$ tests V in the same way. However, in case (c), the integer programming problem has no solution. In other words, the current clique Q is the maximal clique in the global corresponding graph. To repeat these stpdf, the proposed method tries to search for the maximum cliques. Then, this algorithm initializes $Q = \phi$ (case (d)), and repeats those stpdf.

The computational cost of the proposal is the same as RndMCP. The computational time is $\mathbf{C_3}$ and the space cost is $O(\mathbf{C_1}^2)$. However, the extracted uniform tests are not subsets of the $\mathbf{C_1}$ tests assembled by **Step 2**. Therefore, when this algorithm assembles $|C|$ uniform tests, this algorithm requires $O(|C|)$ space cost for storing clique vertices.

5   Experiments

To demonstrate the advantage of our proposal, we conducted an experiment. We compared the number of assembled test forms of our proposal with those of traditional methods [5, 9–11].

We compared each method with the simulated and actual item pools that have 500–2000 items. The items in the simulated item pools have the discrimination parameter a and the difficulty parameter b based on IRT. We set the discrimination parameter a as $\log_2 a \sim N(0, 1^2)$, and the difficultly parameter $b \sim N(0, 1^2)$. Table 1 shows the details of the actual item pools.

We set the test constraints as follows.

1. The test includes 25 items.
2. The allowed numbers of overlapping items are 0 and 10.

The information constraint is described by the lower and upper bounds of the test information function $I(\theta_k)$ and are listed in Table 2.

Table 1. Details of the actual item pool.

Item pool size	Parameter a			Parameter b		
	Range	Mean	SD	Range	Mean	SD
978	0.12–3.08	0.43	0.20	−4–4.55	−0.22	1.16

Table 2. Constraints for test assembly.

I(θ) (Lower bound/Upper bound)				
$\theta = -2.0$	$\theta = -1.0$	$\theta = 0$	$\theta = 1.0$	$\theta = 2.0$
2/2.4	3.2/3.6	3.2/3.6	3.2/3.6	3.2/3.6

We used a time limitation of test assembly of 24 h for all methods. For RndMCP [5] and our proposal, we determined the computational cost constraint $\mathbf{C_1}$ as 100,000, $\mathbf{C_2}$ as 3 h, and $\mathbf{C_3}$ as 24 h. For BST [11] and our proposal, We used CPLEX [3] for the integer programming problem.

Table 3. The numbers of assembled tests for each methods.

item pool size	OC	BST	GA	BA	RndMCP	RIPMCP
500	0	12	3	5	10	18
	5	20	23	96	4380	20,547
1000	0	21	4	6	17	33
	5	40	17	104	46,305	58,760
2000	0	53	8	12	32	69
	5	80	22	104	96,876	102,666
978 (actual)	0	24	9	9	16	35
	5	39	283	371	40,814	55,658

Table 4. The number of assembled tests in 168 h.

	OC	RndMCP	RIPMCP
2000	5	96,949	134,383
	10	99,999	136,318
978 (actual)	5	45,955	96,787
	10	99,999	132,451

In the table, "BST" denotes big shadow method [11], "GA" denotes [10], "BA" denotes [9], and "RndMCP" denotes [5]. Our proposal is listed as "RIPMCP".

Table 3 shows the number of test forms assembled using our proposal and the traditional methods for the item pool size and the overlapping constraint. In traditional methods, with the exception of "OC = 0" cases, RndMCP assembles a greater number of test forms than the other methods. This is because the aim of BST, GA, and BA is not to maximize the number of assembled tests. In the case of "OC = 0," BST assembles a greater number of tests than RndMCP. Moreover, in the case of "item pool size = 2000, OC = 5," the number of assembled tests by RndMCP converged to 100,000. The reasons were that the C_1 size was too small for this test assembly setting.

On the other hand, the proposal assembled a greater number of tests than RndMCP in all cases. In more detail, the difference in the number of tests between RndMCP and our proposal was small in the situation that the number of assembled tests are nearly 100,000. This might be caused by the fact that the integer programming in our proposal takes a lot of time when the number of assembled tests is large. Moreover, the number of assembled test by RndMCP does not exceed C_1; therefore, setting a larger time limit might increase the difference in the number of tests between RndMCP and our proposal in that situation.

To confirm this, finally we compared the number of assembled tests by RndMCP and our proposal, under the situation of setting the time limit as 168 h (7 days). For RndMCP [5] and our proposal, we determine the computational cost constraint C_1 as 100,000, C_2 as 3 h, and C_3 as 168 h (7 days). We examined item pools sizes 2000 and 978 and OC = 5 and 10.

Table 4 lists the number of assembled tests at time 168 h for both methods. Figure 4 plots the number of assembled tests for calculation time in the situation of item pool size 2000 and OC = 5. From Table 4 and Fig. 4, the proposed method can assemble a greater number of tests than RndMCP, and the difference in the number of assembled tests might increase with calculation time. In all situations, the number of assembled tests by RndMCP did not increase with calculation time; however, the number of assembled tests using our proposal did increase.

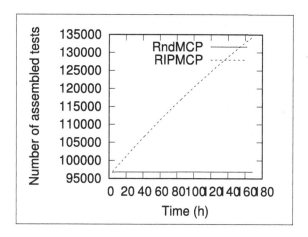

Fig. 4. Relation between the calculation time and the number of assembled tests.

6 Conclusion

We have proposed an algorithm that assembles a greater number of uniform tests than traditional methods. The proposal applies integer programming and the MCP for assembling uniform tests.

To demonstrate the performance of the proposed method, we have conducted an experiment using simulated and actual data. To summarize the results, the proposed method assembled a greater number of uniform tests than the traditional methods. Moreover, the results suggested that the difference in numbers of assembled tests between proposal and Ishii and Ueno's method [5] was increased by extending the calculation time.

Future works will include assessing this method in practical uses, and improving the algorithm to increase the number of assembled tests.

References

1. Baker, F., Kim, S.: Item Response Theory: Parameter Estimation Techniques, 2nd edn. Statistics: A Series of Textbooks and Monographs. Taylor & Francis (2004)
2. Garey, M.R., Johnson, D.S.: Computers and Intractability; A Guide to the Theory of NP-Completeness. W. H. Freeman & Co., New York (1990)
3. ILOG: ILOG CPLEX User's Manual 11.0
4. Ishii, T., Songmuang, P., Ueno, M.: Maximum clique algorithm for uniform test forms. In: The 16th International Conference on Artificial Intelligence in Education, pp. 451–462 (2013)
5. Ishii, T., Songmuang, P., Ueno, M.: Maximum clique algorithm and its approximation for uniform test form assembly. IEEE Trans. Learn. Technol. **7**(1), 83–95 (2014)
6. ISO/IEC: ISO/IEC 23988:2007 Information technology - A code of practice for the use of information technology (IT) in the delivery of assessments (2007)

7. Karp, R.M.: Reducibility among combinatorial problems. Complex. Comput. Comput. **40**(4), 85–103 (1972)
8. Lord, F.M., Novick, M.R.: Statistical Theories of Mental Test Scores. Addison-Wesley Series in Behavioral Science. Addison-Wesley Pub. Co., MA (1968)
9. Songmuang, P., Ueno, M.: Bees algorithm for construction of multiple test forms in e-testing. IEEE Trans. Learn. Technol. **4**, 209–221 (2011)
10. Sun, K.T., Chen, Y.J., Tsai, S.Y., Cheng, C.F.: Creating irt-based parallel test forms using the genetic algorithm method. Appl. Measur. Educ. **2**(21), 141–161 (2008)
11. van der Linden, W.J.: Liner Models for Optimal Test Design. Springer, New York (2005)

Personalized Tag-Based Knowledge Diagnosis to Predict the Quality of Answers in a Community of Learners

Oluwabukola Mayowa Ishola[(⊠)] and Gordon McCalla[(⊠)]

Department of Computer Science,
University of Saskatchewan, Saskatoon, Canada
bukola.ishola@usask.ca, mccalla@cs.usask.ca

Abstract. Professionals in a discipline often interact with other professionals to help them keep up to date in their field, to overcome impasses, to answer questions, in short to meet their knowledge needs. Such professionals are essentially engaged in lifelong learning, and the platform that helps them interact with each other essentially supports a community of professional learners. In our research we have been studying one such community, the community of programmers supported by Stack Overflow (SO), with the ultimate goal of diagnosing the knowledge needs of the SO users in such an open ended and evolving learning environment. In this paper, we report on a study that is a step in the direction of achieving this goal. In particular we diagnosed the knowledge of users in SO to see if their performance level in answering questions could be predicted from their previous behavior. We used a tag-based knowledge model and a Naive Bayes model in making predictions. We measured the success of our predictions using 10-fold cross validation, root mean square deviation, and mean absolute error. Over different sample sizes and different numbers of tags, we achieved prediction accuracy ranging between 84.644% and 91.709%, root mean square error ranging between 0.0517 and .0629, and mean absolute error ranging between 0.011 and .0115. This level of success suggests the potential to provide adaptive feedback about an individual's knowledge needs even before poor answers are provided. The approach has the further advantages of being lightweight (requiring minimal knowledge engineering) and of having the potential to evolve naturally with changes in the learner's knowledge and changes in the disciplinary knowledge.

Keywords: User/learner modelling · Knowledge diagnosis · Lifelong learning · Knowledge needs

1 Introduction

Most software professionals are part of online forums that help them to stay up to date and to overcome problems they may encounter in their professional lives [6]. In effect most users in these support communities are learners helping each other to resolve their

© Springer International Publishing AG 2017
E. André et al. (Eds.): AIED 2017, LNAI 10331, pp. 113–124, 2017.
DOI: 10.1007/978-3-319-61425-0_10

knowledge needs[1]. The overall goal of our research is to provide personalized support to such learners as they interact with peers in such "learning communities". In particular, we want to provide adaptive feedback to learners that would help enhance their interaction within the forum. To this end, we turned to the Stack Overflow (SO) question and answer forum that has been used for years by programmers.

In our previous studies we mined the SO forum with the goal of predicting various aspects of the future knowledge needs of SO users from their past activities within the forum [6, 7]. Our goal was to be able to have the capability to provide immediate support and feedback to users even before these knowledge needs become obvious to them. In the study reported in this paper our aim is to predict a new aspect of SO users: the quality of an individual user's answer performance (whether a user will give good or poor answers to particular questions) even before such answers are provided. This is especially important because we have also discovered there has been a rise in the number of poor answers in SO. Knowing in advance the quality of the answer a particular user may give may help to advise that user (and possibly other users) not only about whether to try to answer a particular question, but also to provide feedback to the user about his or her own weaknesses.

In our study we used a tag-based approach to modelling the knowledge of SO users[2] based on their past performance in answering questions and then predicted the quality of their future answer performance using a tag-based model and a Naïve Bayes model [3]. We evaluated the performance of our model in accurately predicting the performance of each user using 10-fold cross validation. Also, we computed the mean error and the mean absolute error in prediction by comparing the actual accuracy to the predicted accuracy. Results from our study show the effectiveness of our approach in diagnosing the knowledge of users even in an open-ended learning forum like SO.

2 Data Description

In SO, questions and answers can be voted up or voted down by other community members and these votes factor into an overall score earned by the user. In addition, the asker of the question can flag one of the answers as being the most useful which is regarded as the "accepted answer" in SO. Also in SO questions are tagged to indicate the required knowledge needed to answer the question. In this research we mined the tags of answers provided by active SO users to questions asked. We defined active users in this study as those users who have provided at least 200 answers in the forum

---

[1] In this study we define knowledge needs as gaps in the knowledge of the user that might not be obvious to them at the point of providing an answer in the forum. Examples are answers with a score < 0 which according to Table 2 (below) are often indicative of a lack of relevant knowledge about the question.

[2] We will use the term "user" in this paper rather than "learner" when specifically discussing SO users since they are likely not explicitly learners in their own minds. However, in the future most professionals will be using such forums to meet their lifelong learning goals. The term "learner" then will be highly appropriate. Since our research is aimed at helping develop tools for such professional lifelong learners, especially tools that support personalization to each such learner, it is, we believe, deeply and broadly relevant to artificial intelligence in education.

from 2009–2014. The total number of users considered in this study were 8434 users with 3,279,599 question posts, 4,038,969 answer posts containing among them 20,158 distinct tags.

2.1 Data Preprocessing

In predicting the answer performance of users in SO, first we categorized each answer into 5 answer classes, representative of the answer's performance level based on the aggregate score received by the answer as evaluated by other users. The answer classes were discretized using the score requirements for the 4 answer badges as defined in SO which are shown in Table 1 below:

Table 1. Answer badge classification in SO

Badge Name	Score Range
Great answer	$score \geq 100$
Good answer	$25 \leq score < 100$
Nice answer	$10 \leq score < 25$
Teacher	$1 \leq score < 10$

Rather than the awkward SO terminology "*Teacher*", we will refer to the "*Teacher*" answer badge class as "*Satisfactory Answer*" in the rest of this paper. In addition to the 4 badge categories, we created an extra answer class for answers with scores below 0 that we named "*Poor Answer*". In this study, we did not consider answers with score = 0 as the knowledge of the user on such answers could indicate no vote was provided to such answers. We then computed the proportion of the number of accepted answers to the total number of answer classes for each answer category defined above as shown in Fig. 1 below. This is necessary for us to gain insight into the usefulness of the answer classes defined above in assessing the quality of answers.

Figure 1 shows that answers in the answer class "*Great Answer*" are more frequently accepted while answers in the answer class "*Poor Answer*" are rarely accepted. And there is a nice progression in between, with correspondingly higher proportions of "worse" answers not being accepted. This is the expected pattern if the answer classes reflect the quality of the answer.

3   Understanding the Reasons for "Poor Answers"

Next, we studied the distribution of *poor answers* in SO as shown in Fig. 2. The growth in the number of SO users from ∼ 19,000 users in 2009 to ∼ 1.6 million users in 2014 has brought about a corresponding growth in the number of poor answers to questions in the forum as shown in Fig. 2.

Figure 2 shows the rapid growth in the number of *poor answers* in SO in the past five years in each quarter from January 2009 to December 2014. To manage this growth in number of poor answers to questions, it is important to understand the

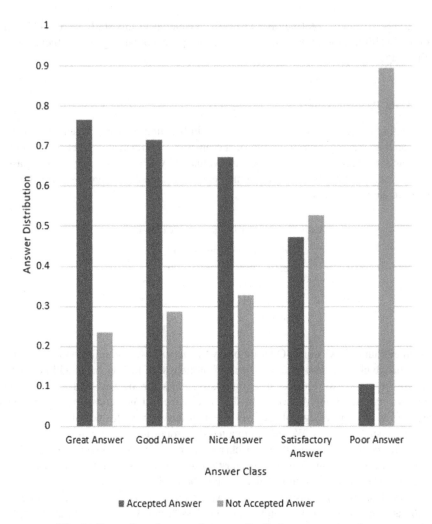

Fig. 1. Proportion of accepted answer distribution per answer class

reasons for *poor answers* in SO and then to take a proactive approach to predicting the quality of answers even before the answers are provided.

In investigating the reasons for *poor answers* in SO, we studied the comments provided by community members to these low quality answers. In SO the comments provided serve as feedback to the user who provided such an answer. We carried out a qualitative analysis of comments (353) provided to *poor answers* with a score of −10 and below (we chose a threshold of −10 since this means at least 10 SO users have ranked the answer as *poor*). The reasons provided for the *poor answers* were manually extracted from the comments. Phrases such as *"misleading answer"*, *"providing off track answers"*, *"solution does not follow best practice"*, *"answer provided does not work in all instances"*, *"misinterpreted question"*, *"recommending a new language different from users' interest"* were the most common kinds of feedback provided to

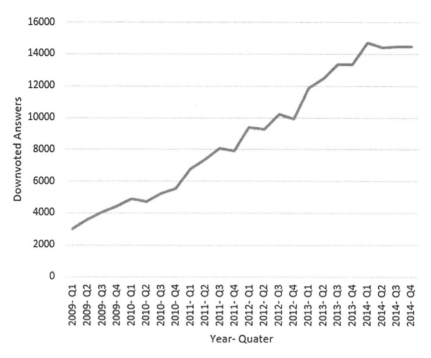

Fig. 2. Poor answer distribution in SO

such poor answers. We counted the occurrence of these common kinds of feedback and the results are shown in Table 2.

Table 2 highlights some of the identified reasons why answers could earn a low score. Importantly, we note that many of these reasons are the result of users providing answers that indicate that they lack relevant knowledge. This points out the importance of diagnosing what the user knows and doesn't know and providing feedback to the user before they create poor answers.

4   Modelling Framework

This section describes in detail the model employed in diagnosing the knowledge of users in SO using tags. In SO, questions are tagged to indicate the required knowledge needed to answer the question. For each question we employed the tags that a question is annotated with as indicative of the knowledge elements required to answer the question correctly. In other studies [8, 9, 12], employing individual model parameters for each knowledge element for each user improves the overall performance of a model. Likewise, in our study for each individual user considered, we predicted the performance of that user to answer a question based on the quality of that user's answers to previous questions. The previous performance of a user was determined by

Table 2. Reasons for down voted answers

Reason for Down Voted Answer	Count	Percentage
providing off track answer	77	21.8130%
misleading answer	70	19.8300%
solution does not follow best practice	38	10.7649%
recommending a new language different from user's interest	21	5.9490%
describing a solution without an example	20	5.6657%
answer provided does not work in all instances	19	5.3824%
answer wrongfully criticizes a product	19	5.3824%
controversial opinion	16	4.5326%
outdated solution	16	4.5326%
code provided contains bug or is incorrect	13	3.6827%
wrong application of knowledge	13	3.6827%
misinterpreted question	11	3.1161%
inefficient answer that does not optimize performance	10	2.8329%
answer provides link to other external sources which are not useful	6	1.6997%
unpopular answer	2	0.5666%
attacking new product or not been open to new discoveries	1	0.2833%
promoting one product over another without sufficient knowledge	1	0.2833%

computing the probability of the answer class distribution for each of the tags represented in their user model[3] using the Naive Bayes model [3] as shown in Eq. (1) below.

$$P_t^u(A = c|Tag_A, Tag_B, \ldots, Tag_N) = P_t^u(A = c) \times \frac{\prod_i^N (P_t^u(Tag_i|A_c))}{\prod_i^N (P_t^u(Tag_i))} \quad (1)$$

where $Tag_A, Tag_B, \ldots Tag_N$ represent the knowledge needed to answer the question (they are the tags the question asker has assigned to the question); $P_t^u(A = c)$ denotes the prior probability that an answer A equals to answer class value c (where c could represent any of the 5 answer classes) for user u at time t; while $P_t^u(Tag_i|A_c)$ is the probability of tag Tag_i at time t given an answer class $A = c$. To maximize the posterior probability, the numerator is maximized since the denominator is common to all the posterior probabilities computed for each answer class. The prior performance of a user for each respective tag in the training dataset is used to initialize the model in predicting the performance of a user in answering a question in the testing set, as shown in Eq. 2 below.

---

[3] The user model contains the questions asked, answers provided, score earned for each question and answer, tags used, and the badges earned. As described in Sect. 2, the score earned for each answer was discretized into the various answer classes to reflect the quality of the answer provided.

$$C_t^u = argmax_c \left[log\left[P_t^u(A = c)\right] + \sum_{i=1}^{N} log\left[P_t^u(Tag_i|A = c)\right] \right] \qquad (2)$$

where C_t^u represents the possible answer performance class outcomes for the particular user we are considering. To avoid creating numbers that are too small to be significant, we perform computation by addition rather than the multiplication used in Eq. (1); hence, we took the log of the right hand side as shown in Eq. (2). The predicted answer class for each answer post for user u would be the answer class with the maximum posterior probability as computed in Eq. (2) above. Upon evidence of the actual performance of the user as seen in the test set, the posterior probability shown in Eq. (1) is recomputed to update the model parameters indicated in (2). This means that as the performance of a user changes for a knowledge element represented by a tag, the tag-based model would adapt accordingly by updating the model parameters employed in computing the posterior probabilities in (2) above. The modelling process described above is applied for all users and the next section describes the procedures taken in validating the model.

5   Validity of the Model and Results

We evaluated the model by studying how well the model performs on varying data points. For instance, we studied the performance of the model by comparing prediction accuracy of the model with different users whose number of answer posts is greater than 1000, answer posts between [500, 1000), and answer posts between [200,500). Also, we studied how well the model performs by comparing the prediction accuracy of the model as the number of tags used in the predictive model varies. In validating the model, we carried out 3 tests. First, we employed 10-fold cross validation to check the stability of our model with varied data sets, a process which also helps to ensure that our model is not prone to over fitting. In carrying out 10-fold cross validation, we divided our data set into 10 randomized subsets. Then one subset was reserved to validate the training set and the remaining 9 subsets were used for training (this implies for each user 90% of their dataset is used for training and 10% was used to evaluate the performance of our model). This process was repeated 10 times using a different subset each time for validation. The prediction accuracy (PA) was thereafter calculated across all randomized testing sets as shown below:

$$PA = \frac{Number\ of\ correct\ predictions}{Total\ number\ of\ predictions} \times 100\% \qquad (3)$$

Using 10-fold cross validation, we also checked the performance of our model on varying numbers of data points, and our results are shown in Table 3:

The results obtained in Table 3 show that the accuracy decreases as the number of posts decreases, although even with users with "only" 200 answer posts we achieved an average of 84.900% accuracy. Table 3 only reflects how the model performs with varying data points for each user but does not show how the model performs with a

Table 3. Prediction accuracy on different user categories

Data Description	Answer posts ≥ 1000	Answer posts ≥ 500 and < 1000	Answer posts ≥ 200 and < 500
Prediction Accuracy	90.897%	86.702%	84.900%

Table 4. Prediction accuracy with varying number of Tag(s)

Data Description	Answer posts ≥ 1000	Answer posts ≥ 500 and < 1000	Answer posts ≥ 200 and < 500
1 Tag	91.709%	87.725%	85.699%
2 Tags	90.978%	86.777%	84.644%
3 Tags	90.753%	86.300%	84.570%
4 Tags	90.521%	86.367%	84.914%
5 Tags	90.753%	86.804%	85.413%

varying number of tags. Table 4 shows the accuracy of our model based on the number of tags present in the question being answered.

Results from Table 4 demonstrate that the model does not show a wide variation in its prediction accuracy even with a varying number of tags. This reinforces the robustness of the tag-based model. In further validating our model, we computed the root mean square deviation (RMSD) as shown in Eq. (4) to check the deviation of the model between the actual answer class probability estimate and the predicted class probability estimate:

$$RMSD = \sqrt{\frac{\sum_{i=1}^{n} \left(y_i - \breve{Y}_i\right)^2}{n}} \tag{4}$$

In this equation y_i represents the actual answer class value estimate, $\breve{Y}_i$ represents the predicted answer class value estimate as obtained from the posterior probability computation in Eq. (2) above, and n represents the number of instances in the testing set. Similarly, the mean absolute error (MAE) is computed as shown in Eq. (5) that measures how close the predictions are to the actual outcomes:

$$MAE = \frac{\sum_{i=1}^{n} \left|\left(y_i - \breve{Y}_i\right)\right|}{n} \tag{5}$$

The results of these calculations for our data are shown in Table 5:

Table 5. Results for RMSD and MAE

Data Description	RMSD	MAE
Answer posts ≥ 1000	0.0629332	0.0109518
Answer posts ≥ 500 < 1000	0.05585143	0.0115118
Answer posts ≥ 200 < 500	0.05169019	0.0110675

Results from Table 5 show that irrespective of the number of the data points employed, the RMSD and the MAE are low, which indicates a small deviation between the actual answer class estimates and the predicted class estimates. These are very good outcomes and show the promise of our tag-based model in making good predictions about the future from the analysis of past behavior.

6 Discussion

The long term goal of our research is to support the lifelong learning of software professionals by providing adaptive feedback to such learners as they interact in an open ended learning environment. In particular in this paper we have been interested in how we might be able to reduce the number of poor answers that users give to questions asked by other users in the Stack Overflow forum, especially important given the growth in the number of poor answers in SO demonstrated in Fig. 2. We first carried out a qualitative study to understand the possible reasons for this rise as shown in Table 2. Results from this analysis reflect that the occurrence of poor answers can largely be attributed to the users themselves lacking relevant knowledge to answer the question. In light of this, we attempted to predict the performance of each user in answering a question by modelling their knowledge based on their previously observed answer performance in SO. If we can predict such performance, we can advise a user in advance as to whether to try to answer a particular question, and possibly also provide feedback on the state of their knowledge at a given time.

Previous work [3, 4] in advanced learning technology has successfully modelled the knowledge of users in well-defined domains where the body of knowledge is not constantly evolving. In the lifelong learning context of our research, this is definitely not the case, as technological advancements are leading to continuous change in knowledge [6]. This creates the need to extend study in knowledge diagnosis beyond intelligent tutoring systems to open ended learning environments. We argue that such open ended environments should use lightweight diagnosis techniques that would work without needing extensive knowledge engineering (and re-engineering) as the user and the disciplinary knowledge changes over time.

To this end, we employed a lightweight tag-based Naïve Bayes model to diagnosing the knowledge of users based on their previous answer performance in SO. As described in Sect. 4 such an approach can yield informative results that shed light on the individual capabilities of each user to answer questions. We argue that our approach scales well in that the performance of the model is fairly good even with lower numbers of data points, as shown in Tables 3, 4 and 5. Moreover, our approach naturally evolves as new tags reflect new knowledge, of the user or of the domain itself. A next step in our research will be to see if a deeper analysis of the poor answers, perhaps through both interaction mining and text mining, will further enhance our ability to predict the occurrence of poor answers. We are also interested in being able to predict which users might be best in answering a question and prompting such users to do so. Ultimately, we hope the results could be employed in a system to provide adaptive feedback to users even before poor answers are given in order to forestall the increasing rise in poor answers in SO.

The obvious limitation to the model described in this study is the need to track the previous answer performance of a user. This means that tags present in a new question which have never been associated with any question a user has answered before, cannot be employed in diagnosing the knowledge of the user for the new question, simply because no data about the new tag exists for that user. Of course, with active users (such as those considered in this study), this limitation was minimal as shown by our results in Tables 3, 4 and 5. Moreover, once the user answers such questions, information concerning the user's capability to answer questions with such a new tag starts to become available, and in this way the model would evolve naturally to model the changing knowledge of the user.

7 Related Work

In our study, we employed a Naïve Bayes model in diagnosing the knowledge of users. The Bayesian model has been employed in modelling skills of users and in inferring learners' attitudes [1, 3]. Bayesian Knowledge Tracing (BKT) is a common model employed in many places, especially in the cognitive tutors [4, 9, 12]. Lee and Brunskill [8] in their application of the BKT model, fitted the model parameters according to individual students. Results from this study show that by integrating individual student parameters rather than using the same set of model parameters, fewer practice opportunities are required for a significant number of students. These studies have successfully predicted the performance of learners in cognitive tutors, but our use of Bayesian approaches in more open-ended domains is a step forward.

Prediction of student performance is one of the oldest applications of data mining in education [5]. Vandamme et al. in 2007 [11] studied the correlation between attributes such as attendance, previous academic experience, and study skills. Students were classified based on their risk level into 'high-risk' for students whose probability of failing is high, 'medium-risk' indicating students who may succeed if appropriate measures were employed, and finally 'low-risk' which shows students with high likelihood of succeeding. This study applied neural networks, as well as random forest and decision tree methods, in predicting the academic performance of students using the variables mentioned above. Similarly, Baradwaj and Pal [2] employed metrics such as attendance, as well as marks from assignments, tests and seminars to predict the final performance of students in higher education using decision tree techniques. Likewise, Romero et al. [10] in their study predicted the final grades of students based on the activities of students in a Moodle-supported course. These previous studies predicted the performance of students within a controlled ITS or a closed classroom learning environment. Our study extends such previous studies by attempting to predict the performance of users in open-ended learning environments.

8 Conclusion

Being able to diagnose the knowledge of learners in an open ended learning environment is the first step in providing personalized support to learners in such environments. This study proposed a lightweight tag-based methodology that is especially promising since lifelong learning support systems are meant to be compatible with ever changing, highly dynamic professional knowledge domains. Such systems cannot rely on the need for vast amounts of ongoing knowledge engineering, ontology building, metadata annotation, or system customization. Beyond just answer prediction, we would also like to use similar lightweight approaches to create an open learner model that could recommend appropriate learning resources (including access to particular peer helpers) that will assist professionals in acquiring missing skills, and possibly will even carry out dynamic instructional planning to support lifelong learners in keeping up to date in the changing and evolving world of professional knowledge.

Acknowledgements. We would like to thank the Natural Sciences and Engineering Research Council of Canada and the University of Saskatchewan for their financial support of the first author.

References

1. Arroyo, I.; Woolf, B.: Inferring learning and attitudes from a Bayesian Network of log file data. In: Proceedings of the 12th International Conference on Artificial Intelligence in Education, Amsterdam, pp. 33–40 (2005)
2. Baradwaj, B.K., Pal, S.: Mining educational data to analyze students' performance. arXiv preprint arXiv:1201.3417 (2012)
3. Conati, C.: Bayesian student modelling. In: Advances in Intelligent Tutoring Systems, pp. 281–299 (2010)
4. Corbett, A.T., Anderson, J.R.: Knowledge tracing: modelling the acquisition of procedural knowledge. User Model. User-Adap. Inter. **4**(4), 253–278 (1994)
5. Desmarais, M.C., Baker, R.S.: A review of recent advances in learner and skill modelling in intelligent learning environments. User Model. User-Adap. Inter. **22**(1–2), 9–38 (2012). Springer, Heidelberg
6. Ishola, O.M., McCalla, G.: Detecting and supporting the evolving knowledge interests of lifelong professionals. In: Verbert, K., Sharples, M., Klobučar, T. (eds.) EC-TEL 2016. LNCS, vol. 9891, pp. 595–599. Springer, Cham (2016). doi:10.1007/978-3-319-45153-4_71
7. Ishola, O., McCalla, G.: Tracking and reacting to the evolving knowledge needs of lifelong professional learners. In: Proceedings of the 6th Workshop on Personalization Approaches in Learning Environments (PALE 2016) at the 24th International Conference on User Modeling, Adaptation, and Personalization (UMAP 2016), pp. 68–73 (2016)

8. Lee, J.I., Brunskill, E.: The impact on individualizing student models on necessary practice opportunities. In: Proceedings of the 5th International Educational Data Mining Society. Chania Greece, pp. 118–125 (2012)
9. Pardos, Zachary A., Heffernan, Neil T.: Modeling individualization in a bayesian networks implementation of knowledge tracing. In: Bra, P., Kobsa, A., Chin, D. (eds.) UMAP 2010. LNCS, vol. 6075, pp. 255–266. Springer, Heidelberg (2010). doi:10.1007/978-3-642-13470-8_24
10. Romero, C., Ventura, S., García, E.: Data mining in course management systems: moodle case study and tutorial. Comput. Educ. **51**(1), 368–384 (2008)
11. Vandamme, J.P., Meskens, N., Superby, J.F.: Predicting academic performance by data mining methods. Educ. Econ. **15**(4), 405–419 (2007)
12. Yudelson, M.V., Koedinger, K.R., Gordon, G.J.: Individualized bayesian knowledge tracing models. In: Lane, H.C., Yacef, K., Mostow, J., Pavlik, P. (eds.) AIED 2013. LNCS (LNAI), vol. 7926, pp. 171–180. Springer, Heidelberg (2013). doi:10.1007/978-3-642-39112-5_18

iSTART-ALL: Confronting Adult Low Literacy with Intelligent Tutoring for Reading Comprehension

Amy M. Johnson[1]([✉]), Tricia A. Guerrero[1], Elizabeth L. Tighe[2], and Danielle S. McNamara[1]

[1] Institute for the Science of Teaching and Learning, Department of Psychology, Arizona State University, Tempe, AZ 85287, USA
{amjohn43,taguerre,dsmcnama}@asu.edu
[2] Department of Psychology, Georgia State University, Atlanta, GA 30302, USA
etighe@gsu.edu

Abstract. There is little empirical research available on the substantial problem of adult low literacy rates, and limited educational technologies are available to address distinct instructional needs of this population. This paper reports on development and testing of a version of Interactive Strategy Training for Active Reading and Thinking (iSTART) for Adult Literacy Learners (iSTART-ALL) We describe modifications of iSTART to accommodate adult literacy learners, including new practice modules (i.e., summarization, question asking), a new library of texts, and an interactive narrative for adult literacy learners to engage in extended practice of reading comprehension strategies. We report results of a study examining reactions to iSTART-ALL and performance data while engaging with the interactive narrative. The attitudinal study, conducted with 38 adult literacy learners, demonstrated generally positive reactions to the narrative. Results also revealed that task performance was strongly related to individual difference scores on reading comprehension assessments, and more so with higher-level comprehension skills than basic word-level skills, providing concurrent validity for the interactive narrative tasks.

Keywords: Intelligent tutoring systems · Interactive narrative · Adult literacy · Reading comprehension · Literacy technology

1 Introduction

The results of the Program for the International Assessment of Adult Competencies (PIAAC) conducted in 2012–2014 revealed that 17% of U.S. adults between 16 and 65 years old scored at or below the lowest level of the literacy scale (https://nces.ed.gov/surveys/piaac/results/summary.aspx). Furthermore, an additional 33% are at level 2, indicating performance well below functional literacy levels. Compared to the international average, the US had a higher percentage of adults performing at the lowest literacy levels. Even though findings such as these demonstrate an alarming need for empirically-based, effectual adult literacy instruction, there is a scarcity of rigorous

© Springer International Publishing AG 2017
E. André et al. (Eds.): AIED 2017, LNAI 10331, pp. 125–136, 2017.
DOI: 10.1007/978-3-319-61425-0_11

research dedicated to this problem. To address this concern, our team set out to identify unique educational needs of adult literacy learners and develop educational technology solutions tailored to those needs. We used an existing intelligent tutoring system for reading comprehension, the Interactive Strategy Training for Active Reading and Thinking (iSTART) as a foundation on which to develop iSTART-ALL for adult literacy learners.

iSTART delivers reading comprehension strategy training and extended strategy practice, using natural language processing to offer automated feedback. Originally developed to provide self-explanation strategy training for high school students, results demonstrate that iSTART improves self-explanation quality and performance on reading comprehension assessments [1, 2]. The iSTART strategies (comprehension monitoring, paraphrasing, prediction, bridging inferencing, elaborating) have shown utility for readers with a wide range of ability [2]; thus, we expected iSTART to be effective for adult literacy learners. However, adult literacy learners have unique educational needs (e.g., low fluency and decoding skills; [3]); thus, we made several modifications and additions to the system. This paper focuses on the development and testing of an interactive narrative called 'Lost in Springdale'. The interactive narrative, or "choose your own adventure" story, offers learners additional opportunities to practice comprehension strategies using varied authentic text artifacts.

1.1 iSTART

iSTART provides reading comprehension training in two phases, *instruction* and *practice*. The instruction phase delivers a series of lesson videos covering self-explanation and five comprehension strategies (i.e. comprehension monitoring, paraphrasing, prediction, elaboration, and bridging). We have recently added summarization strategy lesson videos (i.e., deletion, replacement, main ideas, and topic sentences), as well as instruction on deep-level reasoning questions (i.e., how and why questions). We developed these additional instructional videos with the adult literacy population in mind; however, we expect they will promote reading for younger learners as well. After the instruction phase, learners advance to the practice phase, which offers generative and identification games to practice the reading strategies. Currently, we have practice games only for self-explanation strategies. In the generative games, learners read a text and type self-explanations for target sentences. iSTART provides automated feedback, using a natural language processing algorithm that compares self-explanation content to the target sentences, as well as previous and subsequent text content. In the identification games, learners see example self-explanations (along with the self-explained sentences) and attempt to identify which of the trained self-explanation strategies are used in the self-explanations. Empirical studies have demonstrated the effectiveness of iSTART to improve self-explanation skills and performance on reading comprehension measures [1, 2] as well as science course performance [4]. Results further show that learners of varied reading skills can benefit from iSTART instruction [1, 2], suggesting that the system holds promise for improving reading comprehension for the adult literacy population as well. Nonetheless, as the next section describes, we tailored elements of the system to make it more appropriate for this population.

1.2 Modifying iSTART for Adult Literacy Learners

In order to adapt iSTART more precisely to the needs of adult literacy learners, we applied user-centered design to make several modifications. First, we added strategy instruction for summarization and deep-level reasoning questions, and are in the process of developing practice games for those strategies. Next, we collected a new library of approximately 60 texts that are life-relevant (i.e., technology, health-related issues, family matters) to adult learners. Finally, we created the interactive narrative combining practice for self-explanation, summarization, and question asking.

Summarization and Question Asking Training An analysis of the commonly-used adult literacy assessments [5] suggested that training summarization strategies can promote performance on The Adult Basic Learning Examination (ABLE), the Comprehension Adult Student Assessment System (CASAS), the Test of Adult Basic Education (TABE), and the General Educational Development (GED) exam. The summarization instructional modules present instruction on four effective summarization strategies [6, 7]. Using the *deletion* strategy, learners remove unnecessary (i.e., trivial or redundant) information from the text. The *replacement* strategy involves identifying subordinate items in a list (e.g., apples, oranges, and bananas) and replacing the list with the superordinate category to which they belong (e.g., fruit). Using the *main ideas* strategy, learners identify the key points from the text that should be reflected in the summarization. Finally, learners can either identify or construct their own *topic sentence* to introduce the summary. The instructional videos on summarization include one overview of the strategies to be learned, four lesson videos on the strategies described above, and a recap lesson. These videos range from two to six minutes, for a total of 23.1 min of instructional time. We recorded human narration of the verbal instructional content and used the Prezi presentation software to develop the graphic content.

When learners generate questions about text, they can assess their comprehension of the material, [8, 9] and the process of answering one's own deep-level questions can improve learning [10, 11]. Deep-level questions, which require logical, causal, or goal-oriented reasoning [10], especially promote learning because they help the learner identify gaps in texts and their own comprehension. In fact, research has shown that viewing instructional videos using deep-level questions within dialogues can improve learning [12]. The three question asking instructional videos (1.5 to 5 min each; total time = 7.4 min) focus on instructing learners to generate deep-level reasoning questions, especially *how* and *why* questions concerning the causal mechanisms behind system functioning. The instruction describes the *value* of asking questions, supplies information about *how to apply* question asking strategies, and gives *examples* of deep questions.

New Library of Texts. Research shows that the content of texts plays an important role in interest, engagement and persistence, and learners are especially motivated toward content connecting to their knowledge and values [13, 14]. Furthermore, the average range of reading abilities identified for adult literacy learners is from 3rd to 8th grade. The texts in the previous versions of iSTART are difficult science texts (Flesch-Kincaid grade levels 6 to 14). Thus, we have collected a set of approximately

60 new texts from the California Distance Learning Project (www.cdlponline.org). The texts are simplified news stories on life relevant topics (e.g., housing, family, money) and range in difficulty from 3rd to 8th Flesch-Kincaid grade levels. These new text passages are used for both the generative and identification practice games.

Interactive Narrative. *Lost in Springdale* is an interactive first person narrative during which learners read several life-relevant artifacts and attempt to navigate the seemingly abandoned town of Springdale to find a friend from which they have been separated. In order to complete the narrative, the learner must visit three key locations (i.e., the Mall, School, and Hospital), encountering one Springdale resident at each (i.e., Elliot, Milo, and Violet, respectively). Learners select a character image from three females and three males to represent their friend and name the friend.

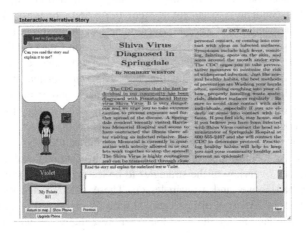

Fig. 1. Screenshot of an artifact from the interactive narrative

Within the narrative, various life-relevant artifacts (e.g., school map, fire extinguisher instructions, update from the Centers for Disease Control [CDC], emails/letters) attempt to serve learning, assessment, and engagement goals. The interactive narrative provides instantiated practice of self-explanation, summarization, and question asking. After reading each artifact, the learner must answer a question, self-explain the text, ask a question about the text, provide a summary, or make a decision on where to go next. We selected life-relevant artifacts which could help learners in developing important life skills related to the three types of literacy identified by the NAAL: prose literacy (e.g., news stories), document literacy (e.g. drug labels), and quantitative literacy (e.g., food labels). Figure 1 is an example artifact in which the learner writes a self-explanation of a news story on a CDC virus update. Character speech is provided visually and auditorily (which can be muted depending on learner preference). For each artifact, the learner receives immediate feedback, including hints and corrective feedback (at bottom-out). As the learner progresses through each of the three primary story arcs, the tasks become more difficult; texts become longer and more complex, and responses change from binary decisions, to four-choice multiple-choice questions, and ultimately, to open-response items (e.g., short answers, self-explanations, and summaries). The system will provide automated feedback for open-response items using natural language processing (NLP) algorithms. The self-explanation assessment algorithm used in other self-explanation activities in iSTART [15] is implemented. We are in the process of developing NLP algorithms for assessing students' summaries and generated questions [16]. When a task is successfully completed, the learner earns points; the number of points depends on the sophistication of the reasoning skill, the type of learner response, and the complexity of the text or image.

Learners' responses to each artifact determine the subsequent flow of the storyline. For example, in the Introduction, the learner must decide whether to stay with the broken down car (while the friend investigates a nearby house), or to go investigate the house (while the friend stays with the car). Which pages are shown subsequently depends on the learner's decision in this situation. Additionally, the learner is given the choice of which segment of the story to read at any time (i.e., Mall, School, or Hospital). The town map is presented after the introduction segment of the narrative, which establishes the overall premise of the story. By clicking on an image that represents a location (e.g., the Mall), the learner can go to a new town location. This design facilitates interactions with our target population by allowing for simple, visual, non-language dependent interface navigation.

Learners have access to a cell phone during the interactive narrative, which provides several assistive and motivational features. First, at predetermined moments in the narrative, the cell phone automatically 'takes photos' of scenes and artifacts, and the system saves the photos to the photo album. Previously-saved photos can be accessed from the cell phone at any time. Next, the cell phone can be used to type electronic notes, which are saved in the phone's notes feature. The cell phone also provides a simple open learner model to track learning progress using two sets of skill-o-meters, one representing mastery of domain knowledge (e.g., health, mechanical skills) and one representing mastery of the reading and thinking skills (e.g., self-explanation, summarization). The fill of each skill-o-meter is determined by the proportion of correct answers for each category. This feature was designed to promote reflection on learning and help plan future behavior in the system. Finally, points scored in the narrative can be used to purchase trendier models of phones. We included this functionality to increase investment toward successful task completion (i.e., to score points) and to investigate off-task behavior and personalization activities.

2   Method

2.1   Participants

Participants included 38 adults recruited from three adult literacy programs in the Southwestern region of the United States and who were paid for their participation. The mean age of the participants was 34 ($SD = 13.22$; range 18–65), and the majority of the participants were female (76.3%). Participants self-identified as Hispanic (57.9%), African American (15.8%), Caucasian (15.8%), and 10.5% as other. Most declared English as their native language (65.8%) while 31.6% identified Spanish and 2.6% as other. Although participants were recruited from General Educational Development preparation classes, they represented a variety of education backgrounds: 52.6% did not graduate high school, 29.0% graduated high school, 7.9% received a GED, 7.9% completed some college, and 2.6% graduated from a 4-year college.

2.2 Measures

Participants completed a series of reading comprehension measures. On the Gates-MacGinitie Reading Comprehension subtest (level 6) [14] the sample performed at a mean grade equivalency of 7.27 (SD = 2.47). By comparison, participants scored a mean grade equivalency of 10.1 (SD = 2.95) on the Gates-MacGinitie Vocabulary subtest [17], indicative that the participants were more able to understand words, and less able to comprehend sentences and connected discourse. Testing also assessed morphological and semantic awareness using the Test of Morphological Structure - Decomposition and Derivation sections [18]. The proportion accuracy was .85 (SD = .17) and .61 (SD = .21) respectively.

iSTART logs participants' behavior throughout interactions with the system, including participant responses to each artifact question. A proportion correct score was obtained by dividing the number of correct responses by number of responses. Further, an analogous proportion correct score was calculated for each story arc.

A post-survey was administered to assess participants' enjoyment of the system and its features (e.g., "I enjoyed reading the story") as well as their engagement in the task (e.g., "I set goals for myself during the story"). Participants answered these survey items on a 5-point Likert Scale. In addition to these overall ratings of the participants' perceptions of the narrative, they also responded to four 4-point Likert Scale items for each of the story arcs: (1) How difficult did you find the tasks you completed in the X (e.g., Introduction)?, (2) How useful did you consider the tasks in the X?, (3) I found the X segment of the story engaging, and (4) After reading the X, I was interested to find out what happened next in the story.

2.3 Procedure

The study was conducted over two sessions. In the first session, participants responded to a battery of reading comprehension measures. Next, the participants viewed six short videos briefly describing self-explanation, summarization, and question asking. In the second session, participants completed the interactive narrative and a post-experience survey. Participants who completed the story ($n = 33$) spent an average of 105.4 min ($SD = 27.2$). Five participants did not finish reading the entire story, spending an average of 122.4 min in the system ($SD = 7.98$). Within individual story arcs, participants' completion times varied: Introduction ($M = 2.9$; $SD = .72$); Mall ($M = 25.2$; $SD = 7.2$); Hospital ($M = 34.5$; $SD = 15.12$); School ($M = 26.2$; $SD = 9.3$); Conclusion ($M = 14.6$; $SD = 4.1$). After completing the interactive narrative, the participants completed questions regarding their perceptions and attitudes.

3   Results

3.1   Perceptions of the Narrative

Results revealed generally positive attitudes toward the interactive narrative. Figure 2 presents frequencies of the responses from Strongly Disagree (1) to Strongly Agree (5) on the five overall perceptions of enjoyment and engagement. A series of one-sample t-tests revealed that mean ratings for each of these items were significantly higher (all p's < .005) than the mid-point of the scale (i.e., 3), indicating that participants leaned toward the 'agree' end of the scale for these positive perception statements about the story. The majority of participants responded either 'agree' or 'strongly agree' to the following statements: (1) I enjoyed reading the story (75.0%), (2) The feedback was helpful (69.4%), (3) The interface had game-like features (62.2%), The environment provided a purpose for my actions (78.4%), The visual parts of the environment made the story more enjoyable (75.7%), The objects in the environment were easy to control (67.6%), I wanted to perform well during the story (81.1%), and I would use this environment to practice other skills (75.7%).

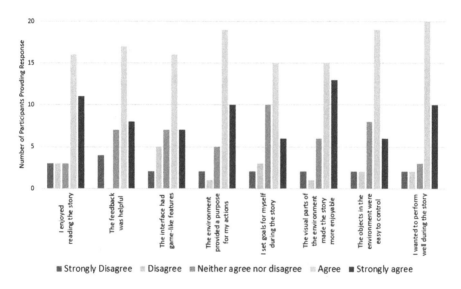

Fig. 2. Overall perceptions of the narrative

We further conducted analyses on participants' perceptions toward the individual story arcs. Figure 3 shows frequencies of responses on the difficulty item, across the story arcs. One-sample t-tests revealed that mean ratings of difficulty were significantly lower than the mid-point of the scale (i.e., 2.5) for all story arcs (all p's < .001).

Figure 4 shows the frequencies of responses for the usefulness item, across story arcs. The one-sample t-tests revealed that mean ratings of usefulness were significantly higher than the mid-point of the scale for each story arcs (all p's < .001). Corresponding analyses were conducted for the engagement (see Fig. 5) and interest (see Fig. 6) items. Results revealed that mean ratings of engagement were significantly higher than the mid-point of the scale for all story arcs (all p's $< .001$), and the same was true for interest ratings (all p's $< .001$).

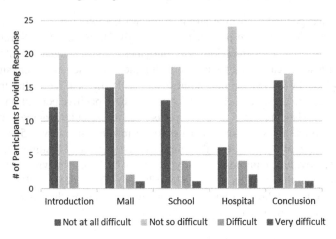

Fig. 3. Difficulty ratings of the story arcs

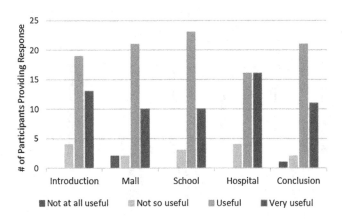

Fig. 4. Usefulness ratings of the story arcs

3.2   Online Performance Measures

Exploration of participants' performance in the system began by examining the percentage correct on artifact items, across each participant's entire session. Overall, participants provided the correct response on a mean of 66.5% ($SD = 8.8\%$) of items. This overall performance indicates that the difficulty of the tasks was acceptable for this population. This performance level seems to contradict the self-reported difficulty ratings reported earlier, indicating generally low ratings of difficulty. Hence, we conducted a series of correlations between the overall percentage correct and the difficulty ratings for the story arcs. None were significant, and all were below .20, which is consistent with research on students' tendency to miscalibrate their performance [19].

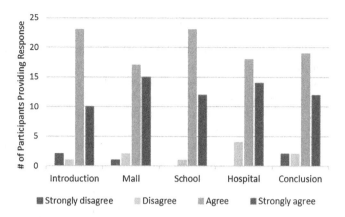

Fig. 5. Engagement ratings of the story arcs

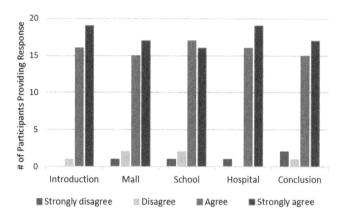

Fig. 6. Interest ratings of the story arcs

Four of the story arcs included items with response accuracy (i.e., which could be scored as correct or incorrect). The Introduction segment did not include any such items. Performance appeared to differ across the four story arcs: M(Mall) = 65.0% (SD = 10.3%), M(School) = 72.7% (SD = 12.0%), M(Hospital) = 68.4% (SD = 14.7%), M(Conclusion) = 61.0% (SD = 16.0%). A repeated-measures ANOVA revealed a significant effect of story arc on these performance scores, $F(3,99)$ = 7.20, $p < .001$, η_p^2 = 0.18. Pairwise comparisons showed that scores were significantly higher for the School arc, compared to the Mall ($p < .001$), and compared to the Conclusion ($p < .001$). Additionally, scores were higher for the Hospital, compared to the Conclusion ($p < .05$). There were no other significant comparisons. We further sub-divided the artifact questions into types of questions. Across the four story arcs containing evaluative questions, 44 questions were multiple-choice items and 8 were select all or drag-and-drop questions. We expected performance to be lower for select all/drag-and-drop questions; results confirmed this: M(multiple-choice) = 72.9%

(SD = 9.2%), M(select all/drag-and-drop) = 30.4% (SD = 20.7%), $t(37)$ = 12.33, $p < .001$, $d = 2.19$.

One of our questions regarded the degree to which performance on the artifact questions within the narrative would correlate with participants' scores on the individual difference measures. Positive correlations would be indicative that the tasks within the narrative were tapping into the comprehension skills targeted in iSTART, and thus provide one source of concurrent validity. To address this question, we conducted a series of bivariate correlations between the individual difference measures in reading (Gates reading, Gates vocabulary, Test of morphological structure – decomposition, and Test of morphological structure – derivation) and the overall narrative performance score, the narrative multiple-choice score, and the narrative select all/drag-and-drop score (see Table 1). Not surprisingly, the correlation between the two Gates measures was strong, as was the correlation between the two morphological structure measures ($r = .79$). Also, the correlation between all narrative items and the ($n = 44$) multiple-choice items was very strong ($r = .95$) compared to the correlation between all items and the ($n = 8$) select all/drag-and-drop items ($r = .43$), primarily because there were more multiple-choice items comprising all items. Of particular interest to our development efforts, the correlation between the Gates reading measure and all narrative items was strong ($r = .60$), indicating that the items in the story are suitably evaluative of reading comprehension ability. Correlations between performance in the narrative and the morphological structure measure, and the Gates vocabulary measure were comparably lower, suggesting that the narrative items relate more toward higher-level comprehension skills than basic word-level skills.

Table 1. Correlations for individual difference measures and narrative performance scores

	2	3	4	5	6	7
1. Gates reading	.614 ***	.431**	.393*	.599***	.493**	.499**
2. Gates vocabulary		.428**	.424**	.411*	.313	.351*
3. TMS-Decomposition			.787***	.264	.189	.244
4. TMS-Derivation				.221	.140	.205
5. All Narrative items					.953***	.431**
6. MC Narrative items						.157
7. SA/DD Narr. items						

*** Significant at the 0.001 level ** Significant at the 0.01 level * Significant at the 0.05 level

Notes: TMS = Test of Morphological Structure; MC = multiple-choice; SA/DD Narr. items = Select All/Drag-and-Drop Narrative Items

4   Conclusions

This paper describes the development of iSTART-ALL for adult literacy learners. We focused the description on design, development, and testing of the interactive narrative developed to provide extended practice of reading comprehension strategies. The narrative, designed as a new practice module in iSTART-ALL instruction, was informed by prior recommendations [20]. We created the learning artifacts in the narrative to target life-relevant skills for low literate adults, and used the following design elements to ensure its effectiveness in improving adults' reading comprehension:

- The storyline is adaptive to learners' decisions
- Learning artifacts are life-relevant to adult learners to develop life skills
- The system uses a variety of interaction methods and response types
- Motivation elements are used to enhance effort and persistence
- An open learner model is used to promote reflection on learning
- Foundational skills (e.g., decoding) are supported with pronunciation scaffolding and auditory text presentation

The results from an attitudinal study conducted with adult literacy learners indicated overall positive perceptions of their experiences with the narrative. Over 60% of the participants responded 'agree' or 'strongly agree' to a series of positive statements about the module. Although the participants tended to rate the segments of the story as not very difficult, performance data within the system indicated a mean percent correct of 66.5%; thus, we believe the difficulty of the items is appropriate for this population. The conclusion story segment appears to be the most difficult, perhaps because it includes items requiring participants to remember what happened in earlier-read segments and to determine the sequence of events that led up to the abandonment of the town. Interestingly, though, students did not rate the conclusion segment as more difficult than the other parts of the story, perhaps because they were not required to read new learning artifacts during the conclusion.

The correlations between the individual difference measures and the online performance data were indicative of strong relations between students' reading ability and narrative performance. This finding establishes tentative concurrent validity for the tasks within the narrative, and further suggests that the tasks provide indicators of reading comprehension abilities. As such, the difficulty of the texts and the question types (e.g., multiple choice vs. open-ended) can potentially be iteratively adjusted according to individuals' performance on the tasks. Future development plans also include refining the NLP assessment algorithms for students' summaries and questions and to use those algorithms to provide automated feedback.

Of course, this study is only a first in a series of those that we envision. Most importantly, empirical evidence of effectiveness is crucial. For example, a study is currently underway to examine the effects of iSTART-ALL on adult learners' motivation and reading comprehension abilities. Nonetheless, the current study provides an important stride and preliminary evidence for the potential promise of iSTART-ALL to meet the unique needs of adult literacy learners.

Acknowledgments. The authors would like to recognize support of the Institute of Education Sciences, U.S. Department of Education, through Grant R305A130124, and the Office of Naval Research, through Grants N00014140343 and N00014172300, to Arizona State University. The opinions expressed are those of the authors and do not represent views of the Institute, the U.S. Department of Education, or the Office of Naval Research.

References

1. McNamara, D.S., O'Reilly, T.P., Best, R.M., Ozuru, Y.: Improving adolescent students' reading comprehension with iSTART. J. Educ. Comput. Res. **34**, 147–171 (2006)
2. Snow, E.L., Jackson, G.T., McNamara, D.S.: Emergent behaviors in computer-based learning environments: computational signals of catching up. Comput. Hum. Behav. **41**, 62–70 (2014)
3. Baer, J., Kutner, M., Sabatini, J., White, S.: Basic Reading Skills and the Literacy of America's Least Literate Adults: Results from the 2003 National Assessment of Adult Literacy (NAAL) Supplemental Studies. NCES (2009)
4. McNamara, D.S.: Self-explanation and Reading Strategy Training (SERT) Improves Low-knowledge Students' Science Course Performance. Discourse Process (in press)
5. Hock, M., Mellard, D.: Reading comprehension strategies for adult literacy outcomes. J. Adolesc. Adult Lit. **49**, 192–200 (2005)
6. Brown, A.L., Campione, J.C., Day, J.D.: Learning to learn: on training students to learn from texts. Educ. Res. **10**, 14–21 (1981)
7. Brown, A.L., Day, J.D.: Macrorules for summarizing texts: the development of expertise. J. Verbal Learn. Verbal Behav. **22**, 1–14 (1983)
8. King, A.: Guiding knowledge construction in the classroom: effects of teaching children how to question and how to explain. Am. Educ. Res. J. **31**, 338–368 (1994)
9. Rosenshine, B., Meister, C., Chapman, S.: Teaching students to generate questions: a review of the intervention studies. Rev. Educ. Res. **66**, 181–221 (1996)
10. Graesser, A.C., Person, N.K.: Question asking during tutoring. Am. Educ. Res. J. **31**, 104–137 (1994)
11. Sullins, J., Craig, S.D., Graesser, A.C.: The influence of modality on deep-reasoning questions. Int. J. Learn. Tech. **5**, 378–387 (2010)
12. Craig, S.D., Sullins, J., Witherspoon, A., Gholson, B.: The deep-level-reasoning-question effect: the role of dialogue and deep-level-reasoning questions during vicarious learning. Cog. Instr. **24**, 565–591 (2006)
13. Au, K.H.P., Mason, J.M.: Cultural Congruence in Classroom Participation Structures: Achieving a Balance of Rights. Discourse Process. **6**, 145–167 (1983)
14. Wigfield, A., Eccles, J.S., Rodriguez, D.: The development of children's motivation in school contexts. Rev. Res. Educ. **23**, 73–118 (1998)
15. McNamara, D.S., Boonthum, C., Levinstein, I.B., Millis, K.: Evaluating self-explanations in iSTART: comparing word-based and LSA algorithms. In: Handbook of Latent Semantic Analysis, pp. 227–241 (2007)
16. Kopp, K., Johnson, A.M., Crossley, S.A., McNamara, D.S.: (accepted) Assessing Question Quality using Natural Language Processing. In: Proceedings of the 18th International Conference on Artificial Intelligence in Education.
17. MacGinitie, W.H.: Gates-MacGinitie Reading Tests. Nelson, Toronto (1980)
18. Carlisle, J.F.: Awareness of the structure and meaning of morphologically complex words: impact on reading. Read. Writ. **12**, 169–190 (2000)
19. Hacker, D.J., Bol, L., Horgan, D.D., Rakow, E.A.: Test prediction and performance in a classroom context. J. Educ. Psychol. **92**, 160–170 (2000)
20. Lesgold, A.M., Welch-Ross, M. (eds.): Improving Adult Literacy Instruction: Options for Practice and Research. National Academies Press, Washington (2012)

Adapting Step Granularity in Tutorial Dialogue Based on Pretest Scores

Pamela Jordan[(✉)], Patricia Albacete, and Sandra Katz

University of Pittsburgh, Pittsburgh, PA 15260, USA
{pjordan,palbacet,katz}@pitt.edu

Abstract. We explore the effectiveness of adaptively deciding whether to further decompose a step in a line of reasoning during tutorial dialogue based on students' pretest scores. We compare two versions of a tutorial dialogue system in high school classrooms: one that always decomposes a step to its simplest substeps and one that adaptively decides to decompose a step based on a student's performance on pretest items that target the knowledge required to correctly answer that step. We hypothesize that students using the two versions of the tutoring system will learn similarly but that students who use the version that adaptively decomposes a step will learn more efficiently. Our results from classroom studies suggest support for our hypothesis. While students learned similarly and with similar efficiency across conditions, high prior knowledge students in the adaptive condition learned significantly more efficiently than high prior knowledge students in the control condition and learned similar amounts.

Keywords: Tutorial dialogue · Adaptive tutoring · Classroom studies

1 Introduction

General ways in which a tutoring system could adapt to support a student's particular needs include deciding: what content the student should focus on, who (student or tutor) should be doing the reasoning involved (e.g. [3]) and when help should be offered to the student (e.g. [12,13]). If we consider an inner and outer loop for a tutoring system [14], adapting what the student should focus on in the outer loop can include problem selection (e.g. [8,11,16]) and in the inner loop can include what level of detail is given in the content presented by the tutor (e.g. [16,18]). In addition, other aspects of the interaction besides the adaptation of domain knowledge have been explored such as how the selected content is presented (e.g. [4,10,18]) and other student characteristics for driving the adaptation besides learning gains have been explored such as learning style (e.g. [10]). This study focuses on what details to cover with the student during the inner loop and adapts what it covers based on the student's pretest performance.

© Springer International Publishing AG 2017
E. André et al. (Eds.): AIED 2017, LNAI 10331, pp. 137–148, 2017.
DOI: 10.1007/978-3-319-61425-0_12

The tutorial dialogue system (Rimac) used in this study [1, 7] decides whether it needs to decompose a task for the learner including: (1) deciding whether to decompose the reasoning needed to answer a post-problem reflection question (RQ), as in Fig. 1, and (2) the granularity of any reasoning discussed. The communicated steps in the reasoning of an expert can abstract over some of the reasoning that leads from one step to the next. The reasoning between those steps has been called microsteps [2] or substeps and is illustrated in Fig. 2.

Prior research challenged the assumption that microstep-based tutoring (best illustrated by human tutoring) is more effective than step-based tutoring. This research has typically been conducted in a nonadaptive context (i.e., students in one condition always experience steps and in the other always experience microsteps). For example, [15] observed that the benefits of microstep-based tutoring relative to less interactive forms of instruction, including step-based tutoring, plateau over time. However, [2] found that augmenting microstep-based tutoring with non-adaptive pedagogical policies that decide, for example, who will cover what (the tutor or the student), is significantly more beneficial for learning than tutoring that addresses steps only. Not surprisingly, [2] also noted that non-adaptive microstep-based discussions between the student and simulated tutor are significantly more time consuming than step-based discussions, which raises the central question addressed in this paper: Can *adaptive* decision-making about whether to address the reasoning between steps improve the efficiency of microstep-based tutoring, without compromising its benefits? We expect that it will. Our prediction is supported by related research which found that a simple, non-adaptive approach to improving the efficiency of microstep-based tutoring (i.e., alternating between problems that involve highly interactive, microstep-based dialogues and non-interactive problems that summarize the line of reasoning that leads to a solution) proved to be as beneficial for learning as an all microstep-based tutoring approach. However, the latter was significantly less efficient than the intervention that shifted between interactive and non-interactive problems [9].

Problem:

Suppose you aim a bow horizontally, directly at the center of a target 25.0 m away from you. If the speed of the arrow is 60 m/s, how far from the center of the target will it strike the target? That is, find the vertical displacement of the arrow while it is in flight.

Assume there is no air friction.

Reflection Question (RQ):

Let's imagine a scenario in which an archer is standing at the edge of a high cliff. He shoots an arrow perfectly horizontally with an initial velocity of 60 m/s off this cliff. During the arrow's flight, how does its horizontal velocity change (increases, decreases, remains the same, etc.)? Remember that you can ignore air resistance.

Fig. 1. An example problem and post-problem reflection question.

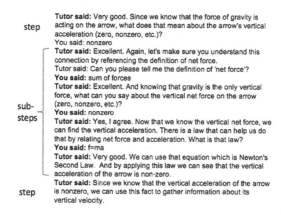

Fig. 2. An example of steps and substeps in a line of reasoning.

We compare two versions of Rimac for high school physics: one that always decomposes successfully co-constructed steps and one that adaptively decides whether to decompose such a step based on students' pretest assessment. The reason for decomposing a successfully co-constructed step is that the student may have contributed a correct answer using incomplete reasoning or may have simply guessed correctly using intuition and thus it could be beneficial to explicitly cover the underlying reasoning with the student. We hypothesize that if our approach to adapting step granularity is effective, then students will learn similarly from using either version of the system but that students who use the adaptive granularity version will learn more efficiently.

The rationale for the hypothesis follows. Students using either version of the system can spend as much time as they need to complete the assigned problems. If the student fails to successfully co-construct a decomposable step, then the system will elicit its substeps so that the student explicitly covers the underlying reasoning with the system. However, if the student succeeds at co-constructing the step, then there is a choice about whether or not to skip eliciting the substeps. When substeps are skipped the student can progress faster through the problem. Thus, if the adaptive system is accurate in its decisions to skip or not, then it should enable a significant number of students to complete the problem faster. Furthermore, if it is not detrimental to have skipped explicit mention of this material, then learning gains for students who used the adaptive system should be similar to learning gains for students who used the nonadaptive system. Our results suggest support for this hypothesis.

2   The Rimac Tutorial Dialogue System

Rimac is a web-based natural-language tutoring system that engages students in conceptual discussions after they solve quantitative physics problems. Similar to Wood's EXPLAIN, QUADRATIC and DATA tutors [16], Rimac decides whether to discuss the line of reasoning (LOR) underlying a correct answer to an RQ and, if so, at what grain size (i.e., it decides whether to decompose a step into simpler substeps). And similar to Wood's DATA tutor, Rimac bases decomposition decisions on pretest assessments. Unlike Wood's tutors, help seeking is not left to the learner in that Rimac and the student are engaged in a discussion of the line of reasoning (LOR) that leads to the answer to a reflection question and the system always helps the student co-construct the next sought step in the LOR. To help the student co-construct the sought step, Rimac uses hint strategies to elicit the step from the student. If the hint fails, and the student is unable to co-construct the step, then the system either offers a more specific hint, decomposes the step further and hints at each of its substeps, or simply completes the step for the student by stating the correct response.

Rimac was built using the TuTalk tutorial dialogue toolkit [6]. Thus the dialogues authored for the system can be represented with a finite state machine. Each state contains a single tutor turn. The arcs leaving the state correspond to possible classifications of student turns. When creating a state, the dialogue author enters the text for a tutor's turn and defines classes of student responses (e.g., correct, partially correct, incorrect).

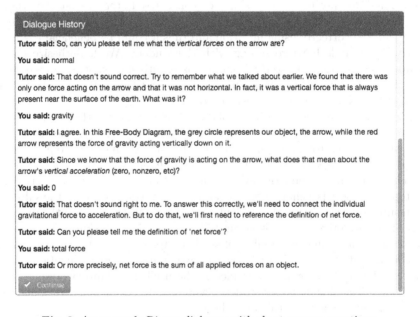

Fig. 3. An example Rimac dialogue with short-answer questions.

Rimac's dialogues were developed to model a directed LOR [5] during which the tutor presents a series of carefully ordered questions to the student. If the student answers a question correctly, he advances to the next question in the LOR. If the student provides an incorrect answer, the system launches a remedial subdialogue and then returns to the main line of reasoning after the subdialogue has completed. If the system is unable to understand the student's response, then it completes the step for the student. Rimac asks mainly short-answer questions to improve recognition of student responses as shown in Fig. 3, which illustrates the system's follow-up to correct, partially correct and incorrect answers.

Rimac's dialogues are structured as hierarchical plan networks where a parent node abstracts over its child nodes [17]. See Fig. 4 for an example of part of a plan network for one of the Rimac dialogues we use in our testing.

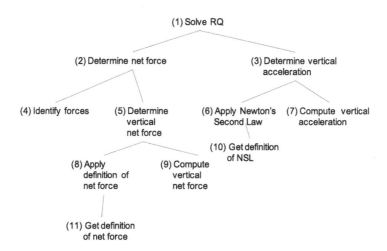

Fig. 4. Extract of plan network for responding to the RQ in Fig. 1.

The adaptive version of Rimac uses a decision algorithm to decide whether, after eliciting a parent node, to expand the parent node and elicit its child nodes. For this study, we selected the nodes where decisions should be made instead of treating each non-leaf node as a potential decision point in order to improve coherency and focus on steps with the greatest potential need for remediation.

For example, in reference to the plan network in Fig. 4, both example dialogues in Fig. 5 first elicit the top child nodes of "(2) Determine net force" and "(3) Determine vertical acceleration" for the parent node "(1) Solve RQ". Neither of the child nodes "(2) Determine net force" and "(3) Determine vertical acceleration" is expanded further in the dialogue example in Fig. 5 (left), which was generated by the adaptive version of the system. Instead, the dialogue moves on to elicit a new sibling node not shown in the plan network. However, in the dialogue example on the right in Fig. 5, the system decides to expand all decomposable nodes further [e.g., "(2) Determine net force" and "(3) Determine vertical acceleration"].

Thus, the dialogues for the adaptive version of the system would range between that shown by the dialogue on the left in Fig. 5, where none of the target parent nodes is expanded, and that shown by the dialogue on the right where the algorithm decides to expand every target parent node.

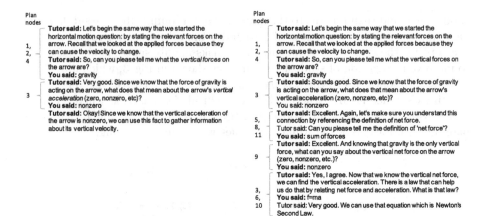

Fig. 5. The dialogue on the left represents the non-expanded network in Fig. 4 (possibly produced by the experimental version of Rimac, during expert performance) and the dialogue on the right represents the fully expanded network (always produced by the control version of Rimac).

3   Adaptive Step Decomposition

The adaptive version of Rimac uses a student model that is initialized with the student's pretest scores for the knowledge components (KCs) that need to be applied to arrive at the correct answer to the reflection questions presented to the student. Currently, Rimac does not update the student model during the discussions since doing so in a computationally feasible way requires exploratory research that we are currently undertaking.

The adaptive version of the system consults the student model at every decision point to predict whether the student is likely to need the current step to be decomposed into simpler steps. Two types of decision points occur: (1) after a reflection question (RQ) is answered by the student and (2) when it is possible to further decompose a step into substeps. In the former case the reflection question is the top node in the plan network and is decomposed by engaging in a discussion of the reasoning with the student (i.e., it elicits some subset of child nodes). For every decision point a set of prerequisite KCs have been identified that are expected to predict whether the student sufficiently knows the knowledge expressed in the child nodes (substeps). The student's pretest scores for that set of KCs are evaluated to decide whether to decompose the node (step).

Let KC_D be the set of KCs associated with decision point D where $KC_d \in KC_D$ is a single KC and let S_D be the set of scores for KC_D where $S_d \in S_D$ is the score for KC_d and is defined as:

$$S_d = 1/n \sum_{i=1}^{n} a_i \qquad (1)$$

a_i is the score $\in [0, 1]$ for a pretest item that tests KC_d and n is the number of test items testing KC_d. Finally, T_D is the score for decision point D where T_D is defined as:

$$T_D = min(S_D) \tag{2}$$

We consider a student with $T_D >= .8$ as very knowledgeable about the content that could be skipped, $T_D >= .5$ as having medium-level knowledge, and $T_D < .5$ as having low-level knowledge. The algorithm applied at each decision point D is defined as:

if RQ node & node correct & $T_D >= .8$ **then**
    do not expand the RQ node
else if RQ node & (node incorrect OR $T_D < .8$) **then**
    expand the RQ node
else if node correct & $T_D >= .5$ **then**
    do not expand the node
else if node incorrect OR $T_D < .5$ **then**
    expand the node
end if

4   Evaluation

A two condition evaluation was performed in which the experimental condition used the adaptive tutor (as described in Sect. 2) and the control condition used the non-adaptation tutor; that is, all students were presented with a dialogue that represented a detailed line of reasoning to discuss the reflection questions. This line of reasoning was the same that was used for students in the adaptive condition when their understanding of the relevant knowledge for the current reflection question was assessed with a probability below 50%.

4.1   Participants

Students from three high schools in the Pittsburgh, PA area were recruited to participate in the study. They were taking the school's regular level physics class (as opposed to an accelerated course) that covered the topics discussed in the system. Students were randomly assigned to the control and experimental conditions and used the system as a homework helper. A total of 80 students were recruited to participate in the study but 7 dropped out. Of the 73 remaining students, one belonging to the control condition was eliminated from the study because she was an outlier with regards to the time she took to complete the problems. Her time on task was more than three times the standard deviation, though her transcript revealed that her session had been similar to that of students who had an average time on task. Of the 72 students included in the study, N = 35 were in the control condition and N = 37 in the experimental condition.

4.2   Materials

Using the control and experimental versions of the tutoring system, students solved two homework problems with a total of five reflection questions on the topic of dynamics. A pretest and isomorphic posttest were developed. The tests consisted of 19 multiple choice questions that were presented online. Students were given 20 min to take the tests in two of the schools and 35 min in the other.[1]

4.3   Protocol

Students started by taking an in-class online pretest. After the pretest, they interleaved solving homework problems on paper with using the system in the following way: first, students solved a problem on paper; second, they viewed a video of the solution to the problem on the system, which contained no reference to any conceptual aspect of the problem; third, they engaged in reflection dialogues with the system which addressed conceptual aspects of the recently solved problem. After all problems and dialogues were completed, students took an in-class posttest. Students completed some problems and dialogues in class and the rest at home; all without assistance from teachers.

4.4   Results

Our main hypothesis is that students will learn equally from both versions of the system but students in the adaptive condition would do so more efficiently. To test this hypothesis, we started by investigating whether students, all together and in each condition, learned from interacting with the system. Then we compared the mean learning between conditions and checked for aptitude treatment interactions. Finally, we compared the mean time on task between conditions. The results of the analysis follow.

Did Students Learn from Interacting with the System? According to paired samples t-tests, the mean scores of the pretest vs. those of the posttest considering all students together and considering subjects in each condition separately were statistically significantly different for all groupings of students. Table 1 shows the results. This suggests that students learned from interacting with the system.

Did One Condition of the System Foster More Learning than the Other? First, we investigated whether students in both groups had comparable incoming knowledge as measured by the pretest. We found a statistically significant difference between the two groups, $t(70) = 2.283$, $p = .03$. To control for the possible

---

[1] The time difference was due to an experimental error. The mean pretest score for students who had longer to take the test ($M = 8.56$, $SD = 2.24$) was statistically significantly lower than the mean pretest score of the students who had less time ($M = 11.43$, $SD = 2.71$), $t(70) = 3.030$, $p = .003$. This suggests that the extra time to take the test did not provide a performance advantage.

Table 1. Pretest vs. posttest scores

Condition	Pretest mean SD (normalized mean SD)	Posttest mean SD (normalized mean SD)	$t(n)$	p
All students	$M = 11.07\ SD = 2.81$ ($M = .58,\ SD = .15$)	$M = 13.32\ SD = 3.24$ ($M = .70,\ SD = .17$)	$t(71) = 8.302$	$<.001$
Adaptive	$M = 11.78\ SD = 2.92$ ($M = .62\ SD = .15$)	$M = 14.03\ SD = 2.98$ ($M = .74\ SD = .16$)	$t(36) = 7.214$	$<.001$
Nonadaptive	$M = 10.31\ SD = 2.52$ ($M = .54\ SD = .13$)	$M = 12.57\ SD = 3.37$ ($M = .66\ SD = .18$)	$t(34) = 4.957$	$<.001$

effect of this difference in incoming knowledge, we compared the effect of condition on posttest scores by performing an ANCOVA with Pretest as the covariate, Condition as the fixed factor, and Posttest as the independent variable. The ANCOVA result suggests that condition had no statistically significant effect on posttest when controlling for the effects of pretest $F(1, 69) = .207, p = .65$. This suggests that students in both conditions learned equally.

Was There an Aptitude-Treatment Interaction? In Other Words, did the Difference in Learning Between Conditions Vary Depending on Students' Prior Knowledge? We studied whether the effectiveness of each version of the system varied depending on students' prior knowledge (as measured by pretest scores)—for example, if the adaptive condition was more effective for high performers than the nonadaptive condition but this trend did not hold for low performers. To this end, a regression analysis was performed using Condition, Pretest, and Condition * Pretest (interaction term) as independent variables and gain as the dependent variable. The regression coefficient of the interaction term was not significant ($t = -.053, p = .96$) suggesting no aptitude-treatment interaction.

Was There a Time on Task Difference Between Conditions? According to an independent samples t-test, the mean time on task of the adaptive condition ($M = 2290.27\,\text{s}$—about 38.17 min, $SD = 943.36\,\text{s}$—about 15.7 min) was smaller though not statistically different from the mean time on task of the nonadaptive condition ($M = 2558.78\,\text{s}$—about 42.65 min, $SD = 1017.25\,\text{s}$—about 16.95 min), $t(70) = 1.162, p = .249$. This suggests that there is not a significant difference in the time students spent solving problems between the two conditions.

Given the possible effects of prior knowledge (as measured by pretest) on time on task, we performed an ANCOVA with pretest score as the covariate, condition as the fixed factor, and time on task as the independent variable. We found no significant effect of condition on time on task when controlling for the effect of prior knowledge, $F(1, 69) = .884, p = 0.35$. This result confirms our finding that students in both conditions took, on average, approximately the same amount of time to solve their homework problems.

An In-Depth Look at Time on Task: Studying Time on Task Differences Between Conditions for High Incoming Knowledge Students. The lack of difference in time on task that was found in the previous section could be due to the fact that students with low prior knowledge in the adaptive condition would go through the system in the same way as the students in the nonadaptive condition; hence their time on task would be expected to be similar. However students in the adaptive condition with high incoming knowledge would not go through unnecessarily long lines of reasoning while solving the problems; they would either go through the expert line of reasoning or skip the reflection question all together and this would tend to make their time on task shorter than that of students in the nonadaptive condition. So we examined whether students with higher incoming knowledge in both groups had a time on task difference and, if so, if they learned the same in spite of this difference. To test this hypothesis we divided the students in each condition into two groups using the median of the condition as the cutting point.[2] We then compared the time on task of students with high pretest scores in both conditions.

For high prior knowledge students, the mean time on task of students in the adaptive condition ($M = 2033.24$ s—about 33.89 min, $SD = 880.27$ s—about 14.67 min) was statistically significantly lower than the mean time on task of students in the nonadaptive condition ($M = 2761.27$ s—about 46.02 min, $SD = 931.66$ s—about 15.53 min). Given the possible differences in pretest scores of both groups (even if all students are in the upper 50th percentile of their conditions) and the effects that prior knowledge could have on time on task, we performed a ANCOVA using condition as the independent variable, pretest score as the covariate, and time on task as the dependent variable, to study the effect of condition on time on task of high incoming knowledge students controlling for the effects of prior knowledge. We found a trend in the effect of condition on time on task when controlling for prior knowledge, $F = 3.710, p = .062$. Both of these results suggest that students in the adaptive condition solved their problems in a more efficient manner, taking less time than students in the nonadaptive condition.

Given this finding we studied whether higher incoming knowledge students performed equally well in both groups. To that end we performed an independent samples t-test, which showed that the mean gain of the adaptive condition ($M = 1.52, SD = 1.63$) was not statistically different from the mean gain of the nonadaptive condition ($M = 2.29, SD = 2.34$), $t(36) = 1.194, p = .24$. These results suggest that students in the adaptive condition with higher incoming knowledge were able to learn as much as similar students in the nonadaptive condition but did so much faster with a mean time on task of about 34 min vs. 46 min for the control condition.

---

[2] In the nonadaptive condition students with scores equal to the median were not included in the high group and in the adaptive condition students with pretest scores equal to the median were included in the high group. This yielded approximately the same amount of students classified as high and low pretesters in each condition.

5   Conclusions and Future Work

We explored the effectiveness of adaptively deciding whether or not to decompose a step in a line of reasoning during tutorial dialogue based on students' pretest performance. We developed two versions of the Rimac system to test its effectiveness: a control version that always decomposes a step regardless of the student's prior knowledge level on the content involved and an experimental version that decides whether or not to decompose a step based on the student's prior knowledge of the content involved in the step.

We found that while all students who used the adaptive system learned similarly and took similar time to complete the tutoring as all students who used the nonadaptive system, high prior knowledge students who used the adaptive system took significantly less time to complete the problems and learned similarly to high prior knowledge students who used the nonadaptive system. This finding supports our hypothesis that students using a system that adapts the granularity of steps will learn more efficiently than students using a system that does not adapt, with no detrimental effect on students' learning gains.

In future work we will test a version of the system in which there are never any decompositions of target nodes that are answered correctly to further test the validity of our hypothesis. We will also explore additional adaptations that traverse the plan network in different ways and the effect of dynamically updating the student model based on the interactions between the student and tutor. After we have fine-tuned and validated our approach, we will explore whether it will transfer to other tutorial dialogue domains.

Acknowledgments. We thank Dennis Lusetich, Svetlana Romanova, and Scott Silliman. This research was supported by the Institute of Education Sciences, U.S. Department of Education, through Grant R305A130441 to the University of Pittsburgh. The opinions expressed are those of the authors and do not necessarily represent the views of the Institute or the U.S. Department of Education.

References

1. Albacete, P., Jordan, P., Katz, S.: Is a dialogue-based tutoring system that emulates helpful co-constructed relations during human tutoring effective? In: Conati, C., Heffernan, N., Mitrovic, A., Verdejo, M.F. (eds.) AIED 2015. LNCS, vol. 9112, pp. 3–12. Springer, Cham (2015). doi:10.1007/978-3-319-19773-9_1
2. Chi, M., Jordan, P., VanLehn, K.: When is tutorial dialogue more effective than step-based tutoring? In: Trausan-Matu, S., Boyer, K.E., Crosby, M., Panourgia, K. (eds.) ITS 2014. LNCS, vol. 8474, pp. 210–219. Springer, Cham (2014). doi:10.1007/978-3-319-07221-0_25
3. Chi, M., VanLehn, K., Litman, D., Jordan, P.: Empirically evaluating the application of reinforcement learning to the induction of effective and adaptive pedagogical strategies. User Model. User Adapt. Interact. **21**(1–2), 137–180 (2011)
4. Di Eugenio, B., Fossati, D., Yu, D., Haller, S.M., Glass, M.: Natural language generation for intelligent tutoring systems: a case study. In: AIED, pp. 217–224 (2005)

5. Evens, M., Michael, J.: One-on-One Tutoring by Humans and Computers. Psychology Press (2006)
6. Jordan, P.W., Hall, B., Ringenberg, M., Cui, Y., Rosé, C.: Tools for authoring a dialogue agent that participates in learning studies. In: Proceedings of AIED 2007, pp. 43–50 (2007)
7. Katz, S., Albacete, P.: A tutoring system that simulates the highly interactive nature of human tutoring. J. Educ. Psychol. **105**(4), 1126 (2013)
8. Koedinger, K., Pavlik Jr., P.I., Stamper, J., Nixon, T., Ritter, S.: Avoiding problem selection thrashing with conjunctive knowledge tracing. In: Proceedings of Educational Data Mining (2011)
9. Kopp, K.J., Britt, M.A., Millis, K., Graesser, A.C.: Improving the efficiency of dialogue in tutoring. Learn. Instr. **22**(5), 320–330 (2012)
10. Latham, A., Crockett, K., McLean, D.: An adaptation algorithm for an intelligent natural language tutoring system. Comput. Educ. **71**, 97–110 (2014)
11. Mitrovic, A., Martin, B.: Scaffolding and fading problem selection in SQL-tutor. In: Proceedings of the 11th International Conference on Artificial Intelligence in Education, pp. 479–481 (2003)
12. Mostow, J., Aist, G.: Giving help and praise in a reading tutor with imperfect listening: because automated speech recognition means never being able to say you're certain. CALICO J. **16**(3), 407–424 (1999)
13. Murray, R.C., VanLehn, K.: Effects of dissuading unnecessary help requests while providing proactive help. In: AIED, pp. 887–889. Citeseer (2005)
14. Vanlehn, K.: The behavior of tutoring systems. Int. J. Artif. Intell. Educ. **16**(3), 227–265 (2006)
15. VanLehn, K.: The relative effectiveness of human tutoring, intelligent tutoring systems, and other tutoring systems. Educ. Psychol. **46**(4), 197–221 (2011)
16. Wood, D.: Scaffolding, contingent tutoring, and computer-supported learning. Int. J. Artif. Intell. Educ. **12**(3), 280–293 (2001)
17. Young, R.M., Ware, S., Cassell, B., Robertson, J.: Plans and planning in narrative generation: a review of plan-based approaches to the generation of story, discourse and interactivity in narratives. SDV – Sprache und Datenverarbeitung. Int. J. Lang. Data Process. **37**(1–2), 41–64 (2013)
18. Zhou, Y., Freedman, R., Glass, M., Michael, J.A., Rovick, A.A., Evens, M.W.: What should the tutor do when the student cannot answer a question? In: FLAIRS Conference, pp. 187–191 (1999)

The Impact of Student Individual Differences and Visual Attention to Pedagogical Agents During Learning with MetaTutor

Sébastien Lallé[1](✉), Michelle Taub[2], Nicholas V. Mudrick[2],
Cristina Conati[1], and Roger Azevedo[2]

[1] University of British Columbia, Vancouver, BC, Canada
{lalles,conati}@cs.ubc.ca
[2] North Carolina State University, Raleigh, NC, USA
{mtaub,nvmudric,razeved}@ncsu.edu

Abstract. In this paper, we investigate the relationship between students' ($N = 28$) individual differences and visual attention to pedagogical agents (PAs) during learning with MetaTutor, a hypermedia-based intelligent tutoring systems. We used eye tracking to capture visual attention to the PAs, and our results reveal specific visual attention-related metrics (e.g., fixation rate, longest fixations) that are significantly influenced by learning depending on student achievement goals. Specifically, performance-oriented students learned more with a long longest fixation and a high fixation rate on the PAs, whereas mastery-oriented students learned less with a high fixation rate on the PAs. Our findings contribute to understanding how to design PAs that can better adapt to student achievement goals and visual attention to the PA.

Keywords: Pedagogical agents · Personalization · Visual attention · Achievement goals · Personality traits · Intelligent tutoring systems

1 Introduction

Pedagogical agents (PAs) are intelligent virtual agents that support learning with intelligent tutoring system (ITS) by providing students with adaptive scaffolding (e.g., hints, feedback) [1–3]. There is extensive evidence that PAs can improve learning with ITS at the cognitive, metacognitive, and affective level, e.g., [1, 2, 4]. However, there is also work showing that PAs' effectiveness can be influenced by student individual differences (e.g., gender, achievement goals, personality traits), e.g., [5–7]. For instance, Duffy and Azevedo [6] showed that student *achievement goals* (motivational goals in learning situations [8]) can influence learning during interaction with the PAs in MetaTutor, an ITS designed to scaffold student cognitive and metacognitive processes [1]. These findings indicate that it is important to investigate how we can design PAs that can enhance student learning by dynamically adapting to the relevant individual differences. However, previous research does not provide guidance on *how* and *when* this personalization should happen.

© Springer International Publishing AG 2017
E. André et al. (Eds.): AIED 2017, LNAI 10331, pp. 149–161, 2017.
DOI: 10.1007/978-3-319-61425-0_13

Other work has used eye tracking to show that student individual differences impact visual attention to PAs, suggesting that changes in visual attention could be leveraged as triggers to provide adaptation [9, 10]. These studies, however, have not linked changes in visual attention with changes in learning. In this paper, we aim to explore the relationship between individual differences, visual attention to PAs and learning, as a step toward understanding how to design PAs that can better adapt to student individual differences and use information on visual attention to PAs to drive this adaptation.

In particular, we extend the work by Duffy and Azevedo [6] by looking at visual attention to PAs in the same ITS, MetaTutor, and by looking at *personality traits* [11] in addition to achievement goals. We track student visual attention to the PAs (simply "attention" from now on) by generating a variety of eye-tracking metrics that capture students' gaze behavior when they are looking at the PAs during learning.

Our results show that eye tracking data reveal specific visual attention-related variables (e.g., fixation rate, longest fixations) on the MetaTutor PAs that can be predictive of learning gains depending on student achievement goals. For instance, we found that performance-oriented students (i.e., students aiming at outperforming others) achieved lower learning when they had lower values for gaze measures indicating attention to the PAs, and higher learning when they had higher values of these measures. Thus, although Duffy and Azevedo [6] found that performance-oriented students can overall learn from the MetaTutor PAs, we actually show that performance-oriented students may benefit from the PAs even further if they receive personalized scaffolding (e.g., prompts to refocus on the PA) delivered when they do not attend to the PAs.

2 Related Work

There is extensive evidence that PAs can impact learning, motivation, self-regulated learning (SRL), and affect when interacting with ITS [1, 2, 4]. Further research has shown that learning with PAs can be modulated by students' individual differences [6, 12]. Duffy and Azevedo [6] showed that student achievement goals can influence learning and the use of SRL strategies while interacting with MetaTutor. In particular, they showed that performance-oriented students benefitted more from the PAs than mastery-oriented students (i.e., students who aims at developing competencies). As detailed in the introduction, we extend this work by investigating whether the effect of achievement goals on learning can be modulated by attention to the PAs. Wang et al. [12] showed that personality traits can influence learning when interacting with a PA teaching domain-specific procedural knowledge. For example, they found that extroverted students benefited from PAs exhibiting a polite behavior [12]. In our work, we investigate whether personality traits also influence learning with MetaTutor's PAs.

There is an extensive body of work showing that students' overall level of attention during learning tasks is critical for effective learning (see [13, 14] for an overview). In the field of ITS, eye tracking has been used to investigate which factors affect user visual attention to salient components of agent-based ITS [9, 10], but these works do not establish a connection with learning outcomes. For example, Conati et al. [9] showed that attention to textual hints provided by a PA in an educational game is influenced by hint timing and types, as well as by students' current game performance and their general attitude toward getting help. In a second example, Taub and Azevedo [10] showed that student prior knowledge affects total time spent looking at Meta-Tutor's learning content and PAs. We extend these previous findings and investigate the relationship between students' attention to the MetaTutor PAs and learning gains.

Eye-tracking has also been used to add real-time adaptive interventions to Guru, an agent-based ITS for learning about biology [3]. In that work, audible prompts were triggered if a student had not looked at the screen for more than 5 s while the Guru PA was providing scaffolding. The prompts were designed to reorient student attention towards the screen, and this work showed that students who received these gaze-reactive feedback learned more. They also showed that the effectiveness of the gaze-reactive prompts was impacted by students' SAT scores. These results provide concrete evidence that feedback guided by student attention can benefit learning, and that the feedback may be more effective if tailored to specific students' differences.

3 MetaTutor

MetaTutor [1] is a hypermedia-based ITS containing multiple pages of text and diagrams, developed to teach students about the circulatory system and how to self-regulate their learning with the assistance of multiple PAs. When working with MetaTutor, students are given the overall goal of learning as much as they can about the human circulatory system. The main interface of MetaTutor (see Fig. 1) includes a table of contents, a timer that indicates how much time remains in the learning session, and an SRL palette where participants can engage in cognitive and metacognitive SRL strategies, with the assistance (i.e., prompts and feedback) of each of four PAs.

All PAs provide audible assistance through the use of a text-to-speech engine (Nuance). Three of the PAs provide prompts and feedback (PF) aimed to scaffold self-regulatory processes. Specifically, Pam the Planner prompts and scaffolds planning processes primarily at the beginning of the learning session by assisting the student in creating subgoals relevant to the overall learning goal (e.g., learning about the path of blood flow or malfunctions of the circulatory system). Mary the Monitor prompts and supports students in their metacognitive monitoring processes (e.g., self-assessment of their progress during learning) that they can use to judge their understanding or relevancy of the content to their subgoals. Sam the Strategizer supports students in applying cognitive learning strategies such as taking notes on the content or summarizing it in their own words. The fourth PA, Gavin the Guide, provides guidance on how to interact with the interface and also administers pretest and posttest questionnaires.

Students can initiate the use of SRL strategies via the SRL palette where they are then provided with feedback on their performance. Alternatively, the system can also prompt the use of SRL strategies using a set of 20 production rules that can be fired based on the student's behavior with the system (e.g., time spent reading a page or number of pages visited). For example, Sam the Strategizer can prompt students to summarize the content of the current page if the students had spent enough time on the page, and Sam would then provide feedback on the student's summary (e.g., that the summary was too short and suggest strategies to improve it). Mary the Monitor can prompt students to monitor their progress toward completion of the current subgoal if the students had read enough relevant pages to complete that subgoal. This would lead to a quiz on the subgoal to gauge how accurate the students' judgment was. Mary would also provide feedback on the results of the quiz, such as suggesting to read more material for the subgoal if they scored less than 60%. High-level rules were also implemented to avoid over-prompting, for instance students would not be prompted to summarize the current page if they already refused to do it, but can be prompted to summarize material on the next page.

Only one of the four PAs remains visible at a time. Thus, when a PA is done talking, it remains visible and silent until a new interaction starts with either the same or another PA. The PAs are visually rendered using Haptek virtual characters, which generate idle movements when the PAs are not speaking (subtle, gradual head and eye movements), as well as lip movements during speech.

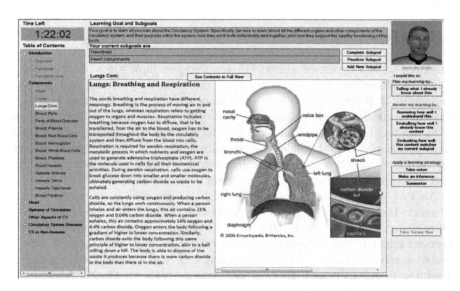

Fig. 1. Screenshot of MetaTutor during the learning session.

4 User Study

The data used for the analysis presented in this paper was collected via a user study designed to gain a general understanding of how students learn with MetaTutor, and how this learning is influenced by a variety of student traits, as well as cognitive, metacognitive and affective factors [1]. The study included the collection of a variety of multi-channel trace data (e.g., eye tracking, log files, physiological sensors), as well as self-report measures for several individual differences. In this paper, we focus on the relationships among two of the tested individual differences (achievement goals and personality traits, described next), attention to the PAs (captured via an eye-tracker), and learning outcome with MetaTutor. There were 28 study participants (66% female, mean age of 20) with complete data that we could use for our analysis. All participants were undergraduate students from a large public university in North America.

4.1 Individual Differences: Achievement Goals and Personality Traits

Achievement goals assess four components of motivation in learning situations: (a) mastery-approach (e.g., goal to develop competence and skills), (b) mastery-avoidance (e.g., goal to avoid a failure to learn a skill), (c) performance-approach (e.g., goal to outperform others), and (d) performance-avoidance (e.g., goal to avoid being outperformed by others) [8]. In this work, we focused only on mastery-approach and performance-approach goals, given that avoidance goals are typically considered less useful to foster effective learning [6]. We used the 12-item Achievement Goal Questionnaire Revised (AGQ-R) [8] to collect achievement goals.

Personality traits are expressed according to the well-established Five-Factor Model [11] in terms of: (a) agreeableness (tendency to be more friendly, considerate of others, altruistic, sympathetic); (b) extraversion (associated with high physical and verbal activity, assertiveness, sociability); (c) conscientiousness (associated with efficiency, determination, responsibility, and persistence); (d) neuroticism (tendency to be temperamental and experience negative moods and feelings, such as anxiety); (e) openness (tendency to prefer novel and broader ideas and experiences, intellectual activities, creativity). We used the 50-item International Personality Item Pool (IPIP) [15] to measure students' personality traits.

4.2 Procedure and Experimental Conditions

The study consisted of two sessions conducted on separate days. During the first session, lasting approximately 30–60 min, students were administered several questionnaires, including the IPIP and AGQ-R discussed in the previous section. Participants were also given a 30-item pretest to assess their knowledge of the circulatory system. During the second session lasting about three hours, students first underwent a calibration phase with the eye tracker (SMI RED 250) as well as a training session on MetaTutor. Each student was then given the overall goal of learning as much as possible about the human circulatory system with MetaTutor and was given 90 min to interact with the system. Finally, students completed a posttest analogous to the pretest, followed by a series of questionnaires about their experience with MetaTutor.

Students were randomly assigned to work with one of two different versions of the system: either a *Prompt and Feedback (PF)* condition (N = 14) or *Control* condition (N = 14). In the PF condition, the PAs exhibited the behavior described in Sect. 3, e.g., they would provide students with prompts and feedback to foster SRL strategies. In the control condition, PAs had a much more passive role. They would not prompt the use of any SRL strategies, and would not provide any form of feedback when students applied these strategies. The only form of verbal interaction with the students would consist of neutral verbal acknowledgement and general advice when students initiated an SRL activity via the SRL palette (also provided to students in the PF condition when they initiate SRL). For instance, if a student initiates the writing of a summary, Sam would say "It looks like you want to summarize. Go ahead and type your summary. Remember to include as much info as you understood." After submission of the summary, Sam would just say "Great! Let's move on" without additional feedback.

5   Gaze Data Processing and AOIs

Gaze data collected during interaction with MetaTutor were exported with the SMI BeGaze 3.5 software in terms of fixations (gaze maintained at one point on the screen for at least 80 ms) and saccades (quick movement of gaze from one fixation to another). To model student attention to the PAs, we defined two Areas of Interest (AOIs) on the PAs (displayed in the upper right corner of the screen, shown in Fig. 1): one when PAs were speaking to the students (*Speaking-AOI*) and one when PAs were present but not speaking (*Silent-AOI*). The Speaking-AOI captures student attention to PAs when it is the most important [3], i.e., when PAs are delivering prompts and feedback to support student learning. The Silent-AOI reveals whether or how students looked at the PAs when they were not delivering any scaffolding.

We processed the gaze data on the two AOIs using EMDAT (available at *github. com/ATUAV/EMDAT*), a gaze data analysis toolkit, to generate a battery of six gaze-based features summarized in Table 1. The gaze features were computed for each of the two AOIs (Speaking-AOI and Silent-AOI) separately, resulting in a total of 2 (AOIs) × 6 (features) = 12 gaze features. We selected these features because they have been extensively used in the fields of psychology and HCI to capture user attention on specific areas of an interface (e.g., [16, 17]). Furthermore, in the field of ITS, fixation duration has been used to capture student attention to textual hints in an educational game [9]. Number of fixations, fixation duration, fixation rate, and longest fixation have been used to predict student learning gains when learning with several learning environments [18, 19], including MetaTutor [20].

Table 1. Description of the six gaze features generated for fixations over each of the Speaking-AOI and Silent-AOI.

Feature	Description	Unit
Number of fixations	Total number of fixations on the AOI	*fixation (fix)*
Proportion of fixations	Number of fixations on the AOI divided by the total number of fixations over the entire MetaTutor interface	–
Fixation *rate*	Total number of fixations on the AOI divided by the total time spent looking at the AOI	*fix/sec*
M and *SD* fixation duration	Mean and standard deviation of the duration of fixations over the AOI	*sec*
Longest fixation	Length of the longest fixation over the AOI	*sec*

6 Data Analysis

Our analysis aims to investigate if and how student attention to MetaTutor's PAs and individual differences (i.e., achievement goals and personality traits) influence learning. The variable we adopt to measure learning in our analysis is *proportional learning gain*, defined as:

$$\frac{posttest\ score\ ratio - pretest\ score\ ratio}{1 - pretest\ score\ ratio} \qquad (1)$$

Table 2 reports statistics for pre- and post-test scores (the highest possible score was 30), as well as for the corresponding learning gains[1].

Table 2. Descriptive statistics for pretest, posttest, and learning gain.

Measures of learning outcomes	M	SD	Median
Pretest	18.6	4.2	19
Posttest	21.4	4	21
Proportional learning gain	15.3	50.2	20

Table 3. Descriptive statistics for students' personality traits (range: 0–50)

Personality traits	M	SD	Median
Extraversion	33.28	9.83	32
Agreeableness	40.89	4.93	39
Conscientiousness	36.88	6.98	38
Neuroticism	28.37	7.93	25
Openness	38.14	5.87	34

Table 4. Descriptive statistics for students' achievement goals (range: 1–5).

Achievement goals	M	SD	Median
Performance-approach	4.27	0.63	4
Mastery-approach	4.05	0.68	4

Tables 3 and 4 report the summary statistics of the data collected on personality traits (Table 3) and achievement goals (Table 4). For our analysis, we discretize each individual difference into two groups. For achievement goals, we assigned students to either a *mastery-approach* or a *performance-approach* group based on their dominant goal (i.e., their highest rated goal orientation from the AG Questionnaire described in Sect. 4.1). For the five personality traits, we assigned students to either low or high levels of each trait using a median split. For instance, students who obtained a score lower than the median for Extroversion are labeled as *introverted*, and students who scored higher than the median are labeled as *extroverted*.

Tables 5 and 6 report descriptive statistics of the eye-tracking features generated for the Speaking-AOI and the Silent-AOI (cf. Sect. 5). We compared the ratio *fixations/time_visible* for both speaking and silent PAs separately, accounting for the

---

[1] The increase from pretest to post-test is statistically significant indicating that MetaTutor is overall effective at fostering learning, as further discussed in [1].

Table 5. Descriptive statistics of gaze features over the Speaking-AOI.

Gaze features	M	SD
Number of fixations	42	45
Proportion of fixation	.002	.002
Fixation rate	.13	.035
Mean fixation duration	.32	.13
Std.dev fixation duration	.27	.18
Longest fixation	1.29	1.15

Table 6. Descriptive statistics of gaze features over the Silent-AOI

Gaze features	M	SD
Number of fixations	181	201
Proportion of fixations	.011	.01
Fixation rate	.029	.03
Mean fixation duration	.31	.12
Std.dev fixation duration	.29	.15
Longest fixation	2.01	1.14

fact that the PAs remained visible much longer when they were silent than when they spoke (1.5 h vs. 22 min on average). The ratio is almost the same (2 fix/min for silent PAs and 1.9 fix/min for the speaking PAs), indicating that students look at the PAs even when they are not providing any support. To ascertain whether there are differences in how attention to speaking vs silent agents affects learning we conducted separate analysis for the corresponding Speaking-AOI and Silent-AOI.

To investigate the impact of individual differences and attention on learning, we used moderate linear regression. We ran 12 different moderate linear regression models, one for each of the six individual differences (achievement goals and five personality traits) and for each of the Speaking-AOI and Silent-AOI[2]. Each model has *proportional learning gain* as the dependent variable, whereas the factors are the six *gaze features* on the AOI, one of the six *individual differences*, and the *group condition* (PF or Control). For post-hoc analysis we ran pairwise *t*-test comparisons, and *p*-values were adjusted with the Holm-Bonferroni approach based on the number of comparisons made.

7 Results

Our statistical analysis uncovered significant[3] interaction effects of *achievement goals* with *longest fixation* ($F_{2,8} = 4.97$, $p = .04$, $\eta_P^2 = .09$) and *fixation rate* ($F_{2,8} = 6.51$, $p = .02$, $\eta_P^2 = .15$) over the Speaking-AOI, as well as an interaction effect of *achievement goals* with *fixation rate* ($F_{2,8} = 5.64$, $p = .03$, $\eta_P^2 = .1$) over the Silent-AOI. No significant effects were found for personality traits and group condition ($p > .05$, small effect sizes [$\eta_P^2 < 0.13$]). We describe the significant effects found below.

Interaction effect of achievement goal with longest fixation over the Speaking-AOI. This interaction effect (shown on Fig. 2) and related pairwise comparisons reveal that performance-oriented students learned more when having a longer

---

[2] We include each of our six individual differences separately in the analysis to ensure that we do not overfit our models by including all factors at once.

[3] We report statistical significance at the .05 level throughout this paper, and effect sizes as small for $\eta_P^2 \geq 0.02$, medium for $\eta_P^2 \geq 0.13$, and large for $\eta_P^2 \geq 0.26$.

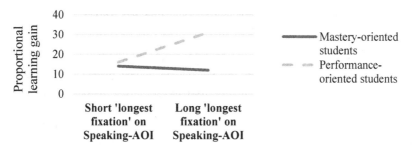

Fig. 2. Interaction effects of achievement goals with longest fixation over the Speaking-AOI on proportional learning gain.

longest fixation compared to when they have a shorter one. There is no such difference for mastery-oriented students.

Interaction effects of achievement with fixation rate over *(i)* the Speaking-AOI and *(ii)* the Silent-AOI. These two interaction effects (shown on Fig. 3 for the Speaking-AOI and Fig. 4 for the Silent-AOI) and related pairwise comparisons reveal similar results. Mastery-oriented students learned significantly less when having a high fixation rate over the PAs rather than a low fixation rate. The effect is reversed for performance-oriented students.

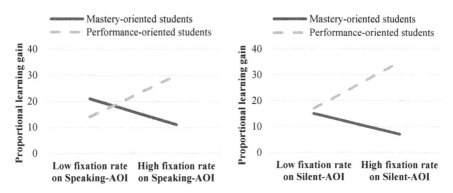

Fig. 3. Interaction effects of achievement goals with fixation rate over the Speaking-AOI on proportional learning gain.

Fig. 4. Interaction effects of achievement goals with fixation rate over the Silent-AOI on proportional learning gain.

Overall, our results show that gaze measures can reveal attention patterns over the PAs that are suboptimal for learning, for students with different achievement goals. Thus, these results identify circumstances that could be the target of personalized support.

Specifically, our results show that *performance-oriented students* learned more when having a long longest fixation and a high fixation rate on the speaking PAs. Long fixations have been linked to higher cognitive processing [21–23]. As such, our findings may indicate that performance-oriented students learned more when they dedicated significantly more cognitive resources to process the scaffolding provided by the speaking PAs. Fixation rate has been linked to a variety of user states and behaviors (e.g., [24, 25]). In particular, a high fixation rate has been linked to less mind wandering (i.e., the unintentional shift in attention from task-related to task-unrelated thoughts) [25]. This could indicate that performance-oriented students who had a high fixation rate over the speaking PAs learned more because they were not mind wandering, consistent with our finding for longest fixations. This suggests that the PAs are useful for the performance-oriented students if they pay attention to them, indicating that these students could benefit from personalized PF that reorient their attention to the speaking PAs when they exhibit gaze behaviors predictive of lower learning gains (no long fixations or a low fixation rate on the PAs).

Performance-oriented students also learned more when having a high fixation rate on the silent PAs. We have no theoretical framework to help interpret these findings, as previous literature has not investigated allocation of attention to PAs not interacting with students. However, these results indicate a significant influence of achievement goal on attention to the PAs, such that even when the PAs were not providing scaffolding, attention to them still predicted higher learning outcomes. Based on this finding, it is worth conducting further analysis to understand how and why those performance-oriented students can still benefit from the PAs who are not speaking.

As for *mastery-oriented students*, our results show that they learned less when having a high fixation rate on the speaking PAs. As previously reported for performance-oriented students, high fixation rates have been linked to less mind wandering. This could indicate that, contrary to performance-oriented students, mastery-oriented students did not benefit from the PAs when attending to them, possibly because they found the scaffolding to be limited or not useful to fulfil their goal of mastering the content. This interpretation is consistent with previous findings showing that mastery-oriented students learned less with MetaTutor and experienced negative affect (e.g., anxiety) [6, 7], and augments these findings by revealing that visually attending to the PAs hinder learning for those students. Although further investigation would be required to understand this finding, it suggests that mastery-oriented students could benefit from personalized support geared toward better supporting their goal. For example, one option is to reduce the amount of current prompts and feedback delivered to them, since they appear to be learning well without the feedback. Alternatively, the PAs could use a different script for these students, which includes emphasizing how prompts and feedback can help them toward achieving their goal of mastering the content.

Mastery-oriented students also learned less when having a high fixation rate on the silent PAs. Similar to the interpretation for performance-oriented students, further investigation is needed to understand this result. Nonetheless, this suggests that a high fixation rate on the silent PAs can predict lower learning outcomes, and thus justifies investigating if and how personalized PFs could be designed to counteract this negative effect on learning.

8 Conclusion

In this work we investigated the relationship between individual differences (achievement goals and personality traits), visual attention to PAs, and learning gains with MetaTutor, a hypermedia-based ITS that fosters self-regulated learning and metacognition during learning about the human circulatory system. We used gaze data to capture visual attention to the PAs by deriving a set of eye-tracking metrics from students' gaze behavior on the PAs.

Overall, our results show that visual attention to the PAs influenced learning gains when the PAs were both providing PF or were visible but silent, depending on students' achievement goals. Such findings provide insight on how motivational goals influence learning with PAs. Furthermore, they suggest how and when scaffolding personalized to motivational goals could be provided. For example, we found that mastery-oriented students did not benefit as much from the PAs when they visually attended to them. This indicates that those mastery-oriented students could benefit from personalized scaffolding geared toward reducing the amount of prompts they receive, when gaze metrics (fixation rate and longest fixation) reveals that they attend to them.

We found no significant effects on learning for personality traits in our analysis. Such effects, however, were found in [12]. These differences call for further studies to better understand when and how personality affects learning with PAs.

Our main avenue for future work is to design and evaluate the personalized prompts suggested by the results in this paper. We are also interested in gaining a better understanding of how students process the MetaTutor's scaffolding, for instance by investigating what parts of the interface they inspect when the PAs are speaking.

Acknowledgements. This publication is based upon work supported by the National Science Foundation under Grant No. DRL-1431552 and the Social Sciences and Humanities Research Council of Canada. Any opinions, findings, and conclusions or recommendations expressed in this material are those of the authors and do not necessarily reflect the views of the National Science Foundation or the Social Sciences and Humanities Research Council of Canada.

References

1. Azevedo, R., Harley, J., Trevors, G., Duffy, M., Feyzi-Behnagh, R., Bouchet, F., Landis, R.: Using trace data to examine the complex roles of cognitive, metacognitive, and emotional self-regulatory processes during learning with multi-agent systems. In: Azevedo, R., Aleven, V. (eds.) International Handbook of Metacognition and Learning Technologies. SIHE, vol. 28, pp. 427–449. Springer, New York (2013). doi:10.1007/978-1-4419-5546-3_28
2. Schroeder, N.L., Adesope, O.O.: A systematic review of pedagogical agents' persona, motivation, and cognitive load implications for learners. J. Res. Technol. Educ. **46**, 229–251 (2014)
3. D'Mello, S., Olney, A., Williams, C., Hays, P.: Gaze tutor: a gaze-reactive intelligent tutoring system. Int. J. Hum.-Comput. Stud. **70**, 377–398 (2012)
4. Heidig, S., Clarebout, G.: Do pedagogical agents make a difference to student motivation and learning? Educ. Res. **6**, 27–54 (2011)

5. Arroyo, I., Woolf, B.P., Royer, J.M., Tai, M.: Affective gendered learning companions. In: International Conference on Artificial Intelligence in Education, pp. 41–48. Springer (2009)
6. Duffy, M.C., Azevedo, R.: Motivation matters: interactions between achievement goals and agent scaffolding for self-regulated learning within an intelligent tutoring system. Comput. Hum. Behav. **52**, 338–348 (2015)
7. Lallé, S., Mudrick, N.V., Taub, M., Grafsgaard, J.F., Conati, C., Azevedo, R.: Impact of individual differences on affective reactions to pedagogical agents scaffolding. In: Traum, D., Swartout, W., Khooshabeh, P., Kopp, S., Scherer, S., Leuski, A. (eds.) IVA 2016. LNCS, vol. 10011, pp. 269–282. Springer, Cham (2016). doi:10.1007/978-3-319-47665-0_24
8. Elliot, A.J., Murayama, K.: On the measurement of achievement goals: critique, illustration, and application. J. Educ. Psychol. **100**, 613 (2008)
9. Conati, C., Jaques, N., Muir, M.: Understanding attention to adaptive hints in educational games: an eye-tracking study. Int. J. Artif. Intell. Educ. **23**, 136–161 (2013)
10. Taub, M., Azevedo, R.: Using eye-tracking to determine the impact of prior knowledge on self-regulated learning with an adaptive hypermedia-learning environment. In: Micarelli, A., Stamper, J., Panourgia, K. (eds.) ITS 2016. LNCS, vol. 9684, pp. 34–47. Springer, Cham (2016). doi:10.1007/978-3-319-39583-8_4
11. Costa, P.T., McCrae, R.R.: Four ways five factors are basic. Personal. Individ. Differ. **13**, 653–665 (1992)
12. Wang, N., Johnson, W.L., Mayer, R.E., Rizzo, P., Shaw, E., Collins, H.: The politeness effect: pedagogical agents and learning outcomes. Int. J. Hum.-Comput. Stud. **66**, 98–112 (2008)
13. Olney, A., Risko, E.F., D'Mello, S.K., Graesser, A.C., Fawcett, J., Risko, E.F., Kingstone, A.: Attention in educational contexts: the role of the learning task in guiding attention. In: Fawcett, J., Risko, E.F., Kingstone, A. (eds.) The Handbook of Attention. MIT Press, Cambridge (2015)
14. D'Mello, S.K.: Giving eyesight to the blind: towards attention-aware AIED. Int. J. Artif. Intell. Educ. **26**, 645–659 (2016)
15. Goldberg, L.R.: A broad-bandwidth, public domain, personality inventory measuring the lower-level facets of several five-factor models. Personal. Psychol. Eur. **7**, 7–28 (1999)
16. Holmqvist, K., Nyström, M., Andersson, R., Dewhurst, R., Jarodzka, H., van de Weijer, J.: Eye Tracking: A Comprehensive Guide to Methods and Measures. Oxford University Press, Incorporated (2015)
17. Lai, M.-L., Tsai, M.-J., Yang, F.-Y., Hsu, C.-Y., Liu, T.-C., Lee, S.W.-Y., Lee, M.-H., Chiou, G.-L., Liang, J.-C., Tsai, C.-C.: A review of using eye-tracking technology in exploring learning from 2000 to 2012. Educ. Res. Rev. **10**, 90–115 (2013)
18. Kardan, S., Conati, C.: Comparing and combining eye gaze and interface actions for determining user learning with an interactive simulation. In: Carberry, S., Weibelzahl, S., Micarelli, A., Semeraro, G. (eds.) UMAP 2013. LNCS, vol. 7899, pp. 215–227. Springer, Heidelberg (2013). doi:10.1007/978-3-642-38844-6_18
19. Peterson, J., Pardos, Z., Rau, M., Swigart, A., Gerber, C., McKinsey, J.: Understanding student success in chemistry using gaze tracking and pupillometry. In: Conati, C., Heffernan, N., Mitrovic, A., Verdejo, M. Felisa (eds.) AIED 2015. LNCS, vol. 9112, pp. 358–366. Springer, Cham (2015). doi:10.1007/978-3-319-19773-9_36
20. Bondareva, D., Conati, C., Feyzi-Behnagh, R., Harley, J.M., Azevedo, R., Bouchet, F.: Inferring learning from gaze data during interaction with an environment to support self-regulated learning. In: Lane, H.C., Yacef, K., Mostow, J., Pavlik, P. (eds.) AIED 2013. LNCS, vol. 7926, pp. 229–238. Springer, Heidelberg (2013). doi:10.1007/978-3-642-39112-5_24

21. Martin, S.: Measuring cognitive load and cognition: metrics for technology-enhanced learning. Educ. Res. Eval. **20**, 592–621 (2014)
22. Chen, S., Epps, J., Ruiz, N., Chen, F.: Eye activity as a measure of human mental effort in HCI. In: International Conference on Intelligent User Interfaces, pp. 315–318. ACM (2011)
23. Irwin, D.E.: Fixation location and fixation duration as indices of cognitive processing. Interface Lang. Vis. Action Eye Mov. Vis. World **217**, 105–133 (2004)
24. McCarley, J.S., Wang, R.F., Kramer, A.F., Irwin, D.E., Peterson, M.S.: How much memory does oculomotor search have? Psychol. Sci. **14**, 422–426 (2003)
25. Smilek, D., Carriere, J.S., Cheyne, J.A.: Out of mind, out of sight eye blinking as indicator and embodiment of mind wandering. Psychol. Sci. **21**, 786–789 (2010)

Automatic Extraction of AST Patterns for Debugging Student Programs

Timotej Lazar$^{(\boxtimes)}$, Martin Možina$^{(\boxtimes)}$, and Ivan Bratko$^{(\boxtimes)}$

University of Ljubljana, Faculty of Computer and Information Science,
Ljubljana, Slovenia
{timotej.lazar,martin.mozina,ivan.bratko}@fri.uni-lj.si

Abstract. When implementing a programming tutor it is often difficult to manually consider all possible errors encountered by students. An alternative is to automatically learn a bug library of erroneous patterns from students' programs. We propose abstract-syntax-tree (AST) patterns as features for learning rules to distinguish between correct and incorrect programs. We use these rules to debug student programs: rules for incorrect programs (buggy rules) indicate mistakes, whereas rules for correct programs group programs with the same solution strategy. To generate hints, we first check buggy rules and point out incorrect patterns. If no buggy rule matches, we use rules for correct programs to recognize the student's intent and suggest missing patterns. We evaluate our approach on past student programming data for a number of Prolog problems. For 31 out of 44 problems, the induced rules correctly classify over 85% of programs based only on their structural features. For approximately 73% of incorrect submissions, we are able to generate hints that were implemented by the student in some subsequent submission.

Keywords: Programming tutors · Error diagnosis · Hint generation · Abstract syntax tree · Syntactic features

1 Introduction

Programming education is becoming increasingly accessible with massive online courses. Since thousands of students can attend such courses, it is impossible for teachers to individually evaluate each participant's work. On the other hand, in-time feedback directly addressing students' mistakes can aid the learning process. Providing feedback automatically could thus greatly enhance these courses.

Traditional programming tutors use manually constructed domain models to generate feedback. Model-tracing tutors simulate the problem-solving *process*: how students program. This is challenging because there are no well-defined steps when writing a program. Many tutors instead only analyze individual programs submitted by students, and disregard how a program evolved. They often use models coded in terms of constraints or bug libraries [10].

Developing a domain model typically requires significant knowledge-engineering effort [4]. This is particularly true for programming tutors, where

© Springer International Publishing AG 2017
E. André et al. (Eds.): AIED 2017, LNAI 10331, pp. 162–174, 2017.
DOI: 10.1007/978-3-319-61425-0_14

most problems have several alternative solutions with many possible implementations [11]. Data-driven tutors reduce the necessary authoring effort by mining educational data – often from online courses – to learn common errors and generate feedback [8,16,17].

In this paper we address the problem of finding useful features to support data mining in programming tutors. To support hint generation, these features must be robust against irrelevant code variations (such as renaming a variable) and relatable to knowledge components of the target skill (programming).

We describe features with *abstract-syntax-tree patterns* that encode relations between nodes in a program's abstract syntax tree. We use patterns that describe a path between pairs of leaf nodes referring to variables or values. By omitting some nodes on these paths, patterns can match different programs containing the same relation. We then induce rules to predict program correctness from AST patterns, allowing us to generate hints based on missing or incorrect patterns.

We evaluated our approach on existing Prolog programs submitted by students during past lab sessions of a second-year university course. For 73% of incorrect submissions we are able to suggest potentially useful patterns – those that the students had actually implemented in the final, correct programs.

The main contributions presented in this paper are: AST patterns as features for machine learning, a rule-based model for predicting program correctness, and hint generation from incorrect or missing patterns in student programs.

2   Background

Several programming tutors generate hints from differences between the student's program and a predefined set of possible solutions. The possible solution strategies for each problem can be given as a set of programs, or specified in a domain-specific language. Both Johnson's Pascal tutor [9] and Hong's Prolog tutor [7] perform hierarchical goal decomposition based on predefined programming *plans* or *techniques* to determine the student's intent. Gerdes et al. use a small set of annotated model programs to derive solution strategies, which function in a similar way [5].

Rivers and Koedinger compare students' programs directly to a database of previous correct submissions [17]. They reduce program variability using equivalence-preserving transformations, such as inlining functions and reordering binary expressions. Hints are generated by suggesting a minimal correct step leading from the current submission to the closest correct program.

Another option is to compare program behavior. Nguyen et al. classify programming mistakes according to results on a preselected set of test inputs [16]. Li et al. generate test cases to distinguish between programs by selecting inputs that exercise different code paths in the program [14]. Such tutors can point out pertinent failing test cases, which can be very helpful.

Constraints [15] encode domain principles using if-then rules with relevance and satisfaction conditions, e.g. "if a function has a non-void return type, then it must have a return statement" [6]. If a program violates a constraint, the tutor displays a predefined message. Le's Prolog tutor improves constraint-based diagnosis by assigning weights to different types of constraints [12].

Jin et al. use *linkage graphs* to describe data dependencies between the program's statements [8]; we use AST patterns in a similar way. Nguyen et al. analyzed submissions in a large machine-learning course to learn a vocabulary of *code phrases*: subtrees of submissions' abstract syntax trees that perform the same function in a given context [16]. By swapping parts between different programs, they built up a search library of functionally equivalent AST subtrees within a given context.

The idea for AST patterns comes from Tregex – *tree regular expressions*, mainly used in the field of natural-language processing [13]. Tregex patterns can encode complex relations between nodes, but can become unwieldy; in this paper we use a simpler s-expression syntax. Another language for describing tree patterns using s-expressions is *trx*, which additionally supports choice, repetition and other operators [1].

3   AST Patterns

In this section we describe AST patterns through examples, while Sect. 4.1 explains how patterns are extracted from student programs. Consider the following Prolog program implementing the relation sister(X,Y)[1]:

```
sister(X,Y):-    % X is Y's sister when:
   parent(P,X),
   parent(P,Y),   % X and Y share a common parent P,
   female(X),     % X is female, and
   X \= Y.        % X and Y are not the same person.
```

Figure 1 shows the program's AST with two patterns. The pattern drawn with blue dotted arrows encodes the fact that the first argument to the sister predicate also appears as the first argument in the call to female. In other words, this pattern states that X must be female to be a sister. We write this pattern as the s-expression

```
(clause (head (compound (functor 'sister') (args var))))
   (compound (functor 'female') (args var)))
```

Every pattern used in this paper has the same basic structure, and describes paths from a clause node to one or two leaf nodes containing variables or values. All patterns in Figs. 1 and 2 are induced from such pairs of nodes. For each leaf we also include some local context, such as the name of the predicate (e.g. parent) and the operators used in unop and binop nodes.

We regard these patterns as the smallest units of meaning in Prolog programs: each pattern encodes some interaction between two objects (variable or value)

---

[1] Binary relations like this one should be read as "X is a sister/parent/... of Y".

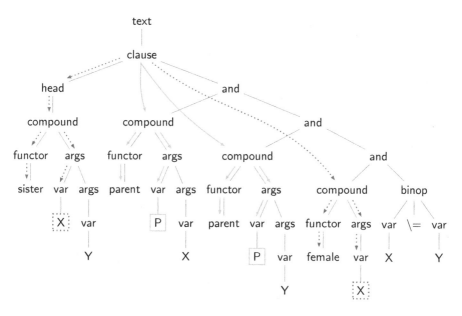

Fig. 1. The AST for the `sister` program, showing two patterns and the leaf nodes inducing them. Solid red arrows equate the first arguments in the two calls to `parent`. Dotted blue arrows encode the necessary condition that X must be female to be a sister. (Color figure online)

in the program. Including more than two leaf nodes in a pattern could make it difficult to pinpoint the exact error when generating hints. Each pattern contains at most two var nodes, so we require they both refer to the same variable – relating two nodes with different variables would not tell us much about the program. We can thus omit actual variable names from patterns.

We handle syntactic variations in programs by omitting certain nodes from patterns. For example, by not including and nodes, the above pattern can match a clause regardless of the presence (or order) of other goals in its body (i.e., with any arrangement of and nodes in the AST). Order *is* important for the nodes specified in the pattern; this is explained below.

The second pattern in Fig. 1, drawn with solid red arrows, encodes the fact that the two calls to `parent` share the first argument. In other words, X and Y must have the same parent P.

```
(clause (compound (functor 'parent') (args var))
        (compound (functor 'parent') (args var)))
```

Patterns describe relations between nodes in a program's AST. Specifically, the pattern $(a\ b\ c)$ means that the nodes b and c are descended from a, and that b precedes c in a depth-first tree walk. In general, an AST matches the pattern (name $p_1 \dots p_k$) if it contains a node n labeled name; the subtree rooted at n must also contain, in depth-first order, distinct nodes n_1 to n_k matching subpatterns p_1 to p_k. The above pattern, for example, matches only the last of the following programs (the first program is missing one call to parent, and the second has different variables in positions encoded by the pattern):

```
% nonmatching          % nonmatching          % matching
sister(X,Y):-          sister(X,Y):-          sister(X,Y):-
   female(X),             female(X),             parent(A,X),
   parent(P,X),          parent(A,X),           female(X),
   X \= Y.               parent(B,Y),           parent(A,Y),
                         X \= Y.                X \= Y.
```

A relation between any two objects in a program is insufficient to reason about the program's behavior on the whole. In the tutoring context, however, there are patterns that strongly indicate the presence of certain bugs. Take for example the following incorrect program to sum a list:

```
sum([],0).             % base case: the empty list sums to zero
sum([H|T],Sum):-       % recursive case:
   sum(T,Sum),         %   sum the tail and
   Sum is Sum + H.     %   add first element (bug: reused variable)
```

This error is fairly common with Prolog novices: the variable Sum is used to represent both the sum of the whole list (line 2), and the sum of only the tail elements (line 3). The last line fails since Prolog cannot unify Sum with a (generally) different value of Sum + H. The program's AST is displayed in Fig. 2.

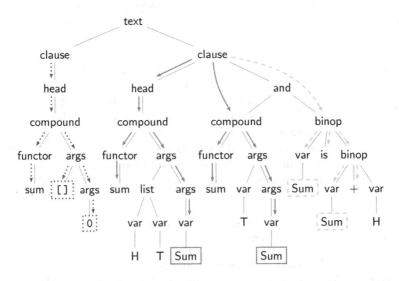

Fig. 2. The AST for the buggy sum program. Dotted arrows relate the correct values in the base case. Solid and dashed arrows denote two patterns describing incorrect reuse of the Sum variable in the recursive case. (Color figure online)

Various patterns capture this mistake. Solid red arrows in Fig. 2 show one example – Sum returned by the predicate should not be the same as the Sum from the recursive call:

```
(clause (head (compound (functor 'sum') (args (args var))))
    (compound (functor 'sum') (args (args var))))
```

The second pattern, drawn with dashed orange arrows in the figure, indicates the likely error in the arithmetic expression:

```
(clause (binop var 'is' (binop var '+')))
```

The leftmost pattern in Fig. 2, drawn with dotted blue arrows, describes the correct relation between the two constants in the base-case rule:

```
(clause (head (compound (functor 'sum') (args [] (args 0)))))
```

We include such patterns in our feature set to cover the base-case clauses in recursive programs, which often include no variables.

4 Method

This section explains the three steps in our approach: discovering AST patterns, learning classification rules for correct and incorrect programs, and using those rules to generate hints.

4.1 Extracting Patterns

We extract patterns from student submissions. As described above, we are only interested in patterns connecting pairs of leaf nodes in an AST: either two nodes referring to the same variable (like the examples in Fig. 1), or a value (such as the empty list [] or the number 0) and another variable/value occurring within the same compound or binop (like the blue dotted pattern in Fig. 2).

We induce patterns from such node pairs. Given the clause (the second occurrence of each variable – A, B and C – is marked with ? for disambiguation)

```
a(A, B):-
    b(A', C),
    B' is C' + 1.
```

we select the following pairs of nodes: $\{A, A'\}$, $\{B, B'\}$, $\{C, C'\}$, $\{B', 1\}$ and $\{C', 1\}$.

For each selected pair of leaf nodes (a, b) we construct a pattern by walking the AST in depth-first order and recording nodes that lie on the paths to a and b. We omit and nodes, as explained in the previous section. We also include certain nodes that lie near the paths to selected leaves. Specifically, we include the functor/operator of all compound, binop and unop nodes containing a or b.

Patterns are extracted automatically given above constraints (each pattern connecting a pair of variables or values). We find that such patterns work well for Prolog. Other languages, however, will likely require different kinds of patterns to achieve good performance.

In order to avoid inducing rules specific to a particular program (covering typos and other idiosyncratic mistakes), we ignore rare patterns. In this study we used patterns that occurred in at least five submissions. These patterns form the feature space for rule learning.

4.2   Learning Rules

We represent students' programs in the feature space of AST patterns described above. Each pattern corresponds to one binary feature with value true when the pattern is present and false when it is absent. We classify each program as correct if it passes a predefined set of test cases, and incorrect otherwise. We use these labels for machine learning.

Since we can already establish program correctness using appropriate tests cases, our goal here is not classifying new submissions. Instead, we wish to discover patterns associated with correct and incorrect programs. This approach to machine learning is called *descriptive induction* – the automatic discovery of patterns describing regularities in data. We use rule learning for this task, because rule conditions can be easily translated to hints.

Before explaining the algorithm, let us discuss the reasons why a program can be incorrect. Our experience indicates that bugs in student programs can often be described by (1) some incorrect or *buggy* pattern, which needs to be removed, or (2) some missing relation (pattern) between objects that should be included before the program can be correct. We shall now explain how both types of errors can be identified with rules.

To discover buggy patterns, the algorithm first learns *negative rules* that describe incorrect programs. We use a variant of the CN2 algorithm [2] implemented within the Orange data-mining toolbox [3]. Since we use rules to generate hints, and since hints should not be presented to students unless they are likely to be correct, we impose additional constraints on the rule learner:

- classification accuracy of each learned rule must exceed a threshold (we selected 90%, as 10% error seems acceptable for our application);
- each conjunct in a condition must be significant according to the likelihood-ratio test (in our experiments we set significance threshold to $p = 0.05$);
- a conjunct can only specify the presence of a pattern (in other words, we only allow feature-value pairs with the value true).

The first two constraints ensure good rules with only significant patterns, while the last constraint ensures rules only mention the presence (and not absence) of patterns as reasons for a program to be incorrect. This is important, since conditions in negative rules should contain patterns symptomatic of incorrect programs.

With respect to the second type of error, we could try the same approach and use the above algorithm to learn *positive rules* for the class of correct programs. The conditional part of positive rules should define sufficient combinations of patterns that render a program correct. It turns out that it is difficult to learn accurate positive rules, because there are many programs that are incorrect despite having all important patterns, because they also include incorrect patterns.

A possible way to solve this problem is to remove programs that are covered by some negative rule. This way all known buggy patterns are removed from the data, and will not be included in positive rules. However, removing incorrect patterns also removes the need for specifying relevant patterns in positive rules. For example, if all incorrect programs were removed, the single rule "true ⇒ correct" would suffice, which cannot be used to generate hints. We achieved the best results by learning positive rules from the complete data set, but estimating their accuracy only on programs not covered by some negative rule.

While our main interest is discovering important patterns, induced rules can still be used to classify new programs, for example to evaluate rule quality. Classification proceeds in three steps: (1) if a negative rule covers the program, classify it as incorrect; (2) else if a positive rule covers the program, classify it as correct; (3) otherwise, if no rule covers the program, classify it as incorrect.

We note that Prolog clauses can often be written in various ways. For example, the clause "sum([],0)." can also be written as

```
sum(List,Sum):- List = [], Sum = 0.
```

Our method covers such variations by including additional patterns and rules. Another option would be to use rules in conjunction with program canonicalization, by transforming each submission into a semantically equivalent normalized form before extracting patterns [17].

4.3   Generating Hints

Once we have induced the rules for a given problem, we can use them to provide hints based on buggy or missing patterns. To generate a hint for an incorrect program, each rule is considered in turn. We consider two types of feedback: *buggy hints* based on negative rules, and *intent hints* based on positive rules.

First, all negative rules are checked to find any known incorrect patterns in the program. To find the most likely incorrect patterns, the rules are considered in the order of decreasing quality. If all patterns in the rule "$p_1 \wedge ...p_k \Rightarrow$ incorrect" match, we highlight the corresponding leaf nodes. As a side note, we found that most negative rules are based on the presence of a single pattern. For the incorrect sum program from the previous section, our method produces the following highlight

```
sum([],0).          % base case: the empty list sums to zero
sum([H|T],Sum):-    % recursive case:
  sum(T,Sum),        %   sum the tail and
  Sum is Sum + H.    %   add first element (bug: reused variable)
```

based on the rule "$p \Rightarrow$ incorrect", where p is the solid red pattern in Fig. 2. This rule covers 36 incorrect programs, and one correct program using an unusual solution strategy.

If no negative rule matches the program, we use positive rules to determine the student's intent. Positive rules group patterns that together indicate a high likelihood that the program is correct. Each positive rule thus defines a particular "solution strategy" in terms of AST patterns. We reason that alerting the student to a missing pattern could help them complete the program without revealing the whole solution.

When generating a hint from positive rules, we consider all *partially matching* rules "$p_1 \wedge ... \wedge p_k \Rightarrow$ correct", where the student's program matches some (but not all) patterns p_i. For each such rule we store the number of matching patterns, and the set of missing patterns. We then return the most common missing pattern among the rules with most matching patterns.

For example, if we find the following missing pattern for an incorrect program implementing the `sister` predicate:

```
(clause (head (compound (functor 'sister') (args var))) (binop var '\=')),
```

we could display a message to the student saying "comparison between X and some other value is missing", or "your program is missing the goal X \= ?".

This method can find several missing patterns for a given partial program. In such cases we return the most commonly occurring pattern as the main hint, and other candidate patterns as alternative hints. We use main and alternative intent hints to establish the upper and lower bounds when evaluating hints.

5   Evaluation

We evaluated our approach on 44 programming assignments. We preselected 70% of students whose submissions were used as learning data for rule learning. The submissions from the remaining 30% of students were used as testing data to evaluate classification accuracy of learned rules, and to retrospectively evaluate quality of given hints. Problems analyzed in this paper constitute a complete introductory course in Prolog, covering the basics of the language.

Table 1 contains results on five selected problems (each representing a group of problems from one lab session), and averaged results over all 44 problems.[2] The second, third, and fourth columns provide classification accuracies (CA) of the rule-based, majority, and random-forest classifiers on testing data. The majority classifier and the random forests method, which had the best overall performance, serve as references for bad and good CA on particular data sets.

For example, our rules correctly classified 99% of testing instances for the `sister` problem, the accuracy of the majority classifier was 66%, and random forests achieved 98%. CA of rules is also high for problems `del` and `sum`. It

---

[2] We report only a subset of results due to space restrictions. Full results and source code can be found at https://ailab.si/aied2017.

Table 1. Results on five selected domains and averaged results over 44 domains. Columns 2, 3, and 4 contain classification accuracies of our rule learning method, majority classifier, and random forest, respectively. Columns 5 and 6 report the number of all generated buggy hints and the number of hints that were actually implemented by students. The following three columns contain the number of all generated intent hints (All), the number of implemented hints (Imp) and the number of implemented alternative hints (Alt). The numbers in the last column are student submission where hints could not be generated. The bottom two rows give aggregated results (total and average) over all 44 domains.

Problem	CA			Buggy hints		Intent hints			No hint
	Rules	Maj	RF	All	Imp	All	Imp	Alt	
sister	0.988	0.719	0.983	128	128	127	84	26	34
del	0.948	0.645	0.974	136	136	39	25	10	15
sum	0.945	0.511	0.956	59	53	24	22	1	6
is_sorted	0.765	0.765	0.831	119	119	0	0	0	93
union	0.785	0.783	0.813	106	106	182	66	7	6
...									
Total				3613	3508	2057	1160	244	1045
Average	0.857	0.663	0.908	79.73	77.34	46.75	26.36	5.55	23.75

is lower, however, for is_sorted and union, suggesting that the proposed AST patterns are insufficient for certain problems. Indeed, after analyzing the problem is_sorted, we observed that our patterns do not cover predicates with a single empty-list ([]) argument, which occurs as the base case in this problem. For this reason, the rule learning algorithm failed to learn any positive rules and therefore all programs were classified as incorrect. In the case of union, many solutions use the cut (!) operator, which is also ignored by our pattern generation algorithm.

We evaluated the quality of hints on incorrect submissions from those student traces that resulted in a correct program. In the case of the sister data set, there were 289 such incorrect submission out of 403 submissions in total.

The columns captioned "Buggy hints" in Table 1 contain evaluation of buggy hints generated from negative rules. For each generated buggy hint we checked whether it was implemented by the student in the final submission. The column "All" is the number of all generated buggy hints, while the column "Imp" is the number of implemented hints. The results show high relevance of generated buggy hints, as 97% (3508 out of 3613) of them were implemented in the final solution; in other words, the buggy pattern was removed.

The intent hints are generated when the algorithm fails to find any buggy hints. The column "All" contains the number of generated intent hints, "Imp" the number of implemented main intent hints, and "Alt" is the number of implemented alternative hints. Notice that the percentage of implemented intent hints is significantly lower when compared to buggy hints: in the case of problem sister 84 out of 127 (66%) hints were implemented, whereas in the case of problem union only 66 out of 182 (36%) hints were implemented. On average, 56% of main intent hints were implemented.

The last column shows the number of submissions where no hints could be generated. This value is relatively high for the is_sorted problem, because the algorithm could not learn any positive rules and thus no intent hints were generated.

To sum up, buggy hints seem to be good and reliable, since they are always implemented when presented, even when we tested them on past data – the decisions of students were not influenced by these hints. The percentage of implemented intent hints is, on average, lower (56%), which is still not a bad result, providing that it is difficult to determine the programmer's intent. In 12% (244 out of 2057) of generated intent hints, students implemented an alternative hint that was identified by our algorithm. Overall we were able to generate hints for 84.5% of incorrect submissions. Of those hints, 86% were implemented (73% of all incorrect submissions).

High classification accuracies for many problems imply that it is possible to determine program correctness simply by checking for the presence of a small number of patterns. Our hypothesis is that for each program certain crucial patterns exist that students have difficulties with. When they figure out these patterns, implementing the rest of the program is usually straightforward.

6   Conclusion

We have used AST patterns as features to describe program structure. By encoding only relations between particular nodes, each pattern can match many programs. AST patterns thus function as a sort of "regular expressions" for trees.

We presented a method for automatically extracting AST patterns from student programs. Our patterns encode relations between data objects in a program, with each pattern connecting either two instances of the same variable, a variable and a value, or two values. We consider such patterns as the atomic syntactic relations in a program, and use them as machine-learning features.

We explained how to induce rules for classifying correct and incorrect programs based on AST patterns. Since the goal of our research is to generate hints, we adapted the CN2 algorithm to produce rules useful for that purpose. We induce rules in two passes: we first learn the rules for incorrect programs, and then use programs not covered by any such rule to learn the rules for correct programs.

Evaluation shows that our patterns are useful for classifying Prolog programs. Other programming languages will likely require different patterns. For example, in commonly taught imperative languages such as Python or Java, each variable can take on different values and appear in many places. Further research is needed to determine the kinds of patterns useful in such situations.

We showed how to generate hints based on rules by highlighting buggy patterns or pointing out what patterns are missing. Evaluation on past student data shows that useful hints can be provided for many incorrect submissions this way.

The quality of feedback could be improved by annotating rules with explanations in natural language. Since patterns and rules are easily interpretable, they can also help when manually authoring tutoring systems, by indicating the common errors and the typical solution strategies for each problem.

In the future we will attempt to improve rule accuracy for certain problems, such as union. This will likely necessitate new kinds of patterns, for example to handle the cut operator. Adapting our methods to handle Python programs will give us some insight into what kinds of patterns could be useful in different situations. Finally, we will implement hint generation in an online programming tutor CodeQ, and evaluate the effect of automatic feedback on students' problem-solving.

References

1. Bagrak, I., Shivers, O.: trx: regular-tree expressions, now in scheme. In: Proceeding of Fifth Workshop on Scheme and Functional Programming, pp. 21–32 (2004)
2. Clark, P., Boswell, R.: Rule induction with CN2: some recent improvements. In: Proceeding Fifth European Conference on Machine Learning, pp. 151–163 (1991)
3. Demšar, J., Curk, T., Erjavec, A., Gorup, Č., Hočevar, T., Milutinovič, M., Možina, M., Polajnar, M., Toplak, M., Starič, A., štajdohar, M., Umek, L., Žagar, L., Žbontar, J., Žitnik, M., Zupan, B.: Orange: data mining toolbox in Python. J. Mach. Learn. Res. **14**, 2349–2353 (2013). http://jmlr.org/papers/v14/demsar13a.html
4. Folsom-Kovarik, J.T., Schatz, S., Nicholson, D.: Plan ahead: pricing ITS learner models. In: Proceeding 19th Behavior Representation in Modeling & Simulation Conference, pp. 47–54 (2010)
5. Gerdes, A., Heeren, B., Jeuring, J., van Binsbergen, L.T.: Ask-elle: an adaptable programming tutor for haskell giving automated feedback. Int. J. Artif. Intell. Educ. https://link.springer.com/article/10.1007/s40593-015-0080-x
6. Holland, J., Mitrovic, A., Martin, B.: J-LATTE: a constraint-based tutor for Java. In: Proceeding 17th International Conference Computers in Education (ICCE 2009), pp. 142–146 (2009)
7. Hong, J.: Guided programming and automated error analysis in an intelligent Prolog tutor. Int. J. Hum.-Comput. Stud. **61**(4), 505–534 (2004)
8. Jin, W., Barnes, T., Stamper, J., Eagle, M.J., Johnson, M.W., Lehmann, L.: Program representation for automatic hint generation for a data-driven novice programming tutor. In: Proceeding of 11th International Conference Intelligent Tutoring Systems, pp. 304–309 (2012)
9. Johnson, W.L.: Understanding and debugging novice programs. Artif. Intell. **42**(1), 51–97 (1990)
10. Keuning, H., Jeuring, J., Heeren, B.: Towards a systematic review of automated feedback generation for programming exercises. In: Proceeding of 2016 ACM Conference on Innovation and Technology in Computer Science Education, pp. 41–46. ACM (2016)
11. Le, N.T., Loll, F., Pinkwart, N.: Operationalizing the continuum between well-defined and ill-defined problems for educational technology. IEEE Trans. Learn. Technol. **6**(3), 258–270 (2013)

12. Le, N.T., Menzel, W.: Using weighted constraints to diagnose errors in logic programming - the case of an ill-defined domain. Int. J. Artif. Intell. Educ. **19**(4), 381–400 (2009)
13. Levy, R., Andrew, G.: Tregex and Tsurgeon: tools for querying and manipulating tree data structures. In: 5th International Conference Language Resources and Evaluation (2006)
14. Li, S., Xiao, X., Bassett, B., Xie, T., Tillmann, N.: Measuring code behavioral similarity for programming and software engineering education. In: Proceeding 38th International Conference on Software Engineering Companion, pp. 501–510. ACM (2016)
15. Mitrovic, A.: Fifteen years of constraint-based tutors: what we have achieved and where we are going. User Model. User-Adap. Inter. **22**(1–2), 39–72 (2012)
16. Nguyen, A., Piech, C., Huang, J., Guibas, L.: Codewebs: scalable homework search for massive open online programming courses. In: Proceeding 23rd International Conference World Wide Web, pp. 491–502 (2014)
17. Rivers, K., Koedinger, K.R.: Data-driven hint generation in vast solution spaces: a self-improving Python programming tutor. Int. J. Artif. Intell. Educ. https://link.springer.com/article/10.1007/s40593-015-0070-z

Dusting Off the Messy Middle: Assessing Students' Inquiry Skills Through Doing and Writing

Haiying Li[✉], Janice Gobert, and Rachel Dickler

Graduate School of Education, Rutgers University,
New Brunswick, NJ 08904, USA
{Haiying.li,Janice.Gobert,
Rachel.Dickler}@gse.rutgers.edu

Abstract. Researchers are trying to develop assessments for inquiry practices to elicit students' deep science learning, but few studies have examined the relationship between students' *doing*, i.e. *performance assessment,* and *writing,* i.e. *open responses,* during inquiry. Inquiry practices include generating hypotheses, collecting data, interpreting data, warranting claims, and communicating findings [1]. The first four practices involve "doing" science, whereas the last involves writing scientific explanations, i.e. arguing using evidence. In this study, we explored whether what students wrote in their constructed responses reflected what they did during science inquiry in the Inq-ITS system. Results showed that more than half of the students' writing did not match what they did in the environment. Findings revealed multiple types of students in the *messy middle*, which has implications for both teacher instruction and intelligent tutoring systems, such as Inq-ITS, in terms of providing real-time feedback for students to address the full complement of inquiry practices [1].

Keywords: Inquiry skills · Explanation skills · Log files · Constructed response · Doing science

1 Introduction

Next Generation Science Standards [1] and a framework for K-12 science education [2] expect students to demonstrate grade-appropriate proficiency in inquiry practices and understanding of core scientific ideas. These inquiry practices can be classified into two major categories: "doing" and "writing" scientific explanations (also called arguments or argumentation). The former consists of procedural knowledge including how to generate a research question, formulate a hypothesis, collect data from an experiment, analyze and interpret data, and select data to warrant claims. The latter involves constructing responses in order to communicate findings and argue a claim using evidence.

The original version of this chapter was revised. The spelling of the third author's name was corrected. The erratum to this chapter is available at https://doi.org/10.1007/978-3-319-61425-0_83

© Springer International Publishing AG 2017
E. André et al. (Eds.): AIED 2017, LNAI 10331, pp. 175–187, 2017.
DOI: 10.1007/978-3-319-61425-0_15

To achieve the expectations of NGSS, researchers have developed intelligent tutoring systems (ITSs) [3] or 3-D videogames [4] to teach and assess science inquiry skills in computer-assisted learning and assessment environments.

These environments stealthily record a myriad of students' actions and behaviors that are saved in the form of log files. Typically, the log files record the forced answers that students select from multiple-choice questions, dropdown menus, clickable buttons, or drag-and-drops. Digital environments also record students' constructed responses, such as scientific explanations written in open response format. For all actions that students make, the log files record the corresponding response time. These log files provide researchers with substantial information on the processes that occur during inquiry as well as during the composition of explanations. Some researchers have examined experimentation data from log files to identify whether students designed controlled experimental trials (e.g., [5, 6]), specifically by changing one target variable at a time [7, 8]. A few researchers have analyzed experimentation data to evaluate performance on constructed causal explanations in the format of multiple-choice questions (e.g., [9]). Other researchers have examined constructed explanations using a content-reasoning matrix assessment framework to explicitly demonstrate the range of students' explanation skills from intermediary or middle knowledge to more sophisticated understanding [10].

Previous studies have primarily concentrated on either inquiry skills (such as experimenting) or written explanation skills. Few studies, to date, have developed an assessment of the full complement of inquiry practices to score student performance that includes both inquiry skills and explanation skills. It is uncertain whether students who are good at designing and conducting experiments can also produce strong scientific explanations, as their writing skills may not be sufficiently developed to do so. Likewise, some students are able to parrot what they have heard or read and can produce satisfactory explanations, but their understanding, as reflected and demonstrated by their experimentation, is lacking. In either case, an assessment could be negatively or positively biased depending on which data are used.

The present study aims to examine whether students' inquiry skills for designing and conducting an experiment reflect their performance on writing scientific explanations within the Inq-ITS system (Inquiry Intelligent Tutoring System; inq-its.org). We use the term "*inquiry skills*" to refer to the behaviors involved in "doing" science that are captured in the log data. These behaviors consist of generating a hypothesis, collecting data, interpreting data, and warranting claims with data. We use the term "*explanation skills*" to refer to the scientific explanations constructed in an open response format. This study will significantly enhance science inquiry assessment for the following three reasons. First, it will provide a panoptic view of students' skills for science inquiry practices by integrating both doing science and writing a scientific explanation into the assessment. This method will allow for a clear investigation of the messy middle [10], as commonly acknowledged by assessment researchers, because using both types of data provides a complementary data set. This will also provide teachers, researchers, students, parents, and stakeholders with a more accurate form of assessment for the full complement of science inquiry practices. Second, Educational Data Mining (EDM), used as an automatic measure of inquiry skills [3], is able to capture student behaviors that are representative of authentic skills for science inquiry. Third, explanation skills are examined at the sublevel of knowledge components (KCs) instead of macro-level KCs to reduce ambiguity for human grading (see Method section for details). Scoring sub-KCs of claim, evidence, and reasoning helps raters avoid subjective bias and judgment when grading, and hence yields higher agreement. For example, we used a general rubric [10] and our rubric with sublevel KCs to score students' reasoning, and interrater reliability as measured by Pearson correlation increased from .55 to .88.

This paper has four sections. First, we briefly review current approaches to the assessment of science inquiry, specifically based on doing science and writing explanations. Second, we describe how to assess inquiry skills and explanation skills in the Method section. Third, we display results and discuss the findings in terms of the relationship between inquiry and explanation skills. Fourth, implications for teachers and researchers are discussed.

1.1 *Doing* Science

Accurate and appropriate assessments can be used to guide teachers in making instructional decisions. The types of assessments adopted in classrooms range from the traditional elicitation-response-evaluation pattern, such as open-ended investigation (e.g., [11]), to newly-emerged assessments (e.g., [12]). Even though the latter form involves thinking and developing knowledge in disciplinary practices, this type of summative assessment could not capture the intermediary processes involved in science inquiry. Formative assessments that occur during the inquiry process allow for adapting and individualizing instruction to improve students' learning.

Many researchers have developed computer-assisted learning and assessment environments to evaluate science inquiry. The computer-assisted assessment saves students' actions and response times in log files. The log files provide not only students' inquiry products, but also their inquiry processes [13]. For example, Gobert et al. [3] developed automated measures for assessing science inquiry skills for designing and conducting experiments using EDM on students' log files. This approach combined text replay tagging and educational data mining to develop a detector to assess science inquiry skills based on what students did during inquiry. Even though log files are collected in a nonintrusive way [14] and provide an informative progression of inquiry practices [3], to date, most researchers do not include performance assessment based on log data. This is probably due to the volume and complexity of log data and the challenge in analyzing it [15]. Instead, most researchers continue to focus on assessments based on a final product.

1.2 Writing Explanations

Scientific explanations in inquiry practices are purported to assess students' core conceptual understandings and reasoning about key scientific ideas used in inquiry [1, 2]. Scientific explanations require students to construct responses that can elicit critical thinking and involve making connections between scientific concepts and evidence [10, 16]. This in turn requires assessment of complex, higher-order cognitive processes [17, 18]. Toulmin's [19] model of argumentation is widely used as a framework for scientific explanations. The modified version consists of three components: claim (a statement that establishes a conclusion for the investigated question), evidence (data or observations that support or refute the claim), and reasoning (the scientific principle that connects data to the claim and makes visible the reason why the evidence supports or refutes the claim) [10, 16]. Prior research has shown that it is difficult for students to communicate their knowledge about science (i.e. articulating and justifying their claims with sufficient and appropriate evidence [20, 21]), distinguish evidence from theory [16], link their claim and evidence to scientific ideas [16], or use evidence to support their claim [22].

Researchers have assessed inquiry by examining content knowledge with procedural understanding [11, 23], content knowledge with reasoning skills [10], or predicting causal explanations generated by multiple-choice questions based on experimentation behaviors [9]. No studies have investigated procedural performance via doing science and performance on causal explanation via writing in science inquiry.

This study investigated three research questions: (1) to what extent do students' inquiry skills reflect their explanation skills? (2) what distribution is displayed in terms of high versus low inquiry skills and high versus low explanation skills? and (3) to what extent does performance on inquiry and explanation differ among the four groups (High-High, High-Low, Low-High, Low-Low with inquiry before explanation)? We hypothesize that inquiry performance can explain part of explanation performance because both of these skills may require certain domain-specific conceptual knowledge. However, as experimentation involves procedural understanding [24], doing experimentation may have its own unique features that do not reflect explanation skills. Similarly, as explanations involve connecting theory with data using reasoning, writing explanations may have unique characteristics involved in coherently synthesizing information. The second question may illustrate that there are some students who have developed good inquiry skills, but are not good at articulating their understanding as represented by their explanation. Many highly spatial science/math students could fall into this category. Under current assessment tests, such as state multiple-choice tests, these students are at risk for being assessed as not knowing science when they are actually highly skilled at conducting key inquiry practices. Conversely, those who are unskilled at inquiry but skilled at writing explanations are likely students who are parroting what they have "learned" in science class. Under current assessment tests, these students are at risk for being assessed as knowing science when their understanding is very superficial.

2   Method

2.1   Participants and Materials

293 middle school students from 18 classes in six public middle schools completed one Inq-ITS density virtual lab (inqits.com). Inq-ITS is a web-based intelligent tutoring and assessment system for Physical, Life, and Earth science that automatically assesses scientific inquiry practices at the middle school level in real time within interactive microworld simulations [3]. Within each microworld, inquiry practices proposed in the

NGSS for middle school are assessed including: hypothesizing, collecting data, analyzing data, interpreting data, warranting claims, and communicating findings. The Density Virtual Lab contained three activities aimed to foster understanding about the density of different liquid substances (water, oil, and alcohol), different amounts of liquid (quarter, half, and full), and different shapes of the container (narrow, square, and wide). This study analyzed the data in the last activity, the shape of the container.

Students completed four stages of inquiry over the course of the Density Virtual Lab, as illustrated in Fig. 1 and also in demos on the Inq-ITS website (inqits.com). During the Hypothesis stage, students used a widget (dropdown menu) to formulate a hypothesis that measured an activity goal. In the Collect Data phase, students used a widget (clickable buttons) to manipulate the independent variables in a simulation while a data table automatically recorded their findings. During the Analyze Data stage, students used a widget (dropdown menu) to state their claim, identified whether or not their claim supported their hypothesis, and selected evidence that supported their claim (clickable). Communicate Findings was the final inquiry stage where students responded to three open response questions in order to explain their claim, evidence, and reasoning for how their evidence supported their claim (writing). The first three stages are involved in doing science and we refer to the skills involved in doing science as inquiry skill. The last stage involves writing a scientific explanation and we refer to the skills involved in writing as explanation skill.

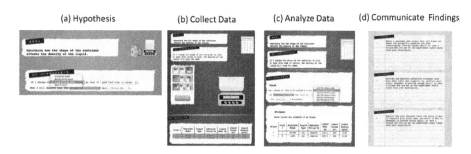

Fig. 1. Stages of the density virtual lab in Inq-ITS.

2.2   Measures

Inquiry skills were measured by four components using educational data mining techniques in Inq-ITS (see [3] for details). Each component contained sublevel KCs: (1) hypothesis (a. the identification of the independent variable (IV) and b. the identification of the dependent variable (DV)), (2) data collection (a. designing controlled experiment, b. testing hypothesis, and c. changing pairwise IV and controlled variable), (3) data interpretation (a. interpreting IV, b. interpreting DV, c. interpreting IV-DV relationship, and d. supporting hypothesis), and (4) warranting claims (a. warranting IV-DV relationship, b. number of single trial, c. supporting hypothesis, and d. all controlled trials). Each sublevel KC was automatically graded with binary scores, 0 for failing or 1 for succeeding at a skill. The inquiry score adopted the total of all the sublevel KC scores, with 0 as the minimum score and 13 as the maximum score.

The scientific explanation consisted of three components: claim, evidence, and reasoning. Each component was graded according to a scoring rubric that was modified based on the previous rubrics used by researchers (e.g., [10]) (see Table 1). The previous rubrics for claim and reasoning classified responses into incorrect or correct, but failed to specify the extent to which the claim was correct or incorrect. Similarly, the previous rubrics for evidence categorized three types of evidence: complete, incomplete, and incorrect. To determine which category evidence belonged to depended on raters' subjective ratings. This ambiguity reduces the agreement among human raters. Since previous coding schemes were too general to apply to Inq-ITS claim, evidence, and reasoning, we created a more specific coding scheme, as displayed in Table 1.

Table 1. Rubrics for scoring claim, evidence, and reasoning.

Type	KC		2 points	1 point	0.5 points	0 points
Claim (0–4)	IV		X	Shape	X	Incorrect IV
	IVR		X	2 shapes	1 shape	Incorrect IVR
	DV		X	Density	X	Incorrect DV
	DVR		X	Stays the same	X	Incorrect DVR
Evidence (0–4)	Sufficient		2 shapes	1 shape	X	No shape
	Appropriate	Mass + Volume	X	Data of mass & volume	Data of mass or volume	Incorrect data
		Density	X	Data of density	X	No density
Reasoning (0–6)	Theory		Mass/volume = density or property of substance	Mass + density or volume + density or partial property	Mass or volume	Incorrect theory
	Connection		X	Data supports/refutes claim	Partial connection	Incorrect connection
	Data	IV/IVR	X	Shape or 2 shapes	1 shape	Incorrect IV/IVR
		DV	X	Density	X	Incorrect DV
		DVR	X	Stays the same	X	Incorrect DVR

Note. 2 shapes = two of three types of shape (narrow, square, wide). 1 shape = any one of three types of shape. Shape means mentioning the word "shape."

In Inq-ITS, the widget claim is constructed with four knowledge components (KCs), IV, IVR (IV relationship, namely, any two of three types of shape; e.g., from narrow to wide), DV, and DVR (DV relationship, namely, state of density; e.g., stays the same). Therefore, the written claim was graded with the same four KCs. Written evidence was graded in terms of sufficiency and appropriateness [21]. Sufficiency was a measure of whether students provided sufficient evidence, namely, whether students specified changing the shape of container from one shape to another. Mentioning only one specific shape was considered insufficient evidence and not mentioning any specific shape was considered incorrect. During data collection, a data table displayed the values for mass, volume, and density for each trial a student ran. Appropriateness was a measure of whether students provided appropriate data, specifically the data for mass, volume, and density. Reasoning was composed of three sublevel KCs: theory, connection of data to theory, and data. Theory referred to whether students stated the nature of density, namely, density is only affected by the property of substance or the ratio of mass to volume. Data referred to whether students generalized the data, such as "The shape of the container does not affect the density of the liquid." Data-Theory connection referred to whether students specified that their data supports or refutes their claim.

Two expert raters discussed the rubrics and then graded for each KC or sublevel KC. The maximum score for claim and evidence was 4 points, respectively. The maximum score for reasoning was 6 points. Thus, the total possible score for explanation was 14 points. Inter-rater reliability was assessed by the intraclass correlation coefficient with a two-way random model and absolute agreement type [25]. The interrater-reliabilities by Cronbach's α were .993, .994, .938 and the intraclass correlations were .986, .988, .882 for claim, evidence, and reasoning, respectively. Then two raters discussed the disagreements and generated agreement scores. The agreement scores were used to compute the total scores of explanation skills.

2.3   Statistical Analysis

The analyses adopted the standardized total scores of inquiry skills and explanation skills. The relationship between inquiry skills and explanation skills was examined using linear regression. We performed K-means cluster analyses ($K = 2$) on the scores for inquiry skills and explanation skills, respectively, and classified students into low versus high for both inquiry and explanation. We performed the Chi-square analysis on inquiry group and explanation group to examine the distribution of students among these four quadrants. Finally, a multivariate general linear model (GLM) was performed to examine the extent to which the performance on inquiry skills and explanation skills differed among these four groups. The two dependent variables were inquiry skills and explanation skills. The independent variable was the four groups: High-High, High-Low, Low-High, and Low-Low with inquiry before explanation.

3   Results and Discussion

3.1   Results of Linear Regression

Results of linear regression showed that the total scores of inquiry skills significantly predicted the total scores of explanation skills, $B = .53$, $t(291) = 10.63$, $p < .001$. Results suggest that inquiry skills could explain 28% of the variance in explanation skills, $R^2 = .28$, $F(1, 291) = 112.99$, $p < .001$. However, the majority of variance (about 72%) in explanation skills could not be explained by inquiry skills. These findings imply that these two types of skills possess unique characteristics that represent unique constructs. The shared variance may represent the shared content knowledge (the relationship between the shape of the container and the density) that students apply when they do science and write an explanation. During experimentation, however, knowledge about doing experiments is needed, such as how to formulate a hypothesis, how to test the hypothesis by designing a controlled experiment, how to collect appropriate and sufficient data, how to generate a claim based on the collected data, and how to warrant a claim. The process of doing experiments involved procedural knowledge, which is unlikely to be captured in a written explanation.

On the other hand, constructing an explanation requires knowledge about logic and writing coherently. For example, students must understand what components should be included in a good claim. Most students did not specify how they controlled the target IV (e.g., The shape did not change density.); thus, generated an incomplete claim. Students needed to report the specific data in the evidence, but they only repeated their conclusion in this section. In reasoning, students needed to specify theory and connect data to theory to further support the claim. In fact, most students were confused by claim, evidence, and reasoning and repeated the same contents in each section. Therefore, writing an explanation requires writing skills, especially in terms of how to generate a coherent and complete claim, sufficient and appropriate evidence, and a theory that links to data to support and validate a claim.

3.2   Results of Chi-Squire

Results of Chi-square showed that inquiry skills and explanation skills were not independent (see Table 2), $\chi^2(1, N = 293) = 6.18$, $p = .013$. Specifically, 46.5% of students with high inquiry skills and 27.1% of students with low inquiry skills wrote a high quality scientific explanation. Moreover, 53.5% of students with high inquiry skills and 72.9% of students with low inquiry skills wrote a low quality scientific explanation. In addition, results showed a subset of the explanation group whose column proportions did not differ significantly from each other at the .05 level. Specifically, 89.8% of students with high explanation skills had high inquiry skills, whereas 10.2% had low inquiry skills. Conversely, 78.9% of students with low explanation skills had high inquiry skills, whereas 21.1% had low inquiry skills. These findings imply that 49.1% of the total students showed "middle" knowledge. Among them, 44.7% had high inquiry skills, but low explanation skills and 4.4% had low inquiry skills, but high explanation skills. 50.9% of the total students showed consistent knowledge: 38.9% achieved both high inquiry and explanation skills and only 11.9% had both poor inquiry and explanation skills.

Table 2. Inquiry group and explanation group ($N = 293$)

		Explanation Skill		Total	χ^2 (df = 1)
		High	Low		
Inquiry skill	High	114 (47.5)	131 (53.5)	245 (100)	6.18[*]
	Low	13 (27.1)	35 (72.9)	48 (100)	
Total		127 (43.3)	166 (56.7)	293	

Note. [*] $p < .05$. Numbers in parentheses are the percentage in each category.

Approximately half of the total students exhibited "middle" knowledge. These students showed intermediary knowledge in terms of inquiry and explanation skills. From the perspective of assessment, if they are assessed based on only one of these skills, they will be mistakenly evaluated. This is true for students who are good at doing science, but not skilled at writing explanations; as well as for students who are good at writing, but not skillful at doing science. If the former group of students is encouraged and trained in writing (or the latter in doing science), then students may have greater opportunity to excel as scientists in the future. However, if they are inaccurately reported as students who are poor at science based on their writing or doing science skills, we may not recognize the potential of a number of promising scientists. Hence, it is very important to assess science inquiry comprehensively with both doing science and writing about science.

3.3   Results of GLM

Table 3 displays the descriptive statistics of inquiry skills and explanation skills among four groups: High-High, High-Low, Low-High, and Low-Low with inquiry before explanation. Results of multivariate general linear model revealed a statistically significant difference in inquiry skills based on group, $F(6, 578) = 230.35$, $p < .001$; $\eta^2 = .705$. Tests of between-subjects effects indicated that group had a statistically significant effect on both inquiry scores ($F(3, 289) = 311.06$; $p < .001$; $\eta^2 = .764$) and explanation scores ($F(3, 289) = 226.64$; $p < .001$; $\eta^2 = .702$). The table below shows that mean scores for inquiry skills were significantly different between any two groups ($p < .001$). Mean explanation scores were also statistically different between any two groups ($p < .001$), except between High-High and Low-High ($p = 1.000$). The pattern of performance of inquiry skills is displayed: High-High > High-Low > Low-High > Low-Low. The pattern of performance of explanation is listed: High-High = Low-High > High-Low > Low-Low.

Table 3. Descriptive statistics

Group	N	Inquiry skills		Explanation skills	
		Mean	SD	Mean	SD
High-High	114	0.63	0.53	0.95	0.56
High-Low	131	0.13	0.40	−0.62	0.52
Low-High	13	−1.24	0.36	0.86	0.37
Low-Low	35	−2.10	0.67	−1.09	0.66
Total	293	0.00	1.00	0.00	1.00

Note. Group displays inquiry skills first, followed by explanation skills.

These findings further indicate that inquiry and explanation skills are differently represented in each group. Specifically, students with high explanation skills could consistently write good explanations irrespective of their inquiry skills. Conversely, students with high inquiry skills could do science better when explanation skills were high than when explanation skills were low. This pattern exists among students whose inquiry skills were low: when their explanation skills were high, they could do better science than when their explanation skills were low (even though their absolute scores remained lower relative to students with high inquiry skills). For students whose explanation skills were low: when inquiry skills were high, they wrote better explanations than when inquiry skills were low. To sum up, if students are good at conducting experiments, these skills are likely to help them yield better performance on writing. Conversely, if students are good at writing scientific explanations, these skills are less likely to help them do better science as writing is the final step and would not impact their inquiry.

4   General Discussion and Implications

In this study, we explored whether what students wrote in their constructed responses reflected what they did during science inquiry in the Inq-ITS system. Results indicated that students' skills at doing science only explained 28% variance in writing an explanation. The 72% of unexplained variance is probably explained by the unique skills involved in writing. Similarly, inquiry skills involved a series of procedural knowledge while doing science. Chi-square analysis demonstrated that nearly half of the students' writing did not match with their "doing". Findings revealed two types of the *messy middle*, which further illustrated that approximately half of the total students were good at doing science, but not good at writing explanations (44.7%). However, there were few students who were good at writing explanations, but not good at doing science (4.4%). Students who were good at both accounted for 38.9%, whereas those who performed poorly on both skills accounted for 11.9%. Multivariate analysis further indicated that each group performed differently on inquiry skills and explanation skills, except for High-High and Low-High groups on explanation skills. Our study dusts off the messy middle knowledge between inquiry skills and explanation skills, unfolds the complex middle knowledge between doing and writing in science inquiry practices, and provides implications for teachers and researchers when they design instruction and assessment for science inquiry.

Our study provides empirical evidence that science inquiry assessment by either doing science or writing scientific explanations does not capture the students' overall inquiry skills. This study explicitly demonstrated that these two skills only shared a small portion of variance because they each involve unique constructs. Only about 40% students developed equivalent, high inquiry skills and explanation skills. Another 10% had equivalent but poor skills. Another half did not develop equivalent skills. Among them, about 45% students failed to write good explanations in their open responses, even though they had designed and conducted a good experiment to test their hypotheses. One possible explanation is that students did not know what information they should put in the claim, evidence, and reasoning in their open responses. Another explanation is that students had not reified what they knew into their mental model of the phenomena under investigation. In this situation, teachers or computer tutors in an ITS could provide scaffolding for students for claim, evidence, and reasoning:

(1) *Claim*. Prompt students that the written claim should be consistent with the experimentation process conducted. Specifically, the written claim should contain the same four components as displayed in the widget claim; (2) *Evidence*. Prompt students to observe how the data table presents data and that the written evidence also needs to display data with the values of mass, volume, and the corresponding density; and (3) *Reasoning*. Scaffold student to understand that reasoning should include a theory that supports the claim, data that supports the claim, and then how data connects to the theory. This scaffolding may lead students to construct deep mental models which reflect both their doing of science and their writing explanations about the phenomena under investigation.

There were a few students who were poor at inquiry skills, but skillful at writing explanations. It is possible that these students were parroting what they had "learned" in science class, but they were not clear about how to "do" science. For these students, it is necessary to scaffold them on procedural knowledge that is required for designing and conducting experiments, such as how to collect controlled trials for a specific research question and how to select appropriate and sufficient data to support a claim.

Students who were poor in both inquiry skills and explanation skills might not have mastered content knowledge or procedural knowledge for conducting a controlled experiment. This means that teachers or a computer tutor should not scaffold students based solely on either doing or writing, but from the inquiry phase where students showed difficulties. Thus, when students successfully complete experiments, they can continue on to their writing. It is better to remind students how information is displayed during experimentation and tell them they could use the same format when writing their explanations. Similarly, when it is time for them to write, they could be reminded of how claim and evidence is presented during experimentation. This scaffolding would enhance students' skills to build connections between doing and writing, and consequently write a good explanation.

This study reveals students' "messy middle knowledge" in science inquiry, which explicitly informs teachers and researchers of the students' complex learning patterns and helps them develop adaptive and individualized instruction, curriculum, or scaffolding. This study also suggests that science inquiry should be interactively assessed by evaluating both inquiry and explanation skills so as to avoid biased judgment. Even though the current study successfully uncovered unequal performance between inquiry and explanation skills, one limitation would be that we focused on the macro-level of inquiry and explanation skills by aggregating the scores of the subskills. In future work, we will further investigate whether the same phenomenon consistently exists by: (1) analyzing the subskills that co-occur in both inquiry and explanation processes, such as claim and evidence, and (2) adding more activities in the analyses. Understanding what, how, and why middle knowledge occurs facilitates adaptive feedback and scaffolding in an ITS.

Acknowledgement. The research reported here was supported by Institute of Education Sciences (R305A120778) to Janice Gobert.

References

1. Generation Science Standards Lead States: Next generation science standards: for states, by states. National Academies Press, Washington (2013)
2. National Research Council: A framework for K-12 science education: practices, crosscutting concepts, and core ideas. National Academies Press, Washington (2012)
3. Gobert, J.D., Sao Pedro, M., Raziuddin, J., Baker, R.S.: From log files to assessment metrics: measuring students' science inquiry skills using educational data mining. J. Learn. Sci. **22**, 521–563 (2013). doi:10.1080/10508406.2013.837391
4. Shute, V.J.: Stealth assessment in computer-based games to support learning. In: Tobias, S., Fletcher, J.D. (eds.) Computer Games and Instruction, pp. 503–524. IAP (2011)
5. Sao Pedro, M.A., Gobert, J., Baker, R.S.: The development and transfer of data collection inquiry skills across physical science microworlds. In: Paper presented at the American Educational Research Association Conference (2012)
6. Sao Pedro, M., Baker, R., Gobert, J., Montalvo, O., Nakama, A.: Leveraging machine-learned detectors of systematic inquiry behavior to estimate and predict transfer of inquiry skill. User Model. User Adap. **23**, 1–39 (2013)
7. Chen, Z., Klahr, D.: All other things being equal: acquisition and transfer of the control of variables strategy. Child Dev. **70**, 1098–1120 (1999)
8. Tschirgi, J.E.: Sensible reasoning: a hypothesis about hypotheses. Child Dev. **51**, 1–10 (1990)
9. Baker, R.S., Clarke-Midura, J., Ocumpaugh, J.: Towards general models of effective science inquiry in virtual performance assessments. J. Comp. Assist. Learn. **32**, 267–280 (2016)
10. Gotwals, A.W., Songer, N.B.: Reasoning up and down a food chain: using an assessment framework to investigate students' middle knowledge. Sci. Educ. **94**, 259–281 (2010)
11. Roberts, R., Gott, R., Glaesser, J.: Students' approaches to open-ended science investigation: the importance of substantive and procedural understanding. Res. Pap. Ed. **25**, 377–407 (2010). doi:10.1080/02671520902980680
12. Roberts, R., Johnson, P.: Understanding the quality of data: a concept map for 'the thinking behind the doing' in scientific practice. Curriculum J. **26**, 345–369 (2015)
13. Rupp, A.A., Gushta, M., Mislevy, R.J., Shaffer, D.W.: Evidence-centered design of epistemic games: measurement principles for complex learning environments. J. Technol. Learn. Assess. **8**, 1–48 (2010)
14. National Research Council: Knowing what students know: the science and design of educational assessment. In: Pellegrino, J.W., Chudowsky, N., Glaser, R. (eds.) National Academies Press, Washington (2001)
15. Quellmalz, E., Timms, M., Schneider, S.: Assessment of student learning in science simulations and games. National Research Council, Washington (2009)
16. McNeill, K., Lizotte, D.J., Krajcik, J., Marx, R.W.: Supporting students' construction of scientific explanations by fading scaffolds in instructional materials. J. Learn. Sci. **15**, 153–191 (2006). doi:10.1207/s15327809jls1502_1
17. Liu, O.L., Lee, H.S., Linn, M.C.: Multifaceted assessment of inquiry-based science learning. Ed. Assess. **15**, 69–86 (2010). doi:10.1080/10627197.2010.491067
18. Martınez-Cortizas, A., Pontevedra-Pombal, X., Garcıa-Rodeja, E., Novoa-Munoz, J.C., Shotyk, W.: Mercury in a Spanish peat bog: archive of climate change and atmospheric metal deposition. Science **284**, 939–942 (1999)
19. Toulmin, S.: The Uses of Argument. Cambridge University Press, Cambridge (1958)

20. Sadler, T.D.: Informal reasoning regarding socioscientific issues: a critical review of research. J. Res. Sci. Teach. **41**, 513–536 (2004)
21. Sandoval, W.A., Millwood, K.A.: The quality of students' use of evidence in written scientific explanations. Cogn. Instruct. **23**, 23–55 (2005)
22. Hogan, K., Maglienti, M.: Comparing the epistemological underpinnings of students' and scientists' reasoning about conclusions. J. Res. Sci. Teach. **38**, 663–687 (2001). doi:10.1002/tea.1025
23. Gobert, J.D., Pallant, A.R., Daniels, J.T.: Unpacking inquiry skills from content knowledge in geoscience: a research and development study with implications for assessment design. Int. J. Learn. Technol. **5**, 310–334 (2010)
24. Glaesser, J., Gott, R., Roberts, R., Cooper, B.: The roles of substantive and procedural understanding in open-ended science investigations: using fuzzy set qualitative comparative analysis to compare two different tasks. Res. Sci. Ed. **39**, 595–624 (2009). doi:10.1007/s11165-008-9108-7
25. Shrout, P.E., Fleiss, J.L.: Intraclass correlations: uses in assessing rater reliability. Psychol. Bull. **86**, 420–428 (1979). doi:10.1037/0033-2909.86.2.420

Impact of Pedagogical Agents' Conversational Formality on Learning and Engagement

Haiying Li[1(✉)] and Art Graesser[2]

[1] Graduate School of Education, Rutgers University,
New Brunswick, NJ 08904, USA
Haiying.li@gse.rutgers.edu
[2] Department of Psychology, University of Memphis,
Memphis, TN 38152, USA
Graesser@memphis.edu

Abstract. This study investigated the impact of pedagogical agents' conversational formality on learning and engagement in a trialog-based intelligent tutoring system (ITS). Participants ($N = 167$) were randomly assigned into one of three conditions to learn summarization strategies with the conversational agents: (1) a *formal* condition in which both the teacher agent and the student agent spoke with a formal language style, (2) an *informal* condition in which both agents spoke informally, and (3) a *mixed* condition in which the teacher agent spoke formally, whereas the student agent spoke informally. Result showed that the agents' informal discourse yielded higher performance, but elicited higher report of text difficulty and mind wandering. This discourse also caused longer response time and lower arousal. The implications are discussed.

Keywords: Agents · Arousal · Engagement · Formality · Mind wandering · Summary writing · Teacher language · Text difficulty · Valence

1 Introduction

The present study investigated the impact of conversational agents' formality on deep reading comprehension and engagement in a trialog-based intelligent tutoring system (ITS). Formality is defined as a language style on a continuum from informal discourse to formal discourse [1]. Formal discourse, either in print or pre-planned oratory, is precise, cohesive, articulate, and convincing to an educated audience. Informal discourse, at the opposite end of the continuum, is used in oral conversation, personal letters, and narratives, which are replete with pronouns, deictic references (e.g., these, those), and verbs with a reliance on common knowledge among speakers and listeners [2]. Mixed discourse is situated between informal and formal discourses, with moderate characteristics of both formal and informal discourses. Formality increases with grade level and informational texts, but decreases with narrative texts [1–3]. The rationale and significance of this study are elaborated below.

Language is one of the most powerful tools that teachers can use to organize and implement instructional activities and engage students in learning [4]. For example, the professional use of words and phrases engages students in active and interested learning

E. André et al. (Eds.): AIED 2017, LNAI 10331, pp. 188–200, 2017.
DOI: 10.1007/978-3-319-61425-0_16

[4]. Teacher language is correlated to student language [5] and reading comprehension [6]. Agent language affects science learning [7, 8]. No studies, to date, however, have studied teacher language as a unit at integrative levels of *vocabulary, sentence, discourse*, and *genre*. Our study is interested in the effect of teacher language at these multiple textual levels on deep reading comprehension and engagement.

1.1   Teacher Language and Formality

Recently, teacher language has been classified into academic versus conversational language and it has increasingly drawn researchers' interest [9]. The majority of studies concentrated on either the relationship between teacher language and student language, or between teacher language and learning performance. For example, researchers reported that students' vocabulary skills were positively correlated with teachers' use of sophisticated, academic vocabulary and complex syntax [5]. The teachers' use of sophisticated, academic vocabulary was correlated to students' reading comprehension performance [6]. Conversely, the experiments that manipulated the computer agent language in the ITS showed that the agent's conversational style (e.g., the 1st and 2nd personal pronoun) yielded better performance on deep learning than the formal style (e.g., the 3rd personal pronoun) [7, 8]. These conflicting findings likely result from inconsistent measures of language: one at the lexical and syntactic levels [6], and one using personal pronouns [7, 8]. Neither measure represented language style as a whole, but rather only one aspect of language. Therefore, a measure of teacher language that comprehensively represents the characteristics of language is needed to further investigate the effect of teacher language on learning.

Academic language and conversational language are at two extreme ends of the formality continuum, where academic language is at one end, namely, formal language and conversational language at the other, namely, informal language) [1]. Academic language and conversational language were measured using automated Coh-Metrix formality scores (cohmetrix.com) [1, 3]. Specifically, academic language or formal language increased with word abstractness, syntactic complexity, expository texts, high referential cohesion, and high deep cohesion. Conversational language or informal language increased with word concreteness, syntactic simplicity, narrative texts, low referential cohesion, and low deep cohesion. Formality was a standardized score ($M = 0$) [1, 3]. High numbers above 0 represented more formal discourse, whereas lower numbers below 0 represented more informal discourse.

Previous research on teacher language has been confined to correlational research [5, 6] due to the difficulty in consistently manipulating teacher language in the traditional classroom setting. Some researchers resorted to a computer-based system to manipulate the computer agent's speaking style, but the manipulation was restricted to personal pronouns (*I* and *you* versus third-person) [7, 8].

The present study designed a causal study to manipulate the language styles of the conversational, pedagogical agents via an ITS, called AutoTutor [10]. Conversational, pedagogical agents are on-screen computer characters that generate speech, facial expr -essions (e.g., eyebrow-raising, eye-moving), and some gestures and facilitate instruction to the learner [11]. AutoTutor helps improve learning by almost one letter grade [10].

The present study designed a trialog between a: teacher agent, student agent, and human learner. The learner in this study is both an active learner, not a vicarious observer who learns from observing how a student agent learns from a teacher agent and overhearing their ensuing dialogues [12].

1.2 Engagement

Engagement has been categorized into three types: emotional, behavioral, and cognitive [13]. Emotional engagement reflected affective states (e.g., mood, affect, interest) and was usually measured by self-reported affective states (valence and arousal) [14]. Behavioral engagement referred to learners' participation and involvement in a learning task (e.g., effort, persistence, attention) and was usually assessed by self-reported mind wandering [14, 15]. Cognitive engagement meant investment in the task (e.g., task management, material mastery) and was usually measured by reading time [15].

Most studies on engagement and reading focused on the impact of text difficulty and/or text preference [14, 15]. Previous research has shown conflicting findings. Specifically, increasing text difficulty was found to be either beneficial [14] or detrimental [15] to engagement and learning. Some findings showed that mind wandering occurred more frequently when students conducted easy rather than difficult tasks [14]. These findings posit the executive-resource hypothesis [16] because mind wandering employed more available resources for task-unrelated thoughts. Other studies have found that participants reported more mind wandering when they read difficult texts than easy texts [15] because mind wandering was the result of executive maintenance failures (control-failure hypothesis) [17]. One possible explanation for these conflicting findings is that studies used different reading materials and experimenter-paced reading. Researchers also found that learners spent more time reading difficult texts [14, 15], but only for texts that they preferred [14].

No studies to date, however, have investigated the impact of teacher language at multi-textual levels on learning and engagement. As teacher language is one of primary tools for teachers in daily instruction, it is worthwhile to understand how teacher language impacts learning and engagement. This understanding will allow for the development of guidance for teachers and researchers on how to use language during instruction.

This study advances research on teacher language in three ways. First, the present study adopts an automated measure of formality to comprehensively measure teacher language [1–3], ranging from lexical and syntactic levels to textbase (e.g., explicit propositions, referential cohesion), situation model (or mental model), discourse genre, and rhetorical structure (the type of discourse and its composition) [1]. This multilevel measure captures teacher language as a whole rather than at separate aspects of one level, such as vocabulary [5–8] or syntax [6]. Second, this study implements a causal design to manipulate teacher language in an ITS. Third, this study bridges the gap between research on teacher language and engagement so as to provide guidance and enhance the awareness of language for teachers and researchers when they design instruction in traditional classroom settings or in computer-assisted learning and assessment environments.

2 Method

2.1 Participants

Participants (N = 240) volunteered for monetary compensation ($30) on Amazon Mechanical Turk, a trusted and commonly used data collection service [18]. The requirement for participants was that they were English learners who aimed to improve English summary writing. The qualified participants were randomly assigned into one of three conditions (formal, informal, and mixed) and completed a 3-hour experiment. Finally, 164 participants completed the experiments due to technical issues. This led to an uneven number of participants in each condition: N = 46 (Age: M = 33.17, SD = 8.77), N = 56 (Age: M = 33.70, SD = 8.92), N = 62 (Age: M = 33.47, SD = 8.76) for formal, informal, and mixed, respectively. 57% were male and 82% obtained a bachelor's degree or above. 71% participants were Asian, 16% white or Caucasian, 7% African American, 5% Hispanic, 2% other. Non-English speakers (89%) had learned English for 14.71 years on average (SD = 9.70).

2.2 Materials

Text. Eight short English texts (195 to 399 words) were selected from the adult literacy repository of materials (http://csal.gsu.edu) with a slight modification, consisting of four comparison texts and four causation texts [19]. Two comparison texts and two causation texts were randomly selected for tests and the balanced 4 by 4 Latin-square designs were applied to control for order effects on pretest and posttest. The remaining four passages were used for training; the same 4 by 4 balanced Latin-square design was applied. The comparison text structure connected ideas by comparing or contrasting two things/ideas/persons or alternative perspectives on a topic and showing how they were similar or different [20]. The causation texts presented a causal or cause-effect relationship between ideas [20]. Text formality of these eight texts tended to be more formal ranging from .12 to .64 according to the Coh-Metrix formality scores. Based on the Flesch-Kincaid grade level, these texts were at the grade level of 8 to 12.

Training. At the beginning of the training session, two conversational agents [11] interactively presented a mini-lecture on signal words that were frequently used in comparison texts (e.g., *similarly, likewise* for similarity and *differ, however* for differences) and causation texts (e.g., *because, since* for cause and *consequence, therefore* for effect). After participants read the passage and reported engagement (see the section of Independent Variables), agents interacted with participants and guided them to apply the summarization strategy to five multiple-choice questions. The application consisted of identifying: (1) a text structure (1 item), (2) the main ideas (1 item), and (3) the important supporting information (3 items). Thus, the summarization strategy was learned and assessed during a one-hour training session in this trialog-based ITS.

2.3   Manipulation

One expert at discourse processing generated agents' conversations in the formal and informal languages, following a five-step tutoring frame, and expectation and misconception-tailored dialogue (EMT) [11, 21]. Then another expert modified conversations based on the context. Table 1 lists an example of conversations that embodied a systematic conversational structure, which is described in Fig. 1. We annotated in brackets-with-italics some of the dialogue move categories. It should be noted that half of the Jordan responses were incorrect. Cristina always had the ground truth. Tim (the participant) needed to determine his answer based on two agents' suggestions. Therefore, the human was an active participant rather than being a merely vicarious observer. This dialogue structure improved student performance and student engagement in learning [22]. Agents delivered the content of their utterances via synthesized speech, whereas the participants clicked on or typed in their responses.

Table 1.   An example of trialog.

Cristina: Tim [*Participant*], can you tell us the text structure of this text? [*Main question*]
Tim: (*Click*) Sequence. [*First trial: Wrong Answer*]
Cristina: Jordan, what do you think of this answer? [*Ask Jordan*]
Jordan: This answer might be correct. [*Jordan's incorrect response*]
Cristina: Signal words help tell the overall text structure. Sometimes, the text organization or even the title helps too. [*Hint*]
Cristina: The author uses the time sequence to talk about Kobe's and Jordan's careers. The author doesn't use sequence to organize the full text. [*Elaboration*]
Cristina: Try again. I will repeat the question. Tim, what is the text structure of this text? [*Repeat Question*]
Tim: (*Click*) Comparison. [*Second trial: Correct Answer*]
Cristina: Tim, you are absolutely right! Jordan, your answer is incorrect! [*Feedback*]
Cristina: The author first generally talks about how Kobe and Jordan are similar and different. Then it talks about them separately in each paragraph. [*Wrap-up*]
Jordan: You can see some signal words show similarities and differences, such as "two" and "different". So the correct answer is comparison. [*Wrap-up*]

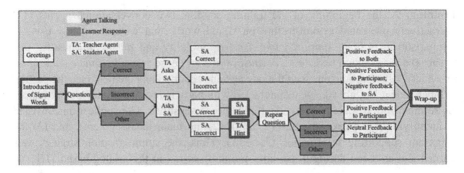

Fig. 1. Trialog moves in conversations. *Note*. Conversations in red box were manipulated. (Color figure online)

The agents' conversations in the trialog were designed in formal and informal language styles that were then assigned to the teacher agent and student agent. The agents' conversations were evaluated by the measure of formality [1, 3]. The mean of agents' formal language was 1.02 and informal, −0.37, which was consistent with humans' perception of formality when they generated conversations. The mixed language was generated by combining the formal language of the teacher agent (Cristina) and the informal language of the student agent (Jordan), and its formality score was 0.12. Based on Graesser et al.'s study [1], the agents' formality in three conditions represents three different levels of formality, ranging from informal to medium to formal. Table 2 illustrates an example of conversations in each condition when agents introduced the functions of signal words. We did not design a mixed condition where an agent's language style changed from formal to informal when common ground increased between agent and learner. The reason was that this design would cause confounds with time. When a significant effect occurred, it would be unclear whether it was caused by language style or by length of time spent learning.

Table 2. Examples of conversations in the formal and informal conditions

Cristina's formal discourse:

The signal words enable readers to determine the text structure, and consequently enhance reading comprehension. Moreover, by using the signal words, the authors guide the readers in the direction that they want them to go. The comparison text consistently compares the similarities and differences of two things or two persons.

Cristina's informal discourse:

Yes, Jordan. The author uses the signal words to lead you in the reading. The signal words help identify the text structure. They help you understand the reading better. The comparison text usually compares how things or persons are similar or different.

Note. It consisted of (A) the teacher agent, Cristina (female), (B) the student agent, Jordan (male), (C) the instruction of the presented question, (D) the text presented with the scroll down button, (E) an input text-box for participants to enter and submit their summaries or choose the answers of multiple choice questions during training, and (F) the self-paced next button.

Fig. 2. Screenshot of Interface.

2.4   Procedure

Participants first took a demographic survey, a pretest, training, and a posttest. There were two passages in the pretest: one comparison and one causation. For each passage, participants first read the passage and then self-reported engagement. Participants then wrote the summary for the passage with the text displayed to them (see Fig. 2). The same procedure was applied to training and posttest as well. However, the training session added instruction of summarization with four texts and accordingly four summaries were written. The summary was short, between 50 and 100 words. The summary required a topic sentence that stated the main idea and important information, and students were meant to use signal words to explicitly express their ideas.

2.5   Dependent Variables and Measures

Summary Writing. The summaries that participants wrote were graded based on the rubric used in the previous studies [23] with a slight modification. The rubric included four elements: (1) topic sentence, (2) content inclusion and exclusion, (3) grammar and mechanics, and (4) signal words of text structures [19]. Each element was assessed on a scale of 0–2 points, with 0 for the absence of target knowledge, 1 for the partial presence of knowledge, and 2 for the complete presence of knowledge.

Four experts whose native language was English (1 male and 3 females) participated in the training for summary grading. At the beginning of training, they discussed each element in the rubrics and then graded three summaries of good, medium, and poor quality. Participants then started three rounds of training. Each round, they graded 32 summaries that were randomly selected from eight texts and then discussed disagreements until an agreement was reached. The average interrater reliabilities for the three training sets reached the threshold (Cronbach $\alpha = .82$). After training, each rater graded summaries for two source texts. There were 1,296 summaries in total.

Engagement. Engagement in this study was measured with the same method that Fulmer et al. [14] adopted. Emotional engagement was measured by affective states that occurred during reading. The participants reported valence and arousal using a circomplex model of affect, called Affect Grid [24]. Figure 3 shows the image of the 9×9 Affect Grid along two dimensions of valence $\times$ arousal. The valence dimension ranges from unpleasant feelings to pleasant feelings (1–9), whereas the arousal dimension ranges from low arousal (i.e., sleepiness) to high arousal (1–9). These two dimensions compressively represent the variations of affective states from positive

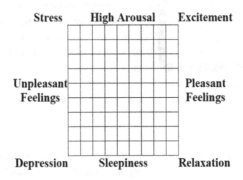

Fig. 3. Affect Grid [14, 24]

(e.g., excitement) to negative (e.g., sadness) valence, and from activating (e.g., excitement) to deactivating (e.g., relaxation) arousal [14].

Behavioral engagement was measured by mind wandering. Participants were given the definition [16]: "At some point during reading, you may realize that you have no idea what you just read. Not only were you not thinking about the text, you were thinking about something else altogether. This is called 'zoning out.'" Participants reported mind wandering once they finished reading by indicating the extent they were conducting off-task behavior during reading. This was reported on a 7-point scale with 1 as mind wandering never occurs and 7 as mind-wandering always occurs.

Cognitive engagement was measured by reading time and summary writing time. Reading time was recorded from displaying the text page to going to next page. Summary writing time was recorded from displaying the summary writing page to the submission of the summary. Both reading time and writing time were self-paced. As previous research has studied the effect of text difficulty on learning and engagement, the present study also included the perception of text difficulty that participants reported with a 6-point scale from very easy (1) to very difficult (6).

The primary independent variable (IV) was agents' formality (formal, informal, and mixed). This study consisted of two types of text structures, comparison and cause-effect, so text structure was also used as an IV. As participants consecutively wrote eight summaries, time phase was used as a repeated measure. We performed the mixed repeated ANOVA with agents' formality as a between-subjects factor, and text structure and time as within-subjects factors. All significance testing was conducted with an alpha level of .05 with Bonferroni correction for multiple analyses.

3   Results and Discussion

Table 3 displays the estimated means (standard errors) of dependent variables in the three conditions. Results showed that participants' summaries were at the medium level, but participants were highly engaged in reading and summary writing. Engagement was represented by moderate valence and arousal, and low mind wandering and text difficulty in all three conditions. Reading time was almost 2 min on average, whereas summary writing time was approximately 7 min on average.

Table 3. Estimated means and standard errors

	Summary	TD (1–6)	Valence (1–9)	Arousal (1–9)	MW (1–7)	RT (Second)	WT (Second)
Formal	4.71(.09)	2.15(.06)	5.84(.12)	6.57(.10)	1.81(.06)	116.31(4.61)	418.05(10.68)
Mixed	4.86(.08)	2.45(.05)	5.73(.10)	6.01(.08)	1.92(.06)	95.63(3.93)	390.52(9.11)
Informal	5.09(.08)	2.42(.05)	5.56(.11)	6.22(.09)	2.08(.06)	113.47(4.18)	441.71(9.68)

Note. TD = Text Difficulty. MW = Mind Wandering. RT = Reading Time. WT = Summary Writing Time. Summary = Summary Writing Scores (0–8 points).

Pearson correlations among dependent variables were performed to examine the relationships between summary writing and engagement after reading but before summary writing. Results displayed that summary scores were significantly but negatively correlated with the perception of text difficulty in three conditions, $r = -.15$, $r = -.19$, and $r = -.11$ for formal, informal, and mixed conditions ($p < .01$), respectively. Participants wrote better summaries for easy texts, which was consistent across the three conditions. Also, summary writing was significantly but negatively correlated with mind wandering in the informal ($r = -.13$, $p < .01$) and mixed conditions ($r = -.15$, $p < .01$), but not in the formal condition. Findings support the claim that mind wandering impaired learning when tasks for the informal and mixed discourses were easier to understand relative to the formal discourse. This finding is inconsistent with previous findings that mind wandering impairs learning when tasks are more difficult [15]. Valence was significantly and positively correlated with learning in the informal condition ($r = .15$, $p < .01$). Reading time before summary writing was significantly and positively correlated with summary scores in the mixed condition ($r = .12$, $p < .01$).

Results also showed that perceived text difficulty was significantly but negatively correlated with arousal ($r = -.19 \sim -.23$) and valence ($r = -.11 \sim -.29$), but positively correlated with mind wandering ($r = .38 \sim .44$) in three conditions with $p < .01$. Findings indicated that difficult texts reduced engagement because the more difficult texts were, the lower arousal and valence were, but the more mind wandering. These findings are consistent with the report that mind wandering occurs with an increase in text difficulty [15]. One possible explanation is that engagement is reduced when readers have difficulty constructing a situation model from the difficult text [15]. These results demonstrated a consistent pattern of engagement in different conditions, but an inconsistent relationship between learning and engagement. The correlation coefficients between summary writing and engagement were small because the engagement was measured before, but not after summary writing.

Mixed repeated ANOVA showed no significant two-way or three-way interactions for learning and engagement. However, there was a significant main effect of agents' formality on summary scores, $F(2, 1248) = 5.25$, $p = 0.005$. Pairwise analyses showed that the participants wrote better summaries when they interacted with agents who spoke the informal discourse than with agents who spoke the formal discourse, Cohen's $d = .63$, $p = 0.004$. This finding is consistent with previous study [7, 8] and suggests that informal discourse is easier to process than formal discourse. The informal style facilitates learners to better understand the instructional content and more successfully apply the newly-learned summarization strategy to summary writing.

Results also demonstrated a significant main effect of agents' formality on text difficulty, $F(2, 1246) = 9.09$, $p < 0.001$. Pairwise analyses showed that participants reported lower text difficulty in the formal condition than in the informal (Cohen's $d = .69$, $p = 0.001$) and mixed conditions (Cohen's $d = .77$, $p < 0.001$). This finding signifies that the agents' formal discourse is more complex and hard to process so as to cause participants to perceive that reading texts are much easier to process relative to listening to agents. Conversely, the informal and mixed discourses are simpler and easier to process, which causes participants to feel that texts are more difficult to read.

Results did not show a significant main effect of agents' formality on valence. Agents' formality, however significantly affected arousal, $F(2, 1246) = 9.66$, $p < 0.001$; mind wandering, $F(2, 1246) = 5.08$, $p = 0.006$; reading time, $F(2, 1248) = 7.45$, $p = 0.001$; and writing time, $F(2, 1248) = 7.45$, $p = 0.001$. Pairwise analyses showed that participants in the formal condition reported higher arousal than in the informal (Cohen's $d = .53$, $p = 0.024$) and mixed (Cohen's $d = .86$, $p < 0.001$) conditions. They reported lower mind wandering in the formal condition than in the informal condition, Cohen's $d = .61$, $p < 0.001$. They spent less time reading text in the mixed condition than in the formal (Cohen's $d = .67$, $p = 0.001$) and informal conditions (Cohen's $d = .57$, $p = 0.001$). They also used less time to write summary in the mixed condition than in the informal condition, Cohen's $d = .71$, $p = 0.001$.

To sum up, participants reported moderate valence and arousal, but low mind wandering and text difficulty, which represented high engagement in three conditions. Mind wandering in the informal condition, however, was higher relative to the formal condition. Interestingly, the time that participants spent reading and writing in these two conditions was not significantly different. One possible explanation, supported by the executive-resource hypothesis, is that informal discourse was easy to understand so after the first time learning summarization strategy, its execution had been automated due to unused executive resources from the primary task [15]. Consequently, mind wandering increased with the simple discourse. Furthermore, reading time and writing time were longer in the informal condition than in the mixed condition. The self-reported affective and behavioral engagement indicated that the agents' informal discourse caused higher mind wandering, which caused longer time on the task [25]. Oppositely, the cognitive engagement measured by reading and writing time showed that longer reaction times often reflected active engagement in tasks [26] due to increased efforts and persistence [27], especially when the task was a high-level processing task of reading [15]. These conflicting findings revealed that the agents' informal discourse helped learners with deeper reading comprehension than the agents' formal discourse. It is likely that participants in the informal condition reported higher mind wandering due to the fast mastery of summarization strategy.

Participants reported higher engagement in the formal condition than in the mixed condition, as indicated by low text difficulty, higher arousal, and longer time spent reading. However, this difference did not occur in summary writing. This finding implies that mind wandering was essential to successful learning. Participants spent longer time reading and writing in the informal condition than in the mixed condition, but their summary writing scores were not significantly different. This finding further demonstrates that even though the time devoted was different, learning was not affected if mind-wandering did not occur.

4   Implications and Future Directions

The present study investigated the impact of agent formality on deep reading comprehension measured by summary writing and engagement in an authentic reading and writing environment. Namely, learners can read and write in their own pace without the constraints to experimenter-paced presentations of text. This self-paced reading will not impact mind wandering during the task [15]. Therefore, the findings more authentically reflect learners' engagement and learning, which provide implications for teachers and researchers. For example, teachers and researchers need to consider the function of teacher language during instruction and the importance of design of teacher language to foster students' deep learning and engagement. The findings can be applied to ITS as more systems have begun using natural language. To sum up, informal discourse may yield more accurate deep learning because it causes high engagement (relatively more effort represented by more response time), even though it leads to lower arousal, higher mind wandering, and higher text difficulty relative to formal condition. The relative mind wandering may elicit more effort and persistence on the high-level cognitive tasks, such as summary writing.

One limitation of the study was that we did not investigate the effect of text difficulty, text interest, or other text characteristics, such as domain-specific versus domain-general texts. These factors may affect learning and engagement along with agents' formality. Another concern was that the experiment lasted more than three hours and participants wrote eight summaries. The long-term studying may have impacted learning and engagement. In the future, the tasks may be allotted into different periods to see whether the same pattern occurs. Moreover, a future study may devise one agent that uses a mixed discourse whose formality falls between formal and informal discourse, as opposed to having the two discourses used by two distinct agents.

Acknowledgement. This work was funded by the Institute of Education Sciences (Grant No. R305C120001). Any opinions are those of the authors and do not necessarily reflect the views of these funding agencies, cooperating institutions, or other individuals.

References

1. Graesser, A.C., McNamara, D.S., Cai, Z., Conley, M., Li, H., Pennebaker, J.: Coh-Metrix measures text characteristics at multiple levels of language and discourse. Elem. School J. **115**, 210–229 (2014). doi:10.1086/678293
2. Li, H., Graesser, A.C., Conley, M., Cai, Z., Pavlik, P., Pennebaker, J.W.: A new measure of text formality: an analysis of discourse of Mao Zedong. Discourse Process. **53**, 205–232 (2016). doi:10.1080/0163853X.2015.1010191
3. Li, H., Graesser, A.C., Cai, Z.: Comparing two measures of formality. In: Boonthum-Denecke, C., Youngblood, G.M. (eds.) 2013 FlAIRS, pp. 220–225. AAAI Press, Palo Alto (2013)
4. Denton, P.: The power of our words: teacher language that helps children learn. Center for Responsive Schools Inc., Turners Falls (2013)
5. Gámez, P.B., Lesaux, N.K.: The relation between exposure to sophisticated and complex language and early—adolescent English—only and language minority learners' vocabulary. Child Dev. **83**, 1316–1331 (2012). doi:10.1111/j.1467-8624.2012.01776.x
6. Gámez, P.B., Lesaux, N.K.: Early-adolescents' reading comprehension and the stability of the middle school classroom-language environment. Dev. Psychol. **51**, 447–458 (2015). doi:10.1037/a0038868

7. Moreno, R., Mayer, R.E.: Personalized messages that promote science learning in virtual environments. J. Educ. Psychol. **96**, 165–173 (2004). doi:10.1037/0022-0663.96.1.165

8. Mayer, R.E.: Principles based on social cues: personalization, voice, and presence principles. In: Mayer, R.E. (ed.) Cambridge Handbook of Multimedia Learning, pp. 201–212. Cambridge University Press, New York (2005)

9. Snow, C.E., Uccelli, P.: The challenge of academic language. In: Olson, D.R., Torrance, N. (eds.) The Cambridge Handbook of Literacy, Cambridge, New York, pp. 112–133 (2009)

10. Graesser, A.C., Chipman, P., Haynes, B.C., Olney, A.: AutoTutor: an intelligent tutoring system with mixed-initiative dialogue. IEEE Trans. Edu. **48**, 612–618 (2005). doi:10.1109/TE.2005.856149

11. Graesser, A.C., Li, H., Forsyth, C.: Learning by communicating in natural language with conversational agents. Curr. Dir. Psychol. Sci. **23**, 374–380 (2014). doi:10.1177/0963721414540680

12. Chi, M.T.H., Roy, M., Hausmann, R.G.M.: Observing tutoring collaboratively: Insights about tutoring effectiveness from vicarious learning. Cog. Sci. **32**, 301–341 (2008). doi:10.1080/03640210701863396

13. Fredricks, J.A., Blumenfeld, P.C., Paris, A.H.: School engagement: potential of the concept, state of the evidence. Rev. Educ. Res. **74**, 59–109 (2004). doi:10.3102/00346543074001059

14. Fulmer, S.M., D'Mello, S.K., Strain, A., Graesser, A.C.: Interest-based text preference moderates the effect of text difficulty on engagement and learning. Contemp. Educ. Psychol. **41**, 98–110 (2015). doi:10.1016/j.cedpsych.2014.12.005

15. Feng, S., D'Mello, S., Graesser, A.C.: Mind wandering while reading easy and difficult texts. Psychon. B. Rev. **20**, 586–592 (2013). doi:10.3758/s13423-012-0367-y

16. Smallwood, J.M., Schooler, J.W.: The restless mind. Psychol. Bull. **132**, 946–958 (2006). doi:10.1037/0033-2909.132.6.946

17. McVay, J.C., Kane, M.J.: Does mind wandering reflect executive function or executive failure? Comment on Smallwood and Schooler (2006) and Watkins (2008). Psychol. Bull. **136**, 188–197 (2010). doi:10.1037/a0018298

18. Buhrmester, M., Kwang, T., Gosling, S.D.: Amazon's Mechanical Turk a new source of inexpensive, yet high-quality, data? Perspect. Psychol. Sci. **6**, 3–5 (2011). doi:10.1177/1745691610393980

19. Li, H., Cai, Z., Graesser, A.C.: How good is popularity? Summary grading in crowdsourcing. In: Barnes, T., Chi, M., Feng, M. (eds.) 2016 EDM, pp. 430–435. EDM Society, Raleigh (2016)

20. Meyer, B.J.F.: Text coherence and readability. Top. Lang. Disord. **23**, 204–224 (2003). doi:10.1097/00011363-200307000-00007

21. Graesser, A.C., Keshtkar, F., Li, H.: The role of natural language and discourse processing in advanced tutoring systems. In: Holtgraves, T. (ed.) The Oxford handbooks of language and social psychology, Oxford, New York, pp. 491–509 (2014)

22. Li, H., Cheng, Q., Yu, Q., Graesser, A.C.: The role of peer agent's learning competency in trialogue-based reading intelligent systems. In: Conati, C., Heffernan, N., Mitrovic, A., Verdejo, M. (eds.) AIED 2015. LNCS (LNAI), vol. 9112, pp. 694–697. Springer, Cham (2015). doi:10.1007/978-3-319-19773-9_94

23. Friend, R.: Effects of strategy instruction on summary writing of college students. Contemp. Edu. Psychol. **26**, 3–24 (2001). doi:10.1006/ceps.1999.1022

24. Russell, J.A., Weiss, A., Mendelsohn, G.A.: Affect Grid: a single-item scale of pleasure and arousal. J. Pers. Soc. Psychol. **57**, 493–502 (1989). doi:10.1037/0022-3514.57.3.493

25. Smallwood, J., Davies, J.B., Heim, D., Finnigan, F., Sudberry, M., O'Connor, R., Obonsawin, M.: Subjective experience and the attentional lapse: task engagement and disengagement during sustained attention. Conscious. Cogn. **13**, 657–690 (2004). doi:10. 1016/j.concog.2004.06.003
26. Smallwood, J.M., Baracaia, S.F., Lowe, M., Obonsawin, M.: Task unrelated thought whilst encoding information. Conscious. Cogn. **12**, 452–484 (2003). doi:10.1016/S1053-8100(03) 00018-7
27. Clifford, M.: Students need challenge, not easy success. Edu. Leadership **48**, 22–26 (1990)

iSTART Therefore I Understand:
But Metacognitive Supports Did not Enhance
Comprehension Gains

Kathryn S. McCarthy[1]([✉]), Matthew E. Jacovina[1], Erica L. Snow[2],
Tricia A. Guerrero[1], and Danielle S. McNamara[1]

[1] Institute for the Science of Teaching and Learning,
Arizona State University, Tempe, AZ, USA
{ksmccarl,Matthew.Jacovina,Tricia.Guerrero,
dsmcnamara}@asu.edu
[2] Center for Technology in Learning, SRI International,
Menlo Park, CA, USA
Erica.Snow@sri.com

Abstract. iSTART is an intelligent tutoring system designed to provide self-explanation instruction and practice to improve students' comprehension of complex, challenging text. This study examined the effects of extended game-based practice within the system as well as the effects of two metacognitive supports implemented within this practice. High school students (n = 234) were either assigned to an iSTART treatment condition or a control condition. Within the iSTART condition, students were assigned to a 2 × 2 design in which students provided *self-assessments* of their performance or were transferred to Coached Practice if their performance did not reach a certain *performance threshold*. Those receiving iSTART training produced higher self-explanation and inference-based comprehension scores. However, there were no direct effects of either metacognitive support on these learning outcomes.

Keywords: Intelligent tutoring systems · Reading comprehension · Strategy-based learning · Metacognition · Game-based practice

1 Introduction

Though reading is an everyday aspect of the classroom, students often struggle to successfully comprehend the kinds of informational texts they encounter in school [1]. Self-explaining, or explaining the meaning of a text to one's self, and self-explanation training have been shown to help students better comprehend these types of text [2]. The current work explores the effects of a self-explanation training system, iSTART, on two learning outcomes: self-explanation score and reading comprehension test performance. More specifically, it investigates the benefits of extended game-based practice and the effect of implementing two metacognitive supports within this practice.

© Springer International Publishing AG 2017
E. André et al. (Eds.): AIED 2017, LNAI 10331, pp. 201–211, 2017.
DOI: 10.1007/978-3-319-61425-0_17

1.1   iSTART

Interactive Strategy Training for Active Reading and Thinking (iSTART) is an intelligent tutoring system (ITS) designed to improve students' reading comprehension abilities through self-explanation training [3]. iSTART teaches five self-explanation strategies (comprehension monitoring, paraphrasing, prediction, elaboration, and bridging) through video lessons, demonstration, and game-based practice [4]. During practice, iSTART uses a natural language processing algorithm to provide students with feedback on the quality of their self-explanations [5].

iSTART training encourages the generation of both bridging inferences that connect information from different parts of the text and elaborative inferences that connect information from the text to prior knowledge. The construction of these inferences supports the development of a more elaborate and coherent mental representation that is necessary for successful reading comprehension [6]. As such, iSTART has been shown to increase the quality of inferences during self-explanation [7] and increase comprehension for both high school and college students [8, 9].

1.2   Game-Based Practice

A common shortcoming of ITSs is that students may lose interest or motivation during the extended training and practice necessary to yield benefits. One way in which this issue has been addressed is through the addition of game-like components to increase

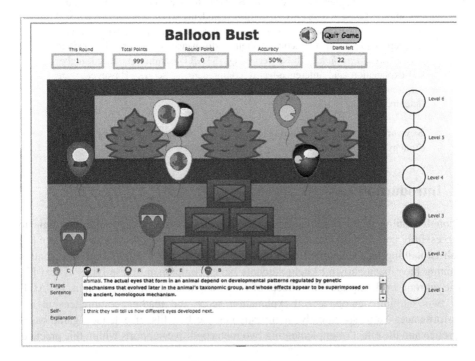

Fig. 1. Balloon bust

engagement and motivation [10]. With this in mind, iSTART has been adapted to include game-based practice activities [11]. Practice includes both identification and generative games. In the *identification practice games*, students are presented with a self-explanation and must determine which strategy was used. For example, in the game *Balloon Bust*, the different strategies are presented on balloons that float around the screen. To earn points, the student must not only identify the correct strategy, but also "throw" the dart at the balloon that represents this strategy (Fig. 1).

More pertinent to the current study are the *generative practice games*. In these two games, *Map Conquest* and *Showdown*, students construct their own self-explanations. In *Showdown*, for example, the student competes against a computer opponent to construct the best self-explanation (Fig. 2).

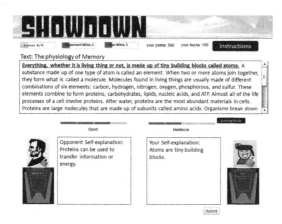

Fig. 2. Showdown

The game-based version of iSTART enhances enjoyment and motivation relative to a non-game-based version [12], and performance within game-based generative practice is correlated with posttest and transfer comprehension scores [13]. The current study furthers the investigation by examining learning outcomes (self-explanation score and comprehension question performance) for students receiving extended game-based practice as compared to students in a non-training control condition.

1.3   Metacognitive Features

Students generally have poor metacognition [14]. Metacognition refers to a person's ability to reflect upon their own knowledge as well as their understanding of a task or task goals. Metacognition can support successful comprehension as it regulates a learner's strategies and efforts [14]. Prompting metacognition has been shown to improve comprehension. Consequently, researchers have encouraged the inclusion of metacognitive supports to increase the efficacy of intelligent tutoring systems [15–17]. These metacognitive supports occur at the global level by prompting self-reflection after the task is completed, but they are also assumed to be beneficial at the local level such as when students are prompted to reflect on their performance during the task [18]. Instructional lessons within iSTART provide instruction on comprehension monitoring, encouraging students to recognize when they do or do not understand the text or parts of the texts; however, there is currently no explicit prompting within the system to encourage students to monitor their performance during self-explanation practice. With this in mind, we developed two interventions designed to support metacognition at both the local and global levels during extended game-based practice.

The first is a *performance threshold* that encourages self-reflection at the global level. Within each generative game, students write between 4 and 10 self-explanations. On each self-explanation, the participant receives a score (0–3). At the end of each game, the student's average self-explanation score is compared to an experimenter-set threshold (2). If this threshold is not met, the student is notified that the score is too low and is then transitioned to Coached Practice, in which a pedagogical agent provides explicit feedback to improve self-explanations. This threshold performance feature has been shown to increase average self-explanation score on the subsequent generative game [19].

The second feature, *self-assessment,* supports local metacognition as it asks the student to reflect on performance on each trial during the task. The self-assessment asks students to rate the quality of each of their self-explanations before receiving feedback from the system. Prior work with this feature indicates that students tend to overestimate their performance on self-explanations, though students with high prior knowledge tend to be more accurate [20].

This study is the first study to examine the effect of both metacognitive supports on posttest performance following extended practice in iSTART. Prior investigations with the performance threshold and self-assessment features have been limited to single sessions in which training was too brief to observe measurable posttest gains. Therefore, the focus of this study is on post-training learning outcomes.

1.4   Current Study

The current study investigated potential comprehension benefits from extended practice in iSTART self-explanation training. It also follows up on previous work exploring the implementation of two metacognitive support features: a performance threshold and a self-assessment rating during practice.

High school students were assigned to either a control condition with no training (n = 116) or an iSTART training condition (n = 118). Within the iSTART condition, we employed a 2 (performance threshold: off, on) × 2 (self-assessment: off, on) between-subjects design.

We compared the quality of participants' self-explanations at pretest and posttest and as well as their comprehension test question performance at pretest, posttest, and on a transfer task. We had two sets of predictions. The first set regarded the use of iSTART compared to the no training condition. We predicted that the extended practice in iSTART's game-based environment would yield improved self-explanation scores from pretest to posttest. We also predicted this practice would yield increased comprehension test performance on both the posttest and transfer test and that this benefit would be most evident for inference-based comprehension questions that assess deeper comprehension.

The second set of predictions pertained to the effects of the performance threshold and self-assessment features embedded within the iSTART training condition. Theories of metacognition generally state that as students gain more information concerning their performance during learning, they are better situated to adapt or change their future learning behaviors and strategies [21]. Accordingly, it might be hypothesized that students exposed to both metacognitive supports would be best situated to adapt or change their behaviors and strategies, and subsequently show superior performance on the posttests. A second competing hypothesis might suggest that the two metacognitive prompts would be redundant. As such, when combined they would not provide unique insights for the student relative to having only one [22]. A third (null) hypothesis comes from skill acquisition theories [23, 24] which place a greater emphasis on the development of the skills necessary to complete the task, rather than on explicit metacognitive interventions. Based on this hypothesis, there were be an overall effect of iSTART in comparison to the control condition, but no effects of metacognitive support conditions.

2   Method

2.1   Participants

Participants were 234 current high school students and recent high school graduates (147 female, 87 male) from the southwestern United States who were financially compensated for their participation in the study. They were, on average 15.90 years old (range 13–20). The sample was 48.7% Caucasian, 23.1% Hispanic, 10.7% African-American, 8.5% Asian, and 9.0% identified as other ethnicities.

2.2   Design and Materials

The study employed a 2(threshold: off, on) × 2(self-assessment: off, on) between-subjects design within those participants who received iSTART as well as a no training control, resulting in five treatment conditions: (1) threshold only (n = 28), (2) self-assessment only (n = 29), (3) threshold and self-assessment (n = 30), (4) neither threshold nor self-assessment (iSTART control, n = 31), and (5) no iSTART training (no training control, n = 116).

Performance Threshold. The performance threshold was designed to support global metacognition. After each self-explanation, participants receive a score of *poor, fair, good,* or *great,* which reflects a numeric score from 0 to 3. Lower scores (zero or one) indicate that the learner has produced an self-explanation that is too short to be of substance or is a restating or paraphrasing of the target sentence. Scores of two or higher reflect that the reader has demonstrated integration of prior knowledge into their response [11]. Given that inferencing and integrating is critical for successful comprehension, the performance threshold was set at 2. This threshold score is consistent with the previous implementation of this feature in iSTART. If the participant's average self-explanation score fell below this threshold at the end of a generative game, a pop-up message would appear (Fig. 3) and they were directed back to Coached Practice for remediation.

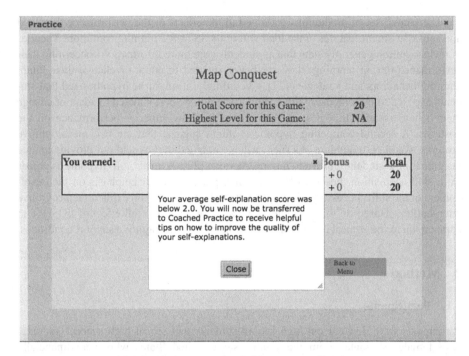

Fig. 3. Performance threshold pop-up notification

Self-assessment. The self-assessment feature was designed to encourage local metacognition. After each self-explanation, the participant was prompted to predict the quality of the self-explanation as *poor, fair, good,* or *great* (again reflected numerically as 0–3) and to rate their confidence in this prediction on the same scale. After making this selection, participants were given the actual self-explanation score.

Pretest and Posttest. The pretest and posttest consisted of two science texts: Red Blood Cells and Heart Disease. The presentation order of the texts as pretest or posttest was counterbalanced across participants. These texts were approximately 300 words and were matched for linguistic difficulty. In each text, participants were prompted to self-explain nine target sentences. After reading, they took a constructed response comprehension test that included four text-based and four bridging inference comprehension questions. Designed to assess more shallow comprehension, text-based questions have answers that can be found in a single sentence in the text. In contrast, bridging inference questions require the reader to connect information across two or more sentences in the text to derive the answer, indicative of deeper comprehension.

Transfer Test. The transfer test was designed to assess the extent to which students could apply the strategies they had learned to a new context. The transfer text, Plant Growth, was longer and more difficult than the Red Blood Cells and Heart Disease texts from the pretest and posttest. Importantly, participants were not prompted to self-explain while they read the transfer text. After reading, participants took another comprehension test that consisted of 10 text-based and 8 bridging inference comprehension questions about this text.

2.3   Procedure

Participants in the iSTART training conditions came into the lab for five sessions. In the first pretest session, participants completed the pretest, including the self-explanations and comprehension questions. Participants were also asked to give basic demographic information and to answer a battery of questions that included prior science knowledge. During the three days of training (three two-hour sessions), participants watched the iSTART video lessons that introduced them to the purpose of self-explanation and the five strategies. After the lessons, participants were transitioned to Coached Practice, a non-game-based activity in which students practice writing self-explanations and receive detailed, formative feedback. After one round of Coached Practice, the participants were allowed to move freely throughout the system to interact with videos, Coached Practice, and the generative and identification games for the remainder of the training sessions. It was during these three training sessions that participants in the performance threshold conditions were transitioned back to Coached Practice if they did not meet the performance threshold and participants in the self-assessment conditions were prompted to rate their self-explanation quality. In the final session, participants completed the posttests and transfer test.

Those in the no training control condition came into the lab for the pretest session and then returned to the lab after a few days ($M = 3.64$, $SD = .95$) to take the posttest.

2.4   Scoring

Using the same scoring algorithm employed within iSTART, each self-explanation in the pretest and posttest (nine in each) was automatically scored from 0–3. We then calculated an average self-explanation score for the entire text.

Three raters scored a subset of 20% of the constructed response comprehension questions for each text achieving high intra-class correlations for all three texts, (Red Blood Cells = .90, Heart Disease = .93, Plant Growth = .94). These raters then scored the remainder of the questions.

3   Results

Analyses of the posttest data indicated no effects of the threshold or self-assessment features on self-explanation scores, posttest comprehension scores, or transfer test comprehension scores (all $Fs < 1.00$, ns). Consequently, the following analyses compare all those who were provided iSTART training to those in the no training control.

3.1   Self-explanations

We first compared pretest average self-explanation scores for those in the iSTART training condition to those in the control condition. Though the difference between the two conditions was not significant, $t(232) = 1.67$, ns, we conducted a two-level analysis of covariance (ANCOVA) which controlled for average self-explanation score at pretest. As shown in Table 1, this analysis indicated that those who received iSTART training received higher average self-explanation scores than those in the no training control condition, $F(1, 231) = 29.78$, $p < .001$, $\eta_P^2 = .11$.

Table 1. Means and standard deviations of self-explanation scores at pretest and posttest

	Self-explanation scores	
	Pretest	Posttest
iSTART (N = 116)	2.30(.55)	2.43(.47)
Control (N = 118)	2.18(.56)	2.02(.63)

3.2   Comprehension Tests

Though students were randomly assigned to condition, there was a significant difference in overall pretest comprehension score between the two conditions, $t(232) = 2.17$, $p < .05$. Consequently, we conducted a 2(treatment: iSTART, control) × 2(question type: text-based, bridging inference) ANCOVA that controlled for overall pretest comprehension score. This analysis indicated no main effect of treatment on posttest comprehension score, $F < 1.00$, ns. There was no main effect of question type, $F < 1.00$, nor was there a significant interaction, $F < 1.00$ (Table 2). Essentially, when the participants were instructed to self-explain, there was no effect of training on the immediate posttest.

To investigate the effect of iSTART treatment on the transfer comprehension test, we conducted a similar 2(treatment: iSTART, control) × 2(question type: text-based, bridging inference) ANCOVA that controlled for overall pretest comprehension score. This analysis revealed no main effect of treatment condition, $F < 1.00$, ns, but a significant main effect of question type, $F(1, 231) = 11.85$, $p < .01$, $\eta_P^2 = .05$, such that students had higher average comprehension scores for the text-based questions than for the inference questions. This was qualified by a significant treatment by question type interaction, $F(1, 231) = 6.65$, $p < .01$, $\eta_P^2 = .03$. As shown in Table 2, there was no effect of iSTART training on text-based comprehension question performance, but those who received iSTART training had a significantly higher average score on the inference comprehension questions than those who received no iSTART training.

Table 2. Means and standard deviations of comprehension test scores from pretest, posttest, and transfer test as a function of question type

	Comprehension scores					
	Pretest		Posttest		Transfer Test	
	Text-based	Inference	Text-based	Inference	Text-based	Inference
iSTART (N = 116)	.55(.27)	.58(.26)	.58(.38)	.58(.27)	.35(.20)	.27(.20)
Control (N = 118)	.49(.31)	.50(.24)	.51(.31)	.55(.28)	.33(.19)	.21(.18)

Comparing iSTART training to a no-training control, iSTART increased the quality of participants' self-explanations at posttest, but had no effect on comprehension test performance. However, in a transfer task in which participants were not explicitly prompted to self-explain, those who had iSTART training yielded deeper comprehension as indicated by higher scores on bridging inference questions.

Consistent with the null hypothesis predicted by a skill acquisition account, there was no effect of either metacognitive support, in isolation or in tandem, on self-explanation score, posttest comprehension, or transfer test comprehension scores.

4 Conclusions

This study explored the benefits of extended game-based practice in iSTART on two posttest learning measures: self-explanation and comprehension. Additionally, it examined the effects of two metacognitive supports implemented within this extended practice.

Consistent with previous research, iSTART training improved high school students' self-explanation quality. Comprehension test scores indicated no effect of iSTART training on a comparable posttest text that prompted for self-explanations. This is a bit surprising, given previous demonstrations of comprehension gains using iSTART [25, 26]. Nonetheless, and perhaps more importantly, there were significant benefits of iSTART training on a more difficult transfer text in which participants were not prompted to self-explain. More specifically, iSTART training enhanced deep comprehension, as indicated by higher scores on bridging inference questions.

The implementation of the metacognitive supports in a 2 × 2 design allowed for the testing of three potential outcomes: an additive effect of having both supports prompting metacognition, an interactive effect in which having both supports would be no more beneficial than having only one support, and a null effect in which the metacognitive supports would show no benefits above and beyond the regular iSTART training. The findings of this study support this final hypothesis, as there were no effects of either the performance threshold or self-assessment. This suggests that the gains in self-explanation quality and comprehension performance are related to consistent practice, rather that the metacognitive interventions that we implemented in this study.

Given that the implementation of these metacognitive supports did not harm performance and have previously showed in-system benefits [19], it is worth continuing to implement their use and to conduct further investigations into how they affect training. One possibility is that the metacognitive supports have an indirect effect such that the performance threshold and self-assessment affect the way the readers interact with the system. Thus, we are investigating how these supports affected in-system performance and how these differences may in turn relate to posttest learning outcomes. For example, these features may increase motivation or enjoyment, which can encourage students to persevere and engage in the long-term practice needed to master complex reading comprehension skills [11, 12, 27]. We are currently analyzing the log data collected during training to explore how these supports affected interactions with the system, such as which games were played or time spent in off-task behaviors, and how differences in these interactions relate to self-explanation and comprehension gains. Importantly however, the manipulation of the metacognitive supports did not affect post-training performance, regardless of students' abilities or reported motivation. Hence, this study provides important information regarding the potential impact of these types of scaffolds, particularly in the context of intelligent tutoring systems that provide adaptive tutoring grounded in skill acquisition theories [28].

Acknowledgments. This research was supported in part by the Institute of Education Sciences (R305A130124). Any opinions, conclusions, or recommendations expressed are those of the authors and do not necessarily represent views of the IES.

References

1. NAEP: The Nation's Report Card: Mathematics and Reading at Grade 12 (2015). https://www.nationsreportcard.gov/reading_math_g12_2015/#reading/acl#header
2. McNamara, D.S.: SERT: self-explanation reading training. Discourse Process. **38**, 1–30 (2004)
3. McNamara, D.S., Levinstein, I.B., Boonthum, C.: iSTART: interactive strategy trainer for active reading and thinking. Behav. Res. Methods Instrum. Comput. **36**, 222–233 (2004)
4. Snow, E.L., Jacovina, M.E., Jackson, G.T., McNamara, D.S.: iSTART-2: a reading comprehension and strategy instruction tutor. In: McNamara, D.S., Crossley, S.A. (eds.) Adaptive Educational Technologies for Literacy Instruction, pp. 104–121. Taylor & Francis, Routledge (2016)
5. McNamara, D.S., Boonthum, C., Levinstein, I.B., Millis, K.: Evaluating self-explanations in iSTART: comparing word-based and LSA algorithms. In: Landauer, T., McNamara, D.S., Dennis, S., Kintsch, W. (eds.) Handbook of Latent Semantic Analysis, pp. 227–241. Erlbaum, Mahwah, NJ (2007)
6. Kintsch, W., Britton, B.K., Fletcher, C.R., Kintsch, E., Mannes, S.M., Nathan, M.J.: A comprehension-based approach to learning and understanding. Psychol. Learn. Motiv. Adv. Res. Theory **30**, 165–214 (1993)
7. Kurby, C.A., Magliano, J.P., Dandotkar, S., Woehrle, J., Gilliam, S., McNamara, D.S.: Changing how students process and comprehend texts with computer-based self-explanation training. J. Educ. Comput. Res. **47**, 429–459 (2012)
8. Magliano, J.P., Todaro, S., Millis, K., Wiemer-Hastings, K., Kim, H.J., McNamara, D.S.: Changes in reading strategies as a function of reading training: a comparison of live and computerized training. J. Educ. Comput. Res. **32**, 185–208 (2005)
9. O'Reilly T., Sinclair, G.P., McNamara, D.S.: iSTART: a web-based reading strategy intervention that improves students' science comprehension. In: Kinshuk Sampson, D.G., Isaías, P. (eds.) Proceedings of the IADIS International Conference Cognition and Exploratory Learning in Digital Age: CELDA 2004. IADIS Press, Lisbon, Portugal, pp. 173–180 (2004)
10. Dickey, M.D.: Engaging by design: how engagement strategies in popular computer and video games can inform instructional design. Educ. Tech. Res. Dev. **53**, 67–83 (2005)
11. Jackson, G.T., McNamara, D.S.: Motivational impacts of a game-based intelligent tutoring system. In: Murray, R.C., McCarthy, P.M. (eds.) Proceedings of the 24th International Florida Artificial Intelligence Research Society (FLAIRS) Conference. AAAI Press, Menlo Park, CA, pp. 519–524 (2011)
12. Jackson, G.T., McNamara, D.S.: Motivation and performance in a game-based intelligent tutoring system. J. Educ. Psychol. **105**, 1036–1049 (2013)
13. Jackson, G.T., Snow, E.L., Varner, L.K., McNamara, D.S.: Game performance as a measure of comprehension and skill transfer. In Boonthum-Denecke C., Youngblood, G.M. (eds.) Proceedings of the 26th Annual Florida Artificial Intelligence Research Society (FLAIRS) Conference. The AAAI Press, Menlo Park, CA, pp. 497–502 (2013)

14. Theide, K.W., Dunlosky, J.: Toward a general model of self-regulated study: an analysis of selection of items and self-paced study. J. Exp. Psychol. Learn. Mem. Cogn. **4**, 1024–1037 (1999)
15. Azevedo, R.: Computer environments as metacognitive tools for enhancing learning. Educ. Psychol. **40**, 193–197 (2005)
16. Azevedo, R., Hadwin, A.F.: Scaffolding self-regulated learning and metacognition–Implications for the design of computer-based scaffolds. Instr. Sci. **33**, 367–379 (2005)
17. Roll, I., Aleven, V., McLaren, B.M., Koedinger, K.R.: Improving students' help-seeking skills using metacognitive feedback in an intelligent tutoring system. Learn. Instr. **21**, 267–280 (2011)
18. Schraw, G.: The effect of metacognitive knowledge on local and global monitoring. Contemp. Educ. Psychol. **19**, 143–154 (1994)
19. Snow, E.L., McNamara, D.S., Jacovina, M.E., Allen, L.K., Johnson, A.M., Perret, C.A., Dai, J., Tanner Jackson, G., Likens, A.D., Russell, D.G., Weston, J.L.: Promoting metacognitive awareness within a game-based intelligent tutoring system. In: Conati, C., Heffernan, N., Mitrovic, A., Verdejo, M. (eds.) AIED 2015. LNCS (LNAI), vol. 9112, pp. 786–789. Springer, Cham (2015). doi:10.1007/978-3-319-19773-9_116
20. Snow, E.L., Jacovina, M.E., McNamara, D.S.: Promoting metacognition within a game-based environment. In: Conati, C., Heffernan, N., Mitrovic, A., Verdejo, M. (eds.) AIED 2015. LNCS (LNAI), vol. 9112, pp. 864–867. Springer, Cham (2015). doi:10.1007/978-3-319-19773-9_134
21. Flavell, J.H.: Metacognition and cognitive monitoring: a new areas of cognitive-developmental inquiry. Am. Psychol. **34**, 906–911 (1979)
22. Roll, I., Aleven, V., McLaren, B.M., Koedinger, K.R.: Designing for metacognition – applying cognitive tutor principles to the tutoring of help seeking. Metacognition Learn. **2**, 125–140 (2007)
23. Healy, A.F., Clawson, D.M., McNamara, D.S., Marmie, W.R., Schneider, V.I., Rickard, T.C., Curtcher, R.J., King, C., Ericsson, K.A., Bourne, L.E.: The long term retention of knowledge and skills. Psychol. Learn. Motiv. Adv. Res. Theory **30**, 135–164 (1993)
24. Ericsson, K.A., Krampe, R.T., Tesch-Römer, C.: The role of deliberate practice in the acquisition of expert performance. Psychol. Rev. **100**, 363–406 (1993)
25. McNamara, D.S., O'Reilly, T., Best, R., Ozuru, Y.: Improving adolescent students' reading comprehension with iSTART. J. Educ. Comput. Res. **34**, 147–171 (2006)
26. Jacovina, Matthew E., Tanner Jackson, G., Snow, Erica L., McNamara, Danielle S.: Timing game-based practice in a reading comprehension strategy tutor. In: Micarelli, A., Stamper, J., Panourgia, K. (eds.) ITS 2016. LNCS, vol. 9684, pp. 59–68. Springer, Cham (2016). doi:10.1007/978-3-319-39583-8_6
27. Jackson, G.T., Boonthum, C., McNamara, D.S.: iSTART-ME: situating extended learning within a game-based environment. In: Lane, H.C., Ogan, A., Shute, V. (eds.) Proceedings of the Workshop on Intelligent Educational Games at the 14th Annual Conference on Artificial Intelligence in Education, AIED, Brighton, UK, pp. 59–68 (2009)
28. McNamara, D.S., Jacovina, M.E., Snow, E.L., Allen, L.K.: From generating in the lab to tutoring systems in classrooms. Am. J. Psychol. **128**, 159–172 (2015)

Inducing Stealth Assessors from Game Interaction Data

Wookhee Min[1(✉)], Megan H. Frankosky[1], Bradford W. Mott[1],
Eric N. Wiebe[1], Kristy Elizabeth Boyer[2], and James C. Lester[1]

[1] Center for Educational Informatics,
North Carolina State University, Raleigh, NC 27695, USA
{wmin, rmhardy, bwmott, wiebe, lester}@ncsu.edu
[2] Department of Computer & Information Science & Engineering,
University of Florida, Gainesville, FL 32601, USA
keboyer@ufl.edu

Abstract. A key untapped feature of game-based learning environments is their capacity to generate a rich stream of fine-grained learning interaction data. The learning behaviors captured in these data provide a wealth of information on student learning, which stealth assessment can utilize to unobtrusively draw inferences about student knowledge to provide tailored problem-solving support. In this paper, we present a long short-term memory network (LSTM)-based stealth assessment framework that takes as input an observed sequence of raw game-based learning environment interaction data along with external pre-learning measures to infer students' post-competencies. The framework is evaluated using data collected from 191 middle school students interacting with a game-based learning environment for middle grade computational thinking. Results indicate that LSTM-based stealth assessors induced from student game-based learning interaction data outperform comparable models that required labor-intensive hand-engineering of input features. The findings suggest that the LSTM-based approach holds significant promise for evidence modeling in stealth assessment.

Keywords: Game-based learning environments · Stealth assessment · Deep learning · Computational thinking · Educational games

1 Introduction

Recent years have seen a growing interest in intelligent game-based learning environments because of their potential to effectively promote learning and engagement [1]. These environments simultaneously integrate the adaptive pedagogical functionalities of intelligent tutoring systems with the engaging interactions provided by digital games [2, 3]. Research has begun to explore student modeling for game-based learning environments including modeling student knowledge [4] and students' progression towards learning goals [5] following work on student-adaptive learning featuring tailored narratives, feedback, and problem-solving support [6].

© Springer International Publishing AG 2017
E. André et al. (Eds.): AIED 2017, LNAI 10331, pp. 212–223, 2017.
DOI: 10.1007/978-3-319-61425-0_18

Stealth assessment [4] is a game-based assessment framework based on evidence-centered design (ECD) [7]. ECD features task, evidence and competency models for diagnostic measurement of multiple aspects of students' proficiency and performance. Built on the three models presented in ECD, stealth assessments utilize a rich stream of student interactions (i.e., an evidence model) with various problem-solving tasks (i.e., a task model) in game-based learning environments, to draw inferences about student knowledge and skills (i.e., a competency model). The evidence model provides the connections between the competency model and the stream of low-level observations, enabling the competency model to update the appropriate competencies related to the task being performed. In contrast to typical formative assessments, stealth assessment has the potential to not only create a valid, reliable evidence model utilizing observed sequences of detailed learning behaviors, but also to perform assessments of a wide range of constructs in an unobtrusive, invisible way, with the aim of providing useful feedback to students and teachers to enhance learning and inform instruction [4, 8].

A key challenge posed by stealth assessment is how to effectively handle both cyclical causalities between actions and events in the gameworld and temporal relationships characterized within learning behaviors. Students are likely to deliberately choose their next action by referring to the current task, their previous actions, and any feedback they received on their previous actions in the gameworld. Despite the popularity of utilizing evidence rules, which define a set of salient features that are indicative of specific student competencies in the evidence model, previous work based on evidence rules often ignores these complex relationships found within student learning behaviors [4, 9, 10]. Furthermore, these features are often hand-engineered, so they are domain expert-dependent, labor-intensive, and domain-specific.

As an alternative to manually devising an evidence model, an approach that automatically extracts patterns and learns predictive features from sequences of raw player actions would be more scalable, less labor-intensive, and would enable the induction of evidence models that directly represent student learning processes without sacrificing causal, temporal relationships. In this work, we investigate long short-term memory networks (LSTMs) [11], a type of gated recurrent neural network, for automating the creation of the evidence model without requiring hand-authored evidence rules and statistical models. LSTMs automatically extract salient features from temporal data and effectively preserve a longer-term memory by operating three gates featured in the network. Results of an evaluation suggest that LSTM-based stealth assessors directly induced from students' interactions with a game-based learning environment show significant promise for stealth assessment.

2 Related Work

Intelligent game-based learning environments are situated at the intersection of (1) digital games that increase students' motivation through rich settings (e.g., compelling plots, engaging characters) in virtual environments, and (2) intelligent tutoring systems that foster students' learning through tailored scaffolding and context-sensitive feedback. Recent work in game-based learning environments explores a broad spectrum of subject matters ranging from high school mathematics [12], to middle school computer science [13], anti-bullying [14], language and culture learning [3], and science inquiry [15], among others.

Stealth assessment can play an important role in game-based learning environments. Previous work on stealth assessment based on evidence-centered design uses sequences of students' interactions with the learning environment to dynamically assess students' knowledge. For stealth assessment, various families of machine learning techniques have been investigated. Kim and colleagues [9] investigated Bayesian network-based evidence modeling, which requires two primary steps: (1) defining targeted competency and observable variables and building a directed graphical model, and (2) specifying the conditional probabilities between parent nodes and corresponding child nodes. Falakmasir et al. presented the SPRING data analysis pipeline that does not require costly domain knowledge engineering [16]. Specifically, SPRING trains two hidden Markov models (HMMs), one for high-performing and the other for low-performing students per game level. Two log-likelihoods of an observed sequence of student events are computed based on the two HMMs, and finally the difference between the two log-likelihoods for each game level is used as an independent variable for a linear regression model that predicts post-test scores. In our previous work, we presented *DeepStealth* [13], a framework based on deep neural networks [17] for stealth assessment. DeepStealth uses a deep feedforward neural network (FFNN)-based evidence modeling approach, in which the multi-level, hierarchical representations of the input data are learned through the training process of deep networks. While the last two approaches have an advantage over the Bayesian network-based approach by requiring less domain expert knowledge for evidence modeling, the competency model (e.g., competency model variables, dependencies between variables) is not designed at the same level of granularity as the Bayesian network and thus provide less fine-grained insight into concept mastery. While DeepStealth uses manually engineered features (e.g., features produced by expert-authored evidence rules), the LSTM-based approach introduced here fully automates the process of evidence modeling by directly utilizing raw game interaction data (i.e., a sequence of low-level actions).

3   ENGAGE Game-Based Learning Environment

ENGAGE (Fig. 1) is a game-based learning environment designed to introduce computational thinking to middle school students. It features a rich immersive 3D storyworld built with the Unity multi-platform game engine. The ENGAGE curriculum was developed by adapting the AP® Computer Science Principles course learning objectives [18] for U.S. middle school students (ages 11–13). A central aim of the curriculum and game-based learning environment is to promote computational thinking and problem-solving processes that involve abstraction and algorithmic thinking, and allow students to effectively use computational tools for data analysis, modeling, and simulations [19]. In addition to providing a foundation for advanced computer science work in high school, the problem-solving activities and computational challenges within the game are designed to increase middle school student's interest in computer science.

Fig. 1. ENGAGE game-based learning environment.

In the game, students play the protagonist who is sent to rescue an underwater research facility. As students progress through the game, they discover that all of the computing devices within the facility have been commandeered by a nefarious researcher. Students navigate through a series of interconnected rooms, each of which presents students with a set of computational challenges they must solve by either programming devices or operating devices in reference to the programs already written for the devices. Programmable devices are programmed using a visual programming language, in which visual blocks are linked together [13]. Finally, support is provided throughout the game by a cast of non-player characters who help progress the narrative and offer clues to assist students in solving the computational challenges.

One of the levels in the game, the Digital World, allows students to explore how binary sequences are used to represent digital data. The work presented in this paper focuses on students' problem-solving activities within this level. To complete a set of binary learning tasks, students must find the binary representation of the base-ten number stored in the binary lock device (Fig. 2, Left). Specifically, students must review an existing program (Fig. 2, Right) associated with the binary lock device, flip

Fig. 2. (Left) A binary lock device that students must unlock. The white tiles indicate the bits are 1, whereas black tiles denote 0. The current binary number is 01110 and the corresponding base-ten number, 14, is displayed on the device as immediate feedback. (Right) The visual programming interface displaying the binary lock's program.

binary tiles on the binary lock device to change the binary sequence (Fig. 2, Left), and execute its program. If the binary sequence matches the base-ten number stored in the program, the current binary lock device opens upon execution and the player can move on to a previously inaccessible area in the room. Through these tasks, students learn about the concept of bits in binary numbers and the weight assigned to each bit.

In this work, we analyze 191 students' interaction data (101 males, 88 females, 2 unreported) from a teacher-led deployment of ENGAGE in four public middle school classrooms. Prior to beginning the Digital World unit, and immediately following the unit, students completed online pre- and post-test assessments measuring computer science attitudes [20], self-efficacy [21], and content knowledge (e.g., binary representation). Students achieved improvements in content knowledge covered in the Digital World unit, and a paired t-test comparing pre-test (M = 0.43, SD = 0.21) to post-test (M = 0.59, SD = 0.24) indicated that students' learning gains were statistically significant with a sizable effect size, $t(185) = 12.25, p < .001, d = .70$, where 186 out of 191 students took both the pre- and post-knowledge tests. These external learning measures are used as predictive features for our evidence models, along with the game interaction data.

4   LSTM-Based Stealth Assessment Framework

For a stealth assessment framework to be scalable to a broad range of learning environments, it must be able to easily accommodate a wide range of domain-specific features. Focusing on this aspect, we first describe how our work is framed in evidence-centered design (ECD) [7] and then turn to our LSTM-based stealth assessment framework. From an ECD perspective, the three models are summarized as follows:

- *Task Model:* We use 11 binary-lock solving tasks from the Digital World unit, the objective of which is finding the binary representation that matches the base-ten number specified in the program.
- *Evidence Model:* Observed sequences of actions in the game reveal students' competencies. A *generic feature set* is used to represent actions. For ENGAGE, there are 19 possible actions, and thus 19 distinct features are used to represent each action using one-hot encoding. In addition to the game interaction evidence, students' five pre-test scores on the knowledge assessment, self-efficacy, and three measures of computer science attitudes are utilized as evidence. An LSTM-based evidence model informs the competency model in order to update students' competency levels.
- *Competency Model:* Following our previous work [13], we examine one competency model variable with respect to students' overall knowledge about binary representation, where the actual labels for their competency levels are acquired from students' post-test performance.

For domain independence, scalability, and robust performance, the evidence model supports a generic feature set as well as missing data. The low-level generic feature set in the evidence model can represent any types of action without being bound to a specific domain, thereby yielding enhanced scalability for the stealth assessment framework. We use a *single* generic feature set to represent actions in this work, but the framework can support multiple feature sets depending on the design of actions in the learning environment (e.g., *"clicking the first binary tile"* can be represented using two distinct feature sets: the action-type feature set that contains *click*, and the action-argument feature set that contains *first binary tile*).

In this work, the binary learning tasks allow 19 possible actions, including 11 *pairing* actions[1] associated with 11 devices described in the task model (e.g., binary lock device in Fig. 2, Left), 5 *bit-click* actions (e.g., clicking a binary tile in Fig. 2, Left), two actions for operating the programming interface (*open* and *close* in Fig. 2, Right), and a *program execution* action to run the device's program.

The evidence model is designed to consider students whose data (either external pre-test scores or task activities) is partially missing. For example, it is possible that a student missed a class and has only partial gameplay data or did not complete some pre-tests prior to playing the game. To formulate the external learning measure evidence from missing pre-test data, we perform mean imputation using a mean score of other students' scores for the specific pre-test. On the other hand, in cases where students did not solve a specific task in the game, the game evidence is generated by linking any observed learning activities, skipping the unsolved tasks. For example, if a student completed only two tasks (T_1 and T_3) and missed one task (T_2) in-between, the activities for T_1 and T_3 are linked to generate a data instance, ignoring T_2. Since it is not uncommon for a student to be absent from class within a multi-week intervention, this specific design for the evidence model is necessary to broaden tailored learning support to all students who participated in the learning activities.

For the competency model, students' competencies are represented by their post-test performance on the knowledge assessment items for binary representations. The competencies are defined based on a tertile split ('high', 'medium', or 'low') with respect to post-test scores on the assessment, and thus this stealth assessment task is cast as a three-class classification problem that predicts one's competency level using an LSTM-based stealth assessor.

4.1 Long Short-Term Memory Networks

Long short-term memory networks (LSTMs) (Fig. 3A) are a variant of recurrent neural networks (RNNs) that are specifically designed for sequence labeling of temporal data. Traditional RNNs have faced significant challenges with respect to vanishing or exploding gradients during training deep networks unfolded in time [22]. The three gating units (input gate, output gate, and forget gate) featured in LSTMs enable modeling long-term dependencies within temporal sequences by allowing gradient information to flow over many time steps. LSTMs have achieved state-of-the-art performance in a diverse set of computational sequence-labeling tasks, including speech recognition and machine translation [23].

---

[1] Within the game, students must pair their virtual in-game computer with devices before they can manipulate or view a device's programs.

In an implementation of LSTMs, the input gate (i_t), forget gate (f_t), candidate value of the memory cell ($\tilde{c}_t$), and output gate (o_t) at time t are computed by Eqs. 1–4, respectively, in which W and U are weight matrices for transforming the input (x_t) at time t and the cell output (h_{t-1}) at time $t - 1$, b is the bias vector of each unit, and σ and *tanh* are the logistic sigmoid and hyperbolic tangent function, respectively:

$$i_t = \sigma(W_i x_t + U_i h_{t-1} + b_i) \tag{1}$$

$$f_t = \sigma(W_f x_t + U_f h_{t-1} + b_f) \tag{2}$$

$$\tilde{c}_t = tanh(W_c x_t + U_c h_{t-1} + b_c) \tag{3}$$

$$o_t = \sigma(W_o x_t + U_o h_{t-1} + b_o) \tag{4}$$

As described in Eq. 5, the current memory cell's state (c_t) is calculated by modulating the current memory candidate value ($\tilde{c}_t$) via the input gate (i_t) and the previous memory cell state (c_{t-1}) via the forget gate (f_t). Through this process, a memory cell decides whether to keep or forget the previous memory state and regulates the candidate of the current memory state via the input gate. Once again, the current memory cell state (c_t) is controlled by the output gate (o_t) to compute the cell activation (h_t) of the LSTM block at time t. This step is described in Eq. 6:

$$c_t = i_t \tilde{c}_t + f_t c_{t-1} \tag{5}$$

$$h_t = o_t \, tanh(c_t) \tag{6}$$

Lastly, we use the final memory cell output vector (h_t) to predict the class label for stealth assessment, which is the competency level of the student. This step is executed in a softmax layer (top-right in Fig. 3A), which is interpreted as a calculation of posterior probabilities of the possible class labels. The LSTM is end-to-end trainable, where all the parameters such as W, U, and b are machine-learned using backpropagation through time.

4.2   Configuring LSTMs for Evidence Modeling

The LSTM's input, x_t, represents the evidence that a student reveals at time t. As noted above, the evidence model considers students' pre-learning measures in addition to actions in the game. These two types of variables feature different dynamics: actions are sequential and discrete, whereas the external learning measures are static and numeric, since they are measured prior to starting the game. Figure 3B describes how we encode these two different types of variables into a trainable input (x_t) at time t. First, we concatenate the integer index of the action at time t (a_t) with the five static external learning measures (e_1–e_5) to generate the original input (*input_t*). While scores for external learning measures (e.g., e_1) can be directly utilized by the LSTMs because their relative, numeric values are meaningful, the action index, a_t, should be reformulated since its discrete value does not represent a magnitude.

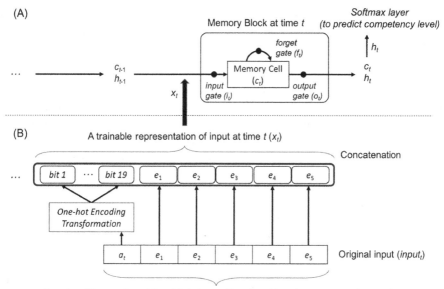

Fig. 3. (A) An illustration of an LSTM memory block that features three gating units and a memory cell [22]. (B) An illustration of how an original input ($input_t$) is transformed to a trainable format (x_t). The discrete action variable, a_t, is one-hot encoded into a 19-dimensional vector using bit 1 to 19, and then the induced vector is concatenated with numeric external learning measure variables (e_1 to e_5) to create the final input, x_t.

To address this issue, we use one-hot encoding to represent actions. One-hot encoding creates a bit vector whose length is the number of the actions, where only the associated action bit is on (i.e., 1), while all other bits are off (i.e., 0). Since we consider 19 distinct actions in ENGAGE, an action (e.g., a_t) is represented with a 19-dimensional vector. The final input (x_t) is generated by concatenating the one-hot encoded action representations with the five external learning measures, and thus the input is a 24-dimensional vector. Like actions in the input, the output of LSTMs should also be represented using one-hot encoding, due to its discrete nature. Since the number of possible competency levels is three in our work, the output is represented using a three-dimensional one-hot vector.

Given this encoding of actions, the next step is to devise an encoding for action sequences. Suppose that a student performed three actions and achieved the competency level, 'high'. We generate x_1, x_2, and x_3 based on our input encoding approach. A naïve method to generate a sequence is creating one from the list of actions, $[x_1, x_2, x_3]$, along with the target label 'high'. Another approach to generate sequences is using *sequence subsampling*. The sequence subsampling method can generate more sequences for the same case. For the same example, a subsampling method can produce three sequences, $[x_1]$, $[x_1, x_2]$, and $[x_1, x_2, x_3]$, all with the same target label of 'high', by accumulating actions sequentially. While the naïve approach creates only one training example (i.e., one sequence), this subsampling approach can create as many training examples as the number of actions per student (three sequences in this example). Since actions in a sequence represent a student's dynamic learning progress to achieve the final competency, we adopt the subsampling method that induces fine-grained training examples.

Finally, as with many other machine learning techniques, an effective configuration of network hyperparameters for LSTMs often must be empirically determined. There are several categories of hyperparameters to consider, including optimization (e.g., optimizer, learning rate), model structure (e.g., the number of hidden units, initialized weights), and training criterion (e.g., regularization terms, loss function) [24]. In this work, we adopt a grid-search on a model structure-based hyperparameter, the number of hidden units, which has the most significant influence on predictive performances of LSTMs among others in student goal recognition work [5]. We explore five values for the hyperparameter: 80, 100, 120, 140 and 160. Other than this, we investigate a single-layer LSTM with a softmax layer for classifying given sequences of actions, adopt a mini-batch gradient descent with the mini-batch size of 128, set the dropout rate [25], a regularization parameter, to 0.75, and utilize categorical cross entropy for the loss function and the Adam stochastic optimizer [26]. Finally, the training process stops early if the validation score has not improved within the last seven epochs. In this work, 10% of the training data is used to determine early stopping, while 90% is utilized for supervised training, leaving the test set purely unseen. The maximum number of epochs is set to 100. For devising LSTM-based evidence models, we use Keras [27], a python-based modular neural networks library.

5 Evaluation

We evaluate evidence models' predictive accuracy with 10-fold student-level cross-validation. The same data split is used for a fair comparison with the competitive baseline approaches. In this empirical evaluation, 191 students' gameplay data along with their external pre-learning measures are investigated, where 35,571 data instances are generated for training LSTM-based evidence models, following the sequence subsampling technique. We compare the LSTM model to the previous state-of-the-art deep feedforward neural network pre-trained with stacked denoising autoencoders (FFNN) [13], support vector machine (SVM), and naïve Bayes model (NB). As discussed, unlike our LSTM models, the three competitive baseline models utilize four salient game features engineered by domain experts, including the number of binary tile flips, the number of binary tile double flips (a binary tile flipped and then immediately flipped again), the number of times the device programs are executed, and the amount of time students spent in the programming interface [13]. Also, for these three baseline models, in case that the gameplay data is partially missing, mean imputation is performed per game feature as done for missing pre-learning measures, since these models take fixed-size inputs. All four evidence modeling approaches utilize the same set of external learning measures as additional evidence.

For each computational approach, the best model configurations are identified in the process of 10-fold cross-validation. Similar to the grid search method applied for the LSTMs, we grid-search a set of hyperparameters for FFNNs, SVMs and NBs.

For FFNNs, we explore two hyperparameters, the number of hidden layers (from one to five) and corruption rate (four randomly chosen values), while freezing some other hyperparameters (e.g., 40 hidden units per layer, softmax for the output activation function). We examine two hyperparameters that are popularly explored for optimization: the penalty parameter (C) and gamma (γ) for SVMs with a radial basis function [28]. C is chosen from $\{1, 10, 50, 100\}$, and γ is chosen from $\{0.0005, 0.001, 0.005, 0.01, 0.05\}$. Finally, for NBs, we investigate two distributions (normal distribution and kernel smoothing density estimate) to fit models for the data.

Table 1. Average accuracy rates of the LSTMs, FFNNs, SVMs, and NBs. {columns : rows} for the four machine learning techniques indicate {number of hidden units}, {number of hidden layers : corruption rate}, {gamma : penalty parameter}, and {distribution}, respectively. The highest accuracy rate is marked in bold for each technique.

LSTMs	80	100	120	140	160
	58.1%	56.1%	58.6%	**63.9%**	60.7%
FFNNs	**1**	**2**	**3**	**4**	**5**
0.20	61.9%	59.1%	56.6%	57.6%	59.7%
0.39	56.6%	61.3%	60.7%	56.5%	55.5%
0.69	59.1%	54.0%	**62.9%**	52.3%	54.5%
0.82	58.1%	59.7%	57.1%	55.0%	49.8%
SVMs	**0.0005**	**0.001**	**0.005**	**0.01**	**0.05**
1	50.8%	55.5%	59.1%	58.1%	56.0%
10	58.6%	59.2%	58.6%	59.2%	58.6%
50	59.2%	**59.7%**	56.6%	57.1%	58.1%
100	59.2%	56.6%	58.7%	58.7%	58.1%
NBs	**Normal**	**Kernel**			
	48.1%	41.6%			

Table 1 reports the average accuracy rates across different hyperparameter configurations for each machine learning technique from cross-validations. Overall, the highest performing LSTMs (the number of hidden units: 140) achieve 63.9% accuracy rate, which outperforms the highest performing models from FFNNs (62.9%), SVMs (59.7%) and NBs (48.1%) as well as the majority class baseline (41.9%).

In addition to the predictive performance improvement, the LSTM-based stealth assessment has two notable benefits over the baseline approaches. First, the capacity to handle various lengths of action sequences, effectively learning sequential patterns, and performing sequence labeling per action points towards LSTMs as being a viable solution for stealth assessment. For instance, as opposed to the FFNN-based approach that takes as input a fixed size of input features generated using the entire sequence of actions, LSTMs can sequentially make a prediction per action, and thus enable dynamic, run-time formative assessments on student competencies. Second, LSTMs directly utilize raw game interaction data dispensing with the need for manually engineering features to induce stealth assessors. This characteristic constitutes considerable benefits over the other models, since the feature engineering process is not only labor and time-intensive, but also impedes scalability of the stealth assessment framework to other learning environments due to the domain-specificity of the engineering process. It is noteworthy that the LSTMs directly utilizing low-level inputs achieve the highest accuracy without leveraging expert knowledge.

6 Conclusions and Future Work

This paper has introduced a novel LSTM-based stealth assessment framework that shows promise for accurately assessing learners' competency levels. Using data collected from multi-week classroom deployments of a game-based learning environment for middle grade computational thinking, we conducted an evaluation of four stealth assessment induction approaches that predict student post-competencies. The results suggest that LSTM-based stealth assessors outperform the previous state-of-the-art approach, deep feedforward neural networks pre-trained with stacked denoising autoencoders, as well as support vector machines and naïve Bayes models, with respect to predictive accuracy of students' post-competencies. This result is notable in that the LSTM-based evidence models were induced directly using raw game interaction data, whereas the other models were devised using domain-expert engineered features. Together with the sequence modeling capability, the LSTM-based stealth assessment framework offers the potential to serve as the foundation for formative assessment that operates dynamically, unobtrusively, and is readily applicable to various learning environments. In the future, it will be important to investigate stealth assessor model optimizations and regularizations for further improving performance and informing decision making for adaptive scaffolding. It will be also important to measure the stealth assessors' early prediction performance to evaluate their capacity for formative assessment. It will also be important to design a granular set of competencies for stealth assessors to be more diagnostic and provide fine-grained pedagogical support to further enhance student learning.

Acknowledgments. This research was supported by the National Science Foundation under Grant CNS-1138497 and Grant DRL-1640141. Any opinions, findings, and conclusions expressed in this material are those of the authors and do not necessarily reflect the views of the National Science Foundation.

References

1. Lester, J., Ha, E., Lee, S., Mott, B., Rowe, J., Sabourin, J.: Serious games get smart: intelligent game-based learning environments. AI Mag. **34**(4), 31–45 (2013)
2. Jackson, T., McNamara, D.: Motivation and performance in a game-based intelligent tutoring system. J. Educ. Psychol. **105**(4), 1036–1049 (2013)
3. Johnson, L.: Serious use of a serious game for language learning. Int. J. Artif. Intell. Educ. **20**(2), 175–195 (2010)
4. Shute, V.J., Ventura, M.: Measuring and supporting learning in games: stealth assessment. In: Computer Games, Simulations & Education. The MIT Press, Cambridge (2013)
5. Min, W., Mott, B., Rowe, J., Liu, B., Lester, J.: Player goal recognition in open-world digital games with long short-term memory networks. In: International Joint Conference on Artificial Intelligence, pp. 2590–2596 (2016)

6. Brusilovsky, P., Millán, E.: User models for adaptive hypermedia and adaptive educational systems. In: The Adaptive Web, pp. 3–53 (2007)
7. Mislevy, R., Steinberg, L., Almond, R.: On the structure of educational assessment. Meas. Interdiscip. Res. Perspect. **1**(1), 3–62 (2003)
8. Rosenheck, L., Lin, C.Y., Klopfer, E., Cheng, M.T.: Analyzing gameplay data to inform feedback loops in The Radix Endeavor. Comput. Educ. **111**, 60–73 (2017)
9. Kim, Y.J., Almond, R.G., Shute, V.J.: Applying evidence-centered design for the development of game-based assessments in physics playground. Int. J. Test. **16**(2), 142–163 (2016)
10. Smith, A., Aksit, O., Min, W., Wiebe, E., Mott, B.W., Lester, J.C.: Integrating real-time drawing and writing diagnostic models: an evidence-centered design framework for multimodal science assessment. In: Micarelli, A., Stamper, J., Panourgia, K. (eds.) ITS 2016. LNCS, vol. 9684, pp. 165–175. Springer, Cham (2016). doi:10.1007/978-3-319-39583-8_16
11. Hochreiter, S., Schmidhuber, J.: Long short-term memory. Neural Comput. **9**(8), 1–32 (1997)
12. Kebritchi, M., Hirumi, A., Bai, H.: The effects of modern mathematics computer games on mathematics achievement and class motivation. Comput. Educ. **55**(2), 427–443 (2010)
13. Min, W., Frankosky, M.H., Mott, B.W., Rowe, J.P., Wiebe, E., Boyer, K.E., Lester, J.C.: DeepStealth: leveraging deep learning models for stealth assessment in game-based learning environments. In: Conati, C., Heffernan, N., Mitrovic, A., Verdejo, M.F. (eds.) AIED 2015. LNCS, vol. 9112, pp. 277–286. Springer, Cham (2015). doi:10.1007/978-3-319-19773-9_28
14. Vannini, N., Enz, S., Sapouna, M., Wolke, D., Watson, S., Woods, S., Dautenhahn, K., Hall, L., Paiva, A., André, E., Aylett, R.: "FearNot!": a computer-based anti-bullying-programme designed to foster peer intervention. Eur. J. Psychol. Educ. **26**(1), 21–44 (2011)
15. Nelson, B.C., Kim, Y., Foshee, C., Slack, K.: Visual signaling in virtual world-based assessments: the SAVE Science project. Inf. Sci. **264**, 32–40 (2014)
16. Falakmasir, M.H., Gonzalez-Brenes, J.P., Gordon, G.J., DiCerbo, K.E.: A data-driven approach for inferring student proficiency from game activity logs. In: ACM Conference on Learning at Scale, pp. 341–349 (2016)
17. LeCun, Y., Bengio, Y., Hinton, G.: Deep learning. Nature **521**(7553), 436–444 (2015)
18. AP® Computer Science Principles Draft Curriculum Framework. http://www.csprinciples. org/. Accessed 05 Feb 2017
19. K–12 Computer Science Framework. http://www.k12cs.org/. Accessed 05 Feb 2017
20. Wiebe, E., Williams, L., Yang, K., Miller, C.: Computer science attitude survey. Comput. Sci. **14**(25), 1–86 (2003)
21. Chen, G., Gully, S.M., Eden, D.: Validation of a new general self-efficacy scale. Organ. Res. Methods **4**(1), 62–83 (2001)
22. Graves, A.: Supervised Sequence Labelling with Recurrent Neural Networks. Studies in Computational Intelligence, vol. 385. Springer, Heidelberg (2012)
23. Schmidhuber, J.: Deep learning in neural networks: an overview. Neural Netw. **61**, 85–117 (2014)
24. Bengio, Y.: Practical recommendations for gradient-based training of deep architectures. In: Montavon, G., Orr, G.B., Müller, K.-R. (eds.) Neural Networks: Tricks of the Trade. LNCS, vol. 7700, pp. 437–478. Springer, Heidelberg (2012). doi:10.1007/978-3-642-35289-8_26
25. Srivastava, N., Hinton, G.E., Krizhevsky, A., Sutskever, I., Salakhutdinov, R.: Dropout: a simple way to prevent neural networks from overfitting. J. Mach. Learn. Res. **15**, 1929–1958 (2014)
26. Kingma, D.P., Ba, J.L.: Adam: a method for stochastic optimization. In: International Conference on Learning Representations (2015)
27. Chollet, F.: Keras. https://github.com/fchollet/keras. GitHub Repository. Accessed 05 Feb 2017
28. Keerthi, S.S., Lin, C.-J.: Asymptotic behaviors of support vector machines with Gaussian kernel. Neural Comput. **15**(7), 1667–1689 (2003)

Supporting Constructive Video-Based Learning: Requirements Elicitation from Exploratory Studies

Antonija Mitrovic[1(✉)], Vania Dimitrova[2,3], Lydia Lau[2],
Amali Weerasinghe[4], and Moffat Mathews[1]

[1] Intelligent Computer Tutoring Group,
University of Canterbury, Christchurch, New Zealand
tanja.mitrovic@canterbury.ac.nz
[2] School of Computing, University of Leeds, Leeds, UK
[3] Leeds Institute of Medical Education, University of Leeds, Leeds, UK
[4] School of Computer Science, University of Adelaide, Adelaide, Australia

Abstract. Although videos are a highly popular digital medium for learning, video watching can be a passive activity and results in limited learning. This calls for interactive means to support engagement and active video watching. However, there is limited insight into what engagement challenges have to be overcome and what intelligent features are needed. This paper presents an empirical way to elicit requirements for innovative functionality to support constructive video-based learning. We present two user studies with an active video watching system instantiated for soft skill learning (pitch presentations). Based on the studies, we identify whether learning is happening and what kind of interaction contributes to learning, what difficulties participants face and how these can be overcome with additional intelligent support. Our findings show that participants who engaged in constructive learning have improved their conceptual understanding of presentation skills, while those who exhibited more passive ways of learning have not improved as much as constructive learners. Analysis of participants' profiles and experiences led to requirements for intelligent support with active video watching. Based on this, we propose intelligent nudging in the form of signposting and prompts to further promote constructive learning.

Keywords: Video-based learning · Intelligent support · Requirements elicitation · Experimental studies · Soft skill learning

1 Introduction

Videos have become the main means for content production and consumption for the millennials and iGeneration. Video-based learning [27] is used in a wide spectrum of instructional settings, ranging from flipped classrooms [15], online learning and MOOCS [10, 23] to informal learning using YouTube. However, watching videos is inherently a passive form of learning; in order to learn effectively, students need to engage with video content [3–6, 13, 20, 27]. Engagement with videos can be facilitated

© Springer International Publishing AG 2017
E. André et al. (Eds.): AIED 2017, LNAI 10331, pp. 224–237, 2017.
DOI: 10.1007/978-3-319-61425-0_19

by embedding interactive activities, such as quizzes and assessment problems [8, 12, 14, 24], or by providing environments for collaborative annotation of videos [3]. Although such strategies increase engagement, they require substantial effort from the teacher during video production, or sophisticated learning environments.

Our approach is to support engagement via interactive notetaking, tapping into learners' familiarity with commenting on videos in social networking sites. For example, in CourseMapper [3], learners can annotate videos, discuss and vote/rate annotations. However, in video annotation environments students annotate videos freely, with no explicit support for personalisation. Our approach differs in that we channel support for interaction with important elements of videos via *aspects*, i.e. micro-scaffolds that direct students' attention on skill-related concepts and foster reflection.

We developed the Active Video Watching (AVW) system [16, 18]. AVW is aimed at soft skills learning (such as communicating, collaborating, critical thinking), which are crucial for employability in the knowledge economy [26]. Videos can be a powerful method for soft skills training [2, 5, 6], where learning requires contextualisation in personal experience and ability to see different perspectives. We conducted two studies using the AVW platform to learn about giving pitch presentations. The findings can inform further improvements of the AVW platform (similar to [22, 25]), and future enhancements with intelligent nudging features to improve learning.

The paper is structured as follows. Section 2 presents AVW and the operationalisation of the ICAP framework for active video watching. The experimental design is presented in Sect. 3, followed by findings and elicited requirements in Sect. 4. Section 5 discusses possible nudging features.

2   Operationalisation of the ICAP Framework for AVW

ICAP Framework. Engagement is crucial for effective learning [4, 19, 27]. In a classroom, the teacher can form judgments about students' levels of engagement. However, engagement in online learning (including learning from videos) is often low, and overt actions students perform are the only source of information about their engagement. The ICAP Framework [4] classifies overt learner behaviours into four type of learning modes, corresponding to different levels of cognitive engagement: Interactive, Constructive, Active and Passive. *Passive* learners are simply receiving information, without performing any additional actions; they might be observing a lecture, reading a book or watching a video, but do not engage further. *Active* learners exhibit additional actions, such as note taking, but those actions simply replicate provided information; for example, writing down lecturer's statements, or rewinding the video to watch important parts multiple times. In the *constructive* mode, the learner generates new information that was not explicitly taught; e.g. summary of points, a concept map, or a self-explanation. In the *interactive* mode, learners engage in discussions with their peers, which allow them to compare and contrast their opinions, and jointly generate solutions to problems. Chi and Wylie [4] provide evidence that as students become more engaged, starting from the passive mode to the interactive mode, the learning effectiveness increases; i.e. Passive < Active < Constructive < Interactive.

AVW Platform. AVW is a controlled video watching environment designed for self-study. It can be customised by the teacher who defines a list of aspects that serve as scaffolds for learning with videos. The choice of aspects should direct the student's attention on skill-related concepts and foster reflection.

AVW offers *Personal Space* and *Social Space* (Fig. 1). Initially students watch and comment on videos individually in the Personal Space, using aspects to tag their comments. The system time-stamps comments (i.e. the time elapsed from the start of video). The student can watch videos multiple times, including rewinding or skipping parts. Once the teacher approves comments for sharing, anonymised comments are available in the Social Space, in which students can browse and rate comments. The students can sort the comments by timestamp or aspect. The teacher defines options for rating to promote deeper reflections. In addition to reading/rating the comments, the students can watch the part of the video associated with a comment.

The AVW platform was instantiated in systems hosted by the Universities of Leeds and Canterbury, respectively. Both instances had identical basic functionality, with the same set of videos and customisation by the teacher. A few small differences include the possibility to add a comment without specifying an aspect in the former instance, while aspects were made mandatory in the latter instance.

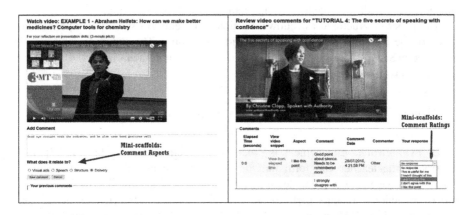

Fig. 1. Adding a comment (Personal Space, left*)*; and rating a comment (Social Space, right).

Operationalising ICAP in AVW. We operationalised the ICAP framework in the context of AVW as follows. Passive Learners are those who watched videos, but have neither manipulated them, or written comments on them. Active Learners are similar in that they do not comment on videos, but manipulate videos (e.g. watching videos multiple times, fast forwarding or rewinding videos). We consider a combined category **Passive/Active Learners (P/AL)** indicating students who watched videos without commenting. **Constructive Learners (CL)** show higher levels of engagement by commenting on videos. Comments, as we will show in Sect. 4, contain remarks on important events in videos, and contain statements showing reflection and self-explanation. AVW does not currently support collaboration between students, and therefore we do not consider the Interactive mode of ICAP. In addition to P/AL and CL, we have also added another mode to characterise students who do not engage in learning at all, i.e. do not watch videos; we refer to them as **Inactive Learners (IL)**.

3   Experimental Design

Aim. We conducted two user studies with undergraduate (UG) and postgraduate (PG) university students using AVW to support soft skill learning, namely giving pitch presentations. Ethical approvals were obtained from the Universities of Leeds and Canterbury. The main aim was to elicit requirements for intelligent support to improve learning with AVW. We investigated four **research questions**:

- *Does AVW support learning?* (if so, which behaviour increases knowledge?)
- *Do micro-scaffolds help* (if so, are there any notable usage patterns)?
- *Do the learner profiles differ* (if so, what are the important differences)?
- *What is the learners' experience with AVW* (are there any critical difficulties)?

Materials. The videos used in the study were carefully selected from YouTube. Four were tutorials on giving presentations, while the other four were actual recordings of pitch presentations (two TED talks, and two 3-minute PhD pitch presentations). The criteria for selecting the videos were: (i) appropriate content (covering opening, closing, structure, delivery and visual aids; or examples of pitch presentations); (ii) no longer than 10 min; (iii) balance of gender for the presenters; (iv) two popular examples and two not so popular (based on the YouTube ratings).

The micro-scaffolds used were related to the target soft skill (Fig. 1). There were three reflective aspects chosen for tutorials: "*I didn't realize I wasn't doing it*" (TA2), "*I am rather good at this*" (TA3), "*I did/saw this in the past*" (TA4); these aspects stimulate learners to recall and reflect on their own experiences. There was one additional aspect, "*I like this point*" (TA1), which allows the learner to externalise learning points. For the example videos, the aspects were: "*Delivery*" (EA1), "*Speech*" (EA2), "*Structure*" (EA3), and "*Visual aids*" (EA4), corresponding to the concepts covered in the tutorials. Ratings in the Social Space also aimed to promote reflection.

We designed three surveys. Survey 1 collected participant's profile (demographic information, background experiences, Motivated Strategies for Learning Questionnaire (MSLQ) [21]); and participants' knowledge of presentations. Survey 2 included the same questions for knowledge of presentations; NASA-TLX instrument [11] to check participants' perception of cognitive load when commenting; Technology Acceptance Model (TAM) [7] to check participants' perceived usefulness of commenting on videos for learning; and questions on usability related to commenting on videos. Survey 3 was similar to Survey 2 but related to rating others' comments.

Procedure. The investigation included two studies (Fig. 2). Study 1 (conducted in March 2016) included PG volunteers recruited via online communities, while Study 2 (conducted in July 2016) included UG engineering students from the University of

Canterbury. The goal of Study 1 was to identify whether learning is happening in AVW. The goals of Study 2 were to identify whether the aspects are effective as micro-scaffolds for reflection, and to identify the effect of rating comments in Phase 2 (Social Space) on learning. Hence in Study 2 there were two conditions: experimental (equivalent to Study 1) and control (used AVW without aspects). Both studies were two weeks long. Week 1: After providing informed consent, the participants took Survey 1, watched and commented on the tutorials, then continued with the examples, and completed Survey 2. Week 2: the participants (except those in control condition) rated comments made by other participants and completed Survey 3.

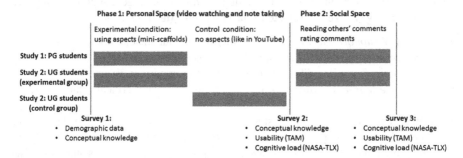

Fig. 2. Outline of experimental set-ups

Assessing Conceptual Knowledge. Each survey contained three questions related to participants' knowledge of presentation skills. Participants had one minute per question to write phrases they associated with (i) structure, (ii) delivery and speech, and (iii) visual aids. We developed an ontology of presentations, consisting of three taxonomies related to these areas. Each response was marked by three independent markers, indicating the number of ontology entities associated with the response. The inter-rater reliability was high: the Krippendorff's alpha was for 0.894 for Study 1, and 0.907 for Study 2. The final scores were confirmed by a fourth marker using the majority vote, or if that was not possible, re-marking the entries.

Participants. Study 1 started with 48 participants, 38 of whom commented on videos and completed surveys (26 females and 12 males; 3 aged younger than 24, 14 aged 24–29, 10 aged 30–35, 5 aged 36–47, and 6 aged 48 or older; 23 with English as first language, while 15 with Asian/European languages as mother tongue; 28 were PhD students and 10 were Masters). In **Study 2**, 37 participants were randomly assigned to either the experimental group (17 males and 2 females) or control group (13 male and 5 female). The majority of participants (83.8%) were aged 18–23. Sixteen Inactive Learners did not use AVW (although some completed all surveys). The remaining students watched the videos, including 8 Passive/Active Learners (4 control, 4 experimental), and 13 Constructive Learners (6 control, 7 experimental).

4 Findings: Recommendations for Intelligent Support

Did AVW Support Learning? Table 1 reports the conceptual knowledge scores from Surveys 1–3. Some participants have not completed all surveys, and therefore we provide the actual numbers of participants who have taken each survey in the table. We found evidence of learning: a repeated measures ANOVA on the conceptual knowledge scores for Study 1 revealed a significant effect overall ($F(2,68) = 6.18$, $p = .003$) with the partial eta squared of 0.15 (medium effect). The pairwise comparison shows there was a significant increase from Survey 1 to Survey 3 ($p = .01$). For constructive participants from Study 2, the Friedman test also revealed a significant difference on conceptual understanding scores ($\chi2(2) = 7.89$, $p = 0.02$). The effect size was large (0.67). There was not enough data to analyse statistical significance of differences for IL and P/AL, but the scores on Survey 3 are lower than earlier scores. Some ILs completed Surveys 2 and 3 without watching any videos; their conceptual knowledge answers contained the same entries, often using irrelevant concepts.

There were no significant differences between CL, P/AL and IL categories on the conceptual knowledge scores from Survey 1, showing that all categories started with similar conceptual knowledge. However, there was a marginally significant difference on the scores for Survey 2 ($H = 3.35$, $p = .09$).

Table 1. Comparing conceptual knowledge by category (scores indicate the number of relevant domain concepts mentioned in the participants' conceptual knowledge answers).

	CL Study 1	CL Study 2	P/AL Study 2	IL Study 2
Pre-test before using AVW (Survey 1)	12.89 (6.44) n = 38	13.62 (4.03) n = 13	11.63 (2.97) n = 8	10.63 (4.95) n = 16
Post-test Personal Space (Survey 2)	13.74 (6.46) n = 38	17 (4.52) n = 10	11.2 (5.45) n = 5	10.13 (4.82) n = 8
Post-test Social Space (Survey 3)	15.86 (6.18) n = 35	18.4 (3.72) n = 5	7.5 (9.19) n = 2	9.5 (6.36) n = 2

In Study 2, there was a significant difference on the conceptual knowledge scores for Survey 2 ($H = 7.25$, $p = .03$), with a significant difference between IL and CL ($p = .03$). We have not compared scores from Survey 3 due to low user numbers. Not all participants engaged in constructive learning, consequently, they did not improve their conceptual knowledge. A large group of participants (43%) from Study 2 have not watched any videos (IL). The percentage of IL in Study 1 is much smaller (20%). We have no data about why ILs have not watched videos. We attribute this to the voluntary nature of the study and demands by other learning activities. In Study 2, 21% of participants watched videos but made no comments (P/AL).

Finding: Only constructive behaviour in both AVW spaces (writing/rating comments) led to increased conceptual understanding. Passive/Active and Inactive behaviour did not lead to increased conceptual understanding.

R1: Further enhance both the Personal Space and the Social Space with intelligent support to foster active video watching that leads to constructive learning behaviour.

Table 2. Comparing control and experimental conditions in Study 2

	Constructive learners		Passive/active learners	
	Control (5)	Exper. (5)	Control (3)	Exper. (1)
Pre-test (Survey 1)	13.2 (3.96)	12.2 (2.28)	11 (2.65)	13
Post-test (Survey 2)	15.8 (2.59)	18.2 (5.98)	12 (6.93)	13
Post-test (Survey 3)	N/A	18.4 (3.72)	N/A	15

Did Micro-scaffolds Help? Study 2 focused on the effect of micro-scaffolds (i.e. aspects and ratings) on learning. The control condition used AVW without micro-scaffolds. Table 2 provides scores for participants who have completed all surveys. The only significant difference on conceptual knowledge scores is for CL from the experimental group ($\chi^2(2) = 7.89$, p = 0.02). The effect size was large (0.667), and the scores from Survey 1 and Survey 3 are significantly different (p = .01).

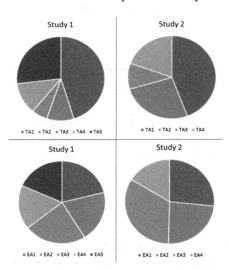

Fig. 3. Percentages of aspects used

Overall, 1029 comments were generated (790 in Study 1 and 239 in Study 2). There was no significant difference between the average number of comments made by CL from Study 1 (19.58, sd = 13.19) and Study 2 (18.38, sd = 16.59). In Study 2, CL from the experimental condition made 12.86 comments (sd = 11.65, range = [1, 29]), while CL from the control group made 24.83 (sd = 20.13, range = [6, 51]). There was no significant difference on the number of comments made by CL from the two conditions. Hence, making comments alone does not contribute to learning; specifying aspects and rating comments is needed. Only 28% of the comments by CL in Study 1 used reflective aspects (TA2, TA3, TA4), while in Study 2 that percentage was 49% (Fig. 3). Study 1 allowed making comments without selecting aspects, and 26.8% of the comments on tutorials (TA5) and 18% of the comments on examples (EA5) were without aspects. As the effect size for CL in Study 1 was medium, versus large effect size in Study 2, the use of aspects and especially reflective aspects lead to increased conceptual knowledge.

The experimental group from Study 2 provided 332 ratings, with two students providing 150 ratings (73 and 77, respectively). In Study 1, AVW did not log who made ratings. Table 3 shows the split of ratings according to categories. The first three ratings trigger learning, as they show that the participant noticed something new in comments, and we label this class as *Trigger Learning*. The other class (*Induce Opinion*) consists of two categories, when participants disagree with comments, or simply state that they like them. Therefore, participants tend to state opinion (although these rating categories were at bottom of the list of categories provided in the interface).

Table 3. Number of ratings on comments – CL engagement in Social Space.

	Rating category	Study 1	Study 2
Trigger learning	This is useful for me	349	122
	I hadn't thought of this	260	23
	I didn't notice this	241	30
Induce opinion	I do not agree with this	213	29
	I like this point	1643	128

Finding: The use of micro-scaffolds (aspects in the Personal Space and ratings in the Social Space) have positive effect on learning. Mandatory use of aspects for all videos and higher usage of reflective aspects in tutorials led to a larger effect size. The use of rating categories was uneven, most referred to state opinion (like/dislike) as opposed to ratings that trigger reflection and further learning.

R2: In the Personal Space, make it mandatory to indicate an aspect when a comment is made. Include intelligent support to encourage students to use a diverse range of aspects, and give preference to aspects that trigger reflection.

R3: In the Social Space, include intelligent support to encourage students to rate comments, and give preference to ratings that trigger reflection.

R4: Include the use of micro-scaffolds in the learner profile that can be used to personalise the intelligent support in both the Personal Space and the Social Space.

Did the Profiles of the Learner Categories Differ? Table 4 presents the basic statistics for the different categories of participants from the two studies. In Survey 1, the participants' profiles were collected, using the Likert scale ranging from 1 (*lowest*) to 5 (*highest*). There was a significant difference on participants' experience in giving presentations ($H = 7.99$, $p = .046$, no significant pairwise differences). There was a significant difference on the use of YouTube ($H = 10.14$, $p = .02$), with significant difference between the constructive participants from both studies ($H = 17.16$, $p = .05$) which is not surprising, as the participants in Study 1 were older than those in Study 2. There was no significant difference on use of YouTube for learning.

Survey 1 contained 46 questions from the MSLQ, with the Likert scale of 1 (*Not at all true of me*) to 5 (*Very true of me*). The MSLQ questions were summarised into ten scales reported in Table 4. The scores for *Task value* are significantly different ($H = 22.39$, $p < .05$), with Study 1 CLs having higher response than (a) A/PL ($H = 25.73$, $p = .011$), (b) CL from Study 2 ($H = 24.89$, $p = .002$), and (c) IL ($H = 20.137$, $p = .009$) respectively. There was a significant difference on *Effort regulation* ($H = 14.6$, $p = .002$), with Study 2 CLs providing higher scores in comparison to IL ($H = 18.92$, $p = .02$) and A/PL ($H = 21.829$, $p = .05$). For *Organisation*

Table 4. Comparing categories of participants (** and * denote significance at the 0.01 and 0.05 level respectively; Kruskal-Wallis with Bonferroni correction for pairwise comparisons).

	Constructive Study 1 (38)	Construct. Study 2 (13)	Pass./Active Study 2 (8)	Inactive Study 2 (16)
Training	2.16 (.95)	1.77 (.59)	1.5 (.53)	1.81 (.75)
Experience*	2.87 (.78)	2.77 (.59)	2.25 (.46)	2.44 (.73)
YouTube*	3.5 (1.11)	4.38 (.65)	4.13 (.64)	4.19 (.98)
YouTube/learning	2.71 (1.01)	2.85 (.89)	2.62 (1.19)	3.25 (1)
MSLQ task value**	4.49 (.38)	3.95 (.4)	3.83 (.53)	4.02 (.45)
MSLQ self-efficacy	3.72 (.56)	3.46 (.72)	3.88 (.56)	3.66 (.4)
MSLQ acad. control	3.91 (.46)	4.04 (.49)	4.25 (.68)	4.22 (.58)
MSLQ intrinsic	4.05 (.52)	3.79 (.35)	3.72 (.68)	3.79 (.51)
MSLQ extrinsic	3.37 (.74)	3.62 (.33)	3.97 (.59)	3.41 (.82)
MSLQ effort regul.**	3.81 (.57)	3.92 (2.28)	3.53 (.54)	3.45 (.55)
MSLQ rehearsal	3.4 (.8)	2.94 (.85)	2.88 (.88)	2.94 (.92)
MSLQ organization**	3.84 (.94)	3.27 (1.25)	2.38 (1.03)	3.02 (1.07)
MSLQ elaboration**	4.13 (.54)	3.67 (.49)	3.63 (.74)	3.55 (.75)
MSLQ self-regul.**	3.56 (.49)	2.82 (.51)	3.31 (.54)	3.23 (.46)

(H = 15.52, p = .001), again the PG students scored significantly higher than A/PL (H = 27.88, p = .005) and IL (H = 17.97, p = .03). Similarly, there were significant differences for *Elaboration* (H = 14.1, p = .003), with PG participants scoring higher than IL (H = 19.48, p = .015), and for *Self-regulation* (H = 21.35, p = 0.), with PG participants scoring higher than CL from Study 2 (H = 30.68, p = 0). These findings show that PG students generally have better learning strategies than P/AL and IL. The only significant differences for the CLs from the two studies were on Task value and Self-regulation.

Finding: Students who are more experienced in the target soft skill are more likely to exhibit constructive learning behaviour. There were differences in MSLQ scales.

R5: Include past experience and MSLQ scales in the learner profile so they can be used to personalise intelligent support in both Personal/Social Space.

R6: Include different strategies for intelligent support. For CL, encourage them to refer to past experience in comment writing and rating. For Passive/Active learners, encourage elaboration, self-regulation, and organisation in comment writing and rating; as well as indicate the task value of active video watching.

R7: Conduct intelligent analysis to further categorise constructive learning in order to identify personalised strategies for this category of learners.

What was the learners' experience with AVW? The participants' perceptions on commenting on the videos (Survey 2) and rating comments (Survey 3) were collected using the NASA-TLX questionnaire on the cognitive workload and the TAM questionnaire measuring perceived usefulness. The participants faced some difficulties.

Cognitive Demand. Four NASA-TLX questions measured: how demanding commenting/rating comments was, how much effort was required, how frustrating the activity was, and how well the participant felt he/she performed (Table 5).

Table 5. Average scores for NASA-TLX cognitive load (Likert scale from 1-*Low* to 20-*High*) and TAM perceived usefulness (Likert scale from 1-*High* to 7-*Low*)

		Constructive Study 1	Constructive Study 2	Passive/active Study 2
NASA-TLX demand	Personal Space	9.89 (4.87)	11.1 (4.95)	10 (7.28)
	Social Space	8.86 (4.84)	9 (4.42)	13.67 (3.21)
NASA-TLX effort	Personal Space	8.55 (4.21)	8.9 (2.99)	7.4 (5.03)
	Social Space	8.37 (4.89)	7.4 (4.34)	15.67 (.58)
NASA-TLX frustration	Personal Space	5.79 (4.49)	8.5 (5.06)	5.8 (5.45)
	Social Space	8.63 (6.17)	8.8 (5.36)	5.67 (6.43)
NASA-TLX performance	Personal Space	12.76 (4.48)	11.5 (5.29)	9.4 (7.7)
	Social Space	10.4 (6.09)	7.6 (3.91)	9.67 (8.5)
TAM usefulness	Personal Space	3.91 (.38)	3 (.89)	3.68 (1.61)
	Social Space	3.33 (1.77)	4.72 (1.35)	3.87 (6.43)

We do not report the scores for Inactive participants, as they have not interacted with AVW. There were no significant differences between the categories on any of the cognitive load values. The participants found commenting on the videos and rating comments moderately demanding. In relation to demand, 45% of Study 1 participants explicitly noted that commenting on videos prompted thinking, which is evidence of the effectiveness of aspects to support reflection. Seven participants stated they made links with their past experience, e.g.: "*I needed to pay proper attention to understand what was explained, to recall my experience, and perceive the usefulness of the tricks and tactics told by the presenter.*"

The participants from Study 1 found rating comments more frustrating than commenting on videos (t = 2.89, p = .007), and stated their performance on rating lower than on commenting (t = 2.14, p = .04). The qualitative feedback on frustration pointed at the large number of comments to be rated, which was time-consuming, as well as the fact that many comments were similar. The participants suggested presenting comments in a structured way, and providing ways to discuss comments with others.

Perceived Usefulness. Table 5 reports the average of five TAM questions related to the perceived usefulness of commenting on video in the Personal Space, and to rating comments in the Social Space. The Kruskal-Wallis test revealed a significant difference on Usefulness for commenting on videos (H = 11.54, p = .01), with a pairwise significant difference between the constructive participants from the two studies (p = .013). The constructive participants from Study 2 found commenting on videos more useful than PG students, which can be explained by the fact that UG students had less experience overall with presentations than PG students. There was no significant difference on Usefulness for rating comments across the categories.

The PG participants found rating comments marginally significantly more useful than commenting (t = 1.95, p = .06), while the CLs from Study 2 ranked them in the opposite way (W = 10, p = .07). The participants were positive about the functionality provided by AVW, and stated that commenting on videos focused attention on important parts of videos, kept them alert and active, and reinforced learning. The majority of participants stated that rating comments supports learning by sharing understanding (when comments are in agreement) and also seeing points from a different perspective. However, 20% of participants did not find rating comments useful; some stated that others' comments were not of good quality, and that presenting comments in a different way (e.g. summary) would be more beneficial.

Finding: Writing comments was cognitively demanding, as participants needed to identify appropriate places in the video and reflect on past experience. Participants found rating comments relatively frustrating; feedback pointed out (i) overwhelming quantity of comments to read and rate; (ii) reading comments of low quality; (iii) seeing many comments similar to one's own; and (iv) lack of structure.

R8: Add means to the Personal Space to aid the reflection process; add means to encourage users to write high quality comments to be used in the Social Space.

R9: In the Social Space, direct learners' attention to high quality comments and to comments that show different perspectives; provide a structure to browse comments.

5   Discussion: Towards Intelligent Nudging

Following the requirements (*R1 to R9*) in the previous section, we identify future enhancements of AVW with intelligent nudging to promote constructive video-based learning. Intelligent nudges are personalised interventions aimed to influence user behaviour towards constructive learning without limiting users' personal choices for engaging in AVW. Following previous research for using nudges in learning environments [22], we consider two types nudges – *signpostings* and *prompts*.

Learner Model. Use explicit profiling by asking students about their experience in the target skill and MSQL scales (*R5*) and implicit profiling from the interaction logs, including number of comments, use of aspects and ratings (*R4*). Machine learning can be used to further characterise constructive learning (*R7*), including clustering of CL and prediction model to identify students likely to be P/AL.

Signposting can be added to both AVW spaces, including: (1) showing '*high attention*' parts of the video which attracted comments by participants to encourage commenting (*R1*), to facilitate reflection (*R8*), and to promote rating comments (*R3*); (2) encourage indication of aspects (*R2*) and use of ratings (*R3*) by showing '*focused attention*' parts in the video where comments/ratings predominantly refer to one specific aspect/rating and '*diverse attention*' parts where a range of aspects are used. The former can prompt the use of a specific aspect/rating while the latter can potentially show multiple perspectives critical for soft skill learning; (3) using *open student models* to aid students' awareness of their engagement together with *open social student models* [1, 9, 17] to allow social comparison to motivate participation (*R2*), foster meta-cognitive activities (*R8*), and indicate the quality of comments (*R8* and *R9*).

Prompts can provide contextualised nudging tailored to the learner's profile and engagement behaviour, including: (1) '*other students made good comments about this part*' - encouraging a participant who has not commented on a part of a video that attracted attention of other students (*R1*) and may suggest possible aspects that others have used (*R2*); (2) '*can you relate to your past experience*' - encourage students to refer to past experiences by using the corresponding aspects/ratings (*R6*) and suggest what other people have said about their past experience; (3) '*have you thought about*' – diversify the use of aspects and ratings when the learner tends to use only a fraction of aspects/ratings (*R2, R3*); (4) '*you may find this useful*' – P/AL can be motivated with tips for organisation, self-regulation, and elaboration, and suggestions how AVW can help with these (R6); (5) '*well done*' – provide positive feedback to recognise both good quality comments (*R8*) and use of a variety of reflective aspects and ratings (*R2, R3*). This requires a deeper analysis of comments, employing the developed ontology to provide words/entities for textual and semantic analysis.

6 Conclusions

The findings from our studies show that when learners engage in commenting on videos and rating others' comments, their conceptual understanding of the target soft skills increases. We reported a number of ways for further enhancements of AVW, using intelligent nudges. Future plans include enhancing AVW and performing more studies focusing on various soft skills.

Acknowledgments. This research was supported by the EU-FP7-ICT-257184 ImREAL grant, a teaching development grant from the University of Canterbury, and a regional grant from Ako Aotearoa.

References

1. Bull, S., Kay, J.: SMILI☺: a framework for interfaces to learning data in open learner models, learning analytics and related fields. Artif. Intell. Educ. **26**(1), 293–331 (2016)
2. Cecez-Kecmanovic, D., Webb, C.: Towards a communicative model of collaborative web-mediated learning. Australas. J. Educ. Technol. **16**(1), 73–85 (2000)
3. Chatti, M.A., Marinov, M., Sabov, O., et al.: Video annotation and analytics in CourseMapper. Smart Learn. Environ. **3**(1), 10 (2016)
4. Chi, M.T., Wylie, R.: The ICAP framework: linking cognitive engagement to active learning outcomes. Educ. Psychol. **49**(4), 219–243 (2014)
5. Conkey, C.A., Bowers, C., Cannon-Bowers, J., Sanchez, A.: Machinima and video-based soft-skills training for frontline healthcare workers. Games Health **2**(1), 39–43 (2013)
6. Cronin, M.W., Cronin, K.A.: Recent empirical studies of the pedagogical effects of interactive video instruction in "soft skill" areas. Comput. High. Educ. **3**(2), 53 (1992)
7. Davis, F.D.: Perceived usefulness, perceived ease of use, and user acceptance of information technology. MIS Q. **13**, 319–340 (1989)

8. Giannakos, M., Sampson, D., Kidziński, Ł.: Introduction to smart learning analytics: foundations and developments in video-based learning. Smart Learn. Environ. **3**(1), 1–9 (2016)

9. Guerra, J., Hosseini, R., Somyurek, S., Brusilovsky, P.: An intelligent interface for learning content: combining an open learner model and social comparison to support self-regulated learning and engagement. In: Proceedings of the 21st International Conference on Intelligent User Interfaces, pp. 152–163 (2016)

10. Guo, P.J., Kim, J., Rubin, R.: How video production affects student engagement: an empirical study of MOOC videos. In: Proceedings of the 1st ACM Conference Learning at Scale, pp. 41–50 (2014)

11. Hart, S.G.: NASA-task load index (NASA-TLX); 20 years later. Proc. Hum. Factors Ergon. Soc. Annu. Meet. **50**(9), 904–908 (2006). Sage Publications

12. Kleftodimos, A., Evangelidis, G.: Using open source technologies and open internet resources for building an interactive video based learning environment that supports learning analytics. Smart Learn. Environ. **3**(1), 1–23 (2016)

13. Koedinger, K.R., Kim, J., Jia, Z., McLaughlin, E., Bier, N.: Learning is not a spectator sport: doing is better than watching for learning from a MOOC learning at scale. In: Proceedings of the 2nd ACM Conference Learning @ Scale, pp. 111–120 (2015)

14. Kovacs, G.: Effects of in-video quizzes on MOOC lecture viewing. In: Proceedings of the 3rd Learning @ Scale, pp. 31–40 (2016)

15. Kurtz, G., Tsimerman, A., Steiner-Lavi, O.: The flipped-classroom approach: the answer to future learning? Eur. J. Open Distance E-learn. **17**(2), 172–182 (2014)

16. Lau, L., Mitrovic, A., Weerasinghe, A., Dimitrova, V.: Usability of an active video watching system for soft skills training. In: Proceedings of the 1st International Workshop on Intelligent Mentoring Systems, ITS 2016, Zagreb (2016)

17. Long, Y., Aleven, V.: Enhancing learning outcomes through self-regulated learning support with an Open Learner Model. User Model. User-Adapt. Interact. **27**(1), 55–88 (2017)

18. Mitrovic, A., Dimitrova, V., Weerasinghe, A., Lau, L.: Reflexive experiential learning using active video watching for soft skills training. In: Chen, W., et al. (eds.) Proceedings of the 24th International Conference on Computers in Education, Mumbai, pp. 192–201, 28 November–2 December 2016. APSCE (2016)

19. Morgan, G., Adams, J.: Pedagogy first: making web-technologies work for soft skills development in leadership and management education. Interact. Learn. Res. **20**(2), 129–155 (2009)

20. Pardo, A., Mirriahi, N., Dawson, S., Zhao, Y., Zhao, A., Gašević, D.: Identifying learning strategies associated with active use of video annotation software. In: Proceedings of the 5th International Conference on Learning Analytics and Knowledge, pp. 255–259. ACM (2015)

21. Pintrich, P.R., De Groot, E.V.: Motivational and self-regulated learning components of classroom academic performance. J. Educ. Psychol. **82**(1), 33 (1990)

22. Thakker, D., Dimitrova, V., Lau, L., Yang-Turner, F., Despotakis, D.: Assisting user browsing over linked data: requirements elicitation with a user study. In: Daniel, F., Dolog, P., Li, Q. (eds.) ICWE 2013. LNCS, vol. 7977, pp. 376–383. Springer, Heidelberg (2013). doi:10.1007/978-3-642-39200-9_31

23. Vieira, I., Lopes, A.P., Soares, F.: The potential benefits of using videos in higher education. In: Proceedings of the EDULEARN14 Conference, pp. 0750–0756. IATED Publications (2014)

24. Wachtler, J., Hubmann, M., Zöhrer, H., Ebner, M.: An analysis of the use and effect of questions in interactive learning-videos. Smart Learn. Environ. **3**(1), 13 (2016)

25. Wang, X., Wen, M., Rosé, C.P.: Towards triggering higher-order thinking behaviors in MOOCs. In: Proceedings of the 6th International Conference Learning Analytics & Knowledge, pp. 398–407. ACM (2016)
26. World Economic Forum Report: What are the 21st-century skills every student needs? (2016). https://www.weforum.org/agenda/2016/03/21st-century-skills-future-jobs-students
27. Yousef, A.M.F., Chatti, M.A., Schroeder, U.: The state of video-based learning: a review and future perspectives. Int. J. Adv. Life Sci. 6(3/4), 122–135 (2014)

Affect Dynamics in Military Trainees Using vMedic: From Engaged Concentration to Boredom to Confusion

Jaclyn Ocumpaugh[1(✉)], Juan Miguel Andres[1], Ryan Baker[1],
Jeanine DeFalco[2], Luc Paquette[3], Jonathan Rowe[4], Bradford Mott[4],
James Lester[4], Vasiliki Georgoulas[5,6], Keith Brawner[6],
and Robert Sottilare[6]

[1] University of Pennsylvania, Philadelphia, USA
jlocumpaugh@gmail.com
[2] Pace University, New York, USA
[3] University of Illinois Urbana-Champaign, Illinois, USA
[4] North Carolina State University, Raleigh, USA
[5] Teachers College, Columbia University, New York, USA
[6] US Army Research Laboratory, Adelphi, USA

Abstract. The role of affect in learning has received increasing attention from AIED researchers seeking to understand how emotion and cognition interact in learning contexts. The dynamics of affect over time have been explored in a variety of research environments, allowing researchers to determine the extent to which common patterns are captured by hypothesized models. This paper present an analysis of affect dynamics among learners using vMedic, which teaches combat medicine protocols as part of the military training at West Point, the United States Military Academy. In doing so, we seek both to broaden the variety of learning contexts being explored in order better understand differences in these patterns and to test the theoretical predictions on the development of affect over time.

1 Introduction

The fundamental role of emotions in learning is well accepted if not fully understood. Though findings of negative correlations between boredom and learning generally replicate [9, 29], other affective states appear to be driven by their context and duration, with confusion appearing to differ in correlation to learning by context [9, 17, 29], possibly mediated by the duration of confusion [20] and what experience induced the confusion [17].

D'Mello and Graesser's theoretical model of affect dynamics, the development of student affect over time [11], as well as their pioneering empirical work in this area [10], has brought needed attention to the study of the affective undercurrents of successful and unsuccessful educational experiences. Over the last decade, researchers have studied affect dynamics both in classroom settings using field observations [5, 16, 29] and laboratory settings using self-report [10, 11, 21].

© Springer International Publishing AG 2017
E. André et al. (Eds.): AIED 2017, LNAI 10331, pp. 238–249, 2017.
DOI: 10.1007/978-3-319-61425-0_20

This research has illustrated several potential benefits to better understanding affect dynamics. First, by understanding affect dynamics, we can understand not just what a learner's affect is right now but what it will be later, helping us predict a learner's eventual outcomes. Understanding the natural developments in affect can help us design interventions that reinforce positive affective transitions and reduce negative transitions. It can also help us to understand the impacts of our interventions better; we should not congratulate ourselves on a positive transition if that transition would have happened with no intervention at all.

However, in order to achieve a theoretical model of affective pathways that will be of broad use, it is important that this data used to inform these models reflects the diverse learning experiences of different learners and different learning contexts (including what learning system is being used). Understanding how affect dynamics vary – and are influenced by – different populations and contexts could be important to fully understanding the processes around affect dynamics. We already know, for instance, that the same affective state can manifest differently in behavioral terms between populations [23]. This current study investigates affect transitions, using data from *in situ* observations of learner affect, among US military cadets using vMedic, a game-based virtual environment that provides training in combat field medicine, representing a different population, domain, and type of interaction than in previous work on affect dynamics. Affective states observed included boredom, confusion, engaged concentration (flow), frustration, surprise and anxiety.

2 Previous Research

2.1 Cognitive-Affective Learning

Researchers have long hypothesized a set of basic emotions (e.g., happiness, sadness, anger, disgust, fear, and surprise, [14]), but, as Table 1 summarizes, those working in education domains typically focus on cognitive/affective states more common to learning contexts and thought to correlate to learning outcomes (e.g., [18]). These typically include boredom, confusion, engaged concentration (the affective state related to Csikszentmihalyi's construct of flow [8]), delight, and frustration, but may also include a range of other states (e.g., [12, 21]).

2.2 Affect Dynamics

One of the more prominent theories about the temporal dynamics of affect is D'Mello and Graesser's [11] hypothesized model of affect dynamics for learning (shown in Fig. 1 and summarized in Table 2). Based largely on Pekrun's [25] control-value theory, this model suggests multiple possible pathways between engaged concentration (Csikszentmihalyi's [8] flow), surprise, confusion, delight, frustration, and boredom. As Fig. 1 illustrates, disequilibrium (experienced as confusion) plays a central role in this model, capturing the longstanding and ever-growing body of work showing the importance of confusion to learning (e.g., [9, 17, 20, 29]).

Table 1. Affective states studied in previous research on affect dynamics in online learning environments. Categories considered in the current study are highlighted in gray.

	D'Mello & Graesser, 2012	D'Mello et al., 2009	McQuiggan et al., 2010	Andres & Rodrigo 2014	Guia et al., 2011	Rodrigo, 2011	Rodrigo et al., 2009	Rodrigo et al., 2010	Bosch & D'Mello, 2013	Baker et al., 2010
Anger		x	x							
Anxiety		x	x							
Boredom	x	x	x	x	x	x	x	x	x	x
Confusion	x	x	x	x	x	x	x	x	x	x
Curiosity		x								x
Delight	x			x	x	x	x	x		
Disgust		x								
Eureeka		x								
Excitement			x							
Fear			x							
Flow	x		x	x	x	x	x	x	x	x
Frustration	x	x	x	x	x	x	x		x	x
Happiness		x								
Neutral		x			x	x	x	x		
Sadness		x	x							
Surprise	x	x			x	x	x	x		x

Fig. 1. D'Mello and Graesser's [11] posited model of affect dynamics during learning, adapted from Control-Value Theory.

Table 2. Summary of D'Mello and Graesser's [11] hypothesized pathways. Pathways hypothesized in Fig. 1 are shown, labeled, in this transition matrix; pathways that are not part of this model are shown in gray-scale.

	to BOR	to ENG	to CNF	to DEL	to FRU	to SUR
fr. BOR						
fr. ENG			1a			1b
fr. CNF		2a		2b	3	
fr. DEL		2c				
fr. FRU	4					
fr. SUR			1c			

Empirical research in affect dynamics, however, has found that other pathways may be common. D'Mello and Graesser [11] report two studies alongside their theoretical model. The first finds that only three of the hypothesized transitions (1a, 2a, and 3) occur at levels above chance, along with one pathway that was not hypothesized (boredom to frustration). The second finds empirical evidence for four of their hypothesized pathways (1a, 2a, 3, and 4), but also evidence for two pathways that were not hypothesized (boredom to frustration as well as frustration to flow). Other studies have also failed to closely match this theoretical model. For example, Rodrigo's [26] study of affect during Mathblaster found compelling evidence for only one of the hypothesized pathways (confusion to flow), and Guia et al. [16] found that in SQL-Tutor the hypothesized pathway of confusion to frustration was less likely than chance, while other hypothesized pathways were not significant at all (Fig. 2).

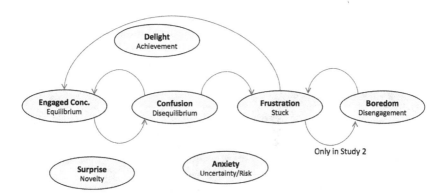

Fig. 2. Pathways found in D'Mello and Graesser's (2012) empirical research.

Much of the other research on affect dynamics has differed from D'Mello and Graesser [11] by including self-transitions (when a learner remains in the same affective state from one observation to the next) in calculations. Baker, D'Mello, Rodrigo and Graesser [2] found that boredom and engaged concentration were likely to be persistent, across three different learning environments. In another study, Rodrigo et al. [30] found only engaged concentration was likely to show persistence, while a similar study by Rodrigo et al. [28] found persistence for boredom, confusion, and engaged concentration. Andres and Rodrigo [1] found persistence for confusion, engaged concentration, and frustration, but Guia et al. [16] found no affective states were significantly more likely than chance to persist.

The picture becomes more complicated when additional affective states are included in the research. For example, Andres and Rodrigo [1] considered all of D'Mello and Graesser's [11] affective categories (boredom, confusion, delight, engaged concentration, delight, frustration, and surprise) when studying Physics Playground [31]), but also added six others (angry, anxious, curious, happy, pride, and sad). Likewise, McQuiggan et al. [21], working in the context of a narrative environment (Chrystal Island), consider ten affective states, including six of those in D'Mello and Graesser's

[11] model (anxiety, boredom, confusion, delight, engaged concentration, and frustration) and four that were not (anger, excitement, fear, and sadness). Coding with expanded lists of affective states may change the base rates of observed affective categories. Furthermore, using expanded lists of affective states may qualitatively change the nature of the coding in ways that are not fully captured by mathematical modeling.

3 Methods

3.1 Learning Environment and Participants

The learning environment observed in this study was vMedic (a.k.a. TC3Sim), a virtual world developed for the US Army by Engineering and Computer Simulations (ECS, Orlando Florida), which provides training in combat medicine and battlefield doctrine around medical first response. The system is administered through the Army Research Laboratory's modular GIFT framework [15]. In this study, 108 West Point cadets (ages of 18–22) were observed using the vMedic system (shown in Fig. 3).

Fig. 3. Screenshot of vMedic scene where learner is expected to treat a combat victim.

3.2 Observation Protocol (BROMP)

While trainees used vMedic, their affective states were observed and recorded using the Baker Rodrigo Ocumpaugh Monitoring Protocol (BROMP 2.0; [24]). BROMP is a momentary time sampling method where learners are observed individually, in a pre-determined order. This ensures that each learner in an observation session is observed at roughly the same frequency as all of his or her peers. Observations are conducted by a BROMP-certified coder using HART, an android application which enforces the sampling method and automatically provides a time stamp for each observation. Observers record two distinct, but simultaneous observations about each learner: his or her behavior (usually on-task, on-task conversation, off-task, or gaming the system) and his or her affective state (usually boredom, confusion, engaged concentration, delight, and frustration). Because of the nature of momentary time sampling methods, affective states which are brief in nature (e.g., Eureka moments) are typically more difficult to capture using BROMP, but it is possible to modify BROMP coding schemes to accommodate relevant constructs that may be environment-specific (e.g., [23]).

In this study two BROMP-certified observers coded for several of the more educationally common affective states (boredom, confusion, engaged concentration, frustration). Additionally, observers coded two constructs that are not typically used in BROMP coding schemes, surprise and anxiety. In this context, surprise reflected novel and unexpected experiences within the virtual world, such as an insurgent appearing from behind a building, rather than reflecting surprise with the learning content. Likewise, anxiety was related to (but distinct from) the observations that were coded as frustration. This distinction reflects previous research on fear and anger (e.g., [19]). vMedic often presents trainees with difficult or unresolvable medical situations, triggering a variety of different affective responses. Affective expressions by a learner that suggested caution or vigilance were coded as anxiety while those that reflected annoyance or defeat were coded as frustration.

3.3   Data and Analysis (D'Mello's L)

In total, 756 of individual observations of affect were recorded: 12 anxiety, 73 boredom, 174 confusion, 435 engaged concentration, 32 frustration, 29 surprise. The number of trainees being coded during these observations varied slightly from one observation session to the next, impacting the time it takes for an observer to return to a given learner. That is, the more learners being observed, the more time between observations of an individual learner, but on average, each learner was observed once every 122 s (stddev = 100.14). In general, the different methods employed for collecting data for affect dynamics research has resulted in data with a variety of characteristics, with some studies using a protocol like this one, leading to regular but fairly lengthy gaps between observations. Other studies have used field observation protocols with many more observers, leading to denser observation but stronger observer effects. Still other studies have used voluntary self-report data, which sometimes is more continuous and other times is more fragmented, depending on the learner's willingness and ability to identify and express their emotions.

In order to examine the common pathways from one affective state to the next, we calculated D'Mello's L, the likelihood that a given affective state will transition to another affective state, [13]):

$$L = \frac{P(NEXT|PREV) - P(NEXT)}{(1 - P(NEXT))}$$

This metric is conceptually similar to Cohen's Kappa, comparing a transition's frequency to the base rate of the affective state that is transitioned into. A value of zero for D'Mello's L indicates that a transition occurs no more frequently than would be expected from the overall proportion of time the destination affective state occurs. Values greater than zero indicate frequencies greater than chance, taking that base rate into account, with a value of one indicating that a specific transition always occurs. Values less than zero indicate a transition that is less likely than chance, with possible values of negative infinity. It is possible to determine whether a transition is statistically significantly more or less likely than chance by calculating a value of D'Mello's L for that transition for each learner, and then comparing those values of D'Mello's L to 0 (chance value) using a t-test for one sample (cf. [5]). Benjamini and Hochberg's [6] post-hoc corrections are used here to adjust for conducting large numbers of comparisons.

4   Results

As discussed above, BROMP observations resulted in 756 observations, corresponding to 450 transitions (e.g., from anxiety to engaged concentration or from engaged concentration to confusion). Table 3 presents totals for each transition, which was then analyzed using D'Mello's L.

Table 3.   Transition matrix for the current study. Anxiety, which was not considered in D'Mello and Graesser's (2012) model, is highlighted in dark gray.

	to ANX	to BOR	to FLO	to CNF	to FRU	to SUR	total	
fr. ANX	0	1	5	1	0	0	7	2%
fr. BOR	1	0	27	175	4	3	210	47%
fr. FLO	4	32	0	61	14	10	121	27%
fr. CNF	2	9	51	0	8	7	77	17%
fr. FRU	2	1	5	4	0	0	12	3%
fr. SUR	0	5	14	4	0	0	23	5%
total	9	48	102	245	26	20	450	
	2%	11%	23%	54%	6%	4%		

Results are presented in Table 4, using the same format as the presentation of previous research findings discussed above, for comparability (plus the category of anxiety – ANX). Only statistically significant results (given post-hoc controls) are reported, and those transitions that are statistically less likely than chance are given in red.

In total, we found 11 statistically significant transitions, but only four (shown in Fig. 4) were more likely than chance. Two of these reflect the hypothesized central role of confusion in learning (engaged concentration to confusion, L = 0.401 and confusion to engaged concentration, L = 0.375). There was also two links that had not been

Table 4. D'Mello's L values for the likelihood of transitions within vMedic. Only statistically significant results given post-hoc controls are reported, with transitions less likely than chance given in red. Pathways that were not predicted in D'Mello and Graesser's [11] model are given in gray, including pathways for anxiety, which are highlighted in darker gray.

	to ANX	to BOR	to FLO	to CNF	to FRU	to SUR
fr. ANX				-0.268		
fr. BOR		-0.135		**0.325**		
fr. FLO		**0.114**	-0.916	**0.401**		
fr. CNF			**0.375**	-0.358		
fr. FRU		-0.078			-0.066	
fr. SUR	-0.022					

previously reported: a transition from engaged concentration to boredom (L = 0.114) and a transition from boredom to confusion (L = 0.325). The link from engaged concentration to boredom suggests that vMedic is relatively unsuccessful at keeping learners engaged in a sustaining fashion (though it is unclear if this is due to features of the game or features of the population using it); however, the link from boredom to confusion suggests that enough events occur during gameplay to prevent boredom from becoming an enduring problem, unlike in other environments (e.g. [2]).

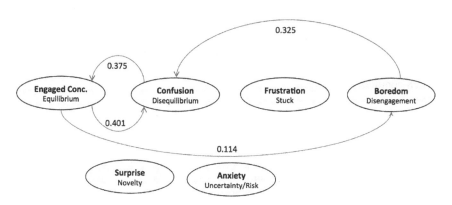

Fig. 4. Pathways found to be (positively) statistically significant in the current study, including the hypothesized loop between flow and confusion and the previously not hypothesized loop between flow and boredom.

Results for transitions that occur at levels below chance are shown in Fig. 5. Note that this figure includes one of the transitions hypothesized in D'Mello and Graesser's [11] model to be more likely than chance, the transition from frustration to boredom. Contrary to that model, this transition was statistically significantly less likely than chance in vMedic, L = −0.078. This result may be due to the population of Army cadets, who may be better able to regulate their responses to otherwise frustrating events than previously studied populations (e.g., middle-schoolers). Learners were also less likely to be anxious after being surprised, and less likely to be confused after being

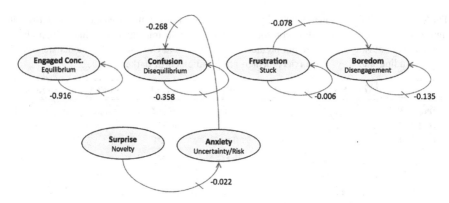

Fig. 5. Pathways found to be statistically less likely than chance in the current study.

anxious, results which are statistically significant despite the relative infrequency of anxiety in this data set.

One additional finding that is curious is the relatively low probability of learners staying in their current affective state, with self-transitions (a transition from a state to itself) being less likely than chance for all four of the most commonly studied affective states (boredom, engaged concentration, frustration, and confusion). This pattern is in contrast to most of the previous work on affect dynamics (e.g., [1, 26, 28, 30]), and may result from a combination between the fast pace of activity in vMedic, where learners switch activities with fairly high frequency, and the sampling rate of the BROMP method. However, it is worth noting that the former is a variable that has not been well controlled for in previous studies and that the latter has also varied widely from one research condition to another.

5   Conclusions

In this paper, we study the dynamics of affect within the simulation vMedic, using BROMP field observation to measure affect, and conducting statistical significance testing on whether the D'Mello's L metric is different than zero across students, to determine which transitions are significantly less or more likely than chance. Our results differ from previous published results and a key theoretical model in showing a link from engaged concentration to boredom, a link from boredom to confusion, and the lack of a hypothesized link from frustration to boredom. In general, the difference of these results from this past work is probably attributable at least in part to differences between the populations (military cadets learning material relevant to their future compared to K-12 populations or undergraduates in lab studies learning material that is relatively arbitrary to them). A military cadet might be expected to have better self-regulatory skill than the other populations studied in the past, preventing frustration from becoming boredom. However, a military cadet might also be less engaged by a game than other populations, leading the fun of the game to quickly turn boring. We also find relatively low persistence of affect between observations, another contrast to past work. We hypothesize that this may be due to the relatively fast pace of change of activities within vMedic compared to many of the other environments studied.

Investigating these hypotheses is a valuable area for future work. But the broader question is: what factors determine the differences in affect dynamics between contexts and studies? With a range of published studies on affect dynamics, we see a range of patterns – and relatively few of those patterns are consistent across studies or consistent with the one theoretical model published (e.g. [11]). Ultimately, it becomes worth asking whether affect dynamics are entirely contextual, or whether there are some patterns that reliably cut across studies. To the extent that affect dynamics *are* contextual, we need to ask what factors in the context best determine the patterns seen – is it the population? The system they are using? The design of the study? The method for measuring affect? The characteristics of individual students?

Determining the answer to these questions will be necessary to achieve the goals originally set for affect dynamics research, including the development of interventions that can improve learning outcomes. They will also allow us to build a more comprehensive theory of how affect develops and unfolds over time.

Acknowledgments. This research was supported by grant by the Army Research Lab #W911NF-13-2-0008.

References

1. Andres, J.M., Rodrigo, M.M.T.: The incidence & persistence of affective states while playing Newton's playground. In: 7th IEEE International Conference on Humanoid, Nanotechnology, Information Technology, Communication & Control, Environment, & Management (2014)
2. Baker, R.S., D'Mello, S.K., Rodrigo, M.M., Graesser, A.C.: Better to be frustrated than bored: the incidence, persistence, and impact of learners' cognitive–affective states during interactions with three different computer-based learning environments. Int. J. Hum Comput Stud. **68**(4), 223–241 (2010)
3. Baker, R.S.J., et al.: The dynamics between student affect and behavior occurring outside of educational software. In: D'Mello, S., Graesser, A., Schuller, B., Martin, J.-C. (eds.) ACII 2011. LNCS, vol. 6974, pp. 14–24. Springer, Heidelberg (2011). doi:10.1007/978-3-642-24600-5_5
4. Baker, R.S.J., Ocumpaugh, J.: Interaction-based affect detection in educational software. In: Calvo, R.A., D'Mello, S.K., Gratch, J., Kappas, A. (eds.) The Oxford Handbook of Affective Computing. Oxford University Press, Oxford (2014)
5. Baker, R.S.J., Rodrigo, M.M.T., Xolocotzin, U.E.: The dynamics of affective transitions in simulation problem-solving environments. In: Paiva, A.C.R., Prada, R., Picard, R.W. (eds.) ACII 2007. LNCS, vol. 4738, pp. 666–677. Springer, Heidelberg (2007). doi:10.1007/978-3-540-74889-2_58
6. Benjamini, Y., Hochberg, Y.: Controlling the false discovery rate: a practical and powerful approach to multiple testing. J. R. Stat. Soc. Ser. B (Methodological) **57**, 289–300 (1995)
7. Bosch, N., D'Mello, S.: Sequential patterns of affective states of novice programmers. In: The 1st Workshop on AI-Supported Education for Computer Science (AIEDCS 2013), pp. 1–10 (2013)

8. Csikszentmihalyi, M.: Flow: The Psychology of Optimal Performance. Cambridge University Press, New York (1990)

9. Craig, S., Graesser, A., Sullins, J., Gholson, B.: Affect and learning: an exploratory look into the role of affect in learning with AutoTutor. J. Educ. Media **29**(3), 241–250 (2004)

10. D'Mello S.K., Craig, S.D., Gholson, B., Franklin, S., Picard, R., Graesser, A.C.: Integrating affect sensors in an intelligent tutoring system. In: Affective Interactions: The Computer in the Affective Loop, pp. 7–13 (2005)

11. D'Mello, S.K., Graesser, A.: Dynamics of affective states during complex learning. Learn. Instr. **22**(2), 145–157 (2012)

12. D'Mello, S.K., Person, N., Lehman, B.: Antecedent-consequent relationships & cyclical patterns between affective states and problem solving outcomes. In: AIED, pp. 57–64 (2009)

13. D'Mello, S.K., Taylor, R.S., Graesser, A.: Monitoring affective trajectories during complex learning. In: Proceedings of the 9th Annual Meeting of the Cognitive Science Study, pp. 203–208 (2007)

14. Ekman, P.: An argument for basic emotions. Cognition Emot. **6**(3–4), 169–200 (1992)

15. Goldberg, B., Brawner, K., Sottilare, R, Tarr, R., Billings, D., Malone, N.: Use of evidence-based strategies to enhance the extensibility of adaptive tutoring technologies. In: Interservice/Industry Training, Simulation, & Education Conference (I/ITSEC) (2012)

16. Guia, T.F.G., Sugay, J.O., Rodrigo, M.M.T., Macam, F.J.P., Dagami, M.M.C., Mitrovic, A.: Transitions of affective states in an intelligent tutoring system. In: Proceedings of the Philippine Computing Society, pp. 31–35 (2011)

17. Lehman, B., D'Mello, S., Graesser, A.: Confusion and complex learning during interactions with computer learning environments. Internet High. Educ. **15**(3), 184–194 (2012)

18. Lehman, B., Matthews, M., D'Mello, S., Person, N.: What are you feeling? Investigating student affective states during expert human tutoring sessions. In: Woolf, B.P., Aïmeur, E., Nkambou, R., Lajoie, S. (eds.) ITS 2008. LNCS, vol. 5091, pp. 50–59. Springer, Heidelberg (2008). doi:10.1007/978-3-540-69132-7_10

19. Lerner, J., Keltner, D.: Fear, anger, and risk. J. Pers. Soc. Psychol. **81**(1), 146 (2001)

20. Liu, Z., Pataranutaporn, V., Ocumpaugh, J., Baker, R.S.J.: Sequences of frustration and confusion, and learning. In: Proceedings of the 6th International Conference on Educational Data Mining, pp. 114–120 (2013)

21. McQuiggan, S.W., Robison, J.L., Lester, J.C.: Affective transitions in narrative-centered learning environments. Educ. Technol. Soc. **13**(1), 40–53 (2010)

22. Ocumpaugh, J., Baker, R., Gowda, S., Heffernan, N., Heffernan, C.: Population validity for educational data mining models: a case study in affect detection. Br. J. Educ. Technol. **45**(3), 487–501 (2014)

23. Ocumpaugh, J., Baker, R.S., Kamarainen, A.M., Metcalf, S.J.: Modifying field observation methods on the fly: metanarrative and disgust in an environmental MUVE. In: Proceedings of PALE 2013: The 4th International Workshop on Personalization Approaches in Learning Environments, pp. 49–54 (2014)

24. Ocumpaugh, J., Baker, R.S., Rodrigo, M.M.T.: Baker Rodrigo Ocumpaugh Monitoring Protocol (BROMP) 2.0 technical and training manual. Technical report. Teachers College, Columbia University, New York. Ateneo Laboratory for the Learning Sciences, Manila (2015)

25. Pekrun, R.: The control-value theory of achievement emotions: assumptions, corollaries, and implications for educational research and practice. Educ. Psychol. Rev. **18**(4), 315–341 (2006)

26. Rodrigo, M.M.T.: Dynamics of student cognitive-affective transitions during a mathematics game. Simul. Gaming **42**(1), 85–99 (2011)

27. Rodrigo, M.M.T., Baker, R.S.J.: Comparing the incidence and persistence of learners' affect during interactions with different educational software packages. In: Calvo, R.A., D'Mello, S. (eds.) New Perspectives on Affect and Learning Technologies, pp. 183–202. Springer, New York (2011)

28. Rodrigo, M.M.T., Baker, R.S.J., Agapito, J., Nabos, J., Repalam, M.C., Reyes, S.S., San Pedro, M.C.Z.: The effects of an interactive software agent on student affective dynamics while using an intelligent tutoring system. IEEE Trans. Affect. Comput. 3(2), 224–236 (2012)

29. Rodrigo, M.M.T., Baker, R.S., Jadud, M.C., Amarra, A.C.M., Dy, T., Espejo-Lahoz, M.B. V., Lim, S.A.L., Pascua, S.A.M.S., Sugay, J.O., Tabanao, E.S.: Affective and behavioral predictors of novice programmer achievement. In: Proceedings of the 14th ACM-SIGCSE Annual Conference on Innovation & Technology in Computer Science Education, pp. 156–160 (2009)

30. Rodrigo, M.M.T., Baker, R.S.J., Nabos, J.Q.: The relationships between sequences of affective states and learner achievements. In: Proceedings of the 18th International Conference on Computers in Education (2010)

31. Shute, V.J., Ventura, M., Kim, Y.J.: Assessment and learning of qualitative physics in Newton's playground. J. Educ. Res. 106(6), 423–430 (2013)

Behavioral Engagement Detection
of Students in the Wild

Eda Okur[(✉)], Nese Alyuz, Sinem Aslan, Utku Genc,
Cagri Tanriover, and Asli Arslan Esme

Intel Labs, Intel Corporation, Hillsboro, USA
{eda.okur,nese.alyuz.civitci,sinem.aslan,utku.genc,
cagri.tanriover,asli.arslan.esme}@intel.com

Abstract. This paper aims to investigate students' behavioral engagement (*On-Task* vs. *Off-Task*) in authentic classrooms. We propose a two-phased approach for automatic engagement detection: In Phase 1, contextual logs are utilized to assess active usage of the content platform. If there is active use, the appearance information is utilized in Phase 2 to infer behavioral engagement. Through authentic classroom pilots, we collected around 170 hours of in-the-wild data from 28 students in two different classrooms using two different content platforms (one for Math and one for English as a Second Language (ESL)). Our data collection application captured appearance data from a 3D camera and context data from uniform resource locator (URL) logs. We experimented with two test cases: (1) Cross-classroom, where trained models were tested on a different classroom's data; (2) Cross-platform, where the data collected in different subject areas (Math or ESL) were utilized in training and testing, respectively. For the first case, the behavioral engagement was detected with an F1-score of 77%, using only appearance. Incorporating the contextual information improved the overall performance to 82%. For the second case, even though the subject areas and content platforms changed, the proposed appearance classifier still achieved 72% accuracy (compared to 77%). Our experiments proved that the accuracy of the proposed model is not adversely impacted considering different set of students or different subject areas.

Keywords: Behavioral engagement detection · Student engagement · Intelligent Tutoring Systems (ITS) · Learning Analytics

1 Introduction

The availability of learning technologies in schools has been rapidly increasing [1]. This increase has resulted in new challenges for teachers: Keeping students engaged in learning tasks while they use their personal computing devices during classes. To this end, a number of educational technology systems have been investigated for providing teachers the data required for monitoring and facilitating student engagement. One example of such systems is Intelligent Tutoring Systems (ITSs) with a major goal to improve student performance by keeping students *engaged* in learning through personalized instruction [2].

Engagement is an important student state to consider in 1:1 learning scenarios [3]. Fredricks *et al.* [4] defined engagement in three different dimensions: Behavioral

© Springer International Publishing AG 2017
E. André et al. (Eds.): AIED 2017, LNAI 10331, pp. 250–261, 2017.
DOI: 10.1007/978-3-319-61425-0_21

engagement, emotional engagement, and cognitive engagement. In contrast to the earlier work on emotional engagement detection [5–8], this paper only focuses on students' behavioral engagement. As cited in [9], "behavioral engagement refers to effort and persistence, with an emphasis on the amount or quantity of engagement rather than its quality" (p. 266). In our research, we operationalized behavioral engagement in two student states: Being *On-Task* vs. *Off-Task*. The definition of this binary problem was well-framed in [10]: *Off-Task* state refers to "...any behavior that does not involve the learning task or material, or where learning from the material is not the primary goal". The definition of the *On-Task* state is just the opposite.

Majority of the current ITSs report behavioral engagement states of students solely based on content platform logs. However, in [11], it is clearly articulated that nonverbal behaviors such as posture and gesture are important cues to understand student states. Therefore, approaches solely relying on logs fail to capture the real picture of students' behavioral engagement. To exemplify, a student can play an instructional video on the computing device while casually conversing with her peers at the same time. Systems relying only on platform logs would report the state of this student as *On-Task* since the video is playing on her device. However, the student is *Off-Task* in reality as a casual conversation between the students is taking place. In this scenario, an investigation of students' body language (e.g., where the student's gaze is focused on, how the body is positioned, whether the student is in front of the computer and looking at the screen etc.) using a camera would give the accurate state of the student. Similarly, in another scenario, the student may be watching a video but it may not be an instructional one. Relying purely on the appearance data in this scenario would also be misleading. Therefore, as also suggested in [12], both context and appearance cues are important to accurately understand different dimensions of students' states.

In the related literature, a number of researchers have investigated students' *On-Task* and *Off-Task* states in 1:1 digital learning. In some studies [13–16], only context and performance logs of a content platform were incorporated; while in others, multi-modal approaches were investigated [2, 5, 6, 17]. Inherently, there are some challenges in both of these approaches. First, once features from a specific content platform are used, the solution becomes irrelevant to other platforms. Moreover, the features defined over the platform's functions could be identical even when the student is not actively using it (e.g., when the student is looking elsewhere). Second, although complex multi-modal systems (e.g., using a specialized chair, leveraging BCI as a modality etc.) can be useful for improving model accuracy, they have many limitations for using in real-world scenarios. These limitations can be both technical (e.g., time synchronization of different types of data) and practical (e.g., it would not be feasible and scalable to collect data from such complex modalities in a real classroom setting).

We believe our novel approach towards understanding behavioral engagement in our research makes the problem still addressable while benefiting from multi-modality in a simple scalable way: A camera and the uniform resource locator (URL) logs. Towards this end, we aim to address the following major research questions: What level of behavioral engagement detection performance can we reach by using a simple and scalable multi-modal approach (i.e., camera and URL logs)? How would this performance change when considering cross-platforms or cross-subjects?

2   Methodology

In this paper, we propose a two-phased system that can detect a student's behavioral engagement (*On-Task/Off-Task*) in a learning activity by incorporating both contextual and visual cues. The overall scheme for the proposed behavioral engagement classifier is given in Fig. 1. As illustrated in the figure, data from two modalities are collected: (1) Contextual information from the device, and (2) upper-body appearance information from the camera. First of all, contextual information (in the form of URL logs) is processed to assess whether the student is actively using the content platform (Phase 1). If not, then the system detects the student's state as *Off-Task*. If content platform is active in learner's device, then the appearance information is utilized to understand whether the student is really consuming the content (Phase 2). For the appearance modality, we trained supervised classifiers for the two-class behavioral engagement problem. Further details of the proposed detection system are provided in the following sub-sections.

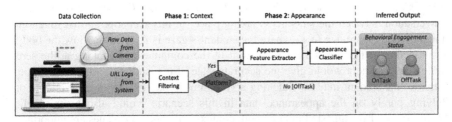

Fig. 1. Overview of two-phased behavioral engagement classification scheme

Data Collection and Modalities

As discussed above, we collected contextual data in addition to the appearance data: Each student used a personal computing device equipped with a 3D camera to individually study on the content platforms. The content was provided by a content platform (Math or English as a Second Language (ESL)), in the form of two section types of *Instructional* (where the students watched instructional videos or read instructional articles) and *Assessment* (where the students solved related questions). To enable applicability to any content platform, we did not employ platform specific information in the system. The content was carefully designed together with the course teachers. In order to diversify the content, we incorporated both easy and difficult content.

For feature extraction of the appearance modality, we utilized a window size of 8-seconds, as in [18] it was empirically defined as suitable for engagement detection. Moreover, we used a sliding window with an overlap of 4-seconds, considering the continuous nature of the video information. Therefore, the frame-wise raw appearance data are segmented into instances (i.e., 8-second windows) and related features are extracted for each instance. For consistency, the context logs are also processed to yield instance-wise contextual information.

Phase 1: Context-Based Behavioral Engagement Filtering

In order to apply context-based information filtering in Phase 1, our data collection application launches the content platform on each student's device, and it monitors the student activity by collecting active URL logs of the foreground application (i.e., the content platform or the web browser). At the start of each session, the students have been informed about their responsibilities to stay within the provided content platform. Based on the platform used, we have a pre-defined structure and possible tags within the URLs: The content platform is given in the *domain name* of URL, whereas the *path* of the URL identifies the subject area (e.g., Math) of lectures the student should be attending. If the currently active URL log of a student does not match with this pre-defined structure and tags, we identify that the student is not following the content. If the student is detected to be *Off-Platform*, then the system predicts the behavioral engagement state of a student to be *Off-Task*. On the contrary, if the student is detected to be *On-Platform*, the system does not immediately assume the behavioral state of the student as *On-Task*, since being on the content platform does not necessarily indicate active involvement with the learning material. As a result, our system transfers those *On-Platform* samples as inputs to the next phase, namely the appearance phase.

Phase 2: Appearance-Based Behavioral Engagement Modeling

For incorporating appearance-based information into behavioral engagement detection, the videos of students were recorded with a 3D camera (i.e., Intel® RealSense™ F200 Camera). The visual data captured included both the RGB and the depth streams of the students' upper body and face. The frame-wise raw data are fed into the camera's SDK (i.e., Intel® RealSense™ SDK [19]), yielding face location, head position and pose, 78 facial landmark localizations, 22 facial expressions, and seven basic facial emotions. In order to inject temporal information into the model, these frame-wise features are then employed in the extraction of *instance-wise* features. For instance-wise feature extraction, conventional time series analysis methods were applied. These are robust statistical estimators (e.g. tri-mean of head velocity), motion and energy measures (e.g. trend of pose energy) and frequency domain features related to head position, pose, facial expressions, and seven basic emotions. In Table 1, groups of instance-wise appearance features are provided to exemplify the utilized feature sets.

Table 1. Instance-wise appearance feature groups

Feature groups (Counts)	Examples
Head position/pose (128)	Max of head acceleration, quartiles of head yaw, etc.
Facial expressions (32)	Eyebrow lowering counts per segment, std. dev. of smile, etc.
Seven basic emotions (28)	Max intensity of sadness, number of joyful segments etc.

As seen in Fig. 1, the extracted instance-wise appearance features are fed into the appearance classifier. For the appearance modality, we employed Random Forest classification method [20], where a multiple number of decision trees are trained using random sets of labeled training data. During testing phase, each tree provides a prediction for the test sample, and the multiple predictions are processed by majority voting to generate a final decision. In our experiments, we trained random forests with

100 trees. Initially, we constructed train and test subsets for each student by randomly dividing that subject's data into 80% (for training) and 20% (for testing) parts, keeping the class distributions as in the original subjective set. Moreover, to handle the data imbalance, we applied 10-fold random selection and reported results averaged over 10-folds. When necessary, we applied leave-one-subject-out to separate training and test subjects.

3 Experiments and Results

Dataset
We ran authentic classroom pilots with 9th grade students (of ages 14–15) in a high school. The pilots were scheduled to run throughout a school semester as part of the curriculum, where we collected data from volunteering students. Each student retrieved the content by using a personal computing device equipped with a 3D camera, allowing us to capture the upper body appearance information, and the contextual data in the form of URL logs. The pilot sessions were organized as two subsequent sessions of 40 min each week (80 min per week). During the pilot sessions, two different class-rooms (i.e., student sets with different overall class profiles) attended the pilot sessions, and one classroom used two different content platforms (Math and ESL). In Math, students watched instructional videos (*Instructional* sections) and solved related questions (*Assessment* sections). In ESL, students read English articles (*Instructional* sections) and answered related questions (*Assessment* sections). Although our proposed behavioral engagement classifier does not employ any information specific to the content platform, we gathered section type information (*Instructional* or *Assessment*) for experimental purposes: We assessed whether the student behavior differs and whether it is beneficial to utilize this information in our system. The distribution of pilot sessions for each classroom and each content platform are summarized in Table 2.

For training supervised models and evaluating the detection performance of our system, it was necessary to obtain ground truth labels for the collected data. For data annotation, we utilized the Human Expert Labeling Process (HELP) [21]: As suggested in HELP, we employed three labelers with expertise on Education or Educational Psychology (i.e., at least a bachelor's degree), who defined segments based on observed state changes and provided *On-Task/Off-Task* labels for each recording. In addition, the labeling tool enabled the labelers to annotate instances as *N/A* (student is not visible, or the session has not started/is over) or *Can't-Decide* (the labeler cannot decide on the behavioral engagement). As explained in HELP, the labelers were given access to both RGB video streams and desktop recordings of the students. To improve the accuracy of labeling, recorded audio data and mouse cursor locations were provided as well. The labeling tool also displays the contextual logs from the content platform (i.e., section types: *Instructional* or *Assessment*), if available. Since the labelers had access to the screen recordings, they were able to interpret the contextual information related to URL logs indirectly when giving labels. As a result, the labelers annotated the whole recordings of students using all available cues. Prior to labeling, training about the process and the tool were given, and example data were shown to the labelers to provide a better understanding of the task. However, no limiting rules were defined (e.g., fist on cheek means boredom), since the annotation process is a very subjective task and we expected them to infer labels just as a teacher would do in a classroom setting.

For model training and testing, the labeling data provided by each labeler were processed and divided into instance-wise labels: For each 8-second window (with an overlap of 4-seconds), a behavioral label was obtained for each labeler. To assess inter-rater agreement measures, we computed Krippendorff's alpha [22] over three labelers for the four labels (i.e., *On-Task, Off-Task, N/A, Can't-Decide*). The inter-rater agreement measures for different combinations of students and content platforms are summarized in the last column of Table 2. As these high inter-rater agreement measures indicate, behavioral engagement can be considered as an objective annotation problem.

Table 2. Summary of pilot sessions

Set name	Classroom ID	Student count	Subject area	Session count	Hours of data	Inter-rater agreement
Set1	1	17	Math	13	113	0.820
Set2	2	11	Math	6	29	0.860
Set3	1	17	ESL	3	29	0.896

The final ground truth labels for each instance were obtained by applying majority voting. Validity filtering [21] was applied to discard any instance with no majority vote. The behavioral engagement label distributions for different sets (different combinations of student set and content platform, as given in Table 2) are illustrated in Fig. 2. As these distributions indicate, students are *On-Task* for a high percentage of the time, and this holds true even for different classrooms and different subject areas.

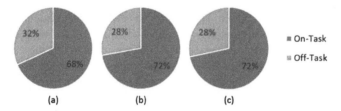

Fig. 2. Behavioral engagement distribution for different combinations of student set and content platform: (a) Set1, (b) Set2, (c) Set3

Context-Based Behavioral Engagement Filtering Results

As explained in detail in Sect. 2, we developed a rule-based detector using the collected URL logs data in the contextual phase (i.e. Phase 1) that has two possible outputs: (1) *Off-Platform* samples, where a student is predicted to be in *Off-Task* state; (2) *On-Platform* samples, where a student can be in *On-Task* or *Off-Task* states which will be detected by the appearance classifier in Phase 2. In this section, we summarize the results of our rule-based contextual model based on URL filtering.

The total number of samples (i.e., instances of 8-s length) identified as *On-Platform* and *Off-Platform* in Phase 1 are summarized for each dataset in Table 3, together with the ground-truth distribution of *On-Task* and *Off-Task* samples. As can be seen in Table 3, only 3% and 5% of the total instances are found to be *Off-Platform* samples by URL log filtering in Set1 and Set2 datasets, respectively. This indicates that most of the time, the students were on the content platform based on their URL logs.

Table 3. Distribution of On/Off-Platform samples detected in Phase 1

Dataset	Ground-truth class	Off-Platform samples	On-Platform samples
Set1	On-Task	64	35663
	Off-Task	1501	16581
	OVERALL	1565	52244
Set2	On-Task	2	11033
	Off-Task	770	4246
	OVERALL	772	15279

Note that in Table 3, there are very few *Off-Platform* samples with ground truth values as *On-Task*. These outlier cases are reflecting very rare situations in which the student is not on the content platform but, for instance, watching a Math-related video on an alternative platform (i.e. YouTube). These limited samples are interpreted as *On-Task* by the labelers, but our rule-based approach predicts *Off-Task* for all *Off-Platform* samples. Since we cannot detect those samples as *On-Task* with rule-based URL filtering, we achieved an overall performance of 97% on *Off-Platform* samples. On the contrary, when we examine the *On-Task* and *Off-Task* class distributions within the *On-Platform* samples, we observe that both states are highly possible. As a result, instead of a rule-based approach, an appearance classifier is necessary to detect *On-Task* and *Off-Task* states for the *On-Platform* samples.

In Table 4, we summarized the F1-scores of our rule-based detector on the *Off-Platform* samples of each dataset. The results indicate that our assumption holds true for most of the *Off-Platform* samples and we have an overall F1-score of 95.9% and 99.7% for Set1 and Set2 datasets, respectively. When we combine these two datasets, we obtain an overall F1-score of 97.2% for our contextual modality in Phase 1. Note that we report F1-score as it incorporates the trade-off between precision and recall.

Table 4. Performance of rule-based URL filtering approach in Phase 1

Ground-truth class	F1-score (%)	
	Set1 (Off-Platform Samples)	Set2 (Off-Platform Samples)
On-Task	0	0
Off-Task	97.91	99.87
OVERALL	95.91	99.74

Appearance-Based Behavioral Engagement Modeling Results

As detailed in Sect. 2, the samples that are detected as *On-Platform* are fed into Phase 2, where appearance-based behavioral engagement classifiers are implemented. For classification, we employed random forests, and for experiments including same classrooms (i.e. student sets) in both training and testing, leave-one-subject-out method is utilized to obtain person-independent (i.e. generic) accuracies. In this section, the classification results are summarized.

First, we investigated the effect of training separate models for different section types (i.e., *Instructional* and *Assessment*) and compared them to a *Single* model. The results of models trained and tested on Set1 are reported in Table 5, where average training set sizes[1], total test set sizes, and the average F1-scores are reported for different models. As these results indicate, for *Assessment* sections, the Off-Task detection rate is slightly lowered. However, this decrease is also related to the limited training set. Considering the overall results, we can say that different sectional models do not yield any prominent improvement over the *Single* one. Therefore, in our further experiments, we utilized the *Single* model approach.

Table 5. Appearance-based behavioral engagement results on Set1

Class	Average train counts			Test counts			F1 (%)		
	Instr	Asses	Single	Instr	Asses	Single	Instr	Asses	Single
On-Task	7128	5360	12488	2979	4148	7127	78.97	84.34	82.21
Off-Task	7128	5360	12488	1896	1417	3313	70.97	65.52	68.77
OVERALL	14256	10720	24976	4875	5565	10440	75.61	78.46	77.33

In order to assess the applicability of our generic behavioral engagement models on a separate classroom, the models trained on data collected in one classroom (Set1) are tested on data collected in the other classroom (Set2). Moreover, we experimented with an augmented set, where we merged the sets of the two classrooms. The results are summarized in Table 6: Considering different classrooms for training and testing resulted in a slight decrease (6%) for the *Off-Task* detection. However, by augmenting the data sets, the *Off-Task* accuracies are improved (by 4.5%).

Table 6. Appearance-based behavioral engagement results for cross-classroom experiments

Train set	Test set	Class	Average train counts	Test counts	F1 (%)
Set1	Set2	On-Task	13268	2210	83.37
		Off-Task	13268	843	62.82
		OVERALL	26536	3053	77.02
Set1 + Set2	Set1 + Set2	On-Task	16076	9337	82.39
		Off-Task	16076	4156	67.42
		OVERALL	32152	13493	77.14

---

[1] Training set sizes differ for each student, as leave-one-subject-out approach is utilized in model training.

Next, we investigated the performance of our appearance-based models on a cross-platform setting, where for training and test sets, different content platforms and subject areas (Math or ESL) are utilized. In this experiment, we trained our appearance classifiers on the datasets where the students were learning Math by watching videos and solving questions, and then tested this appearance model on another dataset where the students were reading English articles and answering questions. The aim was to observe how these changes could affect our system due to the possible behavioral changes (e.g. head movement can be more expectable for the watching, than for the reading). The results are given in Table 7: As changing subject areas can result in behavioral changes (which is visible in the 8% decrease in *Off-Task* accuracies), the promising overall F1-score (∼ 72%) shows the reliable cross-platform applicability of our models.

Table 7. Appearance-based behavioral engagement results for cross-platform experiments

Train set	Test set	Class	Average train counts	Test counts	F1 (%)
Set1 + Set2 (Math)	Set3 (ESL)	On-Task	15891	7575	78.50
		Off-Task	15891	3078	59.30
		OVERALL	31782	10653	71.86

Note that for our appearance modality, the F1-scores of *Off-Task* class are not as good as that of *On-Task*. This indicates that our models cannot cover all possible *Off-Task* scenarios with the extracted appearance features. Visual inspection showed us that we had ill-tracked samples (i.e., successful face detection but wrong face alignment/landmark localization) which were feeding into our classifiers. A substantial set of these samples are labeled as *Off-Task* (i.e., when the student is turning his head right/left with more than certain angle), thus affecting the detection performance of this class.

Overall Behavioral Engagement Results

In this section, the overall system performance results of proposed two-phased behavioral engagement detection are summarized. To obtain the overall F1-scores, *Off-Platform* samples from Phase 1 and the test partition of *On-Platform* samples from Phase 2 are merged. In Table 8, we compare our appearance classifier with the two-phased system to elaborate the benefits of using the context information.

As observed in Table 8, using the two-phased approach and incorporating contextual information even in its simplest form of URL logs is rewarding for the overall system performance in all cases. When we train and test our system on Set1, the F1-score of *Off-Task* was around 69% with appearance classifier and it reaches 77% by incorporating the contextual cues. The overall F1-score is improved from 77% to 80% in this case. When we examine the cross-classroom results (i.e., training on Set1 and testing on Set2), the F1-score of *Off-Task* is improved by 16%, from 63% to 79% with our two-phased approach. The overall F1-score is increased from 77% to 82% for that case. The difference between improvements obtained on Set1 and Set2 stems from the fact that, the number of test samples for *Off-Task* is increased more significantly in Set2 than in Set1 when we use both modalities. Since our contextual phase has a very high performance for the *Off-Task*, the overall system accuracy will further increase if the students become more *Off-Platform*. Finally, when we merge these two classroom datasets, we observe that the F1-score of *Off-Task* increases to 78% from 67%, and the overall F1-score reaches to approximately 80% from 77% using the two-phased model and the appearance model, respectively. We believe that the level of overall systems performance achieved is good enough, since we computed the expected accuracy by chance to be 0.48, observed accuracy (i.e., average recall) to be 0.77, and Cohen's Kappa to be 0.55 for the final models. Note that for Set3 (using a different content platform), the system did not allow the user to leave content. Since there were no *Off-Platform* instances, Set3 was not considered in the overall performance experiments.

Table 8. Overall system performance of two-phased behavioral engagement

Train set	Test set	Class	Appearance			Context + Appearance	
			Average train counts	Test counts	F1 (%)	Test counts	F1 (%)
Set1	Set1	On-Task	12488	7127	82.21	7191	81.82
		Off-Task	12488	3313	68.77	4814	77.16
		OVERALL	24976	10440	77.33	12005	79.75
Set1	Set2	On-Task	13268	2210	83.37	2212	83.33
		Off-Task	13268	843	62.82	1613	79.48
		OVERALL	26536	3053	77.02	3825	81.61
Set1 + Set2	Set1 + Set2	On-Task	16076	9337	82.39	9403	82.08
		Off-Task	16076	4156	67.42	6427	77.61
		OVERALL	32152	13493	77.14	15830	80.09

4   Conclusion and Future Directions

In this paper, we investigated automatic detection of students' behavioral engagement, where the aim is to classify between two states of *On-Task* or *Off-Task*. We proposed a two-phased detection system incorporating both visual and contextual cues. We ran experiments to assess two different test cases: (1) Cross-classroom, to assess how the trained models would perform when tested on a different student profile; (2) Cross-platform, to understand how the appearance models would perform if tested for a different subject area. For the first case, although there is a small performance decrease for the *Off-Task*, the overall accuracy is not affected. For the second scenario, the performance decrease is more evident for the *Off-Task*, as we would expect a behavior change with the learning activity. When the contextual data in the form of URL logs are incorporated, we obtain around 3–5% improvement in overall performance. We expect this improvement to be higher, if the students are not constrained to stay within the content platform during the data acquisition process.

The results showed that the behavioral engagement of students in 1:1 learning scenarios can be detected with generic models, yielding acceptable accuracies. As future work, expanding the student diversity in terms of age groups, and ethnicities provides opportunities for generalizing our existing models. Furthermore, analyzing the engagement patterns and detection performances on different individual characteristics (e.g., gender, highly performing, self-aware, introvert, extravert, etc.) would be useful when constructing a generic and robust classifier.

References

1. Madden, M., Lenhart, A., Duggan, M., Cortesi, S., Gasser, U.: Teens and Technology. Pew Internet & American Life Project, Washington, DC (2013)
2. Woolf, B., Burleson, W., Arroyo, I., Dragon, T., Cooper, D., Picard, R.: Affect-aware tutors: recognising and responding to student affect. Int. J. Learn. Technol. 4(3–4), 129–164 (2009)
3. D'Mello, S., Olney, A., Williams, C., Hays, P.: Gaze tutor: a gaze-reactive intelligent tutoring system. Int. J. Hum. Comput. Stud. 70(5), 377–398 (2012)
4. Fredricks, J.A., Blumenfeld, P.C., Paris, A.H.: School engagement: potential of the concept, state of the evidence. Rev. Educ. Res. 74(1), 59–109 (2004)
5. Bosch, N., D'Mello, S., Baker, R., Ocumpaugh, J., Shute, V., Ventura, M., Wang, L., Zhao, W.: Automatic detection of learning-centered affective states in the wild. In: International Conference on Intelligent User Interfaces (2015)
6. Chen, J., Luo, N., Liu, Y., Liu, L., Zhang, K., Kolodziej, J.: A hybrid intelligence-aided approach to affect-sensitive e-learning. Computing 98(1–2), 215–233 (2016)
7. Alyuz, N., Okur, E., Oktay, E., Genc, U., Aslan, S., Mete, S.E., Stanhill, D., Arnrich, B., Esme, A.A.: Towards an emotional engagement model: can affective states of a learner be automatically detected in a 1:1 learning scenario. In: International Conference on User Modeling, Adaptation, and Personalization - Workshop on Personalization Approaches in Learning Environments (2016)
8. Alyuz, N., Okur, E., Oktay, E., Genc, U., Aslan, S., Mete, S.E., Arnrich, B., Esme, A.A.: Semi-supervised model personalization for improved detection of learner's emotional engagement. In: International Conference on Multimodal Interaction (2016)
9. Reinhard Pekrun, L.L.-G.: Academic emotions and student engagement. In: Handbook of Research on Student Engagement, pp. 259–282. Springer, New York (2012)
10. Rodrigo, M.M.T., Baker, R.S.J.D., Rossi, L.: Student off-task behavior in computer-based learning in the Philippines: comparison to prior research in the USA. Teachers Coll. Rec. 115(10), 1–27 (2013)
11. Grafsgaard, J.F., Wiggins, J.B., Boyer, K.E., Wiebe, E.N., Lester, J.C.: Embodied affect in tutorial dialogue: student gesture and posture. In: International Conference on Artificial Intelligence in Education (2013)
12. Paquette, L., Rowe, J., Baker, R., Mott, B., Lester, J., DeFalco, J., Brawner, K., Sottilare, R., Georgoulas, V.: Sensor-free or sensor-full: a comparison of data modalities in multi-channel affect detection. In: International Conference on Educational Data Mining (2015)
13. Miller, W.L., Baker, R.S., Labrum, M.J., Petsche, K., Liu, Y.H., Wagner, A.Z.: Automated detection of proactive remediation by teachers in Reasoning Mind classrooms. In: International Conference on Learning Analytics and Knowledge (2015)
14. Fancsali, S.E.: Data-Driven causal modeling of "gaming the system" and off-task behavior in cognitive tutor algebra. In: NIPS Workshop on Data Driven Education (2013)
15. Gobert, J.D., Baker, R.S., Wixon, M.B.: Operationalizing and detecting disengagement within online science microworlds. Educ. Psychol. 50(1), 43–57 (2015)

16. Mohammadi-Aragh, M.J., Williams, C.B.: Student attention in unstructured-use, computer-infused classrooms. In: American Society of Engineering Education Annual Conference (2013)
17. Su, Y.N., Hsu, C.C., Chen, H.C., Huang, K.K., Huang, Y.M.: Developing a sensor-based learning concentration detection system. Eng. Comput. **31**(2), 216–230 (2014)
18. Aslan, S., Cataltepe, Z., Diner, I., Dundar, O., Esme, A.A., Ferens, R., Kamhi, G., Oktay, E., Soysal, C., Yener, M.: Learner engagement measurement and classification in 1:1 learning. In: International Conference on Machine Learning and Applications (2014)
19. Intel Corporation: Intel RealSense SDK: Design Guidelines (2014). https://software.intel.com/sites/default/files/managed/27/50/Intel%20RealSense%20SDK%20Design%20Guidelines%20F200%20v2.pdf. Accessed 2016
20. Chen, C., Liaw, A., Breiman, L.: Using Random Forest to Learn Imbalanced Data. University of California, Berkeley (2004)
21. Aslan, S., Mete, S.E., Okur, E., Oktay, E., Alyuz, N., Genc, U., Stanhill, D., Esme, A.A.: Human expert labeling process (HELP): towards a reliable higher-order user state labeling by human experts. In: International Conference on Intelligent Tutoring Systems - Workshops (2016)
22. Krippendorff, K.: Reliability in content analysis. Hum. Commun. Res. **30**(3), 411–433 (2004)

Improving Reading Comprehension with Automatically Generated Cloze Item Practice

Andrew M. Olney[✉], Philip I. Pavlik Jr., and Jaclyn K. Maass

University of Memphis, Memphis, TN 38152, USA
{aolney,ppavlik,jkmaass}@memphis.edu

Abstract. This study investigated the effect of cloze item practice on reading comprehension, where cloze items were either created by humans, by machine using natural language processing techniques, or randomly. Participants from Amazon Mechanical Turk ($N = 302$) took a pre-test, read a text, and took part in one of five conditions, Do-Nothing, Re-Read, Human Cloze, Machine Cloze, or Random Cloze, followed by a 24-hour retention interval and post-test. Participants used the MoFaCTS system [27], which in cloze conditions presented items adaptively based on individual success with each item. Analysis revealed that only Machine Cloze was significantly higher than the Do-Nothing condition on post-test, $d = .58$, $CI_{95}[.21, .94]$. Additionally, Machine Cloze was significantly higher than Human and Random Cloze conditions on post-test, $d = .49$, $CI_{95}[.12, .86]$ and $d = .71$, $CI_{95}[.34, 1.09]$ respectively. These results suggest that Machine Cloze items generated using natural language processing techniques are effective for enhancing reading comprehension when delivered by an adaptive practice scheduling system.

Keywords: Reading comprehension · Natural language processing · Testing effect

1 Introduction

Reading has long been one of the preeminent means of learning new information. Reading to learn necessarily involves comprehension, the process by which information in the text is reconciled with prior knowledge. Theorists differ on the precise mechanisms underlying the role of prior knowledge in reading comprehension, though there is considerable overlap across theories [19]. The differences that exist between theories may be partly attributable to differing ideas about how knowledge is represented and applied. Experimental results, however, have broadly found that prior knowledge exhibits a strong positive effect on reading comprehension [1,3,15]. Prior knowledge also moderates the effect of reading ability on comprehension. When prior knowledge is high, the effect of reading ability on comprehension vanishes [28]. Prior knowledge also influences whether reading ability interacts with text difficulty to influence comprehension [26].

© Springer International Publishing AG 2017
E. André et al. (Eds.): AIED 2017, LNAI 10331, pp. 262–273, 2017.
DOI: 10.1007/978-3-319-61425-0_22

Altogether the evidence suggests that prior knowledge has a central role, if not the central role, in reading comprehension.

If reading to learn requires prior knowledge, but the goal of reading to learn is to acquire new knowledge, then it seems there is a kind of circular causality between knowledge and reading. In educational practice, this relationship becomes apparent when the curricular focus shifts from the mechanics of reading, i.e. decoding fluency, to content area reading with the emphasis on learning from text. This shift is often marked by a sudden drop in reading scores, particularly in students from low income families [5]. Long referred to as the "fourth-grade slump," evidence now suggests that the disparity between learning to read and reading to learn starts much earlier but becomes apparent as tasks and assessments shift from narrative to informational, content-area reading [9,21]. Unfortunately, the fourth-grade slump neither begins in fourth grade, nor does it end there. Rather, the evidence suggests that early differences in reading skill widen over time. Those with high reading comprehension skill read more and become more skilled by practice, a positive-feedback loop [20]. Those with low reading comprehension skill read less, and their slowness in decoding delays identification of words by sight, which delays vocabulary growth, which in turn diminishes comprehension [30].

The importance of reading to learn has led to calls for interventions that embed comprehension activities in the learning of content areas [23]. The advantage of targeting comprehension in content areas is that, in addition to teleological prior knowledge [28], content areas typically have their own specialized vocabulary and style distinct from narrative and informal conversation, making normal mechanisms for acquiring vocabulary and grammar, like implicit learning, less efficient because of children's reduced exposure to content-area text [7,22]. Vocabulary and comprehension are deeply intertwined because text must be decoded, disambiguated, and linked with prior knowledge for comprehension to occur [12]. Multiple studies investigating the impact of unknown words on comprehension suggest that the number of unknown words should be no lower than 1 in 20 if serious comprehension deficits are to be avoided [13], which is roughly less than one unknown word per sentence.

Reading comprehension activities in educational contexts typically center around the instruction and practice of reading strategies. The definition of strategy is wide ranging and can include activities that occur before, during, or after reading of the text. Moreover, the strategies can be covert, artifact-producing, or interactive. For example, of the seven comprehension strategies recommended by the National Reading Panel (NRP) [23], comprehension monitoring and question generation are covert and occur during reading, graphic organizers and summarization are artifact producing and occur after reading, and cooperative learning, question answering, and reciprocal teaching are interactive and occur during reading. Arguably, activities that occur after reading, or tasks that are interactive, fall more into the realm of instructional activities than comprehension strategies. Nevertheless, such activities can be highly effective for increasing comprehension of text. One possible explanation for the effectiveness of these activities is the ICAP Hypothesis [6], which predicts that learning outcomes will follow the order *interactive > constructive > active > passive* because of the cognitive processes required by interactive, constructive, active, and passive activities. Of the NRP comprehension activities, all but monitoring are either constructive or interactive in nature, meaning that they require generating outputs or co-generating outputs, respectively.

Although interactive educational technologies have been developed, most notably in dialogue-based intelligent tutoring systems (ITS) [24], these systems currently have two weaknesses with respect to reading comprehension. First, these systems are primarily content-oriented rather than reading-oriented, meaning that students using the ITS may not do any particular reading during the learning process (though see [14] for a counterexample). Secondly, ITS content must be authored manually, and it is commonly believed that it takes several hundred hours of authoring effort to create one hour of instruction for an ITS using traditional methods [2], though research is beginning to make progress in automated authoring [25]. Because of authoring needs and challenges, it is not currently possible to automatically create a high-quality, interactive ITS for a given piece of text on demand. Accordingly, there are two options for educational technology. First, one could focus on interactive strategy training divorced from content with the aim of strategy transfer to other texts [18]. This is a worthwhile strategy but it does not directly support comprehension of an arbitrary piece of text. Secondly, one could step back from interactive activities and instead focus on constructive activities, which is the focus of the present work.

This paper investigates an automated method for generating cloze items and the effect of practice with these items on reading comprehension. In a cloze task, a participant is asked to restore words that have been deleted from a text. Cloze tasks are well established for both vocabulary and comprehension instruction in addition to vocabulary and comprehension assessment [7,17,23]. Additionally, according to the ICAP theory, practice with cloze items is constructive because students must generate fill-in-the-blank answers, and constructive activities facilitate transfer of learning to novel contexts. In this work our primary research questions are therefore (1) whether practice with machine generated cloze items promotes reading comprehension, (2) whether reading comprehension with machine generated cloze items is equivalent to reading comprehension with human generated or random cloze items, and (3) whether reading comprehension supported by machine cloze practice supports transfer.

2   Method

2.1   Design

This study used a between-subjects design with the following conditions: Do-Nothing, Re-Read, Human Cloze, Machine Cloze, and Random Cloze conditions. All participants took pre-tests and read a text before being assigned to one of the conditions. Therefore, the Do-Nothing condition participants did nothing beyond the pre-test and reading. The Do-Nothing condition can be considered a business as usual control condition, the Re-Read a stronger control condition where reading time is consistent with practice time in the cloze conditions, and Random Cloze another control condition where cloze practice occurs but items may not be optimal. All participants also took a post-test after a 24-hour delay. Test items with simple declarative answers, or *fact* questions, were concept-matched to test items with contextualized application questions, or *transfer* questions, such that a concept either appeared on the pre-test or on the post-test but not both. The purpose of concept matching was to eliminate the possibility that the pre-test cued participants on what to study for the post-test.

2.2   Participants

Participants were recruited through the Amazon Mechanical Turk (AMT) marketplace between September and November of 2016. In this study, participants were required to be English speakers from the U.S. or Canada and required to have completed at least 50 previous AMT tasks with at least a 95% approval rating. Experience/approval criteria were applied to prevent automated programs from attempting the experiment (i.e. "bots") and to ensure quality from human participants. Participants were paid $3 for the first phase of the experiment and $2 for the second phase following the 24-hour retention interval.

Age of participants in years was 18–25 (11%), 26–34 (45%), 35–54 (36%), 55–64 (6%), and over 65 (2%), and participants were slightly more female (52%) than male (47%). Educational attainment of participants included less than high school (<1%), high school (12%), some college (35%), bachelor's degree (43%), and graduate degree (9%). Over 95% of participants reported never having worked in a profession dealing with the circulatory system.

2.3   Materials

A text on the heart and circulatory system was derived from experimental materials used by [33], which used four versions of the text ranging from elementary school to medical school difficulty. The text used in the present study was derived from elementary school level text, with modifications primarily removing the extraneous information present in the original. Examples of removed sentences include motivational/interest statements like "You probably think you know what the heart looks like. But you may be wrong.", statements involving reader-oriented imagery like "You can feel the thumps if you press there with your hand. You can hear them with your ear.", and statements that are thematically relevant but not directly relevant to the functioning of the heart and circulatory system like "When a fire burns, carbon dioxide is formed." Both fact and transfer test items were created from the derived text by matching on a particular concept. For example, the *heart is a pump* concept has the associated fact question "Which component(s) of the circulatory system acts as a pump?" and the associated transfer question "Why doesn't oxygen rich blood flow directly from the lungs to the rest of the body?" A total of 16 concept clusters were created, each having one associated fact and transfer question for a total of 32 questions. All questions were in multiple-choice format.

Cloze items for the three cloze conditions were created either by human, randomly, or by machine using an algorithm described below. Human cloze items were created by the same researcher who derived the text and created the pre- and post-test items. The researcher selected, at their discretion, the sentences capturing the main ideas of the text and the words central to each selected sentence's meaning. The number of sentences (21) and words (53) selected by the human were then held constant in the random and machine generated cloze item conditions. Accordingly, all cloze conditions contained the same number of items, the items in each condition were generated from 21 sentences and 53 words within those sentences, but each condition differed in terms of which 21 sentences and 53 words were selected.

Random cloze items were created by randomly selecting 21 sentences from all sentences in the text and randomly selecting between one and four words in each sentence such that the words were longer than two characters, words did not include "the" or "and," and 53 words were selected in total. The random cloze generation procedure was repeated six times to create six sets of random cloze items, to minimize the chance the effects from this condition were due to an unusual random sample.

Machine generated cloze items were selected by using natural language processing techniques at the word, sentence, and discourse level. Specifically, the entire text was parsed using syntactic, semantic, and discourse parsers [10, 16, 29]. These parsers annotated the text with a variety of information, including part of speech, word form/lemma, named entities, syntactic dependencies, verbal and nominal predicates, argument roles, coreference chains, elementary discourse units, and discourse dependencies. Because no labeled data was available, we used applied intuition and linguistic knowledge to develop a relatively simple heuristic for the selection of sentences and words. Sentences were selected primarily based on the number of coreference chains they contained (at least three) and the length of those chains (at least two). These criteria ensured that only sentences that were well connected to the discourse were preserved. Alternatively these criteria can be considered as argument overlap where anaphora, e.g. pronouns, have been resolved to their referents (cf. [4, 31]). Once selected, sentences were filtered if they consisted of only satellite discourse units, i.e. discourse units that did not carry the core meaning of the discourse relationships in which they participated. Candidate cloze words for these sentences were selected based on whether the word was an argument in a coreference chain, a semantic argument, or a syntactic subject or object with a noun or modified noun part of speech. Final cloze words were chosen from candidates if they did not belong to the 1000 most frequent words of English. For example, in the heart and circulatory system text, excluded candidate words included "heart," "middle," "blood," and "body."

2.4 Procedure

The experiment was delivered through the web interface of the MoFaCTS system [27] to AMT participants. Participants completed informed consent and then took the pre-test. For each participant, 12 concept clusters were randomly selected from a test bank of 16 concept clusters. Four concepts were randomly assigned for pre-test, and eight concepts were randomly assigned for post-test. Since each concept had an associated fact and transfer question, the selection process yielded eight pre-test items and 16 post-test items. Order of items on each test was randomized. After the pre-test, participants read a text on the heart and circulatory system for at least 5 min and up to 10 min if they so chose. After reading the text, each participate completed one of five conditions: Do-Nothing, Re-Read, Human Cloze, Machine Cloze, or Random Cloze. Except for Do-Nothing, each of these conditions lasted from 5 min up to 25 min. Continuing longer than 5 min was purely by participant choice. The text presented in the Re-Read condition was the same as the original text. Participants in the three cloze conditions received items specific to their condition. However all items were adaptively sequenced using the MoFaCTS system based on the success history of each item and model parameters inferred from pilot experimentation. During the cloze conditions, cloze items were presented on the screen and participants were asked to fill in the missing word(s) with a 15 s timeout that was reset whenever the participant typed. After an incorrect response, the correct response was displayed for 8 s. Upon completing their condition, participants were paid for the first phase of the experiment. After a 24-hour retention interval, participants were contacted via email from MoFaCTS to complete the second phase. The second phase consisted of a post-test, consisting of items not selected on the pre-test, presented in random order. Following the post-test, participants completed a demographic survey and were paid for the second phase of the experiment.

3   Results and Discussion

Although 365 participants attempted the experiment, 13 were excluded for various reasons including using a friend's account, server crashes, and collection errors, and 50 were excluded because they did not return for the post-test, i.e. were lost to attrition ($N = 302$). Each condition had approximately the same attrition ($M = 11.6$, $SD = 1.64$), within the acceptable range for attrition and differential attrition for educational research [32]. No outliers were removed or transformed. None of the demographic variables collected (age, gender, educational attainment, professional knowledge of circulatory system) were significantly related to assigned condition under a chi-square test of independence. Table 1 shows the condition sample sizes and means, standard deviations, and 95% confidence intervals for pre- and post-test proportion correct.

Learning outcomes could not be analyzed as normalized gain scores, i.e. $(post - pre)/(1 - pre)$, because this value was undefined for some participants. The choice of analysis between ANOVA on gain scores and ANCOVA on post-test using pre-test as a covariate was informed by recent guidance suggesting that when, as in the present study, differences in pre-test between conditions are substantial, $d = .2$, and correlation between simple learning gains and pre-test

Table 1. Proportion correct

Group	n	Pre-test		Post-test	
		M (SD)	95% CI	M (SD)	95% CI
Do-Nothing	62	.46 (.23)	[.41, .52]	.54 (.20)	[.49, .59]
Re-Read	61	.46 (.19)	[.41, .51]	.57 (.23)	[.51, .63]
Random Cloze	58	.46 (.18)	[.41, .51]	.56 (.18)	[.51, .61]
Human Cloze	60	.51 (.18)	[.46, .55]	.61 (.21)	[.56, .67]
Machine Cloze	61	.50 (.20)	[.45, .55]	.67 (.22)	[.61, .73]

Note: CI = confidence interval.

is large, $r(300) = -.5$, ANOVA on gain scores is more likely to be biased than ANCOVA (see Table 5 of [11]). Therefore ANCOVA was adopted for all analyses. We conducted statistical tests at $\alpha = .05$ to address our research questions.

To answer our first research question, whether practice with machine generated cloze items promotes reading comprehension, we ran an ANCOVA with condition and pre-test proportion correct as predictors and post-test proportion correct as the dependent variable. The model controlled for differences in pre-test across participants so that differences in post-test can be attributed to condition. The ANCOVA revealed a significant main effect of condition, $F(4, 296) = 3.04$, $p = .02$, $\eta_p^2 = .04$, as well as a main effect of pre-test proportion correct, $F(1, 296) = 53.95$, $p < .001$, $\eta_p^2 = .15$. Post hoc comparisons between predicted marginal means using Tukey's HSD revealed that the Machine Cloze had significantly higher post-test proportion correct ($M = .66$, $SE = .03$) than the Do-Nothing condition ($M = .55$, $SE = .03$), $t(296) = 3.21$, $p = .01$, $d = .58$, $CI_{95}[.21, .94]$. No other pairwise comparisons were significant.

An additional exploratory analysis was performed to investigate whether other variables or interactions omitted from the ANCOVA might qualify or limit these results. An exploratory ANCOVA model with condition, text reading time (log transformed), pre-test proportion correct, and all interactions as predictors and post-test proportion correct as the dependent variable was created and refined using backward elimination variable selection based on the Akaike information criterion (AIC). The only significant predictors in the exploratory model were condition and pre-test proportion correct, which were the same predictors in the a priori model. Diagnostic plots revealed no concerning departures from normality, heterogeneity, or violations of independence, suggesting the model was well-fitted.

To answer our second research question, whether reading comprehension with machine generated cloze items is equivalent to reading comprehension with human generated or random cloze items, we ran an ANCOVA with the three cloze conditions, pre-test proportion correct, and variables controlling for the learning experience within the cloze conditions as predictors and post-test proportion correct as the dependent variable. The measured variables controlling for the learning experience within the cloze conditions included proportion correct across trials, number of trials, and time. Because time and number of trials were highly correlated, $r(176) = .94$, and number of trials (log transformed) was more normally distributed than time, trials was included in the model and time was not included. Furthermore, because the learning experience necessarily involves correctness over time, an interaction between number of trials and proportion correct across trials was included. Thus the model controlled for differences in pre-test scores, number of trials, proportion correct across trials, and the interaction of number of trials and proportion correct across trials so that differences in post-test can be attributed to condition.

The ANCOVA revealed a significant main effect of condition, $F(2, 171) = 7.89$, $p < .001$, $\eta_p^2 = .08$, a main effect of pre-test proportion correct, $F(1, 171) = 5.78$, $p = .02$, $\eta_p^2 = .03$, and a main effect of number of trials, $F(1, 171) = 9.80$, $p = .002$, $\eta_p^2 = .05$. A main effect of proportion correct across trials was not significant $F(1, 171) = 1.57$, $p = .21$, but the interaction of proportion correct across trials and the number of trials was significant, $F(1, 171) = 10.27$, $p = .002$, $\eta_p^2 = .06$. Examination of the interaction slope revealed that participants with low proportion correct across a high number of trials fared poorly on post-test proportion correct. Note that while only the main effect of condition was relevant to our hypothesis, the effects of condition, number of trials, and the interaction of the number of trials and proportion correct across trials are statistically significant with Bonferroni adjusted alpha levels of .01 per test ($\alpha = .05/5$). Post hoc comparisons between predicted marginal means using Tukey's HSD revealed that the Machine Cloze had significantly higher post-test proportion correct ($M = .66$, $SE = .02$) than the Human Cloze condition ($M = .58$, $SE = .02$), $t(171) = 2.69$, $p = .02$, $d = .49$, $CI_{95}[.12, .86]$ and significantly higher post-test proportion correct than the Random Cloze condition ($M = .54$, $SE = .02$), $t(171) = 3.88$, $p < .001$, $d = .71$, $CI_{95}[.34, 1.09]$.

An additional exploratory analysis was performed to investigate whether other variables or interactions omitted from the ANCOVA might qualify or limit these results. An exploratory ANCOVA model with condition, text reading time (log transformed), pre-test proportion correct, number of trials, proportion correct across trials, and all two-way interactions as predictors and post-test proportion correct as the dependent variable was created and refined using backward elimination variable selection based on the Akaike information criterion (AIC). The significant predictors in the exploratory model were identical to the a priori model except for the addition of a pre-test proportion correct by number of trials interaction, $F(1, 170) = 5.50$, $p = .02$, $\eta_p^2 = .03$. Examination of the interaction slope revealed that participants with low pre-test proportion correct who experienced a high number of trials fared better on post-test proportion correct while participants with high pre-test proportion correct who experience a high number of trials fared more poorly. Though this interaction is sensible, it should be treated with caution because it was obtained through variable selection [8]. The most useful finding of the exploratory ANCOVA is that it did not alter the significant effect of condition or contrasts found in the a priori ANCOVA. Diagnostic plots revealed no concerning departures from normality, heterogeneity, or violations of independence, suggesting the model was well-fitted.

To answer our final research question, whether reading comprehension with machine generated cloze items supports transfer, we re-ran ANCOVAs with test scores based on the transfer questions alone. An ANCOVA for transfer post-test proportion correct using condition and transfer pre-test proportion correct as predictors yielded virtually the same effects and contrasts as the ANCOVA for all test items. There was a significant main effect of condition, $F(4, 296) = 2.59$, $p = .04$, $\eta_p^2 = .03$, as well as a main effect of pre-test proportion correct, $F(1, 296) = 23.34$, $p < .001$, $\eta_p^2 = .07$. Post hoc comparisons between predicted marginal means using Tukey's HSD revealed that Machine Cloze had significantly higher transfer post-test proportion correct ($M = .61$, $SE = .03$) than the Do-Nothing condition ($M = .50$, $SE = .03$), $t(296) = 2.82$, $p = .04$, $d = .51$, $CI_{95}[.15, .87]$. No other pairwise comparisons were statistically significant. An ANCOVA for transfer post-test proportion correct using the three cloze conditions, pre-test proportion correct, number of trials, proportion correct across trials, and the interaction of number of trials and proportion correct as predictors also yielded virtually the same effects and contrasts as the ANCOVA for all test items. There was a significant main effect of condition, $F(2, 171) = 6.52$, $p = .002$, $\eta_p^2 = .07$, a main effect of pre-test proportion correct, $F(1, 171) = 3.98$, $p = .05$, $\eta_p^2 = .02$, and a main effect of number of trials, $F(1, 171) = 9.13$, $p = .003$, $\eta_p^2 = .05$. A main effect of proportion correct across trials was not significant $F(1, 171) = 0.56$, $p = .46$, but the interaction of proportion correct across trials and the number of trials was significant, $F(1, 171) = 7.45$, $p = .007$, $\eta_p^2 = .04$. Examination of the interaction slope revealed that participants with low proportion correct across a high number of trials fared poorly on post-test proportion correct. Post hoc comparisons between predicted marginal means using Tukey's HSD revealed that the Machine Cloze had significantly higher transfer post-test proportion correct ($M = .61$, $SE = .02$) than the Human Cloze condition ($M = .52$, $SE = .03$), $t(171) = 2.71$, $p = .02$, $d = .5$, $CI_{95}[.13, .86]$ and significantly higher transfer post-test proportion correct than the Random Cloze condition ($M = .49$, $SE = .03$), $t(171) = 3.42$, $p = .002$, $d = .63$, $CI_{95}[.26, 1.0]$.

Our main findings were that the Machine Cloze condition led to superior post-test outcomes relative to other conditions, including Human Cloze when learning experience variables are controlled for, and that these findings hold both overall and for a subset of pre- and post-test questions specifically targeting transfer. The causal mechanism behind the advantage for the Machine Cloze condition is currently unclear. An examination of the Human Cloze and Machine Cloze items revealed 13 sentences in common out of 21. Presumably differences in learning between the Human and Machine Cloze conditions are attributable to the items not shared and their interactions with the items in common. Recall that the primary features for selecting the Machine Cloze sentences were based on coreference chains. Sentences with more chains and with longer chains are more connected to the discourse by virtue of echoing or extending ideas present in other sentences. For the eight items not shared, the sum of Machine Cloze coreference lengths was 221 and the sum of Human Cloze coreference weights was

67, meaning that the Machine Cloze items were approximately three times more connected to the discourse than the Human Cloze items. Whether differences in coreference chains can explain differences in post-test performance is a matter for future research.

4 Conclusion

Results from the study suggest that cloze items generated by machine using natural language processing techniques are effective for enhancing reading comprehension when delivered by an adaptive practice scheduling system. Because such cloze items can be generated automatically, ostensibly for any text, our findings potentially have broad implications for improving reading comprehension in educational settings. An important limitation on these implications, however, is that these results were obtained for a single text only and in comparison to human-generated items by a single individual. It may be that the natural language processing techniques used were particularly suitable to this text and would not be as effective for other texts or that these techniques would not fare as well against items generated by a domain expert. Two important targets for future research are to replicate this finding with other texts in other domains and to better understand the properties of the machine generated cloze items that made them more effective than human generated cloze items.

Acknowledgements. This work was supported by the National Science Foundation Data Infrastructure Building Blocks program (NSF; ACI-1443068), by the Institute of Education Sciences (IES; R305C120001) and by the Office of Naval Research (ONR; N00014-00-1-0600, N00014-12-C-0643; N00014-16-C-3027). Any opinions, findings, and conclusions or recommendations expressed in this material are those of the authors and do not necessarily reflect the views of NSF, IES, or ONR.

References

1. Ahmed, Y., Francis, D.J., York, M., Fletcher, J.M., Barnes, M., Kulesz, P.: Validation of the direct and inferential mediation (DIME) model of reading comprehension in grades 7 through 12. Contemp. Educ. Psychol. **4445**, 68–82 (2016)
2. Aleven, V., Mclaren, B.M., Sewall, J., Koedinger, K.R.: A new paradigm for intelligent tutoring systems: example-tracing tutors. Int. J. Artif. Intell. Educ. **19**(2), 105–154 (2009)
3. Bransford, J.D., Johnson, M.K.: Contextual prerequisites for understanding: some investigations of comprehension and recall. J. Verbal Learn. Verbal Behav. **11**(6), 717–726 (1972)
4. Britton, B.K., Gülgöz, S.: Using Kintsch's computational model to improve instructional text: effects of repairing inference calls on recall and cognitive structures. J. Educ. Psychol. **83**(3), 329–345 (1991)
5. Chall, J.S., Jacobs, V.A.: Writing and reading in the elementary grades: developmental trends among low SES children. Lang. Arts **60**(5), 617–626 (1983). http://www.jstor.org/stable/41961511

6. Chi, M.T.H., Wylie, R.: The ICAP framework: linking cognitive engagement to active learning outcomes. Educ. Psychol. **49**(4), 219–243 (2014). http://dx.doi.org/10.1080/00461520.2014.965823

7. Fang, Z.: The language demands of science reading in middle school. Int. J. Sci. Educ. **28**(5), 491–520 (2006). http://dx.doi.org/10.1080/09500690500339092

8. Harrell, F.: Regression Modeling Strategies: With Applications to Linear Models, Logistic Regression, and Survival Analysis. Graduate Texts in Mathematics. Springer, New York (2001)

9. Hirsch, E.D.: Reading comprehension requires knowledge-of words and the world. Am. Educator **27**(1), 10–13, 16–22, 28–29, 48 (2003)

10. Johansson, R., Nugues, P.: Dependency-based syntactic-semantic analysis with PropBank and NomBank. In: Proceedings of the Twelfth Conference on Computational Natural Language Learning, CoNLL 2008, pp. 183–187. Association for Computational Linguistics, Morristown (2008)

11. Kelly, S., Ye, F.: Accounting for the relationship between initial status and growth in regression models. J. Exp. Educ. **85**(3), 353–375 (2017). http://dx.doi.org/10.1080/00220973.2016.1160357

12. Kintsch, W.: Comprehension: A Paradigm for Cognition. Cambridge University Press, Cambridge (1998)

13. Laufer, B.: Lexical thresholds for reading comprehension: what they are and how they can be used for teaching purposes. TESOL Q. **47**(4), 867–872 (2013). http://www.jstor.org/stable/43267941

14. Leelawong, K., Biswas, G.: Designing learning by teaching agents: the Betty's Brain system. Int. J. Artif. Intell. Educ. **18**(3), 181–208 (2008)

15. Lipson, M.Y.: Learning new information from text: the role of prior knowledge and reading ability. J. Read. Behav. **14**(3), 243–261 (1982)

16. Manning, C., Surdeanu, M., Bauer, J., Finkel, J., Bethard, S., McClosky, D.: The Stanford CoreNLP natural language processing toolkit. In: Proceedings of 52nd Annual Meeting of the Association for Computational Linguistics: System Demonstrations, pp. 55–60. Association for Computational Linguistics, Baltimore, June 2014. http://www.aclweb.org/anthology/pp.14-5010

17. McKeown, M.G., Beck, I.L., Omanson, R.C., Pople, M.T.: Some effects of the nature and frequency of vocabulary instruction on the knowledge and use of words. Read. Res. Q. **20**(5), 522–535 (1985). http://www.jstor.org/stable/747940

18. McNamara, D., Levinstein, I., Boonthum, C.: iSTART: interactive strategy training for active reading and thinking. Behav. Res. Methods **36**, 222–233 (2004). doi:10.3758/BF03195567

19. McNamara, D.S., Magliano, J.: Toward a comprehensive model of comprehension. In: The Psychology of Learning and Motivation, Psychology of Learning and Motivation, vol. 51, pp. 297–384. Academic Press (2009). https://www.sciencedirect.com/science/article/pii/S0079742109510092

20. Mol, S.E., Bus, A.G.: To read or not to read: a meta-analysis of print exposure from infancy to early adulthood. Psychol. Bull. **137**(2), 267–296 (2011)

21. Moss, B.: Making a case and a place for effective content area literacy instruction in the elementary grades. Read. Teach. **59**(1), 46–55 (2005). http://dx.doi.org/10.1598/RT.59.1.5

22. Nagy, W., Townsend, D.: Words as tools: learning academic vocabulary as language acquisition. Read. Res. Q. **47**(1), 91–108 (2012). http://dx.doi.org/10.1002/RRQ.011

23. National Institute of Child Health and Human Development: Report of the National Reading Panel. Teaching children to read: an evidence-based assessment of the scientific research literature on reading and its implications for reading instruction. NIH Publication No. 00-4769, U.S. Government Printing Office, Washington, DC (2000)

24. Nye, B.D., Graesser, A.C., Hu, X.: AutoTutor and family: a review of 17 years of natural language tutoring. Int. J. Artif. Intell. Educ. **24**(4), 427–469 (2014). http://dx.doi.org/10.1007/s40593-014-0029-5

25. Olney, A.M., Brawner, K., Pavlik, P., Koedinger, K.: Emerging trends in automated authoring. In: Sottilare, R., Graesser, A., Hu, X., Brawner, K. (eds.) Design Recommendations for Intelligent Tutoring Systems, Adaptive Tutoring, vol. 3, pp. 227–242. U.S. Army Research Laboratory, Orlando (2015)

26. Ozuru, Y., Dempsey, K., McNamara, D.S.: Prior knowledge, reading skill, and text cohesion in the comprehension of science texts. Learn. Instr. **19**(3), 228–242 (2009)

27. Pavlik, P.I., Kelly, C., Maass, J.K.: The mobile fact and concept training system (MoFaCTS). In: Micarelli, A., Stamper, J., Panourgia, K. (eds.) ITS 2016. LNCS, vol. 9684, pp. 247–253. Springer, Cham (2016). doi:10.1007/978-3-319-39583-8_25

28. Recht, D.R., Leslie, L.: Effect of prior knowledge on good and poor readers' memory of text. J. Educ. Psychol. **80**(1), 16–20 (1988)

29. Surdeanu, M., Hicks, T., Valenzuela-Escarcega, M.A.: Two practical rhetorical structure theory parsers. In: Proceedings of the 2015 Conference of the North American Chapter of the Association for Computational Linguistics: Demonstrations, pp. 1–5. Association for Computational Linguistics, Denver. http://www.aclweb.org/anthology/N15-3001

30. Torgesen, J.K.: Avoiding the devastating downward spiral: the evidence that early intervention prevents reading failure. Am. Educator **28**(3), 6–19 (2004)

31. Vidal-Abarca, E., Martínez, G., Gilabert, R.: Two procedures to improve instructional text: effects on memory and learning. J. Educ. Psychol. **92**(1), 107–116 (2000)

32. What Works Clearinghouse: Assessing attrition bias. Technical report, Institute of Eduation Sciences (2012). https://ies.ed.gov/ncee/wwc/Docs/ReferenceResources/wwc_attrition_v2.1.pdf

33. Wolfe, M.B., Schreiner, M., Rehder, B., Laham, D., Foltz, P.W., Kintsch, W., Landauer, T.K.: Learning from text: matching readers and texts by latent semantic analysis. Discourse Process. **25**(2–3), 309–336 (1998). http://dx.doi.org/10.1080/01638539809545030

Variations of Gaming Behaviors Across Populations of Students and Across Learning Environments

Luc Paquette[1(✉)] and Ryan S. Baker[2]

[1] University of Illinois at Urbana-Champaign, Champaign, IL, USA
lpaq@illinois.edu
[2] University of Pennsylvania, Philadelphia, PA, USA
rybanker@upenn.edu

Abstract. Although gaming the system, a behavior in which students attempt to solve problems by exploiting help functionalities of digital learning environments, has been studied across multiple learning environments, little research has been done to study how (and whether) gaming manifests differently across populations of students and learning environments. In this paper, we study the differences in usage of 13 different patterns of actions associated with gaming the system by comparing their distribution across different populations of students using Cognitive Tutor Algebra and across students using one of three learning environments: Cognitive Tutor Algebra, Cognitive Tutor Middle School and ASSISTments. Results suggest that differences in gaming behavior are more strongly associated to the learning environments than to student populations and reveal different trends in how students use fast actions, similar answers and help request in different systems.

Keywords: Gaming the system · Intelligent tutoring system · Student populations

1 Introduction

Studies of students who "game the system", a disengaged behavior in which students "attempt to succeed in an educational environment by exploiting properties of the system rather than by learning the material and trying to use that knowledge to answer correctly" [1], have shown its relationship with poorer learning outcomes [2–5], increased boredom [6] and lower long-term levels of academic attainment [7]. Research on gaming the system has applied machine learning [1, 8, 9] and knowledge engineering [9–14] approaches to build models able to detect gaming from data sets collected from a specific population of students in a specific learning environment. Although data collected across multiple learning environments provides us with information about how often students typically game different environments, little work has focused on explicitly comparing gaming across environments and populations of students. In one exception, Baker and Gowda [15] compared the incidence of disengaged behaviors across populations of students using Cognitive Tutor Algebra, finding

© Springer International Publishing AG 2017
E. André et al. (Eds.): AIED 2017, LNAI 10331, pp. 274–286, 2017.
DOI: 10.1007/978-3-319-61425-0_23

that the incidence of gaming was different across populations. However, their work did not investigate whether the nature of the gaming behaviors differed across populations.

Recent work in the creation of models of student affect (which are often similar to models of gaming the system) has found that they may not always transfer between different populations of students [16]. By contrast, recent work has suggested that models of gaming the system can, in some cases, function reliably in new learning environments, albeit with some degradation in performance [17]. To better understand this degradation and how we may be able to develop more universal models of this important behavior, we study whether the specific ways that gaming the system manifests varies between environments and populations of students.

In this paper, we study differences in the patterns of gaming behaviors demonstrated by students from three different populations of students using the Cognitive Tutor Algebra [18] environments and within three different learning environments: Cognitive Tutor Algebra [18], Cognitive Tutor Middle School [18] (an earlier version of Cognitive Tutor Bridge to Algebra), and ASSISTments [19]. To do so, we compared the relative frequencies of 13 patterns of actions associated with gaming that were previously identified in a cognitive model of gaming behaviors [20]. Results from our study showed stronger differences in gaming patterns across environments than across student populations, suggesting that the ways that gaming manifests behaviorally are more strongly associated with the environment than with specific student populations.

2   Method

2.1   Model

In previous work, we studied how experts identify whether students are gaming the system by analyzing text replays, textual representations of the students' actions in the learning environments [20]. To do so, we conducted a cognitive task analysis [21, 22] of how an expert identifies behaviors as gaming or not. This was achieved using a combination of active participation [22, 23] (in which the person performing the cognitive task analysis actively participated in the coding of text replays), think aloud observations [24] and interviews to explicate the coding process.

Using this technique, 13 patterns of actions were identified that each captured part of the gaming behavior in Cognitive Tutor Algebra. Those 13 patterns were used to build a cognitive model able to detect gaming from sequences of student actions in the learning environment. In this model, a sequence of actions, called a clip, was classified as gaming the system when the actions it contained matched at least one of the 13 patterns. Table 1 describes the 13 patterns that were identified as gaming (symbolic representations of the patterns are presented in [20]). The most frequent elements of those patterns include: quickly entering answers without thinking, re-entering the same answer in different parts of the problem, entering sequences of similar answers (defined as two consecutive answers with a Levenshtein distance [25] of 1 or 2), quickly asking for help without thinking about what to do next, and moving on to a new part of the problem before correctly solving the part that was previously attempted.

This cognitive model of gaming the system achieved a performance of 0.330 [20] for the Kappa [26] metric, a metric which indicates how much better the model is than chance at identifying gaming behaviors, when applied to an held-out test set. This performance was considerably higher than the previous best model of gaming for Cognitive Tutor Algebra, which obtained a Kappa of 0.24 [27] when cross-validated at the student level, but was less effective than a more recent hybrid model created by improving on the cognitive model using machine learning techniques [28]. This hybrid model combined traditional classification algorithms with the automatic generation and selection of patterns of actions that mirror the structure of those identified during the cognitive task analysis. This model achieved a Kappa of 0.457 under student-level cross-validation [28]. In the current paper, we use the cognitive model for two main reasons. First, the pattern structure of the cognitive model makes it easier to interpret than the hybrid model, an important consideration when comparing gaming behaviors across populations and learning environments. Second, a previous study [17] showed that the performance of the cognitive model was more robust than the hybrid model when applying it to data sets from two new learning environments: the scatter plot lesson in Cognitive Tutor Middle School and ASSISTments.

Table 1. List and descriptions of the 13 patterns contained in our model of gaming the system.

#	Pattern
1	The student enters an incorrect answer and then quickly re-enters the same incorrect answer in a different part of the problem
2	The student enters an incorrect answer, enters a similar and incorrect answer in the same part of the problem and then enters another similar answer in the same part of the problem
3	The student enters an incorrect answer, followed by a similar and incorrect answer and finally re-enters the second answer in a different part of the problem
4	The student quickly enters an incorrect answer, followed by quickly entering a second incorrect answer and then, once again, quickly entering a different answer
5	The student enters an incorrect answer, followed by a similar incorrect answer and then quickly enters a different answer
6	The student asks for help and quickly looks for the answer in the hints provided by the learning environment, enters an incorrect answer and then enters a similar incorrect answer
7	The student enters an incorrect answer, followed by the same incorrect answer in a different part of the problem, followed by the student attempting to answer, or requesting help for, a different part of the problem
8	The student enters a known error (recognized by the system as a "bug"), then re-enters the same answer in a different part of the problem, gets the right answer, and then enters a new bug for a different part of the problem
9	The student enters an incorrect answer, enters a similar incorrect answer and then moves on to a different part of the problem and enters another incorrect answer
10	The student enters an incorrect answer, moves on to a different part of the problem, once again enters an incorrect answer and then enters a similar incorrect answer

(continued)

Table 1. (*continued*)

#	Pattern
11	The student enters an incorrect answer, followed by a similar incorrect answer, doesn't take the time to think about the error before asking for help and finally enters a similar incorrect answer
12	The student asks for help, followed by a sequence of 3 incorrect answers with at least 2 of which are similar to each other
13	The student enters a sequence of 3 incorrect answers, at least 2 of which are similar to each other, and then quickly asks for help without thinking about the errors

2.2 Data

To study differences in the usage of the 13 patterns of gaming the system, we applied the cognitive model from [20] to 6 different data sets. The first three data sets (obtained from the Pittsburgh Science of Learning Center DataShop [29]) were all collected from students using the Cognitive Tutor Algebra digital learning environment [18]. Each data set was collected from one school and represents a different population of students: rural, suburban and urban students. All three schools were located in the same geographical region of the Northeastern United States with the same nearest urban center. Table 2 presents the number of different classes and teachers who used the system in each data set, a summary of the demographic information for the school and the distance between the school and the nearest urban center.

The second group of three data sets was collected from different learning environments: Cognitive Tutor Algebra, Cognitive Tutor Middle School and ASSISTments. The Cognitive Tutor Algebra data set was created by combining the rural, suburban and urban data sets. The Cognitive Tutor Middle School data set was collected from 2 suburban school districts in the Northeastern United States, in the same region as the Cognitive Tutor Algebra data set. The ASSISTments data set was collected from three school districts in a different part of the Northeastern United States. One of the ASSISTments schools was urban and two were suburban. It is important to note that, although the focus of the analysis for those data sets is the learning environment, the population of students will also vary due to the different geographical regions in which those systems are used and the different age groups targeted by each system.

Table 2. Descriptive statistics for each school that used the Cognitive Tutor Algebra system

	Rural	Suburban	Urban
# classes	24	4	11
# teachers	7	3	6
White students	97.51%	97.61%	2.69%
Black students	1.79%	0.46%	96.58%
Hispanic students	0.39%	0.28%	0.24%
Asian/Pacific Islander students	0.08%	1.57%	0.49%

(continued)

Table 2. (*continued*)

	Rural	Suburban	Urban
American Indian/Alaska Native students	0.23%	0.09%	0%
Reading proficient	44.00%	90.80%	31.20%
Math proficient	25.00%	84.00%	21.60%
Economically disadvantaged	26.72%	4.20%	99.30%
Distance from urban center	32.6 mi.	8.6 mi.	0.8 mi.

Each of the data sets were separated into clips on which our model of gaming the system was applied. The result is a list of clips for each student as well as an indicator of whether a clip contained each of the 13 patterns of gaming the system.

For the Cognitive Tutor Algebra and Cognitive Tutor Middle School data sets, clips were created from sequences of at least 5 actions with a minimum duration of 20 s. In cases where the 5 selected actions had a total duration of less than 20 s, additional sets of 5 actions were added until the duration of the clip was greater than 20 s. This is consistent with how clips were created in the data set that was used to develop the model of gaming the system.

Due to differences in how ASSISTments presents problems, clips in ASSISTments were defined using a different structure. Whereas the Cognitive Tutor platform requires students to solve multiple steps before completing a problem, ASSISTments's problems can be solved in one step when the first attempt is correct. Problems are scaffolded through additional sub-questions when the student answers incorrectly. As such, we defined a clip in ASSISTments as starting from the first action on an original unscaffolded problem to the last attempt before the next original problem. For this reason, clips in ASSISTments can be shorter or longer than clips in the Cognitive Tutors.

Table 3 presents the number of actions, clips and students for each data set as well as the average number of clips per student and average number of actions per clip. For each student, in each data set, we computed the *relative percentage* of time each pattern was observed for this student, shown in Table 3. This measure informs us as to which gaming pattern was most common in each data set.

Table 3. Descriptive statistics for our six data sets.

	Algebra - rural	Algebra - suburban	Algebra - urban	Algebra - all	Middle school	ASSIST-ments
# actions	474,150	385,628	1,048,294	1,908,072	865,439	681,105
# clips	80,337	61,510	178,662	320,509	126,434	240,450
# students	352	59	165	576	233	1,367
Avg. clips per student	228.23	1042.54	1082.80	556.44	542.64	175.90
Avg. actions per clip	5.90	6.27	5.87	5.95	6.84	2.83

Table 4. Mean (and *SD*) for the relative percentage of time each pattern was observed.

	Algebra - rural	Algebra - suburban	Algebra - urban	Algebra - all	Middle school	ASSIST-ments
Pattern 1	4.94% (5.87%)	6.48% (3.46%)	4.08% (3.59%)	4.85% (5.13%)	5.33% (4.27%)	4.64% (11.73%)
Pattern 2	25.10% (18.12%)	20.97% (6.94%)	30.98% (21.19%)	26.38% (18.53%)	23.85% (9.90%)	36.17% (18.55%)
Pattern 3	2.17% (3.80%)	2.08% (1.27%)	1.99% (2.10%)	2.11% (3.19%)	2.59% (1.87%)	0.01% (0.17%)
Pattern 4	7.59% (8.48%)	9.74% (4.53%)	5.79% (4.89%)	7.29% (7.34%)	12.98% (6.00%)	5.12% (6.50%)
Pattern 5	18.03% (11.46%)	20.00% (4.85%)	15.38% (10.75%)	17.47% (10.83%)	25.57% (6.47%)	29.38% (15.98%)
Pattern 6	2.73% (3.04%)	2.90% (1.97%)	2.88% (2.47%)	2.79% (2.78%)	1.18% (1.33%)	1.77% (6.51%)
Pattern 7	4.42% (5.66%)	5.22% (2.58%)	5.68% (11.21%)	4.87% (7.52%)	5.97% (6.12%)	0.29% (2.57%)
Pattern 8	1.44% (3.37%)	1.64% (1.47%)	2.57% (9.15%)	1.79% (5.61%)	0.00% (0.00%)	0.00% (0.00%)
Pattern 9	4.57% (5.66%)	4.68% (2.83%)	4.22% (3.41%)	4.48% (4.86%)	8.51% (3.96%)	0.14% (1.28%)
Pattern 10	4.64% (4.48%)	4.83% (2.68%)	4.52% (3.51%)	4.46% (4.06%)	7.90% (3.94%)	5.89% (8.35%)
Pattern 11	5.09% (4.95%)	4.74% (2.49%)	4.52% (3.24%)	4.89% (4.31%)	1.22% (1.88%)	3.30% (7.18%)
Pattern 12	7.06% (7.03%)	5.76% (2.12%)	6.47% (5.50%)	6.75% (6.27%)	3.10% (2.47%)	7.29% (10.40%)
Pattern 13	12.21% (10.27%)	10.96% (3.35%)	10.90% (9.45%)	11.70% (9.55%)	1.82% (2.04%)	5.99% (7.97%)

3   Results

Statistical analyses were conducted to compare the distributions of relative percentages of gaming patterns across populations and learning environments. This allowed us to investigate which gaming patterns were most common in each data set. Due to the non-normal distributions and non-homogeneous variance of our variables, we used Kruskall-Wallis tests, the non-parametric equivalent of ANOVA, to identify main effects across population and environments and Mann-Whitney tests, the non-parametric equivalent of the t-test, to compare pairs of data sets when a main effects were found.

Two different sets of analyses were conducted: (1) relative percentages of patterns across populations in Cognitive Tutor Algebra (Table 5); and (2) relative percentages of patterns across learning environments (Table 6). For each set of analyses, Kruskall-Wallis tests were conducted to identify statistically significant differences across three data sets, followed by Mann-Whitney tests to identify significant differences between pairs of data

Table 5. Diffences in relative percentages of gaming patterns across populations of students. Dashes signify that pairwise comparisons were not conducted when no significant main effect was found. Significant results, after controlling the false discovery rate, are indicated using bold fonts.

	All data	Rural vs. suburban		Rural vs. urban		Suburban vs. urban	
	P	p	r	p	r	p	r
Pattern 1	< 0.001	< 0.001	0.202	0.954	0.003	< 0.001	0.314
Pattern 2	< 0.001	0.455	0.038	< 0.001	0.182	< 0.001	0.254
Pattern 3	0.003	0.02	0.154	0.027	0.099	0.199	0.087
Pattern 4	< 0.001	0.001	0.167	0.074	0.080	< 0.001	0.355
Pattern 5	< 0.001	0.011	0.129	< 0.001	0.159	< 0.001	0.355
Pattern 6	0.156	–	–	–	–	–	–
Pattern 7	< 0.001	< 0.001	0.187	0.006	0.123	0.085	0.116
Pattern 8	< 0.001	< 0.001	0.255	< 0.001	0.224	0.206	0.085
Pattern 9	0.087	–	–	–	–	–	–
Pattern 10	0.559	–	–	–	–	–	–
Pattern 11	0.945	–	–	–	–	–	–
Pattern 12	0.564	–	–	–	–	–	–
Pattern 13	0.085	–	–	–	–	–	–

Table 6. Diffences in relative percentages of gaming patterns across learning environments. Significant results, after controlling the false discovery rate are indicated using bold fonts.

	All data	Algebra vs. Middle School		Algebra vs. ASSISTments		Middle School vs. ASSISTments	
	P	p	r	p	r	p	r
Pattern 1	< 0.001	0.010	0.092	< 0.001	0.304	< 0.001	0.356
Pattern 2	< 0.001	0.494	0.024	< 0.001	0.345	< 0.001	0.313
Pattern 3	< 0.001	< 0.001	0.209	< 0.001	0.714	< 0.001	0.916
Pattern 4	< 0.001	< 0.001	0.408	< 0.001	0.187	< 0.001	0.410
Pattern 5	< 0.001	< 0.001	0.500	< 0.001	0.467	< 0.001	0.134
Pattern 6	< 0.001	< 0.001	0.239	< 0.001	0.379	< 0.001	0.258
Pattern 7	< 0.001	< 0.001	0.165	< 0.001	0.746	< 0.001	0.876
Pattern 8	< 0.001	< 0.001	0.473	< 0.001	0.652	1.000	0.000
Pattern 9	< 0.001	< 0.001	0.461	< 0.001	0.763	< 0.001	0.906
Pattern 10	< 0.001	< 0.001	0.383	0.173	0.032	< 0.001	0.217
Pattern 11	< 0.001	< 0.001	0.426	< 0.001	0.302	0.266	0.028
Pattern 12	< 0.001	< 0.001	0.331	0.002	0.073	0.008	0.067
Pattern 13	< 0.001	< 0.001	0.603	< 0.001	0.366	< 0.001	0.101

sets and to compute effect sizes (reported as the rank-biserial correlation r). Due to the use of many statistical significance tests, the false discovery rate for each set of analyses was controlled using the Benjamini and Hochberg procedure [30].

4 Discussion

4.1 Differences Across Populations of Students

Table 7 summarizes our comparison of the distributions of relative percentages of each pattern of gaming across 3 populations of students using Cognitive Tutor Algebra. Significant main effects were found in 7 out of 13 gaming patterns with less than half of the pairwise comparison showing significant differences (counting pair-wise tests not run due to a non-significant main effect as themselves non-significant). The suburban population of students seemed to differ most in gaming behavior with the highest number of significant pairwise differences found when comparing rural and suburban students and the largest effect size being found when comparing suburban and urban students. Effect sizes were relatively low when comparing rural and suburban students (average $r = 0.182$) and rural and urban students (average $r = 0.157$). The comparison of suburban and urban students resulted in higher size (average $r = 320$ among significant results), but only 4 patterns showed significant differences.

Further inspection of the patterns for which significant differences were found provided us with information about the nature of gaming behaviors across population. The strongest effects were found in relationship to students quickly entering answers. Suburban students more often engaged in gaming that involved quick answers. This was observed for all three patterns that included quick answers (patterns #1, #4 and #5). Urban students also used more quick answers than rural students, but this difference was only significant for pattern #5. Significant differences for pattern #2 revealed that urban students used more long sequences of similar answers when gaming. Finally, significant differences for patterns #7 and #8 suggest that rural students engage less often in gaming that involve reusing the same answer in different parts of the problem.

Table 7. Number of significantly different distributions of relative percentages of gaming pattern across 3 populations of students and average effect size r significant.

	Relative percentages	
	Significant differences	Average r
Main effect	7 out of 13	–
Rural vs. Suburban	6 out of 13	0.182
Rural vs. Urban	5 out of 13	0.157
Suburban vs. Urban	4 out of 13	0.320

4.2 Differences Across Learning Environments

Table 8 summarizes our comparison of the distributions of the relative percentages of each pattern of gaming across Cognitive Tutor Algebra, Cognitive Tutor Middle

School and ASSISTments. Significant main effects were found in all patterns with a large majority of patterns showing significant pairwise comparison. Average effect sizes were also stronger than for populations of students. Overall, Gaming behaviors differed more between ASSISTments and both Cognitive Tutor environments than between Cognitive Tutor Algebra and Cognitive Tutor Middle School.

Significant differences in relative percentages suggested that quick answers were more common in Cognitive Tutor Middle School then in Cognitive Tutor Algebra. Both Cognitive Tutors had more gaming involving quick answers than ASSISTments. This was supported by significant differences in the relative percentages for patterns #1 and #4. However, pattern #5, which also involves quick answers, was more common in ASSISTments. Long sequences of similar answers (pattern #2) were more common in ASSISTments than in other environments and were more common in Cognitive Tutor Algebra than in Cognitive Tutor Middle School. Gaming Patterns which included students reusing the same answer in a different part of the problem tended to occur infrequently in ASSISTments. This is true for 3 out of 4 patterns containing such behaviors (patterns #3, #7 and #8) which had average relative percentages lower than 0.3% (Table 4); only pattern #1 had a higher average relative percentage (4.64%). This is probably because Cognitive Tutors tend to show several problem steps on the screen at once, whereas students complete one problem step at a time in ASSISTments, enabling students to quickly try the same answer in multiple places. Even pattern #1 was seen significantly more frequently in Cognitive Tutors than ASSISTments. Finally, gaming behavior containing help requests were most frequent in Cognitive Tutor Algebra, followed by ASSISTments. Cognitive Tutor Middle School had the least help-related gaming. This was true for 3 out of 4 patterns containing help requests (patterns #6, #11 and #13). However, pattern #11 did not show a statistically significant difference between Cognitive Tutor Algebra and ASSISTments. Pattern #12 was the only help related pattern for which ASSISTments had the highest relative percentage. This may reflect a lower overall rate of gaming for ASSISTments than the Cognitive Tutors, or it may suggest that students using ASSISTments use additional methods for gaming that were not uncovered in the qualitative research (conducted using Cognitive Tutor data) that led to this model.

Table 8. Number of significantly different distributions of relative percentages of gaming patterns across learning envrionments and average effect size r across significant differences.

	Relative percentages	
	Significant differences	Average r
Main effect	13 out of 13	–
CT Algebra vs. CT Middle School	12 out of 13	0.358
CT Algebra vs. ASSISTments	12 out of 13	0.442
CT Middle School vs. ASSISTments	11 out of 13	0.414

5 Conclusion

Results from our study showed significant differences in the nature of gaming behavior demonstrated by different populations of students and in different environments. However, differences between populations tend to be less frequent and weaker than those between environments. We also observed that, when comparing behaviors across learning environments, the degree of similarity between the environments seems to play a factor in the strength of the differences. Indeed, observed differences between the fairly similar Cognitive Tutor Algebra and Cognitive Tutor Middle School were weaker than the differences between either of those environments and ASSISTments.

The presented study allowed us to identify that student behaviors, more specifically gaming the system behaviors, can vary across different data sets. This information is important to consider when building models of student behaviors, whether for gaming the system or for other constructs. Although it is not surprising that students have different behaviors in different learning environments, the possibility of different behaviors across different schools is not as readily apparent. As such, it is important to keep in mind that models created using only a data set limited only to specific schools and/or regions might have biases based on the population of students it includes.

Those biases do not necessarily imply that models of student behaviors are unusable across different data sets. For example, a previous study [17] showed how gaming models were able to transfer, with some limitation, to new data sets. However, those biases could be a factor in the decreased performance we observed when applying our models to some of the new data sets. Similarly, they might explain why the model created solely based on expert knowledge was more stable across data sets than the hybrid model, created using a combination of machine learning and expert knowledge, despite being less accurate on the training data. The improved accuracy the hybrid models achieved within the systems they were created for may be due to them fitting to details of how gaming specifically occurs in that system, rather than capturing more general aspects of gaming behavior. Being aware of such biases in our models will offer us insight that will be useful as we attempt to improve the generalizability of our models of student behaviors, whether developed using knowledge engineering or machine learning approaches.

Our study presents a first step toward understanding how different factors can bias gaming behaviors in intelligent tutoring systems. We showed differences in the frequencies of gaming behavior across systems and populations. However, we did not investigate in detail which specific factors are most strongly associated to those differences (though there is good reason to believe that some of the difference between systems is related to different aspects of their design, specifically whether multiple problem steps are visible at the same time). One interesting direction that this suggests is that it may be possible to better tailor gaming detection for a new system by taking a model such as this one, and determining which behaviors are less feasible within the new system. These behaviors can then be omitted and the predictive strength of the more feasible behaviors can be increased within the model, under the assumption that students who want to game will find an alternate strategy for doing so [cf. 31].

When studying differences across student populations, our first step focused on comparing rural, suburban and urban schools. This was done for multiple varied reasons. First, a study in the field of affect detection [16] provided us with evidence that differences can be observed, even at such a coarse-grained level. Second, the demographic information presented in Table 2 indicates that there are variations in student populations across the different schools we selected. Finally, historically, fine-grained demographic information has usually not been collected in intelligent tutoring system studies. This lack of historical data significantly increases the difficulty of conducting large scale studies across populations of student. In this context, studying school level differences provided a good starting point for our study. Future study will need to ensure that detailed demographic information is collected. The absence of this information may have led to the result we observed, where although the differences between populations were statistically significant, the correlations were stronger between systems than between populations. It is possible that looking at more fine-grained characteristics of the student populations, such as gender, ethnicity or socio economic status, would provide a better fit for the distribution of gaming behaviors across students. Similarly, when studying differences across systems, future study will need to identify defining characteristics of the different systems and study how they are associated with the observed differences in behavior and will need to pay attention to how demographic differences in the populations of students using those learning environments impacts their behaviors. By doing so, we hope that we identify ways to improve the generalization of models of student behaviors, such as gaming the system, across learning systems and student population to speed their adoption by the broader community of learning engineers.

Acknowledgement. We would like to thank PSLC DataShop, Carnegie Learning and the ASSISTments team for providing us with access to student data. We would also like to thank support from NSF #DRL-1535340 and NSF #DRL-1252297.

References

1. Baker, R.S.J., Corbett, A.T., Roll, I., Koedinger, K.R.: Developing a generalizable detector of when students games the system. User Model. User Adap. Inter. **18**, 287–314 (2008)
2. Beck, J., Rodrigo, M.M.T.: Understanding wheel spinning in the context of affective factors. In: Proceedings of the 12th International Conference on Intelligent Tutoring Systems, pp. 162–167 (2014)
3. Cocea, M., Hershkovitz, A., Baker, R.S.J.: The impact of off-task and gaming behaviors on learning: immediate or aggregate? In: Proceedings of the 14th International Conference on Artificial Intelligence in Education, pp. 507–514 (2009)
4. Fancsali, S.E.: Data-driven causal modeling of "Gaming the System" and off-task behavior in cognitive tutor algebra. NIPS Workshop on Data Driven Education
5. Pardos, Z.A., Baker, R.S., San Pedro, M.O.C.Z., Gowda, S.M., Gowda, S.M.: Affective states and state tests: investigating how affect and engagement during the school year predict end of year learning outcomes. J. Learn. Anal. **1**(1), 107–128 (2014)

6. Baker, R.S.J., D'Mello, S.K., Rodrigo, M.M.T., Graesser, A.C.: Better to be frustrated than bored: the incidence, persistence, and impact of learners' cognitive-affective states during interactions with three different computer-based learning environments. Int. J. Hum Comput Stud. **68**, 223–241 (2010)

7. San Pedro, M.O.Z., Baker, R.S.J., Bowers, A.J., Heffernan, N.T.: Predicting college enrolment from student interaction with an intelligent tutoring system in middle school. In: Proceedings of the 6th International Conference on Educational Data Mining, pp. 177–184 (2013)

8. Baker, R.S.J., Mitrovic, A., Mathews, M.: Detecting gaming the system in constraint-based tutors. In: Proceedings of the 18th Conference on User Modeling, Adaptation and Personalization, pp. 267–278 (2010)

9. Walonoski, J.A., Heffernan, N.T.: Detection and analysis of off-task gaming behavior in intelligent tutoring systems. In: Proceedings of the 8th International Conference on Intelligent Tutoring Systems, pp. 382–391 (2006)

10. Beal, C.R., Qu, L., Lee, H.: Classifying learner engagement through integration of multiple data sources. In: Proceedings of the National Conference on Artificial Intelligence, pp. 151–156 (2006)

11. Johns, J., Woolf, B.: A dynamic mixture model to detect student motivation and proficiency. In: Proceedings of the National Conference on Artificial Intelligence, pp. 163–168 (2006)

12. Muldner, K., Burleson, W., Van de Sande, B., VanLehn, K.: An analysis of students' gaming behaviors in an intelligent tutoring system: predictors and impact. User Model. User Adap. Inter. **21**, 99–135 (2011)

13. Aleven, V., McLaren, B.M., Roll, I., Koedinger, K.R.: Towards meta-cognitive tutoring: a model of help seeking with a cognitive tutor. Int. J. Artif. Intell. Educ. **16**, 101–130 (2006)

14. Gong, Y., Beck, J., Heffernan, N.T., Forbes-Summer, E.: The fine-grained impact of gaming (?) on learning. In: Proceedings of the 10th International Conference on Intelligent Tutoring Systems, pp. 194–203 (2010)

15. Baker, R.S.J., Gowda, S.M.: An analysis of the differences in the frequency of students' disengagement in Urban, Rural, and Suburban High Schools. In: Proceedings of the 3rd International Conference on Educational Data Mining, pp. 11–20 (2010)

16. Ocumpaugh, J., Baker, R.S., Gowda, S., Heffernan, N., Heffernan, C.: Population validity for educational data mining models: a case study in affect detection. Br. J. Educ. Technol. **45**(3), 487–501 (2014)

17. Paquette, L., Baker, R.S., de Carvalho, A.M.J.A., Ocumpaugh, J.: Cross-system transfer of machine learned and knowledge engineered models of gaming the system. In: Proceedings of the 23rd Conference on User Modeling, Adaptation and Personalization, pp. 183–194 (2015)

18. Koedinger, K.R, Corbett, A.T.: Cognitive tutors: technology bringing learning sciences to the classroom. In: Sawyer, R.K. (ed.) The Cambridge Handbook of the Learning Sciences, pp. 61–77 (2006)

19. Razzaq, L., et al.: The assistment project: blending assessment and assisting. In: Proc. of the 12 Annual Conference on Artificial Intelligence in Education, pp. 555–562 (2005)

20. Paquette, L., de Carvalho, A.M.J.A, Baker, R.S.: Towards understanding export coding of student disengagement in online learning. In: Proceedings of the 36th Annual Cognitive Science Conference, pp. 1126–1131 (2014)

21. Clark, R.E., Feldon, D., van Merriënboer, J., Yates, K., Early, S.: Cognitive task analysis. In: Spector, J.M., Merrill, M.D., van Merriënboer, J.J.G., Driscoll, M.P. (eds.) Handbook of Research on Educational Communications and Technology, 3rd edn., pp. 575–593 (2008)

22. Cooke, N.J.: Varieties of knowledge elicitation techniques. Int. J. Hum Comput Stud. **41**, 801–849 (1994)

23. Meyer, M.A.: How to apply the anthropological technique of participant observation to knowledge acquisition for expert systems. IEEE Trans. Syst. Man Cybern. **22**, 983–991 (1992)
24. Van Someren, M.W., Barnard, Y.F., Sandberg, J.A.C.: The Think Aloud Method: A Practical Guide to Modeling Cognitive Processes. Academic Press, London (1994)
25. Levenshtein, A.: Binary codes capable of correcting deletions, insertions and reversals. Sov. Phys. Dokl. **10**(8), 707–710 (1966)
26. Cohen, J.: A coefficient of agreement for nominal scales. Educ. Psychol. Measur. **20**(1), 37–46 (1960)
27. Baker, R.S.J., de Carvalho, A.M.J.A.: Labeling student behavior faster and more precisely with text replays. In: Proceedings of the 1st International Conference on Educational Data Mining 2008, pp. 38–47 (2008)
28. Paquette, L., de Carvalho, A.M.J.A, Baker, R.S., Ocumpaugh, J.: Reengineering the feature distillation process: a case study in the detection of gaming the system. In: Proceedings of the 7th International Conference on Educational Data Mining, pp. 284–287 (2014)
29. Koedinger, K.R., Baker, R., Cunningham, K., Skogsholm, A., Leber, B., Stamper, J.: A Data Repository for the Community: The PLSC DataShop. CRC Press, Boca Raton (2010)
30. Benjamini, Y., Hochberg, Y.: Controlling the False discovery rate: a practical and powerful approach to multiple testing. J. Roy. Stat. Soc. B **57**, 289–300 (2003)
31. Murray, C., VanLehn, K.: Effects of dissuading unnecessary help requests while providing proactive help. In: Proceedings of the International Conference on Artificial Intelligence and Education, pp. 887–889 (2005)

Identifying Productive Inquiry in Virtual Labs Using Sequence Mining

Sarah Perez[✉], Jonathan Massey-Allard, Deborah Butler, Joss Ives,
Doug Bonn, Nikki Yee, and Ido Roll

University of British Columbia, Vancouver V6T1Z4, Canada
{sarah.perez,deborah.butler,ido.roll}@ubc.ca,
{jmassall,joss,bonn}@phas.ubc.ca, nikki.yee@alumni.ubc.ca

Abstract. Virtual labs are exploratory learning environments in which students learn by conducting inquiry to uncover the underlying scientific model. Although students often fail to learn efficiently in these environments, providing effective support is challenging since it is unclear what productive engagement looks like. This paper focuses on the mining and identification of student inquiry strategies during an unstructured activity with the DC Circuit Construction Kit (https://phet.colorado.edu/). We use an information theoretic sequence mining method to identify productive and unproductive strategies of a hundred students. Low domain knowledge students who successfully learned during the activity paused more after testing their circuits, particularly on simply structured circuits that target the activity's learning goals, and mainly earlier in the activity. Moreover, our results show that a strategic use of pauses so that they become opportunities for reflection and planning is highly associated with productive learning. Implication to theory, support, and assessment are discussed.

Keywords: Inquiry learning · Sequence mining · Exploratory learning environments · Virtual lab · Self-regulated learning

1 Introduction

Learning science through inquiry has received increased attention over the last two decades [6,8]. However, together with the push for incorporating more inquiry into the STEM curriculum, there has also been criticism of students' ability to manage their learning in exploratory learning environments (ELEs) [7,9,24]. ELEs are open-ended learning environments in which students learn by engaging with complex tasks or problems [1,2]. Certain ELEs, such as virtual labs, provide environments where students design experiments, make measurements, and analyze observations, in order to test hypotheses and uncover the underlying scientific model that governs the behavior of the lab [7]. When designing support in these labs, balancing information giving and withholding is challenging as too much guidance can eliminate the benefits of the exploratory nature of the labs. One viable approach for support is providing adaptive and

© Springer International Publishing AG 2017
E. André et al. (Eds.): AIED 2017, LNAI 10331, pp. 287–298, 2017.
DOI: 10.1007/978-3-319-61425-0_24

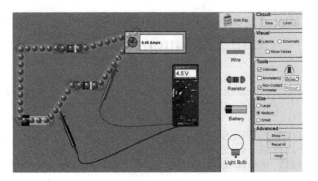

Fig. 1. A screenshot of the CCK virtual lab showing a series circuit with a connected voltmeter and ammeter.

timely feedback. However, this approach requires a learner model that describes which inquiry strategies learners apply when engaging with an ELE and how productive these are in achieving the expected learning outcomes.

Our study aims to identify inquiry strategies used by students in open-ended virtual lab inquiry activities, and to evaluate their relationship with learning outcomes. The virtual lab studied is the DC Circuit Construction Kit (CCK) which is part of the widely used suite of simulations [27]. This lab allows students to simulate DC circuits with various elements such as batteries, wires, light bulbs and resistors. Students can also measure basic physical properties such as current and voltage by connecting voltmeters and ammeters to their circuits (Fig. 1). Our study aims to answer the following research questions:

1. Which sequences of student actions in the virtual lab are associated with learning?
2. How do these change over time during the activity?
3. Which inquiry strategies might these be associated with?

We begin by situating these questions in inquiry learning theories and relevant prior work. We then describe the data collection and the information theoretic sequence-mining approach adapted from Biswas and colleagues [13]. Following the results, we discuss the identified patterns and their contribution to theory, support, and assessment of inquiry learning using virtual labs.

2   Background

Virtual labs are a class of ELEs that facilitate inquiry learning by supporting students as they design experiments, collect measurements, and analyze data, with the goal of uncovering an underlying physical model [7,9]. Virtual labs are typically complex open-ended environments that allow learners to choose from a multitude of different action paths. This characteristic of virtual labs makes the self-regulation of cognitive and metacognitive aspects of a student's inquiry particularly important and challenging. Studies have shown that given proper regulative support (e.g. cognitive tools), inquiry learning can have a positive impact on learning outcomes [12,15,26]. This support can promote scientific inquiry skills such as generating hypotheses, conducting experiments, drawing conclusions [14], as well as key regulative inquiry skills such as planning next steps, monitoring progress and reflecting [18].

Due to the complexity of student interactions with these labs, researchers have been leveraging automated techniques to more efficiently extract the key features of those interactions [4,19]. Many studies have focused on extracting and assessing the behaviors associated with inquiry learning processes in the context of scaffolded activities such as with cognitive tools [11] or with metacognitive support [15]. While these studies capture meaningful skills, these skills are often pre-defined and supported by the environment. Studies on unstructured activities typically focus on predicting learning (with much success) [3,10]. However, these studies often do not focus on understanding the strategies that lead to productive inquiry. Recently, more research efforts have been made towards identifying productive inquiry strategies in more open and minimally supported virtual labs [25]. For example, Bumbacher and colleagues identified three aspects of productive inquiry: focusing on an unfamiliar target element, doing so deliberately, and seeking contrasts [5].

As reflected by the work presented above, our understanding of what strategies are used by learners in relatively unstructured inquiry activities and how effective these strategies are is lacking. Furthermore, extracting such strategies in an automated way from student action paths in unstructured activities remains challenging. In this paper we focus on identifying productive strategies by finding action sequences that differentiate between novices who learn well (termed "intelligent novices" [16]); and novices who learn comparatively less. We do so by applying a combined top-down and bottom-up approach to analyzing student log data. A key component of this approach is our adaptation of a sequence-mining method that was suggested by Biswas and colleagues [13].

3   Methods

3.1   Data Collection

A hundred first year undergraduate students from a Canadian University participated in this study (one student was removed due to technical malfunctions). During the study, students completed two 25-minute activities on circuits using the CCK lab shown in Fig. 1. The first activity focused on light bulbs and the second on resistors. During the first activity on light bulbs, students were randomly assigned to a guided or unguided condition, which differed in the amount of domain level support students were given in the form of worksheets [21]. Condition in the first activity had no effect on learning outcomes in the second activity [21]. Here, we focus on the second activity on the topic of resistors. Students received minimal guidance in the form of an activity sheet with the learning goals of understanding what happens to the current and voltage of a circuit when: (1) the resistance of resistors is changed and, (2) multiple resistors with different resistances are arranged differently. A third and final goal of exploring the properties of different combinations of resistors possessing equivalent resistances was also given. Before and after the activities, students completed pre- and post-tests on both topics. The post-test assessed conceptual understanding of resistors in circuits and was a reliable measure of student's knowledge with a Cronbach alpha of 0.75, which is above the suggested threshold of 0.7. Analysis of identical items between pre- and post-test shows that overall students learned from the activities ($mean \pm sd$: pre: 0.47 ± 0.17; $post$: 0.63 ± 0.23; $t(96) = 5.3$, $p < 0.0005$, Cohen's d = 0.77).

3.2   Identifying Novice Learners

The pre-test score distribution is bimodal, which we used to assign students to either a low- or high incoming knowledge group with 74 and 25 students respectively (low knowledge z-score: -0.5 ± 0.6; high knowledge z-score: 1.5 ± 0.5). Being experts, the 25 students with high incoming knowledge were excluded from the analysis. To identify productive inquiry strategies, we applied a median split to the post-test, distinguishing between students who performed well on the post-test (intelligent novices; Low-High, or LH, with 38 students) as compared to those that did poorly on both tests (Low-Low, or LL, with 36 students). The pre-test did not correlate significantly with post-test scores for low pre-test students ($r_s = 0.06$, $p = 0.63$). Within these groups, students were evenly split between the two conditions of the first activity: 17 out of 36 LL and 21 out of 38 LH were in the guided condition.

3.3   Abstracting Sequences of Actions from Log Data

Our first step was to choose an appropriate representation when parsing the log data. We applied top-down approaches such as think-aloud protocols and expert cognitive tasks analysis as well as bottom-up approaches such as visualizing log data of individual students. For example, screen recordings of students' activity in the virtual lab showed that there were many periods of inactivity and retrospective think-aloud protocols allowed us to label these moments as students taking a pause to either think back and reflect (e.g. while writing down conclusions about experiments), or think forward and plan (e.g. what circuit to build or test next). We defined pauses as inactivity for more than 15 s, based on the long tail of the distribution of time between actions. Changes to this threshold have nearly no effect on relative frequencies of actions.

We then categorized individual log actions into two broad categories: Construct actions and Test actions. Construct actions encompass all actions that change the circuit configuration such as adding or connecting batteries and resistors. Test actions encompass all actions related to connecting a voltmeter or ammeter to the circuit. Other actions such as those relating to the interface (e.g., zooming) were ignored.

Time	Action in logs	Action Type	Block	Sequences		
time bin 1	add battery 1	Construct	C	CPT_1P		
	add wire 1	Construct				
	add wire 2	Construct				
	add resistor 1	Construct				
	connect wire1-battery	Construct				
	connect wire2-battery	Construct				
	connect wire2-resistor	Construct				
	connect wire1-resistor	Construct				
	Inactivity for > 15 sec	Pause	P			
time bin 2	connect voltmeter probes	Test 1 resistor	T_1	PT_1PC	T_1PCT_2	
	connect ammeter probes	Test 1 resistor				
	Inactivity for > 15 sec	Pause	P			
	add wire 3	Construct	C			
	add wire 4	Construct				
	add resistor 2	Construct				
	connect ammeter probes	Test 2 resistor2	T_2			
...		...				

Fig. 2. Log data was parsed by action type and then to blocks of actions. Each student's virtual lab activity log was divided into 4 equal time bins. Here, 3 possible action sequences composed of 4 action blocks each are represented; two of these sequences occur in the first quarter of the activity and one in the second.

Analysis of trace data often focuses on the events alone. However, in this context (as in many other ELEs), the state of the virtual lab affects the outcome or intention of the action [17]. Thus, given the activity's learning goals, we further qualified Test actions with information about the circuits being tested: circuits with only one resistor (T_1), circuits with two resistors (connected in parallel or in series; T_2), and circuits with any other configuration (T_m).

Within the virtual lab there are many ways to achieve a certain effect. For example, students can build the same circuit in any order of actions. Given that we are mainly interested in the final configuration of the circuit to be tested, and less so in the steps that students took to construct it, we collapsed individual actions of the same type into action blocks (Fig. 2). Merging actions of the same type into a block reduces the granularity of the data and facilitates the interpretation of sequences.

3.4 Mining Interesting Sequences of Actions

In order to identify interesting behaviors that could be associated to inquiry strategies, our analysis mines for sequences of actions that are both commonly used by students and highly differentiated in their usage across student groups (LL or LH) and/or activity time. To do so we first extract and collect all unique sequence patterns of two to ten blocks of actions (Fig. 2) for every student (~10,454 different sequence patterns). We limited the length to ten blocks in order to focus on more commonly used sequences. Only sequences that were used at least once by a minimum of 35% of LL or LH students were examined, leaving us with 119 sequence patterns to evaluate.

We then evaluate the interestingness of action sequences based on how their usage differentiates student groups and/or time bins. To do so we (1) bin each student's activity into four bins of equal time length (determined on a per student basis), (2) determine in which time bin each sequence was used for each student (Fig. 2), (3) for each sequence, we count the number of students that used it at least once per group per time bin, and (4) score each sequence based on the added information (or information gain) it provides given how it was used over time and/or by group compared to being used evenly over time and/or by group [13].

After following this sequence mining procedure and scoring the sequences based on their information gain, we produce three rankings of the 119 sequences given how they were used (1) differentially by each group, (2) differentially over time (3) differentially over time and by group. When comparing the use of sequences by learners we report a Pearson χ^2 test. When examining whether specific subsequences were used more frequently by one group, we report their median (mdn) and compare them using a one-tailed Mann-Whitney $(U$; corrected for ties) since the frequency of use of subsequences are not normally distributed.

4   Results

Within the activity, students performed over 400 individual actions each, grouped into 47 ± 16 blocks of actions. All students used Pause, Construct and Test actions more than once throughout the activity. Notably, both groups used Pauses with similar frequency (LL:0.29 ± 0.08, LH:0.31 ± 0.08; $t(35) = 1.11$, $p = 0.27$).

Sequences that Differentiate Learner Groups. Figure 3A shows the use over time of the top six sequences with the highest information gain with respect to differentiating LL and LH student groups. The difference in number of students from each group that used those sequences is statistically significant in all of these cases: more LH do PT_2P, ($\chi^2(1) = 9.5$, $p = 0.002$), PT_2PC, ($\chi^2(1) = 8.8$, $p = 0.003$), T_2PT_2PC, ($\chi^2(1) = 4.2$, $p = 0.04$), and CT_2PT_2P, ($\chi^2(1) = 4.2$, $p = 0.04$), while more LL do $CPCT_2C$, ($\chi^2(1) = 5.3$, $p = 0.02$) and PCT_mCT_mC, ($\chi^2(1) = 5.3$, $p = 0.02$). LH apply PT_2P, PT_2PC, T_2PT_2PC and CT_2PT_2P primarily early on the in the activity; LL apply the sequence $CPCT_2C$ early in the activity and apply the sequence PCT_mCT_mC mid activity (Fig. 3B).

Sequences that Differentiate Time in the Activity. Figure 3B shows two sequences that had a significant amount of information gain with respect to time. Other sequences that ranked highly were quite similar in that they all included testing of a basic single resistor circuit (T_1) and were used by both groups of students in the first or second quarter of the activity. Sequences obtained with the criteria of highest information gain with respect to the interaction of group and time were overwhelmingly dominated by the same sequences obtained with respect to time only.

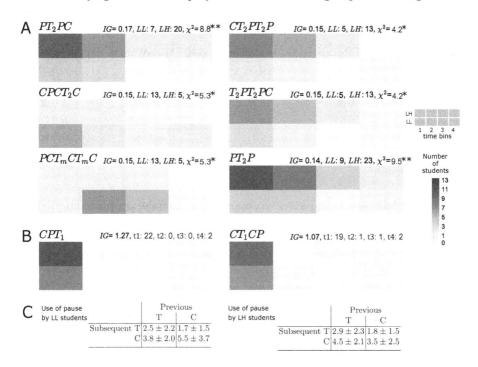

Fig. 3. (A) Top six action sequences with high information gain (IG) by group. The total number of *unique* students in each group using the sequence is indicated above the heatmaps along with chi-squared test of independence values ($* = p < 0.05$, $** = p < 0.01$). (B) Top two sequences with high IG by time. The total number of *unique* students in each time bin using the sequence is indicated above the heatmaps. Colorbar and axes identified on the right are used for both (A) and (B). (C) The mean and standard deviation of counts of uses of Pauses given the previous and subsequent action (normalized given the number of pauses done by each student) for LL and LH.

Building Blocks. All sequences with high information gain across groups are composed of common building blocks that are unique to each group. To better understand the nature of the inquiry strategies these sequences allude to, we first examine their building blocks. Of particular interest are the T_2P building block from LH sequences and the T_2C and T_mC building blocks from LL sequences.

These building blocks were used with a significantly higher frequency by one of the two groups. LH perform the unit T_2P more often than LL (Table 1). Controlling for the use of T_2, LH also followed a T_2 action with a Pause more. LL perform the T_mC unit more frequently than LH. LL Construct more after T_m also when controlling for frequency of T_m. However LL do no use the T_2C unit more often, nor do they Construct more controlling for T_2.

Evaluating Pauses. Pausing after simple tests was found to be very common among LH, yet not among LL. To evaluate whether Pauses are used strategically before or after Construct or Test action blocks of any kind may explain

Table 1. Frequency of use of sequence building blocks.

Building block	Median use (LL)	Median use (LH)	MannWhitney test	p-value
T_2P	0.03	0.06	$U = 848.5$	$p = 0.04$
T_2 followed by P	0.20	0.56	$U = 919.0$	$p < 0.01$
T_2C	0.06	0.05	$U = 639.0$	$p = 0.60$
T_2 followed by C	0.33	0.25	$U = 620.5$	$p = 0.76$
T_mC	0.17	0.11	$U = 508.5$	$p = 0.03$
T_m followed by C	0.57	0.39	$U = 440.5$	$p < 0.01$

whether students are using pauses as opportunities to reflect or plan and predict. Figure 3C shows the count (normalized given the number of pauses done by each student) with which each group uses Pauses as a function of the previous and subsequent action (Test or Construct). We evaluate the dependency of pauses on their context by running a repeated measures ANOVA with a normalized count of pauses as a dependent variable, and three factors as independent variables: the previous action, the subsequent action, and their interaction.

For the LH group, there was a significant main effect for the previous action, where LH students Pause significantly more after Test than after Construct: $F(1,37) = 5.91$, $p = 0.02$, $\eta^2 = 0.14$. There was also a strong main effect for subsequent action, where LH Pause more before Construct than before Test: $F(1,37) = 22.10$, $p < 0.01$, $\eta^2 = 0.37$ (Fig. 3C). There was no significant interaction ($p = 0.93$). Taken together, LH pause either after testing or before constructing, likely to reflect on the previous test and to plan the next circuit.

For LL, there was a main effect on the subsequent action, where LL Pause more before Construct than before Test, $F(1,35) = 37.80$, $p < 0.001$, $\eta^2 = 0.51$ (Fig. 3C). However, there was no significant effect for the previous action, $F(1,35) = 0.90$, $p = 0.35$, $\eta^2 = 0.25$. There was also a significant interaction, $F(1,35) = 9.43$, $p < 0.01$, $\eta^2 = 0.21$; given that Pause before Construct are always more frequent than Pause before Test, interpreting the main effects is possible. The interaction shows that LL pause before constructing mainly if their previous action was also Construct, as opposed to Test (CPC sequence as opposed to TPC). That is, overall, LL do not pause much in relation to testing but mainly do so before a Construct action, and most frequently in the process of building (i.e. between successive Construct blocks).

5   Discussion

The behaviors of novice learners in an inquiry activity were studied using a sequence analysis of actions logged in a virtual lab on DC circuits. The aims of the present study are to identify what action sequences were (a) associated with learning of the domain, (b) used differently over time, as well as to (c) interpret these characteristic action sequences in terms of inquiry learning strategies.

Sequences of Actions Associated with Learning. Our results identify different sequences of actions that were associated with learning. Novice learners that achieved high learning outcomes (LH) engaged in repeated testing-pausing cycles (i.e. T_2PT_2PC and CT_2PT_2P). This strategy is evocative of an efficient inquiry process whereby the students iteratively test and reflect [18]. Importantly, this process was performed by these students on simpler series and/or parallel two-resistor circuits, which are amongst the most useful configurations to test to acquire domain knowledge on basic DC circuits. Thus, intelligent novices were able to infer more meaningfully by pursuing simpler experiments, ones that match their zone of proximal development. The fact that they did so iteratively suggests that these students applied a compare-and-contrast strategy, where they compared two measurements on the same circuit or across two different circuits. This is an effective inductive reasoning strategy in building a mental framework necessary to explain an unknown model [22]. In contrast, LL students built circuits and subsequently measured the properties of these circuits without pausing (e.g. $CPCT_2C$). They also do so iteratively and often on complex circuits (e.g. PCT_mCT_mC). This greater focus on complex circuit configurations that are likely beyond their zone of proximal development likely had a negative impact on their ability to infer meaningful relationships from the learning environment. Furthermore, these students pause while constructing, but rarely pause after testing to reflect on their previous tests.

Sequences of Actions Used Differently over Time. The analysis also found a simple pattern of time dependency: students test the simplest circuits first (e.g. CPT_1 and CT_1CP). Testing such circuits makes sense for these low domain knowledge students, particularly early on in the activity (Fig. 3A). Doing so may be a combination of metacognitive awareness (recognizing one's limitations) and being able to recognize informative configurations in a new domain. This result suggests that effective strategy use has time dependency, but why was this not observed in our analysis beyond the first five minutes? It may be that the first five minutes of problem setup are the most distinct in the learning process. Thus, these patterns showed the highest information gain. Also, it may be that afterwards, learners disperse in their behaviors in a manner that does not converge to common patterns that emerge in the sequence mining method used here.

Interpreting Inquiry Strategies from Sequences of Actions. Finally, we investigated the inquiry strategies that may be associated with the different sequences of actions described. Specifically, we evaluated how the learner groups differ in the way they pause in order to interpret their sequences of actions. Overall, students in both groups pause the same number of times given the number of action blocks in their activity - thus, it is not the frequency of pausing, but rather their context that is associated productive inquiry. Intelligent novices pause primarily before constructing and after testing. Pausing before constructing is likely done to plan for the next experiment. Pausing after testing is done possibly to reflect on the results, take notes, evaluate a new observation, and validate/refine an existing hypothesis, or, having inferred new knowledge from a test, create a new hypothesis. This behavior resembles the use of pauses by novices in intelligent tutoring systems [23]. Novices that had a less productive inquiry paused mostly between construction blocks, indicating they had opportunities to plan with respect to a previous build as opposed to an opportunity to reflect and plan based on previous test. The strategic use of pauses for both reflection and planning is indicative of a stronger regulative inquiry process [18] and is thus likely to play an important role in learning from the activity.

Contributions and Future Work. Overall, we demonstrate how inquiry learning strategies can be studied not only in structured or guided ELEs but also in open-ended virtual labs using a bottom up and top down approach that combines expert cognitive task analysis, think alouds and sequence mining.

We show that intelligent novices strategically use pausing for reflection and planning, which agrees with previous findings that metacognitive skills are a key factor for learning in open virtual labs [15,26]. In addition, we demonstrate that the recurring process of testing and pausing with simple experiments is a powerful inquiry learning strategy. This result shows a striking resemblance to the findings of Bumbacher and colleagues, which most notably associated learning in an open-ended virtual lab activity with focusing on an unfamiliar target element (we do not show this explicitly but we do focus on novice learners), seeking contrasts (similar to the repetitions in the current study) and doing so deliberately (shown as pauses here) [5]. While Bumbacher and colleagues manually coded video data [5], we demonstrate that it is possible to extract inquiry strategies in open-ended virtual labs from log data. Given that the process of analyzing log data can be automated and run in real time, this study supports the idea that inquiry learning can be evaluated as it happens and possibly used to trigger timely support. Our results represent an important step towards informing the design of adaptive feedback and creating responsive simulations that help learners become better scientists [11].

The limitations of this work leave three important questions unanswered. First, the analysis focuses on learners with low prior knowledge. How do high incoming knowledge students engage with the virtual lab? It may be that experts can benefit from patterns that are used by low learners, such as testing complex circuits. If that is the case, then perhaps low learners apply generally good strategies, but fail to adapt their strategies to their low incoming knowledge, in a form of the Kruger-Dunning effect (unskilled and unaware). Secondly, we studied one group of learners using one simulation in a single activity. What is the dependency of these patterns on virtual lab, activity, and population? This will have to be evaluated in additional studies. Lastly, this work shows association, not causation. It would be of interest to evaluate the impact of supporting the identified productive patterns. Can students be taught these skills and what is the best way to do so? Prior evidence shows that following suggestions does not necessary transfer to future learning activities, as students merely do the motions [20]. For example, it is much easier to make someone pause then reflect. How can learners learn to become better scientists? Identifying behaviors of productive learners is an essential step in the right direction.

References

1. Amershi, S., Conati, C.: Automatic recognition of learner groups in exploratory learning environments. In: Ikeda, M., Ashley, K.D., Chan, T.-W. (eds.) ITS 2006. LNCS, vol. 4053, pp. 463–472. Springer, Heidelberg (2006). doi:10.1007/11774303_46

2. Amir, O., Gal, K., Yaron, D., Karabinos, M., Belford, R.: Plan Recognition and Visualization in Exploratory Learning Environments. In: Peña-Ayala, A. (ed.) Educational Data Mining. SCI, vol. 524, pp. 289–327. Springer, Cham (2014). doi:10.1007/978-3-319-02738-8_11

3. Baker, R.S., Clarke-Midura, J., Ocumpaugh, J.: Towards general models of effective science inquiry in virtual performance assessments. J. Comput. Assist. Learn. **32**(3), 267–280 (2016)

4. Berland, M., Baker, R.S., Blikstein, P.: Educational data mining and learning analytics: applications to constructionist research. Technol. Knowl. Learn. **19**(1–2), 205–220 (2014)

5. Bumbacher, E., Salehi, S., Wierzchula, M., Blikstein, P.: Learning Environments and Inquiry Behaviors in Science Inquiry Learning: How their Interplay Affects the Development of Conceptual Understanding in Physics. International Educational Data Mining Society, pp. 61–68 (2015)

6. Council, N.R.: Inquiry and the National Science Education Standards: A Guide for Teaching and Learning. National Academies Press, Washington, DC (2000)

7. De Jong, T., Van Joolingen, W.R.: Scientific discovery learning with computer simulations of conceptual domains. Rev. Educ. Res. **68**(2), 179–201 (1998)

8. European Commission. A Renewed Pedagogy for the Future of Europe, pp. 1–29 (2007)

9. Fan, X., Geelan, D.: Enhancing students' scientific literacy in science education using interactive simulations: a critical literature review. J. Comput. Math. Sci. Teach. **32**(2), 125–171 (2013)

10. Fratamico, L., Conati, C., Kardan, S., Roll, I.: Applying a framework for student modeling in exploratory learning environments: comparing data representation granularity to handle environment complexity. Int. J. Artif. Intell. Educ. **27**, 1–33 (2017)

11. Gobert, J., Sao Pedro, M., Raziuddin, J., Baker, R.: From log files to assessment metrics: measuring students' science inquiry skills using educational data mining. J. Learn. Sci. **22**(4), 521–563 (2013)

12. Holmes, N.G., Day, J., Park, A.H.K., Bonn, D.A., Roll, I.: Making the failure more productive: scaffolding the invention process to improve inquiry behaviors and outcomes in invention activities. Instr. Sci. **42**(4), 523–538 (2014)

13. Kinnebrew, J., Mack, D., Biswas, G.: Mining temporally-interesting learning behavior patterns. In: Proceedings of the 6th International Conference on Educational Data Mining, pp. 252–255 (2013)

14. Löhner, S., Van Joolingen, W.R., Savelsbergh, E.R., Van Hout-Wolters, B.: Students' reasoning during modeling in an inquiry learning environment. Comput. Hum. Behav. **21**(3 SPEC. ISS.), 441–461 (2005)

15. Manlove, S., Lazonder, A.W., de Jong, T.: Trends and issues of regulative support use during inquiry learning: patterns from three studies. Comput. Hum. Behav. **25**(4), 795–803 (2009)

16. Mathan, S.A., Koedinger, K.R.: Fostering the Intelligent Novice: Learning from errors with metacognitive tutoring. Educ. Psychol. **40**(4), 257–265 (2005)

17. Mitrovic, A., Suraweera, P.: Teaching database design with constraint-based tutors. Int. J. Artif. Intell. Educ. **26**(1), 448–456 (2016)
18. Njoo, M., De Jong, T.: Exploratory learning with a computer simulation for control theory: learning processes and instructional support. J. Res. Sci. Teach. **30**(5), 821–844 (1993)
19. Roll, I., Winne, P.: Understanding, evaluating, and supporting self-regulated learning using learning analytics. J. Learn. Anal. **2**(1), 7–12 (2015)
20. Roll, I., Baker, R., Aleven, V., Koedinger, K.R.: On the benefits of seeking (and avoiding) help in online problem solving environment. J. Learn. Sci. **23**(4), 537–560 (2014)
21. Roll, I., Yee, N., Cervantes, A.: Not a magic bullet: the effect of scaffolding on knowledge and attitudes in online simulations. In: International Conference of the Learning Sciences, pp. 879–886 (2014)
22. Shemwell, J.T., Chase, C.C., Schwartz, D.L.: Seeking the general explanation: a test of inductive activities for learning and transfer. J. Res. Sci. Teach. **52**(1), 58–83 (2015)
23. Shih, B., Koedinger, K., Scheines, R.: A response-time model for bottom-out hints as worked examples. In: Handbook of Educational Data Mining, pp. 201–211 (2010)
24. Tobias, S., Duffy, T.M.: Constructivist instruction: Success or failure? Routledge (2009)
25. Uzan, O., Dekel, R., Seri, O., et al.: Plan recognition for exploratory learning environments using interleaved temporal search. AI Magazine **36**(2), 10–21 (2015)
26. van Joolingen, W., de Jong, T.: Model-based diagnosis for regulative support in inquiry learning. In: Azevedo, R., Aleven, V. (eds.) International Handbook of Metacognition and Learning Technologies, pp. 589–600. Springer, NY (2013)
27. Wieman, C.E., Adams, W.K., Perkins, K.K.: PhET: simulations that enhance learning. Science **322**, 682–683 (2008)

"Thanks Alisha, Keep in Touch": Gender Effects and Engagement with Virtual Learning Companions

Lydia G. Pezzullo[1](✉), Joseph B. Wiggins[1], Megan H. Frankosky[2],
Wookhee Min[3], Kristy Elizabeth Boyer[1], Bradford W. Mott[3],
Eric N. Wiebe[4], and James C. Lester[3]

[1] Computer & Information Science & Engineering, University of Florida,
Gainesville, FL 32611, USA
{lpezzullo,jbwiggi3,keboyer}@ufl.edu
[2] Psychology, North Carolina State University, Raleigh, NC 27695, USA
[3] Computer Science, North Carolina State University, Raleigh, NC 27695, USA
{wmin,bwmott,lester}@ncsu.edu
[4] STEM Education, North Carolina State University, Raleigh, NC 27695, USA
wiebe@ncsu.edu

Abstract. Virtual learning companions have shown significant potential for supporting students. However, there appear to be gender differences in their effectiveness. In order to support all students well, it is important to develop a deeper understanding of the role that student gender plays during interactions with learning companions. This paper reports on a study to explore the impact of student gender and learning companion design. In a three-condition study, we examine middle school students' interactions in a game-based learning environment that featured one of the following: (1) a learning companion deeply integrated into the narrative of the game; (2) a learning companion whose backstory and personality were not integrated into the narrative but who provided equivalent task support; and (3) no learning companion. The results show that girls were significantly more engaged than boys, particularly with the narrative-integrated agent, while boys reported higher mental demand with that agent. Even when controlling for video game experience and prior knowledge, the gender effects held. These findings contribute to the growing understanding that learning companions must adapt to students' gender in order to facilitate the most effective learning interactions.

Keywords: Learning companions · Pedagogical agents · Gender · Engagement · Game-based learning

1 Introduction

Pedagogical agents have shown great potential to improve learning experiences [1]. They engage with students on both social and cognitive levels and are well

© Springer International Publishing AG 2017
E. André et al. (Eds.): AIED 2017, LNAI 10331, pp. 299–310, 2017.
DOI: 10.1007/978-3-319-61425-0_25

suited to addressing emotions, beliefs, and attitudes [2]. Among pedagogical agents, virtual learning companions are characterized by sharing the learning experience with the student and taking on the persona of a knowledgeable peer. Learning companions present a promising vehicle for adapting to affective and social needs by virtue of their peer-like role [3].

How best to design learning companions to support and balance these complex needs in different students is a question of growing interest [1,4,5]. The emerging picture is one in which gender, among other factors, consistently drives differences in students' perceptions and outcomes with learning companions [6,7]. Specifically, girls seem to prefer learning companions more than boys do, and to benefit more than boys from the experience [4].

The present work compares two approaches to integrating a learning companion for affective support into a game-based learning environment for middle school science. By comparing two different design approaches with a functionally identical agent, we investigate the research question, *What gender effects are observed on engagement and learning when integrating a virtual learning companion into a game-based learning environment?* By examining the relationship between agent design and student gender, we aim to discover design recommendations for learning companions to better accommodate both male and female students.

2   Related Work

Virtual learning companions act as near-peers to engage students and foster learning [2,8,9]. Virtual learning companions, in contrast to virtual tutors, do not play an authoritative role or pose new learning tasks. Rather, they are designed to experience learning tasks alongside the student and may play a peer or near-peer role. These virtual characters have the potential to motivate learners to persist in the face of failure, in part by improving interest [10] and self-efficacy beliefs [11]. They may promote academic skills through modeling [8], reducing frustration by offering common ground [7], and boosting confidence by affirming and empathizing with the student [11].

Gender is an influential factor in children's interactions with virtual learning companions and more broadly with all virtual agents for learning, with differences in outcomes such as learning, motivation, engagement, and self-efficacy often associated with the learner's gender [6,7,10,11]. While benefits of affect recognition and adaptation have been shown to be effective in educational settings [12,13], pedagogical agents that provide affective support have been shown to be particularly effective for female learners [6], but benefits for both boys and girls have also been established. For example, after interacting with a pedagogical agent for engineering education, both male and female middle school learners showed increased interest and self-efficacy (regardless of the agent's gender), and interacting with a female agent decreased stereotyping among boys [10].

Fig. 1. Game-based learning environment, with the virtual learning companion's image shown as an icon in lower left corner.

3 Game-Based Learning Environment

Prior work on virtual learning companions in other types of learning environments leads us to the current study, which is contextualized within a game-based learning environment for middle school microbiology, CRYSTAL ISLAND [5]. In the learning environment, learners find themselves on a remote island along with a team of research scientists who have been infected by a mysterious illness. Students learn that their mission is to investigate the illness in order to help those who have fallen ill. To accomplish this mission, learners explore the storyworld (Fig. 1) to gather evidence from non-player characters and science texts they find in the game. Through this process, learners refine their hypotheses about the illness and its source, then test the suspected sources of contamination to ultimately solve the science mystery. The game presents significant challenge in terms of both strategy use and hypothesis formation and testing. Extensive classroom studies and empirical investigations have been conducted with this game, and it has been found to provide substantial learning and motivational benefits [5].

4 Learning Companion Design

Our goal in this study was to investigate the ways in which gender differences emerge with two different approaches to integrating a virtual learning companion into the narrative of a game-based learning environment. Accordingly, we

Table 1. Selected equivalent agent dialogue moves in *Diegetic* and *Non-Diegetic* conditions.

Diegetic dialogue move	Non-Diegetic dialogue move
Introduction	
Hi, I'm Alisha!	Hi, I'm Alisha!
I'm a virtual assistant from the CDC. You can talk to me about your ideas as you work on this mission	I'm a virtual assistant, and I'm here to talk with you about your ideas as you play the game
By the way, my communication system is still under development	By the way, my communication abilities are limited
I might not understand some things you say, and I might say some things that don't make sense. But I will do my best!	I might not understand some things you say, and I might say some things that don't make sense. But I will do my best!
Resuming gameplay	
Hi again! I'm excited to get back to this mission. I'm learning a lot!	Hi again! Welcome back to Crystal Island.
Can you remind me about the last thing we were working on together?	Can you tell me about me the last thing you did when you were here last time?
Reassess hypothesis	
Isn't it exciting how each new piece of info can change the whole case?	It sounds like you've noticed how each new piece of information could change the entire problem
Try to keep questioning your hypothesis as we learn new things about this mystery!	Try to keep questioning your hypothesis as you learn new things!

designed two versions of a learning companion named Alisha, which varied in their narrative framing. We refer to the two conditions as *Diegetic* and *Non-Diegetic*, inspired by the narratological term *diegetic* which refers to narrative elements that are part of the internal world of a story, separate from the audience. For example, one character's dialogue with another is diegetic, whereas a narrator addressing the audience is non-diegetic. In the Diegetic condition, Alisha's backstory and interactions are deeply integrated into the narrative of the game. Alisha introduces herself as a friendly artificial intelligence who is still learning a lot about solving science mysteries. The Diegetic design was intended to foster social closeness: this learning companion is situated inside the same storyworld as the student, uses collaborative language relative to the student in that storyworld, and frequently references the agent's backstory and affective state. The Non-Diegetic learning companion had the same physical appearance as the Diegetic companion but did not introduce herself with any backstory and did not use collaborative language such as "we" to indicate that she was experiencing the narrative events alongside the student. Example Diegetic and Non-Diegetic dialogue moves are shown in Table 1. Finally, the *Baseline* condition consisted of the game without any virtual learning companion.

Alisha uses information about the student's gameplay—such as location in the gameworld and scientific texts the student has collected, read, and completed embedded assessments on–to decide when and how to make a dialogue move. When Alisha sends a new message, players receive an alert, which they can ignore or view and respond to using a text chat interface. Although the dialogue moves Alisha made are worded differently across the Diegetic and Non-Diegetic conditions (Table 1), the underlying dialogue goals and the conditions that triggered them were identical. In general, Diegetic dialogue moves address the learner's task while also referring to the learner's role within the story (the mission) and Alisha's role within the story through the use of first-person plural pronouns "we," "us," and "our." Conversely, the Non-Diegetic dialogue moves address only the learner's tasks as posed by the game, not the learner's persona within the narrative. The average number of dialogue moves the agent made in each student's session in the Diegetic ($M = 43.9$, $SD = 20.0$) and the Non-Diegetic ($M = 43.0$, $SD = 18.1$) condition were not statistically different.

Alisha's persona, appearance, and dialogue were designed based on empirical research and a series of focus groups with middle school students. Her dialogue is designed to (1) encourage good problem-solving strategies, (2) mitigate negative affective states [14], and (3) foster a growth mindset [15]. Regarding strategy use, Alisha encourages note taking, reflection, hypothesis forming, and goal setting/planning, drawn from research on self-regulated learning [16] as this skillset has been shown to be an important predictor of success in this learning environment [17]. Alisha uses a mix of questions, hints, and suggestions. For instance, when the story context combined with the learner's typed natural language input trigger one particular dialogue state, the Diegetic agent says, *Let's see how that fits into our mission objectives. That could help us make a plan.* This dialogue move is intended to encourage learners to reflect on their goals when they may be feeling stuck while choosing a next step.

When student dialogue moves or in-game behaviors indicate that the student may be frustrated or bored (two key affective states that have been found to inhibit learning [14]), the agent is designed to offer affective support. The dialogue moves that provide this support are based on approaches used in dialogue design for a successful affective learning companion that conveys empathy and shared experience [7]. For example, if the learner expresses frustration, the Diegetic companion might utilize humor contextualized within her backstory as an artificially intelligent agent who was sent to help the learner. To convey empathy toward the student, the agent might say, *This is a tough mission! My circuits sometimes get fried when I feel like I'm not making progress.*

Growth mindset refers to the implicitly-held belief that intellectual ability can be increased with effort, and this belief shapes learners' motivation and approach to learning [15]. The virtual learning companion is designed to encourage growth mindset by emphasizing strategy and perseverance rather than innate intelligence. For example, the Diegetic companion always follows the *tough mission* move above with growth-mindset promotion: *This is a tough mission! My circuits sometimes get fried when I feel like I'm not making progress. But I know if we keep choosing good strategies, we can help those sick scientists!*

In both the Diegetic and Non-Diegetic conditions, the interface for chatting with Alisha is available to the student at all times except while they are engaged in menu-based interaction with other game characters, and while interacting with scientific texts or embedded assessments. In the Diegetic condition, the student interacts with Alisha via a mobile device to convey the sense of interacting with another persona in the game world (Fig. 2, *left*). In the Non-Diegetic condition, Alisha's dialogue appears with the same look-and-feel as other game interface elements, tooltips, and game menus (Fig. 2, *right*).

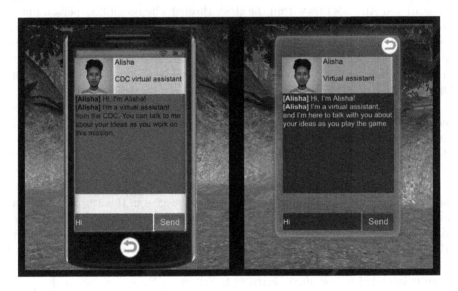

Fig. 2. Dialogue interfaces for the two learning companion study conditions: Diegetic (left) and Non-Diegetic (right)

5   Virtual Learning Companion Study

We hypothesized that gender differences would emerge based on the learning companion condition. To explore this hypothesis, we carried out a three-condition study in six classrooms across two urban middle schools in the United States. A total of 132 students (75 from one school and 57 from another) were randomly assigned into one of the three conditions: Diegetic, Non-Diegetic, or Baseline. Out of the 132 participants, 63 students (48%) identified as female, 54 (41%) as male, 8 (6%) identified as Other, and 7 (5%) students did not report their gender. The mean age was 13.30 years ($SD = 0.76$). One learner did not report race, while 19 (14%) identified as Black or African American, 70 (53%) White or Caucasian, 30 (23%) as other races, and 12 (9%) as more than one race. Most of the students reported prior experience playing games, with only 17 (13%) reporting that they never played. We confirmed using separate one-way ANOVAs that there were no significant between-conditions differences among these students in pretest score or video game play frequency.

In the Diegetic condition there were 23 (61%) female and 15 (39%) male students, while the Non-Diegetic condition had 19 (45%) female and 23 (55%) male students. The Baseline condition included 21 (57%) female and 16 (43%) male students. Participants were given laptops and headphones and played in their regular classrooms and seating arrangements. Each student interacted with the version of the game to which they were randomly assigned for approximately one hour per day for three consecutive days.

Prior to interaction, participants completed a multiple-choice pre-test on the game's science content. After each of the three days of the classroom study, brief surveys were administered, including measures of engagement (the User Engagement Survey [18]) and mental demand (from the NASA Task Load Index [19]). A content knowledge post-test (identical to the pre-test) was administered after gameplay.

6   Results

Using the post-gameplay surveys completed by each student, we test our hypothesis that gender differences would be observed in different agent conditions. We excluded all students ($n = 15$) who either identified their gender as "other" or did not report gender, leaving 117 participants. Several significant differences emerged, which we present here. Normalized learning gain was calculated to obtain a proportional indicator of learning, and is simply referred to in the remainder of this document as learning gain.

Table 2. Descriptive statistics for engagement, learning gain, and mental demand by condition and gender. Starred pairs of means represent significant pairwise comparisons ($p < 0.05$) by Tukey HSD.

Condition		Engagement		Learning gain		Mental demand	
		Female	Male	Female	Male	Female	Male
Diegetic	M	**109.2***	**91.33***	.03052	−.1441	54.52	56.73
	SD	16.11	19.49	.2667	.3213	26.17	32.09
Non-Diegetic	M	104.5	97.17	.1639	.05788	**59.37****	**32.83****
	SD	14.04	15.94	.3515	.4448	24.70	22.27
Baseline	M	102.7	101.2	.02876	.1137	57.05	55.94
	SD	14.04	15.94	.3515	.4448	24.70	22.27
All conditions	M	105.6	96.74	.07016	.01831	56.83	46.31
	SD	16.34	17.83	.2979	.4108	25.45	30.17

First, we evaluated the overall effect of learning companion condition: Diegetic, Non-Diegetic, and Baseline. One-way ANOVAs found no main effect

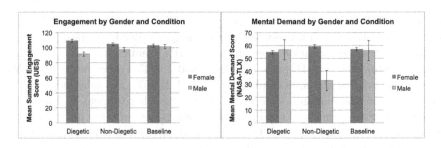

Fig. 3. Mean engagement (left) and mean mental demand (right) by gender and study condition.

of condition on engagement, learning gain, or mental demand. Gender was found as a main effect for both engagement and mental demand: a one-way ANOVA for engagement with gender as a factor found a significant main effect ($F(1,115) = 7.9233$, $p = .0057$) of small-to-medium size ($\omega^2 = .05587$), with girls reporting higher engagement than boys (Table 2). A separate one-way ANOVA found a significant main effect of gender on mental demand ($F(1,115) = 4.1775$, $p = .0432$), of small size ($\omega^2 = .02644$), with girls reporting significantly higher mental demand than boys (Table 2).

To investigate the impact of learning companion condition on learning gain, engagement, and mental demand, we performed 2×3 ANOVAs with gender (male/female) and learning companion condition (Diegetic/Non-Diegetic/Baseline) as the independent variables. The ANOVA found no significant effects on learning gain. With engagement as the dependent variable, we observed a significant main effect of gender ($F(1, 115) = 2.4579$, $p = .0375$) of small-to-medium size ($\omega^2 = .05489$) (Fig. 3, left). Girls from all conditions reported a higher mean engagement score than boys from all conditions (Table 2). Post-hoc Tukey HSD tests showed that the difference between boys' and girls' mean engagement was significant only in the diegetic condition (Diegetic condition: $N_{female} = 23$, $N_{male} = 15$, $p = .0237$). Finally, taking mental demand as the dependent variable, the ANOVA demonstrated a significant interaction of gender and game condition on mental demand ($F(1, 115) = 2.9512$, $p = .0154$) with a moderately small effect size ($\omega^2 = .03733$) (Fig. 3, right). Post-hoc Tukey HSD tests showed that boys in the Non-Diegetic condition reported significantly lower mental demand than girls in the same condition ($p = .0482$).

Overall, boys scored lower ($M = 6.222$, $SD = 2.567$) than girls ($M = 7.270$, $SD = 2.772$) on the content knowledge pre-test ($t(114.3) = -2.1207$, $p = .0361$). Boys also reported more hours per week playing video games ($M = 2.185$ h, $SD = 1.36$) than girls ($M = 1.587$ h, $SD = 1.04$) ($t(98.39) = 2.634$, $p = .0098$). To confirm that neither of these differences explained gender effects, we controlled for pre-test score and video game experience by adding them alongside gender and condition within multiple regression models for engagement and mental demand. The same effects revealed in the ANOVAs held in each model.

7 Discussion

The results suggest that the extent to which a virtual learning companion is integrated into the story of a game-based learning environment has a significantly different impact on boys and girls. We observed significant impacts of gender on engagement and mental demand, but no effect of gender on learning outcome. Girls were more engaged than boys both overall and within the Diegetic condition; mental demand was statistically the same for girls and boys overall and within every condition, except for the Non-Diegetic condition, where boys reported much lower mental demand than girls.

First, we consider the gender difference in engagement, with girls more engaged than boys. While Tukey HSD post-hoc tests did not reveal significant pairwise differences except between boys and girls in the Diegetic condition, visual inspection of the means (Table 2) finds boys and girls reported nearly identical average engagement in the baseline condition and diverged more noticeably in the two learning companion conditions. Based on boys' conversations with the agent (e.g., Fig. 4), one plausible explanation for this pattern is that boys were less engaged by the learning companion's attempts to provide affective support and encouragement to discuss their reasoning. This is consistent with prior studies of learning companions designed to influence affective outcomes [6,7].

Alisha:	Try asking yourself, "Does this fit in with anything else about the mission?"	Alisha:	Try to keep questioning your hypothesis as we learn new things about this mystery!
Kiana:	yes. It fits everything, the people sick claimed to have all eaten breakfast together	Ava:	ok
Emily:	it does....but samonella is still my top pick	Lily:	will you tell me when im right?
Nerea:	YOUR MY FAVORTE	Chloe:	true . thanks Alisha. keep in touch
Carlos:	I asked myself	Isaiah:	(no response)
Ethan:	nah dag	David:	(no response)
Malik:	no	Jacob:	de acuerdo

Fig. 4. Examples of girls' (middle row) and boys' (bottom row) responses to two of Alisha's utterances from the Diegetic condition. All names are pseudonyms.

With regard to mental demand, it is unclear whether a higher rating of perceived mental demand is necessarily a negative reflection on the learning experience, either in terms of user experience (boys' engagement was not affected by condition) or in terms of learning (there were no condition or gender effects on learning gain). A more detailed investigation of this outcome is warranted.

The corollary of these interpretations is that girls were more engaged overall, and no condition showed a dip in girls' engagement. This suggests that our over-arching design choices for both companion versions—to characterize the agent as female, to focus on affective support, and to encourage an ongoing dialogue with the agent—contributed to, or at least did not detract from, girls' engagement in the learning activity.

Key factors that could potentially have driven the observed differences (video game experience, prior content knowledge) significantly differed by gender. However, when we controlled for video game experience and for prior knowledge of the subject matter, we found that neither factor had an effect on the *outcomes* for which we observed the gender effects. This suggests that gender impacts engagement and mental demand above and beyond these gender-linked factors.

Limitations. The condition assignments were not strictly balanced by gender; for example, there were 15 boys and 23 girls in the Diegetic condition. While the statistical tests utilized are fairly robust to these imbalances, it is important to keep them in mind. We also observed social dynamics in which groups of boys disparaged the learning companion and the activity as a whole, which may have influenced a more negative view of the agent among boys. This dynamic seemed much less prevalent or absent among girls. Finally, the mean scores on engagement, learning gain, and mental demand were significantly different between the two schools from which the participants were recruited, and these school-level differences merit further analyses. Further studies are needed to address these limitations.

8   Design Recommendations

This study builds upon the emerging set of design recommendations regarding gender and virtual learning companions. The results suggest that designers of virtual learning companions should consider the following design implications:

1. The extent to which virtual learning companions are integrated into the narrative of a game-based learning environment has important effects on students. Narrative integration may benefit girls more than boys.
2. A learning companion design that is removed from the narrative of a learning environment may reduce mental demand for boys without affecting learning outcomes.
3. Overall, girls may feel more engaged than boys when interacting with virtual learning companions. This may have an important impact on girls' developing academic attitudes toward STEM subjects during a critical time in their lives when many girls lose interest in these subjects or come to believe they cannot succeed in them.
4. In order to achieve the highest possible effectiveness, designers should accommodate for factors driving different needs and expectations, including gender, for instance by giving students options to choose the kind of learning companion they prefer to interact with.

9   Conclusion

Gender is an important factor in children's outcomes with learning companions, but there are many unexplored questions about the role of design choices in gender-related outcome differences. This paper presented a study in which middle school students interacted with one of two differently designed learning companions, or no learning companion. The results indicate that gender indeed has important effects on students' affective experience during learning, and that these effects are not explained by differences that tend to co-occur with gender (such as video game experience). The findings suggest some design elements with gender-related differences in impact, such as a reduction in boys' mental demand when an agent is framed as a part of an interface and an improvement in girls' engagement when an agent is framed as co-experiencing the storyworld alongside them.

Future work should pursue more fine-grained and process-based analyses of gender differences in outcomes with virtual learning companions. The specific design elements of the Diegetic agent that made it so engaging for girls should be explored, as should the relationship between mental demand and other outcomes. Also called for is an investigation of beliefs and attitudes not measured in this study, which may drive differences in outcomes such as those reported here. It will be important to develop a deeper understanding of how virtual learning companions can most effectively support learners of all genders in engaging learning interactions.

Acknowledgements. The authors are grateful for the thoughtful input of the members of the LearnDialogue group. This work is supported by the National Science Foundation through grant CHS-1409639. Any opinions, findings, and conclusions or recommendations expressed in this material are those of the author(s) and do not necessarily reflect the views of the National Science Foundation.

References

1. Schroeder, N.L., Adesope, O.O., Gilbert, R.B.: How effective are pedagogical agents for learning? a meta-analytic review. J. Educ. Comput. Res. **49**(1), 1–39 (2013)
2. Kim, Y., Baylor, A.L.: A social cognitive framework for pedagogical agents as learning companions. Educ. Tech. Res. Dev. **54**(6), 569–596 (2006)
3. Kim, Y., Baylor, A.L.: PALS group: pedagogical agents as learning companions: the role of agent competency and type of interaction. Educ. Tech. Res. Dev. **54**(3), 223–243 (2006)
4. Kim, Y., Baylor, A.L.: Research-based design of pedagogical agent roles: a review, progress, and recommendations. Int. J. Artif. Intell. Educ. (IJAIED) **26**(1), 160–169 (2016)
5. Rowe, J.P., Shores, L.R., Mott, B.W., Lester, J.C.: Integrating learning, problem solving, and engagement in narrative-centered learning environments. Int. J. Artif. Intell. Educ. (IJAIED) **21**(1–2), 115–133 (2011)
6. Arroyo, I., Woolf, B.P., Cooper, D.G., Burleson, W., Muldner, K.: The impact of animated pedagogical agents on girls' and boys' emotions, attitudes, behaviors and learning. In: Proceedings of the IEEE International Conference on Advanced Learning Technology, Athens, GA, pp. 506–510 (2011)

7. Buffum, P.S., Boyer, K.E., Wiebe, E.N., Mott, B.W., Lester, J.C.: Mind the gap: improving gender equity in game-based learning environments with learning companions. In: Proceedings of the 17th International Conference on Artificial Intelligence in Education (AIED), pp. 64–73 (2015)

8. Ryokai, K., Vaucelle, C., Cassell, J.: Virtual peers as partners in storytelling and literacy learning. J. Comput. Assist. Learn. **19**, 195–208 (2003)

9. Cassell, J., Geraghty, K., Gonzalez, B., Borland, J.: Modeling culturally authentic style shifting with virtual peers. In: Proceedings of the 2009 International Conference on Multimodal Interfaces - ICMI-MLMI 2009, pp. 135–142 (2009)

10. Plant, E.A., Baylor, A.L., Doerr, C.E., Rosenberg-Kima, R.B.: Changing middle-school students' attitudes and performance regarding engineering with computer-based social models. Comput. Educ. **53**(2), 209–215 (2009)

11. Woolf, B.P., Arroyo, I., Muldner, K., Burleson, W.: The effect of motivational learning companions on low achieving students and students with disabilities. In: Intelligent Tutoring Systems, pp. 327–337 (2010)

12. Grawemeyer, B., Mavrikis, M., Holmes, W., Gutierrez-Santos, S.: Adapting feedback types according to students affective states. In: Proceedings of the 17th International Conference on Artificial Intelligence in Education (AIED), pp. 586–590 (2015)

13. Grawemeyer, B., Mavrikis, M., Holmes, W., Hansen, A., Loibl, K., Gutiérrez-Santos, S.: Affect matters: exploring the impact of feedback during mathematical tasks in an exploratory environment. In: Proceedings of the 17th International Conference on Artificial Intelligence in Education (AIED), pp. 595–599 (2015)

14. Baker, R.S.J.D., D'Mello, S.K., Rodrigo, M.M.T., Graesser, A.C.: Better to be frustrated than bored: the incidence and persistence of affect during interactions with three different computer-based learning environments. Int. J. Hum. Comput. Stud. **68**(4), 223–241 (2010)

15. Dweck, C.S.: Self-Theories: Their Role in Motivation, Personality, and Development. Essays in social psychology. Psychology Press, New York (1999)

16. Azevedo, R., Cromley, J.G.: Does training on self-regulated learning facilitate students' learning with hypermedia? J. Educ. Psychol. **96**(3), 523–535 (2004)

17. Sabourin, J., Shores, L., Bradford, W., Lester, J.C.: Understanding and predicting student self-regulated learning strategies in game-based learning environments. Int. J. Artif. Intell. Educ. (IJAIED) **23**(1–4), 94–114 (2013)

18. O'Brien, H.L., Toms, E.G.: The development and evaluation of a survey to measure user engagement in e-commerce environments. J. Am. Soc. Inform. Sci. Technol. **61**(1), 50–69 (2010)

19. Hart, S.G., Staveland, L.E.: Development of NASA-TLX (Task Load Index): Results of empirical and theoretical research. Adv. Psychol. **52**, 139–183 (1988)

Hint Generation Under Uncertainty: The Effect of Hint Quality on Help-Seeking Behavior

Thomas W. Price[(✉)], Rui Zhi, and Tiffany Barnes

North Carolina State University, Raleigh, NC 27606, USA
{twprice,rzhi,tmbarnes}@ncsu.edu

Abstract. Much research in Intelligent Tutoring Systems has explored how to provide on-demand hints, how they should be used, and what effect they have on student learning and performance. Most of this work relies on hints created by experts and assumes that all help provided by the tutor is correct and of high quality. However, hints may not all be of equal value, especially in open-ended problem solving domains, where context is important. This work argues that hint quality, especially when using data-driven hint generation techniques, is inherently uncertain. We investigate the impact of hint quality on students' help-seeking behavior in an open-ended programming environment with on-demand hints. Our results suggest that the quality of the first few hints on an assignment is positively associated with future hint use on the same assignment. Initial hint quality also correlates with possible help abuse. These results have important implications for hint design and generation.

Keywords: Intelligent Tutoring Systems · Hints · Help-seeking · Programming

1 Introduction and Related Work

A hallmark of Intelligent Tutoring Systems (ITSs) is their ability to provide next-step help to students while they work on problems. A variety of work has explored how such help can be generated [6,14], how it should be ideally used [2], and its impact on student performance and learning [7,16]. However, this body of work generally makes the assumption that all help provided by the tutor is equally useful and of high-quality. While some work distinguishes between levels of hints (e.g. pointing, teaching and bottom-out hints), each level represents "correct" advice, and is therefore assumed to be useful.

In this paper, we argue that this assumption is not always valid. Increasingly, ITSs employ data-driven hint generation to reduce the need for expensive expert modelling and to target domains where such modelling is difficult [12,14]. While data-driven hints can be designed to meet quality criteria, (e.g. leading to a valid solution), this does not necessarily mean that every hint is useful to every student. In fact, a comparison of various hint generators found high variance in their agreement with expert hints [11]. Even hints engineered by experts are

© Springer International Publishing AG 2017
E. André et al. (Eds.): AIED 2017, LNAI 10331, pp. 311–322, 2017.
DOI: 10.1007/978-3-319-61425-0_26

still subject to the "expert blindspot," where expert domain knowledge fails to translate into pedagogically useful feedback. Further, domains such as open-ended programming are so complex that even the best hints may not account for the diversity of possible solution paths a student might pursue [12]. Outside of ITSs, researchers have found that feedback has widely varying effects on task performance, often negative, depending on a multitude of factors [9], so we might expect similar variability in ITSs.

Because hint quality in open-ended problem-solving domains can be uncertain, it is important to understand its impact on students. In this work, we investigate the effect of hint quality on students' help-seeking behavior in an open-ended programming environment with on-demand hints. Help-seeking plays an important role in student learning in ITSs, and students frequently fail to make good use of help facilities [2]. We present evidence that hint quality does affect both positive and negative help-seeking behaviors.

1.1   Next-Step Hints in ITSs

ITSs traditionally offer next-step hints as support for individual steps within a problem-solving task. Hints can be provided on-demand or in response to an error, immediately or after a delay. ITSs may present multiple levels of a hint, with increasing specificity, and most include some form of "bottom-out" hint, in which the tutor tells the student exactly how to proceed. Hints in ITSs have been historically grounded in a number of theories. Under the ACT-R model [5], hints can turn an otherwise unsolvable problem into a useful worked example. Under a Vygotskian model, hints play a scaffolding role, bridging the gap between a student's knowledge and the requirements of the problem, and keeping the student in the Zone of Proximal Development (ZPD) [10].

Traditionally, next-step hints are generated using an expert model, such as the Model Tracing found in cognitive tutors (e.g. [7]). By modelling the problem domain, the tutor can identify errors in the student's work and suggest next steps, generally using templated messages. More recently, data-driven hint generation techniques such as the Hint Factory [6] have shown that hints can be generated without an expert model using previous students' attempts at a given problem. Data-driven hint generation was first applied to logic proofs [16] and has since seen a number of applications in open-ended programming [11,12,14].

Empirical evaluations of the effect of next-step hints on student learning have shown positive results. Stamper et al. [16] compared students working with and without on-demand hints in the Deep Thought logic tutor across two semesters and found that the hint group completed more of the tutor, had less dropout and had higher final course grades than the control group. Corbett and Anderson [7] compared a variety of help mechanisms in the ACT Programming Tutor, including on-demand hints, and found that students who received any type of feedback during tutoring completed a subsequent programming assessment in significantly less time, with significantly fewer errors. Piech et al. [11] evaluated a number of hint generation policies in the domain of programming based on their agreement with "gold-standard" hints, authored by human experts, and found that their best hint policy achieved 95.9% and 84.6% agreement with the gold standard hints on two assignments. Aleven et al. [3] point out that some of these studies are not truly experimental, and hints may play a less substantial role in learning than previously thought, especially compared to other interventions, such as support for self-explanation.

1.2 Help-Seeking in ITSs

Help-seeking is a self-regulatory skill that plays an important role in learning. It pertains to a student's ability to appropriately seek out and use available help resources when problem solving. In ITSs, researchers have noted that students generally display poor help-seeking behaviors [4]. For example, Aleven and Koedinger [1] found that students using the PACT Geometry Tutor focused primarily on bottom-out hints, skipping through other hint levels on 82%–89% of steps. Wood and Wood [18] studied students working in the QUADRATIC learning environment and found that those with lower prior knowledge were more likely to seek help and benefit from it. However, in a later study of a different system in which they used a pretest to select challenging problems for each student, they found these differences disappeared [17], suggesting that the effect is due to subjective problem difficulty, rather than prior knowledge alone.

Guided by theoretical perspectives and empirical evidence, Aleven et al. developed a model of desired student help-seeking behavior in a cognitive tutor and implemented the Help Tutor, itself a cognitive tutor, to teach the skill of help-seeking [2]. Their model also defined help-seeking bugs, including Help Abuse, in which students misuse or overuse help, and Help Avoidance, in which a student could benefit from help but chooses not to request it. In an empirical evaluation, they found that help-seeking errors negatively correlated with domain learning, that the Help Tutor reduced the incidence of some of these errors, but that it had no impact on domain learning [15]. Aleven et al. also offer useful reviews of help-seeking research in interactive learning environments [2–4].

2   iSnap

The dataset analyzed in this paper comes from students using iSnap [13], an extension of Snap! [8], a block-based programming environment for novices. iSnap augments Snap! with many features of an ITS, including on-demand, data-driven hints, generated using the CTD algorithm [12]. Students request hints by clicking a Help button, after which their code is annotated with multiple hint buttons, each corresponding to a contextual hint generated based on their current code. Hovering over a button highlights the code to which the hint applies.

When a hint button is clicked, all buttons disappear and the student is shown a next-step hint window, which generally suggests a single edit to the student's code, such as inserting, deleting or reordering a code element. The hints are presented visually, as shown in Fig. 1, demonstrating the edit to make. These

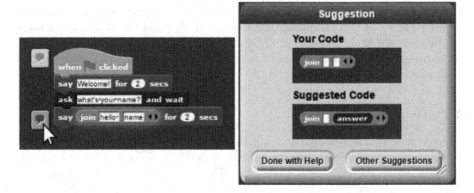

Fig. 1. A student's code is annotated with hint buttons (left). Upon clicking a button, a hint window suggests a change to the student's code (right).

are similar to "bottom-out" hints, in that they tell the student exactly what to do, but they do omit some details, such as variable names and literal values. Students can continue to work with the hint window showing, or they can dismiss it, optionally choosing to re-show the hint buttons. Students can click through multiple hints this way, searching for one that suits their needs.

3   Methods

This study was conducted during an introductory computing course for non-majors, consisting of 68 students, held at a research university during the Fall 2016 semester. During the first half of the course, the lab sections taught the Snap! programming language through a curriculum based on the Beauty and Joy of Computing (BJC) [8]. The course included three in-lab programming assignments, which were completed in class with help available from teaching assistants, interleaved with three homework assignments, which were completed independently. Students completed all work in iSnap, and data-driven hints were available on the 2nd, 3rd, 4th and 5th assignments, shown in Table 1. Hints were generated using data from the Spring 2016 semester.

Before the first hint-enabled assignment, a researcher briefly introduced the hint interface, explaining that the students were encouraged to use hints without any penalty to their grades and that the hints may not be perfect. iSnap reminded students that help was available at the start of each assignment. There was no limit on the number of hints a student could request. iSnap recorded complete logs of hint requests and snapshots of students' code after each edit. Students did not login to use iSnap, so unfortunately we cannot analyze a given student's work over multiple assignments due the anonymous logs.

Using the log data, we identified 642 hint requests (when a hint button was clicked, as in Fig. 1) across the four hint-enabled assignments. For each hint, we calculated how long the hint window was viewed and how long after viewing it

Table 1. For each assignment with hints available, the number of attempts submitted (N), the number of attempts with one or more hint requests (H), the mean grade with SD, and the agreement (κ) for the graders.

Assignment	Type	N	H	Mean grade (SD)	Grader κ
Polygon maker	In-lab	65	11 (17%)	97.5% (9.0%)	0.62
Squiral	HW	60	18 (30%)	78.6% (23.0%)	0.79
Guessing Game 1	In-lab	66	13 (20%)	95.2% (10.8%)	0.81
Guessing Game 2	HW	59	13 (22%)	89.8% (17.8%)	0.63

the student made their next code edit. Because each hint suggested a specific edit to the student's code, we were also able to label each hint as "followed" if the student's code reflected the suggestion within their next 5 edits. Some students viewed a single hint multiple times in a short time span. For example, a student might browse through multiple hints and then return to one to implement it. We considered two hints duplicates for a given student if they suggested the exact same edit, and the student viewed the two hints within 60 s, or without changing their code in between. We merged duplicate hint requests to produce 542 final hint requests, which we used in our analysis. We considered these merged hints to be "followed" if any of their component hints were followed.

3.1 Submission Grading and Hint Rating

For each assignment, we identified 5–6 assignment objectives based on the instructions and the course instructor's grading rubric. Two researchers independently graded each submission, marking each objective as complete or incomplete. The graders discussed disagreements to produce a final grade for each submission, calculated as the percent of objectives completed. Interrater reliability is given for each assignment by Cohen's kappa (κ) in Table 1.

We also developed a detailed hint rating rubric to quantify the quality of iSnap hints.[1] The hint rubric has 3 attributes, each rated 1, 2 or 3, with higher scores being better: *Relevance*, how likely the hint is to address one of the student's current goals; *Progress*, how well the hint moves the student's current code to a correct solution without removing useful code; and *Interpretability*, how easily a novice could understand the intention and value of the hint.

Across all four assignments, a total of 55 assignment attempts included at least one hint request. These may include attempts from the same student on multiple assignments. Of these 55 attempts, 39 (70.9%) included a second hint request, and 29 (52.7%) included a third request. We limited our analysis to the first 2 hints in an attempt, since barely half of the relevant attempts included a third hint request. This resulted in a subset of 94 hints that were selected for rating. Two authors independently rated these hints on each attribute. The raters had access to a snapshot of the student's code when the hint was shown.

---

[1] Complete rubric and dataset available at: http://go.ncsu.edu/aied2017-rubric.

Disagreements were discussed and resolved to produce final ratings. The hint raters achieved squared-weighted Cohen's kappas of 0.857, 0.756 and 0.685 for Relevance, Progress and Interpretability, respectively. This indicates substantial agreement, and while we make no claims that the ratings are objectively "correct," the multiple raters helped to ensure consistent ratings across hints.

4   Analysis

We structured our analysis around the following four research questions, which are addressed in the following subsections:

RQ1. How frequently did students use and follow hints in iSnap?
RQ2. How did hint use relate to student performance on assignments?
RQ3. How did a given hint's quality affect whether it was followed?
RQ4. How did the quality of students' first hints affect their future help use?

4.1   Hint Use in iSnap

With 542 unique hint requests over 250 assignment attempts, students received on average 2.2 hints per assignment. This average is misleading, however, since the number of hints requested per student varied widely. The percentage of students who requested at least one hint on a given assignment ranged from 16.9% to 30.0%, with somewhat higher usage on homework assignments. Despite being introduced to the hint system in class and receiving reminders from iSnap before starting work, the majority of students never used the help on a given assignment. This is consistent with studies of help-seeking in other domains, where hint-usage rates were low. For example, Aleven and Koedinger found hints were used on 22–29% of steps in the PACT Geometry Tutor [1].

Across assignments, 55 attempts (22%) included at least one hint request. Many of these attempts included only 1–2 hint requests (47.3%), but those with 3 or more requests had a median of 16 hint requests per attempt, with a maximum of 68. Of all hints requested, 41.3% were followed. An additional 16.4% of hints were unfollowed but occurred within 1 min of a later hint that *was* followed, indicating that a majority (57.5%) of help requests were closely followed by some resolution. For attempts on any assignment which included at least 1 hint request, we compared the number of hints requested with the percent of hints followed. There is a significant, positive Spearman correlation between the two values ($\rho = 0.552$; $S = 12415$; $p < 0.001$), indicating that students who asked for more hints on a given assignment were also more likely to have followed them.

When a student chose to follow a hint, they took a median 9 s after viewing the hint before making their next edit, compared with 19 s for unfollowed hints. A Mann-Whitney U test[2] showed the difference was significant ($U = 18164$; $p < 0.001$). Students also viewed the hint window for hints they ended up following for less time (Med $= 5$) than those they did not (Med $= 6$), and the difference was significant ($U = 31550$; $p = 0.026$). This suggests that students needed less time to process a hint when they ultimately followed it.

---

[2] The Mann-Whitney U test was used were data were not normally distributed.

4.2   Help Use and Performance

The course from which we collected our data did not include a pre- or post-test on Snap! programming, so we have no measure of learning. Instead, we focus on programming performance on the assignments to evaluate the impact of hints. While this is not a substitute for learning, it does provide insight into how well the hints played their intended role of scaffolding students during programming. Due to the presence of TAs for the in-lab assignments and the high grades students achieved (see Table 1), we focus on the two homework assignments. We defined meaningful hint usage as requesting and following at least one hint, and we labeled attempts with meaningful hint usage as F1, and those without as F0.

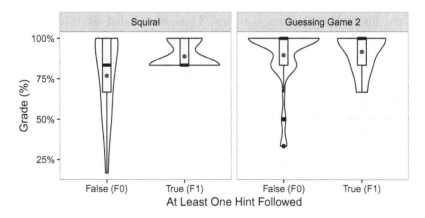

Fig. 2. Violin plots comparing grade distributions for F0 and F1 attempts at both the Squiral (left) and Guessing Game 2 (right) homeworks. Inside each plot is a boxplot, and a red dot indicating average grade. (Color figure online)

Figure 2 shows violin plots of the grade distributions for both homework assignments, comparing F0 and F1 attempts. We can see that F1 attempts perform at least as well as their counterparts, with equal median grades and higher average grades on both assignments. This was not a controlled study, so we can make no claims about the direct effect of hints on performance. However, previous studies have found that students with lower prior knowledge are more likely to request help [18], so if the hints had no effect, we would expect those using them to perform worse, rather than at least as well.

One of the justifications for including hints on a homework assignment is that they allow students to progress when they are "stuck" and do not know how to proceed, allowing them perform adequately on an assignment. We define adequate performance as missing no more than 1 assignment objective (out of 5–6 total). By this definition, 100.0% (9/9) of F1 students performed adequately on Squiral, compared 60.8% (31/51) of F0 students. On Guessing Game 2, 87.5% (7/8) of F1 students performed adequately, as did 88.2% (45/51) of F0 students. Put another way, homework attempts with meaningful hint usage (F1) almost always achieved adequate grades (16/17), and many of the remaining homework attempts (F0) did not achieve adequate grades (26/102). However, different homework assignments do show different impacts of hint use.

The prevalence of students with poor performance and no meaningful hint usage indicates Help Avoidance [2], where students could benefit from using help but choose not to. While there are many things we could do to encourage students to start using the help system, the remainder of this section focuses on how hint quality affects hint use, once students have started using the help.

4.3   Hint Quality and Immediate Hint Use

Our dataset of rated hints consists of 94 hints, the first and second hints requested for each assignment attempt. These were rated on three attributes from 1–3: Relevance, Progress and Interpretability, as described in Sect. 3.1. While these attributes were selected to be relatively independent, we first inspected the relationships among them. Each attribute pair showed a significant positive Spearman's correlation: Relevance and Progress ($\rho = 0.664$; $S = 46454$; $p < 0.001$); Progress and Interpretability ($\rho = 0.777$; $S = 30842$; $p < 0.001$); Relevance and Interpretability ($\rho = 0.632$; $S = 50919$; $p < 0.001$). Due to the high correlations, we also computed a Quality attribute, the sum of the other three, ranging from 3 to 9, and use this for most of our analysis.

An assumption that underlies our investigation is that the quality of data-driven hints is not uniform. We attempted to verify this empirically on our sample of rated hints. While the median Quality ratings for the first and second hints received were high, 7 and 8 respectively, the standard deviations were also high: 2.1 and 2.2, respectively. Out of all 94 rated hints, 30 (31.9%) were rated below the middle possible rating of 6. This suggests that the quality of our sample did vary enough to potentially impact students.

We then investigated the relationship between hint Quality ratings and whether or not a hint was followed. This was in part to confirm the validity of our ratings, since we hypothesize that valid hint ratings would be predictive of whether or not a hint was followed. However, we also note that this *is* an assumption. The theory of ideal help use put forward by Aleven et al. [2] suggests a student *should* evaluate the helpfulness of a hint before applying it, but to our knowledge this has not been investigated empirically in ITSs.

First hints had a median Quality rating of 7, and those with at least that rating were four times as likely to be followed (14/34 = 41.2%) as those with lower ratings (2/21 = 9.5%). Second hints had a median Quality rating of 8, and those with at least that rating were three times as likely to be followed (11/21 = 52.4%) as those with lower ratings (3/18 = 16.7%). Put another way, first hints that were followed had higher Quality ratings (n = 16; Med = 8) than unfollowed hints (n = 39; Med = 7), and a Mann-Whitney U test showed that the difference was significant ($U = 437.5$; $p = 0.018$). For second hints, followed hints were also rated higher (n = 13; Med = 8) than unfollowed hints (n = 26; Med = 6.5), and the difference was significant ($U = 276.0$; $p = 0.001$).

Table 2. Mean attribute ratings (with standard deviation) for first and second hints of attempts with each hint usage label. All hint ratings are summarized at the bottom.

Hint	Label	N	Relevance	Progress	Interpretability	Quality
1	Low	23	1.96 (0.88)	2.13 (0.92)	1.83 (0.72)	5.91 (2.13)
	Med.	15	2.27 (0.88)	2.47 (0.74)	1.80 (0.68)	6.53 (2.13)
	High	17	2.35 (0.70)	2.65 (0.70)	2.12 (0.86)	7.12 (1.90)
2	Low	7	1.57 (0.79)	1.86 (0.90)	1.57 (0.79)	5.00 (2.38)
	Med.	15	2.13 (0.83)	2.53 (0.74)	2.00 (0.76)	6.67 (2.06)
	High	17	2.53 (0.72)	2.71 (0.69)	2.29 (0.77)	7.53 (1.97)
1, 2	All	94	2.18 (0.83)	2.43 (0.81)	1.97 (0.77)	6.57 (2.14)

We conclude that hint quality strongly affects the likelihood that a student will follow a hint, and that the Quality metric is reasonable. Students also have quite high standards for hints they will follow, with median 8 and 8.5 Quality ratings out of a possible 9, for followed first and second hints respectively. While the magnitudes of our ratings are somewhat relative, this is still strong evidence that students are capable of noting and disregarding flawed hints.

4.4   Hint Quality and Future Hint Use

It is encouraging that students can identify and disregard lower quality hints, but what effect does encountering such hints have on a student's future hint use? To answer this question, we labeled each attempt that used hints as Low, Medium or High hint usage, where each label corresponds to a 3-quantile of the number of hints requested for a given assignment. For example, hint requests for the Guessing Game 1 had 3-quantiles [3, 11], so the labels were $n \leq 3$ (Low), $3 < n \leq 11$ (Medium) and $11 < n$ (High), where n is the number of hints requested. Table 2 shows average attribute ratings for the first and second hints per attempt for each usage label. There is a consistent trend of ratings increasing with label, with only one exception for the Interpretability of the first hint.

There was a significant, positive Spearman correlation between an attempt's label and the Quality rating of the first hint received ($\rho = 0.267$; $S = 20322$; $p = 0.049$) and the second hint received ($\rho = 0.409$; $S = 5838$; $p = 0.010$). Additionally, hint Quality ratings had a significant positive Spearman correlation with the percentage of future hints that were *followed* for second hints ($\rho = 0.413$; $S = 2384$; $p = 0.026$) but not first hints ($\rho = 0.201$; $S = 7892$; $p = 0.219$). Together, these findings strongly suggest that better initial hints encourage students to make more use of hints in the future. Another way to interpret this result is that students can somewhat easily be deterred from using hints if they encounter one that does not seem useful. Looking only at the first 2 hints in an attempt, students stop asking for hints after receiving a hint that is at least median Quality only 18.2% of the time (10/55), while they stop 41.0% of the time after lower Quality hints (16/39), over twice as often.

5   Discussion

RQ1. *How frequently did students use and follow hints in iSnap?* Consistent with prior results [1], we found that help use in iSnap was quite low overall. Few assignment attempts included help requests (17–30% across assignments), and many attempts which had help requests only had one or two hints (38–64%). A quarter of student homework attempts missed multiple objectives, but few of these had meaningful hint usage, suggesting Help Avoidance. We could help to address this with a more detailed introduction on iSnap and how to use it effectively, or by offering proactive hints. Under half of hints were followed (41.3%), calling into question the hints' overall utility. However, this result was expected to some extent due to iSnap's UI, which provides students with buttons for all available hints at once, only some of which are likely to address the student's original reason for requesting help.

RQ2. *How did hint use relate to student performance on assignments?* We saw that students who followed at least one hint on homeworks performed at least as well as those who did not and rarely performed poorly. This supports the idea that help in iSnap can improve student performance, at least on some assignments. However, also consistent with the literature, we saw evidence of potential Help Abuse, with some students requesting over a dozen hints on one assignment. Since this behavior is negatively associated with learning [2], improved performance may not lead to improved learning for these students.

RQ3. *How did a given hint's quality affect whether it was followed?* We confirmed our assumption that hint quality does vary considerably among our datadriven hints. We also found empirical evidence to support the intuitive notion that students are more likely to follow higher-quality hints. We saw that the bar is quite high, with followed first and second hints having medium Quality ratings of 8 and 8.5 out of 9. This suggests that anything less than a great hint will go unused more often than not. That has serious implications for the design of data-driven hints, emphasizing the need for a vetting mechanism to ensure lower quality hints are not shown, perhaps using data on which hints have gone unfollowed in the past. However, just as there are many factors that influence a student's willingness to *seek* help in an ITS [4], we should also consider contextual factors besides hint quality that might encourage or discourage students from *following* requested hints, such as student affect.

RQ4. *How did the quality of students' first hints affect their future help use?* The impact of hint quality appears to continue on to later hints, with a positive correlation between the Quality ratings of the first two hints a student receives and the student's later level of hint usage. While we cannot speak directly to the mechanism at work here, it seems likely that a student's interactions with hints establish the student's level of trust in the system, which impacts future hint use. The first few interactions with help may be especially important, though we did not investigate later hints to verify this. Interestingly, we see that higher initial hint quality is predictive of High hint use, which could indicate Help Abuse.

One might hypothesize that students who abuse help are pre-disposed to do so, due to individual factors like prior knowledge and motivation; however, our results suggest that trust in the ITS could also play a role. We currently take no steps to prevent abuse of help in iSnap, but our results suggest this may be necessary to ensure that the majority of a completed assignment is written by the student.

6 Conclusion

In this paper we have presented evidence that in practice, data-driven hints in an ITS for programming vary in quality, which has both an immediate impact on whether students follow hints, and a long-term impact on how many hints they request. This work is novel in that it directly measures hint quality using expert ratings and investigates the impact of hint quality on students. One hypothesis that would explain this impact is that hint quality affects a student's trust in the ITS, and trust affects future help use. This has important implications for the design of ITSs, whether or not they rely on data, since all intelligent systems operate under some degree of uncertainty. Designers should carefully craft ITS help to avoid negative interactions with students, which might mean choosing *not* to offer help in uncertain situations.

This work has several limitations. Our dataset included only one programming course and four assignments, and we cannot claim that the results will generalize to other domains. iSnap differs from traditional ITSs (e.g. Cognitive Tutors) in its lack of a student model and the open-ended nature of the task it supports. It also offers multiple hints at once, giving students some control over the hints they receive, so it is possible student-specific factors played a confounding role in our analysis. Due to the small number of attempts with hint requests, we analyzed hints from different assignments together, but our results in Sect. 4.2 suggest that the assignment may impact how hints affect the student. Additionally, our hint ratings were made by experts, not students, and may be subject to the "expert blindspot." Our analysis was exploratory, and our primary goal was to generate hypotheses, not conclusions. We therefore chose not to correct for multiple significance tests, but this means our results should be interpreted cautiously until they can be confirmed.

While the data analysis we present here is an important first step, future work should employ more detailed methods, such as collecting think-aloud and interview data, to understand how hint quality impacts students' help-seeking behavior, including the mechanisms that translate hint quality into hint usage. While Aleven and colleagues' model of *ideal* help-seeking behavior in a Cognitive Tutor is useful [2], we should also work towards developing a model of how students seek help *in practice*, to design systems which can leverage these behaviors for better learning.

References

1. Aleven, V., Koedinger, K.: Limitations of student control: do students know when they need help? In: International Conference on Intelligent Tutoring Systems, pp. 292–303 (2000)
2. Aleven, V., Mclaren, B., Roll, I., Koedinger, K.: Toward meta-cognitive tutoring: a model of help seeking with a cognitive tutor. Int. J. Artif. Intell. Educ. **16**(2), 101–128 (2006)
3. Aleven, V., Roll, I., Mclaren, B.M., Koedinger, K.R.: Help helps, but only so much: research on help seeking with intelligent tutoring systems. Int. J. Artif. Intell. Educ. **26**(1), 1–19 (2016)
4. Aleven, V., Stahl, E., Schworm, S., Fischer, F., Wallace, R.: Help seeking and help design in interactive learning environments vincent. Rev. Educ. Res. **73**(3), 277–320 (2003)
5. Anderson, J.R.: Rules of the Mind. Lawrence Erlbaum Associates, Hillsdale (1993)
6. Barnes, T., Stamper, J.: Toward automatic hint generation for logic proof tutoring using historical student data. In: International Conference on Intelligent Tutoring Systems, pp. 373–382 (2008)
7. Corbett, A., Anderson, J.: Locus of feedback control in computer-based tutoring: impact on learning rate, achievement and attitudes. In: SIGCHI Conference on Human Computer Interaction, pp. 245–252 (2001)
8. Garcia, D., Harvey, B., Barnes, T.: The beauty and joy of computing. ACM Inroads **6**(4), 71–79 (2015)
9. Kluger, A.N., Denisi, A.: The effects of feedback interventions on performance: a historical review, a meta-analysis, and a preliminary feedback intervention theory. Psychol. Bull. **119**(2), 254–284 (1996)
10. Luckin, R., Du Boulay, B.: Ecolab: the development and evaluation of a Vygotskian design framework. Int. J. Artif. Intell. Educ. **10**, 198–220 (1999)
11. Piech, C., Sahami, M., Huang, J., Guibas, L.: Autonomously generating hints by inferring problem solving policies. In: ACM Conference on Learning @ Scale, pp. 1–10 (2015)
12. Price, T.W., Dong, Y., Barnes, T.: Generating data-driven hints for open-ended programming. In: International Conference on Educational Data Mining (2016)
13. Price, T.W., Dong, Y., Lipovac, D.: iSnap: towards intelligent tutoring in novice programming environments. In: ACM Technical Symposium on Computer Science Education (2017)
14. Rivers, K., Koedinger, K.R.: Data-driven hint generation in vast solution spaces: a self-improving python programming tutor. Int. J. Artif. Intell. Educ. **27**(1), 37–64 (2017). https://link.springer.com/article/10.1007/s40593-015-0070-z
15. Roll, I., Aleven, V., McLaren, B.M., Ryu, E., Baker, R.S.J., Koedinger, K.R.: The help tutor: does metacognitive feedback improve students' help-seeking actions, skills and learning? In: Ikeda, M., Ashley, K.D., Chan, T.-W. (eds.) ITS 2006. LNCS, vol. 4053, pp. 360–369. Springer, Heidelberg (2006). doi:10.1007/11774303_36
16. Stamper, J., Eagle, M., Barnes, T., Croy, M.: Experimental evaluation of automatic hint generation for a logic tutor. Int. J. Artif. Intell. Educ. **22**(1), 3–17 (2013)
17. Wood, D.: Scaffolding, contingent tutoring and computer-supported learning. Int. J. Artif. Intell. Educ. **12**, 280–292 (2001)
18. Wood, H., Wood, D.: Help seeking, learning and contingent tutoring. Comput. Educ. **33**(2–3), 153–169 (1999)

Balancing Learning and Engagement in Game-Based Learning Environments with Multi-objective Reinforcement Learning

Robert Sawyer$^{(\boxtimes)}$, Jonathan Rowe, and James Lester

North Carolina State University, Raleigh, NC 27695, USA
{rssawyer, jprowe, lester}@ncsu.edu

Abstract. Game-based learning environments create rich learning experiences that are both effective and engaging. Recent years have seen growing interest in data-driven techniques for tutorial planning, which dynamically personalize learning experiences by providing hints, feedback, and problem scenarios at run-time. In game-based learning environments, tutorial planners are designed to adapt gameplay events in order to achieve multiple objectives, such as enhancing student learning or student engagement, which may be complementary or competing aims. In this paper, we introduce a multi-objective reinforcement learning framework for inducing game-based tutorial planners that balance between improving learning and engagement in game-based learning environments. We investigate a model-based, linear-scalarized multi-policy algorithm, Convex Hull Value Iteration, to induce a tutorial planner from a corpus of student interactions with a game-based learning environment for middle school science education. Results indicate that multi-objective reinforcement learning creates policies that are more effective at balancing multiple reward sources than single-objective techniques. A qualitative analysis of select policies and multi-objective preference vectors shows how a multi-objective reinforcement learning framework shapes the selection of tutorial actions during students' game-based learning experiences to effectively achieve targeted learning and engagement outcomes.

Keywords: Tutorial planning · Multi-objective reinforcement learning · Game-based learning environments · Narrative centered learning

1 Introduction

Game-based learning environments enable students to engage in rich problem-solving scenarios that enhance student learning. There is compelling evidence that game-based learning environments improve student learning outcomes compared to traditional instructional methods [14, 15]. A key advantage of game-based learning environments is their potential to foster student engagement through features such as 3D virtual worlds and believable characters [6]. However, important questions have been raised about whether specific features of digital games that foster engagement, such as narratives, are beneficial for learning [1]. A one-size-fits-all approach to designing game-based learning environments has significant limitations in terms of balancing effectively between learning and engagement for all students. Recent years have seen

© Springer International Publishing AG 2017
E. André et al. (Eds.): AIED 2017, LNAI 10331, pp. 323–334, 2017.
DOI: 10.1007/978-3-319-61425-0_27

growing interest in *tutorial planners* for game-based learning environments, which personalize game elements to individual students at runtime [4, 16]. Reinforcement learning (RL) techniques have shown particular promise for devising tutorial planners from logs of student interactions with a virtual learning environment [3, 10].

RL-based tutorial planners are often tasked with making personalization decisions that impact both student learning and engagement. Yet, there has been little systematic investigation of *multi-objective RL* techniques for tutorial planning. Multi-objective techniques are particularly relevant to game-based learning environments because there may be tradeoffs between game elements designed to foster learning and game elements designed to foster engagement. Prior work on RL-based planners has typically focused on single-objective reward models [3, 9] and weighted sum-based evaluation functions with author-specified weights [5]. Single-objective RL techniques provide no guarantees about generating policies that balance across multiple objectives. A tutorial planner that is effective for one objective (e.g., learning) may be ineffective for a secondary objective of comparable importance (e.g., engagement). Further, the weight preferences between objectives for a particular game-based learning environment may not be known *a priori*, as they may be dependent upon the educational setting in which a game-based learning environment will be deployed. For example, a tutorial planner intended to support classroom practice before end-of-grade tests might prioritize content learning gains, whereas a game utilized in an after-school setting might optimize engagement and interest in the subject matter.

In this paper, we present a multi-objective RL framework for tutorial planning in game-based learning environments. Using game interaction log data from over four hundred students, we induce a tutorial planner for a game-based learning environment for middle school microbiology education, CRYSTAL ISLAND.

2   Related Work

Data-driven methods for tutorial planning have been the subject of growing interest in recent years. RL techniques have shown particular promise, potentially reducing the need for labor-intensive knowledge engineering processes and large datasets of human demonstrations [3, 5, 10]. Many RL techniques formalize tutorial planning in terms of Markov decision processes, which encode sequential decision-making tasks with stochastic environments and delayed rewards. Chi et al. [3] utilized model-based RL to induce models of pedagogical micro-tactics in a tutorial dialogue system for physics education. More recently, Mandel et al. [16] investigated techniques for offline RL policy evaluation to examine alternate tutorial planning models in the educational game Refraction. Rowe et al. [9] investigated a modular reinforcement learning framework for tutorial planning in educational interactive narratives. Their model, which was evaluated in a classroom study, was found to yield improved student learning behaviors relative to a baseline system [10]. Each of these systems utilized single-objective reward functions to guide RL techniques for inducing tutorial planning models.

In related work on user-adaptive games, Nelson et al. [5] proposed an RL framework for experience management that leveraged a hand-authored evaluation function to personalize events in interactive fiction games. Notably, the evaluation function utilized by Nelson et al. adopted the form of a linear scalarization function with weight preferences. This approach required the system designer to specify weights among objectives prior to training the experience manager. This approach is intuitive, but it is unlikely to generalize effectively across different deployment settings with distinct priorities for users' gameplay experiences.

Multi-objective RL techniques consist of methods for solving a wide array of multi-objective Markov decision processes, with solutions consisting of a single policy or multiple policies depending on the problem context [7]. Recent work by Wiering, Withagen, and Drugan [12] presented a model-based approach for solving deterministic multi-objective Markov decision processes yielding the set of Pareto optimal policies for a given task. Barrett and Narayanan [2] devised a method for calculating all optimal policies for any weight preference vector used in linear scalarization. Their approach enables a system designer to defer specifying weight preferences for each objective until the RL model is deployed, when a specific policy is extracted at run-time by utilizing properties of convex hulls. Multi-objective RL has been applied successfully in a variety of domains, including traffic light control [18] and water reservoir control [17], but to date there has been little work investigating multi-objective RL techniques for educational software.

3   CRYSTAL ISLAND Game-Based Learning Environment

To investigate multi-objective RL for tutorial planning, we utilize a game-based learning environment for middle school microbiology education as a testbed application, CRYSTAL ISLAND. In CRYSTAL ISLAND, students adopt the role of a medical field agent, who has been tasked with investigating a mysterious epidemic on a remote island. The student must determine the source and identity of the illness by interviewing virtual characters, gathering clues, and running tests in a virtual laboratory. As students solve the mystery, they learn relevant microbiology concepts and utilize the scientific method to complete the science problem-solving scenario. CRYSTAL ISLAND has been used by over 4,000 students in middle school classrooms across the United States.

Tutorial planning in CRYSTAL ISLAND encompasses a broad range of possible decisions about scaffolding student learning and tailoring different elements of the game environment. We seek to induce tutorial planning policies directly from a corpus of student interaction data off-line. To address issues of data sparsity, we decompose tutorial planning in terms of several distinct sub-problems, denoted as *adaptable event sequences* (AESs). An AES is an abstraction for one or more recurring tutorial decision-making events that center on a particular facet of the game-based learning environment, such as the behavior of a non-player character, the properties of a virtual object, or the delivery of a scaffolding-related message. We model CRYSTAL ISLAND's tutorial planner with a set of 12 AESs, each separately encoding a series of sequential game events, which interleave with one another and collectively span the game's problem scenario (Fig. 1).

In our multi-objective RL framework, each AES is modeled as a *multi-objective Markov decision process* (MOMDP) with its own state representation, action set, state transition model, and reward model. Every occurrence of an AES corresponds to a decision point for the MOMDP. The possible gameplay adaptations that can be performed by the tutorial planner represent the sets of actions for the MOMDPs. In order to collect a corpus of student interaction data for off-line RL, we deployed CRYSTAL ISLAND to students using a version of the tutorial planner that controls AESs according to a uniform random policy, deliberately sampling the manager's state-action space. As long as each possible combination of gameplay adaptations produces a coherent user experience, we can collect a corpus of student responses to the tutorial planner's decisions for off-line, model-based RL.

Data for inducing tutorial planning policies from student interactions with CRYSTAL ISLAND were collected from two studies. The first study involved 300 students from a middle school and the second study involved 153 students from a different middle school. Students interacted with the game until they solved the mystery, or 55 min elapsed, whichever occurred first. Students completed pre- and post-tests one-week before, and immediately after using the game, respectively. These tests gathered data on students' learning gains, prior gameplay experience, and perceptions of *presence* (i.e., the sense of "being there" in the virtual environment) experienced in the game.

Each student's trace of in-game problem-solving actions was logged, including which AESs they encountered, what actions were performed by the tutorial planner (according to a uniform random policy), and timestamps for all game events. After removing data from participants with incomplete or inconsistent records, the resulting data set consisted of 10,057 instances of tutorial planner decisions, corresponding to approximately 25 gameplay adaptations per player.

Each MOMDP shared the same state representation, which consisted of 8 binary features drawn from three categories: narrative state, gameplay behavior, and player traits. We limited the state representation to 8 binary features to mitigate potential data sparsity issues. The first four features were narrative-focused. Each feature was

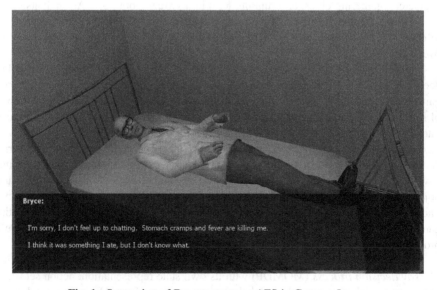

Fig. 1. Screenshot of Bryce symptoms AES in CRYSTAL ISLAND

associated with a salient plot point from CRYSTAL ISLAND's storyline and indicated whether the plot point had been completed thus far. The next two features were computed from a median split on players' microbiology pre-test scores and previous video game experience. The final two features were computed from players' observed gameplay behaviors. Specifically, we computed running median splits on the frequency of students' laboratory testing and book-reading behaviors within CRYSTAL ISLAND. The action sets for the 12 MOMDPs corresponded to the range of gameplay personalization decisions for the associated AESs. The action sets' cardinalities ranged from binary to 6-way decisions.

Table 1. Summary of AESs by type, name, and number of possible actions. R refers to recurring AESs and O refers to AESs that occur once per episode. Asterisks denote policies selected for additional qualitative analysis in the results section below.

AES Type	AES Name	Cardinality	AES Frequency
Scaffolding	Direct Goal	2	R
	Increase Urgency	2	R
	Knowledge Quiz*	2	R
	Record Findings	2	R
	Reflection Prompt	2	R
Information Availability	Bryce Reveal	2	O
	Bryce Symptoms	2	R
	Quentin Reveal	2	O
	Teresa Symptoms*	3	R
Problem Specification	Mystery Solution	6	O
	Test Count*	3	O
	Worksheet Level	3	R

The AESs ranged broadly in terms of how they affected student gameplay, as well as their frequency of occurring during a typical gameplay episode. Detailed information regarding each AES is provided in [8], and these groupings are summarized in Table 1. If the entire tutorial planning task were modeled as a single MOMDP, it would require encoding approximately 1,644,000 parameters to populate the entire state transition model (256 states × 25 distinct actions × 257 states, including the terminal state), although not all state transitions were possible.

Two distinct reward sources were computed using data from the corpus described above to induce RL-based tutorial planning policies. Each MOMDP utilized the same set of two reward models, which were based upon: (1) participants' normalized learning gains, and (2) self-reported presence after gameplay. Both of these reward sources were calculated using data collected from the pre- and post-tests; no incremental rewards were assigned during gameplay.

The first reward source, normalized learning gain, was selected to obtain a tutorial planner that maximized student learning on microbiology content. Normalized learning gain (NLG) is the normalized difference between pre- and post-game science content knowledge test scores, assessed using a 19-item multiple-choice test. We use NLG because it provides a singular metric for student learning that accounts for individual differences in students' prior knowledge, in contrast to alternative metrics like post-test score or un-normalized learning gain. The reward values for NLG were determined by calculating the NLG for each participant at the conclusion of their gameplay episode.

The second reward source was based upon players' self-reported perceptions of presence, as measured by the Presence Questionnaire [13]. Presence refers to a participant's perception of transportation into a virtual environment. We use it here as a proxy indicator for user engagement in the game. Participants completed the Presence Questionnaire after using CRYSTAL ISLAND. The presence reward function was determined by the student's total Presence Questionnaire score divided by the maximum observed score in the corpus. This normalized the presence reward to be in the interval [0, 1] for each student. This objective is important to maximize because fostering engagement is a key motivation of game-based learning environments. These two reward sources reflect each side of the tradeoff between learning and engagement in interactive narrative.

The MOMDPs, one for each AES in CRYSTAL ISLAND, were implemented with a reinforcement learning library written in Python by the first two authors. Policies were induced using a discount rate of 0.9. To encode multiple reward sources for MORL, a vector containing each of the two reward sources was utilized.

4 Multi-objective Reinforcement Learning for Tutorial Planning

Several multi-objective policies were induced for each AES from the corpus of student interaction data using both the NLG and Presence reward sources. A certainty-equivalence model of the environment was created from the state-action transition counts and observed rewards in the training corpus. This is done with the maximum likelihood model of the MOMDP as in [12].

We derive multiple policies per MOMDP using Convex Hull Value Iteration [2]. This method learns the set of all optimal policies for an MOMDP given a model of the environment through operations on convex hulls similar to the classical dynamic programming method of *value iteration* [11]. In Convex Hull Value Iteration, each Q-value is replaced with a set of possible expected reward vectors. If this set is a convex hull, then each possible vector is optimal under some set of preferences over the reward sources, defined as a weight preference vector where the components sum to one. Given a weight preference vector, the best linear scalarized reward Q can be extracted according to the following equation:

$$Q_{\vec{w}}(s, a) = \max_{\vec{q} \in \dot{Q}(s,a)} \vec{w} \cdot \vec{q} \tag{1}$$

where $\vec{w}$ represents the weight preference vector, $\dot{Q}(s, a)$ is the convex set of optimal reward vectors for a state-action pair, and $Q_{\vec{w}}(s, a)$ is the resulting linear scalarized Q-value. Once the Q-values have been scalarized by a weight preference vector, a policy can be obtained greedily by selecting the best action per state, because Q-values take expected discounted future rewards into account. The weight vector is constrained to consist of positive real numbers that sum to one.

Since CRYSTAL ISLAND can be used in many different educational settings (e.g. classrooms, home, after-school clubs), the tutorial planner requires a weight preference vector defined at run-time, which is contingent on the particular educational priorities of the deployment setting. This results in the need for a multi-policy approach that can learn all optimal policies regardless of the preference weight vector that will be utilized at run-time.

In order to evaluate the policies derived from Convex Hull Value Iteration, we used the extraction method from Eq. 1 to generate all distinct policies for each MOMDP. This was performed by generating the convex sets of Q-values for each MOMDP, running a grid search over weight preference vectors to extract their corresponding Q-values, and utilizing greedy selection to derive distinct policies for each MOMDP. Multiple policies were derived for each MOMDP because optimal mappings between states and actions may be dependent on the weight preference vector. Every policy induced with this method is optimal under some subset of the possible weight preference vectors. In the case of tutorial planning in CRYSTAL ISLAND, we considered two reward sources—NLG and Presence—that together sum to 1. In other words, if NLG is the primary reward source, then the secondary objective Presence is assigned a weight of $1 - \text{NLG}$ in the weight preference vector.

5   Evaluation

The multi-objective RL framework yields multiple policies for each AES because a weight preference vector is not specified prior to training the model. Thus, for different specifications of the weight preference vector, different optimal policies can be obtained. The number of distinct policies generated for a single AES from the multi-objective RL procedure varied from a minimum of 3 (Mystery Solution AES) to a maximum of 11 (Reflection Prompt AES), with a median of 7 distinct policies per AES.

In order to evaluate the quality of the policies induced using multi-objective RL, we conducted an analysis of the policies' expected cumulative rewards for each reward component. *Expected cumulative reward* (ECR) is a measure of the average anticipated reward produced by a policy across all possible gameplay episodes and start states [11]. ECR is calculated by taking the product of the expected discounted reward for each start state with the probability of starting in that state. We compare ECR results calculated by each reward source between each set of induced policies. The convex hull of the MOMDP can be visualized by plotting the expected cumulative reward vector for each distinct policy induced for that MOMDP.

Due to space constraints, we focus on presenting results from 3 of the 12 AES convex hulls in this section. These 3 AESs were chosen as representative examples of each of the three AES categories: Scaffolding, Information Availability, and Problem Specification. They serve as two examples of recurring AESs and one example of an AES that occurs once per episode. The Knowledge Quiz AES, a recurring, scaffolding AES, specifies whether to provide a student with an in-game microbiology quiz or not at several specific points in the problem scenario. The Test Count AES, a single-occurrence problem

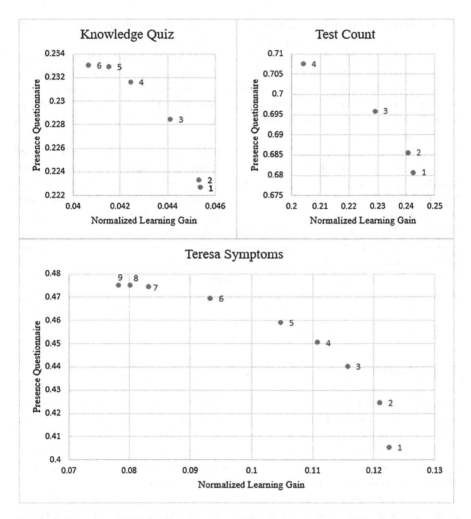

Fig. 2. Scatter plot of ECR vectors for select AESs. X-axis denotes NLG reward values, and y-axis denotes presence reward values.

specification AES, determines whether the student is allotted three, five, or ten initial "scans" with the hypothesis testing equipment in the game's virtual laboratory. The Teresa Symptoms AES, a recurring information availability AES, determines whether a particular non-player character will provide minimum, moderate, or maximum detail regarding her symptoms during a branching conversation with the student.

Figure 2 shows the ECR vectors of distinct policies induced by the multi-objective RL framework for the three selected AESs. The x-axis denotes the NLG ECR value of a policy, and the y-axis denotes the Presence ECR value. A qualitative analysis of policies for each AES reveals how changing the weight preference vector affects action choices for the tutorial planner.

In the Knowledge Quiz AES, as the NLG weight decreases, the induced policies tend to give fewer quizzes to students who have read a higher number of books and have higher prior content knowledge. Because this change of policy comes from decreasing the NLG weight (and therefore increasing the Presence weight), this indicates that presenting the knowledge quizzes may reduce engagement in students who are already familiar with microbiology content, or who are now more knowledgeable from reading the virtual microbiology books. Conversely, this indicates that in-game quizzes may help learning but diminish engagement; it is plausible that quizzes disrupt the flow of gameplay and reduce perceptions of presence in the virtual environment.

In the Test Count AES, the policies induced by weight preference vectors that de-prioritize NLG tend to allot more initial "scans" to students with high number of books read. This indicates that letting students that have already gathered information from reading perform more tests may help engage the students at the cost of decreased learning gains. This may be a way of keeping students engaged by allowing students who have spent time gathering information to form hypotheses continue the problem-solving process by thoroughly testing their hypotheses.

In the Teresa Symptoms AES, policies induced with weight preference vectors that prioritize Presence tended to provide fewer details when students had high prior content knowledge and more detail when students had high prior gameplay experience. This indicates that giving less information to students with high prior content knowledge may help keep them engaged, and it may have also helped engage students who were performing a high number of scans. The lack of information given to a student with high prior content knowledge effectively increases the scenario's difficulty, which may lead to a more appropriate challenge level for a high knowledge student.

In summary, tutorial planning policies are noticeably influenced by the weight assignments in the multi-objective preference vector. In general, increased weight for the NLG reward source corresponds to increased learning support from the tutorial planner. This trend can be observed for both the Knowledge Quiz AES (i.e., more quizzes are given) and Teresa Symptoms AES (i.e., more detailed information is given) with higher NLG weights. The Test Count AES is an exception, where allotting an increased number of tests—an indirect form of learning support—corresponds to a reduction in NLG weight. However, students "earn" additional tests by completing in-game quizzes, so it may be the case that students with fewer allotted tests complete more remedial quizzes, which could be associated with higher learning gains. It should be noted that this trend is only observed for students with a strong tendency toward book reading. This would be consistent with a tutorial planner that seeks to limit guessing behavior to encourage learning among students that have already read the relevant content.

As noted above, each of the policies induced is optimal over some subset of possible weight preference vectors. In Fig. 3, the subsets of weight preference vectors associated with each optimal policy (from the three AESs shown in Fig. 2) are visually represented. The policy numbers corresponding to the hulls from Fig. 2 are centered on the ranges of NLG weights that make those policies optimal. For example, Policy 1 in each AES is the policy that favors NLG most and Presence least. In the Test Count AES, this policy is optimal under all weight preference vectors from NLG = 0.58 to NLG = 1.0 (with the corresponding Presence = 0.42 to Presence = 0.0). This image also shows that Policy 2 for Test Count, Policy 5 for Teresa Symptoms, and Policy 5 for Knowledge Quiz are optimal under a weight preference vector that gives even preference to NLG and Presence, i.e. NLG = Presence = 0.5.

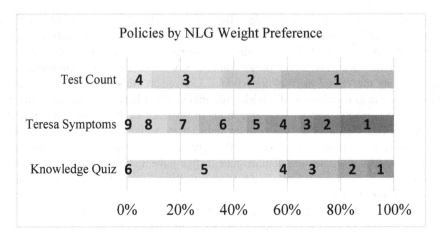

Fig. 3. Policies preferred by various values of NLG weight (with Presence = 1 − NLG) for three different AESs corresponding to policies in Fig. 2.

Next, we statistically compared policies induced for different weight preference vectors using the multi-objective RL framework. To perform this comparison, we conducted a series of paired t-tests, where each pair consisted of the reward-specific ECR values for two different policies associated with a single AES. Each weight preference vector corresponds to a set of policies from the convex hull; the set is comprised of one policy for each AES. Thus, for two distinct weight preference vectors, there are 12 pairs of policies. We calculate the 12 differences between policy ECRs and average (and take the standard deviation of) these ECR differences to compare two distinct preference weight vectors. These tests investigated whether the ECR value for a particular reward source was statistically different across policies induced by two distinct weight preference vectors.

For example, consider the Teresa Symptoms AES and its induced policies: Policy 1 (induced by $w = [1.0, 0.0]$) and Policy 2 (induced by $w = [0.75, 0.25]$). We want to compare NLG ECR values between the two policies. From the data in Fig. 2, we see that NLG ECR of Policy 1 is 0.122 and the NLG ECR of Policy 2 is 0.121, yielding a pairwise NLG difference of 0.001. This difference is averaged with differences between other AESs, providing the mean NLG ECR difference between policies induced by two weight preference vectors.

It should be noted that policies induced using linear scalarization with weights [1.0, 0.0] and [0.0, 1.0] are equivalent to single-objective policies, enabling a statistical comparison between single-objective and multi-objective policies. The results from these paired t-tests are shown in Table 2.

Table 2 indicates that policies induced with different weight preference vectors have significant differences in ECR across both reward sources when paired by AES. A negative Mean Difference represents the case when policies induced by Weight Vector Two are greater than the policies induced by Weight Vector One for that reward source. Results show that the equal-preference policy given by $w = [0.5, 0.5]$ outperforms single-objective policies in the secondary objective, but it does not perform as well on the primary objective.

Table 2. Paired t-tests comparing policies from different weight preference vectors with differences averaged across all AESs.

Weight Vector One	Weight Vector Two	Reward Source	Mean Difference	SD	t (p-value)
[1.0, 0.0]	[0.75, 0.25]	NLG	0.00421	0.00372	3.76 (0.003)**
[1.0, 0.0]	[0.75, 0.25]	Presence	-0.0209	0.0214	-3.25 (0.008)**
[1.0, 0.0]	[0.5, 0.5]	NLG	0.0132	0.00818	4.99 (< 0.001)***
[1.0, 0.0]	[0.5, 0.5]	Presence	-0.0313	0.0258	-4.02 (0.002)**
[0.5, 0.5]	[0.0, 1.0]	NLG	0.0194	0.0248	2.601 (0.025)*
[0.5, 0.5]	[0.0, 1.0]	Presence	-0.00501	0.00554	-3.00 (0.012)*
[0.25, 0.75]	[0.0, 1.0]	NLG	0.00879	0.0182	1.60 (0.138)
[0.25, 0.75]	[0.0, 1.0]	Presence	-0.0001	0.002	-1.53 (0.153)

6 Conclusion

Dynamically balancing between multiple objectives is a key functionality of tutorial planners for a broad range of interactive learning environments ranging from intelligent tutoring systems to game-based learning environments. We have presented a multi-objective reinforcement learning framework for tutorial planning in game-based learning environments that addresses the problem of incorporating multiple reward sources, such as learning and engagement, into a data-driven framework for tutorial planning. Our multi-objective RL framework has been investigated in the context of a game-based learning environment for middle school microbiology education, and it was trained using a corpus of student interaction data from classroom studies involving over 400 participants. Multiple reward sources (i.e., content learning, engagement) were used to define an MOMDP for the game-based tutorial planner. These reward sources were chosen because they typify the educational objectives often discussed in the design of game-based learning environments. An analysis of different tutorial planning policies induced using multi-objective RL indicated that tutorial planners utilizing these policies provide a more balanced expected cumulative reward on multiple objectives compared to single-objective policies. We generated an approximate convex hull of optimal policies for several AESs, yielding sets of tutorial planning policies that optimize multiple dimensions of students' game-based learning experiences. These policies can be selected at deployment time by specifying a weighted preference vector tailored to a particular educational setting.

In future work, it will be important to investigate alternate representations for multi-objective policies using complementary evaluation methods, such as importance sampling. In addition, we plan to explore techniques for incorporating multi-objective tutorial planners into the run-time decision cycles of a range of learning environments, investigating how best to dynamically create personalized learning experiences that are simultaneously effective for learning and engagement. In this work, we have utilized ECR as a preliminary evaluation metric to assess multi-objective tutorial policies. This lays the foundation for conducting follow on studies with human subjects to investigate multi-object tutorial planning in laboratory and classroom settings.

References

1. Adams, D.M., Mayer, R.E., MacNamara, A., Koenig, A., Wainess, R.: Narrative games for learning: testing the discovery and narrative hypotheses. J. Educ. Psychol. **104**(1), 235–249 (2012)
2. Barrett, L., Narayanan, S.: Learning all optimal policies with multiple criteria. In: Proceedings of the 25th International Conference on Machine Learning, pp. 41–47. ACM (2008)
3. Chi, M., VanLehn, K., Litman, D., Jordan, P.: Empirically evaluating the application of reinforcement learning to the induction of effective and adaptive pedagogical strategies. User Model. User-Adap. Inter. **21**(1–2), 137–180 (2011)
4. Lee, S., Rowe, J., Mott, B., Lester, J.: A supervised learning framework for modeling director agent strategies in educational interactive narrative. IEEE Trans. Comput. Intell. AI Games **6**(2), 203–215 (2014)
5. Nelson, M., Roberts, D., Isbell, C., Mateas, M.: Reinforcement learning for declarative optimization-based drama management. In: Proceedings of the 5th International Conference on Autonomous Agents and Multiagent Systems, pp. 775–782. ACM, Japan (2006)
6. Prensky, M.: Digital Game-based Learning. McGraw-Hill, New York (2001)
7. Roijers, D., Vamplew, P., Whiteson, S., Dazeley, R.: A survey of multi-objective sequential decision-making. J. Artif. Intell. Res. **48**, 67–113 (2013)
8. Rowe, J.: Narrative-centered tutorial planning with concurrent markov decision processes. Ph.D. diss., Dept. of Computer Science, North Carolina State University (2013)
9. Rowe, J., Mott, B., Lester, J.: Optimizing player experience in interactive narrative planning: a modular reinforcement learning approach. In: Proceedings of the 10th Artificial Intelligence and Interactive Digital Entertainment Conference, pp. 160–166. Raleigh, NC (2014)
10. Rowe, J., Lester, J.: Improving student problem solving in narrative-centered learning environments: a modular framework. In: Proceedings of the 17th International Conference on Artificial Intelligence in Education, pp. 419–428. Madrid, Spain (2015)
11. Sutton, R., Barto, A.: Reinforcement Learning: An Introduction. MIT Press, Cambridge (1998)
12. Wiering, M., Withagen, M., Drugan, M.: Model-based multi-objective reinforcement learning. In: IEEE Symposium on Adaptive Dynamic Programming and Reinforcement Learning, pp. 1–6 (2014)
13. Witmer, B., Singer, M.: Measuring presence in virtual environments: a presence questionnaire. Presence Teleoperators Virtual Environ. **7**(3), 225–240 (1998)
14. Clark, D.B., Tanner-Smith, E., Killingsworth, S.: Digital games, design, and learning: a systematic review and meta-analysis. Rev. Educ. Res. **86**(1), 79–122 (2015)
15. Wouters, P., van Nimwegen, C., van Oostendorp, H., van der Spek, E.D.: A meta-analysis of the cognitive and motivational effects of serious games. J. Educ. Psychol. **105**, 249–265 (2013)
16. Mandel, T., Liu, Y., Levine, S., Brunskill, E., Popovic, Z.: Offline policy evaluation across representations with applications to educational games. In: Proceedings of the 2014 International Conference on Autonomous Agents and Multi-Agent Systems, pp. 1077–1084. Richland, SC (2014)
17. Castelletti, A., Pianosi, F., Restelli, M.: A multiobjective reinforcement learning approach to water resources systems operation: pareto frontier approximation in a single run. Water Resour. Res. **49**(6), 3476–3486 (2013)
18. Houli, D., Zhiheng, L., Yi, Z.: Multiobjective reinforcement learning for traffic signal control using vehicular ad hoc network. EURASIP J. Adv. Signal Process. **1**, 724035 (2010)

Is More Agency Better? The Impact of Student Agency on Game-Based Learning

Robert Sawyer[(⊠)], Andy Smith, Jonathan Rowe,
Roger Azevedo, and James Lester

North Carolina State University, Raleigh, NC, USA
{rssawyer, pmsmith4, jprowe, razeved, lester}@ncsu.edu

Abstract. Student agency has long been viewed as a critical element in game-based learning. Agency refers to the degree of freedom and control that a student has to perform meaningful actions in a learning environment. While long postulated to be central to student self-regulation, there is limited evidence on the design of game-based learning environments that promote student agency and its effect on learning. This paper reports on an experiment to investigate the impact of student agency on learning and problem-solving behavior in a game-based learning environment for microbiology. Students interacted with one of three versions of the system. In the *High Agency* condition, students could freely navigate the game's 3D open-world environment and perform problem-solving actions in any order they chose. In the *Low Agency* condition, students were required to traverse the environment and solve the mystery in a prescribed partially ordered sequence. In the *No Agency* condition, students watched a video of an expert playing the game by following an "ideal path" for solving the problem scenario. Results indicate that students in the *Low Agency* condition achieved greater learning gains than students in both the *High Agency* and *No Agency* conditions, but exhibited more unproductive behaviors, suggesting that artfully striking a balance between high and low agency best supports learning.

Keywords: Game-based learning · Student agency · Problem-solving behavior

1 Introduction

Intelligent game-based learning environments have been investigated across a broad range of domains [1–3]. By integrating the rich problem scenarios of inquiry learning environments [4] and the adaptive pedagogy of intelligent tutoring systems [5, 6], intelligent game-based learning environments can deliver personalized learning experiences that dynamically scaffold learning and engagement. There is growing evidence to suggest that game-based learning environments can benefit learning, but the relationship between learning and game design is complex [3, 7, 8]. For example, a recent meta-analysis found that while serious games were more effective than conventional instruction methods in terms of learning and retention, they did not increase motivation [3]. Another recent study suggested that popular gamification features (i.e., performance-based rewards) and an award-winning educational game were less effective at promoting transferrable knowledge gains than a non-game environment for algebra education [9].

© Springer International Publishing AG 2017
E. André et al. (Eds.): AIED 2017, LNAI 10331, pp. 335–346, 2017.
DOI: 10.1007/978-3-319-61425-0_28

These findings raise important questions about how intelligent game-based learning environments should be designed in order to realize their envisioned educational potential. At the core of these questions is the degree to which student agency should be incorporated into a game-based learning environment.

A salient feature of intelligent game-based learning environments is their support for *student agency*. In this paper, student agency, which is related to constructs such as control [10], self-determination [11], and self-regulated learning [12], aligns with the definition from the game design literature, which defines *player agency* as the degree of freedom and control that a student has to perform meaningful actions in a virtual environment [13]. For example, if a student observes a location within a virtual environment that she is not permitted to visit, this limitation is a constraint on the student's agency. Similarly, if a student perceives her own in-game actions (e.g., trial and error strategy in testing potential sources of evidence) as having only superficial effects on the game environment, her agency within the game is limited. In contrast, a student who perceives herself as being able to perform any action that she desires in the game world, even if the *actual* range of possible actions is limited, has a high degree of agency, and may have a richer, more meaningful game experience.

For game-based learning environments, the assumption, supported by empirical results, is that increased student agency is associated with higher levels of motivation and involvement with the subject matter, and consequently better learning outcomes [14, 15]. However, there is likely a balance to strike: increasing student agency can give rise to behaviors that are associated with less desirable learning outcomes, as a person exerting low levels of agency may not accurately monitor and regulate their cognitive, metacognitive, and affective processes required for success [16]. This issue is related to critiques of discovery learning [17, 18], which argue that providing too much freedom and too little support leads to students struggling to select, organize, and integrate relevant information in open-ended learning environments. A related concern is the risk of "seductive details," or superfluous features of a learning environment that may distract students from a learning task [19]. Potentially harmful side effects of student agency manifest in game-based learning environments when students devote significant time to off-task behaviors, which are associated with reduced student learning and negative affect [20, 21].

In this study, we investigate the relationship between student agency, learning, and problem-solving behavior in an intelligent game-based learning environment for microbiology education, CRYSTAL ISLAND. Specifically, we examine three distinct versions of CRYSTAL ISLAND. In the *High Agency* version, students can freely explore the game's 3D virtual environment and perform problem-solving actions in any order they choose. In the *Low Agency* version, students must visit a series of in-game locations in a fixed linear sequence, where they must complete a specified set of problem-solving actions in each location before progressing in the game. In the *No Agency* version, students passively watch a video of an expert playing CRYSTAL ISLAND and modeling an "ideal path" for solving the problem scenario. With these conditions we investigate three research questions. First, how do different agency conditions affect learning? Second, for the *High* and *Low Agency* conditions, what problem-solving behaviors in the environment account for the differences in learning between the conditions?

Finally, what effect, if any, does the agency manipulation have on problem-solving behavior in the game environment?

2 Related Work

Designing game-based learning environments that afford high levels of student agency is motivated by the hypothesis that increasing agency will produce higher levels of involvement, interest, and motivation, which will subsequently lead to better learning outcomes. This argument has empirical support, including evidence that increased perceptions of control are associated with higher levels of direct and relative enjoyment and perceived competence [22]. However, it is important that the mechanisms that afford the higher levels of motivation be aligned with the target learning objectives. For example, allowing students freedom to explore might result in them not encountering some elements of the subject matter [17]. Additionally, some students may not be able to properly plan, monitor, and react, rendering them ineffective when given more autonomy in a learning task [12].

High levels of student agency have been a purposeful design feature of several prominent game-based learning environments, such as Quest Atlantis [23] and Virtual Performance Assessments [24]. These games allow students to move freely through a multi-user game world as they gather information through reading scientific texts, interact with virtual characters, form hypotheses, collect data, and synthesize their findings. Studies with iSTART-2 have investigated agency by analyzing students' choice patterns in a game-like environment, finding that student success is closely related to a student's ability to exercise controlled choice patterns, as opposed to disorganized (i.e., random) choice patterns [14]. A study with a previous version of Crystal Island showed that learning gains and in-game problem-solving performance are correlated with several facets of engagement, including presence and perceived interest [15]. In this paper, we extend this line of work by reporting on a study that isolates the effects of game design features intended to manipulate student agency and investigating their impact on student learning and problem-solving behavior.

3 Crystal Island

Crystal Island is a game-based learning environment that integrates science problem solving and literacy education within an interactive science mystery. Students adopt the role of a medical field agent who has been sent to a remote island research station to investigate an epidemic among a team of scientists. Students determine the source and identity of the disease, as well as recommend a treatment plan by exploring the game environment, conversing with non-player characters, running tests in a virtual laboratory, and completing an in-game diagnosis worksheet. The island features several buildings, including an infirmary, dining hall, laboratory, and various residences where the student can gather information and talk to characters. In addition, students read complex informational texts (e.g., in-game books and articles) that describe relevant microbiology concepts about viruses, bacteria, immunization, and how diseases spread.

Students must apply and synthesize microbiology knowledge to successfully diagnose the illness and solve the mystery.

To investigate the effects of agency on student learning, three versions of CRYSTAL ISLAND were developed. In the *High Agency* version, students moved freely throughout the virtual environment after completing a brief gameplay tutorial near the entrance of the island. In this version, students navigated between buildings and interacted with non-player characters and virtual objects at will. In the *Low Agency* version, students investigated the mystery in a fixed order. As shown in Fig. 1, students moved between buildings in a prescribed order: they completed a tutorial near the entrance of the island, then transitioned to the Infirmary, followed by the Living Quarters, Bryce's Quarters, Dining Hall, and the Lab. In each location, students were required to interact with all of the virtual characters, virtual books, and virtual objects in that building before moving on to the next location (Fig. 2). This includes fully traversing dialog trees for each virtual character, as well as reading each of the virtual books and articles in the building, along with their accompanying assessments of reading comprehension. These texts presented information regarding relevant microbiology concepts, which are instrumental to successfully developing hypotheses and solving the mystery. To transition between buildings in the *Low Agency* version, students did not navigate through the outdoor environment but instead utilized a "fast travel" interface; the fast travel interface appeared whenever a student attempted to depart a location (e.g., walking to the exit door), and it provided students with a menu listing available locations to which the student could teleport. Upon completing the initial tour of the five buildings, students were free to return to previously visited buildings, and they continued to use the fast travel interface to transition between locations. Eventually, students returned to the Infirmary to submit their final diagnosis to the camp nurse.

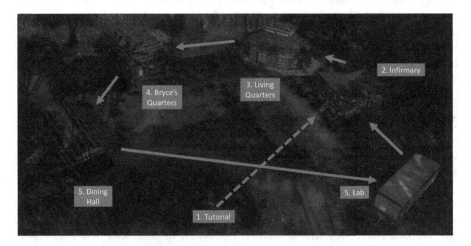

Fig. 1. The "Ideal Path" of CRYSTAL ISLAND

In a third version, the *No Agency* condition, students watched a narrated video of an expert solving the CRYSTAL ISLAND problem scenario. The walkthrough showed the expert exploring each of the buildings, interacting with each of the virtual characters, reading each of the books and articles, and testing each of the relevant virtual objects in the same sequence as prescribed in the *Low Agency* condition.

The CRYSTAL ISLAND problem scenario consisted of three phases of gameplay: (1) Tutorial, (2) Information Gathering, and (3) Diagnosis. Both the *High Agency* and *Low Agency* versions of CRYSTAL ISLAND featured the same gameplay tutorial, which was presented at the start of the game. The two game versions had only minor differences in this phase. Next was the Information Gathering phase, which included the series of gameplay activities occurring after the tutorial and prior to the student's arrival in the virtual laboratory, where she typically conducts a series of tests (i.e., scans) on hypothesized transmission sources of the disease. This phase focused on exploring the virtual environment and gathering information from virtual characters, books, and research articles. This phase unfolded differently between the *Low Agency* and *High Agency* versions: the *Low Agency* version prescribed how the student must complete the phase's gameplay activities, whereas the *High Agency* version permitted the student to complete the phase's gameplay activities in any fashion she chose. After conducting a first test with the laboratory scanning equipment, the Diagnosis phase began. In the *Low Agency* version, the student was permitted to move freely between buildings using the fast travel interface during the Diagnosis phase. In the *High Agency* version, the student could also move freely between buildings, but she must navigate the outdoors 3D environment to reach her destination. The Diagnosis phase concluded after a student had successfully solved the mystery by submitting a correct diagnosis and treatment plan to the camp nurse. We utilized these three gameplay phases in the analysis of students' problem-solving behavior and agency.

Fig. 2. Non-player character and book elements students were required to interact with.

4 Study Description

The study involved 105 college age students randomly assigned to one of the three study conditions: *High Agency*, *Low Agency*, and *No Agency*. Seven students were removed due to partial or missing data. This resulted in 98 students ($M = 20.0$ years old, $SD = 1.74$) of which 59 (60.2%) were female. After removing the students for which not all data had been collected, there were 33 students in the *High Agency* condition, 34 in the *Low Agency* condition, and 31 students in the *No Agency* condition. Students began the session by completing a 20-question multiple choice test assessing their conceptual and application-based understanding of microbiology. Students were then introduced to the game environment and played the game until completing the mystery (approximately 60–90 min). Upon completing the game, students again completed the same microbiology assessment, concluding the experimental session.

5 Results

To better understand the effect of agency on problem solving, we collected high-granularity timestamped game logs for each participant's learning interactions. From these interaction logs, several measures were calculated to summarize how a student interacted with the game environment and provide insight into how the agency manipulation affected their problem-solving behavior. These specific actions are hypothesized to be related to problem solving, as they capture how students gather information (reading books, speaking with non-player characters), organize the information (editing the diagnosis worksheet), and test their hypotheses (scanning objects, submitting the final solution). The measures reported include the number of actions performed and the duration of the actions. The set of actions reported includes conversations with non-player characters (*ConversationCount* and *ConversationDuration*), items scanned in the virtual laboratory *(ScanCount)*, books and articles read *(BooksReadCount, ReadingDuration)*, edits to the diagnosis worksheet (*WorksheetCount, WorksheetDuration*), and number of times the worksheet was submitted (*SubmitCount*). Since students in the *No Agency* condition do not have differences in gameplay actions, the majority of the analysis focuses on the differences in the *High Agency* and *Low Agency* conditions.

Research Question 1: How do different agency conditions affect learning?

To address this research question, we examined students' performance on the multiple-choice microbiology content test administered before and after students' interactions with CRYSTAL ISLAND. Using the pre-test score (Pre-Test) and post-test score (Post-Test), Normalized Learning Gain (NLG) was calculated for each student participating in the study. NLG is the difference between Post-Test and Pre-Test, standardized by the total amount of improvement or decline possible from Pre-Test.

A one-way ANOVA was conducted to compare the effect of agency condition on NLG and revealed a statistically significant effect of agency condition on NLG ($F(2, 95) = 6.47$, $p = 0.0023$). A series of Welch two-sample t-tests, which do not assume equal population variances, was used to conduct a post-hoc analysis of the differences between conditions. The students in the *Low Agency* condition had significantly higher learning gains than students in the *High Agency* condition according to an independent two sample t-test (t = 2.33, p = 0.0231) and in the *No Agency* condition (t = 3.70, p < 0.001). Students in the *High Agency* condition did not exhibit statistically significantly higher NLG than students in the *No Agency* condition (t = 1.17, p = 0.248). Among all the participants, 71 of 98 (72.4%) exhibited positive learning gains, with 25 of the 33 (75.7%) in the *High Agency* condition, 30 of the 34 (88.2%) in the *Low Agency* and 16 of the 31 (51.6%) in the *No Agency* condition having positive learning gains (Table 1).

Table 1. Means (SDs) of Pre-Test, Post-Test, and NLG across conditions.

Condition	Pre-Test	Post-Test	NLG	Participants
All	12.0 (2.79)	14.1 (2.82)	0.255 (0.304)	98
High Agency	12.0 (2.58)	13.7 (3.01)	0.226 (0.315)	33
Low Agency	11.6 (2.88)	14.9 (2.40)	0.390 (0.256)	34
No Agency	12.5 (2.91)	13.5 (2.91)	0.138 (0.290)	31

Research Question 2: *What student problem-solving behaviors in the game environment account for differences in learning between agency conditions?*

Using the cumulative counts and durations of the different actions as predictors of Normalized Learning Gain, a stepwise linear regression with Akaike Information Criterion (AIC) was performed on all of the students to derive a set of significant predictors. AIC tries to minimize the residual sum of squares while penalizing a model with more parameters. This resulted in a linear model with *SubmitCount*, *ScanCount*, *WorksheetDuration*, and *ReadingDuration* as significant predictors of NLG among all 67 participants with an R^2 of 0.296. Two additional linear regressions were then performed using the same features, one using the *High Agency* students and one using the *Low Agency* students. In the *High Agency* model, both *ScanCount* and *ReadingDuration* remain significant predictors of NLG and this model yields an R^2 value of 0.371. In the *Low Agency* model, only *WorksheetDuration* remains significant and the R^2 value of 0.237 is lower than both the all students and *High Agency* models (Table 2).

The sign of the coefficients indicates how the actions are correlated with NLG, keeping all other actions constant. The two coefficients for the *SubmitCount* and *ReadingDuration* are both positive, indicating that more worksheet submissions and more time spent reading books and articles predict higher NLG. *ScanCount* and *WorksheetDuration* have negative coefficients, indicating that more scans and more time spent on the worksheet predict lower NLG. The sign of these coefficients is consistent across the three models with minimal variation in levels of magnitude but moderate variation in levels of significance.

Research Question 3: *How do different levels of student agency affect problem-solving behavior in the game environment?*

For this research question we first considered the effect on time spent in the environment. A one-way MANOVA was conducted to compare the effect of high or low agency on time spent in each interval: Tutorial, Information Gathering, and Diagnosis,

Table 2. Linear regression results predicting NLG from different groups' gameplay actions

	High Agency				Low Agency			
	B	SE B	β	t	B	SE B	β	t
Submit Count	0.018	0.040	0.025	0.453	0.028	0.015	0.099	1.86
Scan Count	−0.008	0.0032	−0.14	−2.62*	−0.0028	0.0032	−0.12	−0.89
Worksheet Duration	−0.027	0.020	−0.070	−1.31	−0.025	0.0099	−0.047	−2.5*
Reading Duration	0.014	0.0047	0.146	2.97**	0.0012	0.0047	0.011	0.257
	$R^2 = 0.371$				$R^2 = 0.237$			

Note: * $p < 0.05$, ** $p < 0.01$

and revealed a statistically significant effect of agency condition on time spent in each interval ($F(3, 63) = 32.2$, $p < 0.001$). Note that *No Agency* is not included here because students in this condition watched the same gameplay video and thus had no variation in duration or gameplay behaviors. A series of Welch's two-sample t-tests was used to conduct a post-hoc analysis of the differences between the two conditions. Because this results in multiple tests for significance, a Bonferroni correction ($\alpha = 0.5/4$) was applied to the significance threshold to account for the familywise error rate.

With respect to the differences between the two gameplay conditions, students in the *Low Agency* condition spent on average 19.0 min more in the game than students in the *High Agency* condition. The majority of the disparity between durations appears in the Information Gathering gameplay phase, the phase in which students in the *Low Agency* condition are restricted from moving on to the next area and thus progressing to the next phase. Overall, students in the *Low Agency* condition spent more than twice the amount of time ($M = 51$ min.) as students in the *High Agency* condition ($M = 23.7$ min.) in the Information Gathering phase (Table 3).

Table 3. Means (SDs) duration per gameplay interval in minutes for the *High Agency* and *Low Agency* conditions

Duration interval	High Agency	Low Agency	t-value (p-value)
All Gameplay	64.7 (18.8)	83.7 (17.7)	−4.50 (< 0.01)
Tutorial	7.75 (3.13)	7.50 (2.63)	0.353 (0.725)
Information Gathering	23.7 (13.4)	51.2 (8.91)	−9.76 (< 0.01)
Diagnosis	32.3 (13.8)	25.0 (14.8)	2.05 (0.0448)

In addition to duration, some of the other differences in gameplay actions can be explained by the structure of the conditions. The *Low Agency* condition required students to read all of the books and talk to all of the characters before progressing, so it is expected that students in the *Low Agency* condition read more books, talked to more characters, and spent more time performing both of these actions as shown in Table 4. A one-way MANOVA was conducted to compare the effect of high and low agency on six gameplay behaviors and revealed a statistically significant effect of agency condition on the behaviors ($F(6, 60) = 5.31$, $p < 0.001$). A post-hoc analysis using Welch's t-tests with a Bonferroni correction revealed the discrepancy between conditions for the actions is manifest most prominently in the Information Gathering phase, when students in the *Low Agency* condition have greater *ConversationCount* ($t = -7.28$, $p < 0.001$), *BooksRead* ($t = -10.4$, $p < 0.001$), spend more time *ConversationDuration* ($t = -8.05$, $p < 0.001$), and *ReadingDuration* ($t = -8.21$, $p < 0.001$).

Table 4. Comparison of actions between Low/High Agency condition (Full gameplay)

Gameplay behavior	High Agency	Low Agency	t-value (p-value)
ConversationCount	47.8 (8.70)	60.6 (14.9)	−4.20 (< 0.01)
BooksRead	22.2 (9.54)	27.4 (7.76)	−2.41 (0.018)
SubmitCount	1.82 (1.34)	3.44 (3.52)	−2.44 (0.017)
ConversationDuration	7.95 (1.54)	10.2 (2.04)	−4.92 (< 0.01)
ReadingDuration	26.0 (10.5)	35.7 (8.71)	−4.06 (< 0.01)
WorksheetDuration	5.42 (2.58)	7.44 (4.87)	−2.08 (0.041)

Once students transitioned from the Information Gathering phase to the Diagnosis phase, they were given full autonomy regardless of condition. Therefore, besides their previous experience in the game (i.e. time spent in Tutorial and Information Gathering), it would be expected that the experiences should be more similar between the two conditions. A one-way MANOVA was conducted to compare the effect of high and low agency on four gameplay behaviors from the Diagnosis phase and revealed a statistically significant effect of agency condition on these gameplay behaviors ($F(4, 62) = 12.87$, $p < 0.001$). A series of Welch's two-sample t-tests with a Bonferroni correction was used to conduct a post-hoc analysis of the differences between conditions.

The differences in key game actions in the Diagnosis phase are summarized in Table 5. These comparisons indicate that students in the *High Agency* condition had higher *BooksRead* and *ReadingDuration* than students in the *Low Agency* condition in the Diagnosis phase. This is likely due to the fact that *Low Agency* students have already read all of the content while *High Agency* students have not necessarily read all of the content prior to scanning their first item, and may be more inclined to seek out information to improve their hypotheses. Also of note is that students in the *Low Agency* condition spent very little time reading books in this phase ($M = 1.07$ min), indicating there were very few instances of returning to review previously read material. The students in the *Low Agency* condition also performed more incorrect worksheet submissions than students in the *High Agency* condition. Since correctly submitting the diagnosis worksheet is the final event required to complete the game, all submissions before the last submission indicate incorrect worksheet submissions. The higher number of *SubmitCount* for the *Low Agency* condition indicates that those students engaged in more guessing than students in the *High Agency* condition. Finally, while *ScanCount* was relatively equal between the two conditions, due to the *Low Agency* students spending less time overall in the Diagnosis phase, their *ScanCount* per minute was significantly higher than the *High Agency* condition. This result further reinforces the view that in the Diagnosis phase, the *Low Agency* students spent the majority of the time scanning objects and guessing solutions rather than conscientious problem solving.

Table 5. Comparison of actions between Low/High Agency condition (Diagnosis phase)

Action type	High Agency	Low Agency	t-stat (p-value)
SubmitCount	1.67 (1.17)	3.06 (3.25)	−2.28 (0.026)
BooksRead	11.5 (9.11)	5.11 (7.79)	3.09 (0.003)
ReadingDuration	10.5 (7.91)	1.07 (0.99)	6.92 (< 0.001)
ScanCount per minute	0.790 (0.364)	1.07 (0.361)	−3.15 (0.002)

6 Discussion

Analysis of the gameplay differences between the *High Agency* and *Low Agency* conditions reveals that many are likely due to the structural design of agency manipulation used in this experiment. However, some of the differences observed cannot be fully explained by the structure of the gameplay in those conditions. This includes the differences in the Diagnosis phase, when students in each condition have the same access to the gameplay environment. In this phase, students in the *Low Agency* condition exhibited undesirable behaviors such as reading fewer books, attempting more incorrect submissions, and performing a higher rate of scans than students in the *High Agency* condition. These behaviors are undesirable because they are indicative of "guess-and-check" problem solving because scans and submissions are attempts at validating a student's hypothesis while lack of reading indicates less informed hypotheses. The difference in these types of behaviors suggests that students in the *Low Agency* condition engaged in more "guess-and-check" problem solving than students in the *High Agency* condition. Additionally, the negative coefficient of *ScanCount* in the linear models supports the notion that testing a large number of hypotheses negatively predicts Normalized Learning Gain, regardless of condition.

While the results presented here suggest that limiting agency can improve performance on cognitive measures, they also suggest that limiting agency can have detrimental effects, such as increased propensity for guessing. The findings support previous work on discovery learning [17, 18] in that it may be beneficial to sacrifice some agency to ensure that students have an opportunity to interact with all content available. Overall, it suggests a need for scaffolding that adaptively promotes the most effective learning interactions rather than forcing all students through the same path. This calls for data-driven techniques for personalizing a game-based learning environment with adaptive agency to encourage learning and reduce guess-and-check problem solving.

7 Conclusion and Future Work

Game-based learning seeks to create learning interactions that are both effective and engaging. A key feature of many game-based learning environments is providing students with the freedom to experience agency by exploring and pursuing tasks in a manner of their choosing, based on a complex set of factors that include individual differences and self-regulatory skills. However, the more freedom that is provided, the less structured the activity becomes, sometimes leading to impoverished learning outcomes. The study presented here investigates the effect of manipulating the amount of student agency on learning.

To test the effect of agency, we conducted a study with three conditions where students were assigned to a *High Agency* condition, a more restrictive *Low Agency* condition, or a *No Agency* condition consisting of watching a video walkthrough of a game-based learning environment. Results showed that while all groups exhibited positive learning gains, the *Low Agency* group had significantly higher normalized learning gains. Regression analyses of students' actions in the game-based learning environment suggest that the strong performance of the *Low Agency* group may be attributed to students' more extensively engaging with instructional materials. Further analyses of gameplay behaviors show that while *High Agency* students exhibited productive behaviors, including completing the activity more efficiently than *Low Agency* students, in the end *Low Agency* students exhibited greater learning gains.

The results suggest two important lines of investigation. First, it will be important to explore the effect of the agency manipulation on students' performance, scientific reasoning, and self-regulated learning including motivational beliefs, metacognitive monitoring, and cognitive and affective engagement [25]. Because a key promise of game-based learning environments is their capacity to enable students to learn through problem-solving episodes that are deeply engaging, it will be important to investigate the motivational impact of varying student agency. Second, the results suggest that there may be a significant benefit to designing in-game scaffolds that adaptively support learning and self-regulatory processes that mediate agency, problem solving, and performance. Well-designed adaptive scaffolding could potentially simultaneously support effective learning interactions and enable students to have a deep sense of autonomy throughout their game-based learning interactions.

Acknowledgments. We would like to thank our collaborators in the Center for Educational Informatics and the SMART Lab at N.C. State University. This study was supported by funding from the Social Sciences and Humanities Research Council of Canada. Any conclusions expressed in this material do not necessarily reflect the views of SSHRC.

References

1. Ventura, M., Shute, V., Kim, Y.: Assessment and learning of qualitative physics in newton s playground Newton's Playground. J. Ed. Res. **106**, 423–430 (2013)
2. Easterday, M.W., Aleven, V., Scheines, R., Carver, S.M.: Using tutors to improve educational games: a cognitive game for policy argument. J. Learn. Sci. pp. 1–51 (2016)
3. Wouters, P., van Nimwegen, C., van Oostendorp, H., van der Spek, E.D.: A meta-analysis of the cognitive and motivational effects of serious games. J. Educ. Psychol. **105**, 249–265 (2013)
4. Sao Pedro, M., Baker, R., Gobert, J., Montalvo, O., Nakama, A.: Leveraging machine-learned detectors of systematic inquiry behavior to estimate and predict transfer of inquiry skill. User Model. User-Adap. Inter. **23**, 1–39 (2013)

5. VanLehn, K.: The relative effectiveness of human tutoring, intelligent tutoring systems, and other tutoring systems. Educ. Psychol. **46**, 197–221 (2011)

6. Koedinger, K., Aleven, V.: An interview reflection on "intelligent Tutoring Goes to School in the Big City". Int. J. Artif. Intell. Educ. **26**, 13–24 (2016)

7. Clark, D., Tanner-Smith, E., Killingsworth, S.: Digital games, design, and learning: a systematic review and meta-analysis. Rev. Ed. Res. **86**, 79–122 (2016)

8. Mayer, R.E.: Computer games for learning: an evidence-based approach (2014)

9. Long, Y., Aleven, V.: Gamification of joint student/system control over problem selection in a linear equation tutor. In: Proceedings of the 12th International Conference on Intelligent Tutoring Systems, pp. 378–387 (2014)

10. Malone, T., Lepper, M.: Making learning fun: a taxonomy of intrinsic motivations for learning. Aptit. learn. instr. **3**, 223–253 (1987)

11. Ryan, R., Deci, E.: Self-determination theory and the facilitation of intrinsic motivation, social development, and well-being. Am. Psychol. **55**, 68–78 (2000)

12. Winne, P., Hadwin, A.: The weave of motivation and self-regulated learning. In: Schunk, D., Zimmerman, B. (eds.) Motivation and Self-Regulated Learning: Theory, Research, and Applications, pp. 297–314. Taylor & Francis, New York (2008)

13. Wardrip-Fruin, N., Mateas, M., Dow, S., Sali, S.: Agency Reconsidered. Breaking New Ground: Innovation in Games, Play, Practice and Theory (2009)

14. Snow, E., Allen, L., Jacovina, M., McNamara, D.: Does agency matter?: exploring the impact of controlled behaviors within a game-based environment. Comput. Educ. **82**, 378–392 (2015)

15. Rowe, J., Shores, L., Mott, B., Lester, J.: Integrating learning, problem solving, and engagement in narrative-centered learning environments. Int. J. Artif. Intell. Educ. **21**, 115–133 (2011)

16. Winne, P., Azevedo, R.: Metacognition. In: Sawyer, K. (ed.) Cambridge Handbook of the Learning Sciences, pp. 63–87. Cambridge University Press, Cambridge (2014)

17. Mayer, R.: Should there be a three-strikes rule against pure discovery learning? The case for guided methods of instruction. Am. Psychol. **59**, 14–19 (2004)

18. Kirschner, P., Sweller, J., Clark, R.: Why minimal guidance during instruction does not work: an analysis of the failure of constructivist, discovery, problem-based, experiential, and inquiry-based teaching. Educ. Psychol. **41**, 75–86 (2006)

19. Harp, S., Mayer, R.: How seductive details do their damage: a theory of cognitive interest in science learning. J. Educ. Psychol. **90**, 414–434 (1998)

20. Baker, R., Moore, G., Wagner, A., Kalka, J., Salvi, A., Karabinos, M., Ashe, C., Yaron, D.: The dynamics between student affect and behavior occuring outside of educational software. In: Proceedings of the 4th International Conference on Affective Computing and Intelligent Interaction, pp. 14–24 (2011)

21. Rowe, J., McQuiggan, S., Robison, J., Lester, J.: Off-task behavior in narrative-centered learning environments. In: 14th International Conference on Artificial Intelligence in Education, pp. 99–106. IOS Press, Brighton (2009)

22. Cordova, D., Lepper, M.: Intrinsic motivation and the process of learning: beneficial effects of contextualization, personalization, and choice. J. Educ. Psychol. **88**, 715–730 (1996)

23. Barab, S., Thomas, M., Dodge, T., Carteaux, R., Tuzun, H.: Making learning fun: quest atlantis, a game without guns. Educ. Technol. Res. Dev. **53**, 86–107 (2005)

24. Baker, R., Clarke-Midura, J., Ocumpaugh, J.: Towards general models of effective science inquiry in virtual performance assessments. J. Comput. Assist. Learn. **32**, 267–280 (2016)

25. Azevedo, R.: Defining and measuring engagement and learning in science: conceptual, theoretical, methodological, and analytical issues. Ed. Psychol. **50**, 84–94 (2015)

Can a Teachable Agent Influence How Students Respond to Competition in an Educational Game?

Björn Sjödén[1,2(✉)], Mats Lind[3], and Annika Silvervarg[4]

[1] Lund University, Lund, Sweden
[2] Halmstad University, Halmstad, Sweden
Bjorn.Sjoden@hh.se
[3] Uppsala University, Uppsala, Sweden
Mats.Lind@uu.se
[4] Linköping University, Linköping, Sweden
Annika.Silvervarg@liu.se

Abstract. Learning in educational games is often associated with some form of competition. We investigated how students responded to winning or losing in an educational math game, with respect to playing with or without a Teachable Agent (TA). Students could choose between game modes in which the TA took a more passive or active role, or let the TA play a game entirely on its own. Based on the data logs from 3983 games played by 163 students (age 10–11), we analyzed data on students' persistence, challenge-seeking and performance during gameplay. Results indicated that students showed greater persistence when playing together with the TA, by more often repeating a lost game with the TA, than a lost game after playing alone. Students' challenge-seeking, by increasing the difficulty level, was greater following a win than following a loss, especially after the TA won on its own. Students' gameplay performance was unaffected by their TA winning or losing but was, unexpectedly, slightly worse following a win by the student alone. We conclude that engaging a TA can make students respond more productively to both winning and losing, depending on the particular role the TA takes in the game. These results may inform more specific hypotheses as to the differential effects of competing and collaborating in novel, AI-supported social constellations, such as with TAs, on students' motivation and ego-involvement in educational games.

Keywords: Educational game · Competition · Teachable agent · Social influence

1 Introduction

Learning with digital educational games is quite different from learning with traditional teaching materials. One aspect is that games usually include an element of explicit competition. Over the course of playing a digital game, the student's success or failure is reflected in terms of scores, rewards, or won and lost games. In effect, the goal of learning becomes increasingly associated with the goal of winning.

© Springer International Publishing AG 2017
E. André et al. (Eds.): AIED 2017, LNAI 10331, pp. 347–358, 2017.
DOI: 10.1007/978-3-319-61425-0_29

A second aspect is that digital games typically include digital characters, that is, avatars or agents, which add a social dimension. Unlike a traditional lecture, where social interactions between teachers and students are quite limited, a game environment with digital characters make a continuously engaging, dynamic social construct with unique affordances for learning. The pedagogical potential of gamification, which includes competitive elements, has for a long time interested researchers [e.g. 1]. However, yet there is relatively little research on the novel social constellations that can be created with digital characters which, guided by AI techniques, act more or less independently to the human player. The effects on student motivation and performance, when students work together with such AI-supported characters for collaboration or competition in educational settings, have only begun to be explored.

In the present study, we address students' learning behaviors in competitive situations in an educational math game, where the student can take on different social roles in relation to the computer player, using the construct of a teachable agent (TA). Although this particular game has been used in schools for more than ten years (see [2] for an overview), many questions remain as to how the game dynamics affect the pedagogical process, especially as to the actions students take in response to the competitive outcomes (i.e. winning or losing) in the game.

For example, is the experience of winning or losing conducive to learning for all students? Do certain social factors (such as playing in teams or pairs) have greater effect on students' performance than others (such as playing alone against an opponent)? Such questions aim to differentiate the effects of specific conditions under which players engage in competition, rather than making overall comparisons between, for instance, competition and collaboration (which addressed in a previous study of this game [3]).

Due to some unique game features, which allowed students to choose between different modes of competition that included or excluded their TA, we could gain insights into these and other pedagogically meaningful aspects of students' game-playing behavior. The empirical basis for our analysis consisted of the accumulated game logs from a large number of played games. A significant advantage of using game logs was that we could retrieve behavioral data on students' in-game choices. When informed by findings from educational research, these data make a contextualized and objective measure of students' learning behavior that complement other, more common measures, such as students' self-reports and post-game questionnaires, which have been used in previous studies.

In sum, this makes the first attempt to use game log data for clarifying meaningful playing patterns with respect to how students respond to winning or losing, in different social constellations with their digital character in the game. Next, we relate previous research that informed our research questions and describe the relevant game features in more detail.

2 Social Motivations from Teachable Agents and Competition

Research over the past decade has produced extensive empirical evidence for the benefits of using teachable agents, or TAs, for learning (e.g. [4–6]). Here, we focus on the motivational effects that a TA may have by virtue of being perceived and treated as a social character. In short, TAs rely upon the idea that students learn better within the context of teaching or tutoring someone else. This pedagogical approach is widely known as Learning-By-Teaching [7]. A TA represents the application of LBT pedagogy in a digital setting. The TA takes the form of a semi-independent or hybrid digital character [5], which produces an output that reflects the student's own knowledge.

It has been suggested that the learning power of TAs can be attributed to the immersive narrative of teaching [4]. In other words, the cognitive effects of using a TA can be seen as fundamentally driven by social attitudes and approaches related to the teacher/student schema. These social mechanisms are reflected in studies, which showed that students spontaneously and easily relate to their TA as a social being, for example by cheering and commenting on it during gameplay [5, 8, 9].

In a competitive context, the social motivations from working with a TA might be even more pronounced. Okita et al. [10] showed that the mere belief in social interaction improved learning in a LBT setting. It has been suggested that TAs are important because of a *protégé effect*[chase], which means that students make greater efforts to learn in order to tutor their TA than they do in order to learn for themselves. In addition, the TA might provide an *ego-protective buffer* against feelings of failure, which particularly benefits low-achieving students [ibid].

We suggest two underlying reasons why the role of a TA might influence the effects of competitive outcomes, while acknowledging that both factors (i.e. playing with/without a TA, and winning/losing, respectively) can have an important motivational impact on students' subsequent behavior and performance.

First, research on motivation suggests that competitive situations generally make people ego-involved, that is, people invest feelings of self-worth in accomplishing the competitive task [11, 12]. Ego-involvement appears particularly important for how people respond to losing [13]. When faced with a choice between repeating the task they failed or taking on a new task, ego-involved losers prefer to repeat the same task in order to recover their feelings of personal failure.

Second, as players form joint constellations (e.g. in pairs), the competition changes from being an individual challenge to becoming a shared challenge against the opponent. Competing together (in this case with a TA) arguably affects one's degree of ego-involvement, due to providing an ego-protective buffer. These findings provide a rationale for hypothesizing that students would take different actions in the game (e.g. persisting in a task or trying out new options) following a loss, depending on whether they played alone or together with their TA.

2.1   Forms of Competition in TA-Based Systems

The present study focused on an adaptation of the Squares Family, a research-based educational math game developed by Pareto [2], which has been extensively played and tested in schools. As far as we are aware, there are only two other, comparable TA-based systems that have demonstrated learning gains through extensive testing with students in authentic classroom settings. These systems are Betty's brain (for an overview, see [4]) and SimStudent (e.g. [6, 14]).

Both Betty's brain and SimStudent do in some, but not all, versions include a competitive Game show module where students can set their TA to challenge the TAs of other students. In one version of Betty's brain, the Game show proved an effective support for students' metacognition and increased their engagement in the software, as reflected in students going back to tutor their TA on the specific subjects it failed in the Game show [15]. In SimStudent, Matsuda et al. [6] evaluated the effects of including an optional competitive Game show where students could have their TAs compete against each other in solving first-order algebraic equations. Students who used the Game show increased their engagement in tutoring the TA. However, there was also a tendency for students to employ an "easy win" - strategy by challenging weaker opponents just in order to win, when having the opportunity to do so.

The examples show that competition can be, but is not necessarily, a positive addition to TA systems. Betty's brain demonstrated positive motivational effects of students having their TA compete against another TA. However, as the SimStudent study showed, if students consider winning more important than learning, the competitive element might have unwanted effects, depending on the game options.

There are some important features that distinguish the educational math game used in the present study from both Betty's brain and SimStudent, with respect to the competitive game modules. First, in the latter systems, submitting the TA to compete was optional – the students did not need to compete with their TA in every game or interaction. Second, the learning-by-teaching context (tutoring the TA) was clearly separated from the competitive context (the Game show) in both systems.

In the Squares Family game, the competitive element was integrated in all modes of playing. The students could not choose to exclude the competition as such, but only the modes or social constellations in which to compete against the computer player (e.g. alone or together with the TA). These included two game modes for tutoring the TA and two game modes with no active tutoring, using the following setup:

In Mode 1, students played alone (thus without a TA), represented only by their own name on-screen. In Mode 2, the student played together with a passive TA, which learned implicitly by observing the student's gameplay and from posing questions about the game. In Mode 3, the TA took a more active role by suggesting game moves. In Mode 4, the TA played a game on its own, letting the student watch its performance, based on how it was tutored in the previous two modes. From the student's perspective, the order of the four modes thus represents a progression from learning the game for oneself (Mode 1) to tutoring a TA (Mode 2 & 3), such that the TA can play independently against the computer (Mode 4). In addition, before each game, the skill level of the opponent (always an impersonal computer), which represented the difficulty level of the game, could be set from 1 (low) to 5 (high).

3 Research Questions

Since competition was always present and as such invariable in the game, we were primarily interested in what choices students made (e.g. which game mode or difficulty level they selected) following different competitive outcomes (winning or losing). Our analysis was guided by three types of educationally relevant behaviors, or constructs, in response to the competitive outcomes. These three constructs concerned students' *persistence* (after losing), *challenge-seeking* (after winning) and *performance* (in terms of an implicitly calculated game score, whether win or loss). Because this was a post hoc study, the purpose of the analysis was not to test particular hypotheses relating to these measures, but rather to clarify to what extent the available data could serve as a basis for formulating meaningful hypotheses that could be tested in future and experimentally controlled studies.

In each case of the three educationally relevant constructs of persistence, challenge-seeking and performance, we aimed to compare how playing with the TA and playing without the TA affected students' choices in the subsequent game. Hence, we formulated three main research questions, Q1–Q3, that could be empirically addressed by extracting and analyzing data from the game logs.

Q1: Are students more likely to repeat a lost game that they played alone, or a lost game that they played with their TA?
Q2: Are students more likely to increase the difficulty level following a win by the TA on its own than following a win either alone, or together with the TA?
Q3: Is student performance when tutoring the TA influenced by the competitive outcomes when the TA plays alone and/or when the student plays alone?

4 Method

4.1 Participants

We analyzed the anonymous game log data from 163 fourth-graders (age 10–11, 81 girls and 82 boys) from nine school classes in a small municipality in South Sweden. The students had played the game as part of their curriculum in mathematics, one lesson (40–50 min) per week for seven weeks, in 2014.

4.2 Instruments

The aim of the Squares Family math game was to train conceptual understanding of the base-10 system using the graphical metaphor of squares and boxes. The game employed a board-game design with playing cards and a shared game board. The game could be played as either an addition or a subtraction game. A game move consisted of picking a card that depicts a certain constellation of squares and boxes, which then add to, or in the subtraction game subtract from, the present squares and boxes on the game board. The goal was to consistently pick the cards that maximize the number of carry-overs (in addition) or borrowings (in subtraction). Each carry-over or borrowing rewarded the player one star. The winner of the game was the player who had gained more points when all cards were finished. The stars and cards of both players are visible at all times, which makes the competitive element quite explicit (see Fig. 1).

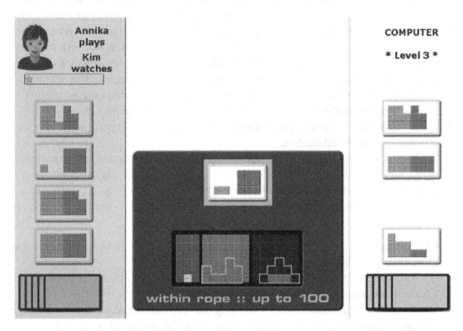

Fig. 1. Gameplay in the Squares Family, with the TA (Kim) in the upper left corner. The computer plays a card representing the number 29, whereas the boxes on the common game board represent 103. The card played by the computer will add nine units to the three units on the game board and thus yield one carry-over, which rewards the computer one point.

4.3   Procedure

In the introductory game session, students were given a short introduction to the game and instructed to first play on their own in Mode 1 (i.e., without the TA). As the students gained knowledge of the game, they were instructed to start tutoring their TA and continue to do so in Modes 2 and 3. A goal was formulated such that students should train their TA so well that it could win over the computer component at the difficulty level 3 or higher (note: the difficulty level could be set from 1–5). The researchers assisted the students in how to begin and interact in the game, but kept direct instructions to a minimum and encouraged them to keep on playing in order to understand more.

Over the following six game sessions, students could play at their own pace. Although we instructed the students to teach their TA carefully (in Modes 2 and 3) before subjecting it to an independent competition against the computer (in Mode 4), students were free to self-regulate how they played the game. In effect, the number of played games in each mode, as well as the difficulty level, varied between students.

4.4 Measures and Data Analysis

In order to identify relevant data from the game logs, we used the following operationalized measures of students' persistence, challenge-seeking and performance.

Persistence was measured in terms of whether the student chose to repeat the same game mode when starting a new game (e.g. playing in Mode 2 immediately following a game in Mode 2, or in Mode 3 immediately following a game in Mode 3).

Challenge-seeking was measured in terms of whether the student selected a higher difficulty level for the computer opponent (1–5) than in the immediate previous game. Notably, the difficulty level defaulted back to 1 after each game, which means that any level set higher than 1 required an active choice by the student.

Performance was measured in terms of the students' quality of gameplay, as represented by the average "goodness value" (0–100) of each card the student selected during a game. Importantly, even though goodness correlates with competitive outcomes (i.e. higher scores are correlated with winning), there are game situations where the player cannot win (for example due to getting "bad" cards) which still reflect the player's ability to choose the best possible alternative among the given options. The goodness value provides a measure of performance, which, over time, reflects the player's learning progression in the game, independent of the number of wins and losses. For details on how the goodness value was calculated, we refer to previous accounts [2].

The game logs contained detailed gameplay data for each individual game played by each individual student. For the present purposes, we extracted data on students' choices of game mode (Mode 1–4), difficulty level (1–5), the average goodness value of each game, and the competitive outcome (win, loss or draw) of each game. We recorded these data in an Excel-file, which was recoded and imported into Matlab®. All subsequent analyses were performed using custom-made Matlab scripts on the imported data. The initial sequence of training games played in Mode 1, by which students learned the very basics of the game, were excluded from the analysis.

5 Results

5.1 General Description and Validation of Measures

The total dataset comprised 3983 games played by 163 students. Thus, every student played the game on average 24.4 times (median 25, range 8–41); not all students were present at all game sessions. There was no correlation between the number of wins or losses and the number of games played per student, which indicates that the competitive outcome did not influence students' decisions to continue playing the game (e.g. to give up) during the study period. There was a small but significant general training effect of playing the game, in terms of a significant correlation between the number of games played and the average goodness values; Pearson $r = .146$; $p = .000$.

As to game performance measured by the average goodness values, we verified that winning was associated with better game performance than losing (thus winning was not only due to chance). Games in which students tutored their TA (Mode 2 & 3) were associated with higher performance than games played without a TA (Mode 1), in accordance with the protégé effect.

5.2   Students' Persistence Following a Loss

Q1: Are students more likely to repeat a lost game that they played alone, or a lost game that they played with their TA?

First, we identified all games where the student lost and was playing in Mode 1, or, lost and was playing in Mode 2 or Mode 3. A total of 90 students had lost at least once in Mode 1 as well as lost at least once in one or both of Mode 2 and Mode 3; this subset of students and games became subject to the subsequent analyses.

Second, we calculated the ratio of repeated games to the number of identified games after a loss, where "repeated" means that the student chose exactly the same game mode following the game mode they had lost (e.g. if a student had lost in Mode 2 and then again chose Mode 2, this would count as a repetition, but not if the same student chose Mode 3). If there were one repetition and one non-repetition, the "repetition ratio" was 1 (repetition)/2 (games) = .5.

The group mean value of this repetition ratio was 0.169 for ($SD = 0.262$) losses in Mode 1 and 0.378 ($SD = 0.220$) for losses in Mode 2 or Mode 3. This difference was substantial; $t(89) = -5.483$, $p = .000$. The effect size, in terms of Cohen's d, was 0.87. This means that there was a differential effect of losing a game in the two conditions, such that students were more likely to persist by repeating a lost game with the TA than repeating a lost game alone.

5.3   Students' Challenge-Seeking Following a Win

Q2: Are students more likely to increase the difficulty level following a win by the TA on its own than following a win either alone, or together with the TA?

First, we wanted to test the assumption that winning a game, compared to losing, had a general effect on increasing the difficulty level in the subsequent game. To investigate this we identified the game immediately following a win or a loss for each student. We counted the number of such games and how many of these games were played with a higher difficulty level. This was done separately for the wins and the losses. One student had no losses and was disregarded, leaving 162 students for analysis. Lastly, we calculated the ratio between the number of opportunities to increase the difficulty level after a win and a loss, respectively, and the number of times this was actually done by each student. For each student we then obtained two numbers representing the probability that this student would increase the difficulty level after a win and after a loss, respectively. The group means value of these probabilities was 0.337 ($SD = 0.216$) after a win, but only 0.154 ($SD = 0.135$) after a loss. This difference was large; $t(161) = -9.849$, $p = .000$; Cohen's $d = -1.01$. Thus, the assumption that students would seek greater challenge after winning was strongly supported.

We identified which students had won games both when their TA played on its own (Mode 4) and when playing alone (Mode 1). There were 83 students who fulfilled these criteria. The games won in Mode 1 or Mode 4 for these students were then selected and the game after each win was further analyzed. We calculated the ratio of games with an increased difficulty level to the total number of selected games in each mode. The group means ratio of increased difficulty levels was 0.3510 (SD = 0.414) for games in Mode 4 and 0.274 (SD = 0.364) for games in Mode 1. A t-test resulted in t (82) = 1.265, p = .21; Cohen's d = 0.20.

Following the same procedure as above, but for games in Mode 2 and Mode 3 (instead of Mode 1), there were 133 students who fulfilled the inclusion criteria for analysis. The group mean ratio of increased difficulty levels was 0.373 (SD = 0.394) following games in Mode 4 and on average 0.280 (SD = 0.220) following games in the tutoring modes. A t-test resulted in $t(132)$ = 2.396, p < .05; Cohen's d = 0.29.

In summary, challenge-seeking was slightly higher following a win by the TA on its own compared to all other game modes and especially in relation to the two tutoring modes. However, more data from each game mode would be required for making specific comparisons of the effect of the TA's wins (Mode 4) to the player winning alone (Mode 1) and winning in a tutoring mode (Mode 2 & 3), respectively.

5.4   Students' Performance Following Different Competitive Outcomes

Q3. Is student performance when tutoring the TA influenced by the competitive outcomes when the TA plays alone and/or when the student plays alone?

To examine this question we looked at sequences where the student had been tutoring the TA (Mode 2 &3), then either played alone against the computer (Mode 1) or let the TA play alone (Mode 4), followed by a game where the student tutored the TA (Mode 2 or 3). For the game(s) in Mode 1 and Mode 4, the competitive outcome was coded using −1 for a loss, 0 for a draw, and +1 for a win. If there were several consecutive games in this mode, a mean value was calculated. To see if the student performed better or worse depending on this competitive outcome, the difference in goodness values for the following tutoring game, in comparison to the previous games in Mode 2 and Mode 3 was calculated. If there were three or more tutoring games, we performed a linear regression analysis to predict the goodness value of the following tutoring game; the predicted value was then compared to the actual value. Linear regression is, however, not robust in the presence of only two values in the presence of randomness and impossible to use with only one value. Therefore, if only two values were present preceding the game played alone, the mean of the two values were used as the best possible predictor. If there was only one value, that value was used.

Each student who had at least one such sequence thus generated two values: one representing the average performance in the games played alone by the student or agent, and one value representing the average difference between the following and preceding goodness values of tutoring games.

With the TA playing alone (Mode 4) as target games, 115 students generated sequences that could be analyzed according to the above scheme. With the student playing alone (Mode 1) as target games, 112 students generated such sequences. These two sets of students were not identical; only 81 students appeared in both sets.

As to the competitive outcomes by the TA alone (Mode 4), we calculated the Pearson correlation between the mean competitive outcome value and the mean goodness value difference for the subset of 115 students. This correlation was very small, $r = -0.0531$ and not significantly different from zero; $t(113) = -0.565, p = .57$. Thus, the competitive outcomes of the TA did not seem to influence the students' performance in the subsequent tutoring games at all.

As to the competitive outcomes by the student alone (Mode 1), we again calculated the Pearson correlation r between the mean competitive outcome value and the mean goodness value difference, but for the subset of 112 students. The correlation was larger, $r = -0.21$, and significantly different from zero; $t(110) = -2.233, p < .05$.

In sum, the competitive outcome in games played by the students alone (Mode 1) seemed to affect students' performance in a subsequent tutoring game (Mode 2 & 3), but not the competitive outcome in games played by the TA on its own (Mode 4). Also, this influence is negative, meaning that the more often the students lost when playing alone, the relatively better they performed in the subsequent tutoring games.

6 Discussion

This study investigated how the motivational effects of competing in an educational game may be affected when students can involve a teachable agent in the competition. A reason for focusing on the TA was that digital characters ideally serve to off-load the negative impact of failure as well as exploit the positive motivation from success. TAs have been shown to be particularly effective in these respects, by exploiting the many positive motivations and responsibilities associated with tutoring someone else.

The most important findings were that we could demonstrate that the TA had immediate and specific influence on students' actual choices while playing the math game. Overall, we found significant effects of students preferring to repeat lost games with their TA over repeating lost games alone. This result is noteworthy with respect to the concept of "ego-involved persistence" from social psychology [12]. Our results point to a contrasting effect of "TA-involved persistence", that is, it might be more important for students to redress their TA's loss than a loss on their own. Together with the positive effects on challenge-seeking – that a win by the TA on its own triggered students to continue on a higher difficulty level – this adds to positive effects of forming an ego-protective buffer when working with a TA [cf. 5].

A more general question concerns how motivated students are by the competitive outcomes in relation to other (and from a learning perspective more relevant) aspects of the game, such as wanting to understand more of the game strategies, making progress in tutoring, getting the math questions right, etc. Some comments made by the students seemed to confirm that winning, at least to some, was an important motivator. For example, when asked after the study what they liked about the game, some students spontaneously said that "winning" was fun or important – one of them adding "it was also fun … that [my TA] was learning". Students' comments and experiences of both the game and the TA make the topic for an on-going study. We found no significant effect of the TA's competitive success on student performance, but some surprising results as to the immediate effects of students' own competitive success. Specifically, worse competitive outcomes (i.e. more losses) when the student played alone correlated with better performance in subsequent tutoring games. This effect would rather be expected from games where the teachable agent, but not the student, played on its own (since watching the TA lose should motivate the student to put more effort into tutoring, according to the general protégé effect). One interpretation is that students made less efforts following a win because they perceived winning as a confirmation of superior competence. By contrast, students would make more efforts following a "bad" game (i.e. losing).

That students were affected by watching their TA win on its own is in itself an interesting finding. It implies that students can be even without being active themselves in the game, and that this kind of automatic gameplay can make a meaningful addition to educational games for increasing student motivation. Specifically, digital characters such as a TA should be considered as a potentially effective means for counteracting negative effects of competition in educational games and other digital learning environments. One message, perhaps for teachers to keep in mind, is that losing is not necessarily negative but can also have a positive effect on students' performance. Another implication is that competitive outcomes should not be taken as a valid indication of a student's competence or general performance level.

The overall conclusions we can draw from this study are necessarily limited by the nature of the data, which were not collected for the purpose of conventional hypothesis testing using experimental controls. As a result of students being largely free to choose game modes and how many games they played during the study period, the dataset was too heterogeneous too allow all, hypothetically relevant comparisons across groups or conditions on an equal statistical basis (e.g. comparing students' choices following a win with an active TA in Mode 3 to playing with a passive TA in Mode 2). This said, experimental rigor should be reasonably balanced with the ecological validity of data in order to be applicable to authentic educational settings [16]. We conceive of the present study as the first step towards scientifically exploring the effects of the novel social configurations that emerge as students engage with AI-supported digital characters in hybrid, competitive and collaborative constellations, in the classroom.

In conclusion, the main contribution of this study was to differentiate some of the effects a TA can have on how students respond to competitive outcomes in an educational game. The results add to the complexity of reasons why constructs such as a TA are effective for learning, particularly with respect to the social motivations involved in responding productively to failure. We demonstrated how such effects can appear in a vast and varied data set, to uncover students' learning behaviors during actual gameplay. Our hope is that these results can inform more specific hypotheses for testing using structured, experimental controls in future studies, while acknowledging the need for ecologically valid data that reflect students' active choices in authentic educational settings.

References

1. Gee, J.P.: What video games have to teach us about learning and literacy. Palgrave Macmillan, New York (2007)
2. Pareto, L.: A teachable agent game engaging primary school children to learn arithmetic concepts and reasoning. Int. J. AI Educ. **24**, 251–283 (2014)

3. Pareto, L., Haake, M., Lindström, P., Sjödén, B., Gulz, A.: A teachable agent based game affording collaboration and competition – evaluating math comprehension and motivation. Educ. Technol. Res. Dev. **60**(5), 723–751 (2012)
4. Biswas, G., Segedy, J.R., Bunchongchit, K.: From design to implementation to practice a learning by teaching system: Betty's brain. Int. J. Artif. Intell. Educ. 1–15 (2015)
5. Chase, C., Chin, D., Oppezzo, M., Schwartz, D.: Teachable agents and the protégé effect: increasing the effort towards learning. J. Sci. Educ. Technol. **18**, 334–352 (2009)
6. Matsuda, N., Yarzebinski, E., Keiser, V., Raizada, R., Stylianides, G.J., Koedinger, K.R.: Studying the effect of a competitive game show in a learning by teaching environment. Int. J. Artif. Intell. Educ. **23**(1–4), 1–21 (2013)
7. Bargh, J., Schul, Y.: On the cognitive benefits of teaching. J. Educ. Psychol. **72**, 593–604 (1980)
8. Lindström, P., Gulz, A., Haake, M., Sjödén, B.: Matching and mismatching between the pedagogical design principles of a maths game and the actual practices of play. J. Comput. Assist. Learn. **27**, 90–102 (2011)
9. Ogan, A., Finkelstein, S., Mayfield, E., D'Adamo, C., Matsuda, N., Cassell, J.: Oh dear stacy! Social interaction, elaboration, and learning with teachable agents. In: Proceedings of the SIGCHI Conference on Human Factors in Computing Systems, pp. 39–48. ACM (2012)
10. Okita, S.Y., Schwartz, D.L.: Learning by teaching human pupils and teachable agents: the importance of recursive feedback. J. Learn. Sci. **22**, 375–412 (2013)
11. Butler, R.: Interest in the task and interest in peers' work in competitive and non-competitive conditions: a developmental study. Child Dev. **60**, 562–570 (1989)
12. Vansteenkiste, M., Deci, E.L.: Competitively contingent rewards and intrinsic motivation: can losers remain motivated? Motiv. Emotion **27**(4), 273–299 (2003)
13. Reeve, J., Deci, E.L.: Elements within the competitive situation that affect intrinsic motivation. Personality Soc. Psychol. Bull. **22**, 24–33 (1996)
14. Matsuda, N., Yarzebinski, E., Keiser, V., Raizada, R., Stylianides, G.J., Cohen, W.W., Koedinger, K.R.: Learning by teaching simstudent – an initial classroom baseline study comparing with cognitive tutor. In: Biswas, G., Bull, S., Kay, J., Mitrovic, A. (eds.) AIED 2011. LNCS, vol. 6738, pp. 213–221. Springer, Heidelberg (2011). doi:10.1007/978-3-642-21869-9_29
15. Chin, D.B., Dohmen, I.M., Cheng, B.H., Oppezzo, M.A., Chase, C.C., Schwartz, D.L.: Preparing students for future learning with teachable agents. Educ. Technol. Res. Dev. **58**(6), 649–669 (2010)
16. Ross, S.M., Morrison, G.R., Lowther, D.L.: Educational technology research past and present: balancing rigor and relevance to impact school learning. Contemp. Educ. Technol. **1**(1), 17–35 (2010)

Face Forward: Detecting Mind Wandering from Video During Narrative Film Comprehension

Angela Stewart[1]([✉]) [iD], Nigel Bosch[2] [iD], Huili Chen[3] [iD],
Patrick Donnelly[1] [iD], and Sidney D'Mello[1]([✉]) [iD]

[1] University of Notre Dame, Notre Dame, IN, USA
{astewal2, sdmello}@nd.edu
[2] University of Illinois at Urbana-Champaign, Urbana, IL, USA
[3] Massachusetts Institute of Technology, Cambridge, MA, USA

Abstract. Attention is key to effective learning, but mind wandering, a phenomenon in which attention shifts from task-related processing to task-unrelated thoughts, is pervasive across learning tasks. Therefore, intelligent learning environments should benefit from mechanisms to detect and respond to attentional lapses, such as mind wandering. As a step in this direction, we report the development and validation of the first student-independent facial feature-based mind wandering detector. We collected training data in a lab study where participants self-reported when they caught themselves mind wandering over the course of completing a 32.5 min narrative film comprehension task. We used computer vision techniques to extract facial features and bodily movements from videos. Using supervised learning methods, we were able to detect a mind wandering with an F_1 score of .390, which reflected a 31% improvement over a chance model. We discuss how our mind wandering detector can be used to adapt the learning experience, particularly for online learning contexts.

Keywords: Mind wandering · Attention aware interfaces

1 Introduction

Consider a situation where you are enrolled in an online anthropology course. Every week, you are assigned a documentary film to watch and discuss in an online forum. Your forum posts are graded based on your demonstration of film comprehension and your ability to relate the subject matter to current cultural trends. While watching this week's documentary on linguistics in early American society, you are initially engaged in the film. However, your thoughts inevitably begin to drift away from task-related thoughts to unrelated thoughts about your grocery shopping list for tonight's dinner. Using your computer's webcam, the online educational interface has been monitoring your facial expressions and detects that you are not attending to the content even though you appear to be looking at the screen. The interface pauses the video and asks you a question about the film's content, which you answer incorrectly. Based on this, the interface provides an explanation to reinforce certain concepts that you were not

© Springer International Publishing AG 2017
E. André et al. (Eds.): AIED 2017, LNAI 10331, pp. 359–370, 2017.
DOI: 10.1007/978-3-319-61425-0_30

attending to, before asking whether you would like to continue viewing the video. This reengages your attention, leading to a deeper understanding of the course content, and consequently a higher score in the course.

Educational interfaces that detect and respond to attentional states, such as the one described above, are on the horizon in the next 5–10 years [1]. Here, we focus on a specific form of inattention, known as mind wandering (MW). MW is a ubiquitous phenomenon where attention unintentionally shifts from task-related to task-unrelated thoughts. The widespread incidence of MW has been documented during a host of real-world activities. In one highly-cited, large-scale study, MW was tracked in 5,000 individuals from 83 countries working in 86 occupations, using an iPhone app that prompted people to report their thoughts at random intervals throughout the day [2]. People reported MW for 46.9% of the prompts, which confirmed numerous lab studies on the pervasiveness of MW (e.g., [3]), which is estimated to occur approximately 20–50% of the time, depending on the person, task, and the environmental context [2, 4].

In addition to being frequent, MW is also detrimental to performance across a number of tasks, such as reading comprehension [5] and retention of lecture content [6]. In fact, a recent meta-analysis of 88 samples indicated a negative correlation between MW and performance across a variety of tasks [7], a correlation which increased in proportion to task complexity. When compounded with its high frequency, MW can have serious consequences on performance and productivity, particularly in learning environments where attention is key to learning and retaining material. Therefore, we believe that next-generation personalized learning technology could benefit from some mechanism to detect and address MW [1]. Of course, an interface must first detect MW before it can respond to it, which is the focus of this work.

As reviewed below, previous work on MW detection, particularly in educational domains, has mainly focused on reading tasks. Here, we focus on MW detection in the novel context narrative film comprehension. Further, for the first, time we consider automated detection of MW from facial features and bodily movements obtained from commercial-off-the-shelf (COTS) webcams.

Related Work. Attention-aware education interfaces are not a new idea. Real-time analysis of eye gaze has been proposed as a way of monitoring and responding to attention [1]. Considerable work has provided offline methodologies to model attention in educational domains; however, real-time attention detection and response systems are still in their infancy [1]. Most work has been limited to eye gaze analysis. We aim to expand work in the field through the use of automatically extracted facial features.

Most of the work on MW detection has been done in the context of reading. These studies use a variety of features, such as eye-gaze [3, 8], reading times [5], and physiological signals [9]. For example, Bixler and D'Mello used eye gaze to detect both probe-caught [3] and self-caught reports [8] of MW during reading. Probe-caught MW reports required users to indicate if they were MW in response to auditory thought probes triggered at pseudo-random intervals during reading. Self-caught reports were obtained whenever users caught themselves MW. The authors achieved above-chance accuracies of 17% to 45% in detecting MW in a user-independent fashion.

Despite their success, these studies have relied on specialized equipment to collect eye-gaze (Tobii TX300). The prohibitive cost or lack of accessibility of these sensors potentially limits wide-spread adoption outside the context of laboratory settings. To address this, some researchers have considered sensor-free MW detection. Reading times have been particular beneficial in this regard. In one study, reading times for individual words were tracked using a word-by-word self-paced reading paradigm [5]. Readers were considered to be MW if they spent too little or too much time on difficult sections of the text, as determined by predetermined thresholds on word length, syllables, and word familiarity. Despite success, an obvious limitation with the use of reading time for MW detection is that such a detector is only applicable while reading.

There has been limited work investigating detection of MW during video watching. Pham and Wang use heart rate to detect MW during videos for massively open online courses (MOOCs) with a 22% above-chance accuracy [10]. They detected heart rate by monitoring fingertip transparency using the back camera of an iPhone. While this method makes use of widely-owned equipment (an iPhone in this case), whether this method can be used on non-mobile devices is an open question.

Mills et al. took a different approach to MW detection in narrative film viewing by using eye-gaze features [11]. They used global and local (context-dependent) features, as well as a combination of the two, to build models to detect MW. Their best models yielded a 29% improvement over chance when using only local features. This work demonstrates the feasibility of detecting MW during film viewing tasks. However, the prohibitive cost of the eye-gaze sensors potentially limit widespread adoption of their method for detecting MW.

Contributions and Novelty[1]. This study reports the development and validation of the first student-independent facial feature-based MW detector during narrative film comprehension. Our work is novel in two respects. First, while previous work has focused on MW in the context of reading, we consider MW detection during narrative film comprehension. This is a challenging domain, because, compared to reading, where there are detectable patterns that might indicate attentional lapses, such unexpected reading times or failing to advance to the next screen, naturalistic film viewing is less interactive, which provides less context information for detecting MW.

Nevertheless, we chose to study this domain because video-based courses, such as MOOCs, are very popular for a variety of students [6]. Although one previous study [10] focused on MW detection while students viewed MOOC-style videos, our present focus is on commercially-produced narrative films, such as historic documentaries, nature films, and fantasy-drama films that might be assigned in history, sociology, and film appreciation courses, amongst others. We focused on these types of films because professional filmmakers employ a host of cinematic devices to direct and engage viewer attention [4]. Furthermore, films contain both audio and visual content, which would presumably keep attention focused [4]. Despite these efforts to engage the

---

[1] A preliminary two-page version of this paper was presented as an Extended Abstract Poster at the 24th Conference on User Modeling, Adaptation and Personalization. The present paper describes the methods in more detail, updated results, and expanded analyses not included in the preliminary paper.

viewer, MW still occurs quite frequently while students watch such films [4] (as well as with typical MOOC-style videos [10]), suggesting that tracking and responding to moments of MW during film viewing could improve online learning from these materials.

Second, previous work has relied on specialized sensors for MW detection, thereby limiting scalability. This work represents the first attempt at a fully automated student-independent detection of MW using face videos recorded from COTS webcams. This also raises some challenges because unlike emotional states, where facial correlates have been investigated for decades and video-based automated affect detection is common [12], the facial correlates of MW have yet to be mapped out. It is also an open question if such correlates exist. For example, as Fig. 1 illustrates, facial expressions corresponding to MW reports (left) appear to be highly similar to when MW was not reported (right). Despite these challenges, if successful, our MW detector should be scalable (because it uses webcams) and more broadly applicable to additional contexts (because it does not rely on any features specific to a particular interaction context, like reading times or click-stream analyses).

Our approach to MW detection entailed collecting videos and self-reports of MW while users watched a short film on a computer screen. We used a self-caught method to detect MW in order to avoid the disruptive effects of thought probes. We extracted facial features and bodily movements from the videos and used supervised classification techniques to build models that identified when users were MW across short time windows. The models were constructed and validated in a student-independent fashion so that they would generalize to new students.

2 Data Collection

Participants were 65 undergraduate students from a medium-sized private Midwestern university and 43 undergraduate students from a large public university in the Southern United States. Of the 108 participants, 66% were female and their average age was 20.1 years. Participants were

Fig. 1. Video frame of participant corresponding to the presence (left) and absence (right) of MW reports.

compensated with course credit. Data from one participant was discarded due to equipment failure.

Participants viewed the narrative film "The Red Balloon" (1956), a 32.5-minute French-language film (with English subtitles). The film has a musical score but only sparse dialogue. This short fantasy film depicts the story of a young Parisian boy who finds a red helium balloon and quickly discovers it has a mind of its own as it follows him wherever he goes. This film was selected because of the low likelihood that participants had previously seen it, and because it has been used in other film comprehension studies [4]. Participants' faces were recorded while they watched the film with a low-cost ($30) consumer-grade webcam (Logitech C270).

Participants were instructed to report MW throughout the film by pressing labeled keys on the keyboard. Specifically, participants were asked to report a task-unrelated thought if they were "thinking about anything else besides the movie." Participants were explicitly instructed to report a task-related interference if they were "thinking about the task itself but not the actual content of the movie." A small beep sounded to register their response, but film play was not interrupted.

It is important to emphasize a couple of points on the self-caught method used to track MW. First, we chose to have participants self-report when they caught themselves MW instead of the more traditional probing method [3] because the probe method has the potential to interrupt the comprehension process (i.e., when participants are not MW and report "no" to the probes) [13]. This is particularly problematic as participants did not have control over the film presentation (i.e., no pausing or rewinding capabilities were available). Additionally, self-caught reports, as opposed to probe-caught reports, are likely to occur at the end of a MW episode when the student became aware that they were not attending to the task at hand. It is unclear, however, if a probe-caught report takes place at the onset or end of MW, or somewhere in between. Furthermore, although the method relies on self-reports, there is no clear alternative because MW is an internal phenomenon. Nevertheless, self-reported MW has been linked to predictable patterns in eye-gaze [14] and task performance [7], providing validity for this approach.

We obtained a total of 845 MW reports from the 108 participants. In this initial work, we do not distinguish between the two types of MW, instead merging the task-unrelated thoughts and the task-related interferences, both of which represent thoughts independent of the content of the film.

3 Machine Learning

Creating Instances of MW. MW reports were sparsely distributed throughout the 32.5 min video. Our first task was to create data instances corresponding to short windows of time preceding MW reports. To ensure that we captured participants' faces while MW and not the act of reporting MW itself (i.e., the preparation and execution of the key press), we added a 3-second offset before each MW self-report. From observing participant videos, this appeared to be sufficient time to prevent detection of the key press. We chose not to use larger offsets because it is not known how long MW lasts and we aimed to avoid removing data from windows where the participant was MW prior to the report.

The next task was to extract instances corresponding to Not MW while ensuring a gap between the MW and Not MW instances to account for the fact that we do not know precisely when MW begins.

The procedure for creating instances was as follows:

1. Add a 3-second offset before the self-caught MW report to account for movement due to reporting.

2. Partition the video between consecutive MW reports into $(t_1 - t_0)/S$ segments, where t_0 and t_1 are the timestamps of consecutive MW reports and S is the segment size. The segment immediately preceding the MW report at t_1 is a MW segment. All other segments between t_0 and t_1 are Not MW segments.

3. Extract features from a window of data of size w, where $w < S$, at the end of each segment generated in the previous step. The remaining time ($S - w$ seconds) in the segment is the gap that is not analyzed.

In this study, we chose a 55 s segment length as it resulted in a MW rate of approximately 20% to 25%, which was consistent with previous research [3]. We explored various windows sizes within the 55-second segment (Sect. 4). The procedure described above is depicted in Fig. 2 using a 45-second windows as an example.

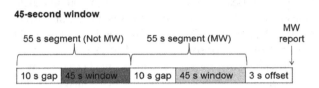

45-second window

Fig. 2. Example of window segmentation approach, using a 45-second widow sizes. Features are extracted from the dark grey (Not MW) and light grey (MW) windows.

We generated a total of 3,370 segments in all. We excluded any instances in which the participants' face was occluded, yielding less than one second of data for the time window. Extreme head pose or position, occlusions from hand-to-face gestures, and rapid movements were common causes of face registration errors. We also experimented with various window sizes. The number of instances (after removing instances with too little valid data) varied as a function of window size (from 2,476 for 10 s windows to 2,734 for 45 s windows). Larger window sizes contained more instances because there was a higher probability that the face was registered for at least one second. MW rates were quite similar across window sizes although there was a slight increase for the longer windows (from .204 for 10 s windows to .221 for 45 s windows).

Feature Extraction and Selection. We used FACET [15], a commercialized version of the CERT computer vision software for facial feature extraction. FACET provides likelihood estimates of the presence of 19 action units (AUs; specifically 1, 2, 4, 5, 6,7, 9, 10, 12, 14, 15, 17, 18, 20, 23, 24, 25, 26, and 28 [16]) as well as head pose (orientation), face position (horizontal and vertical within the frame), and face size (a proxy for distance to camera). Features were created by aggregating FACET estimates in a window of time leading up to each MW or Not MW instance using maximum, median, and standard deviation for aggregation. In all, there were 75 facial features (3 aggregation functions × [19 AUs + 3 head pose orientation axes + 2 face position coordinates + face size]).

We also computed gross body movement present in the videos using a validated motion estimation algorithm [17]. Body movement was calculated by measuring the proportion of pixels in each video frame that differed by a threshold from a continuously updated estimate of the background image generated from the four previous frames. We used the maximum, median, and standard deviation of gross body movement within each window, similar to the method used to compute FACET features.

In all, we extracted 78 features (75 facial features + 3 body movement features). We treated outliers, defined as values greater than three standard deviations away from the mean, with Winsorization, a common outlier handling technique [18]. This technique replaces outliers with the closest non-outlier value, allowing the retention of instances with outliers rather than discarding the entire instance.

We used tolerance analysis to eliminate features with high multicollinearity (variance inflation factor > 5) [19], after which 59 features remained. This was followed by RELIEF-F [20] feature selection (on the training data only) to rank features. Feature selection was performed using nested cross-validation on training data only. In particular, we ran 5 iterations of feature selection within each leave-one-participant-out cross-validation fold (discussed below), using data from a random 67% of students within the training set in each iteration. We retained a proportion of the highest ranked features (with rankings averaged across folds) for use in the models (proportions ranging from .05 to 1.0 were tested).

Classifier Selection and Validation. Informed by preliminary experiments, we selected nine classifiers for more tests (Naïve Bayes, Support Vector Machines, Simple Logistic Regression, LogitBoost, Random Forest, C4.5 trees, Stochastic Gradient Descent, Classification via Regression, and Bayes Net) using the WEKA toolkit [21].

We evaluated the performance of our classifiers using leave-one-participant-out cross-validation. This process runs multiple iterations of each classifier in which, for each fold, the instances pertaining to a single participant are added to the test set and the training set is comprised of the instances for the other participants. This process is repeated for each participant, and the classifications of all folds are weighted equally to produce the overall result. This cross-validation approach ensures that in each fold, data from the same participant is in the training set or testing set but never both, thereby improving generalization to new participants.

We considered the F_1 score for the MW class as our key accuracy measure as MW is the minority class of interest (compared to Not MW). Further, F_1 strikes a balance between precision and recall, and is less susceptible to skew from class imbalance (which is present in the current dataset) than simply measuring recognition rate.

4 Analyses and Results

Varying Window Size. We experimented with window sizes from 10 through 45 s in intervals of 5 s to empirically identify the window size that yielded the highest MW F_1. For the support vector machine (SVM) classifier (the most effective classifier – see below), there was a slight trend in performance of MW F_1 score in favor of larger window size (from .355 for 10-second windows to .390 for 45-second windows). Therefore, all subsequent results focus on the 45-second window size.

Overall Classification Results. The results for the highest MW F_1 model were achieved with an SVM classifier using sequential minimal optimization (SMO) [22] on a data set with 45-second windows where the SMOTE technique [23] was used (on training data only). This model classified 45.1% of the instances as MW. We compared it to a chance (baseline) model that also assigned MW to 45.1% of all instances, but did so randomly. This process was repeated for 1,000 iterations and precision and recall were averaged across iterations. This chance-level method yielded a precision of .221 (i.e. the same as the MW base rate) and recall of .451 (i.e. the same as the predicted MW rate). We believe this chance model to offer a more appropriate comparison than a simple minority baseline that assigns MW to all instances, because a minority baseline would results in an inflated recall (MW precision = .221, MW recall = 1, MW F_1 = .362). Additionally, a majority class baseline would result in a MW F_1 of 0, which is trivial to surpass.

Table 1 shows the results of the SVM classifier compared to the chance model. The key metrics are the precision, recall, and F_1 of the MW class. For completeness, we also provide results for Not MW class and a weighted average of the two (Overall).

Table 1. Results of the SVM classifier with chance values in parentheses

	Precision	Recall	F_1MW
MW	**.290 (.221)**	**.593 (.451)**	**.390 (.297)**
Not MW	.836 (.779)	.589 (.549)	.691 (.644)
Weighted overall	.715 (.656)	.590 (.527)	.624 (.567)

The key result is that the SVM model detected MW at rates that were substantially (31%) greater than the chance model. The SVM model's recall was also double its precision. The model has a similar proportion of hits (.593) and correct rejections (.589). Similarly, we note the model makes the same proportions of misses (.407) and false positive (.411) errors. However, the effect of false positives are exemplified as the model predicts a much higher rate of MW (.451) than the true rate (.221).

Analysis of MW Threshold. SVMs provide an estimate of the model's confidence (on a 0 to 1 scale) that an instance reflects MW. This estimate needs to be converted into a binary decision. In the aforementioned results, any instance that exceeded a confidence of .500 was classified as MW. To determine the optimal threshold that would result in the highest MW F_1, we adjusted the threshold in increments of .100 and computed resultant F_1 scores for MW and Not MW classes (Fig. 3). We note that the MW and Not MW curves in Fig. 3 intersect at a threshold of .370, yielding

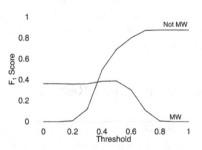

Fig. 3. F_1 scores for MW and Not MW across classification thresholds.

an approximate equal F_1 scores of .380. However, the MW F_1 score, which is our primary metric of interest, peaked at a threshold of .500, which suggests that the default threshold was appropriate for this task.

Feature Analysis. We examined the features used in the SVM model, focusing on the nine features most commonly selected by the RELIEF-F procedure as described in

Sect. 3. Features were analyzed using Cohen's d, which measures the effect size of the difference of each feature across MW and Not MW instances divided by the pooled standard deviation [24]. Positive d-values for a feature indicate an increase in the value of that feature for MW compared to Not MW. We note that effect sizes for most of the features were in the small ($d = .200$) to medium ($d = .500$) range [24], suggesting that no one feature dominated, but a combination of features was needed for MW detection.

With respect to specific features, the median of the face's vertical position ($d = .354$) and size in the screen($d = .272$) were quite predictive of MW. These two features suggest the participant was higher in the frame and closer to the screen. This could be due to participants dozing off and nodding their head when they were MW (based on examination of videos). With the exception of the median of AU7 (lid tightener, $d = .169$) and AU28 (lip suck, $d = .010$), there was less activity in facial features, such as the median of AU5 (upper eye lid raiser, $d = -.305$), AU10 (upper lip raiser, $d = -.193$), AU17 (chin raiser, $d = -.224$), and AU18 (lip puckerer, $d = -.131$), and the max value AU9 (nose wrinkle, $d = -.203$). This indicates that participants adopted more neutral facial expressions when MW, ostensibly because they were not reacting to the unfolding film as thoughts were concentrated inwards.

5   General Discussion

Main Findings. We expanded on previous MW research through our novel use of facial expressions and body movements to detect MW. We were able to detect MW with an F_1 score of .390, a notable 31% improvement over a chance-level model, which yielded an F_1 score of .297. Although we showed that the default threshold of .500 resulted the highest MW F_1, our model had higher recall (.593) than precision (.290), which suggests that it over predicts MW (i.e., more false positives). We should also note that it is possible that the self-reports underestimate the MW rate, either because participants choose not to report MW or because they are unaware that they are MW. Perhaps the truth lies somewhere between the self-reports and computer-estimates of MW.

Our model, shown in Table 1 achieved a 31% improvement over a chance classifier. As a point of comparison, Mills et al. [11] achieved a comparable accuracy of 29% over chance. Note that both chance-level classifiers were computed using the same measure of chance (Sect. 4) and the method for partitioning data into MW and Not MW instances (Sect. 3) was similar, thus providing a basis for comparison. While the accuracy of models in both works is moderate, the improvement over chance demonstrates the feasibility of detecting MW from either eye gaze or facial features. However, Mills et al. used research-grade eye trackers, which might prohibit widespread use of their method, particularly in online educational interfaces where students provide their own equipment. Additionally, their best models used content-dependent features, which might not easily generalize to new stimuli. Thus, our results are significant in that we were able to obtain results similar to the previous state of the art on this dataset, but by using a more scalable (and presumably generalizable) modality.

Generalizability was a key design constraint that guided a number of our decisions. First, we used COTS webcams to afford eventual deployment of our models at scale, thereby allowing us to test generalizability in more diverse contexts. We also restricted ourselves to facial features and bodily movements that were independent of the specific content being displayed on the screen, suggesting that the models should generalize to additional films and perhaps even other interaction contexts. Further, our models were validated in a student-independent manner, which increases our models' ability to generalize to new students. We have even more confidence in the generalization of our models as our data was collected from two universities with very different demographic characteristics. Taken together, these results increase our confidence that the models will generalize more broadly, though this claim requires further empirical validation.

Finally, given the paucity of research, it was unclear if MW manifests via facial expressions. It was therefore quite possible that our entire research endeavor would fail. Fortunately, our findings do indicate that there appear to be generalizable patterns between facial-expressions and MW. Specifically, we found that MW was characterized by vertical head movement and more neutral facial expressions.

Applications. The present findings are applicable to any user interface that involves viewing and comprehending videos. Monitoring MW in this context could greatly inform commercial or educational film makers as to how their films can be improved to better sustain viewers' attention. Segments of film with high rates of detected MW can be edited to better engage viewers.

Media, such as films and recordings of lectures, play a major role in online learning, so our MW detector, which only uses a webcam, can be quite beneficial in that context. One strategy is to assess comprehension of content associated with periods of high MW (as noted by the detector) by asking the student to answer a multiple-choice question or to self-explain the content. Both interleaved questions [25] and self-explanations [26] have been shown to be effective at focusing attention. Students who answer incorrectly will be encouraged to review the material associated with the questions and self-explanation prompts, and can optionally answer follow-up questions, thereby giving them multiple opportunities to correct comprehension deficits attributed to MW.

Our work also has applications in contexts apart from viewing videos.MW has been widely studied during reading using a variety of sensors [3, 8, 9, 14] but not facial features. Facial feature data could supplement existing features to improve MW detection. This also raises the possibility of multimodal MW detection.

Limitations and Future Work. There are a number of limitations with this study. First, our model had a MW F_1 of .390. Although it outperformed a chance model, this performance is moderate at best. The precision was also much lower than the recall, suggesting that caution should be taken when integrating the model into interfaces that sense and respond to MW. In future work, we will aim to improve precision by expanding the feature set and considering skew-sensitive classification methods.

Another limitation of this study is the self-report method which requires users to be mindful of when MW occurs and to respond accurately and honestly. Previous studies have validated the self-report method [7, 14], however, it is possible that some participants may not report MW accurately or honestly. One possibility would be to complement self-reports with observer annotations. However, this assumes that observers can identify when a person is MW, a question that we are investigating in our research.

Finally, although we provided some evidence of generalizability to new users, to further boost our claims of generalizability, data should be collected from more diverse populations apart from undergraduate students. It should also be collected more real-world environments, rather than the lab-setup used here. Generalizability could also be enhanced by studying video-based MW detection in other contexts such as playing interactive games, to better understand how the models generalize to other tasks. Training models on data from multiple domains is also likely to yield more general models.

Concluding Remarks. The ubiquity of webcams has opened up the possibility of advancing research in attentional state estimation, thereby enabling an entirely new generation of attention-aware interfaces, particularly in education. As a step in this direction, we demonstrated the feasibility of using facial features extracted from webcam video to record MW during a narrative film comprehension task. The next step is to close the loop by intervening when MW is detected.

Acknowledgements. This research was supported by the National Science Foundation (NSF) (DRL 1235958 and IIS 1523091). Any opinions, findings and conclusions, or recommendations expressed in this paper are those of the authors and do not necessarily reflect the views of the NSF.

References

1. D'Mello, S.K.: Giving eyesight to the blind: towards attention-aware AIED. Int. J. Artif. Intell. Educ. **26**(2), 645–659 (2016)
2. Killingsworth, M.A., Gilbert, D.T.: A wandering mind is an unhappy mind. Science **330**, 932 (2010)
3. Bixler, R., D'Mello, S.: Toward fully automated person-independent detection of mind wandering. In: Dimitrova, V., Kuflik, T., Chin, D., Ricci, F., Dolog, P., Houben, G.-J. (eds.) UMAP 2014. LNCS, vol. 8538, pp. 37–48. Springer, Cham (2014). doi:10.1007/978-3-319-08786-3_4
4. Kopp, K., Mills, C., D'Mello, S.K.: Mind wandering during film comprehension: the role of prior knowledge and situational interest. Psychon. Bull. Rev. **23**, 842–848 (2015)
5. Franklin, M.S., Smallwood, J., Schooler, J.W.: Catching the mind in flight: using behavioral indices to detect mindless reading in real time. Psychon. Bull. Rev. **18**, 992–997 (2011)
6. Szpunar, K.K., Moulton, S.T., Schacter, D.L.: Mind wandering and education: from the classroom to online learning. Front. Psychol. **4**, 495 (2013)
7. Randall, J.G., Oswald, F.L., Beier, M.E.: Mind-wandering, cognition, and performance: a theory-driven meta-analysis of attention regulation. Psychol. Bull. **140**, 1411 (2014)
8. Bixler, R., D'Mello, S.: Automatic gaze-based detection of mind wandering with metacognitive awareness. In: Ricci, F., Bontcheva, K., Conlan, O., Lawless, S. (eds.) UMAP 2015. LNCS, vol. 9146, pp. 31–43. Springer, Cham (2015). doi:10.1007/978-3-319-20267-9_3
9. Blanchard, N., Bixler, R., Joyce, T., D'Mello, S.: Automated physiological-based detection of mind wandering during learning. In: Trausan-Matu, S., Boyer, K.E., Crosby, M., Panourgia, K. (eds.) ITS 2014. LNCS, vol. 8474, pp. 55–60. Springer, Cham (2014). doi:10.1007/978-3-319-07221-0_7

10. Pham, P., Wang, J.: AttentiveLearner: improving mobile MOOC learning via implicit heart rate tracking. In: Conati, C., Heffernan, N., Mitrovic, A., Verdejo, M.F. (eds.) AIED 2015. LNCS, vol. 9112, pp. 367–376. Springer, Cham (2015). doi:10.1007/978-3-319-19773-9_37
11. Mills, C., Bixler, R., Wang, X., D'Mello, S.K.: Automatic gaze-based detection of mind wandering during film viewing. In: Proceedings of the 9th International Conference on Educational Data Mining. International Educational Data Mining Society, Raleigh (2016)
12. Zeng, Z., Pantic, M., Roisman, G.I., Huang, T.S.: A survey of affect recognition methods: audio, visual, and spontaneous expressions. IEEE Trans. Pattern Anal. Mach. Intell. **31**, 39–58 (2009)
13. Faber, M., Bixler, R., D'Mello, S.K.: An automated behavioral measure of mind wandering during computerized reading. Behav. Res. Methods 1–17 (2017)
14. Reichle, E.D., Reineberg, A.E., Schooler, J.W.: Eye movements during mindless reading. Psychol. Sci. **21**, 1300–1310 (2010)
15. Littlewort, G., Whitehill, J., Wu, T., Fasel, I., Frank, M., Movellan, J., Bartlett, M.: The computer expression recognition toolbox (CERT). In: 2011 IEEE International Conference on Automatic Face & Gesture Recognition and Workshops (FG 2011), pp. 298–305. IEEE (2011)
16. Ekman, P., Friesen, W.V.: Facial action coding system (1977)
17. Westlund, J.K., D'Mello, S.K., Olney, A.M.: Motion tracker: camera-based monitoring of bodily movements using motion silhouettes. PLoS ONE **10**, e0130293 (2015)
18. Dixon, W.J., Yuen, K.K.: Trimming and winsorization: a review. Statistische Hefte **15**, 157–170 (1974)
19. Allison, P.D.: Multiple Regression: A Primer. Pine Forge Press, Thousand Oaks (1999)
20. Kononenko, I.: Estimating attributes: analysis and extensions of RELIEF. In: Bergadano, F., Raedt, L. (eds.) ECML 1994. LNCS, vol. 784, pp. 171–182. Springer, Heidelberg (1994). doi:10.1007/3-540-57868-4_57
21. Holmes, G., Donkin, A., Witten, I.H.: Weka: a machine learning workbench. In: Proceedings of the 1994 Second Australian and New Zealand Conference on Intelligent Information Systems, pp. 357–361. IEEE (1994)
22. Platt, J., et al.: Sequential minimal optimization: a fast algorithm for training support vector machines (1998)
23. Chawla, N.V., Bowyer, K.W., Hall, L.O., Kegelmeyer, W.P.: SMOTE: synthetic minority over-sampling technique. J. Artif. Intell. Res. **16**, 321–357 (2002)
24. Cohen, J.: Statistical Power Analysis for the Behavioral Sciences, 2nd edn. Lawrence Erlbaum, Hillsdale (1988)
25. Szpunar, K.K., Khan, N.Y., Schacter, D.L.: Interpolated memory tests reduce mind wandering and improve learning of online lectures. Proc. Natl. Acad. Sci. **110**, 6313–6317 (2013)
26. Moss, J., Schunn, C.D., Schneider, W., McNamara, D.S.: The nature of mind wandering during reading varies with the cognitive control demands of the reading strategy. Brain Res. **1539**, 48–60 (2013)

Modeling the Incubation Effect Among Students Playing an Educational Game for Physics

May Marie P. Talandron[1,2]([⊠]), Ma. Mercedes T. Rodrigo[1]([⊠]),
and Joseph E. Beck[3]([⊠])

[1] Ateneo de Manila University, Quezon City, Philippines
mmptalandron@cmu.edu.ph, mrodrigo@ateneo.edu
[2] Central Mindanao University, Maramag, Bukidnon, Philippines
[3] Worcester Polytechnic Institute, Worcester, MA, USA
josephbeck@wpi.edu

Abstract. We attempted to model the Incubation Effect, a phenomenon in which a momentary break helps the generation of a solution to a problem, among students playing Physics Playground. We performed a logistic regression analysis to predict the outcome of the incubation using a genetic algorithm for feature selection. Out of 14 candidate features, those that significantly predicted the outcome were total badges earned prior to post-incubation, the problem's level of difficulty, total attempts made prior to post-incubation, and time interval of post-incubation. We found evidence that incubation in the earlier part of the game is more beneficial than breaks at the later part where students may already be mentally exhausted.

Keywords: Incubation effect · Physics Playground

1 Introduction

Setting aside a problem after initial failures may result to solution ideas [2, 3, 10, 14]. This temporary break is termed an incubation period [14] where an internal mental process takes place, associating new information with past information without conscious knowledge or effort [7]. When the student returns to the original problem and solves it, the positive result is called the Incubation Effect (IE). IE has three phases [3]: (1) pre-incubation phase, (2) incubation phase, and (3) post-incubation phase. The pre-incubation phase occurs when the student engages in a problem solving task and gets stuck. Once the student takes a break, this signals the beginning of the incubation phase. The post-incubation phase begins when the learner decides to return to the problem and tries to solve it again.

The positive effect of incubation has led several educators and researchers [5, 7, 11, 16] to integrate breaks or incubation periods into educational activities, yielding positive results. However, the exact factors that lead to successful incubation periods are not well studied. Prior work [1–3, 10, 14] suggests that engaging in a different activity during the incubation produces a better outcome. Some studies [4, 14] suggest that type

© Springer International Publishing AG 2017
E. André et al. (Eds.): AIED 2017, LNAI 10331, pp. 371–380, 2017.
DOI: 10.1007/978-3-319-61425-0_31

and difficulty of the unsolved problems, the length of the time period for problem solving before the incubation period (pre-incubation phase), and the length of the incubation period as factors in the positive result of incubation.

This study continues the work begun in [6] which investigated the incidence of IE in the context of a physics-based problem solving game and found evidence that majority of the students who took a break after being stuck in a particular level were able to solve the problem. The goal of this study is to develop a model that predicts the outcome of incubation by exploring additional features to what has been previously studied as factors that contribute to the positive result of incubation. This study asks the question: What features predict incubation effect or IE-true? The identification of these factors may help designers take advantage of incubation to help improve student's performance.

2 Physics Playground

Physics Playground (PP), originally named Newton's Playground, is a computer-based game designed for students in the secondary level to tackle concepts of qualitative Physics. This two-dimensional game simulates how the physical objects operate in relation to Newton's laws of motion: balance, mass, conservation and transfer of momentum, gravity, and potential and kinetic energy [13]. The game has different problems with varying levels of difficulty and solutions. The main objective for each problem is to guide a green ball to a red balloon. To do this, the players must draw objects (i.e., ramp, lever, pendulum, springboard) using the computer mouse and these objects become part of the game environment. Figure 1 shows an example level of PP which requires a ramp to lead the ball to the balloon. The solution is shown in Fig. 2.

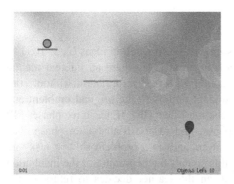
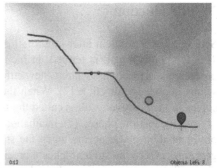

Fig. 1. Example level in Physics Playground.   **Fig. 2.** Example solution using a ramp.

Each level in PP may be solved by drawing levers, pendulums, ramps, and springboards. The player receives either a gold or silver badges once he or she solves a level. A player receives a gold badge if the problem was solved using at or below a par number of objects determined by the game designers. Otherwise, a silver badge is awarded.

3 Methodology

3.1 Data Set

The data was collected from 60 eighth-grade or 2nd year high school students with age ranging from 13 to 18 years old (M = 15.7). Twenty-nine students were from Bakakeng National High School (BNHS), a public junior high school; and 31 from the University of the Cordilleras (UC), a private university, both in Baguio City, Philippines. The students were first asked to take a pre-test, after which they were asked to play Physics Playground for 2 hours. The interactions of each player with PP were tracked and automatically logged into a file. The interaction events examined in this study were:

- *Level Start* – This event indicates the player has started a level.
- *Level End* – This event is generated upon level exit.
- *Badge* – "Gold" or "Silver" indicates the type of badge the player earns after solving a level while "None" indicates that the player failed to solve the level upon exit.
- *Menu Focus* – This event is generated when the main menu switches focus to a new playground or level.
- *Watch Tutorial* – This event is generated when the player watches the tutorial.

After playing, the students were asked to take a post-test.

This same dataset was used to study persistence and wheel spinning. [8] attempted to determine whether greater persistence, as measured within PP, resulted in greater student success. They found that gold and no-badge outcomes were significantly negatively correlated with time spent and significantly positively correlated with number of restarts. This implied that persistence markers might be indicative of both a positive form of persistence as well as the non-learning behaviors. While persistence can be beneficial to students, prolonged persistence actually degenerates into wheel spinning, a phenomenon where the players attempt to solve the problem repeatedly in vain. [9] developed a detector of wheel spinning and found that spending more time in a level and earning a silver badge have both increased the probability of wheel spinning.

3.2 Identifying Incubation Effect

We sorted the data by player, time, and level. IE was identified by mapping the 3 phases with the game events mentioned in the previous section.

- **Pre-incubation Phase** – The player attempts a level, X, indicated by the event 'Level Start' but the player fails and decides to leave the level as indicated by the event Level End – Badge: "None".
- **Incubation Phase** – After leaving level X, the player takes a break and returns to the menu as indicated by the event Menu Focus or plays a different level as indicated by the event Level Start or watches the tutorial.
- **Post-incubation Phase** – The player returns to level X and attempts to solve it again. This is indicated by the event Level Start.

When these 3 phases are present for a certain level, the occurrence is labeled as **Potential IE**. If the player earned a badge, whether gold or silver, during the post-incubation phase, the attempt is considered as **IE-True**. However, if no badge is awarded at the end of the post-incubation phase, it is labeled as **IE-False**.

In [6], the presence of the 3 phases in a level was counted as one Potential IE only regardless of the number of breaks and revisits to Level X. That means there can only be 1 Potential IE per level per player as shown in Fig. 3. In this study, multiple incubation leading to multiple pairs of pre-incubation and post-incubation phases were each considered as multiple Potential IEs as shown in Fig. 4.

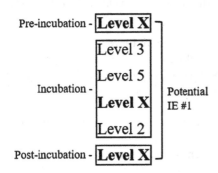

Fig. 3. IE identification in [6]   **Fig. 4.** IE identification in this study

3.3   Features Variables

A total of 14 features were explored as possible factors that predict IE-True and they were categorized based on how they may have affected the outcome of incubation. They are the following:

1. The problem's level of difficulty – [14] considered task difficulty as a possible factor for the occurrence of incubation effect. The designers of PP did not state the level of difficulty of each problem so in order to compute the difficulty level of each problem, an approach based on [13] was used:

$$1 - \frac{\text{Total badges(gold and silver)}}{\text{All attempts}}$$

Based on this computation, the highest possible value is 1 which means no attempt on the level was successful and the lowest possible value is 0 which means all attempts resulted to either a gold or silver badge.

2. Student's prior knowledge – this feature aims to examine if the student's prior knowledge affects the outcome of incubation as reported in [15] where they found that incubation effect is limited to participants with better performance in the initial test conducted. This was computed based on the student's pre-test score over the total number of items.

3. Preparation Period – The meta-analysis of [14] reported that the preparation period, defined as the duration where the problem solver tries and becomes familiar with the problem, had a positive relationship with incubation. They found that longer preparation periods yielded greater incubation effect. In the context of PP, we explored the following features for this category:

   (a) Pre-incubation duration – time (in minutes) the student spent trying to solve the problem on a certain level before taking a break.

   (b) Time interval of incubation – Playing time was divided into four 30-minute intervals. The intervals were labeled in consecutive order (i.e. the first 30 min is labeled as 1, and so on). In order to account for the time difference of incubations occurring in the same interval, the number of minutes was added into the numerical value. For example, if the student started playing at 12:00 and incubation happened at 12:40, the equivalent interval is 2.10. The value "2" was assigned because 12:40 is already in the second 30-minute interval. The ".10" was computed as the difference between 12:40 and 12:30 which is the starting point of the second interval (i.e. 12:00, 12:30, 1:00, etc.). A higher value means the player had a longer preparation period.

   (c) Time interval of post-incubation – this is similar to the previous feature except that the time of post-incubation was coded.

   (d) Total attempts made prior to post-incubation –total number of attempts the student made on all levels from the start of the game up until before the student returned to level X.

   (e) Total badges earned prior to post-incubation –total number of badges the student earned from the start of the game up until before the student returned to level X.

   (f) Overall success rate prior to post-incubation –total number of badges earned prior during post-incubation over the total number of attempts made prior during post-incubation.

   (g) Total Attempts on level X only prior to Post-Incubation –total number of attempts the student made on level X from the start of the game up until the end of the pre-incubation phase.

   (h) IE Number – for cases with multiple breaks, IE number identifies if the post-incubation happened after the first, second, third, or the nth break.

4. Quality of incubation – [2, 14, 15] reported evidence that the length of incubation may improve performance during the post-incubation period and [1–3, 10, 14] claimed that the type of activities during incubation may affect the outcome where incubation period with high cognitive demand tasks resulted to smaller incubation effect. In order to investigate these factors, the following features were explored:

   (a) Incubation duration – time (in minutes) the student spent incubating.

   (b) Number of attempts made on other levels during incubation –total number of attempts the student made to solve other levels during the break from level X.

   (c) Number of badges earned during incubation –total number of badges the student earned during the break from level X.

   (d) Success rate during incubation –total number of badges earned during incubation over the number of levels played during incubation.

3.4 Modeling

We performed a logistic regression analysis to predict the outcome of the incubation. We then performed a feature selection using genetic algorithm to arrive at a parsimonious model. We then performed a student-level cross-validation to ensure that each student's data was entirely either in the testing set or the training set.

4 Results and Discussion

4.1 Incidence of IE and IE Model

A total of 180 incidences of potential IEs were observed in the PP logs. Seventy-seven (43%) of these resulted to either a silver or gold badge and were considered as IE-true. The remaining 103 (57%) were classified as IE-false for not successfully solving the problem during the post-incubation phase. All other attempts without a break were considered as Non-IE and were excluded from the analysis. Out of the 60 players, 37 (62%) exhibited potential IEs with an average of 5 potential IEs per player. These identified players took a momentary break, came back to the level, and tried again. Of the 37 players, there were 34 (92%) who had at least one incidence of IE-true. IE-true and IE-false, labeled as Y_1 and Y_0 respectively, are the dependent variables in the analysis.

The variable's coefficients in Table 1 shows that among the 14 variables, 4 were selected after performing the genetic algorithm feature selection technique.

Table 1. Variable coefficients

Variables	Coefficient	Standard coefficient	Standard error	Wald	p-value
Total badges earned prior to post-incubation	0.164	1.715	0.032	5.185	<0.001
Total attempts made prior to post-incubation	−0.056	−1.268	0.013	−4.220	<0.001
The problem's level of difficulty	−5.726	−0.963	1.709	−3.350	0.001
Time interval of post-incubation	−0.195	−0.233	0.225	−.0867	0.386
Constant	1.389	−0.512	−0.530	−2.623	0.009

In [14], problem-solving ability was a factor that determined the presence of an incubation effect. In the case of PP, the total badges earned prior to post-incubation was an indicator of the student's ability to solve other levels of PP before returning to level X. A higher number of badges prior to the post-incubation period increased the probability of a successful incubation. Students earned significantly more badges prior to post-incubation of IE-True (M = 19, SD = 12) than to IE-False (M = 15, SD = 8) (t(124) = 1.98, two-tailed p < 0.01). Figure 5 shows the number of badges earned prior

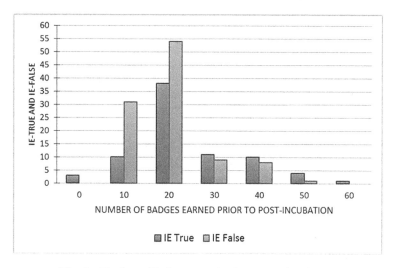

Fig. 5. Number of badges earned prior to post-incubation

to post-incubation divided into buckets of 10 badges each. It can be seen that starting from 30 badges and above, more IE-True occurred than IE-False.

As with the findings of [13], problem task level was among the factors determining the presence of the incubation effect. There were 40 unique levels with an incidence of IE in PP. Two of the levels had a difficulty of 1 meaning no player had earned a badge from attempting to solve the problem while there was 1 level with 0 difficulty, meaning all attempts, whether IE or non-IE, resulted to a badge (M = 35%, SD = 19%). Easier problems increase the likelihood of a successful incubation than problems which are more difficult to solve.

All Potential-IEs had an average of 40 overall attempts from the start of the game until post-incubation of a specific Potential IE (SD = 22). If we examine the number of problem attempts prior to IE-True and IE-False separately, the average number of attempts prior to post-incubation of all IE-True (M = 32, SD = 21) was significantly lower than those of IE-False (M = 46, SD = 22) (t(169) = 1.97, two-tailed p < 0.01).

Moreover, 50 (28%) and 60 (33%) of the post-incubation of all Potential IEs were in the third and fourth 30-minute intervals respectively. As shown in Fig. 6, more IE-False occurred in the second to the fourth intervals while IE-True is more prevalent in the first 30-minute interval.

The negative coefficients of the total attempts made prior to post-incubation and time-interval of post-incubation is surprising because it implies that the more familiar the students were with the environment, the less likely it was for incubation to be successful. This result may be contradictory to the findings of [14] where a longer preparation period resulted to more incubation effects. However, both the badges earned prior to post-incubation and the time interval of post-incubation also mean that the post-incubation occurred at the later part of the game where students might have already felt exhausted. In the study of [1], evidence shows that the benefits of a break "cannot be accounted for in terms of general fatigue". As [3] suggested, an entirely

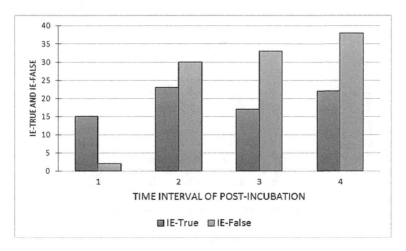

Fig. 6. Post-incubation of IE-true and IE-false in 30-minute time intervals

different activity during incubation may help relieve students' exhaustion and yields a
better outcome but in PP, students were doing similar activities during the break. Aside
from fatigue, students might have also been frustrated in solving the problems at the
later part of the game. A significant relationship was found between the time-interval of
post incubation and the problem's level of difficulty, $r(180) = 0.31$, $p < 0.01$. This
means that the students were trying to solve more difficult problems in the later part of
the game. [12] showed that frustration among students is linked to difficult problems.
Hence, these two factors, fatigue and frustration, might have affected the students'
performance in late-game post-incubation phase which decreased the probability of
successful incubation.

4.2   Validation

The confusion matrix shows the predicted value of IE-true and IE-false of which the
threshold is 0.5. There were 69 incidences of IE-true that were classified correctly and
yields a sensitivity of 90% (recall = 90%, precision = 74%) as shown in Table 2, with
a fair kappa rating of 0.24.

Table 2. Confusion matrix for predicted IE

Observed Y	Predicted Y		Accuracy
	IE-True	IE-False	
IE-True	69	8	90%
IE-False	67	36	35%
Overall accuracy			77%

5 Conclusion, Contributions, and Future Work

This study's goal was to identify the factors that may determine whether an incubation effect will occur or not. We found that a student's problem-solving ability, as represented by the total badges earned prior to post-incubation, and the problem's level of difficulty are factors of successful incubation as reported in [15] and [14], respectively. More importantly, the model showed that incubation or breaks in the later part of the game as well as attempts made prior to post-incubation have a negative relationship with successful incubation. Although these factors mean the students' had a longer preparation period [14] to be familiar with the game, they may also be considered as indication of the students' exhaustion and mental fatigue in the later part of the game where taking a break may not be as effective as it is in the earlier part of the game [1].

Aside from contributing to the existing literature on IE, this study has shown further evidence that incubation is an effective technique to help students who are stuck in a problem [2, 3, 10, 14] as well as possible factors contributing to occurrence of the IE phenomenon. The model may also help designers of game-based learning environments in determining when to inject breaks that would be beneficial to help improve the in-game performance of students. Third, an entirely different activity to give to students during the break may be designed that might help relieve their mental fatigue especially when breaks are given in the later part of the activity.

Further steps for this work may include validation of the model by investigating IE incidence in a different game-based learning environment and looking at the effect of IE not only in the in-game performance but also in learning. It's also worth exploring what activities might be helpful to ease mental fatigue during incubation when students are already exhausted from a series of problem solving tasks.

Acknowledgement. The authors would like to thank Mr. Joshua Martinez and Mr. Jun Rangie Obispo for their valuable contribution in the initial investigation of incubation effect in Physics Playground which paved way for this study. We also would like to thank the Ateneo Laboratory for the Learning Sciences and the Ateneo de Manila University Department of Information Systems and Computer Science. This study was made possible through a grant from the Philippines' Department of Science and Technology Philippine Council for Industry, Energy and Emerging Technology Research and Development entitled "Stealth assessment of student conscientiousness, cognitive-affective states, and learning using an educational game for Physics."

References

1. Ellwood, S., Pallier, G., Snyder, A., Gallate, J.: The incubation effect: hatching a solution? Creat. Res. J. **21**(1), 6–14 (2009)
2. Fulgosi, A., Guilford, J.P.: Short-term incubation in divergent production. J. Creat. Behav. **4**(2), 131–132 (1970)
3. Gilhooly, K.J., Georgiou, G., Devery, U.: Incubation and creativity: do something different. Think. Reason. **19**(2), 137–149 (2013)
4. Kaplan, C.A., Davidson, J.: Incubation effects in problem solving. DTIC Document (1988)

5. Lynch, M.D., Swink, E.: Some effects of priming, incubation and creative aptitude on journalism performance. J. Commun. **17**(4), 372–382 (1967)
6. Martinez, J.C., Obispo, J.R.C., Talandron, M.M.P., Rodrigo, M.M.T.: Investigating the incubation effect among students playing physics playground. In: International Conference on Computers in Education (Mumbai, India, December 2016)
7. Medd, E., Houtz, J.C.: The effects of facilitated incubation on fourth graders' creative writing. Educ. Res. Q. **26**(2), 13 (2002)
8. Palaoag, T.D., Rodrigo, M.M.T., Andres, J.M.L.: An exploratory study of persistence markers within a game-based learning environment. In: International Conference on Computers in Education (China, 2015)
9. Palaoag, T.D., Rodrigo, M.M.T., Andres, J.M.L., Andres, J.M.A.L., Beck, J.E.: Wheel-spinning in a game-based learning environment for physics. Int. Conf. Intell. Tutor. Syst. **2016**, 234–239 (2016)
10. Penaloza, A.A., Calvillo, D.P.: Incubation provides relief from artificial fixation in problem solving. Creat. Res. J. **24**(4), 338–344 (2012)
11. Rae, C.M.: The creative power of doing nothing. Writer **110**(7), 13–15 (1997)
12. San Pedro, M.O.Z., Baker, R.S., Gowda, S.M., Heffernan, N.T.: Towards an understanding of affect and knowledge from student interaction with an intelligent tutoring system. Int. Conf. Artif. Intell. Educ. **2013**, 41–50 (2013)
13. Shute, V., Ventura, M.: Stealth Assessment: Measuring and Supporting Learning in Video Games. MIT Press, Cambridge (2013)
14. Sio, U.N., Ormerod, T.C.: Does incubation enhance problem solving? A meta-analytic review. Psychol. Bull. **135**(1), 94 (2009)
15. Smith, S.M., Blankenship, S.E.: Incubation and the persistence of fixation in problem solving. Am. J. Psychol. **1991**, 61–87 (1991)
16. Webster, A., Campbell, C., Jane, B.: Enhancing the creative process for learning in primary technology education. Int. J. Technol. Des. Educ. **16**(3), 221–235 (2006)

Predicting Learner's Deductive Reasoning Skills Using a Bayesian Network

Ange Tato[(⊠)], Roger Nkambou[(⊠)], Janie Brisson, and Serge Robert

Université du Québec à Montréal, Montreal, Canada
nyamen_tato.ange_adrienne@courrier.uqam.ca,
nkambou.roger@uqam.ca

Abstract. Logic-Muse is an Intelligent Tutoring System (ITS) that helps improve deductive reasoning skills in multiple contexts. All its three main components (The learner, the tutor and the expert models) have been developed while relying on the help of experts and on important work in the field of reasoning and computer science. It is now known that one can't support a student in a learning task without being aware of his level of skills (what he/she knows and what he/she needs to know). Thus, it is important in the setting up of the learner model to consider an efficient mechanism that can both assess and predict her skills. This paper describes the Bayesian Network (that allows real time diagnosis, prediction and modeling of the learner's state of skills) implemented in the learner component of Logic-Muse. We proved that the BN (Bayesian Network) is able to predict with an accuracy near 85%, the answers of learners on different exercises of the domain. Given this result, the system is therefore able to predict the learner's deductive reasoning skills at a given time and help the tutor model for a better assessment and coaching.

Keywords: Intelligent tutoring system (ITS) · Prediction of learner skills · Deductive reasoning skills · Bayesian network

1 Introduction

Logical reasoning is important in everyday life for intellectual self-defense. It is a key component of advanced human cognition and underlies scientific and mathematical thinking. It is also important in computer science since computers are inferential machines (if…then rules) where logic plays a big role. However, logical reasoning is a non-trivial cognitive process that is difficult to be handled. Indeed, cognitive science has shown that human reasoning often differs from the inferences sanctioned by classical logic. A number of questions arise on how to improve human reasoning skills in this area: What are the elements involved in learning logical reasoning skills? What are the strategies to foster the development of logical reasoning skills? How can learning of reasoning skills be automated? Can Intelligent Tutoring Systems (ITS) help? What are the characteristics of an effective ITS in such a context? Logic-Muse is a web-based ITS that aims at combining logical, psychological and computational expertises to build a unique environment for the development of deductive reasoning skills (according toclassical and non-classical logics). This project is mostly inspired bythe following areas:

© Springer International Publishing AG 2017
E. André et al. (Eds.): AIED 2017, LNAI 10331, pp. 381–392, 2017.
DOI: 10.1007/978-3-319-61425-0_32

(1) Psychology: it integrates laypersons inferential reasoning processes; (2) Logic: it treats expertise as formal structures not respected by laypersons. It also makes significant contributions to computer science: to build an ITS based on the previous knowledge and to highlight the metacognitive dimensions of learning. Twoof its three main components (The tutor and the expert models) have been developed while relying on the help of experts and on important work in the field of reasoning and computer science. Predicting a learner' skills is a key feature to adequately respond to his level of knowledge and to improve the learning gain. A learner's state of knowledge is subject to change and competence should be assigned with some degree of certainty, so the learner model can only approximate his actual condition. It is thus important to predict his ability and to support the diagnosis with a formalism that allows uncertain inferences about a learner [15]. Hence, because modeling students' knowledge is a fundamental part of intelligent tutoring systems, we propose an effective BN that can represent and accurately predict learners' skills in deductive reasoning. The diagnosis must be based on the current state of skills but also on the predicted state built from previous behaviors observed during the learning. BNs are quite adequate for the task: they allow to infer the probability of mastering a skill from a specific response pattern [5, 6]. We thus created a BN that allows real-time prediction. Our study aims at providing some relevant information about how such a BNis built includingsome details about the a priori probabilities, the structure of the network and the nodes representing measured skills. We will also present an evaluation of the Network using some relevant data-mining techniques. The results showed that the BN implemented is able to model and predict learner's deductive reasoning skills with an accuracy of about 85%.

The paper is organized as follows: Sect. 2 presents some previous work regarding the uses of a BN in student modeling, Sect. 3 provides a brief review of Logic-Muse design and functionalities. The BN capacity to predict learners' deductive reasoning skills is thoroughly described in Sect. 3 as well as the analysis and interpretation of the results from the validation. The paper ends with a brief recapitulation of the contribution and some issues that we should consider in future works.

2   Related Work

Why build a system for logical reasoning? There are several reasons that triggered us to develop such a system. (1) An important part of human knowledge is related to information processing by reasoning. (2) Logical reasoning plays an important role in daily life. (3) Human reasoning islargely variable and is often non-compliant with the laws of logic. (4) This variation might be due tothe content of the premises, limitations of working memory or the use of other types of inferences (inductive, analogical, abductive) that we call discovery strategies for justifications. (5) Learning to think logically is to learn how information processing works.

The goal of Logic-Muse is to bring together the latest developments in the field of ITS, Cognitive Science and AI (Artificial Intelligence) to build an expert reasoner able to help students improve their logical reasoning skills. ITSs aim at providing every student with an individual and adaptable tutor, and to rely on cognitive diagnosis to determine specific learner' needs. Although many ITSs have been developed since the early 70s, few dealt with logical reasoning as a learning domain [1, 10, 12, 19], and as previously said they are limited in terms of strong semantic grounding in explicit reasoning knowledge structures and lack of metacognitive support in reasoning skills learning. Some eLearning tutorials also exist (e.g. Logic Learning Tools, Logic Tutor and Power of Logic Web Tutor) but fail to explicitly encode the reasoning knowledge and accurately model and predict the student state of knowledge.

The last decade saw a growing interest in theoretically sound approaches of BN in user modeling systems, especially in the field of education [3]. A BN is a probabilistic graphical structure which has proven its efficiency in student modeling in ITS. Using a BN to model students' knowledge is not new. ANDES [4], an ITS that teaches Newtonian Physics viacoached problem solving is the classical instance where an on-line BN is used to carryout long-term knowledge assessment and prediction of the student's action during problem solving. In [2], a BN is used for measuring the level of knowledge of a student (given her/his answers on items) and provides grades accordingly. [16] used BNs for knowledge assessment in a computerized testing system. They built two versions of the BN, one with the help of experts, and the other from data.

A drawback of the previous BN-based ITS is that the predictive power of the BN is usually assessed within the system. Such approach makes it difficult to validate the BN before its implementation within the ITS. In addition, none of the previous researches has proposed an on-line BN that models and predicts student skills in the logical reasoning field. In this paper, we propose not only a Bayesian network of logical reasoning skills built with the participation of experts, but also a data-driven validation framework of its effectiveness.

3   Brief Review of the Design of Logic-Muse

The architecture of Logic-Muse looks like a classical ITS including the three usual components: the expert model, the learner model and the tutor. The expert model has multiple dimensions as shown in Fig. 1. It implements logical reasoning skills and knowledge as well as related reasoning mechanisms (syntactic and semantic rules of the given logical system). The system has a general controller component whichgoal is to select the relevant logical system that should be used in a given problem situation (current problem statement). This is carried out using meta-knowledge that the system uses to find patterns (markers of each logical system provided by the experts) in the situation, offering a good prediction of the needed degree of expressivity which in turn leads to the selection of the appropriate logical system. For each logic (classical, fuzzy, etc.), there is a local controller, which is intended to manage the main domain components of that logic: The model of (valid and invalid) inference rules are encoded as production rules, and the semantic memory of the target logic is encoded in a formal OWL ontology and connected to the inference rules. In each local controller, an algorithm is encoded to select the right reasoning type depending on the problem. The first version of Logic-Muse first version focuses on propositional logic.

Logic-Muse learner model goal is to represent, update and predict the learner state of knowledge based on her/his interaction with the system. It has multiple aspects

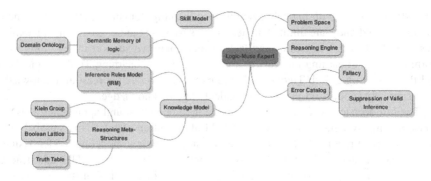

Fig. 1. Global view of the Logic- Muse expert component

including the cognitive part that essentially represents the state of the learner's knowledge (mastery of the reasoning skills in each of the six reasoning situations that have been identified thanks to the experts). The cognitive state is generated from the learner behavior during his interactions with the system, that is, it is inferred by the system from the information available. It is supported by a BN (Fig. 2) based on domain knowledge, where influence relationships between nodes (reasoning skills) as well as prior probabilities are provided by the experts [20]. Some nodes are directly connected to the reasoning activities such as exercises. The skills involved in the BN are those put forward by the mental models theory to reason in conformity to the logical rules. Besides the cognitive aspect, the model has an episodic memory that keeps track of all the exercises performed by the learner. Furthermore, a CDM-Based (Cognitive Diagnosis Models) psychometric model [8, 18] is built using the items bank, a Q-Matrix (items/skills), as well as data from all student responses to items.

The resulting model is part of the learner model as well and allows for initial predictions of the learner strengths and weaknesses regarding the reasoning skills given

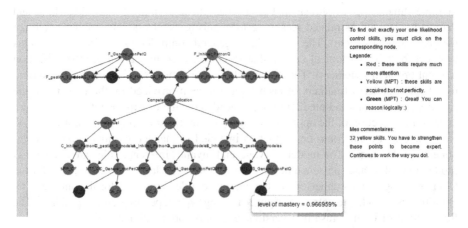

Fig. 2. A visualization of a learner's Bayesian net for deductive reasoning in Logic-Muse Interface. This learner has mastered 4 skills (in bold).

his/her performance on items. More concretely, we predict the probability of a learner mastering the overall competence (root node) via the pre-test results. For this, we use the "posterior" matrix obtained through the CDM. We seek a learner's response pattern, the line of the "posterior" matrix containing the same pattern or a similar pattern. The joint probability matching this pattern, based on the probabilities associated with each skill is used as the a priori likelihood (prior probability) of mastering the root node.

Figure 3 shows a screenshot of a learner's session. On the left, we have the working space where the system presents problems that need to be solved. On the right, we have the space where the tutor can interact with the learner. There are also several tabs providing key tutoring services. In the domain exploration tab, the learner can visualize subsets of the domain ontology to access some relevant information about the domain. In the Metacognition space, the learner can access to his model in different ways. For instance, he can visualize the current state of his knowledge via the BN (Fig. 2). He can also visualize the annotated Boolean lattice as an underlying meta logic structure of the propositional logic, which aim here is to provide some metacognitive supports to some advanced users. At any time during the learning session, the learner can ask the system for help or go through some relevant lessons to the current problem, recommended by the system. The next section will further present the Logic-Muse learner model.

Fig. 3. Screenshot of a learner's session in Logic-Muse

4   Logic-Muse Learner Model

The leaner model allows an ITS to adapt the interaction with its user's specific needs. One of the biggest challenges in designing ITS is the effective assessment, representation and prediction of the student's knowledge state and specific needs in the problem domain based on uncertain information. It is thus important to support the diagnosis with an effective method able to carry out all those challenges. We have developed a BN to represent the user's knowledge as accurately as possible. As previously said, it was built from the domain knowledge analysis, where causal relationships between nodes (reasoning skills) as well as prior probabilities are provided by the experts. In fact, as we planned to cover several logical systems, for every type of logic implemented (propositional logic, first order logic, etc.) there is a BN associated in the learner model. Because the diagnosis and the predictive mechanism stays the same in those different BN, we will just focus on the BN for deductive reasoning in propositional logic.

4.1   The Bayesian Network for the Deductive Reasoning Diagnosis

The nodes in our BN are directly connected to the reasoning activities. The skills involved in the Bayesian network are those put forward by the mental models theory to reason in conformity to the logical rules. This includes the inhibition of exceptions to the premises, the generation of counterexamples to the conclusion and the ability to manage all the relevant models for different problems contexts, the concrete, contrary to fact and abstract informal [14]. We have considered that cognitive parameters and diagnosis can be modeled by random variables. There are two types of nodes: nodes measuring the learner's knowledge or skills (skill nodes), and those containing the evidence, which represent answers to exercises (item nodes).

Skills nodes represent all the skills involved in deductive reasoning learning. They have a continuous probability between 0 and 1 that respectively correspond to the non-acquisition and acquisition of the skill.

Evidences nodes (items nodes) represent learner's answers to problems from the item bank. The evidence nodes are represented by a random variable Q with a Bernoulli distribution. $Q = 1$ means that the student correctly answered the exercise, $Q = 0$ means that the answer is incorrect.

Because deductive reasoning is the main subject to be learnt, it represents the global node of the BN. According to Markovits's theory of developmental reasoning [14], 3 abilities are at play when reasoning with the four logical forms of conditional inferences (Modus Ponendo Ponens (MPP), Modus Tollendo Tollens (MTT), Affirmation of the Consequent (AC) and Denial of the Antecedent (DA)).

- **Inhibition of P and not Q:** This skill enables the reasoner to *inhibit disabling conditions* (possibilities in which P is true et Q is false) that would lead to uncertainty about the conclusions of the valid MPP and MTT inferences.
- **Generation of not P and Q:** This skill will allow the learner to *generate alternative antecedents* (possibilities in which P is false and Q is true) that would lead to the logical answer of uncertainty for the invalid AC and DA.
- **Three mental models management:** This skill will allow the learner to *manage to represent the 3 true possibilities* for the conditional if P then Q: P and Q, not P and not Q, not P and Q.

These threeskills are represented as skill nodes in the BN that are directly connected to inferences (MPP, MTT, AC, DA, also are skills nodes). The structure is replicated in the three different contents of increasing difficulty:

- **Causal familiar:** Real life premises with many ("If I throw a rock at a window, then it will break") and few ("If a finger is cut, the it will bleed") alternative antecedents and many ("If the ignition key is turned, then the car will start") and few ("If one jumps in a pool, then one will be wet") disabling conditions.
- **Causal contrary-to-fact:** Premises contrary to our knowledge of the world ("If afeather is thrownat a window, then the window will break")
- **Abstract:** Premises built with fantasy terms ("If a person morp, it will become plede").

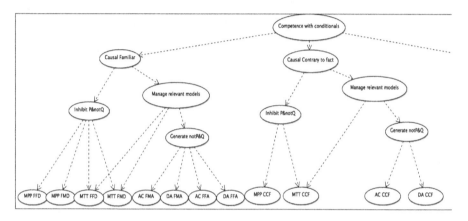

Fig. 4. A part of the BN for the deductive reasoning diagnosis

We denoted 28 skills. The number of items nodes is the size of our item bank on propositional logic. The structure and the prior probabilities of our BN was built according to the underlying developmental theory of reasoning. The system's estimate that a student has acquired a skill is continually updated every time the student gives a first response to a step in the problem. The system then re-computes the probability that the student knew the skill before the answer, using answers as evidence. Exercises are chosen according to these probabilities (the more the probability of a skill node is low, the more likely it is going to be chosen). Figure 4 depicts a small part of Logic-Muse's BN.

4.2 Evaluation Protocol and Results

Learner modeling is valid only if it accurately reflects the learner's progress longitudinally. Evaluation of the inference mechanism addresses the evaluation of the validity of user competences inferred from the input data previously collected. In order to ensure this validity, we assessed the inference capability of our BN. In this section, we present a preliminary formative evaluation of the Network using an incremental cross validation approach. In formative evaluation, researchers examine a system under development, to identify problems and guide modifications [13].

The grading protocol under the cognitive model is as follows: (1) for the assessment of the cognitive model representation (network structure, causal links) we used data mining techniques and the CDM library; (2) for the assessment of the prediction accuracy, we used a prediction procedure with an incremental cross validation.

4.2.1   Network Structure and Causal Links Validation

Data Preparation. The very first step was to preprocess the raw data obtained. For each of the 48 questions of the test, students had to choose between 3 answers (the valid one, the invalid typical one and the invalid a typical one). We created a data-matrix that has 71 rows (for the 71 students) and 48 columns (for the 48 items). The 3 possible answers were encoded as "1" for the valid answer, "0" for both the invalid typical and invalid atypical answers.

Table 1. Correspondence between the 48 questions and skills involved

Question number	Skill involved
47, 42, 37, 36, 32, 27	Abstract MPP
46, 25, 41, 39, 33, 30	Abstract DA
45, 44, 38, 35, 29, 28	Abstract MT
48, 43, 40, 34, 31, 26	Abstract AC
1, 6, 10	MPP with many alternatives
17, 15, 23	MPP with few alternatives
3, 5, 11	MTT with many alternatives
14, 18, 24	MTT with few alternatives
2, 8, 9	AC with many alternatives
16, 19, 21	AC with few alternatives
4, 7, 12	DA with many alternatives
13,20,22	DA with few alternatives

Results and Discussion. We ran the ID3 algorithm available in SPMF datamining toolkit [9] as well as the J48 (Decision tree) algorithm available in Weka datamining toolkit on data. We have executed the decision tree algorithms (ID3 and J48) 48 times by choosing one of the 48 questions as the class to predict at each time. Figure 5 shows the output of J48 algorithm (which is practically the same as the output of the ID3 algorithm) after we chose item 48 as the class to predict.

After consolidation of the results based on different skills (e.g. 48, 43, 40, 34, 31, 26 for abstract skill AC. See Table 1), we drew some conclusions. For example, we concluded that to answer abstract AC problems, the student must have mastered some skills in resolving abstract AC and DA problems. Likewise, if he can answer at least two abstract AC and or DA questions, then he is more likely to perform well on other questions involving these same skills. These results allowed us to validate the skills grouping (Causal familiar, Abstract, etc.) done in the BN and the causal links between those skills but also the Logic-Muse Q-matrix that has been designed by experts. The fact that this matrix is valid simply indicates that the initialisation of the learner model which is done by the CDM using Q-matrix and a dataset (Dina matrix [11]) is based on valid knowledge.

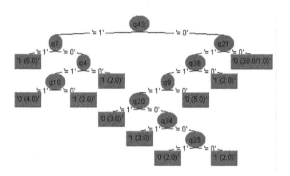

Fig. 5. Decision Tree with Q48 as the class to predict.

4.2.2   Assessment of the BN Prediction Accuracy

A second evaluation that we have conducted on the BN learner model aims at looking how accurate it is when inferring the learners'answers. The goal is to assess the predictive capability (or predictive power) of the BN and its ability to best represent the current skills of a learner. To achieve this, we opted for a prediction procedure [17] and for an incremental cross validation. In the incremental version of k-fold cross valida-tion, the training data increase one by one and the test data decrease one by one. For each of the 71 students who answered on 48 logical reasoning problems, we have compared the real answer of each question with the one predicted by the network. Thus, for each student, we extracted the likelihood of correctly answering question 1 and then we compared it with his actual answer. After that, we introduced his real answer in the network and extracted the likelihood of the second question, which we compared with his answer to that question, and so on.

We randomly pick up 3 students to show the results of the analysis on Fig. 6. We notice on all the students that after an average of 10 to 15 questions answered, the Bayesian network is able to predict the behavior of a learnerwith an accuracy thatrise from 85% to 95%. It shows very good predictive performance as we can see: F-measure is 81%, the Recall is 84% the Precision is 77%. Some errors can be due to the guess (giving a correct answer, despite not knowing the skill) and slip (knowing a skill, but giving a wrong answer) parameters [7]. For example, with student 60 (Fig. 6) we can see that the network predicts he does not have the necessary skill to give a correct answer to question 5, but he did give a correct answer probably because the guess probability of the question 5 is very high (0.809). The same reasoning can be done with students 60 and 67 (Fig. 6) on question 3 which has a slip probability of 0.570.

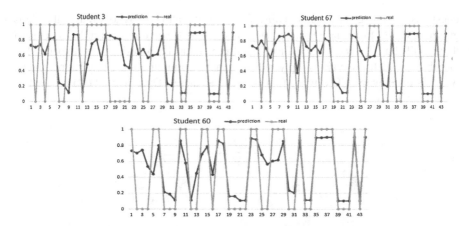

Fig. 6. Comparison between real answers (clear line) and those predicted by the Bayesian network (bold line) for 3 students. The X-axis represents probabilities and the Y-axis the questions.

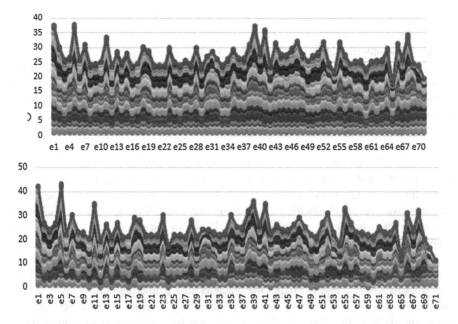

Fig. 7. (a) Real trend (real data) (b) Prediction on all the students. The X-axis represents students and the Y-axis represents questions.

Figure 7 presents the global trend of the network prediction and the real answers. The x-axis represents students and the y-axis the questions (the scales are different in the two figures a and b just because the answers are compressed; In (a) answers are expressed in term of probability and they are expressed in term of 0 or 1 in (b)). One can easily see that the two graphs vary in a similar way. We summarize by saying that the BN implemented gives not only a good representation of the learner's knowledge but it can also predict deductive reasoning skills based on the learner's behaviours. However, we must improve the prior probabilities. Currently, a failure to a question is represented by a probability below 0.6 (see Fig. 7); it would be ideal if this limit could vary according to a specific skill.

5 Conclusion and Future Works

The Bayesian learner modeling presented in this paper contributes to research onprobabilistic user modeling in ITS and specifically in ITS for teaching logicusing a probabilistic framework to perform diagnosis and prediction of learners' deductive reasoning skills. At the same time, a validation framework was proposed for the assessment of the BN out of the target system. This framework allows to validate the effectiveness (pre-diction accuracy, structure,...) of the learner's model without the need of a complete functional system. Thus, the model can first be refined alone before deploying it in the system for further assessment which will lead to a speeding up of the final deployment of the system (less experiments with the global system).

In this paper, we have presented a BN that can realizea faithful representation of the learner's knowledge state and we also prove its predictive efficiency using an incremental cross validation. A number of issues remain to be addressed such as the improvement of the probabilities and the validation of the complete structure of the BN.

Those issues could be addressed by doing a deeper statistical assessment which will be considered after. The prior probabilities in the network will be refined according to the results obtained. Since we plan to launch the use of Logic-Muse starting in autumn 2017, we will conduct the summative evaluation (added value of such a system in the learning of logical reasoning) at that time. The next step will be to make sure that the Logic-Muse Tutor's interventions is based on the BN learner model's predictions.

References

1. Barnes, T., Stamper, J.C.: Automatic hint generation for logic proof tutoring using historical data. Educ. Technol. Soc. **13**(1), 3–12 (2010)
2. Chakraborty, B., Sinha, M.: Student evaluation model using bayesian network in an intelligent e-learning system. J. Inst. Integr. Omics Appl. Biotechnol. (IIOAB) **7**, 2 (2016)
3. Chrysafiadi, K., Virvou, M.: Student modeling approaches: a literature review for the last decade. Expert Syst. Appl. **40**(11), 4715–4729 (2013)
4. Conati, C., Gertner, A.S., VanLehn, K., Druzdzel, M.J.: On-line student modeling for coached problem solving using bayesian networks. In: Jameson, A., Paris, C., Tasso, C. (eds.) User Modeling. ICMS, vol. 383, pp. 231–242. Springer, Vienna (1997). doi:10.1007/978-3-7091-2670-7_24
5. Conati, C., Gertner, A., Vanlehn, K.: Using Bayesian networks to manage uncertainty in student modeling. User Model. User-Adap. Inter. **12**(4), 371–417 (2002)

6. Conati, C.: Bayesian student modeling, in Advances in intelligent tutoring systems. In: Nkambou, R., Bourdeau, J., Mizoguchi, R. (eds.) Advances in Intelligent Tutoring Systems. Studies in Computational Intelligence, vol. 308, pp. 281–299. Springer, Berlin (2010). doi:10.1007/978-3-642-14363-2_14

7. d Baker, R.S.J., Corbett, A.T., Aleven, V.: More accurate student modeling through contextual estimation of slip and guess probabilities in Bayesian knowledge tracing. In: Woolf, B.P., Aïmeur, E., Nkambou, R., Lajoie, S. (eds.) ITS 2008. LNCS, vol. 5091, pp. 406–415. Springer, Heidelberg (2008). doi:10.1007/978-3-540-69132-7_44

8. De La Torre, J.: A cognitive diagnosis model for cognitively based multiple-choice options. Appl. Psychol. Meas. 33(3), 163–183 (2009)

9. Fournier-Viger, P., et al.: SPMF: a Java open-source pattern mining library. J. Mach. Learn. Res. 15(1), 3389–3393 (2014)

10. Galafassi, F.F.P., Santos, A.V., Peres, R.K., Vicari, R.M., Gluz, J.C.: Multi-plataform interface to an ITS of proposicional logic teaching. In: Bajo, J., Hallenborg, K., Pawlewski, P., Botti, V., Sánchez-Pi, N., Duque Méndez, N.D., Lopes, F., Julian, V. (eds.) PAAMS 2015. CCIS, vol. 524, pp. 309–319. Springer, Cham (2015). doi:10.1007/978-3-319-19033-4_26

11. Junker, B.W., Sijtsma, K.: Cognitive assessment models with few assumptions, and connections with nonparametric item response theory. Appl. Psychol. Meas. 25(3), 258–272 (2001)

12. Lesta, L., Yacef, K.: An intelligent teaching assistant system for logic. In: Cerri, S.A., Gouardères, G., Paraguaçu, F. (eds.) ITS 2002. LNCS, vol. 2363, pp. 421–431. Springer, Heidelberg (2002). doi:10.1007/3-540-47987-2_45

13. Mark, M.A., Greer, J.E.: Evaluation methodologies for intelligent tutoring systems. J. Artif. Intell. Educ. 4, 129 (1993)

14. Markovits, H.: On the road toward formal reasoning: Reasoning with factual causal and contrary-to-fact causal premises during early adolescence. J. Exp. Child Psychol. 128, 37–51 (2014)

15. Mayo, D.G., Kruse, M.: Principles of inference and their consequences. In: Corfield, D., Williamson, J. (eds.) Foundations of Bayesianism. Applied Logic Series, vol. 24, pp. 381–403. Springer, Netherlands (2001). doi:10.1007/978-94-017-1586-7_16

16. Millán, E., Jiménez, G., Belmonte, M.-V., Pérez-de-la-Cruz, J.-L.: Learning Bayesian networks for student modeling. In: Conati, C., Heffernan, N., Mitrovic, A., Verdejo, M.F. (eds.) AIED 2015. LNCS, vol. 9112, pp. 718–721. Springer, Cham (2015). doi:10.1007/978-3-319-19773-9_100

17. Nicol, D.J., Macfarlane-Dick, D.: Formative assessment and self-regulated learning: a model and seven principles of good feedback practice. Stud. High. Educ. 31(2), 199–218 (2006)

18. Robitzsch, A., et al.: CDM: cognitive diagnosis modeling. R Package Version 5.5. (2017). Accessed in 9 June 2017. https://cran.r-project.org/web/packages/CDM/index.html

19. Tchetagni, J., Nkambou, R., Bourdeau, J.: Explicit reflection in prolog-tutor. Int. J. Artif. Intell. Educ. 17(2), 169–215 (2007)

20. Tchétagni, J.M.P., Nkambou, R.: Hierarchical representation and evaluation of the student in an intelligent tutoring system. In: Cerri, S.A., Gouardères, G., Paraguaçu, F. (eds.) ITS 2002. LNCS, vol. 2363, pp. 708–717. Springer, Heidelberg (2002). doi:10.1007/3-540-47987-2_71

Group Optimization to Maximize Peer Assessment Accuracy Using Item Response Theory

Masaki Uto[✉], Nguyen Duc Thien, and Maomi Ueno

University of Electro-Communications, Tokyo, Japan
{uto,thien,ueno}@ai.is.uec.ac.jp

Abstract. As an assessment method based on a social constructivist approach, peer assessment has become popular in recent years. When the number of learners increases as in MOOCs, peer assessment is often conducted by dividing learners into multiple groups to reduce the learner's assessment workload. However, in this case, a difficulty remains that the assessment accuracies of learners in each group depends on the assigned rater. To solve that problem, this study proposes a group optimization method to maximize peer assessment accuracy based on item response theory using integer programming. Experimental results, however, showed that the proposed method does not necessarily present higher accuracy than a random group formation. Therefore, we further propose an external rater selection method that assigns a few outside-group raters to each learner. Simulation and actual data experiments demonstrate that introduction of external raters using the proposed method improves the peer assessment accuracy considerably.

Keywords: Peer assessment · Item response theory · Group formation · Rater selection · Ability measurement

1 Introduction

As an assessment method based on a social constructivist approach, peer assessment, which is mutual assessment among learners, has become popular in recent years [1–3]. Peer assessment can provide the following important benefits [1,2,4].

1. Treating assessment as a part of learning, mistakes can come to represent opportunities rather than failures.
2. Assigning rater roles to learners raises their motivation. Moreover, evaluating others enhances learning from others' work, which induces self-reflection.
3. Transferable skills such as evaluation skills and discussion skills are practiced.
4. Feedback from others who have similar backgrounds is readily understood.
5. Even when the number of learners increases extremely as in massive open online courses (MOOCs), feedbacks and assessment can be offered for each learner.

© Springer International Publishing AG 2017
E. André et al. (Eds.): AIED 2017, LNAI 10331, pp. 393–405, 2017.
DOI: 10.1007/978-3-319-61425-0_33

6. When the learners are mature adults, evaluation by multiple raters is more reliable than that by a single instructor.

Therefore, peer assessment has been adopted into various learning and assessment situations (e.g., [1,3,5]).

One important use of peer assessment is providing formative comments to learners to enhance learning [6,7]. For that purpose, peer assessment has usually been adopted into group learning situations such as collaborative learning, active learning, and project-based learning (e.g., [4,7,8]). Another use of peer assessment is summative assessment [7–9]. The importance of this usage has been increasing with the widespread of large-scale e-learning environments such as MOOCs [7,10,11]. In such environments, evaluation by a single instructor becomes difficult because the number of learners increases extremely. On the other hand, peer assessment can be conducted without burdening the learner's assessment workload if learners are divided into small groups, in which the members assess each other, or only a few peer-raters are assigned to each learner [8,9,11]. Furthermore, peer assessment is justified as an appropriate assessment method because the ability of learners would be defined naturally in the learning community as a social agreement [2,12]. From the above points, this study specifically examines the utilization of peer assessment for summative assessment.

Peer assessment, however, has a problem that the assessment accuracy of a learner's ability depends on rater characteristics such as rating severity and consistency [1,2,4,10,11,13]. To solve the problem, item response theory (IRT)[14] models that incorporate rater characteristic parameters have been proposed (e.g., [1,2,13,15]). The IRT models are known to provide higher assessment accuracy than using the average ratings because they can estimate the ability of learners considering rater characteristics [2].

On the other hand, as described before, peer assessment is often conducted by dividing learners into multiple groups to reduce the learner's assessment workload when the number of learners increases. In such cases, a difficulty persists that assessment accuracies of learners in each group depend on the rater characteristics of the group members. For example, when a group consists of inconsistent peer-raters, the assessment accuracy of the learners in the group will be decreased. To resolve that shortcoming, this study develops a group optimization method to maximize the peer assessment accuracy.

Only one report of the relevant literature describes a study [16] that proposed a group formation method particularly addressing peer assessment accuracy. The purpose of the present study is to provide all learners with assessments that are as equivalently accurate as possible. For that purpose, the study proposed a method that forms groups such that each learner is assessed by peer-raters who are as diverse as possible. The method is expected to reduce differences in assessment accuracy among learners. However, the method does not necessarily maximize the accuracy.

To resolve that shortcoming, this study proposes a new group formation method to maximize peer assessment accuracy based on IRT. Specifically, the method is formulated as an integer programming problem that maximizes the lower bound of the Fisher information measure, a widely used index of ability assessment accuracy in IRT, for each learner. The proposed method is expected to form groups so that the learners in the same group can assess each other accurately. However, experimentally obtained results showed that the proposed method does not necessarily provide higher accuracy than a random group formation method. The result suggests that it is generally impossible to assign raters with high Fisher information to all learners when peer assessment is conducted only within a group.

To resolve the problem, the study proposes an external rater selection method that assigns a few outside-group raters to each learner. The proposed method is formulated as an integer programming problem that maximizes the lower bound of the Fisher information for each learner given by assigned outside-group raters. The proposed method is expected to improve the ability assessment accuracy dynamically because learners can be assessed by outside-group raters who can accurately assess them. Through simulation and experiments using actual data, we demonstrate the effectiveness of the proposed method. Although external evaluation is known to be important for organizations, our results justified it from data.

It is noteworthy that many group formation methods have been proposed for improving the effectiveness of collaborative learning (e.g., [17,18]). This study does not specifically examine learning effectiveness. However, the use of groups created using the proposed method are expected to be effective to improve learning because receiving accurate assessment is known to promote effective learning [4]. Therefore, group optimization for improving peer assessment accuracy can be regarded as an important research effort in the field of educational technology.

2   Peer Assessment

One author has developed a learning management system (LMS) called *Samurai* [19]. This study uses the system as a peer assessment platform. Hereinafter, we describe the system structure briefly.

LMS Samurai stores huge numbers of e-learning courses. Each course consists of 15 content sessions tailored for 90-min classes (the units are designated as *topics*). Each topic comprises instructional text screens, images, videos, and practice tests. In some courses, report writing assignments are given to learners. LMS Samurai has a discussion board system that enables learners to submit reports and to conduct peer assessment.

Figure 1 portrays a system interface by which a learner submits a report. The lower half of Fig. 1 presents hyperlinks for other learners' comments. By clicking a hyperlink, detailed comments are displayed in the upper right of Fig. 1. The five star buttons shown at the upper left are used for assigning ratings. The buttons include −2 (Bad), −1 (Poor), 0 (Fair), 1 (Good), and 2 (Excellent). The learner who submitted the report can take the ratings and comments into consideration and rework the report accordingly.

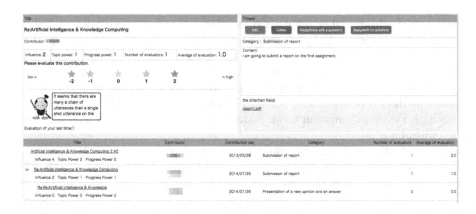

Fig. 1. Peer assessment system.

As described in Sect. 1, peer assessment is often conducted by dividing learners into multiple groups. Peer assessment groups can be described as

$$\boldsymbol{X} = \{x_{igjr} | x_{igjr} \in \{0, 1\}\}. \tag{1}$$

Here, x_{igjr} is a variable that takes the value of 1 if learner $j \in \{1, \cdots, J\}$ and peer-rater $r \in \{1, \cdots, J\}$ are included in the same group $g \in \{1, \cdots, G\}$ for assessment of assignment $i \in \{1, \cdots, I\}$. It takes the value of 0 otherwise.

The rating data $\boldsymbol{U}$ obtained from the peer assessment consist of rating categories $k \in \{1 \ldots, K\}$ given by each peer-rater r to each learning outcome of learner j for each assignment i. Letting u_{ijr} be a response of rater r to learner j's outcome for assignment i, the data $\boldsymbol{U}$ are described as

$$\boldsymbol{U} = \{u_{ijr} | u_{ijr} \in \{-1, 1, \cdots, K\}\}. \tag{2}$$

Here, $u_{ijr} = -1$ denotes missing data. When peer assessment is conducted only among group members, the data u_{ijr} for j and r corresponding to $\sum_{g=1}^{G} x_{igjr} = 0$ are missing data. This study uses five categories $\{1, 2, 3, 4, 5\}$ transformed from the rating buttons $\{-2, -1, 0, 1, 2\}$ in the system.

This study applies item response theory to the peer assessment data for improving the accuracy of learner ability assessment.

3   Item Response Theory

The item response theory (IRT) [14], a test theory based on mathematical models, has been used widely in areas of educational testing. Actually, IRT is known to realize an accurate assessment of learners' ability by facilitating consideration of test item characteristics (e.g., difficulty and discrimination). Traditionally, IRT has been applied to tests of which the responses can be scored automatically as correct or wrong. In recent years, however, application of polytomous

IRT models to performance assessments such as essay tests and report assessment has been attempted.

Peer assessment data U are three-way data, as defined in Sect. 2. However, traditional IRT models are not directly applicable to such multi-way data [1,2]. To resolve that difficulty, IRT models that incorporate rater characteristic parameters have been proposed (e.g.,[1,2,13,15]). The following subsections introduce an IRT model proposed for peer assessment [2].

3.1 Item Response Theory for Peer Assessment

The IRT model for peer assessment [2] has been proposed as a graded response model (GRM). It is a representative polytomous IRT model that incorporates rater characteristic parameters. The model defines the probability that rater r responds in category k to learner j's work for assignment i as

$$P_{ijrk} = P^*_{ijrk-1} - P^*_{ijrk}, \tag{3}$$

$$P^*_{ijrk} = [1 + \exp(-\alpha_i \alpha_r (\theta_j - b_{ik} - \varepsilon_r))]^{-1}, \tag{4}$$

where $P^*_{ijr0} = 1$ and $P^*_{ijrK} = 0$. In those equations, θ_j denotes the ability of learner j; α_r reflects the consistency of rater r; ε_r represents the severity of rater r; α_i is a discrimination parameter of assignment i; and b_{ik} denotes the difficulty in obtaining the score k for assignment i. Here, the order of b_{ik} is restricted by $b_{i1} < \cdots < b_{iK-1}$. Furthermore, $\alpha_{r=1} = 1$ and $\varepsilon_1 = 0$ are given for model identification.

For explanation of the rater parameters, Fig. 2 shows item characteristic curves of two raters with assignment parameters $\alpha_i = 1.5$, $b_{i1} = -1.5$, $b_{i2} = -0.5$, $b_{i3} = 0.5$, and $b_{i4} = 1.5$. The left panel presents item characteristic curves of *Rater 1*, who has $\alpha_r = 1.5$ and $\varepsilon_r = 1.0$. The right panel shows item characteristic curves of *Rater 2*, who has $\alpha_r = 0.8$ and $\varepsilon_r = -1.0$. Figure 2 presents a graph with the horizontal axis showing a learner's ability θ_j. The vertical axis shows the rating probability for each category.

According to Fig. 2, the higher the rater consistency parameter is, the greater the differences in the response probability among the rating categories are. That fact reflects that a rater who has a higher consistency can distinguish differences of performance more accurately and consistently. Additionally, Fig. 2 shows that the item response function of *Rater 1*, who has higher severity, shifted to the right compared to those of *Rater 2*, which means that a higher performance is necessary to obtain a score from *Rater 1* than to obtain the same score from *Rater 2*.

This IRT model is known to realize higher accuracy of ability assessment than the other models when the number of raters increases [2]. This study assumes that a group formation is necessary because of an increasing number of learners (=raters). Therefore, we employ the IRT model.

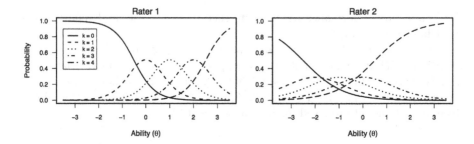

Fig. 2. Item characteristic curves of two raters.

3.2   Fisher Information

In IRT, the standard error of ability estimation is defined as the inverse square root of the Fisher information. Because more information implies less error of measurement, the Fisher information has been widely used as an index of the ability assessment accuracy.

The Uto and Ueno [2] model provides the Fisher information of rater r in assignment i for a learner with ability θ_j as

$$I_{ir}(\theta_j) = \alpha_i^2 \alpha_r^2 \sum_k \frac{\left(P^*_{ijrk-1} Q^*_{ijrk-1} - P^*_{ijrk} Q^*_{ijrk}\right)^2}{P_{ijrk}}, \tag{5}$$

where $Q^*_{ijrk} = 1 - P^*_{ijrk}$.

When peer assessment is conducted among group members, the information for learner j in assignment i is definable by the sum of the information of each rater in the same group as follows.

$$I_i(\theta_j) = \sum_{\substack{r=1 \\ r \neq j}}^{J} \sum_{g=1}^{G} I_{ir}(\theta_j) x_{igjr} \tag{6}$$

A high Fisher information $I_i(\theta_j)$ represents that the assigned raters will accurately assess the ability of learner j. Therefore, if we form groups to provide as much information $I_i(\theta_j)$ to each learner as possible, then the ability assessment accuracy is expected to be improved.

4   Group Optimization Based on Item Response Theory

This study proposes a group formation method to maximize the peer assessment accuracy based on IRT. Specifically, the proposed method is formulated as an integer programming method that maximizes the lower bound of the Fisher information for each learner.

4.1   Group Optimization Method

The group optimization method for assignment i is formulated as shown below.

$$\text{maximize}: \quad y_i$$

$$\text{subject to}: \quad \sum_{\substack{r=1 \\ r \neq j}}^{J} \sum_{g=1}^{G} I_{ir}(\theta_j) x_{igjr} \geq y_i, \qquad \forall j$$

$$\sum_{g=1}^{G} x_{igjj} = 1, \qquad \forall j$$

$$\sum_{g=1}^{G} (1 - x_{igjj}) \sum_{r=1}^{J} x_{igjr} = 0, \qquad \forall j$$

$$n_l \leq \sum_{j=1}^{J} x_{igjj} \leq n_u, \qquad \forall j$$

$$n_l \leq \sum_{g=1}^{G} x_{igjj} \sum_{r=1}^{J} x_{igjr} \leq n_u, \qquad \forall j$$

$$x_{igjr} = x_{igrj}, \qquad \forall g, j, r$$

$$x_{igjr} \in \{0,1\}, \qquad \forall g, j, r$$

The first constraint requires that the Fisher information for each learner j must be larger than a lower bound y_i. The second and third constraints restrict each learner as belonging to one group. The fourth and fifth constraints control the number of learners in a group. Here, n_l and n_u represent the lower and upper bounds of the number of learners in group g. In this study, $n_l = \lfloor J/G \rfloor$ and $n_u = \lceil J/G \rceil$ are used to equalize the number of learners across groups. Here, $\lfloor \ \rfloor$ and $\lceil \ \rceil$ respectively indicate floor and ceiling functions. This integer programming maximizes the lower bound of the Fisher information for each learner. By solving the problem, we will obtain groups that provide as much Fisher information as possible to each learner.

It is noteworthy that the proposed method requires the estimated parameters of the IRT model. This study assumes that provisional values of the parameters can be given. Examples of their estimation are explained in Sect. 7.

4.2   Evaluation of Group Optimization Method

To confirm the effectiveness of the proposed method, the following simulation experiment was conducted.

1. For $J = 30$ and $I \in \{3,5\}$, the true parameters were generated randomly.
2. For each assignment i, learners were divided into $G = \{4,5\}$ groups using the proposed method (designated as $MxFiG$) and a random group formation

Table 1. The average and standard deviation (in parentheses) of the RMSE values in the simulation experiments.

J	I	G			$n^R = 1$		$n^R = 2$		$n^R = 3$	
			RndG	MxFiG	ExRnd	ExFi	ExRnd	ExFi	ExRnd	ExFi
30	3	4	0.368	0.360	0.343	0.297	0.325	0.287	0.318	0.262
			(0.043)	(0.068)	(0.060)	(0.055)	(0.058)	(0.048)	(0.059)	(0.038)
		5	0.438	0.408	0.374	0.321	0.333	0.304	0.306	0.291
			(0.052)	(0.078)	(0.079)	(0.050)	(0.059)	(0.054)	(0.055)	(0.048)
	5	4	0.252	0.264	0.253	0.235	0.230	0.216	0.216	0.197
			(0.025)	(0.065)	(0.072)	(0.044)	(0.057)	(0.034)	(0.057)	(0.037)
		5	0.298	0.307	0.299	0.253	0.259	0.241	0.244	0.225
			(0.043)	(0.045)	(0.045)	(0.051)	(0.048)	(0.039)	(0.038)	(0.037)

method (designated as *RndG*). The proposed method was solved using *IBM ILOG CPLEX Optimization Studio*. A feasible solution is used if the optimal solution could not be obtained within five minutes.

3. Given the created groups and the true model parameters, rating data were sampled randomly.
4. The ability of learners was estimated from the generated data given the true parameters of raters and assignments. The expected a posteriori (EAP) estimation was used for the estimation.
5. The root mean square deviation (RMSE) between the estimated ability and the true ability were calculated.
6. After repeating the procedures described above 10 times, the average and standard deviations of the RMSE values were calculated.

Table 1 presents the results. Table 1 shows that the proposed method did not necessarily outperform the random method. The results suggest the general impossibility of assigning raters with high Fisher information to all learners when peer assessment is conducted only among group members.

To confirm that point, Fig. 3 shows the Fisher information for each learner in groups created using the proposed method, given that $J = 30$ and $G = 5$. In the figure, the horizontal axis shows the ability of learner θ. The vertical axis shows the Fisher information $I_i(\theta_j)$. Each datapoint represents an individual learner; the symbols of the data points represent groups to which each learner belongs. According to Fig. 3, we can confirm that high Fisher information is not necessarily provided to all learners.

5   External Rater Selection

The previous section presented a demonstration that the ability assessment accuracy cannot necessarily be improved if peer assessment is conducted only within a group. To overcome that shortcoming, this study further proposes an external rater selection method that assigns a few outside-group raters to each learner.

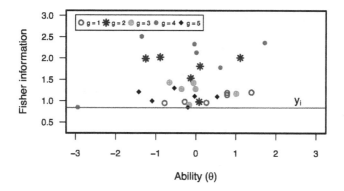

Fig. 3. Fisher information for each learner in groups.

5.1 External Rater Selection Method

The external rater selection method assigns outside-group raters to each learner while providing as much Fisher information as possible. Concretely, the method is formulated as an integer programming problem that maximizes the lower bound of information for learners. Given a group formation X, the proposed method for assignment i is defined as follows.

$$\text{maximize}: \quad y_i$$

$$\text{subject to}: \quad \sum_{r \in C_{ij}} I_{ir}(\theta_j) z_{ijr} \geq y_i, \qquad \forall j$$

$$\sum_{r \in C_{ij}} z_{ijr} = n^R, \qquad \forall j$$

$$\sum_{j=1}^{J} z_{ijr} \leq n^J, \qquad \forall r$$

$$z_{ijj} = 0, \qquad \forall j$$

$$z_{ijr} \in \{0,1\}, \qquad \forall j, r$$

Here, $C_{ij} = \{r \mid r \in \{1, \cdots, J\}. \sum_{g=1}^{G} x_{igjr} = 0\}$ is the set of outside-group raters for learner j in assignment i given a group formation X. Also, z_{ijr} is a variable that takes 1 if rater r is assigned to learner j in assignment i; it takes 0 otherwise. The upper limit number of external raters for each learners is n^R. n^J is the upper limit number of outside-group learners assigned to each rater.

The first constraint indicates that the Fisher information for each learner must exceed a lower bound y_i. The second constraint requires that each learner be evaluated by n^R number of external raters. The objective function is defined as the maximization of the lower bound of the information for learners given by assigned external raters.

The proposed method will assign external raters with high Fisher information to each learner. Therefore, the ability assessment accuracy is expected to be improved dynamically, merely by introducing a few external raters.

5.2 Evaluation of External Rater Selection Method

To evaluate the effectiveness of the proposed method, we conducted similar simulation experiments to those explained in Subsect. 4.2. In this experiment, after forming groups by the proposed group optimization method in Procedure 2, $n^R \in \{1, 2, 3\}$ number of external raters were assigned to all learners. The proposed method (designated as *ExFi*), and a random selection method (designated as *ExRnd*) were used as external rater selection methods. For the proposed method, $n^J = 12$ was given.

The results are presented in the columns of *ExFi* and *ExRnd* in Table 1. Table 1 shows that both external rater selection methods improved the ability assessment accuracy as the number of external raters increased.

A comparison of the results of *ExFi* and *ExRnd* revealed that the proposed method provides higher accuracy in all cases. The results confirmed that introducing the external raters with high Fisher information by the proposed method efficiently improves the accuracy of ability assessment.

6   Actual Data Experiments

Actual data experiments were conducted to evaluate the proposed method.

For the experiments, actual peer assessment data were gathered as follows. (1) 34 university students were collected as participants. (2) They were asked to complete four essay writing assignments that were set in the national assessment of educational progress (NAEP) 2002 [20] and 2007 [21]. (3) After the participants completed all assignments, they were asked to evaluate the essays of all other participants for all four assignments. The assessments were conducted using a rubric that we created based on the assessment criteria for grade 12 NAEP writing [21]. The rubric consists of five rating categories with corresponding scoring criteria.

Using the data, we conducted the following experiments.

1. The parameters in the IRT model were estimated using the Markov chain Monte Carlo algorithm [2].
2. For the number of groups $G \in \{3, 4, 5\}$, groups were formed by *MxFiG* and *RndG*. Then, given the groups formed by *MxFiG*, external raters were assigned by *ExRnd* and *ExFi*.
3. The rating data u_{ijr} were changed to missing data when rater r did not assess learner j's work for assignment i in the formed groups and external rater allocations.
4. Given the parameters of raters and assignments that were estimated in Procedure 1, the abilities of learners were estimated from the missing data.

Table 2. The average and standard deviation (in parentheses) of the RMSE values in the actual data experiment.

J	I	G			$n^R = 1$		$n^R = 2$		$n^R = 3$	
			RndG	MxFiG	ExRnd	ExFi	ExRnd	ExFi	ExRnd	ExFi
34	4	3	0.199	0.214	0.203	0.180	0.191	0.170	0.191	0.130
			(0.027)	(-)	(0.009)	(-)	(0.014)	(-)	(0.012)	(-)
		4	0.241	0.259	0.236	0.210	0.226	0.197	0.208	0.175
			(0.036)	(-)	(0.013)	(-)	(0.014)	(-)	(0.023)	(-)
		5	0.287	0.323	0.295	0.255	0.272	0.206	0.251	0.192
			(0.035)	(-)	(0.024)	(-)	(0.018)	(-)	(0.021)	(-)

5. We calculated the RMSEs between the ability estimated from the complete data and those estimated from missing data.
6. For random methods (*RndG* and *ExRnd*), we repeated the procedure described above 10 times. Then the average and standard deviation of the RMSE were calculated. For proposed methods (*MxFiG* and *ExFi*), we did not repeat the procedure because the optimal solution can be determined uniquely.

Table 2 presents the results. Comparing the group formation methods, the proposed group formation method did not necessarily present higher accuracy than the random method, as was true of the simulation results.

According to the results of the external rater selection methods, the accuracies of both methods increased as the number of external raters increased. Comparison of the selection methods shows that the proposed method revealed higher accuracy than the random method in all cases. Specifically, the proposed method with one external rater revealed almost equivalent accuracy to that of the random method with three external raters. Results show that the proposed method is effective for improving the accuracy of ability assessment.

7   Conclusion

This study proposed methods to improve peer assessment accuracy when the assessment is conducted by dividing learners into multiple groups. Specifically, we first proposed the IRT-based group optimization method, which maximizes the lower bound of the Fisher information for each learner. The experimentally obtained results, however, showed that the proposed method does not necessarily provide higher accuracy than a random group formation method.

To resolve the problem, we further proposed the external rater selection method, which assigns a few outside-group raters to each learner. Concretely, the method was formulated as an integer programming problem that maximizes the lower bound of information provided for learners by assigned outside-group raters. The simulation and actual data experiments demonstrate that introducing a few optimal external raters improved the ability assessment accuracy dynamically. Although external evaluation is generally important for organizations, the results justified it from data.

As described in Subsect. 4.1, the proposed methods require the estimated parameters of IRT models. An approach to estimate the assignment parameters is to use peer assessment data collected from past learners of the same course. To estimate the rater parameters and ability, peer assessment for the first assignment might be conducted using other grouping methods. Given the parameters estimated by the data, the proposed methods are useful from the second assignment. Moreover, re-estimating the parameters after every peer assessment using all previous data will be more appropriate.

In this study, we specifically examined only the peer assessment accuracy. However, as discussed in Sect. 1, the proposed methods would also be effective for learning improvement. Evaluation of that assumption is left as a task for future study.

References

1. Ueno, M., Okamoto, T.: Item response theory for peer assessment. In: Proceedings of IEEE International Conference on Advanced Learning Technologies, pp. 554–558(2008)
2. Uto, M., Ueno, M.: Item response theory for peer assessment. IEEE Trans. Learn. Technol. 9(2), 157–170 (2016)
3. Davies, P.: Review in computerized peer-assessment. Will it affect student marking consistency? In: Proceedings of 11th CAA International Computer Assisted Conference, pp. 143–151(2007)
4. Lan, C.H., Graf, S., Lai, K.R., Kinshuk, K.: Enrichment of peer assessment with agent negotiation. IEEE Trans. Learn. Technol. 4(1), 35–46 (2011)
5. Cho, K., Schunn, C.D.: Scaffolded writing and rewriting in the discipline: a web-based reciprocal peer review system. Comput. Educ. 48(3), 409–426 (2007)
6. Topping, K.J., Smith, E.F., Swanson, I., Elliot, A.: Formative peer assessment of academic writing between postgraduate students. Assess. Eval. High. Educ. 25(2), 149–169 (2000)
7. Moccozet, L., Tardy, C.: An assessment for learning framework with peer assessment of group works. In: Proceedings of International Conference on Information Technology Based Higher Education and Training, pp. 1–5 (2015)
8. Staubitz, T., Petrick, D., Bauer, M., Renz, J., Meinel, C.: Improving the peer assessment experience on mooc platforms. In: Proceedings of Third ACM Conference on Learning at Scale, New York, NY, USA 389–398 (2016)
9. ArchMiller, A., Fieberg, J., Walker, J., Holm, N.: Group peer assessment for summative evaluation in a graduate-level statistics course for ecologists. Assess. Eval. High. Educ. 1–13 (2016)
10. Suen, H.: Peer assessment for massive open online courses (MOOCs). Int. Rev. Res. Open Distrib. Learn. 15(3), 313–327 (2014)
11. Shah, N.B., Bradley, J., Balakrishnan, S., Parekh, A., Ramchandran, K., Wainwright, M.J.: Some scaling laws for MOOC assessments. In: ACM KDD Workshop on Data Mining for Educational Assessment and Feedback (2014)

12. Lave, J., Wenger, E.: Situated Learning. Legitimate Peripheral Participation. Cambridge University Press, New York, Port Chester, Melbourne, Sydney (1991)
13. Eckes, T.: Introduction to Many-Facet Rasch Measurement: Analyzing and Evaluating Rater-Mediated Assessments. Peter Lang Pub Inc., Bern (2015)
14. Lord, F.: Applications of Item Response Theory to Practical Testing Problems. Erlbaum Associates, Mahwah (1980)
15. Patz, R.J., Junker, B.W., Johnson, M.S., Mariano, L.T.: The hierarchical rater model for rated test items and its application to large-scale educational assessment data. J. Educ. Behav. Stat. **27**(4), 341–366 (1999)
16. Nguyen, T., Uto, M., Abe, Y., Ueno, M.: Reliable peer assessment for team project based learning using item response theory. In: Proceedings of International Conference on Computers in Education, pp. 144–153 (2015)
17. Pang, Y., Mugno, R., Xue, X., Wang, H.: Constructing collaborative learning groups with maximum diversity requirements. In: 15th IEEE International Conference on Advanced Learning Technologies, pp. 34–38, July 2015
18. Lin, Y.S., Chang, Y.C., Chu, C.P.: Novel approach to facilitating tradeoff multiobjective grouping optimization. IEEE Trans. Learn. Technol. **9**(2), 107–119 (2016)
19. Ueno, M.: Data mining and text mining technologies for collaborative learning in an ILMS "samurai". In: Proceedings of IEEE International Conference on Advanced Learning Technologies, pp. 1052–1053 (2004)
20. Persky, H., Daane, M., Jin, Y.: The nation's report card: writing 2002. Technical report. National Center for Education Statistics (2003)
21. Salahu-Din, D., Persky, H., Miller, J.: The nation's report card: writing 2007. Technical report. National Center for Education Statistics (2008)

What Matters in Concept Mapping? Maps Learners Create or How They Create Them

Shang Wang[1(✉)], Erin Walker[1], and Ruth Wylie[2]

[1] Computing, Informatics, and Decision Systems Engineering,
Arizona State University, Tempe, USA
{shangwang, Erin.A.Walker}@asu.edu
[2] Mary Lou Fulton Teachers College, Arizona State University,
Tempe, USA
Ruth.Wylie@asu.edu

Abstract. Generative strategies, where learners process the target content while connecting different concepts to build a knowledge network, has shown potential to improve student learning outcomes. While concept maps in particular have been linked to the development of generative strategies, few studies have explored structuring the concept mapping process to support generative strategies, and few studies offer intelligent support. In this work, we present a concept mapping tool that offers navigational support in the form of hyperlinks, where nodes in the concept map are linked to segments of text. We evaluate the effect of the hyperlinks on generative strategies and learning outcomes through a week-long high school study with 32 participants. Our results indicate that proper navigational and visual aid during concept mapping facilitates the development of generative strategies, with implications for learning outcomes. Based on these findings, we propose a constraint-based tutoring system to adaptively support the development of generative strategies in concept mapping.

Keywords: Concept map · Generative strategies · Constraint based model

1 Introduction

Diagrams and mapping tools have been used to improve learning by providing a visual display of information, concepts, and relations between ideas [1, 2]. One such tool is a concept map, which is a graphical representation that illustrates knowledge structures as labelled links (denoting relationships) between various labelled nodes (denoting specific concepts in the knowledge domain) [3]. Although concept maps have been reported to facilitate learning [18], the use of concept maps also comes with drawbacks. The main disadvantage of using concept maps is the complexity of the task and the training required [4]. While previous research has shown the benefits of providing feedback and scaffolding during concept mapping [5], many studies have focused on the quality of the completed map rather than evaluating the process by which it was made. For example, Hirashima assessed the quality of student-generated concept maps by using keyword matching to compare the nodes in the concept map with keywords from the learning content [6]. Others have developed systems to provide immediate

© Springer International Publishing AG 2017
E. André et al. (Eds.): AIED 2017, LNAI 10331, pp. 406–417, 2017.
DOI: 10.1007/978-3-319-61425-0_34

feedback [e.g., 7], but these still focus on the product students create rather than intelligently monitoring the cognitive process.

We argue that it is just as important to consider how the concept maps are created when considering possible forms of intelligent support. For example, in what order are the concept nodes and links created? How much are students comparing concepts while constructing the map? Even two identical maps can result from two completely different strategies, and these strategies might influence learning results. Among different types of learning strategies, generative strategies have shown to have powerful impact on student learning. Generative strategies refer to behaviors and activities that involve the creation of relationships and knowledge networks among different concepts [8]. Research has demonstrated that generative strategies during reading, where learners process the learning content while comparing and connecting different concepts, lead to better learning outcomes than a linear strategy [9]. In addition, prior work suggests that concept mapping can be used as a valuable tool to develop generative strategies [15]. Supporting students in pursuing generative strategies during concept mapping may be highly beneficial.

In this paper, we present our design of a concept mapping environment that is integrated with a digital textbook. The environment is designed to scaffold generative strategies by allowing students to create concept maps directly from the textbook and then use them to navigate to relevant textbook content using a **hyperlink feature**. We hereby propose three hypotheses:

H_1: The hyperlink feature improves learning.
H_2: The hyperlink feature facilitates generative strategies.
H_3: The use of generative strategies predicts learning outcomes.

We investigate our hypotheses through a classroom study with 32 high school students. We discuss the implications of the study findings for developing a system that uses intelligent tutoring to promote generative strategies during concept mapping.

2 Related Work

The introduction of personal computers enabled the development of computer-based concept mapping tools such as CmapTools, Mindmaple, Mind Mapping and Mind Vector. Some of these tools, like CmapTools, have been extensively studied by researchers, and have demonstrated significant advantages over traditional concept mapping tasks [10]. These tools tend to provide features like fast input, easy modification, and map sharing, but do not fully utilize the interactive and intelligent potential of digital platforms to support students.

One way researchers have attempted to use digital technologies to scaffold beneficial learning strategies is by providing concept map based navigation, where students can click on a node in the concept map to navigate to the corresponding page, as opposed to reading the text in a fixed linear order. However, prior research on concept map based navigation failed to demonstrate positive impacts on learning gains [11, 12]. One explanation might be the maps given to student in the above studies are ready-made. Learners confronted with these ready-made maps may initially feel overwhelmed or demotivated by the complexity of the map [13], and thus, the benefits of quick access to relevant content are likely to be diminished by the cognitive load to process ready-made maps. In our work, students use concept maps that they created to navigate to relevant content, reducing the cognitive load of processing an unfamiliar map structure.

Another way researchers have used digital technologies in concept mapping is through the use of artificial intelligence. For instance, Weinbrenner and colleagues designed a system that provides feedback to students by comparing their concept maps with a domain ontology through keyword matching [19]. Similarly, Wu [7] presented a concept mapping environment that provides feedback based on the similarity between a student map and an expert map. These studies highlight the use of feedback in concept mapping, but the feedback given to students is mainly tailored to their final product, that is, the concept maps created by students. Few evaluate the process of constructing the maps. Mayer's work, which directly measured learners' cognitive processing during reading, revealed the importance of different strategies on learning outcomes [9]. In this present work, we evaluate the use of scaffolding to support generative strategies during concept mapping, with the eventual goal of developing adaptive feedback on concept mapping strategies.

3   System Design

In this work, we present an iPad-based interactive concept mapping tool that is integrated with a digital textbook. The tool enables students to create concept maps directly from the textbook content and, in turn, use the created map to access and navigate the content. The system was written in Objective-C, and the content displayed in the book is in.epub format to facilitate importing new materials as necessary. Our system is designed to support students in developing generative strategies during the concept mapping process. The following are the key features of the system:

1. Integrated text and concept map view. Our system has both a textbook view and a concept map view. When students hold the tablet in portrait mode, the system works as a traditional digital textbook. However, when the tablet is in landscape mode, the screen splits into two, with the left side displaying the textbook view and the right side showing the concept map view (see Fig. 1). The dual-window alignment provides quick access to both views for easy comparison between the text and the concept map. The students navigate within the textbook view by swiping left to go forward and right to go back. Since the iPad screen is relatively small, especially when divided in half, we provide students with a concept map preview which indicates where students are within the overall concept map.

2. Concept map construction. To create the concept map, students can add a concept node by long pressing on the word or words in the textbook. This "click-to-add" feature is designed to ameliorate the extraneous effort of typing the concept name on the iPad, while encouraging the cognitively beneficial process of building the knowledge structure. If students want to customize their concept maps by creating nodes that do not come directly from the text, they can add concept nodes by clicking on the "+" icon in the concept map view and using the iPad keyboard to label their nodes. To link concepts, student first long press on a concept node, choose the linking option, and then tap the second node they want to link. Students can then choose a word from a suggested list or type their own word to specify the relationship between the two concepts. Students can delete concepts or the whole map as necessary.

3. Concept map navigation. When a concept node is added to the map, it is hyperlinked to the page in the textbook that was active when it was created. To navigate back to that page, the student can click on the concept. In addition, if the student is navigating using the textbook view (swiping left or right), when the student arrives on a page, the concepts that were created on that page will be highlighted both in the concept map view and in the textbook view. We expect that this hyperlink navigation feature would better support students in pursuing generative strategies by helping them to compare concepts from different segments of text.

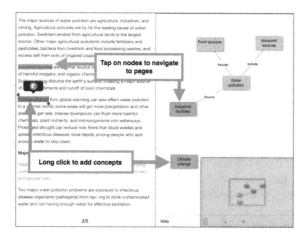

Fig. 1. Our application integrates a concept mapping tool with a textbook. Students can create concept maps directly from the textbook and use the created maps for navigation.

An example of generative strategies in the use of this application would be as follows. A student, Sam, reads the textbook and finds the concept "seed" on page 5. He uses the "click-to-add" feature to add a node named "seed" to the concept map view on the right. He continues to read the textbook. On page 30, where it talks about water pollution, he creates a node "water quality". Sam then realizes water quality might have something to do with the growth of the seed. He taps on the concept map node "seed" and the system navigates back to page 5. He finds that the growth of seeds largely depends on the oxygen level and mineral composition of underground water. He then taps on the node "water quality" and, jumping back to page 30, he finds that the water quality would affect the oxygen level and mineral composition. With this information, he links the concept map nodes "seed" and "water quality" and names the relationship as "depends on". From the example shown above, the hyperlinknavigation feature adds flexibility to the fixed linear textbook structure and enables students to access key information located in different pages of the textbook. These comparisons are critical in developing generative strategies.

4 Study of Hyperlink Feature

We conducted a study to test whether our digital textbook application improves learning (H_1), improves the use of generative strategies (H_2), and whether the generative strategies are related to learning (H_3). We worked with a high school teacher who typically uses concept mapping activities in her classes. In this study, our digital textbook application is used as a substitute to the paper-and-pencil based tools typically used for the concept mapping activity. During the study, students read a textbook chapter and, over the course of 5 classroom periods, constructed a concept map to represent the knowledge structure of the chapter. We investigated students' interactions with the system and their corresponding learning outcomes.

4.1 Method

We recruited 32 participants from a high school 12th grade earth sciences class. All participants had previous experience with concept maps. The application was installed on an iPad 2 Air, with a 9.7-inch display and a multi-touch interface. The learning material consisted of a chapter from the 15th edition of *Living in the Environment: Principles, Connections, and Solutions*, the textbook that was being used in the class. The textbook displayed in the application was manually edited by us to fit the screen of the iPad. The original chapter had 27 pages and the iPad version had 58 pages.

Students were assigned to two conditions (hyperlink and non-hyperlink) via a randomized block design to control for pretest score. All students worked individually and kept his or her iPad for the duration of the study. Students in the hyperlink condition used the system described above. They were able to create concept maps from the book and tap on the nodes to navigate to the related pages, with relevant words in the textbook and concept map nodes highlighted. Students in the non-hyperlink condition used the same system, but with no hyperlink navigation or highlighting on words and concept map nodes.

Students began the study with a pretest, which was taken on a Thursday. The intervention, in which students used our application, began the following week on a Monday, and lasted 20 min per day for 5 consecutive days. On the first day, all of the participants were given a 10-minute in-app training session (tailored to condition) where they learned about how to use the application features through a step-based tutorial. Our intervention was integrated into normal classroom practice and was part of the broader unit on earth sciences taught by the teacher. Therefore, each day after using our system to create their concept maps, students received a related lesson from their teacher and continued to engage with related content on Monday and Tuesday the following week. Similarly, if students finished creating their concept map before the end of the fifth day, they worked on related content the teacher had prepared (e.g., an online reading task). The posttest was given on the Wednesday after the study was completed. During the study, all students' actions were logged and the final concept maps were uploaded to a server for analysis.

4.2   Measures

Learning. The pretest consisted of 30 multiple choice questions covering the whole chapter, and was designed by the high school teacher. The posttest consisted of the same questions as the pretest but in a different order. This was in accordance with the common practice of the classroom teacher, who constructed similar pre and posttests for every unit she taught. Learning results are measured by normalized gains [21].

Generative Strategies. We model generative strategies using three variables.

1. *Backnavigation.* A back navigation is the count of times a student navigates back a previous page after reading forward in the text. Several "back" actions in a row are counted as a single back navigation, but once the learner moves forward again, the next time they go back, a new back navigation will be counted. This captures when learners make comparisons between current concepts and previously recalled ones.
2. *Cross links.* We computed the number of cross links by counting the times two concept nodes that are created from two different pages are linked. This measure reveals that learners are establishing relationships among concepts located on different pages of the textbook. The higher number of cross links a student has, the more comparisons the student is making.
3. *Context switch.* Our log file records whether a student is interacting with the textbook view or the concept map view, so we are able to model how many times students' attention switches from the textbook view to the concept map view. A high number of context switches from a student is an indication that the student is frequently referring to the textbook and comparing it with the concept map while constructing it, which indicates generative strategies.

Using the above three variables, we computed an overall generative score that quantifies generative strategies as a whole by: (1) using *min–max* normalization [22] to rescale the three variables into [0, 1], and (2) averaging the three rescaled values to get an overall generative score, also between 0 and 1.

Concept Map Properties. We also computed three basic properties of the students' concept maps themselves:

1. *Total node.* The total number of concept nodes in the concept map.
2. *Total link.* The total number of links in the concept map.
3. *Link/node ratio.* Link/node ratio is computed as the number of concept links over the number of concept nodes in a given map. The link/node ratio indicates the overall connectivity of a concept map. The higher the link/node ratio is, the more connected a concept map is.

Student Activities. Finally, we computed three variables from the log data that reflected student activity within the application.

1. *Total actions.* Total action is the total number of actions for each student.
2. *Navigation actions.* Navigation actions include turning pages and using hyperlink for navigation.
3. *Hyperlink navigation actions.* A hyperlink action is when a student clicks on a hyperlinked concept map node for navigation.

4.3   Results

Overview of Student Activity. In this section, we first present an overview of how students used our system to create concept maps for learning. As discussed in the method, not all students engaged in concept mapping for all study days, either due to being absent or completing the activity early. The actual attendance days are not significantly different between conditions, $F(1, 28) = 1.579$, $p = 0.219$. 23 students attended for 5 days (11 in the hyperlink condition, 12 in the non-hyperlink condition) and 7 students attended for 4 days (4 in the hyperlink condition, 3 in the non-hyperlink condition). Students who attended 5 days performed marginally less total actions than those who attended 4 days ($p = 0.063$). Two students (one in each condition) who attended less than 3 days are excluded from analysis.

Next, we looked at the basic properties of the concept maps that students produced (see Table 1). Overall, students created a mean of 40.90 nodes ($SD = 19.75$) and a mean of 37.80 links ($SD = 19.14$). We conducted a MANOVA with condition as the independent variable and number of concept nodes, number of concept links, and link/node as dependent variables. There was no significant difference between condition on the overall model ($F(3, 25) = 0.303$, $p = 0.823$, Wilks' $\lambda = 0.965$, partial $\eta^2 = 0.035$), and no significant effects of condition on the individual dependent variables.

Table 1. Variables for modeling concept map outcomes

Condition	#Concept nodes		#Concept links		#Link over node	
	Mean	SD	Mean	SD	Mean	SD
Hyperlink	42.42	18.91	38.40	19.48	0.91	0.16
Non-hyperlink	39.60	21.15	37.20	19.45	0.93	0.11

As a proxy for student engagement, we examined whether student activity varied across conditions. We first examined whether the hyperlink feature influenced the total navigation and total actions. A one-way ANOVA revealed that there was no significant difference between condition on total actions performed ($F(1, 28) = 2.081$, $p = 0.160$), with the hyperlink condition having a mean of 371.80 actions ($SD = 108.55$) and the non-hyperlink condition having a mean of 452.93 actions ($SD = 188.83$). Similarly, there was no difference in number of navigation actions ($F(1, 28) = 2.705$, $p = 0.111$), with the hyperlink condition conducting on average 191.53 actions ($SD = 82.79$) and non-hyperlink conducting 276.33 actions (SD = 181.74). Students used the hyperlink navigation actiona mean of 23.25 times, which is 12.14% of the total navigation actions taken.

H1: The hyperlink feature improves learning. Our hypothesis when designing the hyperlink feature was that the use of the hyperlink feature facilitates students in making connections between concepts, and thus, improves learning. To evaluate this hypothesis, we conducted a two-way repeated-measures ANOVA with condition as a between-subject variable and test time as a within-subject variable. Results show that both conditions demonstrated significant learning results ($F(1, 28) = 50.244, p < 0.001$), but there was no significant difference between conditions ($F(1, 28) = 0.18, p = 0.68$). Pretest and posttest results are shown in Table 2.

Table 2. Pre and posttest scores.

Condition	Pretest		Posttest		Normalized gain	
	Mean	SD	Mean	SD	Mean	SD
Hyperlink	13.71	3.79	18.93	4.08	0.34	0.16
Non-hyperlink	13.40	4.12	19.47	3.77	0.33	0.21

H2: The hyperlink feature facilitates generative strategies. The primary prediction in our work is that the navigational support and highlighting of key information in both views provided by the hyperlink feature would yield more connections among different concepts as well as more references and comparison between the textbook and the concept maps. Table 3 shows three indicators of generative strategies and the overall generative score.

We conducted a MANCOVA with the above features of generative strategies as dependent variables, and condition as an independent variable. We used total actions as a covariate, as a proxy for how active students were when interacting with the application. The overall model was significant between conditions, $F(3, 25) = 13.74$, $p = 0.001$, Wilks' $\lambda = 0.537$, partial $\eta^2 = 0.463$. Looking at the individual variables, back navigation ($F(1, 27) = 10.993, p = 0.003$, partial $\eta^2 = 0.289$) and context-switch ($F(1, 27) = 15.785, p < 0.001$, partial $\eta^2 = 0.369$) were significantly higher in the hyperlink condition. However, number of cross-links was not significantly different between conditions ($F(1, 27) = 3.768, p = 0.063$, partial $\eta^2 = 0.122$). Overall, the hyperlink feature significantly increases the use of generative strategies.

Table 3. Variables for modeling generative strategies

Condition	Back navigation		Cross-links		Context switch		Overall generative score	
	Mean	SD	Mean	SD	Mean	SD	Mean	SD
Hyperlink	34.67	11.41	13.73	10.06	114.40	55.92	0.43	0.18
Non-hyperlink	26.93	14.03	10.47	8.13	63.60	23.77	0.28	0.15

H3: The use of generative strategies predicts learning outcomes. Here, we examine whether the use of generative strategies relates to learning outcomes. We represent generative strategies using the overall generative score metric, introduced in the measures section. We conducted a generalized linear mixed model with condition, overall generative score (centered by mean) and the interaction of condition and overall generative score as independent variables, and learning gain as a dependent variable. We found that the interaction between condition and overall generative score significantly affects learning gain ($F(1, 26) = 6.26$, $p = 0.019$). To explore this interaction, we performed a correlation between generative behavior and normalized gain for each condition. For the hyperlink condition, generative behaviors are positively correlated with learning ($r(13) = 0.623$, $p = 0.013$). For the non-hyperlink condition, generative behavior does not predict learning ($r(13) = -0.302$, $p = 0.274$). Thus, the more generative strategies students use, the higher their learning gain, but only in the hyperlink condition.

5   Discussion

Our study aims to evaluate how our concept map learning environment assists student in the development of generative strategies. In a study with 30 high school students, we found that the use of the hyperlink feature increases generative behaviors. While these generative behaviors were related to learning in the hyperlink condition, they were not in the non-hyperlink condition.

Students in the hyperlink condition were more likely to exhibit generative strategies within our system, comparing and connecting concepts in different segments in the book, as well as relating the concept map with the textbook. Students in the non-hyperlink condition were more likely to process the textbook material in a given linear order. The fact that hyperlink students performed significantly more generative learning behaviors reinforces our hypothesis that the navigational support and visual comparison of key information facilitates students in comparing and establishing connections among concepts across pages.

Research has demonstrated that use of these generative strategies have the potential to improve learning [14]. This is indeed what we find within the hyperlink condition, as students who exhibit more generative strategies score better on a multiple choice test. However, this is not the case in the non-hyperlink condition. We argue that benefits of generative strategies come with drawbacks, as comparing and connecting concepts located in different pages requires extraneous effort, especially when students are not provided with proper visual aids and navigational support. Unlike previous research on generative strategies, where the content used was pretty simple, consisting of only a few pages [9, 16], the reading material in our study consisted of 58 pages that students read over 5 days, imposing a much higher cognitive load. While students in the hyperlink condition are able to use to the concept map to view relevant resources, students in the non-hyperlink condition are challenged with additional effort when comparing different concepts. It is not only physically demanding, as they have to flip through several pages manually, but also cognitive challenging due to the complex content structure. The benefits of using generative strategies are more likely to be hindered by the high cognitive load caused by the inefficient navigation. Thus, to see the benefits of generative strategies, proper visual aids and navigational support need to be given to students.

Our study has some limitations. The total sample size of the study is 32, with 30 used for analysis. Although the results suggest a significant difference in the generative learning behaviors between conditions, the overall effect might be not representative of the population due to the insufficient sample size. In addition, following the teacher's regular practice, the pre and posttests consist of the same questions in different orders, and thus there may have been a testing effect. Further, to adapt the class schedule, our study lasted 20 min per day for 5 days, leaving the students another 20 min for other class activities like group projects, presentations, etc. These additional resources might have caused unpredictable variance within the learning effects. Nevertheless, we believe our results point to the need for future research on how generative strategies can be supported within interactive learning environments.

6 Building an Intelligent Model

Based on our results, we can build an intelligent model that assesses in real-time whether a student is pursuing generative strategies. The core part of our system is the constraint modeler, which compares student interactions with a set of pre-defined constraints and determines what constraint students violate. Based on the overall generative score metric developed above, we propose potential constraints as follows:

1. $x\%$ of the links in the concept map are cross links.
2. Student navigates to previous pages after reading y pages consecutively.
3. Student adds concept map nodes after reading z pages.
4. Student switches attention between concept map and textbook after k actions.
5. Student uses the hyperlink feature every t actions.

Here, variables x, y, k, z, t depend on the learning context, for example, total pages of the textbook, learning proficiency of students, learning period, and objectives. Within our context, we can infer some possible values based on the behavioral data from the hyperlink condition. In the hyperlink condition, the average cross link percentage is 44.73. Thus, we can use 44.73 as a base value for x. Depending on different goals and objectives, these parameters can be varied. For example, a base value for x is 44.73, but when assisting students with less experience with generative strategies, we can lower x to prevent the system from giving extensive feedback. Based on the discussion above, we believe that it may be highly beneficial to provide feedback based on these constraints. In our system, constraints are evaluated after every student action and a student model is updated in real time. Feedback is given when the student model exceeds a certain threshold. For example, if a student constantly reads consecutively without navigating back, which violates constraint 3, a possible feedback message would be "I noticed you've been reading for a while. Are there any important concepts that you would like to add to the concept map?"

Our proposed system leverages research on constraint-based tutoring systems [20] to offer an efficient way of modeling generative learning in concept mapping, but differs from traditional constraint-based models (CBM) in the ways constraints are used and feedback is given. Traditional CBMs are developed based on Ohlsson's theory of learning from performance errors [17] and constraints are assessed during each problem solving state and feedback is given after each task. However, providing feedback on generative strategies might be more helpful if it's immediate, that is, as students are constructing the concept map. Therefore, in our system, constraints are used to evaluate student behaviors and we update the student model in real time.

In this work, we have discussed how navigational support and visual aids in concept mapping supports generative learning. The strength and novelty of our system lies in its ability to facilitate student in comparing and connecting concepts across pages. Although our study has some limitations, our results indicate that the hyperlink feature facilitates generative strategies, and the use of generative strategies in concept mapping relates to more learning when proper navigational aid is given. Based on these findings, we propose a constraint based feedback system that has the potential to support students in developing generative leaning strategies. These findings suggest future promising opportunities for developing adaptive technologies to support generative strategies during a variety of learning activities.

Acknowledgment. We thank the high school teacher that collaborated with us for her kind help with this work and all the students that participated in our high school study. This research was funded by NSF CISE-IIS-1451431 EAGER: Towards Knowledge Curation and Community Building within a Post digital Textbook.

References

1. Vekiri, I.: What is the value of graphical displays in learning? Educ. Psychol. Rev. **14**(3), 261–312 (2002)
2. Winn, W.: Learning from maps and diagrams. Educ. Psychol. Rev. **3**(3), 211–247 (1991)
3. Novak, J.D., Cañas, A.J.: The theory underlying concept maps and how to construct and use them (2008)
4. Davies, M.: Concept mapping, mind mapping and argument mapping: what are the differences and do they matter? High. Educ. **62**(3), 279–301 (2011)
5. Chang, K.-E., Sung, Y.-T., Chen, S.F.: Learning through computer-based concept mapping with scaffolding aid. J. Comput. Assist. Learn. **17**(1), 21–33 (2001)
6. Hirashima, T., Yamasaki, K., Fukuda, H., Funaoi, H.: Kit-build concept map for automatic diagnosis. In: Biswas, G., Bull, S., Kay, J., Mitrovic, A. (eds.) AIED 2011. LNCS, vol. 6738, pp. 466–468. Springer, Heidelberg (2011). doi:10.1007/978-3-642-21869-9_71
7. Wu, P.-H., et al.: An innovative concept map approach for improving students' learning performance with an instant feedback mechanism. Br. J. Educ. Technol. **43**(2), 217–232 (2012)
8. Grabowski, B.L.: Generative learning: past, present, and future. In: Jonassen, D.H. (ed), Handbook of research for educational communications and technology, pp. 897–913 (1996)
9. Ponce, H.R., Mayer, R.E.: Qualitatively different cognitive processing during online reading primed by different study activities. Comput. Hum. Behav. **30**, 121–130 (2014)

10. Cañas, A.J., et al.: CmapTools: a knowledge modeling and sharing environment. Concept maps: theory, methodology, technology. In: Proceedings of the first international conference on concept mapping, vol. 1 (2004)
11. Zeiliger, R., Reggers, T., Peeters, R.: Concept-map based navigation in educational hypermedia: a case study. In: Proceedings of ED-MEDIA, vol. 96 (1996)
12. Puntambekar, S., Stylianou, A., Hübscher, R.: Improving navigation and learning in hypertext environments with navigable concept maps. Hum.-Comput. Interact. **18**(4), 395–428 (2003)
13. Kinchin, I.M.: If concept mapping is so helpful to learning biology, why aren't we all doing it? Int. J. Sci. Educ. **23**(12), 1257–1269 (2001)
14. Wittrock, M.C.: Generative learning processes of the brain. Educ. Psychol. **27**(4), 531–541 (1992)
15. Ritchie, D., Volkl, C.: Effectiveness of two generative learning strategies in the science classroom. Sch. Sci. Math. **100**(2), 83–89 (2000)
16. Doctorow, M., Wittrock, M.C., Marks, C.: Generative processes in reading comprehension. J. Educ. Psychol. **70**(2), 109 (1978)
17. Ohlsson, S.: Learning from performance errors. Psychol. Rev. **103**(2), 241 (1996)
18. Nesbit, J.C., Adesope, O.O.: Learning with concept and knowledge maps: a meta-analysis. Rev. Educ. Res. **76**(3), 413–448 (2006)
19. Weinbrenner, S., Engler, J., Hoppe, H.U.: Ontology-supported scaffolding of concept maps. In: Biswas, G., Bull, S., Kay, J., Mitrovic, A. (eds.) AIED 2011. LNCS, vol. 6738, pp. 582–584. Springer, Heidelberg (2011). doi:10.1007/978-3-642-21869-9_108
20. Mitrovic, A., Koedinger, K.R., Martin, B.: A comparative analysis of cognitive tutoring and constraint-based modeling. In: Brusilovsky, P., Corbett, A., Rosis, F. (eds.) UM 2003. LNCS, vol. 2702, pp. 313–322. Springer, Heidelberg (2003). doi:10.1007/3-540-44963-9_42
21. Hake, R.R.: Interactive-engagement versus traditional methods: a six-thousand-student survey of mechanics test data for introductory physics courses. Am. J. Phys. **66**(1), 64–74 (1998)
22. Jain, A., Nandakumar, K., Ross, A.: Score normalization in multimodal biometric systems. Pattern Recogn. **38**(12), 2270–2285 (2005)

Reliability Investigation of Automatic Assessment of Learner-Build Concept Map with Kit-Build Method by Comparing with Manual Methods

Warunya Wunnasri$^{(\boxtimes)}$, Jaruwat Pailai, Yusuke Hayashi,
and Tsukasa Hirashima

Graduate School of Engineering, Hiroshima University, Higashihiroshima, Japan
{warunya,jaruwat,hayashi,tsukasa}@lel.hiroshima-u.ac.jp

Abstract. This paper describes an investigation into the reliability of an automatic assessment method of the learner-build concept map by comparing it with two well-known manual methods. We have previously proposed the Kit-Build (KB) concept map framework where a learner builds a concept map by using only a provided set of components, known as the set "kit". In this framework, instant and automatic assessment of a learner-build concept map has been realized. We call this assessment method the "Kit-Build method" (KB method). The framework and assessment method have already been practically used in classrooms in various schools. As an investigation of the reliability of this method, we have conducted an experiment to compare the assessment results of the method with the assessment results of two other manual assessment methods. In this experiment, 22 university students attended as subjects and four as raters. It was found that the scores of the KB method had a very strong correlation with the scores of the other manual methods. The results suggest that automatic assessment of the Kit-Build concept map can attain almost the same level of reliability as well-known manual assessment methods.

Keywords: Concept map assessment method · Kit-Build concept map · Reliability

1 Introduction

Concept maps were developed in 1972 in Novak and Musonda's research program [1] which investigated changes in children's knowledge of science. Novak and Musonda's research was based on the learning psychology of Ausubel et al. [2] which discussed the assimilation of new knowledge into existing knowledge by learners. A concept map represents conceptual understanding via connections and links between concepts. A concept in a concept map can be a term or symbol that is enclosed in a box, and a link is a line that is connected to two concepts. A linking word is a word on the link that represents the relationship between concepts. To build the concept map, creators have to organize their knowledge following their target. They can limit the scope of their concept map by constructing a concept map for answering the focus question. Then the

© Springer International Publishing AG 2017
E. André et al. (Eds.): AIED 2017, LNAI 10331, pp. 418–429, 2017.
DOI: 10.1007/978-3-319-61425-0_35

creators build a concept list from the main idea of the content and they order these concepts from general to more specific aiding in hierarchical construction. Proposition of the concept map, or unit of meaning, can be constructed from linking two or more concepts via a proper relationship. The concepts should be ordered by placing the general concept in the top hierarchy and specific concepts at the bottom [3]. Moreover, concept maps can help learners to significantly reduce their learning cognitive load, because concept maps assist in the integration of knowledge and facilitate learners in their independent learning and thinking [4]. Due to these characteristics, concept map is used to organize and represent knowledge extensively.

Afterward, the concept maps are used in a classroom situation for checking learners' understanding. Several educational researchers proposed the concept map assessment method for checking learners' understanding. These assessment methods, which are processed manually, are reasonable for evaluating concept maps, but they entail high costs, such as time and human workload, for scoring each concept map. Hence, an automatic concept map assessment is proposed for decreasing time cost and human workload.

The Kit-Build concept map (KB map) is a framework to realize automatic concept map assessment [5, 6]. In the KB map framework, a learner builds a concept map by using only a provided set of components, referred to as the set "kit". Instant and automatic assessment of a learner-build concept map, realized in this framework, is referred to as the "Kit-Build method" (KB method). In this framework, the set of components are made by decomposing a concept map that is built by a responsible teacher. This map is called the "teacher-build map". The responsible teacher is requested to build the teacher-build map as a criterion to assess a learner's compre-hension for a specific topic or teaching. Then, a learner is requested to build a concept map to express his/her comprehension for the same topic or teaching. Because all components of the learner-build map are the same as the teacher-build map, automatic assessment of a learner-build map is realized by comparing the learner-build map with the teacher-build map. KB map and assessment methods have already been practically used in classrooms in various schools, for example, in science learning in elementary schools [7, 8], geography in junior high schools [9], and the learning of English as a second language [10].

These practices have shown that the KB map is suitable for use in teaching situation where the instructor gives directions followed by instructor's interpretation. However, we have not previously compared the KB method with other well-known manual methods that are accepted as reliable. Although the automatic assessment method has advantages over manual assessment, for example, real time assessment/feedback, load reduction of the rater/teacher, etc., the reliability of automatic assessment requires investigation. In this study, the results of manual methods were assumed to be reliable and we compare the assessment results of the KB method with the assessment results of two other manual assessment methods. As the two manual methods, (1) structural scoring proposed by Novak and Gowin [11] and (2) relational scoring proposed by McClure and Bell [12] were adopted. We conducted an experiment where 22 university students were designated as subjects and four were designated as raters. The results of the experiment showed that the scores of the KB method had a statistically significant correlation with the scores of the other manual methods. The results suggest that automatic assessment using the KB method can attain almost the same level of reliability as well-known manual methods.

2 Overview of the Concept Map Assessment Method

2.1 Manual Concept Map Assessment Methods

A manual concept map assessment method is used by a human who can understand the meaning of words in the concept map well. The human is often called a "rater". In this study, we focus on the methods that pay attention to the structure of a concept map and the meaning of the proposition of a concept map.

Several concept map assessment methods evaluate the concept map by investigating the structure of the map, such as, the levels of the hierarchy, the characteristics of the branch, etc. In this study, we focus on the structural scoring of Novak and Gowin [11] as a typical structural method. This method gives high scores for each correct level of the hierarchy and each valid crosslink because ordering the concepts into the hierarchy, and connecting the crosslinks, can facilitate the constructor's creative thinking. However, structural scoring, which tends to score the structure more than the meaning, may be the cause of substantial meaning-leakage in a concept map.

Many manual assessment methods which pay more attention to the meaning of a proposition for scoring the concept map, rather than the structure, have been proposed. They focus on language and understanding of the representation. These meaningful methods always have a printed set of criteria as the rubric for assessing knowledge and giving feedback. From investigating various meaning methods, we focused on the relational scoring from McClure and Bell [12], which is referred to as relational scoring in this paper, and is a common concept map assessment method. In the study by McClure et al. [13], they requested 63 students to construct concept maps by using 20 provided concepts, creating their own linking words. Then, 12 raters scored individual maps by assessing each proposition on the concept map separately. The rater awarded scores of zero to three points for each proposition based on the suitability of the meaning of the proposition. The authors claimed that this method has the highest reliability when using the criteria map, (teacher-build map), using the holistic method and the structural method as comparisons (Novak and Gowin structural scoring). The authors confirmed this result by using the g-coefficient value. Based on these considerations, we have designed an experiment for testing the reliability of a manual method, similar to the experiment of McClure et al. We have selected the structural scoring proposed by Novak and Gowin, and the relational scoring proposed by McClure and Bell, to compare with the KB map proposed in the current study.

2.2 Kit-Build Concept Map and Automatic Assessment

The Kit-Build concept map framework is one of the automatic concept map assessment methods that use a teacher-build map to compare with the learner-build map by using exact matching at the propositional level. It is utilized in the form of a learning task or exercise for checking learners' comprehension of a topic that they have already learned. The task of the KB map is separated into two subtasks. The first is the segmentation task where a teacher is requested to prepare the teacher-build map, which is an expression of an eligible comprehension of the topic for the teacher. An example of the teacher-build map is illustrated in Fig. 1. After submitting the teacher-build map to the server, the teacher-build map is extracted to be the kit that contains a list of concepts and relationships from the teacher-build map. The kit from the teacher-build map in Fig. 1 is shown in Fig. 2. Moreover, this kit is provided to help learners to reduce their cognitive load more than the traditional concept map, where they must create all components themselves. Using the kit, the learners are required only to recognize the components.

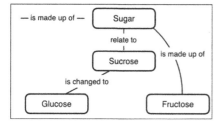

Fig. 1. Teacher-build map

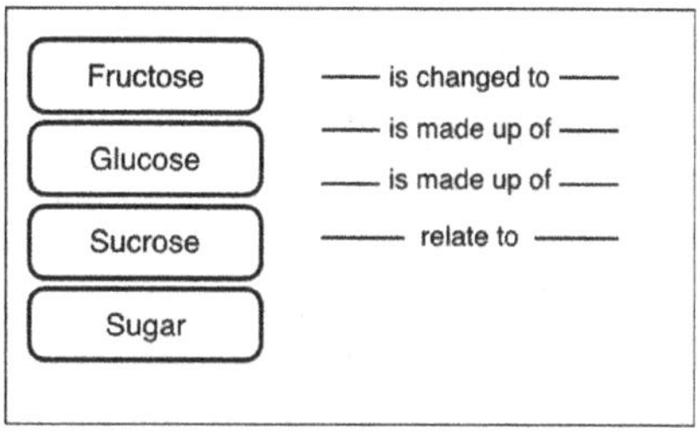

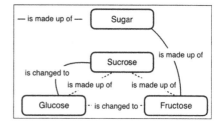

Fig. 2. Kit

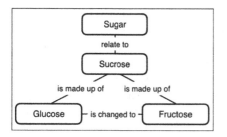

Fig. 3. Learner-build map

Fig. 4. Difference map

The second task is called the structuring task. Learners are given the learning task of reconstructing a concept map by using the kit, creating a map which is referred to as the learner-build map (Fig. 3). After the learner-build maps are uploaded to the server, the KB map will evaluate learner-build maps by exactly matching each learner's proposition with the teacher-build map's proposition. For example, the relationship between the concepts "Sugar" and "Sucrose" is checked. If the relationship is identified as "related to," the score for this learner-build map will increase by one point. In the case of the concepts "Sucrose" and "Glucose," if the learner connected them by using the relationship "is changed to," this does not exist in the teacher-build map. Following the teacher-build map, the relationship of this proposition should be "is made up of", so this proposition is not awarded any point from the system. This corresponds to the scoring by propositional level exact matching method. This method makes the KB map different from the manual methods which allow learners to create their own linking words, preventing the learner-build map from being straightforwardly compared with the criteria map. The manual methods require time for considering the meaning of each proposition carefully. After checking the connections of the learner-build maps by the propositional level exact matching, the system will generate a score in a percentage format. The instructor can also investigate learners' misunderstanding individually as a difference map and can find the overview of all learners by overlaying all learner-build map, as the group map, and the group-goal difference map on the analysis screen of the KB. In the difference map, three types of error link are represented as shown in Fig. 4. The lacking link, which is represented by a dashed line, is a link that exists in the teacher-build map but does not exist in learner-build map. The excessive link, which is shown as a solid line, is a link that occurs in learner-build map but does not occur in the teacher-build map. Lastly, a solid line that is not connected to any concepts in the learner-build map is the leaving link. The instructor can use these links to find the holistic leaking understanding of all learners. Following the KB map framework's ability, the instructor can use the KB map to check understanding of individuals or groups of learners, and can use the diagnosis result to discuss with learners the meaning of each of the error links. After error link analysis, the instructor can adjust the teacher-build map or teach learners about the content that learners have not understand completely.

In the other automatic methods, only a list of concepts is provided to learners. Because these methods also allow learners to create their own linking words, they cannot compare a learner-build map with the criteria map straightforwardly. Hence, they require synonym word matching, which is very flexible for evaluation using the meaning of words, but which has not yet reached a sufficient level of accuracy. In contrast, the KB map provides the kit which can be assessed by using the propositional level exact matching and can create informative diagnosis results. Moreover, the KB map can provide the group map and group-goal difference map, which can support the instructor in analyzing comprehension in both an individual learner and as an overview of the whole class. These are the prominent advantages of the KB map when it is utilized in a classroom situation.

3   Research Methodology

To confirm the reliability of the KB map, we designed an experimental procedure to compare the KB map and the manual methods in terms of their ability to assess the comprehension of learner on atopic. Usually, the KB map is used in teaching situations, however, it is desirable to ensure that the KB map as can be used in a reading situation also. Hence, the experiment was designed to operate in two learning situations. Moreover, to compare the difference between the KB map and the manual method, the important attributes of the concept map assessment method are shown in Table 1.

Two typical scoring methods, which are widely used for assessing concept maps, namely the structural scoring as structural level analysis, and the relational scoring as propositional level analysis, were chosen for comparison. The manual method is inferred from the research of McClure et al. [13], who provided a list of concepts to learners and requested that they construct concept maps by creating linking words themselves. The synonym matching method was used for evaluating the meaning of each proposition. However, the KB map provides both the concepts and the linking words, which are decomposed from the teacher-build map, to learners. Thus, the automatic exact matching method can be used for checking the correctness of each proposition.

Table 1. Comparison between the attributes of each concept map assessment method

Assessment method	Assessment			Provided items	
	Raters	Level of analysis	Matching method	Concepts words	Linking words
Structural scoring	Manual	Structural	Synonym	Provided	Not provided
Relational scoring	Manual	Propositional	Synonym	Provided	Not provided
Kit-Build concept map	Automate	Propositional	Exact	Provided	Provided

3.1 Subjects

Subjects for this study were recruited from university students who possessed a good level of English. The 22 students, who were volunteers from various education fields, were given the role of learners. They were given introductory training in concept maps before participating in the experiment. Four students, who were familiar with the use of the concept map and understood the content of the experiment material well, were assigned as raters. These raters were given an explanation of the procedure of each assessment method, and they were required to study the procedures carefully before scoring the learner-build map. In addition, one graduate student was assigned the role of instructor. The instructor was required to prepare the article and teaching material for the experiment and the instructor was also required to construct the teacher-build map following specific instructions. In this study, the article "Sugar", which uses common explanatory words, was chosen for the learning process. This article contained three sections, each covering one third of a page, defined as the introduction to sugar, types of sugar and how sugar is produced [14].

3.2 Map Production

Initially, the instructor chose a 1,594 word article, prepared the teaching materials and built the teacher-build map. The teacher-build map contained 15 concepts and 16 relationships. In the study, learners were requested to read the article in ten minutes, and they were then provided with the list of concepts. Next, they were required to create linking words by themselves for the construction of a concept map in 15 min using the CMapCloud application [15], as illustrated in Fig. 5. These learner-build maps were scored by the two manual methods. The learners were then asked to construct a concept map again in 15 min by integrating the kit of the KB map, which provided both a list of concepts and a list of linking words. The initial representation of the KB map in this experiment is shown in Fig. 6. After the learners had completely connected the propositions and uploaded their map to the server, these learner-build maps were evaluated using the KB map assessment method based on exact matching at the propositional level.

After the reading session concluded, the instructor taught learners based on the same reading article but following the instructor's interpretation using 16 slides delivered over ten minutes. Afterward, learners were required to construct the learner-build maps following the same procedure as in the reading situation, namely, constructing learner-build maps by creating linking words by themselves and integrating the kit to create a learner-build map using the KB map. When learners completed all learner-build map construction, they were asked to answer a questionnaire. The procedure of this experiment is displayed in Fig. 7.

Fig. 5. CMapCloud screen

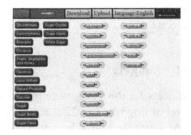

Fig. 6. Kit-Build concept map screen

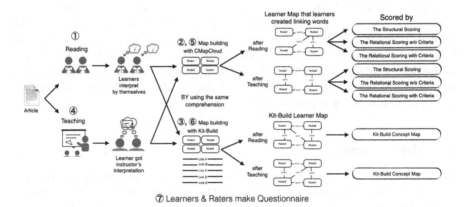

Fig. 7. Experiment procedure

3.3 Concept Map Scoring by Manual Methods

The concept maps, which were constructed using CMapCloud, were scored by three manual methods that contained, (a) the Novak and Gowin structural scoring (the structural scoring), (b) the McClure and Bell relational scoring without the criteria map (the relational scoring without criteria map) and (c) the McClure and Bell relational scoring with criteria map (the relational scoring with criteria map). The raters were required to read the instructions of each assessment method carefully without time restrictions. The score of the manual methods was normalized to a percentage score by using the perfect score for each method. After the scoring was completed, the raters were requested to complete the questionnaire. Procedures for each method were prepared based on the description in [13]. The reliability of the results of the manual methods is discussed in Sect. 4.

3.4 Questionnaires

The questionnaires were assigned to both raters and learners to assess their familiarity with concept mapping and their opinion of the experiment. For the raters, the questionnaire contained two parts. The first part of the questionnaire assessed their familiarity with the concept map and with the content of the article. The questionnaire also asked about their disposition when they were scoring the concept maps. The second part of the questionnaire requested raters to rank each scoring method in four aspects covering (i) hardness of decision, (ii) use of memory, (iii) time taken and (iv) reasonableness of the score.

For the learners' questionnaires, the aim was to assess their background in concept mapping and in the content of the article. A further aim was to understand how their experiences differed when constructing the concept maps by creating their own linking words and when using the KB map.

4 Experimental Results and Discussion

4.1 Correspondence of the KB Map and the Manual Method

The Reliability of the Manual Method
To confirm the KB map's reliability as a framework for assessing learners' comprehension of a topic by comparing with reliable manual methods, we aim to first investigate the reliability of the manual methods. The scores from three manual methods: (a) the structural scoring, (b) the relational scoring without criteria map and (c) the relational scoring with criteria map, were used to perform generalizability analysis through the GNOVA software [16] which returns the g-coefficient, as used in the reliability investigation by McClure et al. [13]. The g-coefficient is analogous to the reliability coefficient in classical test theory [17].

Table 2. The g-coefficient for each manual method and the study of McClure et al. [13]

	Current study		McClure's
	Reading	Teaching	
Structural scoring	0.7520	0.9029	0.23
Relational scoring w/o criteria	0.8659	0.8540	0.51
Relational scoring w/criteria	0.8874	0.9133	0.76

In this study, we interpret the g-coefficient as an estimate of score reliability assuming a single rater which shows the consistency of each scoring method as shown in Table 2. All values of G-coefficient of the current study are higher than values reported in McClure et al. [13]. Then, the scoring with the criteria map resulted in the highest score reliability in both reading and teaching situations, which is consistent with the investigation of McClure et al. which indicated that the relational scoring method is reliable in assessing the concept map. Based on these results, we concluded that the manual assessment conducted in this research is reliable and it is possible to evaluate reliability of KB map by comparing with the results of the manual assessment. As for the reason why the g-coefficient obtained in the current study is higher than that obtained by McClure et al. we guess that the current study was conducted with a smaller number of subjects and raters, that is, 12 raters in McClure et al., and 4 raters in the current study.

The Reliability of KB Method

To confirm the reliability of the KB map, a comparison between the KB map's result and the reliable manual method's result is required. The Pearson's correlation was computed using the R programming language and the correlation value is shown in Table 3. Following the strength of the correlation from Evans [18], the relational method with criteria map, which achieved the highest reliability score, has a very strong correlation with the KB map in both reading and teaching situations. This is because raters use the criteria map as a frame for their scoring, in a similar way to the teacher-build map used in the KB map. For the remaining methods, the results from the relational scoring without criteria map have a very strong correlation in the reading situation and strong correlation in the teaching situation. This is because the procedure of relational scoring without the criteria map is too wide for meaningful evaluation of the learner-build maps, which are constructed for checking the understanding following a specific teaching situation. The structural scoring has a strong correlation with the KB map in both situations, even though structural scoring scores the concept map by giving precedence to the structure of the concept map, which is a different approach compared to the KB map.

The results above suggest that the KB map can assess learners' comprehension of a topic as well as the manual concept map assessment methods. If the manual methods give a relatively high score to a learner, the KB map also has a high possibility of giving a relatively high score to the learner. In addition, learners who get a relatively low score from the manual methods, also have a high possibility of getting a relatively low score from the KB map. As indicated by the high correlation value, the KB map is reliable, and is comparable to the manual methods, in identifying learners' comprehension for a topic and evaluating the concept map.

Table 3. The correlations in scores between each manual method and the KB method

	KB in reading	KB in teaching
Structural scoring	0.7360	0.7360
Relational scoring w/o criteria	0.8532	0.7371
Relational scoring w/criteria	0.8671	0.8165

Note: Calculated Pearson product correlations are statistically significant as indicated by p-value < 0.01

4.2 Results of Questionnaire

Two sets of questionnaires were used in this study. The first questionnaire was for learners after they completed all of their tasks, this is presented in Table 4. From the learners' questionnaire analysis, learners who did not have existing knowledge about the learning material before obtained a good understanding of the content after reading. In addition, the learners could accept the instructor's interpretation clearly after they received an explanation in the teaching situation. When learners constructed their learner-build map by creating their own linking words, most of them concluded that they could represent their understanding adequately; similarly, users of the kit KB map were able to express their understanding appropriately. This summary suggests that the KB map is appropriate to use in supporting learners to express their understanding, and that it produces similar results to using the concept map where the linking words are created freely.

Table 4. A part of the learners' questionnaire

	Strongly disagree	Disagree	Neutral	Agree	Strongly agree
Learners know about concept map before	9%	14%	9%	55%	14%
Learners know about material before	18%	27%	9%	41%	5%
Learners can represent their understanding by using CMapCloud	0%	5%	18%	73%	5%
Learners can represent their understanding by using KB map	0%	5%	0%	36%	59%

For the raters' questionnaire, all raters identified their familiarity with using the concept map and their understanding of the learning material as strong confident. In the raters' ranking of the manual methods, which is illustrated in Fig. 8, the structural scoring was the hardest assessment method, because the rater had to decide on the suitability of each hierarchy and crosslink. Conversely, it was easiest to use the relational scoring with criteria map since the criteria map could be used as a guide for scoring. For the cost of scoring, the raters noted that the structural scoring and the relational scoring without criteria map used their memory load and time more than the relational scoring with criteria map. This was because of the difficulty in thinking about the learner-build map structure and recalling how previous learner-build maps were scored. For this challenge, the criteria map can help the scoring of the learner-build map by using the relational scoring with the criteria map. In the final question, the raters were requested them to rank the most reasonable method in their opinion. The relational scoring with criteria map achieved the highest rating. This ranking corresponds with the comparison between six concept map assessments by McClure et al. [13]. Hence, the strong correspondence between the KB map and the relational scoring with criteria map confirms that the propositional level with exact matching of the KB map is a reliable method to assess the efficiency of learning and the KB map can be used as an alternative automatic method for assessing the concept map.

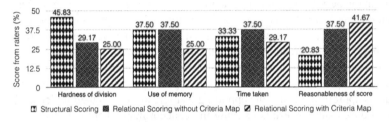

Fig. 8. A part of the score from the raters' questionnaire

5   Conclusion

This study investigates the reliability of the KB map in terms of its ability to identify the efficiency of learning. An experiment was designed to compare the KB map with three manual concept map assessment methods in reading and teaching situations. Selected manual methods contained structural scoring, (which investigates the composition of the concept map straightforwardly), relational scoring without the criteria map, and relational scoring with the criteria map. The relational scoring gives precedence to the meaning of propositions and is reasonable for evaluating understanding from a concept map, but requires expert checking and significant time input for scoring. These manual methods provide flexible and meaningful concept map assessment, and their reliability is widely accepted. However, they are inconvenient due to the limited class time that instructors have to complete a unit of instruction. In this study, the KB map was compared with the manual methods to test the assumption that the KB map is reliable in identifying the efficiency of learning. From this study, the results show a strong and significant correlation between the KB map and the manual methods in both the teaching and reading situations. The KB map has the highest correlation with the relational scoring with criteria map, achieving the most reliability score (g-coefficient) in both learning situations. Moreover, the learner-build map scores of the KB map were similar to the manual methods. Based on these results, it is concluded that the reliability of the KB map assessment is comparable to the manual methods.

References

1. Novak, J.D., Musonda, D.: A twelve-year longitudinal study of science concept learning. Am. Educ. Res. J. **28**(1), 117–153 (1991)
2. Ausubel, D.P., Novak, J.D., Hanesian, H.: Educational Psychology: A Cognitive View, 2nd edn. Holt, Rinehart and Winston, New York (1978)
3. Novak, J.D., Cañas, A.J.: Technical Report IHMC CmapTools. Institute for Human and Machine Cognition, Ocala (2008)
4. Hu, M.L.M., Wu, M.H.: The effect of concept mapping on students' cognitive load. World Trans. Eng. Technol. Educ. **10**(2), 134–137 (2012)
5. Hirashima, T., Yamasaki, K., Fukuda, H., Funaoi, H.: Kit-Build concept map for automatic diagnosis. In: Biswas, G., Bull, S., Kay, J., Mitrovic, A. (eds.) AIED 2011. LNCS, vol. 6738, pp. 466–468. Springer, Heidelberg (2011). doi:10.1007/978-3-642-21869-9_71
6. Hirashima, T., Yamasaki, K., Fukuda, H., Funaoi, H.: Framework of Kit-Build concept map for automatic diagnosis and its preliminary use. Res. Pract. Technol. Enhanced Learn. **10**(1), 1–21 (2015)
7. Sugihara, K., Osada, T., Nakata, S., Funaoi, H., Hirashima, T.: Experimental evaluation of Kit-Build concept map for science classes in an elementary school. In: Proceedings of Computers in Education 2012, pp. 17–24. National Institute of Education, Singapore (2012)
8. Yoshida, K., Sugihara, K., Nino, Y., Shida, M., Hirashima, T.: Practical use of Kit-Build concept map system for formative assessment of learners' comprehension in a lecture. In: Proceedings of Computers in Education 2013, pp. 906–915. Asia-Pacific Society for Computers in Education, Bali (2013)
9. Nomura, T., Hayashi, Y., Suzuki, T., Hirashima, T.: Knowledge propagation in practical use of Kit-Build concept map system in classroom group work for knowledge sharing. In: Proceeding of International Conference on Computers in Education Workshop 2014, pp. 463–472. ICCE 2014 Organizing Committee, Nara (2014)
10. Alkhateeb, M., Hayashi, Y., Hirashima, T.: Comparison between Kit-Build and Scratch-Build concept mapping methods in supporting EFL reading comprehension. J. Inf. Syst. Educ. **14**(1), 13–27 (2015)
11. Novak, J.D., Gowin, D.B.: Learning How to Learn. Cambridge University Press, New York (1984)
12. McClure, J.R., Bell, P.E.: Effects of an Environmental Education Related STS Approach Instruction on Cognitive Structures of Pre-service Science Teachers. State University, Pennsylvania (1990)
13. McClure, J.R., Sonak, B., Suen, H.K.: Concept map assessment of classroom learning: reliability, validity, and logistical practicality. J. Res. Sci. Teach. **36**(4), 475–492 (1999)
14. Klaus, R.: Sugar (2013). http://www.english-online.at/biology/sugar/sugar-carbohy-drate-that-gives-us-energy.htm. Accessed 01 Aug 2016
15. The Institute for Human and Machine Cognition. (2014). Cmap Cloud & CmapTools in the Cloud. http://cmap.ihmc.us/cmap-cloud/. Accessed Aug 2016
16. Brennan, R.L.: Elements of Generalizability Theory. American College Testing Program (1983)
17. Webb, N.M., Shavelson, R.J.: Generalizability theory: overview. In: Everitt, B.S., Howell D.C. (eds.) Encyclopedia of Statistics in Behavioral Science, vol. 2, pp. 717–719. Wiley, Chichester (2005)
18. Evans, J.D.: Straightforward Statistics for the Behavioral Sciences. Brooks/Cole, Boston (1996)

Characterizing Students' Learning Behaviors Using Unsupervised Learning Methods

Ningyu Zhang$^{(\boxtimes)}$, Gautam Biswas, and Yi Dong

Department of Electrical Engineering and Computer Science,
Institute for Software Integrated Systems, Vanderbilt University,
1025 16th Avenue South, Nashville, TN 37212, USA
{ningyu.zhang,gautam.biswas,yi.dong}@vanderbilt.edu

Abstract. In this paper, we present an unsupervised approach for characterizing students' learning behaviors in an open-ended learning environment. We describe our method for generating metrics that describe a learner's behaviors and performance using Coherence Analysis. Then we combine feature selection with a clustering method to group students by their learning behaviors. We characterize the primary behaviors of each group and link these behaviors to the students' ability to build correct models as well as their learning gains derived from their pre- and post-test scores. Finally, we discuss how this behavior characterization may contribute to a framework for adaptive scaffolding of learning behaviors.

Keywords: Open-ended learning environments · Coherence analysis · Learner behaviors · Unsupervised learning · Feature selection

1 Introduction

Open-ended learning environments (OELEs) provide learners with an authentic and meaningful learning experience by engaging them in problem-solving activities that combine constructing, testing, and revising their evolving solutions [1]. However, novice learners often face difficulties in developing and applying the knowledge and strategies they need to succeed [2], and, therefore, may need scaffolding and feedback to develop these proficiencies [5].

Our research group has developed CTSiM – an OELE that promotes synergistic learning of science and computational thinking (CT) concepts using a "learning by modeling" approach. In CTSiM, students build their simulation models using an agent-based, block-structured visual language and are provided with additional tools to help them test and verify their models [3, 4]. Pre- and post-tests in previous studies conducted with CTSiM have demonstrated that students show significant learning gains in the science content knowledge as well as CT skills. However, we have also documented a number of difficulties that middle school students face in developing and applying their domain knowledge and computational modeling skills as they construct their science models in CTSiM [4]. Students employ a variety of strategies to support their learning and model building tasks, yet suboptimal strategies often hinder their learning experience and add to their difficulties in building correct models. To help

© Springer International Publishing AG 2017
E. André et al. (Eds.): AIED 2017, LNAI 10331, pp. 430–441, 2017.
DOI: 10.1007/978-3-319-61425-0_36

students overcome these difficulties, we have found it important to develop adaptive feedback mechanisms that are built upon automated detection, identification, and assessment of students' learning behaviors [4].

In this paper, we discuss an exploratory machine learning approach to identify learner behaviors and present a case study to determine the effectiveness of this approach. Section 2 of the paper introduces the learning activities students can perform in CTSiM. Section 3 presents the metrics that form the feature space characterizing students learning behaviors, followed by feature selection and the application of a clustering algorithm to find groups of prevalent learner behaviors. Section 4 introduces the experimental setting from which we collected student activity data for this analysis, and results of applying our unsupervised learning method to these data. Finally, Sect. 5 discusses how the characteristic learning behavior may form a framework for adaptive scaffolding in CTSiM.

2 The Learning Environment

Students' learning and model building activities in CTSiM involve a mixture of five primary activities: (1) viewing and acquiring information about domain content and CT-related concepts from hypertext resource libraries; (2) constructing an abstract conceptual model of the science scenario using an agent-based framework (which defines the relevant properties and behaviors associated with the agents that operate in that environment); (3) building computational models of agent behaviors using a block-structured visual language; (4) executing their models to analyze the behaviors generated as NetLogo simulations [7]; and (5) verifying the correctness of their models by comparing them to the behaviors generated by an expert model that runs synchronously with theirs. The model building and behavior comparison interfaces are illustrated in Fig. 1, and more details of the CTSiM system that has been successfully deployed in middle school science classrooms can be found in [3, 4].

In previous classroom studies with CTSiM, we have deployed a learning progression that consists of two introductory training activities and three primary modeling activities. In a typical study, students become familiar with the system interfaces and functionality by constructing agents that draw shapes and spirals to learn basic kinematics. The three learning units cover modeling tasks in two science topics: (1) advanced kinematics (unit 3), where students model a rollercoaster car moving along a track, and (2) ecology, where students first build a macroscopic model of a fish tank (unit 4) followed by a microscopic model (unit 5). In the macroscopic model, students implement behaviors for fish and aquatic plants as well as the food chain. However, this model is unstable. Realizing this, in unit 5 students add microscopic phenomena involving bacteria and the waste cycle to build a sustainable model of the fish tank ecosystem. Previous studies have shown that students synergistically learn science and CT concepts through their model building activities in CTSiM [3, 4].

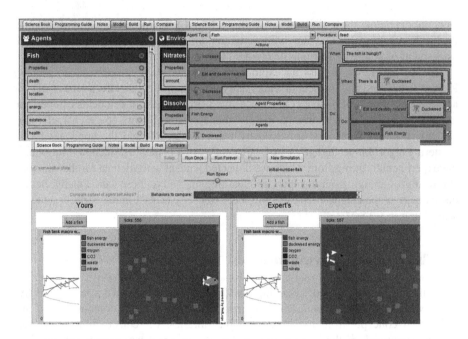

Fig. 1. CTSiM: conceptual, computational, and behavior comparison interfaces.

3 Methods

When building models in CTSiM, students adopt different learning and problem-solving strategies, and therefore, demonstrate a variety of learning behaviors. Rather than designing our feedback mechanisms based on individual behaviors and strategies, our approach has been to form aggregate characterizations of student behaviors and to develop adaptive scaffolding mechanisms that are tuned to these aggregated grouping of behaviors. To accomplish this, we first describe student behaviors based on a number of metrics that are related to a task model we have created to analyze student work in CTSiM. Given this feature space of metrics, we apply a feature selection method to select the metrics that are most relevant to grouping students by their relevant behavior characteristics, and then apply the K-means clustering algorithm to group students by common behavior characteristics. We describe this approach in greater detail below.

3.1 Deriving Measures that Describe Student Learning Behaviors

In previous work, we have developed Coherence analysis (CA) as a general model-driven analytical framework for analyzing students' learning and problem-solving behaviors in OELEs [5, 6]. CA and performance metrics together define the feature space for describing students learning behaviors in the system. Our theory-driven framework adopts a top-down approach to identify students' actions in an OELE into one of three task types: (1) *information acquisition* (IA), (2) *solution construction* (SC), and (3) *solution assessment* (SA) [5]. Each of these task categories can be hierarchically broken down into subtasks, with the leaves of the hierarchy representing individual actions that students can perform in CTSiM. IA tasks cover searching, identifying, and comprehending information necessary for building and correcting models in relevant resource library pages. SC tasks involve constructing and refining the conceptual and computational models. An SC action represents edits to the conceptual or computational models, e.g., adding a property to an agent or removing a block from the agent. SA tasks cover running simulations with the student-constructed computational model and comparing model behaviors to an expert model's behavior as described in Sect. 2. Students are free to perform activities in any order, and tracking how they combine and switch between activities informs us of their learning and problem-solving strategies [5].

In [5], we defined a performance measure for an action as a unary relation called *effectiveness*, which captures whether the action contributes to a correct solution. For example, adding a correct component to or removing an incorrect component from the computational model represent an effective action. Going beyond individual actions, the CA framework defines a *support* relation between two actions x and y, $x \rightarrow y$ (i.e., y follows x), if the subsequent action y uses information generated by the prior action x, x provides support for y, and y is supported by x [5]. We apply CTSiM's CA frame work to specify a set of 22 measures that describe a student's use of learning strategies. In addition to the unary and binary measures defined above, we use a third set of measures called *proportional*, which capture the percentage of a specific type of action in the task hierarchy. For example, *Compare Percentage* describes the proportion of students' model comparison actions in the total number of actions they perform.

3.2 Selecting Features and Generating Clusters

Of the 22 CA measures that we defined, it is likely that some of them have relatively small variance across the set of students. Since these measures would not provide much information toward differentiating students according to their behaviors, we decided to apply a feature selection method that retained only those measures that contributed significantly to generating the clusters.

We used a Sparse Clustering method for feature selection [8] as a pre-processing step before running the K-means clustering algorithm. Sparse Clustering adaptively chooses a subset of the features using a LASSO-type penalty with the Gap statistics as the criterion for the selection of features [8]. Instead of assigning weights to all features, we tweaked the algorithm in the following manner: for a number of clusters K ($2 \leq K \leq 10$), sort and select the features by the weight assigned to them for the current number of clusters, K. Continue until the sum of the feature weights exceeds 90% of the weight bound [8] for the current K. After working across all cluster numbers, we took the union of all of the selected features by the procedure above. The value 10 is an empirical cut-off value for the maximum number of clusters, taking into account that smaller number of clusters reduces the complexity in interpreting the data, and also because our dataset included 98 students. After the pre-processing step, we ran the K-means clustering algorithm on the selected feature set, varying K from small to large numbers. Much like ensemble methods, we used the majority vote on the number of clusters indicated by 30 well-established validity indices (e.g. Dunn, Calinski and Harabasz) [9]. Following this, we identified the unique learning behaviors that characterized each of the clusters, using t-tests to establish the significance of those features in comparison to the rest of the data. We then used the significant features that distinguished each to the clusters to profile students learning behaviors for those clusters. We ran analyses on data collected from a classroom study with 98 students from a middle school in Nashville, TN. The metrics that formed the feature space for characterizing students' behaviors are presented in Table 1.

Table 1. CA metrics and descriptions (*. Selected by feature selection algorithm)

CA metric	Category	Description
Domain read time *CT read time	Unary	The time (in seconds) a student spends on reading domain or CT content pages
Domain IA coherence CT IA coherence	Binary	The percentage of the supported domain or CT reading actions
*Conceptual model edit *Computational model edit	Proportional	The percentage of conceptual or computational model edits in a student's total actions
Conceptual edit effectiveness Computational edit effectiveness	Proportional	The percentage of a student's effective (reducing the model distance) conceptual or computational model edit actions
Conceptual edit coherence Computational edit coherence	Binary	The percentage of a student's supported conceptual or computational model edit actions
*Average conceptual edit size *Average computational edit size	Unary	The average number of consecutive conceptual or computational model edit actions
*Test percentage *Compare percentage	Proportional	The percentage of model test or model comparison actions
*Compare model in parts	Proportional	The percentage of comparisons that explicitly chooses a subset of the agent's behavior(s) for comparison with the expert model
IA to SC transition IA to SA transition *SC to IA transition *SC to SA transition *SA to IA transition *SA to SC transition	Binary	The transitions from one category of learning activity to another. These metrics provide information on the source of coherence given to an action as well as show a flow of learning activities

4   Classroom Study and Results

The study conducted in a 6th-grade classroom (11–13-year-olds) was administered daily for three weeks during the students' one-hour science class. On day 1, all participants took paper-and-pencil based pre-tests on (1) kinematics, (2) ecology, and

(3) CT topics. On day 2, all students had a short lecture on agent-based modeling concepts and the CTSiM learning environment. On day 3, students worked together as a class on Unit 1 (drawing equilateral polygons). On day 4, students worked individually on Unit 2 (drawing spirals shapes). Students then worked individually on Unit 3, building the rollercoaster model on days 5 and 6. On day 7, students took the kinematics post-test and the first CT post-test. On days 8–12, students worked individually to model the ecological processes in a fish tank ecosystem, first a macroscopic model (Unit 4), and then an added on the microscopic model (Unit 5). Finally, all students took the ecology post-test and the second CT post-test. Due to space limitations, this paper only discusses our analysis of data for the rollercoaster and macroscopic fish tank activities.

Pre- and post-test results showed that participants had significant learning gains in kinematics and ecology, as well as in computational thinking skills. Table 2 summarizes the pre-test and post-test scores for kinematics, ecology, and CT. Because students took two post-tests in CT (one after Rollercoaster and one after the Fish tank modeling activity), we used the first post-test as the pre-test scores to block the residual influence from the rollercoaster unit and investigate the effect from the fish tank modeling activity individually. On an aggregated level, the participants showed significant learning gains for kinematics and ecology science content, as well as CT concepts and skills on all assessments. A more detailed analysis of the synergistic learning gains of the domain and CT contents was reported in [4].

Table 2. Means (and standard deviations) of assessment scores

Assessment	Pre-test	Post-test	t-statistic	p-value	Cohen's d
Kinematics	14.71 (6.76)	19.17 (6.95)	4.55	<0.00001	0.83
CT 1	2.87 (2.36)	3.98 (2.47)	3.21	0.002	0.52
Ecology	8.45 (4.31)	22.41 (9.52)	13.22	<0.00001	1.68
CT 2	3.98 (2.47)	4.81 (2.36)	2.40	0.02	0.48

4.1 Cluster Analysis Results for the Rollercoaster Modeling Activity

We applied the K-means clustering algorithm on the subset of metrics picked by feature selection (using the procedure in Sect. 3.2 and the optimal cluster size of 6). The Euclidean metric was used as the distance measure, and 1000 random restarts were performed to mitigate the effects of initial cluster center selection. Table 3 summarizes the mean values (and standard deviations) of the metrics for all of the derived clusters.

We also used the clustering results to compare the learning performance of the clusters. Table 4 presents the learning performance measures: learning gains from the pre- to post-tests (Domain and CT), and the model distance from the student-build models to the canonical expert model (conceptual and computational). Model distances closer to 0 represent better modeling performance.

With the approach described in Sect. 3.2, we used the most significant features to label the individual clusters as the following. Cluster 1: the *CT learners* ($n = 2$). Students in this cluster spent the largest amount of time ($p < 0.00001$) viewing the

Table 3. Cluster means of the rollercoaster modeling activity (*. p < 0.05)

Metrics	CT learners (n = 2)	Aimless comparators (n = 24)	Efficient learners (n = 2)	Non-strategic testers (n = 18)	Tinkerers (n = 36)	Unsystematic builders (n = 16)
CT read	1474*(506)	11 (24)	105 (139)	28 (45)	56 (110)	34 (59)
Conc. edt %	8.8 (4.8)	4.0* (1.9)	10.2 (6.3)	6.3 (3.1)	5.0* (2.1)	11.7* (7.5)
Comp. edt %	23.0 (1.2)	22.9* (4.9)	45.5(14)	28.9 (5.1)	35.3 (5.3)	47.4* (6.6)
Concep. Size	6.0 (2.4)	8.7 (3.9)	10.5 (0.7)	5.3* (2.7)	8.1 (4.2)	6.4 (3.2)
Comp. size	4.4 (0.8)	4.4* (0.8)	5.0 (1.4)	3.9* (0.6)	6.0* (1.1)	6.7* (2.1)
Test %	48*(10.7)	34.2 (4.5)	16.5* (4.6)	44.4* (6.0)	34.7 (4.3)	29.7* (5.5)
Compare %	17.1 (15)	37.4* (6.3)	6.8 (1.4)	16.8* (4.9)	21.4 (5.0)	8.7* (3.4)
Compare part	13.8 (19.5)	34.0* (5.2)	58.3*(11.8)	20.4*(12.9)	31.9* (8.2)	15.6*(13.9)
SC to IA %	1.9 (0.6)	0.3* (0.4)	3.5* (3.7)	1.1 (1.3)	0.6 (0.8)	0.7 (0.7)
SC to SA %	16.3 (6.5)	20.5* (4.4)	11.7 (3.8)	21.3* (3.8)	14.1* (2.6)	12.4* (4.3)
SA to IA %	0.7 (0.3)	0.4 (0.4)	8.7* (1.4)	0.8 (0.5)	0.7 (1.0)	0.8 (1.3)
SA to SC %	6.8 (2.3)	7.3* (1.6)	25* (2.7)	12.2 (3.7)	9.8* (2.4)	18.4* (5.5)

Table 4. Means (and standard deviations) of learning performance by cluster in RC

Cluster	Domain gain	CT gain	Conc. dist.	Comp. dist.
Efficient learners (n = 2)	11.00 (8.49)	3.00 (1.41)	9.50 (0.71)	12.00 (0)
Tinkerers (n = 36)	4.99 (5.05)	1.44 (2.27)	8.44 (1.96)	13.5 (11.3)
Non-strat. testers (n = 18)	5.50 (6.40)	0.64 (2.05)	8.39 (1.54)	14.00 (8.93)
Unsys. builders (n = 16)	3.59 (6.22)	1.09 (1.27)	9.38 (1.96)	12.44 (5.15)
A. comparators (n = 24)	3.52 (3.73)	0.73 (2.46)	8.08 (1.77)	15.83 (11.28)
CT learners (n = 2)	−2.75 (0.35)	2.00 (0)	7.00 (0)	19.50 (3.54)
All students (n = 98)	4.46 (5.39)	1.11 (2.12)	8.49 (1.84)	14.09 (9.84)

programming guide pages in CTSiM. They expended significant effort in testing the computational models (mean = 48%, $p = 0.015$, averaging 116 actions). This cluster was the only group that had negative learning gains on the kinematics test, and their final computational model distance was the largest. However, their CT gain was high and their conceptual model distance was the smallest.

Cluster 2: the *aimless comparators* ($n = 24$). Students in this cluster had the smallest percentage of conceptual model edit actions ($p = 0.0047$, averaging 125 actions) and computational model edit actions ($p < 0.00001$, averaging 187 actions). They also had the fewest transitions between SC-IA actions ($p = 0.015$). Interestingly, the effort they put into comparing their simulation results to the expert simulation was also the highest ($p < 0.00001$, averaging 210 actions). In addition, their comparisons were finer grained ($p = 0.0064$) as 37.4% of the comparisons were performed in parts. The aimless comparators also had a high SC-SA transition rate ($p < 0.0001$), yet the SA-SC transition was very low ($p < 0.00001$). In other words, the aimless comparators did not seem to come back to refer to the resources even when they had errors in their models. It is also noteworthy that students in this cluster performed the largest number of actions (*mean* = 555, $p < 0.0001$) among all groups. In sum, as indicated by the unbalanced transitions between SC and SA actions, the aimless comparators frequently utilized the model comparison activities but were not effective in using the feedback from the comparison. Meanwhile, they had below average learning performance even though their pre-test scores were above average.

Cluster 3: the *efficient learners* ($n = 2$). Students in this cluster had the lowest percentage of actions testing their computational model ($p < 0.001$, averaging 23 actions) yet they applied the comparing model in parts strategy most frequently ($p < 0.001$). In addition, they had the highest SC-IA ($p < 0.0001$), SA-IA ($p < 0.00001$), and SA-SC ($p < 0.001$) transitions, which indicates that they frequently referred to the resource libraries in problem solving and actively modified their models based on the comparison results. They also made the fewest number of total actions (*mean* = 130, $p < 0.001$). The efficient learner cluster achieved the highest learning gains in both kinematics and CT. They had the lowest computational model distance, yet their conceptual model distance was the highest. This inconsistency can be explained by two of their CA metrics *Conceptual Model Edit Percentage* and *Average Conceptual Edit Size*: 10.2% of their total 130 actions (≈ 13.3) were conceptual model edit actions, and the average edit chunk size was 10.5. This indicates that the cluster finished the conceptual model in one attempt and did not see the need to come back and revise it. Perhaps, because of their better understanding of the content, they did not need the conceptual model as a scaffold for model building.

Cluster 4: the *non-strategic testers* ($n = 18$). The most distinguishing characteristics of this cluster was the high percentage of model testing ($p < 0.00001$, averaging 172 actions), relatively low percentage of model comparisons ($p = 0.027$, averaging 70 actions), and low strategic use of model comparison ($p < 0.001$). This cluster had the highest SC-SA transition rates (*mean* = 21.3%, $p < 0.0001$) yet the SA-SC transitions were around the average, indicating that the students tested their model very often, but did not edit the model frequently after the testing. Therefore, we might characterize their behaviors as trial-and-error rather than strategic. Additionally, this group was not very active; their total number of actions were small (*mean* = 252, $p < 0.001$). In terms of performance, the non-strategic testers had above average gains in kinematics and the lowest gains in CT, but heir model distances were below average.

Cluster 5: the *tinkerers* ($n = 36$). This cluster had a low percentage of conceptual model edits ($p = 0.03$, averaging 19 actions). They had frequent applications of the compare model in parts strategy ($p = 0.017$) and relatively low SC-SA transitions ($p < 0.0001$), which indicates that their SA actions were less frequent yet fine-grained. The tinkerers were balanced on the other measures. Because of these traits of the cluster, we adopt a definition of tinkering similar to [10], i.e., tinkerers used just-in-time planning and active exploration to make the most of the feedback from the environment. Therefore, *tinkerers* differ from the users who haphazardly perform trial-and-error strategies and those who purposelessly game the system. The tinkerers were the only group that performed better than the average in all of the measures, indicating those who tinkered systematically with extensive interactions with the learning environment might benefit more than those who adopt the ad hoc learning strategies.

Cluster 6: the *unsystematic builder* ($n = 16$). Students in this cluster had the highest number of SC actions (averaging 23 and 122 actions with both p-values <0.0001). Yet they tested and compared their models infrequently ($p < 0.00001$, averaging 79 actions, and $p = 0.027$, averaging 23 actions, respectively). They also had the lowest percentage of comparison in parts ($p = 0.007$) and the lowest SC-SA transition rate ($p < 0.00001$). The behaviors of this cluster were the opposite of the aimless comparators' yet the two clusters both had below average learning gains. This cluster also had the biggest final conceptual model distance ($p < 0.034$) compared to the rest of students.

4.2   Cluster Analysis of the Fish Tank Macro Modeling Activity

We used the same validity indices on the data collected from the fish tank macro modeling activity to evaluate the optimal cluster size, which was also 6. The significant characteristics of the rollercoaster clusters were preserved in the fish tank unit, and we labeled the six distinct profiles the same except for the *dedicated comparators*. In both units, (1) the CT learners had long CT reading times but low percentages in computational model edits, comparisons, and low SA-SC transition rates. (2) The comparators had the highest percentage in comparisons and SA-SC transition rates but the lowest percentages in SC actions. (3) The efficient learners had the highest SA-SC transition rates and highly strategic use of comparisons, also featuring the lowest total actions and percentages of SA actions. (4) The non-strategic testers had the highest percentage of model tests yet low percentage in model comparisons and the fewest usage of the compare model in parts strategy. (5) The tinkerers had high computational model edit percentages, strategic use of comparisons, and the highest SA to SC transition rates as well as the lowest percentage of testing actions. Finally, (6) the unsystematic builder had very high percentages in SC actions as well as lower percentage and coherence in SA actions.

We named the comparators in the fish tank unit *dedicated* because their model comparison effort became finer grained as the *Compare Model in Parts Percentage* rose from 34% to 66%, and their learning gains in ecology were better than kinematics. We believe this is related to the increase in difficulty level for the fish tank modeling activity – as the trial-and-error strategies became less likely leading to building correct models, the importance of learning and taking hints from the behaviors of the *expert model* increased.

In terms of learning performance in the ecology unit, (1) the CT learners had the highest learning gains in CT and almost the lowest learning gains in ecology. Their conceptual model distance was larger than the average, and they had the greatest computational model distance. (2) The dedicated comparators had the smallest model distance in the conceptual models ($p < 0.01$). Their gain in ecology and the computational model distance were also better than the average. (3) The efficient learners showed the highest learning gains in ecology, and the difference was significant ($p < 0.01$). By looking at this cluster, we realize that the most successful learners overcame model building challenges early to generate succinct and efficient solutions. They achieved the highest learning performance both in the system and in the paper-based tests, even though they started with lower pre-test scores. (4) The non-strategic testers had the lowest learning gains in ecology ($p = 0.01$) and the biggest distances in both the conceptual ($p < 0.001$) and computational ($p = 0.005$) models. (5) The tinkerers achieved the smallest computational model distance and their performance was around the average in other measurements. (6) The unsystematic builders were close to the average on all measures.

4.3   Transition Between Clusters Across Modeling Activities

Finally, we investigated how individual student's behaviors changed across the two model building activities. We found that students' problem-solving approaches fluctuated as the domain of the content and difficulty level of the units changed. We hypothesized (see previous work [4, 11, 12]) that students would develop their IA, SC, and SA skills as well as learn strategies as they progressed through units, and this would result in better performance and also a better use of learning strategies in subsequent units. To understand how students' learning behaviors changed across units of different domains, we analyzed students' transitions from the RC to the Fish Macro unit.

Table 5. Across-unit cluster transitions

Rollercoaster	Fish Macro					
	CT learner	Dedicat. comparator	Efficient learner	Non-strategic tester	Tinkerer	Unsystematic builder
CT Learner	0	2	0	0	0	0
A. comparator	2	19	0	1	2	0
Effi. learner	1	0	0	0	0	1
Non-str. tester	0	4	0	5	0	9
Tinkerer	0	16	4	3	6	7
Unsys. builder	0	1	3	4	6	2

As shown in Table 5, 32 of 98 students ($\approx 33\%$) remained in the same cluster. For the 66 students who made a transition, 45($\approx 68\%$) transferred to clusters with better learning performance. The sizes of better performing clusters increased as the efficient learner cluster increased from 3 to 7, and the dedicated comparators were 18 more than the aimless comparator; meanwhile, the sizes of worse performing clusters decreased: unsystematic builders shrank from 39 to 19, and nonstrategic testers decreased from 19 to 13. Additionally, the tinkerers who had average learning performance reduced from 36 to 14, as 20 tinkerers transferred to better-performing clusters (4 efficient learners and 16 dedicated comparators). Therefore, students adopted more strategic and coherent learning strategies in the fish tank unit. The two CT learners became dedicated comparators in the Fish tank macro unit. The majority of aimless comparators (19 of 24) maintained similar learning behaviors and became dedicated comparators. None of the comparators became the worst performing unsystematic builder. The learning performance of students who transferred to be a better or worse cluster and those who remained the same cluster are summarized in Table 6.

Table 6. Learning performance by transition type

Type	Domain gain	CT gain	Conc. dist.	Comp. dist.
Transfer better ($n = 64$)	15.75 (7.98)	0.83 (1.68)	35.83 (3.29)	52.95 (32.45)
Transfer worse ($n = 21$)	10.95 (7.28)	0.85 (1.51)	39.4 (4.05)	76.3 (23.24)
Remain ($n = 13$)	10.42 (7.38)	0.96 (2.16)	37.5 (3.28)	62.08 (38.42)

This result shows that not only did students transition to better performing clusters, but their overall performance in the model building also improved. However, deeper analyses may need to be conducted to better understand how students' performance and behaviors transition over shorter time periods, e.g., from day to day, so that we may design adaptive feedback mechanisms to support their learning.

5 Discussion and Conclusions

We have presented a combined study of learner behaviors and performance that demonstrates that the clusters are indicative of students' performance in modeling and pre-post learning gains. As a result, the study of each cluster's specific learning characteristics provides us many insights into how we may design adaptive scaffolds for each cluster. We are integrating our methods of deriving CA metrics and clustering into the latest version of CTSiM so that the six behavior types indicated by our clusters reported in this paper can be used to characterize and analyze students' learning behaviors online. We are also working on enhancing the adaptive feedback functionality of CTSiM by delivering suggestions of learning strategies via conversations using a pedagogical software agent. For example, while it is less advisable for the rest of the clusters, trial-and-error strategies could be helpful for the CT learners to get more engaged in learning. It is meaningful to encourage the CT learners to more actively edit their models and make more comparisons with the expert model. We believe the cluster-specific feedback generated with this approach is more holistic and effective compared to performing anomaly detection on multivariate behavioral measurements because the latter assumes that closeness to the means indicates good learning behaviors and lacks the semantics describing the relationship between the measurements.

In this paper, we have presented our generalizable approaches to (1) define actions in an OELE, (2) measure the coherence between students' actions using Coherence Analysis, and (3) selecting the most significant metrics that characterize students' learning behaviors. By analyzing students' specific learning behaviors, we gained insights into distinct behaviors and strategies that students employ. In addition, we showed that students who had a good understanding of the learning tasks and solved problems strategically performed better than ad hoc learners. Finally, we found that a majority of students autonomously improved their learning behaviors and use of strategies in later units.

Acknowledgements. This work has been supported by NSF Cyberlearning Grant #1441542.

References

1. Land, S.: Cognitive requirements for learning with open-ended learning environments. Educ. Tech. Res. Dev. **48**(3), 61–78 (2000)
2. Winslow, L.E.: Programming pedagogy—a psychological overview. ACM SIGCSE Bull. **28**(3), 17–22 (1996)
3. Sengupta, P., et al.: Integrating computational thinking with K-12 science education using agent-based computation: a theoretical framework. Educ. Inf. Technol. **18**(2), 351–380 (2013)
4. Basu, S., Biswas, G., Kinnebrew, J.S.: Learner modeling for adaptive scaffolding in a computational thinking-based science learning environment. User Model. User-Adapt. Interact. (2017). doi:10.1007/s11257-017-9187-0
5. Kinnebrew, J., Segedy, J.R., Biswas, G.: Integrating model-driven and data-driven techniques for analyzing learning behaviors in open-ended learning environments. IEEE Trans. Learn. Technol. (2017). doi:10.1109/TLT.2015.2513387
6. Segedy, J.R., Kinnebrew, J.S., Biswas, G.: Using coherence analysis to characterize self-regulated learning behaviours in open-ended learning environments. J. Learn. Anal. **2**(1), 13–48 (2015)
7. Wilensky, U.: NetLogo. Center for Connected Learning and Computer-Based Modeling. Northwestern University, Evanston, IL. https://ccl.northwestern.edu/netlogo/
8. Witten, D.M., Tibshirani, R.: A framework for feature selection in clustering. J. Am. Stat. Assoc. **105**(490), 713–726 (2010)
9. Charrad, M., et al.: NbClust: an R package for determining the relevant number of clusters in a data set. J. Stat. Softw. **61**(6), 1–36 (2014)
10. Berland, M., et al.: Using learning analytics to understand the learning pathways of novice programmers. J. Learn. Sci. **22**(4), 564–599 (2013)
11. Basu, S., Sengupta, P., Biswas, G.: A scaffolding framework to support learning of emergent phenomena using multi-agent based simulation environments. Res. Sci. Educ. **45**(2), 293–324 (2015)
12. Basu, S., Biswas, G.: Providing adaptive scaffolds and measuring their effectiveness in open-ended learning environments. In: 12th International Conference of the Learning Sciences Singapore, pp. 554–561 (2016)

Poster Papers

Student Preferences for Visualising Uncertainty in Open Learner Models

Lamiya Al-Shanfari[1](✉), Chris Baber[1], and Carrie Demmans Epp[2]

[1] School of Engineering, University of Birmingham, Birmingham, UK
{lsa339, c.baber}@bham.ac.uk
[2] Learning Research and Development Center, University of Pittsburgh,
Pittsburgh, USA
cdemmans@pitt.edu

Abstract. User preferences for indicating uncertainty using specific visual variables have been explored outside of educational reporting. Exploring students' preferred method to indicate uncertainty in open learner models can provide hints about which approaches students will use, so further design approaches can be considered. Participants were 67 students exploring 6 visual variables applied to a learner model visualisation (skill meter). Student preferences were ordered along a scale, which showed the size, numerosity, orientation and added marks visual variables were near one another in the learner's preference space. Results of statistical analyses revealed differences in student preferences for some variables with opacity being the most preferred and arrangement the least preferred. This result provides initial guidelines for open learner model and learning dashboard designers to represent uncertainty information using students' preferred method of visualisation.

Keywords: Uncertainty · Visualisation · Open learner models · Dashboards

1 Introduction

Communicating information about data uncertainty could increase user trust in system results and support decision making [1]. While evaluating the use of variables to represent uncertainty in other disciplines has been performed, few studies in educational contexts have explored how to communicate model uncertainty. The systems that indicate model uncertainty use visual variables such as value, size, position and added marks to indicate uncertainty [2]. Visual variables are classified into two techniques to indicate uncertainty: (i) intrinsic techniques alter the existing display to indicate uncertainty using visual variables such as opacity, colour value, colour hue and saturation; and (ii) extrinsic techniques add objects to the display to represent uncertainty such as glyphs, dots or lines [1]. Although some research shows participants can prefer a method for indicating uncertainty that is not necessarily the most effective [3], there are studies showing that participants accurately retrieved the information depicted by uncertainty using their preferred method [4]. To our knowledge, exploring students' preferred method for visualising uncertainty in open learner models (OLM) has yet to be explored. Here, we address this gap by providing a study evaluating six visual

© Springer International Publishing AG 2017
E. André et al. (Eds.): AIED 2017, LNAI 10331, pp. 445–449, 2017.
DOI: 10.1007/978-3-319-61425-0_37

variables that were applied to a skill meter to show model uncertainty. This evaluation [5] ranked the students' preferred method on a scale from most to least preferred. Our selection of the studied visual variables was based on the percentage of use of the variables reported to effectively communicate uncertainty from an analysis of 50 visualisations [2]. Also, we took into account the design of the visual variables that could fit in OLMlets' skill meters [6]. These skill meters use colours for each level of knowledge (green is known, red is misconception and grey is unknown concepts). All variables had to be capable of communicating three levels of uncertainty (low, medium and high). Two variables were selected from those that were used to communicate uncertainty in 100% of the studied visualisations (added marks and arrangement). Numerosity and opacity were selected from variables with usage above 80% and less than 100%, and orientation and size were selected from variables that were used in less than 80% and more than 50% of the visualisations. Figure 1 shows the six visual variables applied to the selected learner model visualisation (skill meters) that represents the level of knowledge for three topics, which should allow the levels of uncertainty to be easily compared.

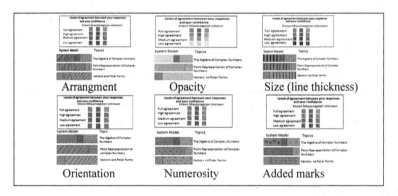

Fig. 1. Six visual variables applied to a skill meter learner model to indicate uncertainty. (Color figure online)

The uncertainty represented in the model is based on the level of agreement between the system's perception of the students' level of knowledge and students' confidence about the correctness of their answers, the lower the agreement (i.e., higher conflict) the higher the uncertainty. For example, consistently arranged lines show low levels of uncertainty, the messier the lines the higher the uncertainty. Opacity shows higher uncertainty through higher transparency. Increasing the size or line thickness shows higher uncertainty. Using the orientation visual variable, the degree of line rotation shows different levels of uncertainty, with vertical lines showing higher uncertainty. In numerosity, more dots indicate higher uncertainty than fewer dots. Using added marks, each element that has the same marks has the same level of uncertainty. In this study, our aim is to identify students' preferred uncertainty visualisation method for OLMs (skill meters).

2 Methods

An exploratory study was run with 67 students (45 undergraduate, 22 MSc). Participants were asked to complete a questionnaire that had 15 paired comparison questions. Questions about student gender and experience with OLMs were included. Participants received a brief presentation from the researcher about the meaning of the visual variables that were used to indicate uncertainty. This was to ensure that participants understood the role of the visual variables applied to the learner model visualisation so their choices were based on their preferences rather than their comprehension, although these two variables cannot be completely disentangled. The order of presentation for the paired comparison items were randomised to prevent order effects. Each student compared a series of 15 pairs of OLM visualisations where they indicated the visualisation that they preferred within each pair. This was a forced-choice task so no equal judgments were allowed. Applying Thurstone's Paired Comparison Method [5], a 6×6 matrix was constructed by assigning a score for each prefered method from the paired comparison data to the top row associated for the prefered visual variable. Data was then divided by the number of responses (1005) and normalised using z-transform. Calculating the sum of each z-score for each column associated with each visual variable shows the preference score for that variable. The visual variables were ordered on a scale from most to least prefered. A Friedman test was used to identify differences in preference between visual variables. Wilcoxon Signed-ranks tests were used to show differences in preferences between pairs of visual variables. Among the 67 (female, $n = 18$; male, $n = 45$) participants, 41 had previously used OLMs and 22 had not used OLMs. The background questions were skipped by 4 students.

3 Results

The paired comparison method shows that the most preferred visual variable was opacity and the least preferred was arrangement. Figure 2 shows the visual variables ordered along a scale from most to least preferred. The Friedman test showed a significant difference in preference score between the visual variables, $\chi^2(5) = 104$, $p < .001$. Wilcoxon Signed-ranks tests showed strong evidence that opacity ($Mdn = 5$) is preferred over every other visual variable: arrangement ($Z = -6.66$, $p < .001$, $r = .81$, $Mdn = 0$), size ($Z = -4.81$, $p < .001$, $r = .59$, $Mdn = 2$), orientation ($Z = -4.13$, $p < .001$, $r = .5$, $Mdn = 3$), numerosity ($Z = -4.08$, $p < .001$, $r = .5$, $Mdn = 3$) and added marks ($Z = -3.95$, $p < .001$, $r = .48$, $Mdn = 3$).

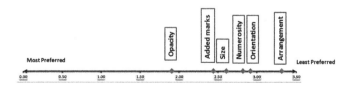

Fig. 2. Preferred measurement scale for visual variables.

It also showed arrangement was significantly less preferred than size ($Z = -5.69$, $p < .001$, $r = .7$), orientation ($Z = -6.15$, $p < .001$, $r = .75$), numerosity ($Z = -5.8$, $p < .001$, $r = .71$) and added marks ($Z = -5.14$, $p < .001$, $r = .63$). There were no significant differences in preference between size, orientation, numerosity and added marks. We can see that students preferred opacity (i.e., an intrinsic technique) as it is the only variable that indicates uncertainty by altering the existing fill colour of the skill meter without adding a new object such as a shape, dot or line. The least preferred choice was arrangement: this shows that students' preference was lower for unorganised lines (e.g., arrangement) than organised lines (e.g., orientation or size/line thickness).

4 Discussion and Conclusion

Our exploration showed that students preferred an intrinsic technique (e.g., opacity) to indicate uncertainty. This preference was stronger than that for all other visual variables which used extrinsic techniques. To our knowledge, our study is the first to evaluate student preferences for the manipulation of visual variables to represent uncertainty within OLMs. Our study provides evidence that students prefer to use visualisations which give them an overview rather than specific views of data. It also confirms the popularity of using opacity to indicate uncertainty [1]. Similar to other studies of user preferences outside of education, students preferred well-structured representations of uncertainty over the less well-organised representations [3]. In this study, 'arrangement' was the least preferred method for indicating uncertainty. Further studies need be done to understand the factors that influence preferences. Moreover, other visual variables and other types of learner model visualisations can be explored in order to develop guidelines that can inform designers of OLMs and other forms of educational reporting when visualising model uncertainty is important for supporting learner decision making. Finally, we can explore the use of visualisation in real learning situations.

References

1. Kinkeldey, C., MacEachren, A.M., Schiewe, J.: How to assess visual communication of uncertainty? a systematic review of geospatial uncertainty visualisation user studies. Cartographic J. **51**(4), 372–386 (2014). Taylor & Francis
2. Demmans Epp, C., Bull, S.: Uncertainty representation in visualisations of learning analytics for learners: current approaches and opportunities. IEEE Trans. Learn. Technol. **1382**(3), 242–260 (2015)
3. Boukhelifa, N., Bezerianos, A., Isenberg, T., Fekete, J.D.: Evaluating sketchiness as a visual variable for the depiction of qualitative uncertainty. IEEE Trans. Vis. Comput. Graph. **18**(12), 2769–2778 (2012)
4. Gerharz, L., Pebesma, E.: Usability of interactive and non-interactive visualisation of uncertain geospatial information. In: Reinhardt, W., Krüger, A., Ehlers, M. (eds), Geoinformatik 2009 Konferenzband, 223–230 (2009)

5. Thurstone, L.L.: A law of comparative judgment. Psychol. Rev. **34**(4), 273–286 (1927)
6. Bull, S., Jackson, T., Lancaster, M.: Students' interest in their misconceptions in first-year electrical circuits and mathematics courses. Int. J. Electr. Eng. Educ. **47**(3), 307–318 (2010)

Intelligent Augmented Reality Tutoring for Physical Tasks with Medical Professionals

Mohammed A. Almiyad[1], Luke Oakden-Rayner[2], Amali Weerasinghe[1(✉)], and Mark Billinghurst[3]

[1] Department of Computer Science,
University of Adelaide, Adelaide, SA, Australia
mohammed.almiyad@gmail.com , amali.weerasinghe@adelaide.edu.au
[2] Department of Radiology, Royal Adelaide Hospital,
Adelaide, SA, Australia
[3] Department of Computer Science,
University of South Australia, Adelaide, SA, Australia

Abstract. Percutaneous radiology procedures often require the repeated use of medical radiation in the form of computed tomography (CT) scanning, to demonstrate the position of the needle in the underlying tissues. The angle of the insertion and the distance travelled by the needle inside the patient play a major role in successful procedures, and must be estimated by the practitioner and confirmed periodically by the use of the scanner. Junior radiology trainees, who are already highly trained professionals, currently learn this task "on-the-job" by performing the procedures on real patients with varying levels of guidance. Therefore, we present a novel Augmented Reality (AR)-based system that provides multiple layers of intuitive and adaptive feedback to assist junior radiologists in achieving competency in image-guided procedures.

Keywords: Intelligent tutoring system · Augmented reality · Percutaneous radiology

1 Introduction

Augmented Reality (AR) seamlessly overlays 3D virtual images onto real world objects, and so is well suited for supporting training on physical tasks [3]. For example, AR systems could superimpose 3D graphics over a patient back showing lumbar levels [2]. However, the learning support provided by AR applications is currently limited to a checklist of tasks to be completed and is not customized to the learner needs. In contrast, intelligent tutoring systems (ITSs) have demonstrated their ability to significantly improve learning in a wide range of domains including Mathematics, Physics, Computer Science and Literacy [7]. Despite this, supporting training in physical tasks has been limited. The overarching goal for this research is to explore how the strengths of AR and ITS technologies can be combined to support personalized learning in the medical domain.

© Springer International Publishing AG 2017
E. André et al. (Eds.): AIED 2017, LNAI 10331, pp. 450–454, 2017.
DOI: 10.1007/978-3-319-61425-0_38

The MAT (Motherboard Assembly Tutor) is one of the few attempts to incorporate AR into an ITS [8]. The ITS module was developed based on ASPIRE, which is an authoring tool for ITS. The system consisted of a motherboard surrounded by AR tracking markers, with an AR application that could identify and track each component to guide and teach motherboard assembly. The ITS then displayed relevant real-time feedback messages on top of the AR view. Results of a small study showed improved learning performance for students compared to those who used the same AR-based system without the ITS component. Further research has investigated the efficiency of AR-based intelligent tutoring systems in military tasks [5].

In this paper we present initial work on a novel AR-based system that provides multiple layers of intuitive and adaptive feedback to assist radiology trainees in achieving competency in imaging guided procedures.

2   Medical Imaging Guided Interventional Procedures

Interventional procedures often require some form of guidance to track the needle trajectory through the human body. Such guidance usually includes radiation exposure such as x-ray or computed tomography (CT) scanning. Due to the fact that the radiologist needs to estimate the insertion angle visually, which is prone to human error, multiple repositioning of the needle need to be carried out in order to reach the targeted area. This causes increased patient discomfort, risk of infection, and radiation dose as each attempt requires further imaging to assess the needle position.

The number of repositioning attempts and radiological exposures vary between experienced and non-experienced practitioners, and having an experienced (or senior) practitioner results in to less radiation exposure. The proposed system aims to make use of 3D object tracking and virtual image feedback, to guide and reduce the number of interventions.

AR technology has been researched to assist medical procedures in previous work. Although the results of transferring clinical settings to AR systems might be inconclusive [4], several research attempts have shown that using AR to assist practitioners improves the efficiency and quality of interventional procedures [1,6].

3   System Architecture

The system consists of three main modules: the ITS module, the AR module, and the Interface Module. Figure 1 illustrates those modules along with the technology and hardware used (given in the upper part of each module).

The ITS module consists of three layers. The first layer presents feedback about the needle angle and depth, providing intuitive guidance during the procedure. The second layer displays instructional feedback during the procedure in the form of pop-up messages based on predefined conditions by analyzing the real-time data acquired by the AR system. For example, when the time spent is

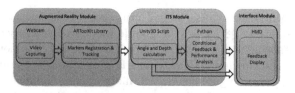

Fig. 1. The system architecture

longer than the pre-defined, feedback is provided by the ITS module. The third layer provides an opportunity for longitudinal performance analysis by aggregating data obtained during multiple procedures in a personalized dashboard. Performance in multiple relevant metrics (such as time taken per procedure) is tracked, enabling to understand the strength and weaknesses of a group of trainees at the same stage of training.

The AR module registers and tracks needle movements by using fiducial markers. The tracking data is then processed by the ITS module to generate the angle and the depth of the needle. The algorithm for calculating the angle and depth uses the ARToolKit[1] tracking library, where one marker is fixed at the top of the needle and another marker is based on a flat surface representing the back of a patient. The angle is calculated by the difference between these two markers' orientation and the depth is calculated using Pythagorean theory.

The Interface module visualizes feedback. The feedback visualization for the angle consists of a protractor-like background, a needle, and a value. The needle rotates dynamically to represent the actual needle rotation and the value of the angle is displayed accordingly. The depth graphics consist of a layered background, a symbolic needle, and a text value. In addition to those two continuous feedback, pop-up messages are initiated from the ITS module.

Previous work with AR in medical procedures have attempted to display three dimensional overlays that represent needle paths and anatomy registered to the patient body [1], but our feedback from radiologists has suggested that this is hard to use, not useful for the task and non-intuitive. Instead, our simplified heads-mounted display is easy to interpret and intuitive for the trainees.

4   Preliminary Experiments

We have conducted a preliminary experiment to assess the first layer of ITS feedback; the real-time feedback on needle angle. We compare the AR-ITS system against current practice, where an expert practitioner estimates the angle based on his own judgment.

The components used in the experiment setup consisted of a flat penetrable surface, a needle, two markers, a webcam, a computer, and a head-mounted display (HMD). The measured angle was determined using a protractor and an electronic ruler-angle tool.

---

[1] http://www.artoolkit.org.

Table 1. Experimental results

Tested angels (°)	Expert estimation	AR guidance
	Mean error (°)	Mean error (°)
0.00	1.00	1.00
20.00	2.50	0.25
40.00	4.00	2.00
60.00	1.50	4.00
Average	2.25	1.81

Table 1 compares needle insertion angles by an expert radiologist and by a user of the AR system. Two needle insertions were attempted at each angle in each group, the mean error is shown in the table. The results show a similar range of variation, with the AR system guidance appearing to outperform visual expert estimation at angles less than sixty degrees.

5 Summary

We present preliminary work on an AR based ITS for guiding and teaching needle insertion skills to highly-trained medical professionals. Our initial evaluation provides evidence for face validity, as the AR system is capable of providing feedback on needle angle to that of an expert radiologist, which is the most critical component that distinguishes learners from experts. By providing certainty of the angle of insertion, the system would be able to reduce needle repositioning and increase confidence for trainees.

We have implemented the system, which will provide real-time feedback to trainees to guide their learning. We plan to begin user testing in simulated procedures in the near future and eventually with real patients.

References

1. Abe, Y., Sato, S., Kato, K., Hyakumachi, T., Yanagibashi, Y., Ito, M., Abumi, K.: A novel 3D guidance system using augmented reality for percutaneous vertebroplasty: technical note. J. Neurosurg. Spine **19**(4), 492–501 (2013)
2. Ashab, H.A.D., Lessoway, V.A., Khallaghi, S., Cheng, A., Rohling, R., Abolmaesumi, P.: An augmented reality system for epidural anesthesia (area): prepuncture identification of vertebrae. IEEE Trans. Biomed. Eng. **60**(9), 2636–2644 (2013)
3. Azuma, R.T.: A survey of augmented reality. Presence Teleoperators Virtual Environ. **6**(4), 355–385 (1997)
4. Barsom, E., Graafland, M., Schijven, M.: Systematic review on the effectiveness of augmented reality applications in medical training. Surg. Endosc. **30**(10), 4174–4183 (2016)

5. LaViola, J., Williamson, B., Brooks, C., Veazanchin, S., Sottilare, R., Garrity, P.: Using augmented reality to tutor military tasks in the wild. In: Interservice/Industry Training, Simulation, and Education Conferernce (I/ITSEC), Orlando, FL, USA, pp. 1–10 (2015)
6. Rosenthal, M., State, A., Lee, J., Hirota, G., Ackerman, J., Keller, K., Pisano, E.D., Jiroutek, M., Muller, K., Fuchs, H.: Augmented reality guidance for needle biopsies: an initial randomized, controlled trial in phantoms. Med. Image Anal. 6(3), 313–320 (2002)
7. VanLehn, K.: The relative effectiveness of human tutoring, intelligent tutoring systems, and other tutoring systems. Educ. Psychol. 46(4), 197–221 (2011)
8. Westerfield, G., Mitrovic, A., Billinghurst, M.: Intelligent augmented reality training for motherboard assembly. Int. J. Artif. Intell. Educ. 25(1), 157–172 (2015)

Synthesis of Problems for Shaded Area Geometry Reasoning

Chris Alvin[1(✉)], Sumit Gulwani[2], Rupak Majumdar[3],
and Supratik Mukhopadhyay[4]

[1] Bradley University, Peoria, IL, USA
`calvin@bradley.edu`
[2] Microsoft Research, Redmond, WA, USA
`sumitg@microsoft.com`
[3] Max Planck Institute for Software Systems, Kaiserslautern, Germany
`rupak@mpi-sws.org`
[4] Louisiana State University, Baton Rouge, LA, USA
`supratik@csc.lsu.edu`

Abstract. A shaded area problem in high school geometry consists of a figure annotated with facts such as lengths of line segments or angle measures, and asks to compute the area of a shaded portion of the figure. We describe a technique to generate fresh figures for these problems. Given a figure, we describe a technique to automatically synthesize shaded area problems. We demonstrate the efficacy of our synthesis techniques by synthesizing problems from fresh figures as well as figures from a corpus of problems from high-school geometry textbooks.

1 Introduction

A *shaded area problem* in high school geometry is composed of a geometric figure, a set of geometric facts (e.g., lengths, angles) about that figure, and a shaded region in the figure whose area is to be computed (see Fig. 1). The ability to synthesize new and meaningful problems is important in large-scale online geometry education: new, synthesized figures can be provided to students as exercises and the difficulty of these problems can be tuned based on the history of previous problems encountered.

We describe a tool that can automatically synthesize shaded area geometry problems in two steps. First, given a set of "basic" shapes (e.g., triangles, circles, etc.), it composes them (e.g., one shape inside another, one shape sharing a side with another, etc.) using a template-based approach to generate a geometric figure. Second, it adds assumptions and a goal to the synthesized figure to create new shaded area problems that use facts about the entire figure. Internally, we represents deductions about area facts as well as all possible algebraic decompositions as a directed hypergraph as shown in Fig. 1. It then acquires the area of regions in the figure as a linear combination of areas of other regions [1].

© Springer International Publishing AG 2017
E. André et al. (Eds.): AIED 2017, LNAI 10331, pp. 455–458, 2017.
DOI: 10.1007/978-3-319-61425-0_39

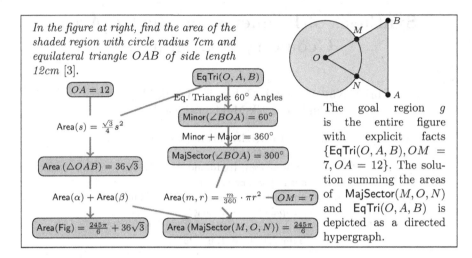

Fig. 1. Example shaded area problem and solution

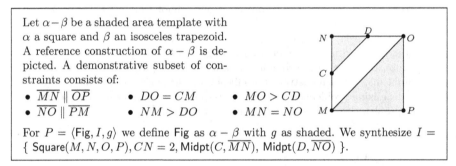

Fig. 2. $\alpha - \beta$ composition and generated problem

2   Figure Synthesis

Composition Templates. Given a set of shapes, we wish to combine those shapes into a meaningful configuration for a shaded area problem. We compose shapes as a linear combination—a template for combining shapes and computing the corresponding area of a region. Let α and β be shapes. The *shaded area addition operation* $\alpha + \beta$ refers to α being appended to β so that α and β share more than a single snapping point and $\alpha \cap \beta = \emptyset$. Since α and β are disjoint, $\mathsf{Area}(\alpha + \beta) = \mathsf{Area}(\alpha) + \mathsf{Area}(\beta)$. The *shaded area subtraction operation* $\alpha - \beta$ refers to β being situated on the interior of α where all snapping points of β align with snapping points of α (see Fig. 2); hence, $\mathsf{Area}(\alpha - \beta) = \mathsf{Area}(\alpha) - \mathsf{Area}(\beta)$.

3   Problem Generation

For a shaded area problem $P = \langle \mathsf{Fig}, I, g \rangle$ with figure Fig, we generate a minimal set of facts for I using an iterative, constraint-driven approach. For each shape

α in Fig, we use the underlying coordinates to *strengthen* the general shape from an implicit fact to an explicit fact about Fig: $\alpha \in \mathcal{I}(\mathsf{Fig})$ to $strong\,(\alpha) \in \mathcal{E}(\mathsf{Fig})$ where $strong : \mathcal{I}(\mathsf{Fig}) \rightarrow \mathcal{E}(\mathsf{Fig})$ is a function that elevates a shape from a general polygon to a specific polygon (e.g., quadrilateral may strengthen to a rectangle). Strengthening a shape α adds constraints on measures, such as length, to an implicit fact characterizing α; strengthening maps an implicit fact (ordered geometry [5]) to an explicit fact (Euclidean geometry).

We now consider how to select which length facts shall be used to compute the area of each shape α for P. Each shape $\alpha \in S$ has an associated set of constraints $K_{strong(\alpha)}$ guided by $strong\,(\alpha) \in \mathcal{E}(\mathsf{Fig})$. For example, with a quadrilateral Q, recognizing $strong\,(Q)$ as a rectangle means we have the opposing sides of $strong\,(Q)$ are congruent and parallel. For sides of rectangle $strong\,(Q)$, γ_i, $K_{strong(Q)} = \{\gamma_1 = \gamma_3, \gamma_1 \parallel \gamma_3, \gamma_2 = \gamma_4, \gamma_2 \parallel \gamma_4\}$. See Fig. 2 for an example of constraints attributed to a shaded area template subtraction operation.

To define I as a minimal set of assumptions, we use the shaded area solution equation E for region g which is a linear combination of areas of regions: $\mathsf{Area}\,(g) = E$. We first construct the set of dependent variables D_g required to calculate $\mathsf{Area}\,(g)$ using E. That is, for each shape $s \in E$, $\mathsf{Area}\,(s)$ is computable if the associated set of parameters P_s are deducible in $\mathcal{C}$ or calculable using $\mathcal{E}(\mathsf{Fig})$ thus satisfying the constraints K_s for each shape s. So $D_g = \bigcup_{s \in E} P_s$. We construct a minimal set of facts I iteratively where, initially, $I = \emptyset$.

1. Randomly select and remove a variable $v \in D_g$.
2. Add v to I: $I := I \cup \{v\}$.
3. Add the shape $strong(s)$ associated with v to I: $I := I \cup \{strong(s)\}$.
4. Query $\mathcal{E}(\mathsf{Fig})$ to identify if the current known set of values in I can be used to calculate any other dependent variables in D_g, updating D_g accordingly.
5. If Fig and I together do not logically entail E, go to step 1.

The set I then contains a minimal set of assumptions required to calculate $\mathsf{Area}(g)$ and the result is a shaded area problem $P = \langle \mathsf{Fig}, I, g \rangle$. Example synthesized problems are shown in Fig. 1 and Fig. 2.

4   Experimental Results

In this analysis we consider the set of shapes which include squares, rectangles, and right triangles. We used the midpoints of segments as snapping points. We consider each of the templates listed in Table 1 with the set of shapes {Square, Rectangle, RightTriangle}. For each template, we generated a minimal set of assumptions using the technique described in Sect. 3. Under these conditions, we generated 3533 figures with corresponding mean 16.5 (std. dev. 34.1) problems. As a benchmark, we ran our algorithms on a set of textbook problems consisting of 102 existing figures taken from standard mathematics textbooks and workbooks from the United States [2, 4, 6–8] as well as from the Indian Class X exam [3]. We used a uniform set of shape axioms and geometric axioms for all experiments. Using the 102 existing textbook figures, we show the effectiveness

Table 1. Figure and problem synthesis: $\alpha, \beta, \gamma \in \{\mathsf{Square}, \mathsf{Rectangle}, \mathsf{RightTriangle}\}$: mean (standard deviation)

Template	Figures	Generated problems
$\alpha \pm \beta$	119	4.71 (5.25)
$\alpha - (\beta - \gamma)$	505	37.2 (73.40)
$(\alpha - \beta) - \gamma$	705	26.0 (31.24)
$(\alpha - \beta) + \gamma$	623	14.4 (19.99)
$\alpha + \beta + \gamma$	994	6.49 (1.83)
$(\alpha + \beta) - \gamma$	587	8.79 (5.88)
	3414	16.65 (34.63)
Overall	3533	16.51 (34.12)

of our problem synthesis algorithm with a mean of 256.7 (1040.3) problems per figure. Most figures result in fewer than 25 generated problems while some figures result in thousands of problems [1]. The distributions of problems generated from fresh figures and existing figures are right-skewed. Numerically, synthesized figures result in a mean of 16.51 (34.12) interesting problems compared to mean 10.28 (15.61) interesting problems for existing figures (both without circles). We conclude that the figure synthesis technique described in Sect. 2 is equally effective for problem synthesis as compared to using existing figures [1].

5   Conclusions

We have presented techniques to efficiently synthesize new shaded area problems using template-based specifications of shapes and a calculational logic framework to reason about geometric facts. Our experiments show we are able to synthesize many problems of similar complexity to high school geometry textbooks.

References

1. Alvin, C., Gulwani, S., Majumdar, R., Mukhopadhyay, S.: Technical report: synthesis of problems for shaded area geometry reasoning (2017). http://hilltop.bradley.edu/~calvin/papers/aied-full.pdf
2. Boyd, C.J., et al.: Geometry (NJ Edition). Glencoe/McGraw-Hill, New York (2006)
3. CBSE, India (2012). http://cbse.nic.in/
4. Chew, T.: Singapore Math Challenge (Grade 5+). Frank Schaffer Publications, Greensboro (2008)
5. Coxeter, H.: Introduction to Geometry. Wiley, Hoboken (1969)
6. Holt, R., Winston: Holt Geometry: Homework and Practice Workbook. Holt, Rinehart and Winston, Orlando (2007)
7. Jurgensen, R., Brown, R., Jurgensen, J.: Geometry. Houghton Mifflin Company, Boston (1988)
8. Larson, R., Boswell, L., Kanold, T., Stiff, L.: Geometry. McDougal Littel, Evanston (2007)

Communication Strategies and Affective Backchannels for Conversational Agents to Enhance Learners' Willingness to Communicate in a Second Language

Emmanuel Ayedoun$^{(\boxtimes)}$, Yuki Hayashi, and Kazuhisa Seta

Graduate School of Humanities and Sustainable System Sciences,
Osaka Prefecture University, Osaka, Japan
eayedoun@ksm.kis.osakafu-u.ac.jp

Abstract. Willingness to Communicate (WTC) in a second language (L2) is believed to have a direct and sustained influence on learners' actual usage frequency of the targeted language. To help overcome the lack of suitable environments to increase L2 learners WTC, our approach is to implement a WTC model based conversational agent. In this paper, we propose a dialogue management model based on set of communication strategies and affective backchannels in order to foster the agent's ability to carry on natural and WTC friendly conversations with L2 learners. We expect that combining communication strategies with affective backchannels can empower conversational agents to the extent to effectively help L2 learners recover from eventual communication pitfalls and create a warm conversation atmosphere.

Keywords: Willingness to communicate in L2 · Conversational agents · Communication strategies · Affective backchannels · Intelligent tutoring

1 Introduction

One of the fundamental goals of second language (L2) learning is to provide learners the ability to communicate effectively using their L2 when given the opportunity to do so. MacIntyre et al. [1] found that the key factor to ensure such communicative readiness is the willingness to communicate (WTC) and therefore suggested that increasing learners' WTC should be the goal of L2 learning. Moreover, they proposed a pyramidal heuristic model of variables affecting WTC in which it appears that the environment in which learners experience or practice the L2 plays an important role in motivating them to actively take part or not in L2 conversation. L2 communication is also problematic in most of cases mainly because it involves learners' ability to communicate within restrictions on their own vocabulary, grammar, etc., so that unlike communication between L1 learners, breakdowns or pitfalls in communication occur more often here.

In this paper, we propose and implement a dialogue management model, based on a set of specific conversational strategies, namely communication strategies and affective backchannels in order to foster dialogue agents' ability to carry on WTC effective conversations with learners in an English as a Foreign Language (EFL) context.

© Springer International Publishing AG 2017
E. André et al. (Eds.): AIED 2017, LNAI 10331, pp. 459–462, 2017.
DOI: 10.1007/978-3-319-61425-0_40

2 Conversational Strategies to Increase WTC

In our previous work [2], we built a dialogue agent based conversational environment aiming to increase L2 learners' WTC and which architecture is described in Fig. 1 (top). An evaluation of the system demonstrated its potential to simulate efficiently natural conversations in a specific context as well as the feasibility of improving learners' WTC using a computer-based environment. We also found that learners faced sometimes difficulties in understanding or answering to the dialogue agent, which led to breakdowns during the interactions. From these findings, we deduced that a good level of conversation smoothness and warmness, to be achieved by implementing strategies to keep the conversation going on especially when learners face some difficulties, is desirable since it may contribute to creating a friendly conversational environment and reduce learners' anxiety.

In this paper, we propose a dialogue management model based on a set of two categories of conversational strategies namely "communication strategies" (CS) and "affective backchannels" (AB). The model aims first, by the way of CS to foster conversational agents' ability to autonomously detect and robustly handle learners' pitfalls in L2 communication, making possible achievement of more or less smooth interaction between L2 learners and conversational agent. Secondly, by the way of AB, this model aims to make possible achievement of a warm interaction where learners will feel less anxious about L2 communication and progressively get confidence about their own linguistic proficiency.

Communication Strategies (CS): CS are defined by Dörnyei and Scott [3] as "a systematic technique employed by a speaker to express his or her meaning when faced with some difficulty". These difficulties might arise both from the speaker (lack of linguistic resources) or from the interlocutor (impossibility to understand the speaker). The use of CS might help dialogue agents not only to overcome their own difficulties (impossibility to understand learners' utterances) but also and more importantly to handle more effectively learners' communication pitfalls (difficulty in understanding or answering to the agent's utterances) during conversations. When learners know that they can rely on a supportive dialogue agent to help them recover from difficulties, they may feel a "sense of security" that can reduce their communication apprehension, leading to a higher level of WTC. In the present study, we targeted about nine strategies among those defined in the comprehensive review of definitions and taxonomies of CS [3]. The strategies were selected according to two criteria: their effectiveness towards encouraging WTC and the feasibility of their implementation from the technical standpoint.

Affective Backchannels (AB): Backchannels are generally defined as a type of short utterances or feedbacks such as *uh-huh, yeah,* … given by the listener to show interest, attention or a willingness to keep the communication channel open. They play an important role in human agent conversation, as mentioned by Smith et al. [4]. Moreover, as stressed by McCroskey [5], the degree of attention that learners get from their interlocutors might be one of the causes of the communication apprehension that they

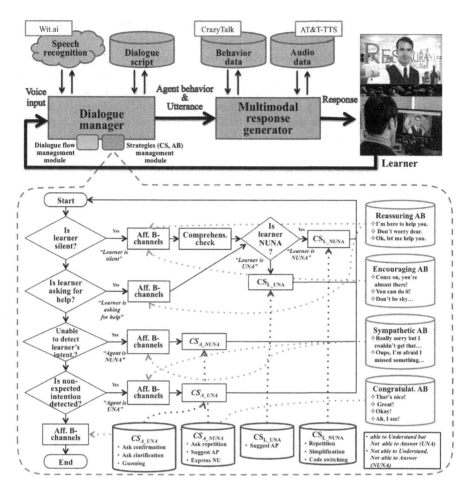

Fig. 1. System architecture (top), dialogue management flow based on AB and CS (bottom)

feel. Thus, L2 learners who do not get enough supportive feedbacks from their interlocutors may easily perceive themselves as being incompetent communicators and therefore tend to be reticent to communication. All this gives much evidence that it might be effective for conversational agents intending to enhance learners' WTC to be able to convey a sufficient amount of interest or sympathy to learners during the interaction since doing so might contribute to create a WTC friendly atmosphere. In order to achieve such empathetic support, we identified and defined a set of backchannels that we call affective backchannels (AB). To cover a wide range of situations the learner can be in, four categories of AB were defined, namely *Congratulatory*, *Encouraging*, *Sympathetic* and *Reassuring* AB.

3   Conversational Strategies Enhanced Dialogue Management

The set of conversational strategies that we implemented are based on the possible dialogue states or type of pitfalls that learners or the system itself often falls into. As described in Fig. 1 (bottom), the dialogue management routine goes from Start to End (top to bottom of the figure) passing through checking of the different possible dialogue states represented in the diamond symbols. The occurrence of each of such dialogue states automatically leads to triggering of adapted conversational strategies (as indicated in square symbols) that are pull out from their respective databases (as shown by dotted lines) in order to keep the learner motivated using AB (represented in pink colored database symbols), and try to move the dialogue forward using CS (represented in blue colored database symbols). We expect that the modular and domain independent nature of the proposed dialogue management model will not only facilitate its reusability across different dialogues domains, but will also make easier the development of conversational systems that are fully adapted to L2 learners from the WTC standpoint.

4   Conclusion and Future Research Directions

Most of traditional spoken dialogue interfaces dedicated to second language learning seem to not explicitly take into consideration aspects related to learners' WTC in a second language. In this paper, we described a dialogue management model based on a set of communicative and affective conversational strategies (CS and AB) aiming to empower conversational agents in order to foster L2 learners' WTC in an EFL context.

A pilot evaluation of the proposed method has suggested that the model and especially the usage of AB might be really effective in motivating L2 learners towards communication. Future research should be directed to evaluating in more details effects associated with each strategy (CS and AB), and determining approaches for strengthening the impact of these strategies in enhancing L2 learners' WTC.

References

1. MacIntyre, P.D., Clément, R., Dörnyei, Z., Noels, K.A.: Conceptualizing willingness to communicate in a L2: a situational model of L2 confidence and affiliation. Mod. Lang. J. **82**(4), 545–562 (1998)
2. Ayedoun, E., Hayashi, Y., Seta, K.: Web-services based conversational agent to encourage willingness to communicate in the EFL context. J. Inform. Syst. Educ. **15**(1), 15–27 (2016)
3. Dörnyei, Z., Scott, M.L.: Communication strategies in a second language: definitions and taxonomies. Lang. Learn. **47**(1), 173–209 (1997)
4. Smith, C., Crook, N., Dobnik, S., Charlton, D.: Interaction strategies for an affective conversational agent. Teleoperators Virtual Environ. **20**, 395–411 (2011). MIT Press
5. McCroskey, J.C.: Willingness to communicate, communication apprehension, and self-perceived communication competence: conceptualizations and perspectives. In: Daly, J., et al. (eds.) Avoiding Communication: Shyness, Reticence, and Communication Apprehension, pp. 75–129. Hampton Press, Cresskill (1997)

A Multi-layered Architecture for Analysis of Non-technical-Skills in Critical Situations

Yannick Bourrier[1,2(✉)], Francis Jambon[2], Catherine Garbay[2], and Vanda Luengo[1]

[1] UPMC – LIP6, Paris, France
{yannick.bourrier,vanda.luengo}@lip6.fr
[2] UGA – LIG, Grenoble, France
{francis.jambon,catherine.garbay}@imag.fr

Abstract. In most technical domains, non-technical skills have an influence on a worker's performance. Studies have shown that these skills are most influential during critical situations, where usual technical procedures cannot be successfully applied. This article describes the challenges raised by the diagnosis of non-technical skills during critical situations inside a virtual environment, and presents the first steps of this diagnosis task, namely the evaluation of a learner's perceptual and gestural performance using a neural network.

Keywords: Ill-defined domains · Non-technical skills · Critical situations · Neural networks

1 General Approach

Non-technical skills (NTS) are defined as 'the cognitive, social, and personal resources skills that complement technical skills, and contribute to safe and efficient task performance" [1]. Their influence on technical activity is bigger during critical situations [1]. The objective of our Intelligent Learning Environment (ILE) is to provide relevant learning situations for NTS training. To reach this goal, a first step is the diagnosis of a learner's NTS level. However, given that NTS can only be observed in perceptions and gestures, they overlap with technical skills. Thus, the diagnosis of NTS in an ILE is an ill-defined task [2, 3]. Our solution is to adopt a hybrid approach [4], combining expert knowledge and data mining knowledge. Its first objective is the performance analysis of a learner's performance inside contextually similar critical and non-critical situations (i.e. situations equal in all aspects except for criticality), as we expect the performance gap to be a strong marker of NTS influence. This should be true if the learner's technical skill level does not change through the learning session, which is an acceptable hypothesis since our ILE focuses on non-novices. To evaluate the perceptual and gestural performance, two neural networks are trained from high level indicators extracted from the learner's activity traces.

This research was supported by the MacCoy-Critical project (ANR-14-CE24-0021).

© Springer International Publishing AG 2017
E. André et al. (Eds.): AIED 2017, LNAI 10331, pp. 463–466, 2017.
DOI: 10.1007/978-3-319-61425-0_41

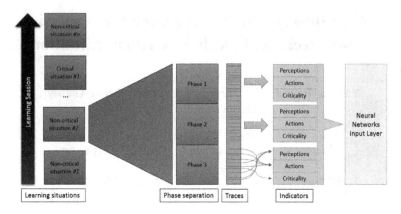

Fig. 1. General view of the performance evaluation architecture. The same process can be applied to the previous and following situations.

Figure 1 is an overview of the architecture. A learning session is constituted of several learning situations which can be critical or not; it is at this level that performance analysis is done. Each learning situation is separated into phases. High level indicators are extracted for each phase and constitute the neural networks input layers.

To separate a learning situation between phases, we use the notion of precursor, which [5] describe as "an element foreshadowing a hazard". For each situation, the domain experts identify a situation precursor, whose evolution will trigger reactions from the learner which may or may not be appropriate. Each different state of a precursor changing the situation characteristics, the number of phases is the number of different precursor states. From this separation we extract domain dependent, high level indicators (e.g.: number of perceptions made during a phase, average intensity of brakes…) from symbolic rules applied to the learner's activity traces, providing information with regards to the learner's perceptions, actions, and the state of the world in which these perceptions and actions are done (we name this information "criticality indicators"). This dimension-reduction process is necessary to analyze a learner's performance in many critical situations and inside different technical domains. To identify contextually similar critical and non-critical situations, we assume that the same technical skills are applied during the two if they have comparable precursor's states, and when the criticality associated to these states is less important in the later. For example, a pedestrian about to cross the road can be the precursor of a situation which is critical (if this behavior is unpredictable), or not (if this behavior is obvious).

We use supervised learning regression techniques to train two neural networks to rate a learner's perceptual and gestural performance in non-critical situations, from the evaluation of an expert. We hold that for contextually similar situations, the network structure can also be used for performance evaluation in the critical situation, thanks to transfer learning mechanisms [6]. This choice is to compensate for the low number of critical situations in comparison to non-critical ones, and for the fact that each critical situation once experienced by a learner has its criticality factor defused.

2 Proof of Concept and Conclusions

We generated data simulating drivers' behaviors in the form of high level indicators of perceptions, actions, and criticality, as shown in Fig. 2, commonly used by experts to analyze drivers' performance [5], in two driving situations, one of them being critical, Both situations ask for the driver to react to a crossing pedestrian (the situation precursor), but while the intention of the pedestrian is obvious in the non-critical situation, it is unclear during the critical situation. Both situations are separated into two phases as proposed in part 1, a first phase where the individual has not started to cross, a second phase starting when crossing begins, and require the learner to stop the car before impact. We generated 1000 runs representing the full spectrum of driver's actions with regards to the handling of the non-critical situation. These runs were then clustered using k-means, and the average values of each indicator, for each cluster, were provided to an expert who classified them from worse to best, separately for perceptions and actions. Once this rating was achieved and since our VE is targeted towards non-novice users, we deleted most of the clusters which resulted in the driver not stopping. Only two of these clusters were kept, the first one had all its values at 0, and the second one was kept to simulate a driver denying priority to the pedestrian. The neural networks input layer were constituted of 9 values for each phase, each corresponding to an indicator, and the target values were the associated expert's rankings. The networks were trained for regression learning since their aim was to predict a continuous value corresponding to learner's performance. The output layer was therefore comprised of a single node for both networks. 10% of the base was kept for validation. The mean squared error (MSE) for both networks during validation was of 0.0151 which was close to the MSE of 0.0126 observed during training.

Once the networks had been trained from learner behavior on a non-critical situation we could observe the networks' abilities to transfer the approximated structure to the critical situation. To do so, we asked the expert to describe a set of realistic learners' behaviors during the previously described critical situation and to range them from

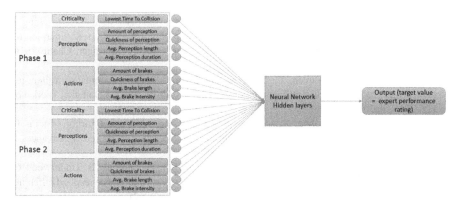

Fig. 2. Input layer, structure and target value of the neural network used for performance evaluation. As justified in part 1, two neural networks were trained separately for perception rating and action rating. Here the Time To Collision variable plays the role of criticality indicator.

worst to best. We generated indicators matching each of these behaviors and fed them as input to both neural networks for performance prediction. Because there was no target value associated to each of these behaviors, the networks could only deliver a performance estimation based on the structure learnt previously from the non-critical situation. The neural network ranked the behaviors the same as the expert for action performance, but showed some differences with regards to perception performance (the 4 worst rankings were in a different order). We assume that this is because two different tasks were asked to the expert; to rank separately perceptions and actions during the non-critical situation, and to rank performance globally during the critical situation. These results suggest that the structure learnt by the neural network, from the evaluation of an expert in non-critical situations, can be transferred to critical situations, given that the two situations present similarities.

Facing the ill-defined problem of TS and NTS overlapping, we have presented a neural-network based hybrid approach for performance analysis of a learner's perceptions and actions during critical situations inside a VE, a necessary first step towards NTS diagnosis. Because critical situations can only be experienced once for a given learner, we trained the neural network on contextually similar non-critical situations before using it to evaluate a learner's performance in critical situations, hypothesizing that transfer learning could allow the network to provide valid performance evaluations in both cases. The first experimental results suggest that transfer learning was efficient given our conceptual hypothesis. In the future, we will compare performance in non-critical situations and critical situations for specific learners using real data. We expect this comparison to be the basis of non-technical skills diagnosis, given other factors such as the technical knowledge of the learner, the situation's criticality, or physiological elements such as heart rate variation or skin conductance.

References

1. Flin, R., Yule, S., Paterson-Brown, S., Maran, N., Rowley, D., Youngson, G.: Teaching surgeons about non-technical skills. Surgeon 5(2), 86–89 (2007)
2. Bourrier, Y., Jambon, F., Garbay, C., Luengo, V.: An approach to the tel teaching of non-technical skills from the perspective of an ill-defined problem. In: Verbert, K., Sharples, M., Klobučar, T. (eds.) EC-TEL 2016. LNCS, vol. 9891, pp. 555–558. Springer, Cham (2016). doi:10.1007/978-3-319-45153-4_62
3. Lynch, C., Ashley, K., Aleven, V., Pinkwart, N.: Defining ill-defined domains; a litera-ture survey. In: Proceedings of Intelligent Tutoring Systems for Ill-Defined Domains Workshop, ITS 2006, pp. 1–10 (2006)
4. Fournier-Viger, P., Nkambou, R., Nguifo, E.M.: Building intelligent tutoring systems for ill-defined domains. In: Nkambou, R., Bourdeau, J., Mizoguchi, R. (eds.) Advances in Intelligent Tutoring Systems. Springer, Heidelberg (2010)
5. Crundall, D., Chapman, P., Trawley, S., Collins, L., Van Loon, E., Andrews, B., Underwood, G.: Some hazards are more attractive than others: drivers of varying experience respond differently to different types of hazard. Accid. Anal. Prev. 45, 600–609 (2012)
6. Pan, S.J., Yang, Q.: A survey on transfer learning. IEEE Trans. Knowl. Data Eng. 22(10), 1345–1359 (2010)

Conceptual Framework for Collaborative Educational Resources Adaptation in Virtual Learning Environments

Vitor Bremgartner[1(✉)], José de Magalhães Netto[1], and Crediné Menezes[2]

[1] Federal University of Amazonas, Manaus, Brazil
vitorbref@gmail.com
[2] Federal University of Rio Grande do Sul, Porto Alegre, Brazil

Abstract. Frequently, the existing resources in Virtual Learning Environments (VLEs), used in distance education courses and blended, are presented in the same way for all students. This may complicate the effective learning process of each student. In order to solve this problem, the approach adopted in this paper is based on a framework called ArCARE, which allows adaptation of resources for students in VLEs, allowing the construction of his knowledge, using multi-agent system technology that handles open learner model ontology. These ArCARE resources are recommendation and adaptation of collaborative activities such as pedagogical architectures for the students have a more effective learning of particular course content. Results obtained in a Computational Thinking course show the feasibility of the proposal.

Keywords: Collaborative learning · Virtual Learning Environments · Adaptation of resources · Software agents

1 Introduction

Distance Education is a modality widely used in the teaching-learning processes. To support the distance education or blended courses there are educational environments as Virtual Learning Environments (VLEs). In addition, there are VLEs that use Artificial Intelligence (AI), especially regarding the possibility of flexible teaching-learning processes to students, in which the learning environment is able to adapt its resources presented according to the student's needs [1]. Tools in AI field, such as ontologies and software agents, can act integrated into these VLEs, becoming responsible for this intelligence layer and making use of a learner model [1, 2].

However, despite the increasing use of educational environments, they usually offer learning resources in the same way for all students (one-size-fits-all form), resulting that the learning cannot become effective for all because of several cognitive characteristics that each student has. Thus, the approach adopted as a proposal to solving this problem is based on a framework called ArCARE (Conceptual Framework of Educational Resources Adaptation in VLEs), being a strategy that allows adaptation of resources for students during the course, using multi-agent system technology that

© Springer International Publishing AG 2017
E. André et al. (Eds.): AIED 2017, LNAI 10331, pp. 467–471, 2017.
DOI: 10.1007/978-3-319-61425-0_42

handles a learner model ontology which consists of several students' characteristics, such as interests, competencies, skills, history of student performance in activities, frequency, and learning styles. The IMS LIP standard [3] was used to integrate all these characteristics. The ArCARE adaptation resources are recommended based on collaborative learning, for example, Pedagogical Architectures (PAs) containing proposals for collaborative activities. PAs can be defined as the construction of pedagogical strategies that is based on a certain theory and its assumptions in order to assist in the effectiveness of learning mediated by digital technologies of communication and information as VLEs and web conferencing tools. The construction of the pedagogical strategy involves, however, the formation of an interdisciplinary group with the participation of professionals of education and computing areas [4]. In addition, the learner model is dynamically changed during the course, through the student interactions with the VLE. The learner model is also presented to the student, being an Open Learner Model (OLM).

2   ArCARE Architecture

The ArCARE architecture is shown in Fig. 1. This framework constitutes the personalization process of VLE through adaptation and recommendation of educational resources, depending on the characteristics of the student. This architecture is composed of three fundamental components: resource adaptation module, VLE database and user action space. The resource adaptation module contains the entire layer of intelligence provided by ArCARE. It consists of two groups of agents: those who control and handle the learner model and the agents who are responsible for adapting resources of the educational environment from the student data. The resource adaptation module has also the OLM ontology. The VLE database contains all data regarding the educational environment. It is shown in the architecture of Fig. 1 that the database has information about the history of user interactions, OLM information, resources, courses and their Learning Units (LUs). It's in the VLE database that the resource adaptation module operates. In turn, user action space refers to users' interactions with the educational environment. Such actions are recorded in the VLE database.

In this framework, we believe that users (students, teachers) are always in interaction with the VLE (1). The student accesses resources, updates his registration data, performs activities proposed by the teacher and accesses his MAA in order to know his performance throughout the course in order to make self-reflections. The teacher can prepare courses, LUs, showed in (6), activities, post grades, insert resources in the repository (8) of the VLE, and perform other actions according to his assignments. In our conceptual framework we defined that the student needs to have his initial profile, i.e., data that compose his initial model, aiming the environment begin to be adapted, instead of the VLE wait for several students' interactions. For this purpose, the first interactions of students with the VLE are registered (2). In addition, his usage history of the environment in past courses is obtained (9) in case of the student has previously used the VLE. With this information, the OLM begins to be formed (3), which is updated in every student interaction within the VLE by the learner model agents (4). To manipulate the students' data, these agents use an ontology that describes the model, the OLM ontology (5), which contains rules for message exchanging between agents, as well as definitions and rules that are part of the learner model. In addition, in the OLM, we have the *resource model*, which, in general, consists of the most relevant data regarding the resources to be used in the adaptation process in the VLE. In turn, resource adaptation agents (7) represented by ellipses, allow the adaptation and selection of resources that are stored in the VLE database (8) that they consider most appropriate for each student in the course using student data (3) and the OLM ontology (5). Finally, these resources are presented for students (8) use them in the VLE (1). It is noticed that this resource recommendation process can be seen as a continuous process, since new resources are showed each time the learner model is updated.

As Fig. 1 shows, there are two types of agents: learner model and adaptation resources agents. The first type of agents were developed in the JADE [5] and the latter in JADEX [6] frameworks. The learner model agents handle the students' data and their learner models in the VLE database, doing updates. In turn, the adaptation resource agents, from the data obtained from the learner model, will select collaborative resources contained in the repository (which is in the VLE database), e.g., PAs, to adapt the VLE. Finally, the student accesses VLE with its adapted content, and he can access his OLM. Students can also interact with each other, doing collaborative activities in VLE.

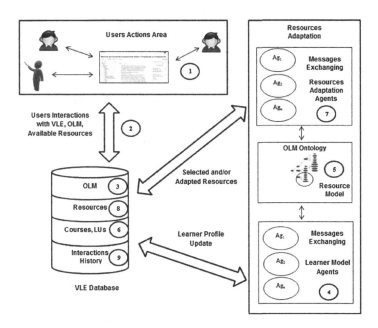

Fig. 1. ArCARE architecture.

3   Applying the Framework in a Classroom

As case study of our work, we used ArCARE on a course of Computational Thinking (CT) offered in blended form. This CT course was held with 38 Higher education students in Mechatronics of Federal Institute of Amazonas, Campus Manaus Distrito

Industrial (IFAM-CMDI). In the practice adopted in this work, the student must solve the proposed problems reflecting on what are the right actions and which programming structures are needed. And when an inadequacy arises, students can test and debug a new procedure, searching for a better result. For this work we used the Moodle VLE [7]. Furthermore, in the VLE were created 3 questionnaires for students answer at the beginning of the course. The questionnaires are: (1) Index of Learning Styles [8] (2) Honey-Alonso Learning Styles Questionnaire, adapted from Honey-Mumford [9]; (3) The pre-test itself, as mentioned previously. In this test scenario we used Pedagogical Architectures and peer correction. The agents made the choice of students to correct the work of their colleagues, based on their profiles. Students of different profiles were chosen to form their peers of performer-evaluator within the activities. The OLM must be easily understood by the student. So, Fig. 2 shows an example of OLM presented to a student, which is the result of student answers to the questionnaires. The presented graph shows the skills of a student in the Computational Thinking course.

In this work, the PA used was *thesis debate*. In this architecture, the intention is stimulate the participants, from their prior knowledge, extend and deepen their knowledge through interactions with peers, following a certain dynamic. In these interactions, which are performed through text production, the participants display their convictions on certain thesis proposed by mediator. After getting the initial profile of each student from the learning styles questionnaires, PAs-based adapted activities were recommended according to their profiles. In the Workshop activity, adaptation occurs firstly using a heuristic in which students in pairs for a thesis debate can be formed with students of heterogeneous profiles. Initially, the profiles were distinguished by learning styles, next interests. Importantly, these activities recommendations are made by Resources Adapter Agent. It can be seen in these initial tests that successful adaptations are being obtained with the ArCARE approach.

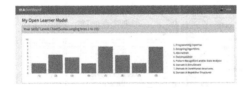

Fig. 2. Presenting OLM to students.

4 Conclusions

This paper has shown the ArCARE framework, which is a model of adaptation of resources in VLEs based on Pedagogical Architectures and collaborative learning. This strategy allows for greater customization of resources based on the characteristics of the students. The adaptation process described in the conceptual model increases the collaborative learning through interaction between students of the same course or discipline and interaction of students within the VLE. The initial tests showed that PAs recommendations is a solution that can help build the student's knowledge in a useful and effective way. The approach of multi-agent system, plus the OLM, can be applied to other VLEs, since the agents and educational environment can share the same database.

References

1. Bremgartner, V., Netto, J.M., Menezes, C.S.: Adaptation resources in virtual learning environments under constructivist approach: a systematic review. In: Proceedings of 45th IEEE Frontiers in Education Conference, El Paso, USA (2015)
2. Fröschl, C.: User modeling and user profiling in adaptive e-learning systems. Master's thesis. Institute for Information Systems and Computer Media, Graz University of Technology, Graz, Austria (2005)
3. LIP. learner information package specification 1.0.1. www.imsglobal.org/profiles/lipinfo01. html#5.1/
4. Tavares, L.O., Menezes, C.S., Nevado, R.A.: Pedagogical architectures to support the process of teaching and learning of computer programming. In: Proceedings of 42th IEEE Frontiers in Education Conference, Seattle, USA (2012)
5. JADE: Java Agent Development Framework. www.jade.tilab.com/
6. JADEX Active Components. www.activecomponents.org/bin/view/About/Features
7. Moodle: a free, open source course management system for online learning. www.moodle. org/
8. Soloman, B.A., Felder, R.M.: Index of learning styles questionnaire. www.engr.ncsu.edu/ learningstyles/ilsweb.html
9. Honey and Mumford's Learning Styles Questionnaire. www.nwlink.com/~donclark/hrd/ styles/honey_mumford.html

Minimal Meaningful Propositions Alignment in Student Response Comparisons

Florin Bulgarov[✉] and Rodney Nielsen

University of North Texas, Denton, TX, USA
florinbulgarov@my.unt.edu , rodney.nielsen@colorado.edu

Abstract. In an intelligent educational system, automatic sentence alignment has a pivotal role in determining a foundation for clustering, comparing, summarizing and classifying responses. In this paper, we go beyond sentence alignment by splitting the reference and the student responses into single clauses, which are then aligned using fine-grained semantic components (facets). This detailed analysis will enable automated educational systems to become highly scalable, domain-independent and to enrich the classroom experience. The results are very promising, showing a significant increase in terms of F_1-score, compared to the best performing baseline.

Keywords: Educational systems · Alignment · Student responses

1 Introduction

The research presented in this paper provides an architecture and foundation for understanding student responses to questions by using a novel approach to align the concepts or propositions contained in a student response with those in the teacher reference answer, or another student response. Several major benefits can be achieved with a proper alignment of the student's concepts. This alignment can facilitate student response clustering, response summarization, paraphrase detection or assessment, among others.

To align the student's response, we make use of Minimal Meaningful Propositions (MMPs) [2]. MMPs have recently been introduced as being a decomposition of text into the set of propositions that individually represent single minimal claims or arguments that cannot be further decomposed without losing contextual meaning. We present an automated method for aligning MMPs from two different texts. This will allow us to make thorough analogies between two text sources and make decisions about their similarity or entailment at a finer-grained level.

Outside of the education field, sentence alignment has been studied in the literature with important implications in fields such as document summarization [1,6], machine translation [10], rewriting systems and paraphrasing [3]. However, most systems have used simple feature sets such as lexical similarity or length

© Springer International Publishing AG 2017
E. André et al. (Eds.): AIED 2017, LNAI 10331, pp. 472–475, 2017.
DOI: 10.1007/978-3-319-61425-0_43

correlations [4,5]. Our novel approach for aligning sentences (or MMPs) relies on the fine-grained information contained in facets and on general relations between the two MMPs.

2 Related Work

The most predominant area where alignment has been used is machine translation, where sentence aligned bilingual corpora are a crucial resource [10]. However, documents in a bilingual corpus are generally closely aligned, whereas in monolingual corpora, sentences encounter a much lower level of alignment, with similar content being expressed using very different words, grammatical form or sentence ordering. As a consequence, many of the simple methods that proved to work well in bilingual datasets, such as sentence length correlations, lexical similarity, word overlap [4,5], are less likely to be effective on monolingual sentence pairs.

Another area where sentence alignment has been shown to be important is text summarization. For example, Marcu [6] proposes a cosine-based metric with the goal of aligning human-written summaries with full documents. Barzilay and Elhadad [1] propose a method for aligning sentences for learning text-to-text rewriting rules. In [7], the authors are improving the state-of-the-art by using a simpler, more robust algorithm with a TF-IDF ranking, treating each sentence as a separate document. Although alignment in text summarization is fundamentally similar to aligning MMPs, there are important differences. Summarization is generally based on well structured formal news sentences; whereas, even our teacher responses are frequently ungrammatical and middle school student responses are extremely colloquial. This changes the dependencies between the words and makes it difficult to detect and compare important semantic information. Furthermore, the unaligned MMP pairs are still likely to contain overlapping words or information from the question, since students will often talk about very related topics using words taken directly from the question. Perhaps, more importantly in our context, not all aligned MMPs have a paraphrase relation – an aligned student response MMP might contradict the reference answer MMP or express a related misconception.

3 Data

The dataset, first introduced in [2], consists of questions asked in real classrooms, each coming with a reference answer and a set of student responses (for more details, see [2]). Annotators established the proper entailment relations between each pair of *reference response MMP* and *student response – understood, misunderstood* or *did not address*. For the first two labels, an evidence from the student response was mandatory – the piece of text that motivated their decision. The alignment labels were automatically created by splitting the student response into MMPs and using the evidence provided by the annotators at the previous step. If the student MMP contained the evidence, it was marked as aligned. The dataset contains a total of 92378 instances, with only about 5% of the them being labeled as *aligned*.

4   MMP Alignment

Given a question, a reference answer and a student response, the goal is to align each student response MMP with the appropriate reference answer MMP, if such a valid alignment exists. This task is important not only for aligning pairs of MMPs that address the same concept or idea, but also to identify cases where we have one or more reference answer MMPs with no corresponding MMP in the student's response. In such cases, we can draw the conclusion that the student did not address that specific aspect of the reference answer.

4.1   Classification

An instance in our model is represented by two MMPs, one extracted from the reference answer and the other from the student's response. We follow a supervised approach to classify the MMP pairs as either *aligned* or *not-aligned* by employing a Random Forest model trained on 254 features. The first 48 features describe general relations between the two MMPs, such as the overall similarities between words, dependencies, Pointwise Mutual Information (PMI), etc. The other subset of features is extracted based on the governors, modifiers and relations of the most likely aligned facets. The most likely aligned facets are chosen based on the highest PMI scores between the governors and modifiers of all facets. Our decision to use facet information was motivated by their granularity level, allowing us to pinpoint the most likely understood relation between two MMPs.

4.2   Results

Because only about 5% of the instances are in the positive (aligned) class, we balanced the *training* set so that the weight of the negative instances is equal to the weight of the positive instances. The test set was maintained at its original unweighted class distribution.

Two baselines were computed to validate our method. In the *Word Overlap Baseline*, we remove stop words, stem remaining words and compare the number of overlapping words between the MMPs with a threshold t. The threshold was tuned on the development set by computing the average number of overlapping words for the positive class ($t = 1.5$). A second baseline (i.e., *Baseline Features*) contains 10 features, such as: length of each MMP in words and in characters, number of overlapping words (original and stemmed), and the BLEU scores for $n = 1, 2, 3,$ and 4 [9]. Naïve Bayes was the classifier chosen for this task as it reported the highest performance.

The results for the positive class are shown in Table 1. As can be seen, our proposed method performs significantly better than the two baselines, achieving an F_1-score 172% higher than the best performing baseline. We can see that

Table 1. MMP alignment results

	Prec.	*Rec.*	F_1-score
Word overlap	0.087	0.435	0.146
Baseline features	0.175	0.211	0.191
Alignment	**0.774**	**0.392**	**0.520**

our MMP alignment method has a high precision, but the recall is significantly lower. This is due to the low percentage of aligned instances in the dataset, which leads to our classifier overpredicting instances in the negative class. However, out of the instances predicted as being aligned, most of the predictions were correct, hence the high precision.

For the two baselines, we can observe that the recall is higher than precision, meaning that the models return too many false positives. This is understandable since, although a reference answer MMP may not be addressed, the student will likely discuss related topics using close words, confusing the classifiers. This issue does not occur in our proposed method, since our features do a much better job of differentiating between aligned and not aligned instances.

5 Conclusions and Future Work

This paper makes use of Minimal Meaningful Propositions in order to break down complex structures and to perform a fine-grained analysis of the student and teacher authored answers in an educational system. We presented a novel sentence alignment algorithm based on semantic facets. The algorithm's goal is to map MMPs from the instructor's reference response to those in the student's answer, addressing the same concepts or ideas. The results were encouraging, significantly outperforming two baselines.

Acknowledgements. This research was supported by the Institute of Education Sciences, U.S. Department of Education, Grant R305A120808 to University of North Texas. Opinions expressed are those of the authors.

References

1. Barzilay, R., Elhadad, N.: Sentence alignment for monolingual comparable corpora. Association for Computational Linguistics (2003)
2. Godea, A., Bulgarov, F., Nielsen, R.: Automatic generation and classification of minimal meaningful propositions in educational systems. In: COLING 2016 (2016)
3. Ibrahim, A., Katz, B., Lin, J.: Extracting structural paraphrases from aligned monolingual corpora. Association for Computational Linguistics (2003)
4. Kaufmann, M.: JMaxAlign: a maximum entropy parallel sentence alignment tool. In: COLING (Demos), pp. 277–288 (2012)
5. Lamraoui, F., Langlais, P.: Yet another fast, robust and open source sentence aligner. Time to reconsider sentence alignment. In: XIV Machine Translation Summit (2013)
6. Marcu, D.: The automatic construction of large-scale corpora for summarization research. ACM (1999)
7. Nelken, R., Shieber, S.M.: Towards robust context-sensitive sentence alignment for monolingual corpora. In: EACL (2006)
8. Nielsen, R.D., Ward, W., Martin, J.H.: Recognizing entailment in intelligent tutoring systems. Natural Lang. Eng. **15**(04), 479–501 (2009)
9. Papineni, K., Roukos, S., Ward, T., Zhu, W.J.: BLEU: a method for automatic evaluation of machine translation. Association for Computational Linguistics (2002)
10. Steinberger, R., Pouliquen, B., Widiger, A., Ignat, C., Erjavec, T., Tufis, D., Varga, D.: The JRC-Acquis: a multilingual aligned parallel corpus with 20+ languages. arXiv preprint arXiv:cs/0609058 (2006)

Does Adaptive Provision of Learning Activities Improve Learning in SQL-Tutor?

Xingliang Chen, Antonija Mitrovic$^{(\boxtimes)}$, and Moffat Mathews

Intelligent Computer Tutoring Group,
University of Canterbury, Christchurch, New Zealand
Xingliang.chen@pg.canterbury.ac.nz,
{tanja.mitrovic,moffat.mathews}@canterbury.ac.nz

Abstract. Tutored Problem Solving (PS), worked examples (WE) and Erroneous Examples (ErrEx) have all been proven to be effective in supporting learning. We previously found that learning from a fixed sequence of alternating WE/PS pairs and ErrEx/PS pairs (WPEP) was beneficial for students in comparison to learning from a fixed sequence of PS and WEs [1]. In this paper, we introduce an adaptive strategy which determines which learning activities (a WE, a 1-error ErrEx, a 2-error ErrEx or a problem to be solved) to provide to the student based on the score the student obtained on the previous problem. We compared the adaptive strategy to the fixed WPEP strategy, and found that students in the adaptive condition significantly improved their post-test scores on conceptual, procedural and debugging questions.

Keywords: Intelligent Tutoring Systems · Worked examples · Erroneous example · Problem solving · Adaptive strategy · SQL-Tutor

1 Introduction

A worked example consists of a problem with its solution and additional explanations. Numerous studies have compared the effectiveness of learning from WEs with unsupported problem solving [4, 11], showing the advantage of WEs for novices. Studies also show the benefits of learning from WEs and tutored problem solving in Intelligent Tutoring Systems (ITSs) [6, 9]. These studies showed that WEs result in shorter learning times, but commonly there is no difference in the knowledge gain compared to learning from tutored problem solving. Contrary to that, Najar and Mitrovic [10] compared learning from alternating example and problem pairs (AEP) to problem solving only (PO) and worked example only (EO) in SQL-Tutor, a constraint-based tutor for teaching database querying. The results indicated that both advanced students and novices learned more from the AEP condition. Furthermore, the AEP condition outperformed the PO condition in conceptual knowledge acquisition.

In contrast to WEs, erroneous examples present incorrect solutions and require students to find and fix errors. Erroneous examples may help students to become better at evaluating problem solutions. Große and Renkl [3] found the learning benefits of ErrExs for students with a high level of prior knowledge. Durkin and Rittle-Johnson [2] found that studying from both WEs and ErrExs resulted in higher declarative and

© Springer International Publishing AG 2017
E. André et al. (Eds.): AIED 2017, LNAI 10331, pp. 476–479, 2017.
DOI: 10.1007/978-3-319-61425-0_44

procedural knowledge gain compared to correct examples only. Our previous study [1] compared a fixed sequence of alternating WE/PS pairs and ErrEx/PS pairs in SQL-Tutor. The results showed students who studied with ErrExs showed better performance on problem solving than students who learned from WEs and problem solving. Additionally, correcting erroneous examples led to better learning outcomes on debugging and problem solving skills.

In this study, we investigated the effects of using an adaptive strategy to present WE, ErrEx or PS. We expected the adaptive strategy to be superior to a fixed sequence of WE/PS and ErrEx/PS pairs, and students who worked with the adaptive strategy would improve their conceptual, procedural and debugging knowledge.

2 Adaptive Strategy and Experiment Design

Our adaptive strategy is designed to select a learning activity for a student based on cognitive efficiency (CE). Kalyuga and Sweller [5] computed CE as $P \div R$, where P is performance (measured as the number of steps students needed to solve the problem), and mental effort R (self-reported by students). In our study, students were asked to rate the mental effort on a 9-point Likert scale after each learning activity (*How much effort did you invest to complete this activity?*). A student's performance P on a problem was represented by the score for the first submission on the problem. In constraint-based tutors, domain knowledge is represented as a set of constraints [8]. A solution is incorrect when it violates one or more constraints. Therefore, the solution can be scored based on the violated or satisfied constraints as $C = 1 - C_v/C_r$, in where C_v represents the number of violated constraints, and C_r represents the number of relevant constraints for the student's solution. However, this simple calculation does not produce accurate scores when there are several violated constraints that come from the same mistake. To deal with this situation, we used Eq. 1 instead.

$$C = \begin{cases} log_{(1/C_r)}(C_v/C_r/2) & 0 < C_v < C_r \\ 1, & C_v = 0 \\ 0, & C_v = C_r \end{cases} \tag{1}$$

Equation 2 calculates the solution score P as the sum of scores for all clauses the student specified (there are 6 clauses in the SQL *Select* statement). If a particular clause is empty in the student's solution, its score is 0. The clause weight (w_i) is calculated from the number of constraints that exist for a clause (C_{ci}) and the number of constraints relevant for the ideal solution of the problem (C_t), as $w_i = C_{ci}/C_t$.

$$P = 9 \sum_{i=1}^{6} w_i C_i \tag{2}$$

Same as in [5], the critical level of cognitive efficiency is defined as $CE_{cr} = P_{max} \div R_{max}$, where $P_{max} = R_{max} = 9$. We regarded $CE > CE_{cr}$ as the high cognitive efficiency; thus students who solved a problem with $CE > 1$ were expected to be able to solve the next problem without any preparation tasks. A student whose CE is between 1 and 0.75 receives a problem as the preparation task. A 2-error or 1-error ErrEx is provided to a student if his/her CE is between 0.75 and 0.25 respectively. A student receives a WE before the next problem if CE is below 0.25.

The study was conducted in a single, 100 min long session with SQL-Tutor [7]. The learning materials used in the study consisted of ten pairs of isomorphic activities, which could be problems to solve, worked examples or erroneous examples. The pairs were presented in a fixed order of increasing complexity.

At the beginning of the session, the students took an online pre-test, which took about 10 min. Then they were assigned randomly to one of the conditions. The control condition received 20 learning activities, presented in a fixed order of alternating WE/PS and ErrEx/PS pairs (5 WEs, 5 ErrExs, and 10 problems in total). The experimental group received the same ten pairs of activities, with the first element of which is a preparation task, and the second element is a problem to be solved. The preparation task could be skipped (for students who are performing well on problem solving), or a WE, 1-error or 2-error ErrEx (as described above). Since the preparation tasks were selected adaptively, the experimental group participants could receive fewer than 20 learning activities, based on their performance during problem solving. Students took an online post-test once they completed all learning activities.

3 Results and Discussion

The participants were 64 volunteers from an introductory database course at the University of Canterbury. The average score on the pre-test was 63.81% (sd = 15.17). Twenty-one students were excluded from the analysis since they did not complete all phases of the study. The remaining 43 students scored 65.76% (sd = 14.66) on the pre-test, and 87.14% (sd = 11.36) on the post-test.

Table 1. Detailed scores on the pre-/post-test

Group	Questions	Pre-test	Post-test	W, p
Control (21)	All questions	68.81 (14.16)	85.74 (13.31)	207, .001
	Conceptual	58.73 (11.3)	95.24 (7.72)	231, .000
	Procedural	87.58 (16.46)	86.11 (24.13)	ns
	Debugging	61.12 (29.24)	75.87 (21.51)	138, .083
	Time used	14.37 (5.84)	6.91 (3.93)	9, .000
Exper. (22)	All questions	62.84 (14.85)	88.47 (9.24)	253, .000
	Conceptual	53.03 (15.16)	93.18 (12.24)	253, .000
	Procedural	82.77 (18.95)	96.59 (5.7)	146, .001
	Debugging	52.73 (23.76)	75.64 (23.26)	253, .000
	Time used	13.22 (4.88)	9.17 (3.96)	31, .003

There were 21 students in the control and 22 in the experimental group (Table 1). The students in both the control group (W = 207, p < .005) and the experimental group (W = 253, p < .001) improved significantly between pre-test and post-test scores, as confirmed by the Wilcoxon singed-rank test. We also performed a deeper analysis of the pre/post-test questions. Questions 1 to 6 measured conceptual knowledge, questions 7 to 9 focused on procedural knowledge, and the last two questions measured debugging knowledge. In the experimental group, there were significant differences between pre-test and post-test scores on conceptual questions ($W = 253$, $p < .001$), procedural questions ($W = 146$, $p < .005$) and debugging questions ($W = 233$, $p < .001$). However, in the control group, only the score on conceptual questions ($W = 231$, $p < .001$) increased significantly between pre-test and post-test.

Several interesting research questions remain to be answered. This study shows that our adaptive strategy was effective in selecting learning activities in the domain of SQL queries. It would be informative to evaluate this strategy in other instructional domains, to test its generality. We also plan to compare the adaptive condition to a condition in which students can select learning activities to work on by themselves. Moreover, it would be interesting to investigate whether the adaptive strategy provides different benefits to students with different levels of prior knowledge.

References

1. Chen, X., Mitrovic, A., Mathews, M.: Do erroneous examples improve learning in addition to problem solving and worked examples? In: Micarelli, A., Stamper, J., Panourgia, K. (eds.) ITS 2016. LNCS, vol. 9684, pp. 13–22. Springer, Cham (2016). doi:10.1007/978-3-319-39583-8_2
2. Durkin, K., Rittle-Johnson, B.: The effectiveness of using incorrect examples to support learning about decimal magnitude. Learn. Instr. **22**(3), 206–214 (2012)
3. Große, C.S., Renkl, A.: Finding and fixing errors in worked examples: can this foster learning outcomes? Learn. Instr. **17**(6), 612–634 (2007)
4. Kalyuga, S., Chandler, P., Tuovinen, J., Sweller, J.: When problem solving is superior to studying worked examples. J. Educ. Psychol. **93**(3), 579 (2001)
5. Kalyuga, S., Sweller, J.: Rapid dynamic assessment of expertise to improve the efficiency of adaptive e-learning. Educ. Technol. Res. Dev. **53**(3), 83–93 (2005)
6. McLaren, Bruce M., Isotani, S.: When is it best to learn with all worked examples? In: Biswas, G., Bull, S., Kay, J., Mitrovic, A. (eds.) AIED 2011. LNCS, vol. 6738, pp. 222–229. Springer, Heidelberg (2011). doi:10.1007/978-3-642-21869-9_30
7. Mitrovic, A.: An intelligent SQL tutor on the web. Artif. Intell. Educ. **13**, 173–197 (2003)
8. Ohlsson, S.: Constraint-based student modeling. In: Greer, J.E., McCalla, G.I. (eds.) Student Modelling: The Key to Individualized Knowledge-Based Instruction, vol. 125, pp. 167–189. Springer, Heidelberg (1994)
9. Schwonke, R., Renkl, A., Krieg, C., Wittwer, J., Aleven, V., Salden, R.: The worked-example effect: not an artefact of lousy control conditions. Comput. Hum. Behav. **25**(2), 258–266 (2009)
10. Najar, A.S., Mitrovic, A.: Examples and tutored problems: is alternating examples and problems the best instructional strategy? Res. Pract. Technol. Enhanced Learn. **9**(3), 439–459 (2014)
11. van Gog, T.: Effects of identical example–problem and problem–example pairs on learning. Comput. Educ. **57**(2), 1775–1779 (2011)

Constraint-Based Modelling as a Tutoring Framework for Japanese Honorifics

Zachary T. Chung[1(✉)], Takehito Utsuro[1], and Ma. Mercedes Rodrigo[2]

[1] University of Tsukuba,
Tennodai 1-1-1, Tsukuba, Ibaraki Prefecture, Japan
chung.zachary.md@alumni.tsukuba.ac.jp
[2] Ateneo de Manila University,
Katipunan Ave., Loyola Heights,
Quezon City, Philippines

Abstract. Japanese honorifics establish the social and working relationship of people and it is indispensable in a conversation. In this research, we examine the use of Constraint-Based Modelling (CBM) and its implementation for developing a tutoring system for Japanese honorifics. We focus on implementing CBM for one form of honorifics called sonkeigo and we represent its formation through constraints. We demonstrate an implementation of a reading assistant tutor using CBM for rewriting sonkeigo expressions to their regular form and vice-versa by pattern matching via constraints.

Keywords: Constraint-Based Modelling · Japanese Honorifics · Intelligent Tutoring Systems

1 Japanese Honorifics

Japanese honorifics, known as keigo, is a set of grammatical and lexical elements used by Japanese speakers to show politeness [1]. There are two ways this is expressed in Japanese. One way is to elevate the status of an addressee, such as a superior using expressions called *sonkeigo*[1]. The other way is to use *kenjougo*[2], where the speaker lowers oneself or lowers the same in-group members of the speaker, to elevate the addressee indirectly. By using a combination thereof, people show respect according to their social relationship and distinguish whether they have a personal or professional relationship with others.

In this research, we focus on *sonkeigo*. *Sonkeigo* is always used to describe the addressee and never one's own actions. With *sonkeigo*, the sentence subject is the addressee and the verb of the sentence must either be in the *naru* form or the *nasaru* form.

---

[1] *Sonkeigo* is also known as the honorific polite form or the exalted form.
[2] *Kenjougo* is also referred to as the humble form.

© Springer International Publishing AG 2017
E. André et al. (Eds.): AIED 2017, LNAI 10331, pp. 480–484, 2017.
DOI: 10.1007/978-3-319-61425-0_45

2   Constraint Based-Modelling

According to Ohlsson, the learning process is in two phases: Error Recognition and Error Correction [6]. An Intelligent Tutoring System (ITS) may play the role of a mentor and identify errors for a student. These errors are corrected in context so the student can learn when and where to apply a solution correctly [3]. The idea of CBM is to equip a tutor with a set of constraints for a target domain, and to inform the learner about his constraint violations. This is important for students lacking declarative knowledge because they are unable to detect errors themselves [3]. Constraints in CBM represent both the domain and student knowledge, where each constraint represents an important concept of the underlying domain [2].

A CBM constraint is an ordered pair with an associated feedback message.

$$(C_r, C_s)$$

C_r is the relevance condition, which describes when the constraint is applicable. C_s is the satisfaction condition, which specifies tests to check solution validity. If C_r is satisfied in a problem state, in order for that problem state to be correct, it must also satisfy C_s. Otherwise, feedback is provided depending on which constraints had their satisfaction condition violated [4,5].

CBM is computationally simple because it does not require an expert model and can be implemented by pattern matching; student diagnosis is performed by using constraints to compare a student's solution to a specified ideal correct solution [5]. CBM can also support multiple solutions because constraints can be made to identify alternative constructs in solutions that are equally valid [4]. CBM also assumes that diagnostic information lies with the problem state and not the solution process. Hence, the learner is free to make any solutions as long as the learner never reaches a state defined to be wrong.

3   Designing and Applying Constraints

To create constraints for CBM to handle *sonkeigo*, we observed sentences with this honorific form as reference from the Balanced Corpus of Contemporary Written Japanese (BCCWJ)[3]. We focused our constraint creation on verbs that appears on the N4 level of the Japanese Language Proficiency Test; this is the level when students begin learning Japanese honorifics. For these verbs, there are three types that each need to be handled separately. These are *suru*-verbs ("サ変動詞"), *u*-verbs ("五段動詞") and *ru*-verbs ("一段動詞"). We created a constraint per conjugation of each verb type except for the past tense conjugation

---

[3] Balanced Corpus of Contemporary Written Japanese (BCCWJ) contains approximately 104.3 million words from 11 sources such as books, magazines, newspapers, white papers, textbooks, PR sheets, Yahoo! Chiebukuro, Yahoo! Blog, poems, the law, national parliament meeting records. See for more information: http://pj.ninjal.ac.jp/corpus_center/bccwj/en/.

of *u*-verbs because it has five irregular conjugations, each needing a separate constraint. In our implementation, these constraints are represented as tokens; each morpheme, the smallest unit of speech, has a unique token assigned except for the verb itself. The verb is only assigned a general token, unique enough to separate its conjugation types. For 25 variants of *sonkeigo* expressions based on BCCWJ data, we had to create 37 constraints. Combining the 37 constraints with 346 verbs, replacing each token with its original morpheme, the system theoretically creates 12,802 unique patterns for constraints.

In CBM, the constraints are used to validate learner input. For example, if the learner is tasked to rewrite the verb " 使う " (tsukau, lit. to use) using *sonkeigo*, which is in " 基本形 " or the dictionary form, we expect the learner to rewrite the verb either as お使いになる , お 使いなさる or お使いになられる (o-tsukai-ni-narareru) (see Fig. 1). Next, assuming that the learner inputs "お使いになる", the system checks if each morpheme matches a pattern in the constraint. If all the morphemes match to a constraint satisfaction condition, the learner's solution is deemed correct (see Fig. 1).

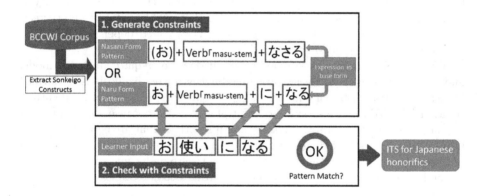

Fig. 1. Constraint generation and checking

4   System Design

The system developed is shown in Fig. 2 and operates according to Fig. 3. Upon user input of a sentence and the desired conversion mode, whether from *sonkeigo* to regular or vice-versa, the system parses the input using MeCab[4], a morphological analyzer, and identifies the target verbs for rewriting (1). In this process, relevant constraints are checked and pre-applied to each verb (2) and the system displays them on the user interface (3). The learner is tasked to rewrite the identified verbs; upon submission, the system parses the rewritten verbs (4)

---

[4] MeCab was used with UniDic instead of the IPA dictionary. UniDic is maintained by the National Institute for Japanese Language and Linguistics (NINJAL), Center for Corpus Development. See: http://pj.ninjal.ac.jp/corpus_center/unidic/.

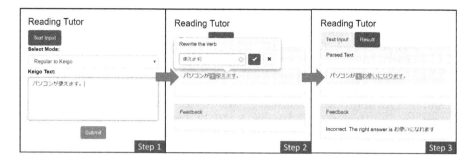

Fig. 2. Tutor interface

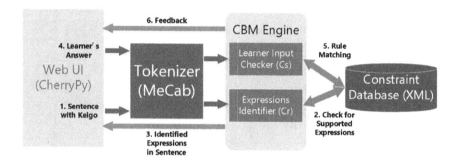

Fig. 3. System design

and performs pattern matching with the appropriate constraints (5). If the constraint satisfaction conditions are fulfilled, the system informs the learner that his answer is correct or otherwise, it is incorrect (6).

5 Conclusion

In this research, we demonstrated a proof-of-concept system that CBM can be used to create a tutor for Japanese honorifics. By using MeCab to break honorific expressions to morphemes, assigning tokens and implementing rule-based pattern matching against constraints, we created a tutor for checking rewrites of *sonkeigo* expressions to their regular forms and vice-versa.

References

1. Makino, S., Tsutsui, M.: Dictionary of Basic Japanese Grammar. The Japan Times, Tokyo (2009)
2. Martin, B.: Constraint-based modeling: representing student knowledge. NZ J. Comput. **7**, 30–38 (1999)

3. Mitrovic, A., Koedinger, K.R., Martin, B.: A comparative analysis of cognitive tutoring and constraint-based modeling. In: Brusilovsky, P., Corbett, A., Rosis, F. (eds.) UM 2003. LNCS, vol. 2702, pp. 313–322. Springer, Heidelberg (2003). doi:10.1007/3-540-44963-9_42

4. Mitrovic, A., Martin, B., Suraweera, P.: Intelligent tutors for all: the constraint-based approach. IEEE Intell. Syst. **22**(4), 38–45 (2007)

5. Mitrovic, A., Mayo, M., Suraweera, P., Martin, B.: Constraint-based tutors: a success story. In: Monostori, L., Váncza, J., Ali, M. (eds.) IEA/AIE 2001. LNCS, vol. 2070, pp. 931–940. Springer, Heidelberg (2001). doi:10.1007/3-540-45517-5_103

6. Ohlsson, S.: Learning from performance errors. Psychol. Rev. **103**(2), 41–262 (1996)

Teaching iSTART to Understand Spanish

Mihai Dascalu[1,2(✉)], Matthew E. Jacovina[2], Christian M. Soto[3],
Laura K. Allen[2], Jianmin Dai[2], Tricia A. Guerrero[2],
and Danielle S. McNamara[2]

[1] Faculty of Automatic Control and Computers,
University "Politehnica" of Bucharest,
313 Splaiul Independenței, 60042 Bucharest, Romania
mihai.dascalu@cs.pub.ro
[2] Institute for the Science of Teaching and Learning,
Arizona State University, PO Box 8721111, Tempe, AZ 85287, USA
{matthew.jacovina,laura.k.allen,jianmin.dai,
taguerre,dsmcnama}@asu.edu
[3] Department of Spanish, University of Concepción,
Psycholinguistics Area, Victor Lamas 1290, Concepción, Chile
christiansoto@udec.cl

Abstract. iSTART is a web-based reading comprehension tutor. A recent translation of iSTART from English to Spanish has made the system available to a new audience. In this paper, we outline several challenges that arose during the development process, specifically focusing on the algorithms that drive the feedback. Several iSTART activities encourage students to use comprehension strategies to generate self-explanations in response to challenging texts. Unsurprisingly, analyzing responses in a new language required many changes, such as implementing Spanish natural language processing tools and rebuilding lists of regular expressions used to flag responses. We also describe our use of an algorithm inspired from genetics to optimize the Fischer Discriminant Function Analysis coefficients used to determine self-explanation scores.

Keywords: Reading comprehension · Natural language processing · Intelligent tutoring systems · Optimizing score prediction

1 Introduction

Intelligent tutoring systems (ITS) provide students with automated instruction and feedback based on their performance and current level of understanding [1]. Providing this adaptive instruction can present a number of challenges for developers, particularly for ITSs that target ill-defined domains such as reading comprehension and writing. In these domains, assessment is highly complex and depends on myriad factors related to the individual student, the task properties, and the specific types of errors that are made. One assessment technique that has been used in these domains is Natural Language Processing (NLP) techniques. In particular, NLP has been used to analyze students' written responses as a means of measuring their performance across multiple domains, such as writing ability and reading comprehension [2–4].

© Springer International Publishing AG 2017
E. André et al. (Eds.): AIED 2017, LNAI 10331, pp. 485–489, 2017.
DOI: 10.1007/978-3-319-61425-0_46

Despite their success, these algorithms are limited in their ability to generalize to multiple languages. This poses problems, as quality reading comprehension instruction is needed for students across multiple languages. In this paper, we describe the process of adapting a web-based reading comprehension tutor, iSTART, such that it is fully available in Spanish. In particular, we describe the process of refining the NLP algorithm that guides scoring and feedback in the system, and outline several of the techniques that we considered and used throughout this translation process.

iSTART (Interactive Strategy Training for Active Reading and Thinking) is a web-based ITS that provides adolescent students with instruction and practice on reading comprehension strategies. In particular, iSTART focuses on strategies for generating high quality *self-explanations* during the reading process [5]. An algorithm scores the quality of these self-explanations on a scale from 0 (response is too short or nonsensical) to 3 (response makes global connections, often bringing in information from beyond the text) in terms of how well students are using the self-explanation strategies [3]. This scoring algorithm relies on a combination of word-based measures and Latent Semantic Analysis (LSA) to provide scores on each generated self-explanation [3].

2   iSTART-E: iSTART en Español

There is increasing evidence that students in Spanish-speaking countries struggle to demonstrate proficiency on standardized assessments of reading comprehension and writing skills [6]. In response to this issue, several educational technologies have been developed to target Spanish literacy [7, 8], and have been shown to improve students' performance on reading comprehension tasks [9]. However, much more work is needed to better promote ITSs in Spanish-speaking countries, including empirical examinations of the similarities and differences in these systems across English- and Spanish-speaking populations.

In light of this goal, we have worked to develop a Spanish version of the iSTART system – iSTART-E [10]. Similar to any large translation project, there were numerous important decision points, ranging from how to translate the instructional materials to be understandable for the widest range of Spanish speakers, to the selection of practice texts that would be contextually meaningful for many Spanish speakers. We outline in Table 1 important steps that had to be made to develop iSTART-E, as well as the specific techniques used to implement these changes.

In addition, we implemented an evolutionary algorithm [11] based on meta-heuristics inspired from genetics, more specifically bio-inspired processes such as selection, mutation and crossover in order to improve the accuracy of iSTART-E's scoring algorithm. In general, genetic algorithms provide a high degree of flexibility in generating high-quality solutions to search and optimization problems: hence, their applicability to our task. The purpose of the designed algorithm was to determine the optimal Discriminant Function Analysis (DFA) coefficients that create the best mapping between the scores of Spanish self-explanation translations and those already computed for English. The previously mentioned coefficients represent the Fischer

Table 1. Encountered challenges and provided solutions.

Challenge	Implemented solution
Providing a new dictionary of words	Upon manual review, we selected the dictionary found at http://www.winedt.org/dict.html which includes low-frequency, scientific words
Introducing a new list of stop words	The stop words list from Snowball (http://snowball.tartarus.org/algorithms/spanish/stop.txt) was expanded to include words describing numbers and interjections (e.g., "bah")
Correcting misspelled words	Instead of the Soundex algorithm available for English, we implemented a rule matching algorithm that relies on the Levenshtein edit distance
Tagging important words from practice texts	The Stanford Core NLP for Spanish (http://stanfordnlp.github.io/CoreNLP) was integrated and used to identify content words (i.e., nouns, verbs, adjectives, adverbs)
Normalizing words to allow for comparisons	Our static lemmatizer based on predefined transformation http://www.lexiconista.com/datasets/lemmatization/ automatically changes word forms to their corresponding inflectional form, i.e. lemma
Building an LSA space in Spanish	The LSA space was built using Apache Mahout with the lemmatized corpus provided by El Grupo de Interés en el Análisis de la Semántica Latente (http://elsemantico.es/index.html)
Translating regular expressions	The algorithm uses regular expressions to identify various types of self-explanations and to flag special types of responses. Manual corrections were made due to language specificities
Iterative testing	We manually translated 2,982 English self-explanations from the identification mini-games into Spanish. Distributions of the various components captured by the algorithms (e.g., matching content words; LSA cosine values) and repeated measures ANOVAs for each component across the two languages helped us identify discrepancies

classification coefficients corresponding to the three discriminant functions that are currently used in the automated iSTART English scoring mechanism [3].

3   Results and Discussion

At the start of the development of the iSTART-E Spanish algorithm, we calculated agreement between the English and Spanish algorithms on a preliminary set of 588 self-explanations (i.e., a subset of the self-explanations that were used to tune the scoring algorithm using the genetic algorithm). The exact agreement was 43.46% and the adjacent agreement was 84.35%. These agreement scores are a baseline, albeit imperfect, to compare our agreement results following the techniques and solutions described in this paper along with other bug fixes and refinements.

A total of 1,638 out of the 2,982 self-explanations, that were manually translated from English, were not flagged to receive special feedback and were included in the follow-up analyses. Before using the new (genetic) algorithm, but after implementing the changes described in Table 1, the exact accuracy was 64.90% with 89.87% adjacent accuracy. After applying the evolutionary algorithm with all considered optimizations, we obtained an exact accuracy of 69.5% with 94.10% adjacent accuracy, an increase in terms of aligning Spanish self-explanations to the corresponding English scores.

Although the correspondence between the Spanish and English scoring algorithms has improved from the initial accuracy, several concerns still exist. Broadly, we note that it will never be possible to perfectly align the iSTART system across the two languages – particularly with respect to the scoring algorithms. For instance, our scoring systems must rely on different LSA spaces that consist of completely different text sources. Moreover, refining the pre-processing stage for Spanish also creates potential differences between the algorithms.

In sum, the optimization of a scoring algorithm for a different language poses many challenges, but is not insurmountable. The complete transformation of a system such as iSTART into a new language requires attention to detail and sufficient input from numerous sources that are sensitive to changes in the language.

Acknowledgements. This work was partially funded by the FP7 2008-212578 LTfLL project, by University Politehnica of Bucharest through the "Excellence Research Grants" Program UPB–GEX 12/26.09.2016, as well as by the Institute for the Science of Teaching & Learning (IES R305A130124) and the Office of Naval Research (ONR N000141410343 and ONR N00014-17-1-2300).

References

1. VanLehn, K.: The behavior of tutoring systems. Int. J. Artif. Intell. Educ. **16**, 227–265 (2006)
2. Boonthum, C., McCarthy, P.M., Lamkin, T., Jackson, G.T., Magliano, J., McNamara, D.S.: Automatic natural language processing and the detection of reading skills and reading comprehension. In: Proceedings of FLAIRS. AAAI Press, Palm Beach, FL (2011)
3. McNamara, D.S., Boonthum, C., Levinstein, I.B., Millis, K.: Evaluating self-explanations in iSTART: comparing word-based and LSA algorithms. In: Landauer, T.K., McNamara, D.S., Dennis, S., Kintsch, W. (eds.) Handbook of Latent Semantic Analysis, pp. 227–241. Erlbaum, Mahwah (2007)
4. Allen, L.K., Snow, E.L., McNamara, D.S.: Are you reading my mind? Modeling students' reading comprehension skills with natural language processing techniques. In: 5th International Conference on Learning Analytics and Knowledge, LAK 2015, pp. 246–254. ACM, Poughkeepsie (2015)
5. Jackson, G.T., McNamara, D.S.: Motivation and performance in a game-based intelligent tutoring system. J. Educ. Psychol. **105**, 1036–1049 (2013)
6. Programme for International Student Assessment (PISA): PISA 2015 Results in Focus. OEDC Publishing (2016)

7. Vidal-Abarca, E., Gilabert, R., Ferrer, A., Ávila, V., Martínez, T., Mañá, A., Llorens, A.C., Gil, L., Cerdán, R., Ramos, L., Serrano, M.A.: TuinLEC, an intelligent tutoring system to improve reading literacy skills/ TuinLEC, un tutor inteligente para mejorar la competencia lectora. Infancia y Aprendizaje **37**, 25–56 (2014)

8. Véliz, M., Osorio, J.: Desarrollo de un software para el desarrollo de la capacidad de lectura crítica. RLA: Revista de lingüística teórica y aplicada, vol. 39, pp. 203–220 (2001)

9. Ponce, H.R., López, M.J., Mayer, R.E.: Instructional effectiveness of a computer-supported program for teaching reading comprehension strategies. Comput. Educ. **59**(4), 1170–1183 (2012)

10. Soto, C.M., McNamara, D.S., Jacovina, M.E., Snow, E.L., Dai, J., Allen, L.K., Perret, C.A., Johnson, A.M., Russell, D.G.: iSTART-E: Desarrollando un tutor inteligente para la comprensión lectora de estudiantes de habla hispana. In: García, M. (ed.) Proceedings of FLAIRS. AAAI Press, Orlando, FL (2015)

11. Mitchell, M.: An Introduction to Genetic Algorithms. MIT Press, Cambridge (1996)

Data-Driven Generation of Rubric Parameters from an Educational Programming Environment

Nicholas Diana[1]([✉]), Michael Eagle[1], John Stamper[1], Shuchi Grover[2],
Marie Bienkowski[2], and Satabdi Basu[2]

[1] Human-Computer Interaction Institute, Carnegie Mellon University,
5000 Forbes Avenue, Pittsburgh, PA 15213, USA
`ndiana@cmu.edu, meagle@cs.cmu.edu, john@stamper.org`
[2] SRI International, 333 Ravenswood Avenue, Menlo Park, CA 94025, USA
`{shuchi.grover,marie.bienkowski,satabdi.basu}@sri.com`

Abstract. We demonstrate that, by using a small set of hand-graded students, we can automatically generate rubric parameters with a high degree of validity, and that a predictive model incorporating these rubric parameters is more accurate than a previously reported model. We present this method as one approach to addressing the often challenging problem of grading assignments in programming environments. A classic solution is creating unit-tests that the student-generated program must pass, but the rigid, structured nature of unit-tests is suboptimal for assessing more open-ended assignments. Furthermore, the creation of unit-tests requires predicting the various ways a student might correctly solve a problem – a challenging and time-intensive process. The current study proposes an alternative, semi-automated method for generating rubric parameters using low-level data from the Alice programming environment.

Keywords: Programming · Automatic assessment · Alice · Educational data mining

1 Introduction

Manually grading programming assignments is often a time-consuming and labor-intensive process. Instructors often employ Automated Assessment Tools (AATs) to increase the efficiency and consistency of the grading process. However, the rigid evaluation criteria used by most AATs are often unable to assess more open-ended programming assignments, such as those seen in the Alice programming environment [3].

One potential approach is natural language processing (NLP). Wang et al. showed that NLP could reliably detect constructs like creative problem-solving in open-ended questions [4]. As part of our previous work, we developed a predictive NLP model of students' final grades. These NLP approaches may provide a method for automating the grading of open-ended programming assignments,

© Springer International Publishing AG 2017
E. André et al. (Eds.): AIED 2017, LNAI 10331, pp. 490–493, 2017.
DOI: 10.1007/978-3-319-61425-0_47

but they often fail to provide an interpretable justification for the automatically-generated grades. In the current study, we expand the grain-size of our features from an NLP term to a small object that we call a code-chunk. Using this larger grain-size, we demonstrate that: (1) we improve the accuracy of our predictive models, and (2) we increase the interpretability of the key features of our model. This second result is particularly important because it allows us to compare the semantic quality of these data-driven features against the real, human-generated rubric used to generate the students' final grades.

2   Methods

Our methodology can be roughly separated into to two stages. First, we transformed the raw, low-level log data into small objects that we call *code-chunks*. Second, we tested two methods for selecting code-chunks that may be predictive of student success: seed-based selection and L1 regularization.

2.1   Data

The data used in the current study were originally collected by Werner et al. [5]. The hand-graded rubric scores serve as the ground truth that we can use to both train and evaluate our models. We used a subset of the original data ($N = 227$), excluding students who worked on the assessment more than 5 min longer than the 30 min allotted or with missing, ambiguous, or incorrect grade or log data.

Diana et al., describes a method for transforming linear log data into hierarchical code-states [1]. These *code-states* are created for each step in a student's log file, approximating a snap-shot of the student's program at each step. The result is a list of cumulative code-states for each student that are both more readable and more amenable to analyses.

Each level of the code-state object is translated into a single-level code-chunk. Note if a parameter is equal to an array or child object, that parameter is ignored. Instead of nesting code-chunks, a new code-chunk containing the parameters of the child element is created.

2.2   Feature Selection

We compared two methods for selecting code-chunks that may be predictive of final grade: selecting code-chunks prior to the regression and selecting code-chunks (as features) within the regression.

In the first method, we selected potentially useful code-chunks by first dividing the sample of student data into two groups along a final grade threshold: high-performing students ($finalgrade \geq threshold$) and low-performing students ($finalgrade < threshold$).

Once two groups of students had been established, we compared the relative frequencies of code-chunks between groups. This was done by first generating a list of all possible code-chunks. Then we count each occurrence of each chunk for each of the two groups. Finally, we use a chi-squared test to determine if each chunk has a significantly higher or lower frequency in the high-performing group than in the low-performing group. These significantly more or less frequent chunks serve as the features for our grade-prediction model. Finally, we generated a linear model using all features as input to serve as a baseline.

In the second method, we used L1 regularization to select features via a lasso regression. The lasso reduces features by encouraging weights to shrink to zero. Features with a weight of zero are effectively dropped from the model, reducing the number of features [2].

2.3   Model Parameters and Cross-Validation

Unless otherwise stated, all models were generated by using 20% of the data for training the model and 80% of the data for testing the model. While the models generally perform better with a larger training set, the purpose of this paper is to provide a method for reducing instructor work. As such, limiting our training set to 20% (approximately 45 students) provides some external validity for the results we report.

We compare each of these models using Root Mean Square Error (RMSE). Each reported RMSE value is the standardized average of a Stratified Shuffle-Split Cross-Validation (Folds = 100). Before cross-validation in the seed-based feature selection method, each student was labeled either a high or low-performing student according to their grade and the specified threshold. Then, for each fold the data were divided into roughly equal groups, preserving the ratio of high to low-performing students across groups. The python package scikit-learn was used for cross-validation, linear regression, and lasso regression.

3   Results

3.1   Linear and Lasso Regression

A linear model was generated to test the effect of organizing features as code-chunks (as opposed to the vocabulary of terms used in the previously reported NLP model). We found that the model using all code-chunks as features was more accurate (RMSE = 0.266) than the previously reported NLP model (RMSE = 0.384) at predicting final grades.

The features used in our seed-based feature selection method were selected by comparing the relative frequency of high-performing vs. low-performing code-chunks. We used a chi-squared test to determine if the frequencies between groups were significantly different ($p < .05$). On average, a very small percentage (0.016%) of code-chunks met this criteria for each fold.

Several linear models were generated to test the effect of our seed-based feature selection approach at different final grade thresholds. We explored the range of final grades from 20–30 (66–100%) as final grade thresholds and generated a linear model for each value in that range. A final grade threshold of 30 had the lowest score (RMSE = 0.273) while a threshold of 26 had the highest score (RMSE = 0.331).

A lasso regression model ($\alpha = 0.25$) was generated to test the effect of using L1 regularization to select features (code-chunks) rather than selecting them using the seed-based, chunk frequency method described above. We found that the lasso regression model was more accurate (RMSE = 0.235) than both a linear model using the same input features (all code-chunks) (RMSE = 0.266) and a linear model using the pre-selected seed-based features (RMSE = 0.273).

On average the lasso regression (M = 14.45, SD = 2.87) selected significantly more features ($p < .001$) than the frequency-based feature selection method (M = 10.12, SD = 1.90). There was also a moderate correlation ($r^2 = 0.686$) between the weights of features shared by both models.

4   Discussion and Conclusion

We found that both methods of feature selection produced models that were more accurate than the previously reported predictive model. This suggests that the increased context provided by the larger grain-size of a code-chunk results in better features and a more predictive model, supporting our first hypothesis.

With respect to our second hypothesis, that increasing the granularity of features will increase the interpretability of the model, we found that several highly-weighted code-chunks present in both feature selection methods shared a resemblance to the human-generated rubric parameters.

By transforming low-level log data from a programming environment into context rich code-chunks, we were able to: (1) increase the accuracy of our predictive model (with respect to a previously reported model that used smaller-grained, NLP terms as features), and (2) draw comparisons between our data-driven rubric parameters and human-generated rubric parameters.

References

1. Diana, N., Eagle, M., Stamper, J., Grover, S., Bienkowski, M., Satabdi, B.: An instructor dashboard for real-time analytics in interactive programming assignments (2016)
2. Friedman, J., Hastie, T., Tibshirani, R.: The Elements of Statistical Learning. Springer series in statistics, vol. 1. Springer, Berlin (2001)
3. Pausch, R., Burnette, T., Capehart, A.C., Conway, M., Cosgrove, D., DeLine, R., Durbin, J., Gossweiler, R., Koga, S., White, J.: A brief architectural overview of Alice, a rapid prototyping system for virtual reality (1995)
4. Wang, H.C., Chang, C.Y., Li, T.Y.: Assessing creative problem-solving with automated text grading. Comput. Educ. **51**(4), 1450–1466 (2008)
5. Werner, L., Denner, J., Campe, S.: The fairy performance assessment: mea-suring computational thinking in middle school. In: Proceedings of the 43rd ACM Technical Symposium on Computer Science Education - SIGCSE 2012, pp. 215–220 (2012)

Exploring Learner Model Differences
Between Students

Michael Eagle[1]([⊠]), Albert Corbett[1], John Stamper[1],
Bruce M. McLaren[1], Ryan Baker[3], Angela Wagner[1],
Benjamin MacLaren[1], and Aaron Mitchell[2]

[1] Human-Computer Interaction Institute, Carnegie Mellon University,
Pittsburgh, USA
{meagle,corbett,jstamper,bmclaren,
awagner,maclaren}@andrew.cmu.edu
[2] Department of Biological Sciences, Carnegie Mellon University,
Pittsburgh, USA
apml@andrew.cmu.edu
[3] Graduate School of Education, University of Pennsylvania, Philadelphia, USA
ryanbaker@gmail.com

Abstract. Bayesian Knowledge Tracing (BKT) has been employed successfully in intelligent learning environments to individualize curriculum sequencing and help messages. Standard BKT employs four parameters, which are estimated separately for individual knowledge components, but not for individual students. Studies have shown that individualizing the parameter estimates for students based on existing data logs improves goodness of fit and leads to substantially different practice recommendations. This study investigates how well BKT parameters in a tutor lesson can be individualized ahead of time, based on learners' prior activities, including reading text and completing prior tutor lessons. We find that directly applying best-fitting individualized parameter estimates from prior tutor lessons does not appreciably improve BKT goodness of fit for a later tutor lesson, but that individual differences in the later lesson can be effectively predicted from measures of learners' behaviors in reading text and in completing the prior tutor lessons.

Keywords: BKT · Genetics · Machine learning · Student modeling

1 Introduction

Learner models of domain knowledge have been successfully employed for decades in intelligent tutoring systems (ITS), to individualize both curriculum sequencing [1–4] and help messages [5, 6]. Bayesian methods are frequently employed in ITSs to infer student knowledge from performance accuracy, as in the citations above, as well as in other types of learning environments [7], and Bayesian modeling systems have been shown to accurately predict students' tutor and/or posttest performance [1, 3, 8, 9].

These models generally individualize modeling parameters for individual knowledge components (KCs, also referred to as skills) [10], but not for individual students.

© Springer International Publishing AG 2017
E. André et al. (Eds.): AIED 2017, LNAI 10331, pp. 494–497, 2017.
DOI: 10.1007/978-3-319-61425-0_48

Several studies have shown that individualizing parameters for students, as well as for KCs, improves the quality of the models [1, 11–13]. These approaches to modeling individual differences among students have monitored student performance after the fact, in tutor logs that have been previously collected to derive individualized student parameters for the tutor module(s). While these efforts have proven successful, they don't achieve the goal of dynamic student modeling within an ITS, since estimating and using individualized parameters concurrently within a tutor lesson is quite difficult. In this paper we examine how well individual differences in student learning in a lesson of the Genetics Cognitive Tutor [8] can be predicted ahead of time from two types of prior online activities: reading instructional text and solving problems in prior tutor lessons. In the following sections we describe Knowledge Tracing, the on-line student activities, the predictors derived from students' reading and prior tutor activities, and our success in using these predictors to model individual differences in the tutor.

Bayesian Knowledge Tracing (BKT) estimates the probability that a student knows each of the knowledge components (KC) in a tutor lesson. It employs a two-state Bayesian learning model – at any time a student either knows or does not know a given KC – and employs four parameters, which are estimated separately for each KC. BKT is employed in Cognitive Tutors to implement *Cognitive Mastery*, in which the curriculum is individualized to afford each student just the number of practice opportunities needed to enable the student to "master" each of the KCs, which is generally operationalized as a 0.95 probability that the student has learned the KC.

Individual Differences. Knowledge Tracing and Cognitive Mastery generally employ best-fitting estimates of each of the four parameters for each individual KC but *not* for individual students. In this work, we incorporate individual differences among students into the model in the form of individual difference weights. Following Corbett and Anderson [1], four best-fitting weights are estimated for each student, one weight for each of the four parameter types, wL_0, wT, wG, wS.

In this paper we focus on four types of BKT models for the third lesson in a Genetics Cognitive Tutor curriculum on *genetic pathways analysis* to examine how well IDWs in a tutor lesson can be predicted from prior online activities. The four models are: (1) a standard BKT model (SBKT) with no individualization, (2) a model with best-fitting IDWs for lesson 3 (BFIDW-L3), (3) models with best-fitting IDWs from prior lessons, and (4) a model with predicted individual difference weights derived from earlier activities. We compare how much each of the three types of individualized models improves upon the non-individualized SBKT fit (1).

In an earlier study, Eagle et al. [14] estimated individual difference weights for the first lesson in this curriculum before students began using the tutor lesson, based on six measures of students' reading performance and six measures of students' pretest performance. The predicted IDW model was about 40% as successful as the best-fitting IDW model. In a second study, Eagle et al. [15] examined how well individual difference weights for the second lesson in the curriculum can be predicted from the same 12 reading and pretest measures, along with 10 measures derived from lesson 1: the 4 best-fitting IDWs from lesson 1, and 6 other measures of student performance in the lesson. In this study, the predicted IDW model was about 60% as successful as the best-fitting model. The predicted model improved the goodness of fit by 4.1%, reducing RMSE from 0.413 to 0.396, while the BFIDW model reduced RMSE by 6.8% 0.385. This study found that reading measures remained useful as predictors of IDWs across all these models, but that pretest measures became much less important as tutor-performance measures were incorporated into the models.

2 Discussion and Conclusions

We examine how well we can predict IDWs in lesson 3 with the same types of reading measures as in [14, 15] along with an expanded set of tutor performance measures. This study examines methods for predicting individual difference weights for students in BKT learning parameters (intercept and rate) and performance (guess and slip) for the third lesson in a Cognitive Tutor curriculum. This is an important issue because integrating IDWs into an intelligent tutor lesson is easier if the IDWs can be assigned before the student starts working in the lesson. We evaluate the different estimated IDWs by examining how well they fit student performance in Lesson 3, compared to (1) standard SBKT with no IDWs, and (2) a model with best-fitting weights for Lesson 3.

We find that directly applying the best-fitting IDWs from either of two prior lessons in the curriculum, or from both lessons combined, does not appreciably improve goodness of fit for Lesson 3, compared to the SBKT model. In contrast, estimating lesson-3 IDWs from measures of students' prior reading performance, and performance in the two prior tutor lessons, is more successful; it is 60% as successful as the best-fitting Lesson-3 IDW model in improving the goodness of fit compared to the SBKT model.

Several secondary conclusions emerge. First, a prior study [15] obtained very similar success in predicting IDWs based on reading performance, pretest performance and a smaller set of tutor performance measures. This study demonstrates that IDWs can be successful predicted without including pretest measures. This is potentially important since pretests may not be available in online learning environments. Second, among reading time measures and a wide range of tutor performance measures, no category of measures emerged as an especially strong predictor of Lesson 3 IDWs; instead it appears that predictive success depends on a broad range of predictor variables. Finally, reading time measures prove to be useful predictors of students' problem-solving behaviors in a subsequent tutor lesson, including reading time measures for text on a topic unrelated to that tutor lesson. This suggests that the reading time measures may reflect knowledge-acquisition strategies, as well as any knowledge acquired.

Acknowledgements. This research was supported by the National Science Foundation via the grant "Knowing What Students Know: Using Education Data Mining to Predict Robust STEM Learning", award number DRL1420609.

References

1. Corbett, A.T., Anderson, J.R.: Knowledge tracing: modeling the acquisition of procedural knowledge. User Model. User-Adap. Inter. **4**, 253–278 (1995)
2. Mayo, M., Mitrovic, A.: Optimising ITS behaviour with Bayesian networks and decision theory. Int. J. Artif. Intel. Educ. **12**, 124–153 (2001)
3. Shute, V.: Smart: student modeling approach for responsive tutoring. User Model. User-Adap. Inter. **5**(1), 1–44 (1995)
4. Ritter, S., Yudelson, M., Fancsali, S., Berman, S.: How mastery learning works at scale. In: Proceedings of the Third ACM Conference on Learning @ Scale, pp. 71–79 (2016)
5. Ganeshan, R., Johnson, W.L., Shaw, E., Wood, B.P.: Tutoring diagnostic problem solving. In: Gauthier, G., Frasson, C., VanLehn, K. (eds.) ITS 2000. LNCS, vol. 1839, pp. 33–42. Springer, Heidelberg (2000). doi:10.1007/3-540-45108-0_7
6. Conati, C., Gertner, A., VanLehn, K.: Using Bayesian networks to manage uncertainty in student modeling. User Model. User-Adap. Inter. **12**, 371–417 (2002)
7. Pardos, Z., Bergner, Y., Seaton, D., Pritchard, D.: Adapting Bayesian Knowledge Tracing to a massive online course in edX. In: Proceedings of the Sixth International Conference on Educational Data Mining, pp. 137–144. (2013)
8. Corbett, A., MacLaren, B., Kauffman, L., Wagner, A., Jones, E.A.: Cognitive tutor for genetics problem solving: learning gains and student modeling. J. Educ. Comput. Res. **42**(2), 219–239 (2010)
9. Gong, Y., Beck, J., Heffernan, N.: Comparing knowledge tracing and performance factor analysis by using multiple model fitting. In: Aleven, V., Kay, J., Mostow, J. (eds.) ITS2010 Intelligent Tutoring Systems. LNCS, vol. 6094, pp. 35–44. Springer, Heidelberg (2010)
10. Koedinger, K., Corbett, A., Perfetti, C.: The knowledge-learning-instruction (KLI) framework: bridging the science-practice chasm to enhance robust student learning. Cogn. Sci. **36**(5), 757–798 (2012)
11. Lee, J., Brunskill, E.: The impact of individualizing student models on necessary practice opportunities. In: Yacef, K., Zaiane, O., Hershkovitz, A., Yudelson, M., Stamper, J. (eds.) EDM2012 Proceedings of the 5th International Conference on International Educational Data Mining Society, pp. 118–125 (2012)
12. Pardos, Z.A., Heffernan, N.T.: Modeling individualization in a Bayesian networks implementation of knowledge tracing. In: Bra, P., Kobsa, A., Chin, D. (eds.) UMAP 2010. LNCS, vol. 6075, pp. 255–266. Springer, Heidelberg (2010). doi:10.1007/978-3-642-13470-8_24
13. Yudelson, M.V., Koedinger, K.R., Gordon, G.J.: Individualized Bayesian knowledge tracing models. In: Lane, H.C., Yacef, K., Mostow, J., Pavlik, P. (eds.) AIED 2013. LNCS (LNAI), vol. 7926, pp. 171–180. Springer, Heidelberg (2013). doi:10.1007/978-3-642-39112-5_18
14. Eagle, M., Corbett, A., Stamper, J., McLaren, B., Wagner, A., MacLaren, B., Mitchell, A.: Estimating individual differences for student modeling in intelligent tutors from reading and pretest data. In: Micarelli, A., Stamper, J., Panourgia, K. (eds.) Intelligent Tutoring Systems: 13th International Conference Proceedings, pp. 133–143. Springer, New York (2016)
15. Eagle, M., Corbett, A., Stamper, J., McLaren, B., Baker, R., Wagner, A., MacLaren, B., Mitchell, A.: Predicting individual differences for learner modeling in intelligent tutors from previous learner activities. In: Aroyo, L., D'Mello, S., Vassileva, J., Blustein, J. (eds.) Proceedings UMAP 2016, pp. 55–63. Association for Computing Machinery, New York (2016)

Investigating the Effectiveness of Menu-Based Self-explanation Prompts in a Mobile Python Tutor

Geela Venise Firmalo Fabic[(⊠)], Antonija Mitrovic,
and Kourosh Neshatian

Department of Computer Science and Software Engineering,
University of Canterbury, Christchurch, New Zealand
geela.fabic@pg.canterbury.ac.nz,
{tanja.mitrovic,kourosh.neshatian}@canterbury.ac.nz

Abstract. *PyKinetic* is a mobile tutor for Python, which offers Parsons problems with incomplete lines of code (LOCs). This paper reports the results of a study in which we investigated the effect of menu-based self-explanation (SE) prompts. Students were asked to self-explain concepts related to incomplete LOCs they have solved. The goals of the study were (1) to investigate whether students are learning with PyKinetic and (2) to determine the effect of SE prompts. The scores of participants have significantly improved from the pre-test to the post-test. There was also a significant difference on the post-test scores of participants from the experimental group compared to the control group. In future work, we aim to add other activities to PyKinetic, and introduce a student model and a pedagogical model for an adaptive version of PyKinetic.

Keywords: Mobile Python tutor · Self-explanation · Parsons problems

1 Introduction

Parsons problems are puzzle-like exercises consisting of a set of randomized lines of code to be rearranged in the correct order to produce a desired outcome [1]. These problems are usually solved by drag and drop actions which make them more suitable for smartphones than program writing exercises. Previous work on Parsons problems in a mobile tutor were reported by Karavirta et al. [2], for Android and iOS.

Self-explanation (SE) is an activity which aims to engage the student in reasoning about elements of a problem which are not directly presented, to promote deeper learning [3]. SE prompts were first introduced as open-ended questions, which encourage learners to think without any set limitations. Other forms of SE prompts have emerged: open-ended, focused, scaffolded, resource-based and menu-based prompts [4]. Johnson and Mayer found that menu-based SE prompts were more effective than open-ended SE prompts in a game-like application about electrical circuits [5]. The authors explained that menu-based SE may have increased the effectiveness of learning because they minimize extraneous cognitive load while fostering germane load.

© Springer International Publishing AG 2017
E. André et al. (Eds.): AIED 2017, LNAI 10331, pp. 498–501, 2017.
DOI: 10.1007/978-3-319-61425-0_49

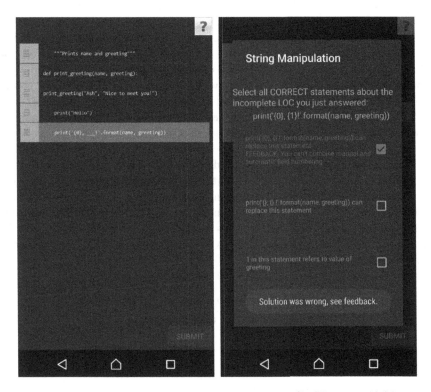

Fig. 1. A Parsons Problem with Incomplete LOCs (left); SE prompt (right)

We present PyKinetic, a mobile Python 3.x tutor for novices aimed as a complement to traditional lectures [6, 7]. PyKinetic provides Parsons problems with incomplete LOCs. Parsons Problems in PyKinetic are completed by dragging and dropping
single LOCs in the correct order. An incomplete LOC is completed by long-clicking on
a LOC to select it (highlighted in blue in Fig. 1, left), and tapping the selected LOC to
choose the right answer from provided options. All incomplete LOCs must be
answered correctly before the solution to the Parsons problem can be submitted. In the
situation illustrated in Fig. 1 (left), SUBMIT is disabled as the student has not completed the selected line. Once the student completes the line, he/she is given an SE
prompt (Fig. 1 right). Each SE prompt allows only one attempt. Feedback "Correct!
Great job!" is displayed when an SE prompt is answered correctly. If the learner's
answer is incorrect, an explanation is shown for all wrong options (right screenshot in
Fig. 1).

2   Evaluation, Findings and Conclusions

The version of PyKinetic used in the study contained 15 problems, which had between
3 and 16 LOCs, with a maximum of 3 incomplete LOCs. The problems were presented
in a fixed order of increasing difficulty. The first two problems were given as practice.

There were 22 SE prompts in total: 14 conceptual questions and 8 procedural questions. There were two conditions in the study: the experimental group received menu-based SE prompts after completing incomplete LOCs, while the control group did not. Our first hypothesis was that all participants, irrespective of the group, would improve their Python skills by interacting with PyKinetic (H1). Secondly, SE prompts would help experimental group participants learn more than control group (H2).

We recruited 83 participants: 70 students enrolled in introductory programming courses from two universities (University of Canterbury and Ateneo de Manila University), as well as 13 high school students from a Digital Technology class from a local high school. The study was approved by the high school and the Human Ethics Committees of both universities. The participants were randomly assigned into the experimental or control group. Each student participated in a group session that lasted for 1.5–2 hours. A 15-minute pre-test was administered first (on paper), after which the participants interacted with PyKinetic. This was followed by a 15-minute post-test. The pre/post-test each had eight questions: six conceptual questions and two procedural questions.

Table 1. Pre/post test scores (%) (* denotes significant differences)

	Experimental (36)	Control (40)	U, p
Pre-test	64.75 (18.52)	66.01 (12.34)	ns
Post-test	75.86 (16.15)	70.56 (14.37)	U = 529.5, p = .047*
Improvement	$z = -3.315, p = .001$	$z = -2.45, p = .014$	
Cohen's d	d = .64	d = .34	
Pre-test Conc.	62.40 (19.05)	63.41 (14.31)	ns
Post-test Conc.	75.71 (16.91)	69.19 (16.71)	U = 550, p = .077
Impr. Conc.	$z = -3.221, p = .001$	$z = -2.37, p = .018$	
Pre-test Proc.	71.82 (26.98)	74.42 (19.48)	ns
Post-test Proc.	76.17 (21.42)	74.58 (19.95)	ns
Norm. Gain	14.94 (77.79)	4.82 (63.71)	U = 530, p = .048*
Time/problem (min)	4 (1.57)	3.18 (1.13)	U = 502, p = .023*

We had to eliminate the data related to seven participants because of incomplete logs due to network issues. The analyses presented in the paper were performed on the data collected from the remaining 76 participants. The populations from the three institutions had comparable levels of pre-existing knowledge as there was no significant difference on their pre-test scores. Table 1 reports the pre/post-test scores of the two groups on all questions, and on conceptual/procedural questions separately. We used the paired non-parametric Wilcoxon Signed Ranks test to verify hypothesis H1. Both groups have significantly improved between pre- and post-test overall (the *Improvement* row), and on conceptual questions (the *Impr. Conc.* row), but there was no significant improvement on procedural questions only. These results show that there is enough evidence to accept our first hypothesis H1, which was that PyKinetic help improve Python skills of the participants.

Table 1 also reports the results of the Mann Whitney U test for checking significant differences between the groups. There was no difference on the pre-test scores, but the experimental group performed better on the post-test ($p < .05$, $U = 529.5$). There was also a significant difference on the normalized gain ($p < .05$, $U = 530$). Both groups had a positive Cohen's d effect size, but the effect size was higher for the experimental group. These results provide evidence to accept our second hypothesis H2, which was that SE prompts would help experimental group participants learn more than the control group. The experimental group participants spent significantly more time per problem in comparison to the control group, which was expected, as they needed to answer SE prompts ($p < .05$, $U = 502$).

Therefore, both groups improved their performance after interacting with PyKinetic. The participants who received SE prompts performed better on the post-test than the participants who did not self-explain. This result is consistent with work by Johnson and Mayer [5], who also found menu-based SE prompts to be effective in increasing learning in a game-like environment. Our study shows that menu-based SE prompts are also effective on a mobile platform. Future work includes adding more problems, and developing other kinds of activities for PyKinetic. We also endeavor to complement PyKinetic with a student model and a pedagogical model, towards an adaptive version of PyKinetic with personalized problem selection and feedback.

References

1. Parsons, D., Haden, P.: Parson's programming puzzles: a fun and effective learning tool for first programming courses. In: Proceedings of the 8th Australasian Conference on Computing Education, vol. 52, pp. 157–163. Australian Computer Society, Inc. (2006)
2. Karavirta, V., Helminen, J., Ihantola, P.: A mobile learning application for Parsons problems with automatic feedback. In: Proceedings of the 12th Koli Calling International Conference on Computing Education Research, pp. 11–18. ACM (2012)
3. Chi, M.T., Bassok, M., Lewis, M.W., Reimann, P., Glaser, R.: Self-explanations: how students study and use examples in learning to solve problems. Cogn. Sci. **13**(2), 145–182 (1989)
4. Wylie, R., Chi, M.T.H.: 17 the self-explanation principle in multimedia learning. In: Mayer, R.E. (ed.) The Cambridge Handbook of Multimedia Learning, pp. 413–432. Cambridge University Press, Cambridge (2014)
5. Johnson, C.I., Mayer, R.E.: Applying the self-explanation principle to multimedia learning in a computer-based game-like environment. Comput. Hum. Behav. **26**(6), 1246–1252 (2010)
6. Fabic, G., Mitrovic, A., Neshatian, K.: Towards a mobile Python tutor: understanding differences in strategies used by novices and experts. In: Proceedings of the 13th International Conference on Intelligent Tutoring Systems, vol. 9684, pp. 447–448. Springer (2016)
7. Fabic, G., Mitrovic, A., Neshatian, K.: Investigating strategies used by novice and expert users to solve Parson's problem in a mobile Python tutor. In: Proceedings of the 9th Workshop on Technology Enhanced Learning by Posing/Solving Problems/Questions PQTEL 2016, pp. 434–444. APSCE (2016)

Striking a Balance: User-Experience and Performance in Computerized Game-Based Assessment

Carol M. Forsyth[1(✉)], Tanner Jackson[1], Del Hebert[1], Blair Lehman[1], Pat Inglese[1], and Lindsay Grace[2]

[1] Educational Testing Service, Princeton, NJ, USA
{cforsyth, gtjackson, dhebert, blehman, pinglese}@ets.org
[2] School of Communication, American University, Washington, D.C., USA
grace@american.edu

Abstract. Game-based assessment (GBA) is a new frontier in the assessment industry. However, as with serious games, it will likely be important to find an optimal balance between making the game "fun" versus focusing on achieving the educational goals. We created two minigames to assess students' knowledge of argumentation skills. We conducted an iterative counter-balanced pre-survey-interaction-post-survey study with 124 students. We discovered that game presentation sequence and game perceptions are related to performance in two games with varying numbers of game features and alignment to educational content. Specifically, understanding how to play the games is related to performance when users start with a familiar environment and move to one with more game features, whereas enjoyment is related to performance when users start with a more gamified experience before moving to a familiar environment.

Keywords: Serious games · Assessment · Cognitive load

1 Introduction

In the age of technology, we are now able to create assessments that are more interactive, engaging and potentially even motivational. Among these assessments are game-based assessments (GBA) created to motivate students and reduce anxiety to gain a better measure of student knowledge. Although very little research has been conducted on GBA's, much research has been conducted on serious games for learning rather than assessment [1–3]. The idea of serious games is to motivate students to want to learn academic material. However, the research is contradictory as to whether the game-like aspects aid in the processing of educational material or simply distract the student [2, 3]. The explanation for this contradiction is that additional game features may require cognitive resources that are needed for addressing the educational material, which aligns to Cognitive Load Theory [4], suggesting that only a limited amount of cognitive resources are available at any given time. Therefore, if resources are consumed by game features, then fewer resources are available for educational material.

E. André et al. (Eds.): AIED 2017, LNAI 10331, pp. 502–505, 2017.
DOI: 10.1007/978-3-319-61425-0_50

This conflict could be resolved by aligning the game features to the educational material [5], such that cognitive resources consumed by game features are minimized.

We created two assessment minigames that assess aspects of argumentation skills with varying numbers of game features and alignment to content, which are played in 5–10 min in attempts to reduce cognitive load and allow for students to play multiple games in one sitting. The two games developed are Robot Sorter (RS) and Text Persuasion (TP). RS has multiple game features and assesses the skill of providing "evidence for claims". In this game, students are first presented with a claim and then a robot presents evidence that is either supportive (a "pro") or not-supportive (a "con") of this claim, and the student must sort the robot appropriately. TP has very few game features and assesses "appeal building skills". The interface was designed to resemble that of text messaging on smart phones and makes the game mechanics straight-forward for students because it is familiar to students and aligns to real world activities. The two key differences between RS and TP are the number of game features and alignment of game mechanics to the educational material. In the current study, we are investigating the relationship between performance and perceptions of these two games.

2   Methods

After informed consents were signed, 124 students at two middle schools, one in the Mid-West and one in the Mid-South USA, were randomly assigned to a counter-balancing order of pre and post-surveys as well as game-play sequence and completed the nine activities depicted in Fig. 1.

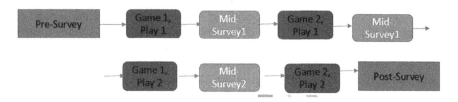

Fig. 1. Study design

The mid surveys (Mid-Survey 1 and 2) had two 9-point scale items (valence and arousal), and 11 items on a 6-point scale (e.g. were the games engaging/frustrating/fun). The post-survey asked participants the same questions as in Mid-Survey 2 (with three additional questions comparing liking of the two games). In addition, there were comprehension questions on the post-survey and pre-survey that are not included in this study.

3 Analyses and Results

Analyses were conducted in two separate stages. First, we replicated a finding from pilot data suggesting that the sequence of game-play (TP First or RS First) would relate to how much students liked each game. We discovered a significant interaction between the perceptions of "fun" on the mid-surveys and game-play sequence $(F_{3,121} = 10.99, p < .001$, partial $\eta^2 = .22)$ showing higher levels of perceived fun or liking for TP, the more familiar, well-aligned game with fewer game features than RS, the game with more game features which are less aligned to the academic content. Therefore, we conducted separate analyses for the two sequences of game presentation in our second set of analyses. Specifically, for each game-play sequence, we conducted a Principal Component Analysis (PCA) with Direct Oblimin Rotation on the non-comprehension oriented post survey questions assessing the user experience. Then, we performed Pearson correlations between the resulting principal components (PC) and the game performance scores for each game-play sequence independently.

3.1 Performance and Perceptions: TP First

For those who played TP first, the PCA converged after nine iterations and resulted in four PC's accounting for 74.10% of the variance. Based on the loadings of the included items, the four components were named "Enjoyment", $(R^2 = .37)$ with high loadings of items such as fun playing the game, "Straight-forward game-play", $(R^2 = .19)$ with high loadings on items suggesting understanding how to play the game, "Feels like Work" $(R^2 = .11)$ with high loadings on the item suggesting the game felt like work, and "Frustrated" $(R^2 = .07)$ with high loadings on the question suggesting the games were frustrating.

Next, Pearson correlations were performed between the PCs and the average performance based on the proportion of correct over total number of decisions made for each of the two games. For students who played TP first, the "Straight-Forward Gameplay" component was significantly correlated with the first game-play of TP (game-play 1, $r = .287, p < .05$). This relationship became even stronger for TP after students interacted with RS (TP game-play 2; $r = .494, p < .01$). Perhaps simply understanding the game was more important than liking the game after interacting with a game that had multiple game features but was less enjoyable.

3.2 Performance and Perceptions: RS First

For those who played RS first, the PCA converged after 18 iterations revealing three components accounting for 67.9% of the variance. The first component, "Enjoyment" $(R^2 = .41)$ included high loadings on items such as finding the game fun to play, the second component of "Straight-forward game-play" $(R^2 = .18)$ included high loadings on items regarding understanding the game, and the third component of "Liked TP" $(R^2 = .09)$ included high loadings on items about enjoying playing TP.

Next, Pearson correlations were performed between the PCs and the performance on the games. The correlational analysis suggests that only "Enjoyment" was significantly positively correlated with performance in each game-play of RS (play 1: $r = .273$, $p < .05$; play 2: $r = .255$, $p < .05$). Interestingly, "Straight-Forward Game-Play" was no longer significantly correlated with performance in TP after playing RS first. However, "Liked TP" was significantly correlated with performance in the first game-play of TP after playing RS ($r = .255$, $p < .05$).

4 Discussion

Overall, we discovered that the sequence of game-play presentation and game perceptions are related to performance in two different GBAs. Furthermore, we discovered correlational evidence that participants may prefer a GBA with more familiar game mechanics that are aligned with an enjoyable real world task (TP) compared to a game with more game features but is not aligned to a real world task (RS). Game-play experiences that were optimal for game performance varied across the two games and changed based on the game sequence presentation which is important because multiple games are intended to be played in one sitting. When TP was played first, straight forward game-play, characterized by a higher level of understanding the game but a more neutral affective response, was highly correlated with better performance on TP. In contrast, when students played RS first, enjoyment became more important and was positively correlated with performance for both game-plays of RS. There was also a significant relationship between the component characterized by liking TP and TP performance when RS was played first. This is in contrast to the correlation between straight-forward game-play and performance on TP, when TP is played first. Thus, the game- play sequence altered students' perceptions of the games, and the relationship between perceptions and performance. These results suggest that the alignment, number of the game features, and sequence of game-play are important to the relationship between perceptions and performance. In future directions, we plan to test these findings with an empirical design where we specifically alter the features of each game.

References

1. Shaffer, D.W.: How Computer Games Help Children Learn. Palgrave, New York (2007)
2. Jackson, G.T., McNamara, D.S.: Motivation and performance in a game-based intelligent tutoring system. J. Educ. Psychol. **105**, 1036–1049 (2013)
3. McQuiggan, S.W., Rowe, J.P., Lee, S., Lester, J.C.: Story-based learning: the impact of narrative on learning experiences and outcomes. In: Woolf, B.P., Aimeur, E., Nkambou, R., Lajoie, S. (eds.) 9th International Conference on Intelligent Tutoring Systems. LNCS, vol 5091, pp. 530–539. Springer, Heidelberg (2008)
4. Sweller, J.: Cognitive load during problem solving: effects on learning. Cogn. Sci. **12**, 257–285 (1988)
5. Gee, J.P.: What video games have to teach us about learning and literacy. Comput. Entertainment (CIE) **1**, 20 (2003)

Interactive Score Reporting:
An AutoTutor-Based System for Teachers

Carol M. Forsyth[1(✉)], Stephanie Peters[1], Diego Zapata-Rivera[1],
Jennifer Lentini[1], Art Graesser[2], and Zhiqiang Cai[2]

[1] Educational Testing Service,
660 Rosedale Rd., Princeton, NJ 08540, USA
{Cforsyth, speters, dzapata, jlentini}@ets.org
[2] The University of Memphis, 202 Psychology,
Memphis, TN 38104, USA
{graesser, zcai}@memphis.edu

Abstract. Teachers often have difficulties understanding many aspects of score reports for assessments, thus hindering their ability to help students. Computerized environments with natural language conversations may help teachers better understand these reports. Thus, we created a tutor on score reports for teachers based on the AutoTutor conversational framework, which conventionally teaches various topics to students rather than teachers. We conducted a pilot study where eight teachers completed interaction with the tutor, providing a total of 98 responses. Results revealed specific ways the framework may be altered for teachers as well as teachers' overall favorable attitudes towards the tutor.

Keywords: Intelligent Tutoring System · Score reports · Teacher education

1 Introduction

Information about student performance is often shared with the academic community with statistical notation that may be incomprehensible or even meaningless to the ones making decisions in real students' lives, such as teachers, administrators, parents and, students [1]. Thus, we created an Intelligent Tutoring System (ITS) to teach teachers about score reports focusing on the concept of measurement error, a topic that has been identified as a source of common misconceptions for teachers interpreting score reports [2]. To create this tutor, we based the conversations on the conversational framework of AutoTutor, an ITS with natural language conversations between an artificial agent and human student, that has successfully taught topics such as computer literacy and physics to students, but not yet deployed to teachers (for a review see [3]). The current study investigates the extent to which the AutoTutor framework can classify teacher responses accurately and assess teacher's attitudes in hopes of eventually deploying the system to help teachers learn.

© Springer International Publishing AG 2017
E. André et al. (Eds.): AIED 2017, LNAI 10331, pp. 506–509, 2017.
DOI: 10.1007/978-3-319-61425-0_51

1.1   A Score Reporting Tutor Using AutoTutor

The AutoTutor conversational framework was developed based on a fine-grained analysis of human-to-human expert tutoring sessions referred to as Expectation-Misconception Tailored dialog (for review [3]). The basic premise is that there is a main question asked at the beginning of each conversation with a corresponding expected answer (typically 3–7 sentences) that the human respondent is supposed to articulate. An example main question may be "The score reports show that Li has a math score of 200 and Susan has a score of 190. Based on the information, what can we say about Li's and Susan's math scores?". If the human is unable to answer this question, the artificial agent helps the respondent to articulate this answer with scaffolding such as pumps (e.g., "um, anything else?"), hints or broad clues, timely feedback (e.g., "good job!" or "no, not quite."), misconception correction, prompts eliciting a specific word or phrase, and assertions explaining the correct answer. The typical progression of these discourse moves includes a pump → hint → prompt → assertion cycle after the human responds to the main question. The amount of scaffolding is adaptive and depends on individual knowledge, thus a high-knowledge teacher may only answer the main question whereas a low-knowledge teacher may complete part of or the entire scaffolding cycle.

The teacher input must be analyzed accurately and matched to a pre-defined expectation (or misconception) for an artificial agent to provide the appropriate scaffolding. This Natural Language Processing (NLP) is accomplished through a combination of an algorithm for capturing world knowledge referred to as Latent Semantic Analysis (LSA; for a review see [4]), and regular expressions [5] that define key words, phrases, and syntactic compositions that represent the meaning of the sentence. We used this framework to create a tutor for helping teachers interpret score reports. To create this tutor, we used a tool referred to as the AutoTutor Script Authoring Tool for Assessment (ASATA). This tool allows one to easily author AutoTutor conversation scripts, by providing a basic interface consisting of talking heads, a text box, and a place for displaying pictures (e.g. a bar chart with error bars). Scripts were designed based on common teacher misconceptions about the concept of measurement error [2]. The tutor starts the conversation by showing a particular case based on a common misconception and engages the teacher in a conversation. The four conversations programmed for the score reporting tutor centered on four main themes about measurement error: (a) confidence bands, (b) variation, (c) overlapping confidence bands, and (d) meaningful differences. The purpose of the current study was to examine initial responses given by the teachers and examine teachers' impressions for eventual refinement of the system.

2   Methods

Participants included eight adults with prior or current teaching experience with K-12 students. After signing an informed consent, teachers completed a pre-interaction survey and a comprehension questionnaire about measurement error. Participants then proceeded through the four conversations designed to teach about measurement error. During these conversations, each of the eight participants completed conversational paths with varying amounts of scaffolding and provided a total of 98 responses. Upon completion of the conversations, participants responded to the post-interaction survey focusing on attitudes towards and perceived learning within the system in addition to a parallel form of the comprehension questionnaire. The focus of this investigation is on teacher responses to the system and answers to the post-interaction survey questions about teacher's attitudes towards the system.

3 Analysis and Results

3.1 Tutor Performance with Teachers

Rating Teacher Responses. Across all four conversations, 98 teacher responses were evaluated across a multitude of various conversational paths. Accuracy levels of the 98 responses were rated by two human raters on a 0–1 scale with a high-level of inter-rater agreement (90.82% agreement). High agreement was also found when comparing the computer evaluation to one of the human ratings (80.62% agreement). We then inspected the 98 responses for inconsistencies between raters (who judged correctness on a partial scale) and the computer (which classified responses) for any themes or interesting findings that might be important for potential improvements to the system.

Partial Prompt Answers. Across the four conversations, teachers gave 30 responses to a total of five prompts. On one prompt, three out of five participants, who answered this prompt, provided responses that were processed as good answers, but our human raters both judged these answers to be only partially correct. Prompts are not currently calculated as partially correct in the AutoTutor framework. Although this was discovered for one prompt, we suspect that developing a metric for partial correctness in prompts may be helpful for teachers. This is a change that we can easily implement in future versions of the system with ASATA.

Bad Questions. Across four conversations, we discovered nine questions (with a corresponding 15 responses) where it appears the questions or hints could be reformulated to elicit better responses. For example, in Conversation 2, the main question focuses on why scores are not precise and error/confidence bars are necessary. One of the hints was the following: "I think that it has something to do with the test-takers and test questions." Four out of eight of the responses to the hints were binary such as "yes" or "I agree." Furthermore, two out of eight participants asked "What's the question?" In traditional AutoTutor, this would be classified as a meta-communicative statement similar to "Please Repeat." However, this classification was only implemented for main questions and not hints in the Score Report Tutor, as in some other AutoTutor systems. Thus, we may also need to consider adding this classification to responses to hints in this tutor focusing on teachers.

Attitudes. Teacher participants were asked a total of eight questions (four on perceived learning and four on impressions of the system). Each question was scored on a four-point Likert Scale ranging from "Strongly Disagree" to "Strongly Agree". In total, 62.8% of participants rated "Agree" or "Strongly Agree" to statements that reflect favorable interactions with the tutor.

4 Discussion

The current work takes the initial step in an iterative process to develop a novel application for Intelligent Tutoring Systems with natural language conversations. In the past, these systems have been developed for student learning or individual training situations (e.g., military). However, we have not yet discovered a system in the literature that teaches teachers. In effort to leverage artificial intelligence capabilities and the success of the AutoTutor framework to teach teachers, the current study focuses on evaluating the initial design and collecting preliminary evidence for how the system design is experienced by the teacher audience.

A key aspect of the current work is that there is initial evidence showing that teachers can receive appropriate feedback with this ITS, based on the high computer-human agreement level on the classification accuracy. Furthermore, we discovered issues that emerged from teachers' interactions with artificial agents including questions that did not elicit the intended response (e.g., yes/no questions) and potentially a need for partial prompts. We found reports of somewhat positive attitudes but still inconclusive results overall in regards to teacher attitudes. We certainly cannot generalize any of our findings due to the low sample size. However, in future work, we will iteratively refine the tutor based on these results and deploy to a larger number of teachers. Thus, the current research is a first step towards building a conversational tutor that may help teachers better understand score reports, which is imperative to proper use of assessment results which will benefit teacher instruction and ultimately student learning.

References

1. Zapata-Rivera, D., Katz, R.I.: Keeping your audience in mind: applying audience analysis to the design of interactive score reports. Assess. Educ. Principles Policy Pract. **21**, 442–463 (2014)
2. Zapata-Rivera, D., Zwick, R., Vezzu, M.: Exploring the effectiveness of a measurement error tutorial in helping teachers understand score report results. Educ. Assess. **21**(3), 215–229 (2016)
3. Graesser, A.C., D'Mello, S.K., Hu, X., Cai, Z., Olney, A., Morgan, B.: AutoTutor. In: McCarthy, P., Boonthum-Denecke, C. (eds.) Applied Natural Language Processing: Identification, Investigation, and Resolution, pp. 169–187. IGI Global, Hershey (2012)
4. Landauer, T., McNamara, D.S., Dennis, S., Kintsch, W.: Handbook of Latent Semantic Analysis. Erlbaum, Mahwah (2007)
5. Jurafsky, D., Martin, J.: Speech and Language Processing. Prentice Hall, Englewood (2008)

Transforming Foreign Language Narratives into Interactive Reading Applications Designed for Comprehensibility and Interest

Pedro Furtado[✉], Tsukasa Hirashima, and Yusuke Hayashi

Hiroshima University, 1 Chome-3-2 Kagamiyama,
Higashihiroshima, Hiroshima Prefecture, Japan
gabrielpff2@gmail.com
http://www.lel.hiroshima-u.ac.jp/

Abstract. This study reports on the design and use of a second language reading application for enhanced comprehension and pleasure reading. The application combines short narratives with dialog construction tasks. Quantitative reading comprehension scores were compared between reading by using the application and reading by using regular text and it also evaluates qualitatively how users perceived the application. Preliminary results indicate that the software was successful in improving reading comprehension by guiding user behavior through its design. However, not all students were optimistic about the application as a learning tool given its implicit approach. How the work stands in relation to extensive reading is also discussed.

Keywords: CALL · DBGL · Dialog construction · Text comprehension · Extensive reading · Foreign language · L2 reading

1 Introduction

Language acquisition gains from foreign language reading have been shown in past research many times ([5,6], etc.). Pleasure reading, often using narratives, where readers engage in reading as a leisure activity, allows for reading of large volumes of content, which leads to high gains in language acquisition, but shows various problems, like in the time it takes to show those gains or in the acquisition of infrequent vocabulary [1,2]. Present research shows that the higher the understanding of the text, the higher the language acquisition gains, so higher understanding could be used to overcome the problems in pleasure reading. For example, higher understanding results in incidental vocabulary learning needing less repetitions in order to be effective. Computer-assisted language learning applications have tried to increase the gains of reading through various means but, in exchange, not being focused on recreation, they have trouble motivating students to read large volumes of content [3,4]. The problem is that, currently, present research has shown no activity that allows for pleasure reading while offering deeper understanding to overcome its shortcomings.

© Springer International Publishing AG 2017
E. André et al. (Eds.): AIED 2017, LNAI 10331, pp. 510–513, 2017.
DOI: 10.1007/978-3-319-61425-0_52

Our research hopes to fill that gap by creating an application that is designed to support comprehensibility and interest, which results in better language acquisition, while still being designed to use narratives to more easily allow for pleasure reading by using a structure similar to the one used in certain games. This similarity is merely structural and not based on extraneous gamification mechanics, like achievements or leader-boards, and it has been designed for taking in to account both cognition and motivation.

The application uses a combination of text and image to tell a story while also allowing users to create dialogs and then experience those created dialogs. The design of the dialog construction and its feedback is made to induce a behavior that best benefits learners who are having trouble in either comprehensibility or interest, in order to increase overall understanding of the text and help users with foreign language acquisition.

2   Methodology

Our software solution has two alternating parts:

1. Narrative segments where text is presented linearly;
2. Dialog construction segments.

For the dialog construction segments, users only construct what one character says, while what the other character says is fixed. After building it, the constructed dialog will be displayed to the user. However, should the user construct something that is not consistent with the story, then that dialog will self-adapt to offer feedback on why it is not consistent. This adaptation is based on adding a reaction to show why the user's mistake does not make sense in that context and a clue on what would be appropriate to say in that moment. Both the reaction and the clue are prepared beforehand.

When designing dialog construction activities to have influence in textual comprehension, the requirements below were found to be important:

1. The text is challenging enough for the reader that he cannot create the dialog on his first try;
2. The user actually reads the software feedback on his mistakes;
3. The feedback is helpful enough that after reading and pondering on it, they are able to move closer to create an appropriate dialog.

3   Preliminary Experiment and Results

3.1   Experiment Description

12 students from a Japanese University's Undergraduate Courses were divided into two groups, group A and group B. Both groups were asked to interact with the application and with a digital text document. Group A interacted with the application containing content 1 and, afterwards, read a document containing

content 2. Group B interacted with a text document containing content 1 and with the application containing content 2. Both content 1 and content 2 had between 15 and 20 lines of text and have had certain words replaced with dummy words. Both groups then were asked to answer the same questions of reading comprehension and of dummy word partial meaning acquisition.

Both contents had two dialog construction activities each. Going through them usually took participants between 10 and 15 min, with application use taking up more time, since users had to create the appropriate dialog. For this experiment we considered that there was no significant gap in difficulty between content 1 and content 2 and also that, since doing the application and the text does not take a lot time, the order of application-text and text-application will not significantly influence the score.

The questions both groups had to answer were divided into a remembering section, a textual interpretation section and partial dummy word comprehension section.

In the remembering section users were asked to write as much as they could remember with as much detail as possible. The textual interpretation section asked questions about the content such as "did Brian ever get angry in the story? If yes, why did he get angry?". The third section showed a small excerpt from the text which contained dummy words and asked questions related to the meaning of the words. For example, "what is the meaning of the word proard? Describe it to the best of your abilities. A vague description and guessing are both fine". Afterwards, 7 of the users were asked to answer a user perception survey.

We expect that scores related to content in the application will be higher than the ones related to textual content. For user perception, we expect for users to be positive towards the software.

3.2 Results

Of the 12 participants, only one participant scored higher by reading the text than by using the application. If it is assumed that there is no difference between the reading condition and the application condition, the probability that of 12 people 11 would score higher is 0.0063 ($p < 0.01$) by a double-sided binomial test. The results point in a positive direction. Average score and standard deviation of each group, and for the combined group, can be seen on Table 1. Calculating

Table 1. "Average scores and standard deviation for the two groups and for the combination of the groups"

	Application	Text
Group A	0.78 (SD 0.08)	0.53 (SD 0.18)
Group B	0.77 (SD 0.17)	0.44 (SD 0.21)
Combined	0.78 (SD 0.13)	0.48 (SD 0.20)

Cohen's d, for the combined group gets us an effect size of 1.78. Though the number of participants has been small to generalize, the results are promising.

As for the user perception survey results, the following trends were found:

1. in the area of interest, all users except for one had a positive opinion towards the application, with over half of the users completely favoring the application over text;
2. On perceived comprehensibility and perceived learning, half of the users had a positive opinion while the other half had a neutral opinion;
3. On usability, one user found the application a little bit hard to use, while the vast majority thought the application was easy to use;

4 Conclusion(s)

Although it's only preliminary results with a small sample size, this application has succeeded in offering a gain in reading comprehension while still having narrative content for pleasure reading. Further experimenting should be able to present an even stronger argument in favor of this design.

User's higher comprehensibility when using the application can be attributed to being able to read the feedback information to solve the dialog assembling problems. This suggests that users were performing according to our expectations, indicating that our efforts to create an activity that can only be practically solved by displaying reading and pondering on feedback have been successful. While this sort of approach is not the best for every type of application, when we talk about reading, which follows a linear path, this approach can be very successful.

Acknowledgements. This work was partially supported by JSPS KAKENHI Grant Number 26280127 and 15H02931.

References

1. Cobb, T.: Computing the vocabulary demands of L2 reading. Lang. Learn. Technol. **11**(3), 38–63 (2007)
2. Harris, S.: The role of extensive reading in the development of second language proficiency in secondary level education (2001)
3. Wang, Y.H.: Promoting contextual vocabulary learning through an adaptive computer-assisted EFL reading system. J. Comput. Assist. Learn. **32**(4), 291–303 (2016)
4. Wang, Y.H.: Developing and evaluating an adaptive business english self-learning system for EFL vocabulary learning. In: Mathematical Problems in Engineering 2014 (2014)
5. Yamashita, J.: Extensive reading and development of different aspects of L2 proficiency. System **36**(4), 661–672 (2008)
6. Yang, A.: Reading and the non-academic learner: a mystery solved. System **29**(4), 451–466 (2001)

Exploring Students' Affective States During Learning with External Representations

Beate Grawemeyer[1(✉)], Manolis Mavrikis[2], Claudia Mazziotti[3],
Alice Hansen[2], Anouschka van Leeuwen[4], and Nikol Rummel[3]

[1] BBK Knowledge Lab, Birkbeck, University of London, London, UK
beate@dcs.bbk.ac.uk
[2] UCL Knowledge Lab, Institute of Education, University College London,
London, UK
{m.mavrikis,a.hansen}@ioe.ac.uk
[3] Institute of Educational Research, Ruhr-Universität Bochum,
Bochum, Germany
{claudia.mazziotti,nikol.rummel}@rub.de
[4] Faculty of Social and Behavioral Science, Utrecht University,
Utrecht, Netherlands
A.vanLeeuwen@uu.nl

Abstract. We conducted a user study that explored the relationship between students' usage of multiple external representations and their affective states during fractions learning. We use the affective states of the student as a proxy indicator for the ease of reasoning with the representation. Extending existing literature that highlights the advantages of learning with multiple external representations, our results indicate that low-performing students have difficulties in reasoning with representations that do not fully accommodate the fraction as a part-whole concept. In contrast, high-performing students were at ease with a range of representations, including the ones that vaguely involved the fraction as part-whole concept.

1 Introduction

The aim of our research is to gain insights into students' learning processes in order to inform the design of technology that is able to assist students during learning and enhances their learning experience and performance. We are particularly interested in the impact of students' affective states during learning fractions with multiple external representations.

External representations (such as diagrams) are powerful aids to reasoning and problem solving (e.g. [2,8]). Suthers [9] outlines how the choice of an external representation can influence an individual's conception of a problem, how it triggers an internal mental representation, and hence the ease of finding a solution to the problem. More specifically, in the domain of fractions, many studies show that learning with multiple external representations supports students' conceptual knowledge [7].

© Springer International Publishing AG 2017
E. André et al. (Eds.): AIED 2017, LNAI 10331, pp. 514–518, 2017.
DOI: 10.1007/978-3-319-61425-0_53

It is well understood that during learning students are experiencing a range of affective states [3]. While positive affective states (such as surprise, satisfaction or curiosity) contribute towards learning, negative ones (including frustration or disillusionment at realising misconceptions) can undermine learning. Any learning experience is typically full of transitions between positive and negative affective states.

In this paper, we explore students' affective states while they are performing fractions tasks with different types of external representations.

2   User Study

We conducted a user study that included the iTalk2Learn platform with the exploratory learning environment *Fractions Lab*.

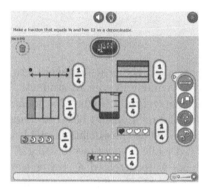

Fig. 1. Exploratory learning environment. **Fractions Lab**.

Figure 1 shows the *Fractions Lab* interface of the exploratory learning environment. The learning task is displayed at the top of the screen. Students are asked to solve the task by selecting a representation (from the right-hand side menu). The students are able to choose between the following external representations to answer the fractions task: rectangle, set, number-line, and liquid.

The external representations differed in the way how they be express a part-whole fraction concept. For example, the part-whole concept of fractions is explicitly included within the rectangle representation, as the area in itself represents one and the colour within the area represents a part of the whole fraction, which is similar to the number-line, where the numbers explicitly say that the number-line starts with zero and ends with one. In contrast, the elements within sets can be seen as discrete entities instead of being a part of the whole group of sets within the fraction. This is similar to the liquid representation as there is no clear separator of the liquid for the value of the numerator. Only the scale on the right hand side of the liquid gives and indication about the actual value of the numerator.

While students are interacting with the learning environment they are asked to talk aloud about their reasoning process. This is used to detect and analyse student's speech in near real time (c.f. [6]). The analysis of the speech and students' interaction with the exploratory learning environment are used to detect their affective states. Adaptive support is provided based on students' affective states [4].

In this user study reported here, we are interested in exploring how students' affective state and their interactions with the different external representations relate to each other. 41 participants took part in the study. They were all primary school students, aged between 8 and 10 years old. Students engaged with fractions tasks in the iTalk2Learn platform for 40 minutes. During this time all the interactions with the external representations in *Fractions Lab*, as well as the students' affective states, were stored in a database. After the 40 minutes, students completed an online questionnaire that assessed their knowledge of fractions (a post-test).

3   Results

Students' performance based on the post-test score was on average 3.83 (SD = 1.46; min = 0; max = 6). A medium split of students' post-test score resulted in a high- and low-performance group (high: 27 students; low: 14 students).

In order to investigate the relationship between students' affective state and their representational usage we used association rule learning (e.g. [1]) over the data set that was gathered while students were using *Fractions Lab*.

Only very few students were detected as being *bored* or *frustrated* (bored: 1.3%; frustrated: 4.9% of all cases) and there was no automatic detection of *surprise*. To further analyse our data we combined the affective states of boredom and frustration into a new variable called 'negative' as those were negative affective states. The resulting graphs of the association rule learning for low- and high-performing students can be seen in Fig. 2. It is a graph-based visualisation with variables and rules as vertices, which are connected by directed edges [5].

Figure 2 shows that for low-performing students some representations were only associated with one affective state, like liquids or sets who are associated with *confusion*. However, other representations, such as rectangles and number-lines were associated with several affective states, like being *in flow* and *confusion*. In contrast, for high-performing students the liquid representation is associated with being *in flow*. Rectangles, number-lines and sets were mainly associated with being *in flow* and *confusion* in the high-performing group.

Overall, the association rule graphs show that high-performing students were in flow with a wider range of representations than the low-performing group, including the representations that only vaguely include the part-whole fraction concept (sets and liquids).

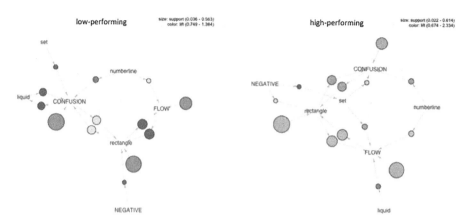

Fig. 2. Association rule graph for low- and high-performing students.

4   Discussion and Conclusion

Our results indicate that low-performing students have difficulties in reasoning with representations that do not fully accommodate the fraction as a part-whole concept. In contrast, high-performing students were at ease with a range of representations, including the ones that only vaguely represented the fraction as a part-whole concept. This might imply that the internal mental image of fractions in high-performing students might be richer than the internal mental representation of fractions in low-performing students as it might include extra knowledge about the part-whole concept of fractions.

Although some of the findings may appear retrospectively intuitive, confirming them with data and automating the detection process will enable the provision of more targeted support.

References

1. Bazaldua, D.L., de Baker, R.S.J., Pedro, M.O.S.: Comparing expert and metric-based assessments of association rule interestingness. In: Proceedings of EDM (2014)
2. Cox, R.: Representation interpretation versus representation construction: an ILE-based study using switchERII. In: Proceedings of AIED, pp. 434–441
3. D'Mello, S.K., Lehman, B., Pekrun, R., Graesser, A.C.: Confusion can be beneficial for learning. Learn. Instr. 29(1), 153–170 (2014)
4. Grawemeyer, B., Mavrikis, M., Holmes, W., Gutiérrez-Santos, S., Wiedmann, M., Rummel, N.: Affective learning: Improving engagement and enhancing learning with affect-aware feedback. User Model. User-Adap. Inter. - Special Issue on Impact of Learner Modeling (2017)
5. Hahsler, M., Chelluboina, S.: Visualizing association rules: introduction to the R-extension package arulesViz (2011). R project module
6. Janning, R., Schatten, C., Schmidt-Thieme, L.: Perceived task-difficulty recognition from log-file information for the use in adaptive intelligent tutoring systems. Int. J. Artif. Intell. Educ. 26(3), 855–876 (2016)

7. Rau, M.A., Aleven, V., Rummel, N.: Intelligent tutoring systems with multiple representations and self-explanation prompts support learning of fractions. In: Proceedings of AIED, pp. 441–448 (2009)
8. Stenning, K.: Seeing Reason: Image and Language in Learning to Think. Oxford University Press, Oxford (2002)
9. Suthers, D.D.: Towards a systematic study of representational guidance for collaborative learning discourse. J. Univ. Comput. Sci. **7**(3), 254–277 (2001)

Enhancing an Intelligent Tutoring System to Support Student Collaboration: Effects on Learning and Behavior

Rachel Harsley[1]([⊠]), Barbara Di Eugenio[1], Nick Green[1],
and Davide Fossati[2]

[1] Department of Computer Science, University of Illinois at Chicago,
Chicago, IL, USA
{rharsl2,bdieugen,ngreen21}@uic.edu
[2] Department of Math and Computer Science, Emory University,
Atlanta, GA, USA
davide.fossati@emory.edu

Abstract. In this study we explore how different methods of structuring collaborative interventions affect student learning and interaction in an Intelligent Tutoring System for Computer Science. We compare two methods of structuring collaboration: one condition, unstructured, does not provide students with feedback on their collaboration; whereas the other condition, semistructured, offers a visualization of group performance over time, partner contribution comparison and feedback, and general tips on collaboration. We present a contrastive analysis of student interaction outcomes between conditions, and explore students reported perceptions of both systems. We found that students in both conditions have significant learning gains, equivalent coding efficiency, and limited reliance on system examples. However, unstructured users are more on-topic in their conversational dialogue, whereas semistructured users exhibit better planning skills as problem difficulty increases.

Keywords: Collaborative intelligent tutoring system · Feedback · Pair programming · Collaboration · Data structures · CS1 · CS2

1 Introduction

Though the historic focus of intelligent tutoring system (ITS) development has been toward one-on-one tutoring, in more recent years, several one-on-one tutoring systems have been extended to support collaborative learning [2–4]. ITS researchers are motivated by the established benefits of collaborative learning as documented in computer supported collaborative learning (CSCL) and other literature. These include learning for transfer, use of higher level skills such as meta-cognition, and learning gains that exceed the best of individual learners [4]. However, it is well accepted that effective collaboration and student learning does not necessarily follow simply by placing students in groups. Instead, much CSCL

© Springer International Publishing AG 2017
E. André et al. (Eds.): AIED 2017, LNAI 10331, pp. 519–522, 2017.
DOI: 10.1007/978-3-319-61425-0_54

research has examined how collaborative activities can be designed and structured in order to facilitate the most desirable outcomes. Moreover, we recognize that the role of the tutor in structuring collaboration can widely range from limited structure with no collaboration feedback to high structuring with role definitions, group formation, and even timing of communication [1].

Our study contrasts two distinct methods of supporting collaboration through an ITS. In one condition, unstructured, students do not receive feedback on their collaboration, while in the second condition, semistructured, the tutor provides automated feedback regarding performance and participation. In this study, we collected over 39,000 interactions from 41 students who used the system to solve computer science coding problems. Analysis of student learning gain and behaviors allowed us to further understand the effect of collaborative intelligent tutor (CIT) design choice. There were significant differences in their example and tutorial use, time to start problems, and dialogue-based activity.

2   Experiment and Analysis

An experiment involving student participants was conducted in a second year Computer Science programming course. Our experiments ran over four different sessions of the course. At the onset of the experiment, students chose their own partners. Then, the pair was randomly assigned to either the unstructured or semistructured condition. Each pair was stationed at a single workstation and individually equipped with a headset. They were given 40 min to work with the system. Our current analysis focused on students who, along with their partner, were new to the system (no prior experience with other ChiQat versions) and who had consented to the study (n = 41).

We performed unpaired t-tests between every collected feature across conditions. For example, we compared the time used to start problem one in the unstructured condition versus the semistructured condition. This analysis allowed us to establish how different methods of structuring collaboration guidance affect the pair's interaction between themselves and the system. Overall, we found that the conditions were similar in terms of example use and coding efficiency. However there were distinct differences in student dialogue, tutorial use, and time taken to start writing code. Specifically, unstructured users had more on-topic conversation and used the lesson tutorial more. Furthermore, semistructured users also took time to plan before beginning more difficult problems. We attribute these observed differences to the alterations in the system structuring which effect collaborative interaction.

There were several key distinctions between the conditions in terms of linguistic features. To begin, students in the unstructured condition spoke significantly more than the semistructured students and averaged around 2,700 words per session. Also, t-test comparison revealed that students in the unstructured version used both a significantly higher volume and proportion of domain related words. This suggests that students in the semistructured condition were more off-topic, however, as mentioned, this was not detrimental to their learning.

There was not a significant difference between conditions on time spent with worked out examples. Neither was there a difference in the amount of examples requested. Furthermore, our measures of coding efficiency showed no significant differences. These included the number of operations required to reach a successful solution, the number of undo/redo operations, the number of problem restarts, the number of programming errors, and the number of bad submissions. Overall, both conditions allowed pairs to benefit from having an external meta-cognizer in terms of avoiding errors and relying less system guidance.

Students in the unstructured condition viewed the lesson tutorial significantly more than students using the semistructured version ($p < .001$). Once students first begin the lesson, the tutoring system invites them to do the tutorial. The tutorial provides students with information on navigating the interface and the relationship between their code and its visual representation. Our hypothesis is that the semistructured students felt more pressure to perform (in terms of code submissions and other actions) once presented with the collaboration panel also at the onset of the exercise. Conversely, unstructured students felt more relaxed and able to explore the system.

The difference in the total time to start all problems and the average time to start per problem was trending towards significance with unstructured students taking more time. The time to start a problem is the time spent between when the problem is introduced and when students submit their first line of code. We use the time to start as an intuitive approximation for planning time. Moreover, given our audio analysis, this time was indeed most often spent discussing the meaning of the problem and proposing an approach to reach a solution. Students in the unstructured condition did take significantly more time to start problem one ($p < .05$, $t = 2.51$). In general, students took a similar amount of time to start problems two and three. However, in problems four and five, semistructured

48:	Alright. Delete the node from l.
62:	Delete the node, the node, delete the node from l
48:	that is pointed to by P.
48:	OK. So, we have to delete this one.
62:	What? I don't understand. Delete the node.
48:	We are deleting.
62:	From L that is pointed to by P.
48:	Yeah so it is asking what node.
62:	So it's like the the last time
48:	Yes, but this time we have two lists. Or something.
48:	I don't know.
48:	So, uh.
48:	I'm trying to think like if is there an easier way of doing this rather then create a temp node?
48:	I think so.
48:	No.
48:	It must be the same thing.
48:	We have to walk through the axis and have to make this point to this one.
48:	So it's the same thing as the last time. Pretty much.
[Begins coding]	

Fig. 1. Excerpt of student dialogue at the beginning of problem four in the semistructured condition.

students took significantly more time before they began to code($p < .05$, $t = -2.08$, $t = -2.15$ *respectively*). Each problem was given in order of difficulty and students were required to solve each problem in order to advance the lesson. Students from both conditions averaged completion of around four problems. Figure 1 provides an excerpt of student planning in the semistructured condition at the onset of a problem.

3   Conclusions and Future Work

In this paper we compare the effects of collaborative intelligent tutoring system design choice on students' interaction and learning process. We developed two collaborative versions of our ITS for CS Education. The semistructured version provides automated feedback on student collaboration through visualization of group performance, individual contribution, and peer review. The unstructured version allows students to work in pairs and does not offer feedback on their collaboration. We discovered that added collaborative feedback can promote planning before problem solving. Moreover, in comparing the effects of the two collaborative systems, there was a significant difference in students' dialogue features such as the frequency of domain-related word use.

Our next step of analysis will explore which factors of interaction contribute to learning from a modeling perspective. We will then use these findings as motivation for the development of an additional tutoring system that supports effective collaborative learning.

Acknowledgments. This work was supported by the Abraham Lincoln Fellowship 2015–2016 from the University of Illinois at Chicago, and grant NPRP 5–939–1–155 from the Qatar National Research Fund.

References

1. Harsley, R.: Towards a collaborative intelligent tutoring system classification scheme. In: Proceedings of the 11th International Conference on Cognition and Exploratory Learning in the Digital Age (Celda 2014), Porto, pp. 290–291, October 2014
2. Magnisalis, I., Demetriadis, S., Karakostas, A.: Adaptive and intelligent systems for collaborative learning support: a review of the field. IEEE Trans. Learn. Technol. **4**(1), 5–20 (2011)
3. Olsen, J.K., Aleven, V., Rummel, N.: Adapting collaboration dialogue in response to intelligent tutoring system feedback. In: Conati, C., Heffernan, N., Mitrovic, A., Verdejo, M.F. (eds.) AIED 2015. LNCS, vol. 9112, pp. 748–751. Springer, Cham (2015). doi:10.1007/978-3-319-19773-9_107
4. Walker, E., Rummel, N., Koedinger, K.R.: Integrating collaboration and intelligent tutoring data in the evaluation of a reciprocal peer tutoring environment. Res. Pract. Technol. Enhanc. Learn. **04**(03), 221–251 (2009)

Assessing Question Quality Using NLP

Kristopher J. Kopp[1]([⊠]), Amy M. Johnson[1], Scott A. Crossley[2],
and Danielle S. McNamara[1]

[1] Department of Psychology, Arizona State University, Tempe, AZ 85287, USA
{Kjkopp,amjohn43,Danielle.McNamara}@asu.edu
[2] Department of Applied Linguistics/ESL, Georgia State University,
25 Park Place, Atlanta, GA 30303, USA
scrossley@gsu.edu

Abstract. An NLP algorithm was developed to assess question quality to inform feedback on questions generated by students within iSTART (an intelligent tutoring system that teaches reading strategies). A corpus of 4575 questions was coded using a four-level taxonomy. NLP indices were calculated for each question and machine learning was used to predict question quality. NLP indices related to lexical sophistication modestly predicted question type. Accuracies improved when predicting two levels (shallow versus deep).

Keywords: Intelligent tutoring systems · Artificial intelligence · Natural language processing · Educational technology design · Question classification

1 Introduction

iSTART (Interactive Strategy Training for Active Reading and Thinking) is an ITS that provides instruction on self-explanation strategies and generative strategy practice with immediate feedback using natural language processing (NLP; [1]). Research indicates that iSTART improves learners' ability to construct quality self-explanations and increases reading comprehension [2]. Similar to self-explanation, question asking is an effective reading strategy and asking deep (i.e., questions that get at a deeper form of knowledge) rather than shallow questions during reading improves reading comprehension [3]. Researchers have created systems to *generate* questions for learners to answer during learning [4]. However, to our knowledge, no systems are available to *assess* the quality of questions that readers ask *during* reading.

Our goal is to create a mechanism to *provide feedback on questions* students ask while reading. The first step is to create an algorithm to classify deep vs. shallow level questions. Readers were explicitly instructed to ask questions and human coders applied a classification scheme modified from Graesser and Person question taxonomy [5] to classify the questions, producing the data for the development of the NLP algorithm described in this study.

© Springer International Publishing AG 2017
E. André et al. (Eds.): AIED 2017, LNAI 10331, pp. 523–527, 2017.
DOI: 10.1007/978-3-319-61425-0_55

2 Method and Results

Two hundred thirty-three participants were recruited using the Amazon Mechanical Turk online research service. Participants read three short, simplified news articles that included three to seven pre-identified target sentences (164 total) for which participants produced questions. The dataset included 4,575 questions. Our coding scheme ranged from (1) very shallow to (4) very deep. Two trained researchers coded 60% of the data set each, with 20% overlap to establish the interrater reliability: kappa$_{(linear\ weighted)}$ = .84, r = .67, 82% exact agreement, and 92% adjacent agreement. Remaining differences between the coders were resolved.

Each question was run through a number of NLP tools including the Tool for the Automatic Analysis of Lexical Sophistication (TAALES) [6], the Tool for the Automatic Analysis of Cohesion (TAACO) [6] and the Constructed Response Analysis Tool (CRAT) [7]. We used the indices reported by the NLP tools to predict human scores (1 through 4) for the corpus of questions. Indices reported that lacked normal distributions were removed. A MANOVA was conducted using the NLP indices as dependent variables and the four categories of questions as independent variables. A DFA retained 28 variables (see Table 1 for the MANOVA results for variables retained in the DFA). The majority of these variables were related to lexical sophistication. The DFA correctly allocated 1904 of the 4575 questions in the total set, $\chi2$ (df = 9, n = 4575) = 669.567, p < .001, accuracy = 41.6%. A leave-one-out cross-validation (LOOCV) analysis allocated 1834 of the 4575 texts, accuracy = 40.1%. Agreement between the human and the model produced a kappa$_{(linear\ weighted)}$ = 0.21. A similar analysis was conducted using two categories (shallow vs. deep) of questions as the independent variables. The DFA retained 14 variables (see Table 2) which were also mostly related to lexical sophistication. The DFA correctly allocated 2817 of the 4575 questions in the total set, $\chi2$ (df = 1, n = 4575) = 245.063, p < .001, accuracy = 61.6%. A LOOCV analysis correctly allocated 2794 of the 4575 texts, accuracy = 61.1%. Agreement between the human and the model produced a kappa$_{(linear\ weighted)}$ = 0.23.

Table 1. List of indices and MANOVA results for four category analysis

Index	Greater at deeper level±	F	Partial N^2
Proportion of bigrams COCA (70,000 words)	Yes	39.247**	0.025
Average lexical decision accuracy	Yes	30.276**	0.019
Lemma TTR (content words)	Yes	24.608**	0.016
Log content word range COCA news	Yes	18.724**	0.012
Lemma overlap between question and text	Yes	18.945**	0.012
Mean combined concreteness score	Yes	18.634**	0.012
Word frequency: Thorndike Lorge (all words)	No	15.015**	0.010
Word frequency (log): BNC spoken content words	Yes	14.082**	0.009

(continued)

Table 1. (*continued*)

Index	Greater at deeper level±	F	Partial N^2
Word frequency (log): COCA spoken content words	Yes	10.377**	0.007
Proportion of bigrams COCA (80,000 words)	No	10.964**	0.007
Lemma TTR (news words)	Yes	6.965**	0.005
Proportion of bigrams COCA (50,000 words)	Yes	7.105**	0.005
Mean COCA bigram log frequency score	Yes	8.030**	0.005
Lemma TTR (COCA fiction)	Yes	7.967**	0.005
Standardized naming RT	No	5.911**	0.004
Bigram proportion score COCA (100,000 words)	Yes	6.374**	0.004
Lemmas TTR (magazine words)	Yes	5.944**	0.004
Semantic variability of contexts	Yes	6.352**	0.004
Lemma TTR (academic words)	No	3.949*	0.003
Lemma TTR (all words)	Yes	5.016*	0.003
Bigram proportion score BNC written words	Yes	4.044*	0.003
TTR for questions (content words)	Yes	4.098*	0.003
Academic bigram association strength (COCA)	Yes	5.085*	0.003
Bigram proportion score COCA (60,000 words)	No	3.436*	0.002
Lemma proportion COCA (fiction)	Yes	2.477*	0.002
Word frequency: COCA academic function words	No	3.094*	0.002
Word frequency: COCA spoken content words	Yes	2.967*	0.002
Log academic word range COCA (all words)	No	2.772*	0.002

$*p < .05$, $**p < .01$; TTR = type-token ratio
± Yes indicates average value for deep questions (level 3 and 4) was above the overall mean

Table 2. List of indices and MANOVA results for two category analysis

Index	Greater at deeper level±	F	Partial N^2
Average lexical decision accuracy	Yes	86.186**	0.018
Mean combined concreteness score	Yes	38.952**	0.008
Word frequency (log): BNC spoken (all words)	Yes	37.730**	0.008
Word frequency: Thorndike Lorge (all words)	No	31.145**	0.007
Word frequency (log): COCA spoken content words	Yes	24.156**	0.005
Word range COCA news (content words)	Yes	23.446**	0.005

(*continued*)

Table 2. (*continued*)

Index	Greater at deeper level±	F	Partial N^2
Content words TTR	Yes	21.350**	0.005
Semantic similarity across words in question	Yes	14.107**	0.003
Standardized naming reaction time across all participants for this word	No	14.244**	0.003
Word frequency (log): BNC (all words)	No	9.924*	0.002
Lemma TTR	Yes	7.480*	0.002
Lemma proportion COCA	No	7.397*	0.002
Bigram proportion score BNC written words	Yes	5.767*	0.001
Bigram proportion score COCA (60,000 words)	No	4.911*	0.001

$*p < .05$, $**p < .01$; TTR = type-token ratio
± Yes indicates average value for deep questions (level 3 and 4) was above the overall mean

3   Conclusions

The most predictive indices related to lexical sophistication and lexical and semantic overlap. Deeper level questions contained less sophisticated words and greater lexical and semantic overlap both within the question and with the text. They included words with higher accuracies on lexical decision tests, more frequent words, less specific words, and more concrete words. Deeper level questions contain words that are easier to process and more familiar allowing for better comprehension of the question. The current study takes strides towards automating classifications of question quality and contributes to the improvement of an existing ITS with the objective of enhancing reading comprehension for a wide range of readers [4]. Our hope is that future work that builds on this foundation will be beneficial to the development of other ITSs and a variety of computer-based learning environments.

Acknowledgments. This research was supported in part by the Institute for Educational Sciences (IES R305A130124) and the Office of Naval Research (ONR N00014-14-1-0343 and ONR N00014-17-1-2300). Any opinions, findings, and conclusions or recommendations expressed are those of the authors and do not necessarily reflect the views of IES or ONR.

References

1. McNamara, D.S.: Self-explanation and reading strategy training (SERT) improves low-knowledge students' science course performance. Discourse Process. **38**, 1–30 (2015)
2. McNamara, D.S., O'Reilly, T.P., Best, R.M., Ozuru, Y.: Improving adolescent learners' reading comprehension with iSTART. J. Educ. Comput. Res. **34**(2), 147–171 (2006)
3. Cerdán, R., Vidal-Abarca, E., Martínez, T., Gilabert, R., Gil, L.: Impact of question-answering tasks on search processes and reading comprehension. Learn. Instr. **19**(1), 13–27 (2009)

4. Graesser, A. C., Jackson, G.T., Mathews, E.C., Mitchell, H.H., Olney, A., Ventura, M., Chipman, P., Franceschetti, D., Hu, X., Louwerse, M.M., Person, N.K.: Why/autotutor: a test of learning gains from a physics tutor with natural language dialog. In: Proceedings of the Twenty-Fifth Annual Conference of the Cognitive Science Society, pp. 1–6 (2003)
5. Graesser, A.C., Person, N.K.: Question asking during tutoring. Am. Educ. Res. J. **31**(1), 104–137 (1994)
6. McNamara, D.S., Allen, L.K., Crossley, S.A., Dascalu, M., Perret, C.A.: Natural language processing and learning analytics. In: Siemens, G., Lang, C. (eds.) Handbook of Learning Analytics and Educational Data Mining (in press)
7. Crossley, S., Kyle, K., Davenport, J., McNamara, D.S.: Automatic assessment of constructed response data in a chemistry tutor. In: Barnes, T., Chi, M., Feng, M. (eds.) EDM 2016, pp. 336–340. International Educational Data Mining Society, Raleigh (2016)

The Effect of Providing Motivational Support in Parsons Puzzle Tutors

Amruth N. Kumar[(⊠)]

Ramapo College of New Jersey, Mahwah, USA
amruth@ramapo.edu

Abstract. In response to student feedback on a tutor on Parsons puzzles on the programming concept of sequence, we incorporated three features meant to improve the motivation of the student solving the puzzles. We compared the performance of students before and after introducing these features. We found that introduction of motivational supports did not affect pre-post improvement, and therefore, the amount of learning. Students who were provided motivational supports spent more time per puzzle than those who were not.

Keywords: Parsons puzzle · Programming · Tutor · Evaluation

1 Introduction

Parsons puzzles have been gaining popularity as a mechanism for teaching programming concepts. In a Parsons puzzle [1], the student is presented a problem statement, and the program written for it. The lines in the program are provided in random order. The student must re-assemble the lines in their correct order.

Epplets (epplets.org) are a suite of tutors that we developed to help students learn programming concepts in C++/Java by solving Parsons puzzles. Each tutor in the suite presents puzzles to the student, has the student solve the puzzles, and provides feedback if the solution is incorrect.

We first deployed the tutors in fall 2015. They were used by students in the introductory programming course from six different undergraduate institutions in fall 2015 and spring 2016. The feedback provided by this user group included that they needed better motivational supports when solving puzzles with the tutors. In particular, they wanted the tutors to provide them a better sense of progressing through the material. In response, we incorporated the following features into the tutors before re-deploying them in fall 2016:

1. When each puzzle was first presented, the tutor listed the number of lines in the puzzle and therefore, the number of drag-and-drop actions with which students should aim to solve the puzzle;
2. In addition to summarizing each drag-and-drop action taken by the student as feedback, the tutor also enumerated the action, e.g., the enumeration **3** in:
   3. "Moved from problem to solution at line 8: `double loan;`"
   So, students could keep track of the number of actions they had already taken and the number of actions remaining to solve the puzzle;

© Springer International Publishing AG 2017
E. André et al. (Eds.): AIED 2017, LNAI 10331, pp. 528–531, 2017.
DOI: 10.1007/978-3-319-61425-0_56

3. After the student had solved each puzzle, the tutor displayed the progress of the student, i.e., the number of puzzles the student had solved.

These features track progress, one of the three components of gamification, and thereby provide extrinsic motivation [2]. We evaluated the effect of providing these features on the learning of students by comparing the data collected in fall 2015-spring 2016 (control group before the features were introduced) with that collected in fall 2016 (experimental group after the features were introduced). The tutor we used for this study was on the programming concept of sequence.

The Protocol: The tutor administered pre-test-practice-post-test protocol:

- **Pre-test:** This consisted of one puzzle. If the student solved the puzzle correctly, the tutor ended the session. If the student solved the puzzle partially or incorrectly, the tutor scheduled additional puzzles as practice.
- **Adaptive Practice:** The tutor presented additional puzzles until the student had mastered the concept of sequence.
- **Adaptive Post-test:** After the student had demonstrated mastery during practice, the tutor presented a post-test puzzle. If the student solved it correctly, the session was terminated. Otherwise, the student was returned to solving additional practice puzzles, followed by a repeat post-test.

The entire protocol was limited to 30 min. It was administered by the tutor seamlessly, back-to-back with no breaks in between the three stages.

The Subjects: The subjects were students in the introductory programming course. In fall 2015 and spring 2016, the tutor was used by students from 6 undergraduate institutions. In fall 2016, it was used by students from 12 institutions – both high schools and undergraduate institutions. The students used the tutor over the web as after-class assignment, on their own time.

The Design: We considered the following dependent variables:

1. The number of puzzles solved: students solved only one puzzle during the pre-test and post-test, but solved multiple puzzles during adaptive practice.
2. The average score per puzzle solved during pre-test, practice and post-test. Each puzzle has only one correct solution. A puzzle containing n lines of code can be solved with n drag-and-drop actions. Allowing for unintentional mistakes, a student who solved a puzzle with 1.1n or fewer actions was given full credit. Thereafter, partial credit was awarded inversely proportional to the number of unnecessary actions taken by the student. The normalized score on each puzzle, calculated by dividing the number of student actions (after negative grading) by the number of lines in the puzzle, ranged from 0 to 1.0 per puzzle.
3. The average time spent per puzzle during pre-test, practice and post-test.

2 Data Analysis and Results

Univariate ANOVA analysis of the score on the pre-test puzzle showed no significant difference between control and experimental groups [$F(1,186) = 2.883$, $p = 0.091$]. So, the two groups were comparable. However, ANOVA analysis of the time taken to solve the pre-test puzzle yielded a significant difference between the two groups [$F(1,185) = 5.972$, $p = 0.015$]: experimental group solved the puzzle significantly faster (312.4 ± 46.145 s at 95% confidence interval, $N = 62$) than control group (436.73 ± 66.553 s, $N = 124$). *So, whereas the control and experimental groups were comparable in terms of prior preparation, experimental group solved the pre-test puzzle significantly faster than control group.*

Mixed factor ANOVA analysis with pre-post as within-subjects factor and treatment (without versus with motivational support) as between-subjects factor yielded:

- Significant main effect for pre-post [$F(1,134) = 500.583$, $p < 0.001$]: the score for the two groups combined improved from 0.2708 ± 0.053 on the pre-test to 0.9495 ± 0.0185 on the post-test. *So, the tutor was effective at helping students learn to solve Parsons puzzles.*
- Significant main effect for treatment [$F(1,134) = 1569.136$, $p < 0.001$]: experimental group scored higher than control group on both the pre-test (0.3368 ± 0.0995 versus 0.2392 ± 0.0635 for control) and the post-test (0.9530 ± 0.2816 versus 0.9478 ± 0.1937 for control), although the difference between the two groups on the pre-test was not itself statistically significant.

But, the interaction between pre-post and treatment was not significant. So, *the introduction of motivational supports did not affect pre-post improvement, and therefore, the amount of learning.*

Similar mixed factor ANOVA analysis of the time spent per puzzle yielded:

- Significant main effect for pre-post [$F(1,133) = 150.639$, $p < 0.001$]: the time spent by the two groups combined decreased from 357.25 ± 36.205 s on the pre-test to 96.69 ± 11.322 s on the post-test. *So, after practicing with the tutor, students were able to solve the puzzle significantly faster.*
- Significant main effect for treatment [$F(1,133) = 440.564$, $p < 0.001$]: experimental group solved the pre-test puzzle a lot faster (281 ± 35.14 s) than control group (394.12 ± 49.32 s), thereby averaging faster times on pre- and post-test puzzles combined.
- The interaction between pre-post and treatment was significant [$F(1,133) = 11.061$, $p = 0.001$]: the pre-post improvement was greater for control group (from 394.12 ± 49.32 to 91.51 ± 13.62 s) than experimental group (from 281 ± 35.14 to 107.42 ± 20.18 s). While experimental group students would have spent a few seconds to read the screen that displayed the progress of the student after each puzzle, that alone could not have accounted for the 16 additional seconds experimental group students took on the post-test puzzle than control group students. Since students were made aware upfront of the minimal number of actions needed to solve each puzzle, and all their actions were enumerated, these motivational supports may have had the adverse effect of making experimental students more cautious, and hence, slower when solving the puzzles. This hypothesis bears further testing.

One of the feedback comments provided by students in fall 2015-spring 2016 was that they had to solve too many puzzles during the adaptive practice session. So, we reduced the mastery criteria used for adaptive practice: whereas students had to solve at least 2 puzzles and score at least 80% in fall 2015-spring 2016, in fall 2016 they had to solve at least one puzzle and score at least 60%.

Univariate ANOVA analysis with the number of practice puzzles solved as the dependent variable and treatment as the fixed factor yielded a significant main effect for treatment [$F(1,169) = 3.774$, $p = 0.054$]: control group solved 7.95 ± 1.298 puzzles during adaptive practice whereas experimental group with reduced mastery criteria solved 5.89 ± 1.218 puzzles. *So, students solved fewer practice puzzles with reduced mastery learning criteria*, but this was to be expected.

Univariate ANOVA analysis of the score per practice puzzle yielded no significant main effect for treatment: control group scored 0.7948 ± 0.0232 whereas experimental group scored 0.7657 ± 0.0413 per practice puzzle. However, based on the assumption that learning improves with the number of puzzles solved, we re-ran ANCOVA analysis with the number of practice puzzles solved as a covariate. The main effect for treatment was now significant [$F(2,169) = 3.19$, $p = 0.044$]. *So, after accounting for the fewer puzzles solved by the experimental group based on reduced mastery learning criteria, experimental group still scored less per puzzle during adaptive practice than control group.*

Similarly, univariate ANOVA analysis of the time spent per practice puzzle yielded no significant main effect for treatment: control group spent 158.258 ± 15.626 s per puzzle whereas test group spent 165.71 ± 32.96 s. When we re-ran the analysis with the number of practice puzzles solved as a covariate, the main effect was significant [$F(2,167) = 6.522$, $p = 0.002$]. *So, after accounting for the fewer practice puzzles solved by the experimental group, experimental group spent more time per puzzle than control group.* However, the difference of 7 s between the two group means can be explained as the time spent by experimental group viewing the progress screen displayed after each puzzle.

We plan to repeat this evaluation with larger sample sizes and better-matched student groups.

Acknowledgments. Partial support for this work was provided by the National Science Foundation under grants DUE-1502564 and DUE-1432190.

References

1. Parsons, D., Haden, P.: Parson's programming puzzles: a fun and effective learning tool for first programming courses. In: Proceedings of the 8th Australasian Conference on Computing Education (ACE 2006), vol. 52, pp. 157–163. Australian Computer Society, Inc., Australia (2006)
2. Glover, I. Play as you learn: gamification as a technique for motivating learners. In: Proceedings of the World Conference on Educational Multimedia, Hypermedia and Telecommunications 2013, Chesapeake AACE (2013)

Assessing Student Answers to Balanced Tree Problems

Chun W. Liew[✉], Huy Nguyen, and Darren J. Norton

Department of Computer Science, Lafayette College,
Easton, PA 18042, USA
{liewc,nguyenha,nortondj}@lafayette.edu

Keywords: Computer science · Data Structures · Learning process

1 Introduction

Problems in the domain of balanced binary tree operations usually involve the students constructing a sequence of transformations to insert or delete a value. An Intelligent Tutoring System (ITS) in this area must be able to perform automated assessment of student performance even if there can be multiple correct solution sequences and the input is graphical in nature. Previous works involve either generating all possible solutions and finding the closest match with the student's answer [1] or restricting the student's inputs to one predefined solution [3]. This paper describes a more flexible approach that uses domain knowledge along with a very small restriction on the input method to determine (1) accurately the correctness of the answer and (2) the location and type of the first error in the answer.

2 Red-Black Trees

A red-black tree is a self balancing binary search tree that has the following properties [4]:

1. The nodes of the tree are colored either red or black.
2. The root of the tree is always black.
3. A red node cannot have any red children.
4. Every path from the root to a null link contains the same number of black nodes.

   The top-down algorithm to insert or delete a value from a red-black tree starts at the root and, at every iteration, moves down to the next node, which is a child of the current node. At each node, it applies one or more transformation rules so that when the actual insertion (or deletion) is performed no subsequent actions are needed to maintain the tree's properties. Other types of balanced trees also use a similar approach. In our work we used red-black tree as an exemplar to evaluate our ideas and implementations, but they should be applicable to balanced trees in general.

© Springer International Publishing AG 2017
E. André et al. (Eds.): AIED 2017, LNAI 10331, pp. 532–535, 2017.
DOI: 10.1007/978-3-319-61425-0_57

3 Our Approach

An essential constraint in the assessment environment is that the system does not provide any hints about the correctness of the answer or any intermediate states. We developed a web interface that displays a "blank" binary tree of 31 nodes, i.e., the interface looks like a sheet of paper with an outline of a binary tree that is 5 levels deep. The student submits an answer tree by entering the value and color of every non-empty node.

In grading the answer, we take an approach similar to [2], which involves developing a solution module that for any problem will generate a solution in canonical form using only primitive operators. The system also has a list of transformations that can potentially belong to a different solution; these are used to modify the canonical version into any other equivalent form, eliminating the need to generate all possible solutions and instead relying on heuristics to find the closest match to the student's answer. The grading algorithm for both insertion and deletion operations is as follows (Fig. 1).

1. retrieve the problem (the sequence of numbers to be inserted)
2. generate a correct solution which consists of the transformations (and resultant trees) for each number to be inserted
3. set the current subproblem to the first subproblem (insertion of the first number)
4. retrieve the generated solution to the current subproblem
5. retrieve the corresponding answer submitted by the student
6. compare the solution and answer trees for each subproblem. If the last tree in each sequence matches, the subproblem has been solved correctly by the student. Otherwise, the student is assigned a partial score based on what has been correctly solved to this point (including the subproblems prior to the current one)

Fig. 1. Grading algorithm for insertion

Once the assessment module has detected that the final state in the student's answer is different and therefore incorrect, it goes on to determine (1) where the first error occurred and (2) the type of error made. Figure 2 describes this procedure. Currently the algorithm can detect insertion errors in *color flip, single rotate, double rotate* and *insert*. It can also detect deletion errors in *drop and rotate, single rotate, double rotate, recolor root* and *delete*.

4 Evaluation

The system was evaluated on 30 students in a Data Structures class in Fall 2016, with 120 answers recorded. The evaluation had the following steps:

1. Week 1 - lectures on the material (2.5 h)
2. Week 2, day 1 - pre-test (0.5 h)
3. Week 2, day 1 - use of tutoring system (1 h)
4. Week 2, day 2 - post-test (0.5 h)

1. retrieve the current subproblem (insertion or deletion of a value)
2. generate the sequence of solution trees for the current subproblem
3. retrieve the sequence of trees submitted by the student
4. set the current tree to the first tree in each sequence (generated and submitted)
5. compare the current tree from the student with the trees in the generated sequence
6. if there is a match, set the current trees to the next tree after the trees match and repeat with step 5 until all the trees in the student's sequence have been compared.
7. otherwise, an incorrect transformation was applied. Terminate the algorithm and return the type of transformation that was attempted.

Fig. 2. Finding The Error In The Tree: starting with the first tree in the student's answer, compare with the first tree in the generated solution. Repeat until there is a tree in the student's answer that does not map to the generated trees even with transformations. Use heuristics to try and categorize the error.

The pre and post tests were identical and contained 4 questions, each composed of the insertion (deletion) of 4 to 6 numbers. The students used a web browser to take the pre and post test using the assessment interface described in the previous section.

Tables 1 and 2 show a breakdown of the errors made for insertion and deletion problems. Our algorithm could effectively identify the first error 78% of the time in insertion problems and 63% in deletion problems. The portion of unrecognized errors were due to either the students combining multiple steps or performing completely incorrect transformations.

The system performs comparably to a human grader and can effectively recognize most single errors. Currently it is unable to detect the combination of more than one errors or assign partial credit if one step is incorrect but subsequent steps are correct based on the resulting tree. Furthermore, we encountered difficulty in determining whether the errors were in identifying the current node or the applicable transformation. These are important features to be added in the next iteration.

Table 1. Distribution of errors made in insertion - pre and post test

	Color flip	Single rotate	Double rotate	Insert	Unrecognized
Pre test	54.9%	3.7%	8.5%	10.9%	22.0%
Post test	29.4%	8.6%	27.6%	12.0%	22.4%

Table 2. Distribution of errors made in deletion - pre and post test

	Drop rotate	Single rotate	Double rotate	Recolor root	Delete	Unrecognized
Pre test	30.7%	14.5%	6.5%	1.6%	9.7%	37%
Post test	45.7%	8.7%	4.3%	0%	2.2%	39.1%

5   Conclusion

This paper has described our approach to automated assessment of graphically inputted answers to red black tree insertion and deletion problems. The approach has been successful in distinguishing between correct and incorrect answers and also in generally identifying the location and type of error. There are still additional features that we intend to implement that would help us to develop a more effective tutoring system that is customized to the individual student.

References

1. Liew, C., Shapiro, J.A., Smith, D.: Determining the dimensions of variables in physics algebraic equations. Int. J. Artif. Intell. Tools **14**(1&2), 25–42 (2005)
2. Liew, C., Shapiro, J.A., Smith, D., McCall, R.J.: Understanding student answers in introductory physics courses. In: Luckin, R., Koedinger, K.R., Greer, J. (eds.) Artificial Intelligence in Education: Building Technology Rich Learning Contexts That Work, July 2007
3. Liew, C.W., Xhakaj, F.: Teaching a complex process: insertion in red black trees. In: Conati, C., Heffernan, N., Mitrovic, A., Verdejo, M.F. (eds.) AIED 2015. LNCS, vol. 9112, pp. 698–701. Springer, Cham (2015). doi:10.1007/978-3-319-19773-9_95
4. Weiss, M.A.: Data Structures & Problem Solving Using Java, 3rd edn. Pearson Education Inc., Boston (2011)

A Comparisons of BKT, RNN and LSTM for Learning Gain Prediction

Chen Lin[✉] and Min Chi[✉]

The Department of Computer Science, North Carolina State University,
Raleigh, USA
{clin12,mchi}@ncsu.edu

Abstract. The objective of this study is to develop effective computational models that can predict student learning gains, preferably as early as possible. We compared a series of Bayesian Knowledge Tracing (BKT) models against vanilla RNNs and Long Short Term Memory (LSTM) based models. Our results showed that the LSTM-based model achieved the highest accuracy and the RNN based model have the highest F1-measure. Interestingly, we found that RNN can achieve a reasonably accurate prediction of student final learning gains using only the first 40% of the entire training sequence; using the first 70% of the sequence would produce a result comparable to using the entire sequence.

Keywords: LSTM · RNN · BKT · Learning gain prediction

1 Introduction

A number of studies have shown that the effectiveness of any learning environment varies greatly based on individual differences such as motivation, aptitude, and incoming competence, etc. [1]. Thus, it is essentially important to track whether a student has embarked upon a unprofitable learning experience and to identify such an individual as early as possible so adaptive remediation can be offered. However, it is often very hard to do so because many factors may impact whether a student would learn, yet those factors are not fully understood. As a result, much student modeling research focused on modeling student knowledge competence level over time such as Bayesian Knowledge Tracing (BKT) [2]. Nonetheless, a student with high knowledge level does not mean that the student benefited from the learning environment; the student may already have high competence before he/she starts use the system.

To fully honor the promise of the learning environment, the main objective in this study is to predict student learning gains on Intelligent Tutoring Systems (ITSs). As far as we know, little research has done in this direction, probably because predicting learning gains is much more challenging than predicting student knowledge level. While it is often reasonable to assume that a student who have done well so far would continue to do well in the final exam, it is unclear

© Springer International Publishing AG 2017
E. André et al. (Eds.): AIED 2017, LNAI 10331, pp. 536–539, 2017.
DOI: 10.1007/978-3-319-61425-0_58

what factors impact student learning gains. Previous research used *Learning Gain (LG)* = *post − pre* or $NLG = \frac{(post-pre)}{(1-pre)}$ (pre and post are defined as a students' pretest score before training and posttest score after training respectively; 1 is the maximum score one can get) to measure learning gain. Both LG and NLG are biased against students with High pretest scores in that it is often harder for them to obtain the same LG and NLG scores as their peers with Low pretest scores. Therefore, we proposed Quantized Learning Gain (QLG) by dividing students into "low", "medium" and "high" groups using 33rd and 66th percentile based on their pretest and posttest scores. *Low* QLG students are defined as those who either down-graded their group from pre- to posttest, or remained in "low" or "medium" groups even though their performance can be improved; the rest are labeled as "High" QLG.

2   Methods and Training Data

Proposed Methods include the classic BKT models, Recurrent Neural Network (RNN) [4] and Long Short Term Memory (LSTM) [5]. BKT [2] is the classic approach for student modeling. It leverages student performance (i.e., correct, incorrect) over time to updates estimations of student knowledge level. Intervention-BKT is a variation of BKT by incorporating instructional interventions within its framework and it has been shown to outperform conventional BKT in various prediction tasks [3]. For BKT family variation models, we have tried the basic BKT model and the mixed model combining Intervention-BKT and BKT. For both models, we used either performance, response time, or a combination of both as observations. Thus we have a total of six BKT models.

Compared to BKT-based models, RNN exhibits greater flexibility: it allows multivariate inputs and does not require any explicit encoding of domain concepts, thus requiring near-to-zero human expert involvement. LSTM is a special type of RNN that contains a system of gating units that controls the flow of information. LSTM has been shown to learn long-term dependencies more easily than vanilla RNN [6]. It has been shown that both RNN and LSTM out-performed the conventional BKT model [5]. For RNN and LSTM, the system-student interaction tuples were converted into a sequence of input vectors. The system learns and passes information across many steps to predict QLG at the final step. A sequential *target replication* (TR) technique inspired by [7] was implemented in our study, where the final target was copied at each sequence step, providing a local error signal. Models with TR were named RNN-TR and LSTM-TR respectively. For both RNN and LSTM, Different combinations of layers (1 or 2) and nodes (50, 100, 150, or 200) were tested. As LSTM contains more parameters, a dropout rate of 0.2 was applied between a LSTM layer and a final dense layer. All of these experiments were conducted using Kera's implementation and trained to 100 epochs with a 100 mini-batch size.

Training Dataset was collected from training 524 students on a probability tutor called Pyrenees. The training was assigned as their final homework in the undergraduate Discrete Mathematics course at the Department of Computer Science at North Carolina State University from 2014–2016. Students were required to complete 4 phases: (1) pre-training, (2) pretest, (3) training and (4) post-test. All students received the same 12 training problems in the same order. Pretests and post-tests were graded in a double-blind manner by a single experienced grader. The scores were normalized using a range of [0, 1].

3 Result

Comparisons among BKT, RNN and LSTM: Two RNNs and two LSTMs were compared against a series of BKT family models and a majority baseline on predicting QLG. Table 1 shows our 10-fold cross validation accuracy, precision, recall and F1-measure results. Note that for our task, detecting *Low* QLG is more important. Our results showed that all the BKT-based, RNN, and LSTM models outperformed the majority baselines. Given the limited space, only the best model among BKT family models were reported as shown in row 2 in Table 1. Generally speaking, the RNN, RNN-TR, LSTM models outperformed the best BKT-based models while LSTM-TR has a worse recall and F1-measure than the BKT family models. Among RNN family models, LSTM achieves the highest accuracy; LSTM-TR has the highest precision rate, and RNN-TR achieves the best recall and F1-measure. Without the replicating target technique, both RNN and LSTM have similar results; whereas using target replication technique improves the recall and F1-measure for RNN, but not for LSTM.

Early Detection of Low QLG: Given that RNN-TR achieves the highest Recall and F1-measure, we investigated its performance in early detection. In Fig. 1, the line with triangular points represents the F1-measure and the line with circular points represents accuracy. They are both measured at every 10% increment of the sequence length. From 10% to 40%, both accuracy (0.52 to 0.64) and the F1-measure (0.65 to 0.72) increase significantly; from 40% to 70%, the increase becomes moderate (0.64 to 0.66 for accuracy; 0.72 to 0.74 for F1-measure); from 70% to the remainder of the sequence, the increase is only slight (0.66 to 0.67 for accuracy; 0.74 to 0.75 for F1-measure). The results indicate that a good prediction of QLG can be achieved by using the first 40% of the entire sequence and that using the first 70% of the entire sequence is as good as using the entire sequence.

Table 1. Prediction results for all 11 models

	Model	Accuracy	Precision	Recall	F1-measure
1	Majority	0.528	0.587	0.595	0.591
2	Best BKT family	0.642	0.648	0.821	0.724
3	RNN	0.669	0.668	0.841	0.744
4	RNN-TR	0.667	0.658	**0.874***	**0.750***
5	LSTM	**0.670***	0.670	0.837	0.744
6	LSTM-TR	0.648	**0.678***	0.734	0.705

best model marked in **bold** and *

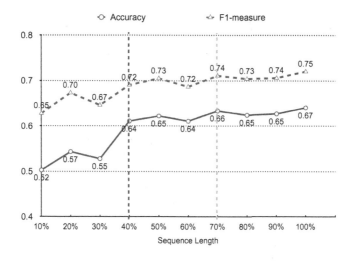

Fig. 1. Accuracy and F1-measure for RNN Prediction Using Partial Sequence

4   Discussion

This study compared a majority baseline model, a series of BKT family models and four RNN/LSTM family models to predict students' QLG. Our results suggest that both all models outperformed Majority baseline and LSTM achieved the highest accuracy whereas RNN-TR, a RNN model with target replicate technique, achieved the highest recall and F1-measure. Furthermore, the performance of using RNN-TR to perform early detection of students who may have a *low* QLG was explored. We found that the model can achieve reasonably good result when using only the first 40% of the entire student log sequence.

References

1. Merrill, D.C., et al.: Effective tutoring techniques: a comparison of human tutors and intelligent tutoring systems. J. Learn. Sci. **2**(3), 277–305 (1992)
2. Corbett, A.T., Anderson, J.R.: Knowledge tracing: modeling the acquisition of procedural knowledge. User Model. User Adapt. Interact. **4**(4), 253–278 (1994)
3. Lin, C., Chi, M.: Intervention-BKT: incorporating instructional interventions into bayesian knowledge tracing. In: Micarelli, A., Stamper, J., Panourgia, K. (eds.) ITS 2016. LNCS, vol. 9684, pp. 208–218. Springer, Cham (2016). doi:10.1007/978-3-319-39583-8_20
4. Mikolov, T., Karafiát, M., Burget, L., Cernocký, J., Khudanpur, S.: Recurrent neural network based language model. In: Interspeech, vol. 2, p. 3, September 2010
5. Piech, C., Bassen, J., Huang, J., Ganguli, S., Sahami, M., Guibas, L.J., Sohl-Dickstein, J.: Deep knowledge tracing. In: Advances in Neural Information Processing Systems, pp. 505–513 (2015)
6. LeCun, Y., Bengio, Y., Hinton, G.: Deep learning. Nature **521**(7553), 436–444 (2015)
7. Lipton, Z.C., et al.: Learning to diagnose with LSTM recurrent neural networks. arXiv preprint (2015). arXiv:1511.03677

Uncovering Gender and Problem Difficulty Effects in Learning with an Educational Game

Bruce McLaren[1]([⊠]), Rosta Farzan[2], Deanne Adams[3],
Richard Mayer[4], and Jodi Forlizzi[1]

[1] Carnegie Mellon University, Pittsburgh, PA, USA
bmclaren@cs.cmu.edu
[2] University of Pittsburgh, Pittsburgh, PA, USA
[3] University of Notre Dame, South Bend, IN, USA
[4] University of California, Santa Barbara, Santa Barbara, CA, USA

Abstract. A prior study showed that middle school students who used the educational game *Decimal Point* achieved significantly higher gain scores on immediate and delayed posttests of decimal understanding than students who learned with a more conventional computer-based learning tool. This paper reports on new analyses of the data from that study, providing new insights into the benefits of the game. First, females benefited more than males from the game. Second, students in the game condition performed better on the more difficult intervention problems. This paper presents these new analyses and discusses why the educational game might have led to these results.

Keywords: Educational games · Mathematics learning · Educational data mining

1 Introduction

Research is still needed to determine the conditions under which game-based learning can be effective [1]. A meta-review of over 1000 educational game studies advises that more *value-added studies* of educational games be conducted, that is, research that carefully identifies the features and conditions that lead to the successes and failures of educational games [2]. This paper is a step in that direction. Using a successful educational game, *Decimal Point*, we investigate the conditions that lead to learning. In a prior study *Decimal Point* was shown to lead to more learning and was more enjoyable to students than a more conventional computer-based learning tool [3]. In this paper, we report on new analyses that shed light on who benefitted from the game and under what conditions.

Decimal Point (Fig. 1) is a single-player game based on an amusement park metaphor, targeted at middle-school students learning decimals. Students play a series of *mini-games* in different theme areas of the amusement park that are targeted at decimal misconceptions. There is no scoring and no leader board; students simply make their way through the park and are congratulated upon finishing.

© Springer International Publishing AG 2017
E. André et al. (Eds.): AIED 2017, LNAI 10331, pp. 540–543, 2017.
DOI: 10.1007/978-3-319-61425-0_59

The "Space Raider" mini-game of Fig. 2 is targeted at the common misconception in which students think longer decimals are larger than shorter decimals (e.g., 0.634 > 0.82). The student tries to shoot the alien ships in the requested order (i.e., smallest to largest). If they make mistakes, they are prompted to correct their solution by dragging and dropping the decimals to the correct sequence. The various mini-games challenge students with other types of decimal problems, as well, including placing a point on a number line and adding decimals. After playing a mini-game and correctly solving the problem, the student is prompted to explain his or her solution [4], by choosing possible self-explanations from a multiple-choice list.

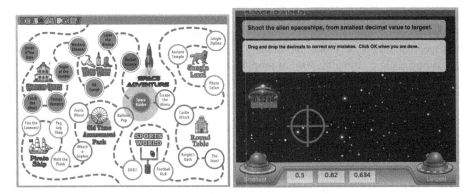

Fig. 1. Map of the *Decimal Point* game   **Fig. 2.** The "Space Raider" mini-game

As a comparison to the game, students use a conventional, non-game version of the decimal instructional materials that employs a more standard user interface for solving decimal problems. As with the mini-games, after solving a problem the student is prompted to explain his or her solution in the same way that the mini-games prompt students for self-explanation.

A classroom study of *Decimal Point* is presented in [3]. The study involved more than 150 sixth grade students at two schools, comparing students who played the *Decimal Point* game to learn decimals with students who learned decimals with the more conventional computer-based learning tool. The same 48 decimal problems were presented to students in the same order across the conditions, except that students in the game condition solved problems using the mini-games, while students in the non-game condition solved the problems using the conventional instructional software. Students in both conditions took a pretest, posttest, and delayed posttest (comprising 61 items). A survey, completed after the intervention, had 11 5-point Likert scale questions ("Strongly agree" (1) to "Strongly disagree" (5)) related to the categories of Lesson Enjoyment, Ease of Interface, and Feelings of Math Efficacy. Summary of the results [3]: students in the game condition learned significantly more and had significantly more positive feelings about their experience. Also, low prior knowledge learners benefited significantly more from the game.

2 Exploring Gender and Problem Difficulty Effects

In this work, we raised new research questions and conducted new analyses of the data from our prior study. *RQ1: Is the learning benefit of playing the Decimal Point game more, less, or the same for female students as for male students?* *RQ2: Did the Decimal Point game lead to students performing better, and potentially learning more, from the more difficult problems in the intervention?* We wondered whether females, in particular, might benefit from the game. One could argue that games are more likely to benefit males who more frequently identify themselves as gamers and are more frequent game players [5]. Yet, there is evidence that gender does not play a role, especially when games rely on fostering intrinsic motivation [6]. It is also important to understand how games facilitate learning of more complicated materials. As the difficulty level of problems grows, engagement with the materials might drop. Thus, engagement might be more important for difficult problems. Games could help by providing a more engaging way to grapple with difficult problems.

157 students participated in the study with the gender distribution as follows:

Game (70) – 39 females, 31 males; *Non-Game* (87) – 49 females, 38 males.

To address *RQ1* we conducted a regression analysis to predict the relationship between the intervention and learning outcomes for female vs. male students. The results of the main effect in the regression model confirmed the prior learning results cited above. The results for immediate and delayed posttests by gender are summarized in Fig. 3(a) and (b). In terms of both immediate posttest and delayed posttest, there is a significant interaction effect of game condition with gender.

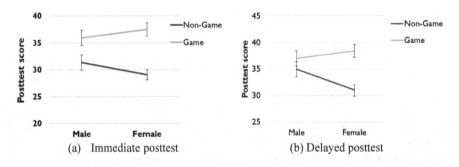

Fig. 3. Interaction effect of game with gender on learning outcomes

Even though both male and female students performed significantly better under the game condition on the immediate posttest, the effect size for the female students is higher ($d = .59$ vs. $d = .39$). For the delayed posttest, while male students did not perform differently with or without game, female students performed significantly better under the game condition ($d = .71$).

To address *RQ2*, we first conducted a subjective evaluation with 3 middle school math teachers of problem difficulty. The teachers rated the 48 intervention problems on a 5-point Likert scale: 1 - "Very Easy"; 5 - "Very Difficult". Using this data, we judged a problem as difficult if the average rating of the 3 teachers was above 3, and easy if the average rating was less than or equal 3. 27 of the problems were judged as easy, 21 as difficult. To then assess the impact of the game on difficult vs. easy problems, we conducted a regression analysis of the relationship between the intervention conditions on the number of errors students made on each problem.

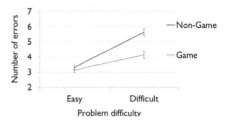

Fig. 4. Interaction of difficulty level of problem with number of errors on each problem

There is a significant interaction of the game condition and the difficulty level of the problem on the number of errors students make at the problem level. The interaction effect is presented in Fig. 4. For the easy problems, the game does not influence the number of errors the students make; however, for difficult problems, the game leads to students making significantly fewer errors ($d = .09$).

Our new data analyses answered our two new research questions. First, females benefited more from the game than males. This result may be related to the fact that game achievement is not a focus of *Decimal Point*. Prior research suggests that male players can be particularly attracted to games of achievement, while achievement does not appear to be a key factor in engaging female players [7]. Second, the game appears to have made difficult problems more tractable, as the game group made significantly fewer errors on the difficult problems in the intervention than the non-game group. Better performance on the difficult problems may be a result of students' higher level of engagement with the game. Games may be a way to engage students in continuing to higher levels of mastery, even in the face of difficult problems.

References

1. Mayer, R.E.: Computer Games for Learning: An Evidence-Based Approach. MIT Press, Cambridge (2014)
2. Clark, D.B., Tanner-Smith, E.E., Killingsworth, S.S.: Digital games, design, and learning: a systematic review and meta-analysis. Rev. Ed. Res. **86**(1), 79–122 (2016)
3. McLaren, B.M., Adams, D.M., Mayer, R.E., Forlizzi, J.: A computer-based game that promotes mathematics learning more than a conventional approach. Int. J. Game Based Learn. (IJGBL) **7**(1), 36–56 (2017). doi:10.4018/IJGBL.2017010103
4. Chi, M.T.H.: Self-explaining expository texts: the dual processes of generating inferences and repairing mental models. In: Glaser, R. (ed.) Advances in Instructional Psychology, pp. 161–238. Lawrence Erlbaum Associates, Inc., Mahwah (2000)
5. Lenhart, A., Smith, A., Anderson, M., Duggan, M., Perrin, A.: Teens, Technology and Friendships. Pew Research Center (2015)
6. Habgood, M.P.J., Ainsworth, S.: Motivating children to learn effectively: exploring the value of intrinsic integration in educational games. J. Learn. Sci. **20**(2), 169–206 (2011)
7. Inkpen, K.: Three important research agendas for educational multimedia: Learning, children, and gender. In: AACE World Conference on Educational Multimedia and Hypermedia, vol. 97, pp. 521–526 (1997)

Analyzing Learner Affect in a Scenario-Based Intelligent Tutoring System

Benjamin Nye[1]([✉]), Shamya Karumbaiah[2], S. Tugba Tokel[3], Mark G. Core[1],
Giota Stratou[1], Daniel Auerbach[1], and Kallirroi Georgila[1]

[1] Institute for Creative Technologies, University of Southern California,
Los Angeles, USA
{nye,core,stratou,auerbach,kgeorgila}@ict.usc.edu
[2] College of Information and Computer Sciences,
University of Massachusetts Amherst, Amherst, USA
shamya@cs.umass.edu
[3] Department of Computer Education and Instructional Technology,
METU, Ankara, Turkey
stugba@metu.edu.tr

Abstract. Scenario-based tutoring systems influence affective states
due to two distinct mechanisms during learning: (1) reactions to performance feedback and (2) responses to the scenario context or events.
To explore the role of affect and engagement, a scenario-based ITS was
instrumented to support unobtrusive facial affect detection. Results from
a sample of university students showed relatively few traditional academic affective states such as confusion or frustration, even at decision
points and after poor performance (e.g., incorrect responses). This may
show evidence of "over-flow," with a high level of engagement and interest but insufficient confusion/disequilibrium for optimal learning.

1 Introduction

Emotions and affective reactions provide insight into the processes of academic
cognition, perceptions, and mental events that cannot be directly measured. A
growing amount of literature has studied academic emotions during computer-
based learning, with affect measured using techniques such as self-report, human
observation, text analysis, facial cues, speech analysis, physical sensors (pressure,
conductance), and inferences from patterns of learner task behavior. Within
the space of learning environments that have been studied, some consensus has
emerged about the utility of four key cognitive-affective states: engagement/flow,
confusion/disequilibrium, frustration, and disengagement/boredom [2].

Scenario-based intelligent tutoring systems (ITS), such as role-playing and
simulations, have unique issues that make them more complex with respect to
academic emotions. First, tutoring behavior (e.g., feedback) is often distinct
from the reactions and consequences that occur during the scenario itself. Second, scenario-based learning is more likely to have a continuous assessment space

E. André et al. (Eds.): AIED 2017, LNAI 10331, pp. 544–547, 2017.
DOI: 10.1007/978-3-319-61425-0_60

(e.g., partial credit). Scenario-based tutors can also cause real or perceived time-pressure, such as ongoing system dynamics (e.g., flight simulators) or expectations (e.g., conversational norms). These issues result in a trade-off between balancing the sense of immersion in the scenario against breaking flow to encourage reflection on one's actions.

Affect has not been extensively studied in scenario-based ITS. Research on the Crystal Island ITS studied affect through behavioral patterns (e.g., time/interaction-based engagement) and building self-report into in-scenario interactions [6,7]. Replicating prior work, engagement was associated with better learning outcomes [7]. However, this methodology was limited in that it did not allow continuous moment-to-moment measures of multiple facets of affect. This is important, because it is not well-established that these four affective states operate identically during scenarios as compared to more abstract learning tasks. For example, emotions that might be considered analogous to engagement (e.g., "invigoration") have sometimes shown the opposite of expected effects, and been associated with higher cognitive load and worse retention of skills on later tests for skills such as medical interventions [3].

The goal of this work was to observe the relationship of emotions to other components of the experience (e.g., correctness of answers, student traits) in a scenario-based ITS. Overall, while certain results replicate insights from prior work (e.g., confusion preceding incorrect answers), as a whole this research indicates that scenario-based tutoring may display different patterns of affect than observed in a traditional ITS.

2   Data Collection and Methodology

Data was collected on learners using the Emergent Leader Immersive Training Environment (ELITE)-Lite system, which was instrumented to collect a corpus of 30–60 min video logs of student interaction via laptop web cameras. ELITE is a scenario-based ITS which uses multiple-choice-based role-playing interactions to train basic counseling skills and practice them with a virtual human, while a virtual coach pro-actively provides hints and feedback [4]. An overview of experimental procedure, overall learning gains, the impact of hints, and student traits has been previously reported [1]. Data for 39 participants at a private university in California was collected across two randomly-assigned conditions with one condition always giving hints/feedback for mixed answers (Always-Mixed-Guidance) and the other never giving hints/feedback for mixed (No-Mixed-Guidance). Of these 39 participants (10 female), the majority of participants identified as Asian/Pacific Islander (33).

We use the acronym C-CERT to refer to commercial video analysis software based on the Computer Expression Recognition Toolbox [5], which performs real time facial expression recognition. C-CERT processed the video logs outputting evidence levels for 20 facial action units (AUs) and prototypical expressions such as Confusion, Frustration, Sadness, Joy, Anger, and Fear. A sweep examining various block sizes (1s to 5s) was briefly explored and 3s found to be the most interpretable. Observed rates of emotions such as frustration, and overt inattention were so rare that C-CERT data was reduced to a more limited set of categories, including only Baseline, Confusion, and Other, where Other was calculated as the maximum of all other remaining C-CERT emotions.

3   Results and Analysis

Means of the emotion categories showed that there were high evidence levels for Baseline (0.92, SD = 0.52), relatively low levels of Other emotions (0.25, SD = 0.44) and the mean for Confusion was negative (−0.7, SD = 0.68) suggesting absence. As would be expected, Pearson's correlations showed significant pairwise correlations between each emotion overall (p < 0.01 for all). Baseline was negatively correlated with Confusion (r = −.35) and Other (r = −.88), with Confusion positively correlated with Other (r = .36).

Under Pearson's correlations adjusted for repeated measures, few self-reported traits showed statistically significant results for this sample size, with only Experience and Anxiety (e.g., test anxiety) notable. Experience was positively correlated with Baseline (r = .40, p < .01) and negatively with Other (r = −.40, p < .01). Lack of anxiety was negatively correlated with Confusion (r = −.34, p < .05), with students who reported more academic anxiety also showing more confusion.

Compared to overall affect, affect around responses showed lower levels of Baseline (0.64, SD = 0.57) and higher Confusion (−0.41, SD = 0.70), with Other remaining similar (0.20, SD = 0.44). Pearson's correlations showed significant pairwise correlations (p < .00) that followed the same trends as the overall affect: Baseline was negatively correlated with Confusion (r = −.40) and Other (r = −.72), with Confusion positively correlated with Other (r = .47). Both overall and around responses, Baseline and Other showed no effect by condition (i.e., no difference despite more/less hint support). However, around student responses, Confusion showed statistically significant differences, with more Confusion in the No-Mixed-Guidance condition with fewer hints (F(1, 37) = 6.25, p < .01).

To look at this further, a paired t-test was conducted for each emotion covering 3s Before and 3s After of Correct, Incorrect, and Mixed answers. Confusion was significantly higher Before Incorrect versus Before Correct (t(39) = 3.75, p < .00) and also higher After Incorrect versus After Correct (t(39) = 3.67, p < .00). Confusion was also higher when comparing Incorrect and Mixed for Before (t(39) = 3.75, p < .00) and After (t(39) = 3.48, p < .00). Conversely, Other was higher Before Correct than Before Incorrect (t(39) = 2.31, p < .03). In general, this confirms that participants who showed confusion were less likely to respond correctly. However, analyses found that answer correctness was a weak predictor of After Confusion ($R^2 = 0.1$; 10-fold subject-level CV). This finding was similar for Baseline ($R^2 = 0.1$) and Other ($R^2 = 0.06$).

Regression analysis results, examining the extent to which Correctness of the answers could be predicted from Before Confusion, Before Other, Before Baseline, Time Taken, and Whether the Question had been seen before, indicated a statistically significant model ($R^2 = .05$, F $(5,1953) = 20.13$, p $< .00$). By comparison, adding a parameter for Question Difficulty raised fit to $R^2 = 0.18$ with 88% of variance explained loaded on Difficulty. As such, regression models indicate that the added predictive value of Confusion for Correctness may be limited.

4 Discussion and Conclusions

Overall, learners in the ELITE-Lite scenario-based ITS showed relatively low levels of affect and a Baseline facial state was dominant. Given the available data, we cannot exclude the possibility that the particular subject population showed particularly flat affect. However, while that may play a role, we believe that the primary cause for the limited incidence of academic emotions was due to sense of flow in the scenario. Considering the low levels of confusion, near-absence of frustration, and no signs of overt disengagement, evidence indicates that learners were in an engaged/equilibrium state as per D'Mello and Graesser's model [2]. This state might be thought of as "over-flow," where learners are engaged in the experience and content, but float past their failures and potential impasses.

Acknowledgment. The effort described here is sponsored by the U.S. Army Research Laboratory (ARL) under contract number W911NF-14-D-0005. Any opinion, content or information presented does not necessarily reflect the position or the policy of the United States Government, and no official endorsement should be inferred.

References

1. Core, M.G., Georgila, K., Nye, B.D., Auerbach, D., Liu, Z.F., DiNinni, R.: Learning, adaptive support, student traits, and engagement in scenario-based learning. In: Interservice/Industry Training, Simulation, and Education Conference (I/ITSEC) (2016)
2. D'Mello, S., Graesser, A.: Dynamics of affective states during complex learning. Learn. Instr. **22**(2), 145–157 (2012)
3. Fraser, K., Ma, I., Teteris, E., Baxter, H., Wright, B., McLaughlin, K.: Emotion, cognitive load and learning outcomes during simulation training. Med. Educ. **46**(11), 1055–1062 (2012)
4. Hays, M.J., Campbell, J.C., Trimmer, M.A., Poore, J.C., Webb, A.K., King, T.K.: Can role-play with virtual humans teach interpersonal skills? In: Interservice/Industry Training, Simulation, and Education Conference (I/ITSEC) (2012)
5. Littlewort, G., Whitehill, J., Wu, T., Fasel, I., Frank, M., Movellan, J., Bartlett, M.: The computer expression recognition toolbox (CERT). In: IEEE International Conference on Automatic Face and Gesture Recognition, pp. 298–305 (2011)
6. Robison, J., McQuiggan, S., Lester, J.: Evaluating the consequences of affective feedback in intelligent tutoring systems. In: Affective Computing and Intelligent Interaction ACII 2009, pp. 1–6. IEEE (2009)
7. Rowe, J.P., Shores, L.R., Mott, B.W., Lester, J.C.: Integrating learning, problem solving, and engagement in narrative-centered learning environments. Int. J. Artif. Intell. Educ. **21**(1–2), 115–133 (2011)

Proficiency and Preference Using Local Language with a Teachable Agent

Amy Ogan[1(✉)], Evelyn Yarzebinski[1], Roberto De Roock[2],
Cristina Dumdumaya[3], Michelle Banawan[3],
and Ma. Mercedes Rodrigo[3]

[1] Human-Computer Interaction Institute,
Carnegie Mellon University, Pittsburgh, USA
{aeo,eey2}@cs.cmu.edu
[2] National Institute of Education,
Nanyang Technological University, Singapore, Singapore
robert.deroock@nie.edu.sg
[3] Department of Information Systems and Computer Science,
Ateneo de Manila University, Quezon City, Philippines
cedumdumaya@usep.edu.ph, mpbanawan@addu.edu.ph,
mrodrigo@ateneo.edu

Abstract. With a teachable agent system and a set of linguistically diverse comparison prototypes, we explore questions of proficiency with and preference for local language agents in two sites in the Philippines. We found that students in a higher-performing school produce more English-language math explanations at a faster rate than students in a lower-performing school, who were more proficient in their local language. However, these students preferred the English-language agent, while students in the higher-performing school had equal preference for agents who communicates in the local language. These findings demonstrate the complex interactions between language and engagement in AIED systems.

Keywords: Natural language dialogue · Code-switching · Teachable agent · Culture

1 Introduction and Background

Around the world, many governments designate English as a medium of instruction for students whose home language may not be English, including Tanzania, Bangladesh, and Singapore. While these policies are carefully enacted to offer certain desirable opportunities to students [1], they may conflict with other student needs. Personalized learning technologies offer an opportunity to bridge the gap between the official medium of instruction and students' home language, while adapting to individual students' needs and preferences.

Whether acknowledged or implicit, the many AIED systems that utilize natural language have embedded design decisions regarding the way they engage in dialogic interactions with students even when the domain content is math or physics. Several

© Springer International Publishing AG 2017
E. André et al. (Eds.): AIED 2017, LNAI 10331, pp. 548–552, 2017.
DOI: 10.1007/978-3-319-61425-0_61

such AIED systems have already waded purposefully into this space. For example, working with an agent that spoke in African-American Vernacular English led to more gains in science reasoning for African-American students than working with one that spoke in mainstream English [2]. Mohammed et al. allowed university students to select the amount of local Trinidad and Tobago dialect their system would use, and found that a majority of students preferred the dialect-enabled system and wanted to control the localization [3]. These two example systems raise two critical issues that could underlie the success of a personalized approach: student proficiency and student preference.

We investigate these issues in the Philippines, where over 170 distinct languages are spoken and many students are tri-lingual. Language is thus a particularly complex issue for instruction closely tied to broader debates about national identity. The Philippines 1974 Bilingual Education Policy (BEP) integrated English and Filipino into instruction, but specified that mathematics be English-only from as early as Grade 3. Amamio [4] surveyed attitudes of students and teachers toward English and Filipino in instruction, finding that both preferred English, demonstrating the prestige associated with the language. However, a wealth of research indicates that children learn best in their home languages (e.g. [5]), including gains in mathematics problem solving [1].

Previous work found that a quarter of students in a Philippines site used a local language when responding to a teachable agent, even though the agent only spoke English [6]. Use of local language was associated with lower prior knowledge in math, and expressed frustration or lack of knowledge. With this same teachable agent and a set of linguistically diverse comparison prototypes, in two distinct Filipino sites, we ask:

RQ1:   What is the relation between proficiency with and preferences for language variation with natural language embodied learning companions?

RQ2:   To what extent do these issues generalize across linguistically diverse settings?

2   Method

We conducted our study in two distinct sites in the Philippines: "Manila," a public school in the capital and largest city, and "Davao," a university-associated school in Davao City. We recruited students age 13–15 (53 in Manila, 68 in Davao) currently enrolled in Algebra I. Students first took a pretest, then used the system to "tutor" their teachable agent in mathematics problems over Days 2–4 for approximately 60 min per day, then took an isomorphic posttest on Day 5. Students tutored using natural language self-explanations (SEs) to the agent in the SimStudent system which we coded with a modified version of the manual in [7]. "Code-Switching" was labeled 0 for English-only input, and 1 otherwise. "Quality of mathematical content" included codes for 0: none; 1: vague; and 2: elaborated. Cohen's Kappa for these codes was high: κ(Code-Switching) = 98.9%, and κ(Quality) = 82.5%. Researchers additionally observed and took structured field notes to gain insight into how the students interacted with the system.

Next, we recruited 12 students in Manila and 10 in Davao to engage with two new prototype agents. These prototypes were simplified versions of SimStudent in which students engaged in the same types of math interactions, for 5 min. The first prototype used the local language that students were expected to be most comfortable with outside of class. The second prototype spoke in English like SimStudent, but the agent had a "robot-like" character rather than a human representation. We interviewed the students about their preferences for engaging with these agents, and their own language backgrounds and preferences. We additionally conducted semi-structured interviews with an administrator in each site regarding class-room language use and expectations.

3 Results

We first investigated whether students learned the math content. A t-test shows lower pre-test scores in Manila (M = 2.76, SD = 3.46) than Davao (M = 7.70, SD = 2.16), (t(54) = 6.054, p < 0.001). However, learning gains achieved across sites were statistically equivalent (M_{Manila} = .83, SD_{Manila} = 1.27; M_{Davao} = .70, SD_{Davao} = 1.74) (t(54) = 0.304, p > 0.05).

Next, we investigated students' choice of language in their interactions with the system. 20% of students in Manila used local language, compared to only 6% of students in Davao. The amount of local language in Manila (M = 10%, SD = 31%) was significantly different from that in Davao (M = 1%, SD = 11%), t(342) = −4.74, p < 0.001). Levene's test was significant, so df were adjusted from 601 to 342.

A χ^2 test to determine if students used language differently across sites when they interacted with the system shows that in Manila, local language SEs contained a greater proportion of elaborated mathematical explanations than those in English only, and that a greater proportion of local language SEs contained mathematical explanations (vague or elaborated) than no math content (X^2(2, N = 280) = 9.9355, p < 0.01). The Manila administrator confirmed that students were most comfortable in Tagalog, explaining a joke that students get "nosebleeds" when confronted with a pure English conversation.

In contrast, English-only SEs in Davao were most likely to be elaborated mathematical explanations, while no local language SEs contained any mathematical content. Instead, they expressed frustration with their agent, e.g., "you should have learned algebra early on"[1] A χ^2 test demonstrated that these differences are significant: X^2(2, N = 323) = 32.289, p < 0.001. The Davao administrator suggested that this use of local language "shows how they are when they are talking with people outside the classroom ... when they feel free..."

We next investigated students' preferences. Manila students reported a strong preference (64%) for the English-language prototype, with only 9% of respondents preferring local language. Participant 4 M relayed that it was important for him to improve his English, and Participant 6 M explained that while he speaks Filipino best, "when we have mathematics equations and problems, it's in English, and it's more understandable than Tagalog." However, in Davao, students showed an almost evenly split preference for the local-language prototype (30%) over the current SimStudent

---

[1] kasi dapat natuto ka ng maaga ng algebra.

(30%) or the robot-embodied prototype (40%). Participant 5D, who felt strongest in English but mostly speaks Bisaya at home, preferred the local language agent not due to language proficiency, but because it felt more relatable: "Ahh, like it's also human, because we are using the same language[2]". In fact, the Davao administrator, when asked whether being able to speak English is prestigious for these students, suggested that "we observed that when they do, their friends would say 'What's with you, why do you speak English?'[3]" This attitude demonstrates a dichotomous perspective of English simultaneously being commonplace for many students, while at the same time is stigmatized as belonging to the "overachievers".

4 Discussion and Conclusion

In this work, we found evidence for distinct differences in proficiency with language and preference for system language across higher performing vs. lower performing schools and by region/language group. Manila students were more likely to use local language in their dialogue with the system than Davao students, and when they did they elaborated more on the mathematical content compared to their English explanations. Alternatively, Davao students did math almost exclusively in English. Importantly, the proficiency students displayed did not match their preferences for system interactions in either site. Students from Manila provided cognitively-focused explanations for their English-language preference, such as the need to improve their English, although students' strongest language generally was Tagalog. They saw English as prestigious. Instead, Davao students suggested that the local language agent was more "human-like" and relatable, emphasizing the rapport-building capacity of embodied agents which may support deeper motivational pathways for students.

These findings emphasize a related conclusion to [5] that detecting and adjusting to local language could support learning gains in AIED systems, but contextualizes that conclusion to account for students' beliefs about whether and how they learn best. This work highlights opportunities for language personalization in learning environments.

Acknowledgments. We thank the Jacobs Foundation and ALLS, DISCS, & ACED of Ateneo de Manila.

References

1. Ruiz, R.: Reorienting language-as-resource. In: Petrovich, J. (ed.) International Perspectives on Bilingual Education: Policy, Practice, and Controversy. IAP, pp. 155–172 (2010)
2. Finkelstein, S., Yarzebinski, E., Vaughn, C., Ogan, A., Cassell, J.: The effects of culturally congruent educational technologies on student achievement. In: Lane, H.C., Yacef, K., Mostow, J., Pavlik, P. (eds.) AIED 2013. LNCS, vol. 7926, pp. 493–502. Springer, Heidelberg (2013). doi:10.1007/978-3-642-39112-5_50

---

[2] Ahh, ano, parang tao na rin, kay pareho man kami ng language na gigamit.

[3] "ano ka man oi, English-English ka man?".

3. Mohammed, P., Mohan, P.: Dynamic cultural contextualisation of educational content in intelligent learning environments using ICON. Int. J. Artif. Intell. Educ. **25**(2), 249–270 (2015)
4. Amamio, L.: Attitudes of students, teachers and parents of RVM schools in metro Manila toward English and Filipino as media of instruction. (Unpublished Thesis) Presented to the UST Graduate School, Manila, Philippines (2000)
5. Dekker, D., Young, C.: Bridging the gap: The development of appropriate educational strategies for minority language communities in the Philippines. Curr. Issues Lang. Plann. **6**(2), 182–199 (2005)
6. Yarzebinski, E., Ogan, A., Rodrigo, M.M.T., Matsuda, N.: Understanding students' use of code-switching in a learning by teaching technology. In: Conati, C., et al. (eds.) AIED 2015. LNAI, vol. 9112, pp. 504–513. Springer, Cham (2015). doi:10.1007/978-3-319-19773-9_50
7. Rodrigo, M.M.T., Geli, R., Ong, A., Vitug, G., Bringula, R., Basa, R., Matsuda, N.: Exploring the implications of tutor negativity towards a synthetic agent in a learning-by-teaching environment. Philippine Comput. J. **8**, 15–20 (2013)

LiftUpp: Support to Develop Learner Performance

Frans A. Oliehoek[3]([✉]), Rahul Savani[3], Elliot Adderton[2], Xia Cui[3],
David Jackson[3], Phil Jimmieson[3], John Christopher Jones[1],
Keith Kennedy[4], Ben Mason[1], Adam Plumbley[3], and Luke Dawson[2]

[1] LiftUpp Limited, Liverpool, UK
[2] School of Dentistry, University of Liverpool, Liverpool, UK
[3] Department of Computer Science, University of Liverpool, Liverpool, UK
`fao@liverpool.ac.uk`
[4] Clinical Trials Research Centre, University of Liverpool, Liverpool, UK

1 Introduction

The last two decades have seen enormous progress in both theories and technology to support learner progress. However, many of the Artificial Intelligence in Education (AIED) techniques are difficult to apply in workplace-based educational settings, such as dentistry. Such settings put high demands on e-infrastructure, because they require intelligent systems that can be used in the workplace every day, and can also fuse many different forms of assessment data together. In addition, such systems should be able to enhance student development through personalised real time feedback (in dentistry education, for example, from both staff and patients) to drive learner self-reflection. Moreover, the information these systems provide must be reliable to facilitate defensible decisions over individual student progress to protect the public [2].

In this paper, we describe LiftUpp, a system developed at the School of Dentistry at the University of Liverpool, which has been specifically designed to meet these demanding requirements.

2 An Overview LiftUpp

LiftUpp is a digital educational platform designed to support quality-assured assessment, feedback, curriculum design and mapping. Its design is grounded in pedagogy and directly addresses the issues of complex data collection, clearing the way for applying AI and data-driven improvements to workplace-based education. It is the most sophisticated digital educational platform

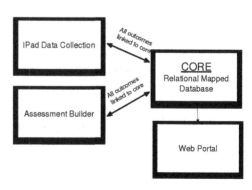

Fig. 1. A graphical overview of LiftUpp.

© Springer International Publishing AG 2017
E. André et al. (Eds.): AIED 2017, LNAI 10331, pp. 553–556, 2017.
DOI: 10.1007/978-3-319-61425-0_62

for workplace-based assessment available in dentistry, and is currently deployed in 70% (10 out of 14) of UK dental schools, as well as in veterinary medicine, physiotherapy, nursing and other healthcare sectors.

An overview of the LiftUpp platform is given in Fig. 1. The figure shows how the 'core', which contains the learning outcomes of the entire program (both internal as well as those of external stakeholders such as accreditation bodies) interacts with several modules, which currently comprise: an assessment building module (with support for exam setting, QA, blueprinting, psychometrics, reviewing, results, feedback); an iPad-based data collection module; and a web portal (system administration, data analysis, collation and display).

3   Data Collection for Workplace-Based Education

A salient feature of LiftUpp is the level of detail with which assessment data are recorded, and its ability to connect these results to learning outcomes, making it the first platform capable of fully programmatic assessment: all assessments are deliberately designed to develop and demonstrate learning outcomes. In the extreme, the importance of individual assessments vanishes: they just supply data on learner performance with respect to learning outcomes. In this paradigm, progression is based on *performance stability* and not on passing single tests, which is much better aligned to the needs of the real-world workplace [2].

However, to realise this, one significant challenge lies in effectively managing data components from multiple sources. For dentistry, this required the collection of daily observational data from 300 students in the workplace in 20 different sites, from 100 different staff, spanning 149 learning outcomes, along with data from other forms of assessment. While this is challenging by itself, it is further complicated by the inherent difficulty of objectively assessing the quality of treatments performed by students while in the work place.

To overcome this, LiftUpp uses the combination of a 6-point grading scale and a 'work flow model' of data collection [1], in which assessors only have to record what they see (rather than being pressurised into 'ticking all the boxes'). This approach was initially rolled out using paper forms that were replaced by an iPad app in 2010. The app, shown in Fig. 2a, is tailored to make sure data collection is a straight forward as possible: it is designed for easy navigation during observations, it deals with all possible work flows and uses location information to automatically select the relevant work flows, and it provides a convenient interface for attendance monitoring of students as well as staff sign in, enabling staff to cover for a colleague.

4   Data Fusion, Visualization and Use

While advanced AI techniques have the potential to radically improve the development of student performance, the current system already benefits from the collected data in various ways. Here, we briefly itemise these ways, for more information please see [3]:

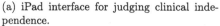

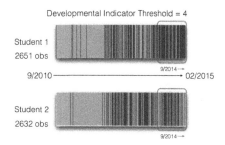

(a) iPad interface for judging clinical independence.

(b) *Barcodes* visualise consistency. (grey indicates sessions with an below-expectation observation.)

Fig. 2. Collection and visualization of data.

- Quality Assurance for Curriculum and Assessment Design. Due to all exam questions and work-based observations being coupled to learning outcomes, it is possible to automatically verify if the requirements of accreditation bodies are satisfied.
- Progress Monitoring. Displaying data in a manner that is simple for both the learner and the staff to understand is challenging. A major step forwards was the definition of what we have termed 'sessional consistency': the fraction of a student's sessions that meets a desired performance threshold level. To represent this sessional consistency visually we developed the 'barcode' view. Figure 2b shows two examples of barcodes.
- Adaptive Instructional Planning. The insight that LiftUpp provides about the students performance is used to decide which students will benefit most from additional practice opportunities, while other students are put in 'holding patterns', which means that the frequency of their workplace-based assessment is reduced or shifted towards less resource-limited treatments.
- Feedback for Students and Observers. Liftupp provides feedback to both students and observers about their performance.

5   Deployment and Effectiveness

LiftUpp has been in use in the School of Dentistry at the University of Liverpool since 2009, and has made an unprecedented impact on the student experience. This is perhaps most clearly expressed by the student satisfaction ratings (as measured by the national student satisfaction (NSS) survey), shown in Fig. 3. The figure clearly shows improvements over all four categories, especially satisfaction with respect to 'assessment & feedback' and 'organization & management', which have improved markedly since the introduction of LiftUpp.

The breadth and quality of the collected data is high and has helped to improve administration. We estimate that LiftUpp has saved approximately £150,000 in administration costs. Moreover, the data has been used successfully in several legal cases where students have challenged decisions, including via the Office of the Independent Adjudicator and the General Dental Council.

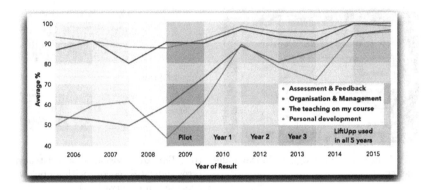

Fig. 3. Student satisfaction ratings since the introduction of LiftUpp.

This success has caused other dental schools to take interest and LiftUpp is now deployed in 70% of UK dental schools. Moreover, in recent years there has also been interest from other workplace-based disciplines, leading to deployments in veterinary medicine, physiotherapy, nursing and other healthcare courses.

6   Conclusions and Future Research Directions

In this paper, we presented some of the challenges addressed by LiftUpp for supporting the development of learners' performance in dentistry. In particular, it addresses the difficulties that one faces in terms of data collection when trying to apply data-driven approaches as developed in the AIED community to educational programs based on workplace-based assessment. In addition, LiftUpp makes some first but effective steps in dealing with the resulting data fusion problem for a variety of uses, ranging from quality assurance, to various forms of feedback and instructional planning. Moreover, the years in which the system has been employed has now generated a wealth of data that may serve as the basis for better data fusion techniques and thus form the basis of many future directions of research, such as advanced statistical methods for data fusion, interpretation and calibration, adaptive tutoring and personalised feedback and student advice.

References

1. Dawson, L., Mason, B., Balmer, M.C., Jimmieson, P.: Liftupp: a technology enhanced framework for the continuous development, measurement, and exploration of professional competence (In preparation)
2. Dawson, L., Mason, B., Bissell, V., Youngson, C.: Calling for a re-evaluation of the data required to credibly demonstrate a dental student is safe and ready to practice. Eur. J. Dent. Educ. **21**, 130–135 (2017)
3. Oliehoek, F.A, Savani, R., Adderton, E., Cui, X., Jackson, D., Jimmieson, P., Jones, J.C., Kennedy, K., Mason, B., Plumbley, A., Dawson, L.: Liftupp: Support to develop learner performance. arXiv (2017)

StairStepper: An Adaptive Remedial iSTART Module

Cecile A. Perret[✉], Amy M. Johnson, Kathryn S. McCarthy,
Tricia A. Guerrero, Jianmin Dai, and Danielle S. McNamara

Institute for the Science of Teaching and Learning,
Arizona State University, Tempe, AZ 85287, USA
{cecile.perret,amjohn43,ksmccarl,taguerre,
jianmin.dai,dsmcnama}@asu.edu

Abstract. This paper introduces StairStepper, a new addition to Interactive Strategy Training for Active Reading and Thinking (iSTART), an intelligent tutoring system (ITS) that provides adaptive self-explanation training and practice. Whereas iSTART focuses on improving comprehension at levels geared toward answering challenging questions associated with complex texts, StairStepper focuses on improving learners' performance when reading grade-level expository texts. StairStepper is designed as a scaffolded practice activity wherein text difficulty level and task are adapted according to learners' performance. This offers a unique module that provides reading comprehension tutoring through a combination of self-explanation practice and answering of multiple-choice questions representative of those found in standardized tests.

Keywords: Intelligent tutoring systems · Game-based learning · Reading comprehension · Strategy based learning · Reading assessment · System adaptivity

1 Introduction

Reading comprehension is a difficult skill to master, yet it is an essential skill for success in school, careers, and daily life [1, 2]. Unfortunately, most students are not proficiently literate, with only 37% of 12th grade students at or above proficiency [3]. Literacy rates continue to be problematic in adulthood: recent data revealed that 40% of adults in the United States scored below functional literacy levels 1.

A common way of assessing literacy is through standardized tests that rely on students reading passages and answering multiple-choice questions [4]. Extended practice is necessary to achieve success on these tests. Intelligent tutoring systems (ITS) provide extended practice with individualized automated, adaptive instruction and feedback that can supplement classroom instruction [5].

One example of such a program is Interactive Strategy Training for Active Reading and Thinking (iSTART), an ITS that provides reading comprehension strategy training and practice geared toward complex texts. Within iSTART learners self-explain texts and receive automated feedback on the quality of their self-explanation (SE). This training increases inferencing skills, which supports deeper text comprehension [6, 7].

© Springer International Publishing AG 2017
E. André et al. (Eds.): AIED 2017, LNAI 10331, pp. 557–560, 2017.
DOI: 10.1007/978-3-319-61425-0_63

iSTART includes instructional scaffolds such as animated lesson videos, guided practice, and game-based practice [8]. Additionally, the system utilizes natural language processing (NLP) algorithms to assess the quality of the learners' SEs and to drive feedback.

StairStepper is a recent addition to iSTART, developed to provide an additional source of instruction for less-skilled readers. In particular, Stairstepper targets adult literacy learners whose reading proficiency is comparable to students at the 3rd to 8th grade levels. By contrast, iSTART involves reading texts that are appropriate for high school and college students. Hence, one objective was to include reading practice for these less-skilled readers. A second objective was to include practice with short passages and corresponding multiple-choice questions that mimic the types of reading tasks in standardized tests. While multiple-choice questions tend not to reveal deep text comprehension, they are tasks that students are expected to perform well, and are often used in high-stakes testing to estimate reading ability. StairStepper is not intended to be used in isolation, but rather to supplement the existing SE and comprehension strategy instruction already found in iSTART, such that students receive training and practice to develop both test-taking skills and deeper text comprehension.

2   StairStepper

StairStepper is a game-based practice module in which learners ascend a staircase of increasingly difficult texts. Students climb up the stairs when they answer questions about the text successfully, and go down the stairs when they do not. Students are also asked to self-explain texts when their performance drops. The goal is to reach the top step by successfully answering comprehension questions for the most difficult texts.

StairStepper adapts to learners' performance through scaffolded SE practice and by adjusting text difficulty depending on comprehension question scores. SE prompts are scaffolded (no prompt, prompt without feedback, prompt with feedback) based on students' multiple-choice comprehension question performance. This approach is intended to help learners increase their awareness of when self-explanation may benefit comprehension, and in turn, train learners to self-explain without being prompted.

The module comprises 162 expository texts, varying in difficulty (appropriate for grades 1–12), length (ranging from 7–80 sentences), and topic matter (history, sports, science, and life-relevant). This library was extracted from public websites[1,2] to afford extended practice using a diverse set of texts found in typical reading assessments. Four raters ranked the texts into levels, iteratively sorting subsets of the texts according to their relative difficulty. Raters repeated this procedure until they agreed on the texts' rankings. This process yielded 13 levels with at least five texts per level. Texts in the first level were discarded because they were too short to support comprehension questions, yielding a final set of 12 levels. These difficulty rankings correlated with Flesch-Kincaid Grade Level ($r = .79$) and with Dale-Chall readability ($r = .77$).

---

[1] http://www.ereadingworksheets.com/e-reading-worksheets/online-reading-tests/.

[2] http://mrnussbaum.com/readingpassageindex/.

Each text is followed by multiple-choice comprehension questions (4–20 per text) retrieved from the same sites as the texts. Questions that were ambiguous or not related to text material were removed. The questions were manually categorized as text-based (N = 677; i.e., answers found within one sentence), bridging (N = 160; inferences made across two or more sentences), or elaboration (N = 144; inferences made between text information and prior knowledge). The proportion of each type of question was 35–45% text-based, 45–55% bridging, 8–10% elaboration for texts (n = 78) at level 8 and up. The lower levels were dominated by text-based questions (70–100%) and fewer bridging and elaboration questions (around 15% each). Therfore, only the more difficult texts (levels 8 and up), were piloted via Mechanical Turk. Participants (n = 259) read and answered the multiple-choice questions for a randomized subset of 20 texts. These data were used to further revise the question set. Questions with 0% accuracy (N = 6 of 818) were removed. Experimenters then correlated text performance with participants' average scores. Three of the 78 texts were removed that did not correlate with individuals' average score due to ceiling effects. Note that each difficulty level reflected text difficulty, not the difficulty of any given question. However, there were more deep comprehension questions (bridging and elaboration) for higher level texts.

There are four parameters that can be set by the experimenter: initial text difficulty level (default value = 5); threshold for question accuracy (default value = 0.75), use of SE score in determining scaffolding/difficulty level (default is off), and threshold for SE score (default value = 2.0). Each learner begins StairStepper by reading a text at the pre-set initial difficulty level (e.g., level 5), and then answers multiple-choice comprehension questions for that text. In order to ascend a stair, learners must receive a comprehension score at or above the question accuracy threshold; in our described scenario, the learner would next read a text at difficulty level six. If the comprehension score is below this threshold, the learner would be prompted to self-explain the subsequent text and then answer corresponding questions. If on this text, the learner still does not meet the comprehension threshold, the text difficulty level would decrease and the learner would self-explain the next text with feedback. Using an NLP algorithm, the system scores SEs from 0 to 3. Learners receive 3 points for SEs that successfully bridge information across multiple sentences in the text and with prior knowledge. The score is intended to offer feedback to students about their SEs so that they might improve as they moved forward through the module. This provides additional support for deeper text comprehension, thus facilitating question answering. Regardless of whether the learner is at the scaffolding level that provides feedback, they always see their score for each SE. This process allows learners to receive sustained remedial SE practice tailored to their specific needs.

3   Conclusion

The StairStepper module was developed to help improve reading comprehension skills of adult literacy learners and prepare learners for standardized assessments. Because standardized testing is commonly used to determine graduation from and admittance to education programs, performance on the tests is crucial to success in school, careers, and daily life. Hence, StairStepper was developed to provide learners with practice using SE to support comprehension (when needed) and practice answering reading comprehension questions similar to those observed in standardized tests.

We have begun testing the benefits of using StairStepper as a form of extended and remedial practice. Next steps include development of an NLP algorithm to reliably estimate the difficulty of new texts using the StairStepper rating system, allowing researchers and educators to add texts and have them automatically assigned to the appropriate (relative) difficulty level. Such an algorithm is necessary because texts and question difficulty in various tests are each leveled according to different standards and methods, and thus one algorithm is necessary for this particular module.

Future work will examine the relations between SE skills and comprehension accuracy for adult literacy learners. This project contributes a necessary technology to address the dearth of computer-based literacy education for adult literacy learners.

Acknowledgments. This research was supported in part by the Institute of Education Sciences (R305A130124) and the Office of Naval Research (N00014140343 and N000141712300). Any opinion, conclusion, or recommendation expressed are those of the authors and do not represent views of the IES or ONR.

References

1. Geiser, S., Studley, R.: UC and the SAT: predictive validity and differential impact of the SAT I and SAT II at the University of California. University of California, Office of the President (2001)
2. Powell, P.R.: Retention and writing instruction: implications of deliberate practice for academic performance. Contemp. Educ. Psychol. **30**, 96–116 (2009)
3. NAEP: The Nation's Report Card: Mathematics and Reading at Grade 12 (2015). https://www.nationsreportcard.gov/reading_math_g12_2015/#reading/acl#header
4. NACAC: Report of the commission on the use of standardized tests in undergraduate admission. National Association for College Admission Counseling (2008). https://eric.ed.gov/?q=ED502721&id=ED502721
5. Crossley, S.A., McNamara, D.S. (eds.): Adaptive Educational Technologies for Literacy Instruction. Taylor & Francis, Routledge, New York (2016)
6. McNamara, D.S.: Self-explanation and reading strategy training (SERT) improves low-knowledge students' science course performance. Discourse Processes (2015)
7. McNamara, D.S., O'Reilly, T.P., Best, R.M., Ozuru, Y.: Improving adolescent learners' reading comprehension with iSTART. J. Educ. Comput. Res. **34**, 147–171 (2006)
8. Jackson, G.T., McNamara, D.S.: Motivation and performance in a game-based intelligent tutoring system. J. Educ. Psychol. **105**, 1036–1049 (2013)

AttentiveLearner^2: A Multimodal Approach for Improving MOOC Learning on Mobile Devices

Phuong Pham and Jingtao Wang$^{(\boxtimes)}$

Computer Science and LRDC, University of Pittsburgh, Pittsburgh, PA, USA
{phuongpham, jingtaow}@cs.pitt.edu

Abstract. We propose AttentiveLearner^2, a multimodal mobile learning system for MOOCs running on unmodified smartphones. AttentiveLearner^2 uses both the front and back cameras of a smartphone as two complementary and fine-grained feedback channels in real time: the back camera monitors learners' photoplethysmography (PPG) signals and the front camera tracks their facial expressions during MOOC learning. AttentiveLearner^2 implicitly infers learners' affective and cognitive states during learning by analyzing learners' PPG signals and facial expressions. In a 26-participant user study, we found that it is feasible to detect 6 types of emotion during learning via collected PPG signals and facial expressions and these modalities are complement with each other.

Keywords: Mobile learning · Intelligent tutoring systems · Massive open online courses · Multimodal interaction

1 Introduction

By 2016, Massive Open Online Courses (MOOCs) have attracted over 700 universities and 58 million registered learners worldwide. To facilitate learning on-the-go, major MOOC providers, e.g. Coursera, edX, and Udacity, have launched their mobile apps. Despite the popularity and rapid growth, today's MOOCs still suffer from low completion rates (e.g. 5.5% as reported in [1]), low engagement, and little personalization. These challenges are caused, at least in part, by the limited interactions between instructors and learners in MOOCs. Other than activity logs [4] and surveys, there is little information from students to instructors representing the learning progress.

We propose AttentiveLearner^2 (Fig. 1), an emotion-aware multimodal intelligent learning system for MOOCs running on unmodified smartphones. AttentiveLearner^2 builds upon and extends AttentiveLearner [6] by Pham and Wang. Similar to AttentiveLearner, AttentiveLearner^2 uses on-lens finger gestures to control video playback (i.e. covering and holding the back camera lens to play a tutorial video, while uncovering the lens to pause the video) and implicitly sense learners' photoplethysmogram (PPG) signals. Going beyond AttentiveLearner, AttentiveLearner^2 leverages the front camera for real-time facial expressions analysis (FEA). By using a combination of PPG signals and facial expressions, AttentiveLearner^2 infers learners' affective and cognitive states during learning. We intentionally choose a superscripted

© Springer International Publishing AG 2017
E. André et al. (Eds.): AIED 2017, LNAI 10331, pp. 561–564, 2017.
DOI: 10.1007/978-3-319-61425-0_64

2 (pronounced as "*square*") in project name to emphasize that: (a) AttentiveLearner^2 is a major upgrade of AttentiveLearner [6]; and (b) it leverages two independent channels of signals, i.e. PPG and FEA, to model and understand learners. AttentiveVideo [5] is another relevant research project. In comparison, AttentiveVideo focuses on detection emotional responses to mobile ads, which is around 30 s long while MOOC videos usually last 3 to 20 min. Although previous research explored the use of PPG [6] and FEA [2] in learning environments, to the best of our knowledge, AttentiveLearner^2 is the first mobile learning system that supports both real-time PPG sensing and FEA on unmodified smartphones for MOOCs.

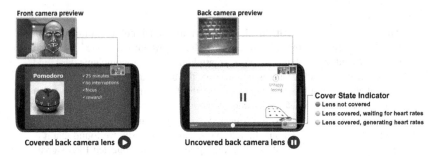

Fig. 1. AttentiveLearner^2 uses both the front and the back cameras as feedback channels: back camera for PPG sensing and front camera for facial expression analysis (FEA).

2   Design of AttentiveLearner^2

2.1   On-Lens Video Control

AttentiveLearner^2 uses tangible, on-lens finger gestures for video control: i.e. covering and holding the back camera lens play a lecture video while uncovering the lens pauses the video (Fig. 1). We utilize the *Static LensGesture* [7] for lens-covering detection.

2.2   Double-Camera Tracking System

AttentiveLearner^2 implicitly senses the PPG signals from a learner's fingertip while she is watching a tutorial video. The underlining working mechanism is: the come and withdrawal of fresh blood in every cardiac cycle change the learner's skin transparency color. These transparency changes (PPG signals) are highly correlated to heart beat cycles (NN intervals) and can be detected by the back camera. AttentiveLearner^2 uses *LivePulse* [3] to extract NN intervals from the detected PPG signals.

AttentiveLearner^2 also uses the front camera to monitor the learner's facial expressions during the tutorial video. In this paper, we employ *Affdex* (http://affectiva.com) as the facial expression analysis library.

2.3   Emotion Inference Algorithms

AttentiveLearner[2] uses SVM with RBF kernels to detect learner's emotions while watching tutorial videos. We use leave-one-participant-out cross validation method.

AttentiveLearner[2] uses both global and sliding local windows to extract PPG signals and facial expression features (Fig. 2). In this project, we evaluate three different feature sets: PPG, FEA, and fusion feature set. The PPG feature set contains 8 dimensions of Heart Rate Variability (HRV): (1) AVNN (average NN intervals); (2) SDNN (standard deviations of NN intervals); (3) pNN10; (4) rMSSD; (5) SDANN; (6) SDNNIDX; (7) SDNNIDX/rMSSD; (8) MAD (median absolute deviation). In total, there are 16 PPG features (8 global features and 8 local features). With FEA features, we propose Action Unit Variability (AUV) capturing the dynamic of each facial expression output value from *Affdex*: (1) AVAU (average action unit value); (2) SDAU (3) MAXAU (the maximum value of action unit value during the video); (4) rMSSD; (5) SDAAU; (6) SDAUIDX; (7) SDNNIDX/rMSSD; (8) MAD. To balance with the PPG feature set, the FEA feature set selects the top 16 AUV features. Lastly, the feature fusion set selects 8 top PPG features and 8 top FEA features. All feature selections were done using univariate ANOVA as in [2].

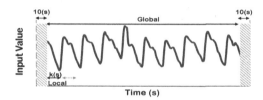

Fig. 2. PPG and FEA features are extracted from each video using global and local windows.

3   User Study

We conducted a within-subject user study to evaluate the feasibility of detecting emotions from PPG signals and facial expressions via unmodified smartphones. There were 26 participants (8 females) joining the user study. Each participant watches three tutorial videos (6 min/video) about Astronomy, Learning Science, and Programming. After each video, participants answered an emotion survey (7-point Likert scale format) about 6 different emotions: *boredom, confusion, curiosity, frustration, happiness,* and *self-efficacy*. We turned each emotion into a binary classification problem using thresholding, i.e. ratings smaller than 4 are negatives, otherwise positives.

Table 1 shows the detection performance of three feature sets and the majority vote baseline. AttentiveLearner[2] achieved high performance as all our models outperformed the baseline. Moreover, we found PPG signals and facial expressions are complement each other. If FEA features can win in 3 emotions (Confusion, Happiness, and Self-efficacy), PPG features are the best solution for Curiosity, and feature fusion can improve detection performance for Boredom and Frustration.

Table 1. Accuracy (Acc) and Kappa of prediction models.

Emotion	Majority	PPG		FEA		Feature fusion
	Acc	Kappa	Acc	Kappa	Acc	Kappa	Acc
Boredom	70.51%	0.35	78.21%	0.56	84.62%	0.57	83.33%
Confusion	74.36%	0.30	78.21%	0.65	88.46%	0.54	84.62%
Curiosity	56.41%	0.46	74.36%	0.41	71.79%	0.43	73.08%
Frustration	78.21%	0.22	80.77%	0.69	91.03%	0.71	91.03%
Happiness	52.56%	0.41	70.51%	0.61	80.77%	0.61	80.77%
Self-efficacy	70.51%	0.38	79.49%	0.70	88.46%	0.67	87.18%

4 Conclusions and Future Work

We introduced AttentiveLearner^2, a multimodal emotion-aware interface for mobile MOOC learning on unmodified smartphones. In a 26-participant user study, we found that by taking advantages from two modalities, AttentiveLearner^2 achieved higher detection accuracy than models using only one modality across 6 different emotions. More importantly, these results were achieved on unmodified smartphones which supports the scalable deployment of AttentiveLearner^2. In the future, we plan use the inferred emotions to improve learner's outcomes and engagement.

References

1. Chuang, I., Ho, A.D.: HarvardX and MITx: Four Years of Open Online Courses – Fall 2012-Summer (2016). https://papers.ssrn.com/sol3/papers.cfm?abstract_id=2889436
2. D'Mello, S.K., Graesser, A.: Multimodal semi-automated affect detection from conversational cues, gross body language, and facial features. User Model. User-Adap. Inter. **20**(2), 147–187 (2010)
3. Han, T., Xiao, X., Shi, L., Canny, J., Wang, J.: Balancing accuracy and fun: designing camera based mobile games for implicit heart rate monitoring. In: Proceedings of the 33rd Annual ACM Conference on Human Factors in Computing Systems, pp. 847–856. ACM (2015)
4. Kim, J., Guo, P.J., Seaton, D.T., Mitros, P., Gajos, K.Z., Miller, R.C.: Understanding invideo dropouts and interaction peaks in online lecture videos. In: Proceedings of the First ACM Conference on Learning@ Scale Conference, pp. 31–40. ACM (2014)
5. Pham, P., Wang, J.: Understanding emotional responses to mobile video advertisements via physiological signal sensing and facial expression analysis. In: Proceedings of the 22nd International Conference on Intelligent User Interfaces, pp. 67–78. ACM (2017)
6. Pham, P., Wang, J.: AttentiveLearner: improving mobile MOOC learning via implicit heart rate tracking. In: Conati, C., Heffernan, N., Mitrovic, A., Verdejo, M.F. (eds.) AIED 2015. LNCS, vol. 9112, pp. 367–376. Springer, Cham (2015). doi:10.1007/978-3-319-19773-9_37
7. Xiao, X., Han, T., Wang, J.: LensGesture: augmenting mobile interactions with back-of-device finger gestures. In: Proceedings of the 15th ACM on International Conference on Multimodal Interaction, pp. 287–294. ACM (2013)

Automated Analysis of Lecture Video Engagement Using Student Posts

Nicholas R. Stepanek$^{(\boxtimes)}$ and Brian Dorn

University of Nebraska at Omaha, Omaha, USA
{nstepanek,bdorn}@unomaha.edu

Abstract. This work explores the feasibility of a learning analytic that would provide high level engagement data to instructors based on students' text artifacts in online learning systems. Student posts from an online lecture video system were collected and manually coded by engagement using the ICAP framework. Analyses show what features are most indicative of engagement and the performance of using a neural network to classify posts by engagement.

1 Introduction

With the rise in popularity of MOOCs and online systems for delivering course content, research into analyzing enormous sets of student log data has become increasingly prevalent. Commonly, these systems store fine grained click-level data about student usage, leaving the door open for a myriad of in-depth analyses, such as developing performance prediction models with video viewing behaviors [1] or demographics and study strategies [2]. Studies like these give insights into how students use MOOCs and similar systems, but one goal when analyzing this data should be to impact instruction. Research in learning analytics, the measurement, collection, analysis, and reporting of data about learning and their contexts [3], can do this by delivering information to instructors in real time.

The purpose of this study is to further the creation of a learning analytic that will provide student engagement data to instructors using text artifacts in video lecture systems. Information about how engaged students are with lecture videos is something instructors using such a system have commonly asked for during interviews [4]. In MOOCs, online courses, or flipped classes, instructors often have no measure of student engagement during the lecture process as in traditional classroom settings, and rely on analytics to help inform class intervention.

In this work, we manually code two course data sets of text artifacts created by students in a lecture video system based on their engagement with the course content. Taking inspiration from Wang, Wen, and Rosé [5], this study applies their coding rubric derived from the ICAP framework which categorizes student behavior into four tiers of engagement [6]. We then generate and filter a list of features for training and testing a neural network for performance evaluation. Specifically, we ask what features are most indicative of engagement, and is the application of machine learning to categorizing student engagement feasible?

© Springer International Publishing AG 2017
E. André et al. (Eds.): AIED 2017, LNAI 10331, pp. 565–569, 2017.
DOI: 10.1007/978-3-319-61425-0_65

2   Related Work

With the large amounts of student-generated data stored in MOOCs and other learning systems, analyzing this data has become a major area of research. One popular form of analysis is predicting student success [1,2], and often these studies find that students who are more active or engaged in the system have more success. Some systems such as Course Signals have implemented similar predictors, and allow students to see if they are at risk of failing, as well is informing instructors [7]. Course Signals was found to get students more engaged, suggesting that instructor awareness of engagement can better enable them to create interventions. Less common than these studies have been ones analyzing the text artifacts produced by students, which may provide more direct insight into how students are thinking about the course material. Recent examples include using activity data and language processing for performance prediction [8] and applying machine learning to predict cognitive presence from student posts [9].

This work leverages the ICAP framework, "A taxonomy that differentiates four modes or categories of engagement, based on the overt behaviors displayed or undertaken by students" [6]. The four categories are *interactive, constructive, active*, and *passive*, where *interactive* behaviors are the most engaged and *passive* behaviors the least. In a study of MOOC student posts, Wang et al. developed a coding rubric for categorizing text artifacts within the ICAP framework [5].

3   Methodology

This study utilizes TrACE, an asynchronous collaborative media platform used to deliver lecture video content at multiple universities. Instructors teaching flipped and online courses upload videos to TrACE, and students view them while collaborating by posting annotations at spatial and temporal locations on the videos. Click-level log data is stored about students' usage of the system, and learning analytics that synthesize this data into more interpretable information are provided to instructors. Annotations from sections of two courses, "Introduction to Computer Programming" and "Introduction to Web Development" were collected and stored as two data sets. In total, there were 2861 and 1464 annotations respectively. The courses contained 25 and 30 videos respectively, after leaving out the first syllabus video of each course.

All annotations were manually coded using the same coding rubric developed by Wang et al. [5]. In our analyses, three categories of annotations are considered, *A2, active* posts that do not mention course content, *A1, active* posts that refer to course content, and *C, constructive* posts that go beyond course content. Three coders were used in total, two coders on each data set with one coder working on both. Unweighted Cohen's kappa was used to ensure intercoder reliability before coding the entire data sets. The data set for "Introduction to Computer Science" received a kappa of 0.82 on 9.0% of the dataset, indicating strong agreement. The data set for "Introduction to Web Development" received a kappa of 0.84 on 6.8% of the dataset, indicating strong agreement. To begin analysis, features were generated on each dataset. 9 natural language features were used: length (words), number of sentences, complexity (ARI), sentiment, whether the post contained a question, contained code, was a reply to an instructor, was a reply to a student, and contained a link. Then, the most popular words in each data set after removing stop words were added as bag-of-words features.

4   Results and Discussion

Table 1 shows the resulting F values (degree of variance) for our 9 natural language features from MANOVAs on the programming and web development data sets, with engagement category as the independent variable and features as dependent variables. All of the natural language features we chose to include had significantly varied means between engagement groups, in this context meaning that those features are indicative of engagement. Not shown are the MANOVA results for bag-of-words features, though in the top 10 words ranked by F value on each data set, the majority of words were course "keywords" such as "variable" and "java" for programming. Answering the first research question, what features are most indicative of engagement, length and complexity are most indicative and sentiment not as indicative. Course "keywords" were the most important bag-of-words features, and future work should test using a keyword feature in place of bag-of-words features to make this model more generalizable.

Table 2 contains the metrics calculated from our performance evaluation of a multilayer perceptron being trained and tested to categorize annotations within our three engagement categories. For these tests, we generated 10 randomly stratified samples for each data set, stratified by video so each sample was representative of discourse throughout the course. Features that were not marginally significant in the MANOVA ($p < 0.1$) were filtered out of the feature set. The performance evaluation shows good results overall, but the classification of C annotations is poor, specifically for the web development data set. We hypothesize that this result is at least in part due to sample size. Only 146 and 349

Table 1. MANOVA F values for natural language features. All $p < 0.0001$.

Feature	Programming dataset F	Web development dataset F
Length	455.26	162.28
Complexity	323.20	138.37
Question	279.86	83.03
Reply to instructor	132.36	114.31
Code	115.27	15.39
Link	78.25	53.43
Reply to student	70.81	17.70
Sentences	44.93	35.01
Sentiment	34.85	16.62

Table 2. Classifier metrics, averaged from 10 randomly stratified samples.

Metric	Programming dataset	Web development dataset
Overall Accuracy	**80.03% ($\sigma = 1.95\%$)**	**74.06% ($\sigma = 1.68\%$)**
A1 Precision	77.81% ($\sigma = 3.77\%$)	71.39% ($\sigma = 4.82\%$)
A1 Recall	78.18% ($\sigma = 4.47\%$)	79.20% ($\sigma = 3.50\%$)
A2 Precision	83.44% ($\sigma = 3.10\%$)	78.29% ($\sigma = 3.51\%$)
A2 Recall	90.04% ($\sigma = 2.02\%$)	79.87% ($\sigma = 4.64\%$)
C Precision	76.54% ($\sigma = 11.71\%$)	64.35% ($\sigma = 17.23\%$)
C Recall	52.45% ($\sigma = 7.60\%$)	25.25% ($\sigma = 7.00\%$)

annotations in the web development and programming data sets were categorized as C respectively. The programming dataset with a larger sample size of C posts performed much better in that category than the web development data set, suggesting that this may be the issue. Answering the second research question, is this model feasible, these results suggest that it is. To build a system like this and develop learning analytics from it, future work should further investigate generalizing the model so that it can be used on multiple courses (instead of using separate models for each course), iterate on the feature set, and evaluate performance on more data from different fields of study.

Acknowledgements. This work is funded by National Science Foundation grant IIS-1318345. Any opinions, findings, or recommendations expressed in this material are those of the authors and do not necessarily reflect the views of the NSF.

References

1. Brinton, C., Chiang, M.: MOOC performance prediction via click stream data and social learning networks. In: 2015 IEEE Conference on Computer Communications (INFOCOM), pp. 2299–2307 (2015)
2. Breslow, L., Pritchard, D.E., DeBoer, J., Stump, G.S., Ho, A.D., Seaton, D.T.: Studying learning in the worldwide classroom: research into edXs first MOOC. Res. Pract. Assess. **8**(1), 13–25 (2013)
3. Ferguson, R.: Learning analytics: drivers, developments and challenges. Int. J. Technol. Enhanced Learn. **4**, 304–317 (2012)
4. Elson, J.S.: Formative assessment in an online asynchronous learning environment. University of Nebraska at Omaha (2016, Unpublished master's thesis)
5. Wang, X., Wen, M., Rosé, C.P.: Towards triggering higher-order thinking behaviors in MOOCs. In: Proceedings of the Sixth International Conference on Learning Analytics and Knowledge, pp. 398–407, Edinburgh, United Kingdom (2016)
6. Chi, M.T.H., Wylie, R.: The ICAP framework: linking cognitive engagement to active learning outcomes. Educ. Psychol. **49**(4), 219–243 (2014)
7. Arnold, K.E., Pistilli, M.D.: Course signals at purdue: using learning analytics to increase student success. In: Proceedings of the 2nd International Conference on Learning Analytics and Knowledge, pp. 267–270 (2012)

8. Crossley, S., Paquette, L., Dascalu, M., McNamara, D.S., Baker, R.S.: Combining click-stream data with NLP tools to better understand MOOC completion. In: Proceedings of the 6th International Conference on Learning Analytics and Knowledge, pp. 6–14 (2016)

9. Kovanović, V., Joksimović, S., Waters, Z., Gasević, D., Kitto, K., Hatala, M., Siemens, G.: Towards automated content analysis of discussion transcripts: a cognitive presence case. In: Proceedings of the 6th International Conference on Learning Analytics and Knowledge, pp. 15–24 (2016)

A Study of Learners' Behaviors in Hands-On Learning Situations and Their Correlation with Academic Performance

Rémi Venant[1], Kshitij Sharma[2], Pierre Dillenbourg[2], Philippe Vidal[1], and Julien Broisin[1(✉)]

[1] Université Paul Sabatier, Toulouse, France
{remi.venant,philippe.vidal,julien.broisin}@irit.fr
[2] Ecole Polytechnique Fédérale de Lausanne, Lausanne, Switzerland
{kshitij.sharma,pierre.dillenbourg}@epfl.ch

Abstract. This study analyzes students' behavior in our remote laboratory environment and aims at identifying behavioural patterns during a practical session that lead to better learning outcomes, in order to predict learners' performance and to automatically guide students who might need more support. Based on data collected from an experimentation conducted in an authentic learning context, we discover recurrent sequential patterns of actions that lead us to the definition of learning strategies as indicators of higher level of abstraction. Results show that some of the strategies are correlated to the learners' performance at the final assessment test. For instance, construction of a complex action step by step, or reflexion before submitting an action, are two strategies applied more often by learners of a higher level of performance than by others. These findings led us to instrument for both students and instructors new guiding and tutoring tools in our remote lab environment.

1 Introduction

Research on predictors of success in learning has been a hot topic for decades [1]. Predictors are information about learners and include work style preference, self-efficacy [2], or background and expectations [3]. However, the development of Educational Data Mining and Learning Analytics provides new capabilities to explore learners' behavior and to study its influence on their performance.

In the field of virtual and remote laboratories, interactions between students and apparatus are behavioral data that can be used as inputs for the above techniques. Based on data resulting from an experimentation conducted in a real setting, we adopt sequential pattern mining approaches to investigate learners' behaviors during practical sessions and to discover sequences of actions, or learning strategies, that are representative of their level of performance.

2 Experimental Settings

The experimentation involved 85 first year students enrolled in an introductory course on Shell commands, and was conducted for 3 weeks. Learners had a

© Springer International Publishing AG 2017
E. André et al. (Eds.): AIED 2017, LNAI 10331, pp. 570–573, 2017.
DOI: 10.1007/978-3-319-61425-0_66

24-7 access to our remote lab dedicated to computer education to complete their tasks. This web-based environment offers on-demand virtual resources and features advanced learning capabilities [4]. Basically, each learner is provided with her own set of resources and can interact with it through a web-based Terminal. The learning features include real-time communication, collaborative work, awareness tools, as well as tools for deep analysis of working sessions.

These features are made possible thanks to a learning analytics framework able to collect most of users' interactions with the platform. Our analysis focus on the Shell commands submitted by learners, where a total number of 9183 xAPI statements was collected. Our objective was to explore these interactions to investigate their possible correlation with the assessment score (AS) which denotes the score learners got at the final assessment test. Also, as the distribution of AS made appear three distinct categories of AS (i.e., low - L, medium - M, and high - H), we also studied correlations with these categories (AScat).

3   Pattern Mining Analysis

3.1   Nature of Actions

To go further our learning context, we applied a pattern mining analysis not on commands themselves, but on their nature, their relationships, and the result of their execution. Our analysis identified 8 exclusive natures of actions: *Sub_S*, *Sub_F*, *ReSub_S*, *ReSub_F*, *VarSub_S*, *VarSub_F*, *Help* and *NewHelp*. The natures *Sub_** refer to an action whose type is different than the previous one, and which is evaluated as right (*Sub_S*) or wrong (*Sub_F*). The natures *ReSub_** consider an action that is identical to the previous one (i.e., same type and parameters), while the natures *VarSub_** represent a command of the same type than the previous one, but with different parameters. Finally, *Help* depicts an action of help seeking about the type of the previous action, while *NewHelp* indicates a help access without relation with the previous action.

3.2   Patterns of Actions

To discover statistically significant sequences of actions, we analyzed two- and three-length sequences and applied to each sequence an analysis of variance (i.e., one-way ANOVA) for AScat, and a Pearson correlation test for AS. We identified 13 significant patterns, most of them being used more often by high- and medium-level students than by others, and presenting a significant weak (i.e., $0.1 < |r| < 0.3$) or medium (i.e., $0.3 < |r| < 0.5$) correlation with AS. Also, the patterns present common semantics depicting students' behaviors: they can be viewed as learning strategies followed by learners to solve a problem.

3.3   Learning Strategies

paginationStarting from the 13 significant patterns, we specified 7 learning strategies: *confirmation, progression, success-then-reflexion, reflexion-then-success, fail-then-reflexion, trial-and-error,* and *withdrawal. Confirmation* is the successful resubmission of the same action, while *progression* depicts a sequence of successful actions of the same type, but whose parameters are different. *Success-then-reflexion* expresses a successful action, followed by access to a related help. Conversely, *reflexion-then-success* appears when students first access help of a certain type of action, and then submit the matching action successfully. *Fail-then-reflexion* shows a help access related to an action that failed. Finally, *withdrawal* matches with an action of a different type than the previous one whose submission failed. Analysis results of each strategy are exposed in Table 1.

Table 1. Analysis of learning strategies

	Trend of use	ANOVA p-value	r	cor. p-value
Confirmation	∅	0.745	0.108	0.321
Progression	**H,M > L**	**0.001**	**0.294**	**0.006**
Success-then-reflexion	**H > L**	**0.010**	**0.282**	**0.008**
Reflexion-then-success	**H > L**	**0.015**	**0.242**	**0.026**
Fail-then-reflexion	∅	0.020	**0.273**	**0.011**
Trial-and-error	∅	0.341	−0.050	0.670
Withdrawal	∅	0.457	−0.004	0.968

The strategies *Progression, success-then-reflexion, reflexion-then-success* and *fail-then-reflexion* present significant results. The first three ones allow to cluster students in a category of performance, and seem to be traits of behavior of high- and medium-level students. Under the *progression* strategy, high-level students seem to decompose their problem in steps of increasing complexity. The three others strategies are related to reflexion through the use of help.

Also, the 4 above strategies are all positively correlated to AS: the results do not reveal particular behaviors of low-level learners. Another interesting result is the *withdrawal* strategy, which is applied homogeneously by all students and thus irrelevant to predict performance or to take a decision.

4   Results Exploitation

The results of our analysis allow for on-the-fly detection of learners' behaviors and open the door for new opportunities. Indeed, the continuous improvement of TEL-based systems, according to experimental findings resulting from their usage, is a critical part of the re-engineering process [5]. Applied to learning analytics, this enhancement cycle makes it possible to discover new design patterns and to generate new data for research about and improvement of TEL [6].

Thus, with respect to the above methodology, we integrated into our remote lab two new features built on two distinct design patterns. The first feature relies on an intelligent tutoring system (ITS) able to guide learners during their practical sessions according to the learning strategies they follow. For instance, when a learner fails several times to execute a command, the ITS suggests her to read the matching manual so that she becomes engaged in the reflexion-then-success strategy leading to better performance. The second design pattern is an awareness system intended for teachers and highlighting students that seem to present weaknesses. For instance, if several learners follow the withdrawal strategy on the same command, the system notifies the teachers so they can make a collective intervention. These new features are already implanted into our system and will be evaluated in the near future to assess their impact on both learners' and teachers' behaviors.

5 Conclusion

The study of this paper aimed at revealing relationships between learners' behaviors during practical learning situations, and their academic performance. We adopted a sequential pattern mining approach to reveal correlations between learning strategies we identified and high-level students. The data we analyzed only relate to interactions between learners and the resources required to achieve the practical work; some works are in progress to extend our analysis model to other tracking data collected by the system in order to analyze in depth their causal nature, but also to compute a predictive model reducing failing rate. These data include social traces resulting from cooperative and collaborative tasks that will allow to study new research questions about learners' behavior in practical work situation, in a socio-constructivism context.

References

1. Blikstein, P.: Using learning analytics to assess students' behavior in open-ended programming tasks. In: Proceedings of the 1st International Conference on Learning Analytics and Knowledge, pp. 110–116. ACM (2011)
2. Wilson, B.C., Shrock, S.: Contributing to success in an introductory computer science course - a study of twelve factors. In: Proceedings of the 32nd SIGCSE Technical Symposium on Computer Science Education, pp. 184–188. ACM (2001)
3. Rountree, N., Rountree, J., Robins, A., Hannah, R.: Interacting factors that predict success and failure in a CS1 course. ACM SIGCSE Bull. 36(4), 101–104 (2004)
4. Broisin, J., Venant, R., Vidal, P.: Lab4CE: a remote laboratory for computer education. Int. J. Artif. Intell. Educ. 27(1), 154–180 (2017)
5. Corbière, A., Choquet, C.: Re-engineering method for multimedia system in education. In: Proceedings of the Sixth IEEE International Symposium on Multimedia Software Engineering, pp. 80–87. IEEE (2004)
6. Inventado, P.S., Scupelli, P.: Data-driven design pattern production: a case study on the ASSISTments online learning system. In: Proceedings of the 20th European Conference on Pattern Languages of Programs. ACM (2015)

Assessing the Collaboration Quality in the Pair Program Tracing and Debugging Eye-Tracking Experiment

Maureen Villamor[1,2(✉)], Yancy Vance Paredes[1,3],
Japheth Duane Samaco[1], Joanna Feliz Cortez[1], Joshua Martinez[1,4],
and Ma. Mercedes Rodrigo[1]

[1] Ateneo de Manila University, Quezon City, Philippines
yancyvance@gmail.com, joannafelizcortez@gmail.com,
joshuamartinez1978@gmail.com,
japheth.samaco@obf.ateneo.edu,
mrodrigo@ateneo.edu
[2] University of Southeastern Philippines, Davao City, Philippines
maui@usep.edu.ph
[3] Ateneo de Davao University, Davao City, Philippines
[4] Ateneo de Naga University, Naga City, Philippines

Abstract. We assessed the extent of collaboration of pairs of novice program-mers as they traced and debugged fragments of code using cross-recurrence quantification analysis (CRQA). Specifically, we compared which among the pairs collaborated the most given a particular task. This was also a preliminary study that looked for patterns on how the pairs categorized according to expertise collaborated. We performed a CRQA to build cross-recurrence plots using the eye tracking data and computed for the CRQA metrics, such as recurrence rate (RR), determinism (DET), entropy (ENTR), and laminarity (LAM) using the CRP toolbox for MATLAB. Findings showed that Pair 3, which consisted of both high-performers, collaborated the most because of its highest RR and DET. However, its highest ENT and LAM implied that Pair 3 struggled the most in program comprehension. We found also that all the pairs as assessed through their RR's started with low values, peaked in the middle, declined, and increased again when the task was about to end, regardless of how well partners knew each other prior to the task. This could mean that at the start the pairs were still independently assessing how to approach the task, then they started to collaborate once comfortable but then worked independently again in an attempt to finish.

Keywords: Eye-tracking · Collaboration · Cross-recurrence quantification

1 Introduction

Prior studies have shown that the coupling of eye gaze between collaborating partners may be an indicator of quality interaction and better comprehension [1] and that joint attention, and more generally, synchronization between individuals is essential for an effective collaboration [2].

© Springer International Publishing AG 2017
E. André et al. (Eds.): AIED 2017, LNAI 10331, pp. 574–577, 2017.
DOI: 10.1007/978-3-319-61425-0_67

Cross-recurrence quantification analysis or CRQA [3] is used to quantify how frequently two systems exhibit similar patterns of change in time. It forms a cross-recurrence plot (CRP), which permits visualization of recurrent state patterns between two time series. Analysis using CRP's is considered a good way to characterize quantitatively the patterns between the eye-movements of two people looking at the same stimulus. Hence, it can be used to measure how much and when two subjects look at the same spot [4].

This paper used CRQA to assess collaboration of pairs of novice programmers in the act of tracing fragments of code and debugging in a remote pair programming eye-tracking setup. Specifically, it attempted to answer the following research questions: (1) Which among the pairs collaborated the most?; and (2) Is there a pattern of collaboration inherent to pairs of (a) both high-performing students, (b) both low-performing performing students, and (c) high- and low-performing students?

2 Methods

The study was conducted in one private university in the Philippines. Eight (8) pairs of students who had taken the college-level fundamental programming course were recruited to participate in this study. After passing the eye-tracking calibration test, they were asked to take the written program comprehension test to determine their level of programming knowledge and skills. The actual eye-tracking experiment followed where pairs were shown 12 programs with known bugs and were asked to mark the location of the bugs with an oval. There was no need to correct the errors. The pairs were told to work and collaborate with their partners on the problems and should communicate only via a chat program.

The number of fixations per program were separated and saved on separate files. The CRP toolbox [3] for MATLAB was used to generate the cross-recurrence plots and the CRQA metrics. The process of constructing a CRP is described in [5] and the definitions of the different CRQA metrics can be found in [3].

3 Results and Discussion

Pair 3, which consisted of both high-performers, seemed to have collaborated the most because it had the highest RR, DET, ENTR, and LAM. Its highest RR and DET indicated that it was the most closely coupled and had shared the most similar scan-paths. However, its highest RR and DET might be a direct consequence of having more fixations points. Its highest ENTR and LAM implied that it struggled most in program comprehension due to their complex scanpaths and their tendency to stay on certain regions of the code. Pair 3 solved the least number of programs, which confirmed that it might indeed struggled in program comprehension.

To seek for patterns of collaboration, the pairs were categorized according to expertise. Of the eight (8) pairs, four (4) had both high-performing students, one (1) had both low-performing students, and three (3) were mixed pairs. The remainder of the text will refer to these categories as BH, BL, and M respectively. The CRQA metrics per program were averaged according to these relationships to get the aggregated values, which were then examined to find differences among the categories. This entailed looking at incidences of high and low values of the CRQA metrics. A value was considered high if it was equal to or greater than the mean plus one SD; and low, otherwise. Table 1 shows the descriptive values of the aggregated CRQA metrics per program.

Table 1. Descriptive values of the CRQA metric per program.

CRQA Metric	Mean	SD	Min	Max	Low <=	High >=
RR	0.0899	0.0318	0.0402	0.1788	0.0581	0.1217
DET	0.3529	0.0742	0.1963	0.5170	0.2787	0.4270
ENTR	0.5820	0.1888	0.2592	0.9549	0.3932	0.7708
LAM	0.4073	0.1334	0.0433	0.6634	0.2738	0.5407

Findings showed that all of the high RR's were found in the middle programs and the last program. The RR's of BH, BL, and M pairs started low, with no value exceeding the mean. It peaked when it reached the middle programs. In program no. 9, the RR's started to decline and increased again in program no. 12. This indicated that all the pairs had more recurrent fixations in the middle of the task. This could also possibly mean that at the onset the pairs were still strategizing how to approach the task so fixations were all over the screen. Once they agreed and picked up their rhythm, the RR's increased. Towards the end, the RR's dropped perhaps due to time constraints. In program no. 12, however, the RR's increased again, suggesting that they concentrated and collaborated again to finish the last program upon realizing that they still had enough time left to finish the task.

As per DET, BH pairs had the most occurrences of high DET and did not have any low DET. BL pairs had the most occurrences of low DET with only two instances of high DET, both were found in the middle. M pairs only had one low and high DET each and the rest were average. This implied that BH pairs shared more similar scanpaths. It could be that the high-performers are more experienced and strategic in locating program bugs, which possibly resulted to more matching scanpaths. Low-performers either have less experience in locating bugs or have more difficulty in program comprehension, which could be the reason why BL pairs had the least matching scanpaths because they were just fixating anywhere on the screen hoping that they could spot the error/s. They, however, improved their collaboration in the middle, but then it declined towards the end due to time constraints. For M pairs, a leader-follower tandem could be possible (probably the high-performer leading the low-performer) since most of their DET were average.

For ENTR, BH pairs had average to high ENTR from the beginning up to the middle programs. Towards the end, its ENTR dropped. BL and M pairs had fluctuating ENTR. This could mean that BH's scanpath patterns for locating bugs became predictable as they progressed towards the end. BL and M pairs, on the other hand, had varying scanpath patterns possibly indicating the use of trial-and-error strategy.

For LAM, BL and M pairs had low and high LAM values, which spanned from the beginning to the end but with BL pairs having more high and low LAM. BH pairs only had high LAM in the middle programs. This implied that BL pairs encountered more problems in understanding the programs requiring them to spend more time in certain regions of the code. Both BL and M pairs also struggled with program comprehension in the last program. BH pairs only struggled with program comprehension in the middle programs. Since most of the high LAM values were found in the middle, this suggested that these programs in the middle were more complicated as regarded by all pairs.

4 Summary and Conclusion

This paper aimed to assess who among the pairs collaborated the most regardless of expertise and seek out patterns of collaboration inherent to pairs categorized according to expertise. Results showed that Pair 3 consisting of both high-performers collaborated the most due to its highest RR and DET. However, its highest ENTR and LAM indicated that they also struggled the most in dealing with the programs.

All the pairs regardless of expertise had more recurrent fixations in the middle of the task. BH pairs shared more similar scanpaths, had more predictable debugging strategies, and struggled less in program comprehension. BL pairs shared the least matching scanpaths. A leader-follower pattern could be seen in M pairs. Both BL and M pairs used trial-and-error strategy for locating bugs and encountered more problems in program comprehension.

Acknowledgments. The authors would like to thank Ateneo de Davao University for allowing us to conduct the eye-tracking experiment and to Private Education Assistance Committee of the Fund for Assistance to Private Education for the grant entitled "Analysis of Novice Programmer Tracing and Debugging Skills using Eye Tracking Data."

References

1. Richardson, D.C., Dale, R.: Looking to understand: the coupling between speakers' and listeners' eye movements and its relationship to discourse comprehension. Cogn. Sci. **29**(6), 1045–1060 (2005)
2. Pietinen, S., Bednarik, R., Glotova, T., Tenhunen, V., Tukiainen, M.: A method to study visual attention aspects of collaboration: eye-tracking pair programmers simultaneously. In: Proceedings of the 2008 Symposium on Eye Tracking Research & Applications, pp. 39–42. ACM (2008)
3. Zbilut, J.P., Giuliani, A., Webber, C.L.: Detecting deterministic signals in exceptionally noisy environments using cross-recurrence quantification. Phys. Lett. A **246**(1), 122–128 (1998)
4. Nüssli, M.-A: Dual eye-tracking methods for the study of remote collaborative problem solving. École Polytechnique Fédérale de Lausanne (2011)
5. Jermann, P., Mullins, D., Nüssli, M.-A., Dillenbourg, P.: Collaborative gaze footprints: correlates of interaction quality. In: Proceedings of the Computer Supported Collaborative Learning (CSCL) Conference 2011, vol. 1. International Society of the Learning Sciences (ISLS) (2011)

EMBRACE: Applying Cognitive Tutor Principles to Reading Comprehension

Erin Walker[1(✉)], Audrey Wong[1], Sarah Fialko[2],
M. Adelaida Restrepo[3], and Arthur M. Glenberg[2]

[1] Computing, Informatics, and Decision Systems Engineering,
Arizona State University, Tempe, USA
{erin.a.walker,aewong}@asu.edu
[2] Department of Psychology, Arizona State University, Tempe, USA
{sfialko,aglenber}@asu.edu
[3] Department of Speech and Hearing Science,
Arizona State University, Tempe, USA
marestre@asu.edu

Abstract. Reading comprehension is a critical skill, and one where dual language learners can fall behind compared to native English speakers. We developed EMBRACE, an intelligent tutoring system to improve reading comprehension of dual language learners. Based on theories of embodied cognition, EMBRACE tutors children on how to create cognitive simulations of text content. We describe the implementation of EMBRACE and show how it is closely aligned to principles posed by Anderson and colleagues in 1995 for the design of cognitive tutors, a type of intelligent tutoring system.

Keywords: Embodied cognition · Cognitive tutors · Reading comprehension

1 Introduction and Related Work

Many children who learn English as a second language (dual language learners, or DLLs) tend to perform poorly in English reading comprehension compared to their monolingual counterparts [1]. Our research explores the way in which intelligent tutoring systems (ITSs) can help DLLs develop their reading comprehension skills. ITSs understand the ways in which students solve problems and provide tailored help and feedback [2]. Developing an ITS for reading comprehension has several challenges. Unlike problems in math or science, in which students typically employ a small set of skills to follow a clear path to a correct answer, problems in reading relate to several complex interconnected skills that are highly context dependent [3]. Nevertheless, there have been several ITSs developed for language learning, including REAP [4], iSTART-2 [5], ITSS [6], and Project LISTEN's Reading Tutor [7].

In this paper, we describe *EMBRACE*, an ITS for DLL reading comprehension. Like iSTART-2 and ITSS, *EMBRACE* instructs children on reading comprehension strategies, and provides them with immediate feedback on their strategies. Like REAP and The Reading Tutor, *EMBRACE* tracks student comprehension skills, and uses this information to give vocabulary or syntax feedback and select subsequent learning

© Springer International Publishing AG 2017
E. André et al. (Eds.): AIED 2017, LNAI 10331, pp. 578–581, 2017.
DOI: 10.1007/978-3-319-61425-0_68

activities. *EMBRACE*'s approach is unique in how it uses the reading comprehension strategy of cognitive simulation to model ideal performance and provide support.

2 *EMBRACE* Implementation

EMBRACE draws from an embodied cognition approach that posits that language comprehension is a cognitive simulation process [8]. The primary goal of *EMBRACE* is to teach children how to engage in this simulation process. The application is an interactive storybook on the iPad with a library of narrative and expository texts, of five to seven chapters. In each chapter, each page has images depicting a scene and sentences are displayed in a text box. Students tap on a "Next" button to advance from sentence to sentence. The current sentence is displayed in either blue (manipulation sentence) or black (non-manipulation sentence). For manipulation sentences, children read the sentence and then perform the action using the story images. Children touch an image to select it and drag it to the desired position, moving one object to another object or location. When the user makes an error, a noise is played, and moved objects are reset.

EMBRACE provides children with direct feedback on their simulations. Suppose the child is trying to comprehend the highlighted sentence in Fig. 1, "*Sofia grabbed the bowl of red chilis and gave it to her mother to grind them.*" If the child moves Sofia to the bowl, then Sofia and the bowl together to the mother, these actions provide evidence that the child can identify Sofia, and understands the vocabulary words "bowl" and "mother." However, if the child moves Sofia to the money on the table, this would indicate that the child successfully identified Sofia, but not the words "bowl" or "money". In contrast, if the child moves the bowl to Sofia, this may mean that the child understands both vocabulary words, but misunderstands the syntax of the sentence. To determine whether the child has made a vocabulary or a syntax error, the application divides each sentence into manipulation steps, and each manipulation step into the

Fig. 1. EMBRACE. Students move images corresponding to the highlighted sentence.

object to be moved (the source), and the destination object or location (the destination). It tracks the current manipulation step, and assesses the child's actions based on whether the source (vocabulary error), the destination (vocabulary error), or the sequence of actions (syntax error) is incorrect. Using this information, *EMBRACE* updates assessments of the child's vocabulary and syntax skills. Vocabulary skills are further divided into specific words (e.g., bowl, money), whereas syntax skills are divided into simple, medium, and complex, mapping to the syntactic complexity of the current sentence. Values of skills range from 0 to 1, and represent an estimate of the probability that students have mastered a particular skill. Extending our example, if the child moves Sofia to the money, the skill associated with Sofia would increase, while the skills associated with bowl and money would decrease. These adjustments are made using a Bayesian knowledge tracing algorithm [9], and it is possible for multiple skills to be adjusted as a result of a single action.

Based on the updating skills, *EMBRACE* gives the child vocabulary and syntax feedback if a skill related to that error decreases, and falls below a feedback threshold (set to 0.50). Thus, students only receive feedback if there is a reasonable probability that they have not yet mastered the skill. *EMBRACE* provides vocabulary feedback by playing a feedback noise and temporarily highlighting the correct objects involved in the step. The system provides syntax feedback by playing a feedback noise and reading the sentence out loud to the child.

EMBRACE additionally adapts the learning activity in two ways based on the child's skills. First, each chapter begins with a list of target vocabulary words that are introduced in the text (called the vocabulary preview). The user taps on each word to hear its pronunciation and definition and to see the corresponding image. Vocabulary previews are adapted by adjusting the list of words that appear in the beginning of each chapter. The list always starts with new words and definitions introduced in the chapter and difficult words from the previous chapter. Additional words are added to the list if they: (a) appeared in a previous chapter, (b) appear in the following chapter, and (c) have a skill value below a threshold of 0.80. At most, eight words appear in this list to not overwhelm the child. Second, syntax is adapted by adjusting the complexity of sentences at the beginning of a chapter. For example, if a medium complexity version of a sentence was, "He carried the full milk bucket to the cat," the complex version might be, "Then, he carried the milk bucket, that was full of milk, to the cat." By default, the user starts at medium complexity for the first chapter of a story. Afterwards, if her simple syntax skill is below 0.90 or her medium syntax skill is below 0.40, then the following chapter will switch to mostly simple sentences. If her medium syntax skill is below 0.90 or her complex syntax skill is below 0.40, then the chapter will switch to mostly medium sentences. Otherwise, the chapter will switch to mostly complex sentences. All thresholds were assigned through piloting and testing the application, to trigger feedback at reasonable times.

3   Discussion and Conclusions

In this paper, we described *EMBRACE,* an ITS for DLL reading comprehension of primary school children. Historically, building ITSs has been challenging for reading comprehension, because of the complexity and contextual embeddedness of the skills involved. However, *EMBRACE* is a traditional implementation of an ITS, and fulfills Anderson and colleagues' [2] eight basic principles of tutor design. In *EMBRACE*, we decomposed the task into production rules related to the manipulation actions (Principle 1), made the manipulation goals evident to the students (Principle 2), and ground instruction in the specific context of the stories (Principle 3). From a theoretical perspective, embodied cognition is highly congruent with traditional cognitive tutoring approaches in that it allows for fine-grained modeling and immediate feedback. Further, *EMBRACE* provides immediate feedback on vocabulary and syntax skills (Principle 6), adjusts the amount of feedback based on student skills (Principle 8), adapts the complexity of the texts based on student skills (Principle 5), and presents students with additional vocabulary mapped to vocabulary skills they have not yet mastered (Principle 7). *EMBRACE* is novel in the way it coaches children on the reading comprehension strategy of simulation, but also helps them acquire the content-specific vocabulary and syntax skills that form the foundation for reading comprehension. By centering our ITS on the concept of simulation (reified through manipulation actions), it was possible to fulfill many of Anderson and colleagues' [2] cognitive tutor principles. We see a lot of promise in this approach for improving the reading comprehension skills of young DLLs using personalized learning.

Acknowledgments. This research was supported by NSF Grant # 1324807. Thanks to James Rodriguez, Jithin Roy, and Ashley Adams.

References

1. National Center for Education Statistics: National Assessment of Educational Progress (NAEP) 2015 Reading Assessment [Data file] (2015). http://nces.ed.gov/nationsreportcard/subject/publications/stt2015/pdf/2016008AZ4.pdf
2. Anderson, J.R., Corbett, A.T., Koedinger, K.R., Pelletier, R.: Cognitive tutors: lessons learned. J. Learn. Sci. **4**(2), 167–207 (1995)
3. Jacovina, E.J., McNamara, D.S.: Intelligent tutoring systems for literacy: existing technologies and continuing challenges. In: Atkinson, R. (ed.) Intelligent Tutoring Systems: Structure, Applications and Challenges. Nova Science Publishers Inc, NY (2016)
4. Heilman, M., Collins-Thompson, K., Callan, J., Eskenazi, M.: Classroom success of an intelligent tutoring system for lexical practice and reading comprehension. In: INTERSPEECH (2006)
5. Levinstein, I.B., Boonthum, C., Pillarisetti, S.P., Bell, C., McNamara, D.S.: iSTART 2: improvements for efficiency and effectiveness. BRM **39**, 224–232 (2007)
6. Meyer, B.J., Wijekumar, K.K., Lin, Y.C.: Individualizing a web-based structure strategy intervention for fifth graders' comprehension of nonfiction. J. Ed. Psych. **103**(1), 140 (2011)
7. Mostow, J., Nelson-Taylor, J., Beck, J.E.: Computer-guided oral reading versus independent practice: comparison of sustained silent reading to an automated reading tutor that listens. J. Educ. Comput. Res. **49**, 249–276 (2013)
8. Glenberg, A.M., Gallese, V.: Action-based language: a theory of language acquisition, comprehension, and production. Cortex **48**(7), 905–922 (2012)
9. Corbett, A.T., Anderson, J.R.: Knowledge tracing: modeling the acquisition of procedural knowledge. User Model. User-Adap. Inter. **4**(4), 253–278 (1994)

Effects of a Dashboard for an Intelligent Tutoring System on Teacher Knowledge, Lesson Plans and Class Sessions

Françeska Xhakaj[✉], Vincent Aleven[✉], and Bruce M. McLaren[✉]

Human-Computer Interaction Institute,
Carnegie Mellon University, Pittsburgh, PA, USA
{francesx, aleven, bmclaren}@cs.cmu.edu

Abstract. Even though Intelligent Tutoring Systems (ITS) have been shown to help students learn, little research has investigated how a dashboard could help teachers help their students. In this paper, we explore how a dashboard prototype designed for an ITS affects teachers' knowledge about their students, their classroom lesson plans and class sessions. We conducted a quasi-experimental classroom study with 5 middle school teachers and 8 classes. We found that the dashboard influences what teachers know about their students, which in turn influences the lesson plans they prepare, which then guides what teachers cover in a class session. We believe this is the first study that explores how a dashboard for an ITS affects teacher's knowledge, decision-making and actions in the classroom.

Keywords: Intelligent Tutoring Systems · Dashboard · Data-driven instruction · Teachers' use of data · Learning analytics

1 Introduction

Although it is by now well established that Intelligent Tutoring Systems (ITS) can enhance student learning [4], ITSs are rarely designed for teachers or with teachers in mind. For example, when a student is not progressing well in the ITS, the teacher might be able to help the student move forward. A dashboard could alert the teacher to such a situation, and more generally, a dashboard could inform the teacher about the students' abilities and performance in the ITS. Almost no work has focused on creating and studying a teacher dashboard for an ITS. Much research focuses on evaluating dashboards for other types of learning technologies, and on studying whether dashboards are useful to teachers [6, 7]. Further, while many dashboards are used in real-time, during a class session, teachers might also use a dashboard in other scenarios, such as when preparing for a class session. Kelly et al. (2013) studied how a teacher used a report on students' performance in a web-based homework system to decide what parts of the homework to review in class, with positive effects [3]. Our study is different in that it uses a fully featured rather than a simplified ITS, involves more teachers and students, a different dashboard design and use scenario (namely, for lesson planning rather than homework review), and different data analysis approach.

© Springer International Publishing AG 2017
E. André et al. (Eds.): AIED 2017, LNAI 10331, pp. 582–585, 2017.
DOI: 10.1007/978-3-319-61425-0_69

In this work, we present our findings from a quasi-experimental classroom study in which 5 middle school teachers, with 8 classes in total, used a dashboard prototype for an ITS. We investigate the effect of the dashboard on teacher practices, and we focus on a scenario in which teachers use a dashboard with analytics from an ITS to prepare for, and then conduct, a class session following sessions during which students worked with the ITS.

2 Methodology

2.1 Formative Evaluation of the Dashboard in the Classroom

We conducted a quasi-experimental study to address the research question: *How does the dashboard affect teacher practices in the classroom?* The study is part of our user-centered design process for Luna, a high-fidelity dashboard prototype we created [1, 2, 9]. Luna was used in conjunction with Lynnette, an ITS that helps middle school students (grades 6–8) learn to solve linear equations in mathematics [5, 8]. Luna presents teachers with data about their students' performance in Lynnette, at the class and individual level. The analytics that Luna presents include information on students' skill mastery, misconceptions, and progress and time in the ITS.

Experimental Design. Five middle school teachers from two suburban U.S. schools took part in the study. The experiment had two conditions, control (9 classes) and experimental (8 classes). In this paper, we present data from the experimental classes only. First, students worked for 60 min in Lynnette. This work generated the data to be displayed on the Luna dashboard. Next, teachers were asked to use Luna and to think out loud as they prepared for a class session. These preparatory sessions lasted 20 min and were video-recorded. Subsequently, teachers conducted class sessions based on their lessons plans. During the class sessions (40 min each), 2–4 coders (undergraduate students and staff from our institution) took observational notes using a tool with predefined categories of observations. They also took free-form notes.

2.2 How Does the Dashboard Affect Teacher Practices in the Classroom?

We investigated how the dashboard affected teachers and their practices in the classroom, specifically: what teachers learned from the dashboard, their lesson plans, and their classroom sessions.

Teacher's Updated Knowledge. We analyzed the video recordings of the teacher preparation sessions to study how Luna affects teacher knowledge. From these video recordings, we distilled and paraphrased the statements teachers made while studying information presented by Luna. We distinguished four categories of statements, characterized by (a) whether the statements conveyed knowledge the teacher had *before* inspecting Luna or knowledge they became aware of *while* inspecting Luna, and (b) whether these statements referred to the class overall or to individual students. From the analyses of the teacher's updated knowledge, we found that Luna's information affected the teachers' knowledge. To varying degrees, this information (1) confirmed what the teacher already knew, (2) surprised or rejected what the teacher knew, (3) added to what the teacher knew, about the class overall and about individual students.

Lesson Plan. To explore how the knowledge teachers gained from the dashboard may have influenced their lesson plans, we analyzed the lesson plans that teachers created as they prepared with Luna. We distilled and paraphrased the main ideas teachers were focusing on or wrote down during the preparation sessions, based on the video recordings of these sessions. The lesson plans specified the topics along with the exercises (if any) that teachers were going to cover in the class session, as well as their plans to interact with individual students, when applicable. We investigated how the information gleaned from Luna affected the teacher's lesson plan, by matching each of the statements in the lesson plan with information (in the form of statements) that teachers learned from Luna. This matching procedure was applied only to statements in which teachers explicitly said they were going to cover a topic or problem in the class session because of some information from Luna. We found that many of the statements and knowledge teachers gain from Luna is accounted for in various ways in their lesson plans, in particular knowledge about where students are struggling.

Class Session. We tracked whether teachers covered in class what they had planned in their lesson plans, using the notes taken during the class sessions by the coders. Part of the knowledge and statements teachers gain from Luna that makes it to their lesson plans also gets accounted for and reaches students in the class session.

3   Discussion

We examine and trace the influence of a dashboard for an ITS on teachers and their practices in the classroom. Our study is, to the best of our knowledge, the first to investigate effects of a dashboard in this manner.

Our findings show that Luna affects teachers' knowledge both at the class and individual level. In turn, the teacher's updated knowledge prompts them to adapt or change their lesson plan and what they decide to cover in class. Furthermore, teachers implement in the class session planned statements they learned from Luna. This is important, as ultimately, what teachers cover during the class session is what students get exposed to and what affects their learning. Overall, Luna provided useful information to teachers on how their students were learning with the ITS, affected their decision-making and planning for the class session, both with respect to the class as a whole and to individual students. Luna also influenced what happened during the class sessions.

Generally, we can conclude that the information that Luna provides (namely skill mastery information, occurrence of misconceptions and students time and progress in Lynnette), at the class and individual level, is helpful to teachers as they prepare for a class session and guides the lesson plans they create and the way they conduct the class sessions. More generally, the study provides strong evidence that a dashboard with information generated by an ITS can be a useful tool for teachers.

Acknowledgments. We thank all the teachers, schools and students who took part in our study, Gail Kusbit, Kenneth Holstein, the coders and graders for the project. NSF Award #1530726 supported this work.

References

1. Aleven, V., Xhakaj, F., Holstein, K., McLaren, B.M.: Developing a teacher dashboard for use with intelligent tutoring systems. In: Proceedings of the 4th International Workshop on Teaching Analytics, IWTA 2016 at the 11th European Conference on Technology Enhanced Learning, EC-TEL 2016, Lyon, France, 13–16 September 2016
2. Holstein, K., Xhakaj, F., Aleven, V., McLaren, B.M.: Luna: a dashboard for teachers using intelligent tutoring systems. In: Proceedings of the 4th International Workshop on Teaching Analytics, IWTA 2016 at the 11th European Conference on Technology Enhanced Learning, EC-TEL 2016, Lyon, France, 13–16 September 2016
3. Kelly, K., Heffernan, N., Heffernan, C., Goldman, S., Pellegrino, J., Goldstein, D.S.: Estimating the effect of web-based homework. In: Lane, H.C., Yacef, K., Mostow, J., Pavlik, P. (eds.) AIED 2013. LNCS, vol. 7926, pp. 824–827. Springer, Heidelberg (2013). doi:10.1007/978-3-642-39112-5_122
4. Kulik, J.A., Fletcher, J.D.: Effectiveness of intelligent tutoring systems: a meta-analytic review. Rev. Educ. Res. **86**(1), 42–78 (2016)
5. Long, Y., Aleven, V.: Mastery-oriented shared student/system control over problem selection in a linear equation tutor. In: Micarelli, A., Stamper, J., Panourgia, K. (eds.) ITS 2016. LNCS, vol. 9684, pp. 90–100. Springer, Cham (2016). doi:10.1007/978-3-319-39583-8_9
6. Martinez-Maldonado, R., Yacef, K., Kay, J., Schwendimann, B.: An interactive teacher's dashboard for monitoring multiple groups in a multi-tabletop learning environment. In: Cerri, S.A., Clancey, W.J., Papadourakis, G., Panourgia, K. (eds.) ITS 2012, vol. 7315, pp. 482–492. Springer, Heidelberg (2012)
7. Mazza, R., Dimitrova, V.: CourseVis: a graphical student monitoring tool for supporting instructors in web-based distance courses. Int. J. Hum. Comput. Stud. **65**(2), 125–139 (2007)
8. Waalkens, M., Aleven, V., Taatgen, N.: Does supporting multiple student strategies lead to greater learning and motivation? Investigating a source of complexity in the architecture of intelligent tutoring systems. Comput. Educ. **60**, 159–171 (2013)
9. Xhakaj, F., Aleven, V., McLaren, B.M.: How teachers use data to help students learn: contextual inquiry for the design of a dashboard. In: Verbert, K., Sharples, M., Klobučar, T. (eds.) EC-TEL 2016. LNCS, vol. 9891, pp. 340–354. Springer, Cham (2016). doi:10.1007/978-3-319-45153-4_26

Dynamics of Affective States During MOOC Learning

Xiang Xiao, Phuong Pham, and Jingtao Wang[(✉)]

Computer Science and LRDC, University of Pittsburgh, Pittsburgh, PA, USA
{xiangxiao,phuongpham,jingtaow}@cs.pitt.edu

Abstract. We investigate the temporal dynamics of learners' affective states (e.g., *engagement, boredom, confusion, frustration*, etc.) during video-based learning sessions in Massive Open Online Courses (MOOCs) in a 22-participant user study. We also show the feasibility of predicting learners' *moment-to-moment* affective states via implicit photoplethysmography (PPG) sensing on unmodified smartphones.

Keywords: Massive Open Online Courses · Intelligent Tutoring Systems · Physiological signals · Affective computing

1 Introduction

Learning is an affectively charged experience. Previous studies have shown that learners experience a rich diversity of affective states, including *engagement, boredom, confusion, curiosity, happiness*, and *frustration* in the process of learning. Affective states can significantly influence learners' motivations, behaviors, and even learning outcomes [3]. Researchers have conducted systematic studies to understand [2], detect [3, 6], and adapt to [5] learners' affective and cognitive states in computer-mediated learning systems. Both the occurrence of learning-centered affective states and the dynamic temporal transitions between them [2] have been studied in complex learning environments, i.e., solving multi-step, time-consuming questions. Nevertheless, little work has been done to understand the dynamics of affect in Massive Open Online Courses (MOOCs) to date. Different from the *interactive* experiences in Intelligent Tutoring Systems (ITS), students in MOOCs learn primarily via *passive* video-watching. As a result, many findings in the complex learning domain might not be applicable to MOOC learning.

In this paper, we investigate the temporal dynamics of learners' affective states during short video-based MOOC learning sessions. Through a 22-participant user study, we quantify both the frequency of occurrence and the dynamic transitions of common affective states during MOOC learning. This work extends the model of affect dynamics in complex learning proposed by D'Mello et al. [2] to MOOC contexts. Moreover, we explore the feasibility of predicting a learner's *moment-to-moment* affective states by analyzing her PPG signals implicitly captured by the built-in camera of smartphones during MOOC learning.

© Springer International Publishing AG 2017
E. André et al. (Eds.): AIED 2017, LNAI 10331, pp. 586–589, 2017.
DOI: 10.1007/978-3-319-61425-0_70

2 Methodology

Twenty-two college students (10 females) participated in our study to investigate the dynamics of affective states in video-based MOOC learning sessions. Participants took a mini MOOC course (the introductory section of the Coursera course "Cryptography") with three lecture videos (30 min in total). To collect learners' moment-to-moment affective states during learning, we asked participants to provide judgment of their affective states at fixed affect judgment points in the video when the video paused automatically. Affect judgment points were either at the end of each concept or after the instructor asked a question and sought answers from the audience. The intervals between two consecutive judgment points ranged from 21 s to 80 s (average 42 s). There were 47 affect judgment points in total across the whole lecture. At each affect judgment point, participants were provided with a checklist of nine states (*engagement, boredom, confusion, frustration, surprise, delight, curiosity, happiness,* and *neutral*) to mark along with definitions of each state. These states were reported to occur during learning with technology [2, 3]. Participants were also asked to rate the level of valence (displeasure to pleasure) and arousal (deactivation to activation) they experienced using the Self-Assessment Manikin's (SAM) [1].

While participants were watching the lecture videos, we also recorded their PPG signals using the LivePulse [4] application running on a Nexus 5 smartphone.

3 Result

3.1 Affective States in MOOCs

A total of 1034 self-reported affect judgments were collected from the 22 participants. There were 35.7% instances of *engagement*, 13.2% *boredom*, 14.5% *confusion*, 2.3% *frustration*, 1.6% *delight*, 2.0% *surprise*, 11.8% *curiosity*, 3.4% *happiness*, and 15.6% *neutral*. A repeated measures ANOVA on the distribution of affective states indicated a statistically significant difference, $F(8, 168) = 21.8$, $p < 0.0001$. *Engagement* was the most frequent affect, followed by *boredom, confusion, curiosity,* and *neutral*. Unlike complex learning, *frustration* had low frequency during the MOOC learning session. There were also only a few occurrences of *delight, surprise,* and *happiness*.

To identify the frequently occurring transitions between affective states, we used the transition likelihood metric L in [2] to compute the likelihood of transitions from one state to another state. Our investigations focused on the frequently occurring states (*engagement, boredom, confusion, curiosity,* and *neutral*) and *frustration*, a primary negative affect in learning [2, 3]. To determine the significance of transitions between two affective states, we first calculated the transition likelihood for each transition per participant. Then, we used one-sample t-tests to check the significance of the transitions. Figure 1 presents the descriptive statistics for the likelihood that each of the 6 investigated affective states immediately follows another.

Different from the affect dynamics in complex learning [2], we observed that the *engagement→boredom* transition was significant. This finding suggests that learners in MOOC contexts are more likely to enter *boredom* than they are in complex learning.

Moreover, we did not observe a strong *confusion* → *engagement* transition as in complex learning [2]. Based on participants' subjective feedback, the occurrences of *confusion→engagement* in MOOCs depend more upon the content and flow of the video than upon the learners actively figuring out the problem themselves (as in complex learning). Because of this large reliance on the content and flow of the video, learners tend to remain confused if their questions or doubts are not answered in the video.

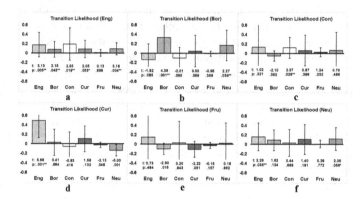

Fig. 1. The likelihoods that each state immediately follows (a) *engagement* (b) *boredom* (c) *confusion* (d) *curiosity* (e) *frustration* (f) *neutral*.

3.2   PPG Signals and Moment-to-Moment Affective States

With the data collected in the study, we also investigated the feasibility of detecting learners' moment-to-moment affective states using the PPG signals collected by the built-in camera of smartphones. For each subject[1], we extracted heart rate variability (HRV) [6] features from the PPG signal segment right before each affect judgment point, and used these features to predict the learner's affective state at that judgment point. To have a long enough PPG sequence to make an accurate prediction and reduce the carry-over effect, we removed those affect judgment points which were too close to the previous affect judgment point (interval < 30 s), leading to a total of 33 affect judgment points per participant. We used LivePulse algorithm [4] to extract RR-intervals from each PPG signal segment. 11 dimensions of HRV features were then calculated based on these RR-intervals: (1) AVNN; (2) SDNN; (3) rMSSD; (4–7) pNN5, pNN10, pNN20, pNN50; (8) MAD; (9) SDANN; (10) SDNNIDX; and (11) rMSSD/SDNNIDX. Definitions of these features can be found in [5, 6]. For each participant, all features were rescaled to [0, 1].

Using self-reported affect judgments as the gold standard, we performed the following detection tasks: (1) detecting whether the learner is in an *engagement, boredom,* or *confusion* state (yes or no, binary classification); (2) detecting whether the learner is

---

[1] We removed data from S1 and S4 in this analysis because the PPG data collected from these two subjects were incomplete.

in a negative state (low valance); and (3) detecting the occurrence of critical events which are marked by strong emotions (high arousal values). We used the Support Vector Machine (SVM) with a radial basis function (RBF) kernel to build the classifiers. We built both user-independent models and user-dependent models. The user-independent models were built using the data from all subjects and were evaluated via leave-one-subject-out evaluation. User-dependent models were built for each participant individually and evaluated with 10-fold cross-validations. Table 1 lists Kappa's best performance for each classification task. The Kappa score indicated a clear relationship between learners' affective states and their PPG signals.

Table 1. The performance of different moment-to-moment affective state prediction tasks

Detection	User-independent		User dependent	
	Accuracy	Kappa	Accuracy	Kappa
Engagement	70.8%	0.151	62.0%	0.277
Boredom	83.6%	0.077	83.7%	0.139
Confusion	80.1%	0.070	83.7%	0.205
Negative events (low valence)	85.5%	0.107	85.0%	0.182
Critical events (high arousal)	84.8%	0.233	84.6%	0.285

4   Conclusion

This paper presents a 22-subject study to understand the dynamic transitions of affective states during video-based MOOC learning. We also show the feasibility of using implicit PPG sensing to detect moment-to-moment affective states. This research is an initial step towards a holistic understanding of learners' affective states during typical video-based MOOC learning sessions.

References

1. Bradley, M.M., Lang, P.J.: Measuring emotion: the self-assessment manikin and the semantic differential. J. Behav. Ther. Exp. Psychiatry **25**(1), 49–59 (1994)
2. D'Mello, S.K., Graesser, A.C.: Dynamics of affective states during complex learning. Learn. Instr. **22**(2), 145–157 (2012)
3. Graesser, A.C., D'Mello, S.K., Strain, A.C.: Emotions in advanced learning technologies. In: Pekrun, R., Linnenbrink-Garcia, L. (eds.) International Handbook of Emotions in Education, pp. 473–493. Routledge, New York (2014)
4. Han, T., Xiao, X., Shi, L., Canny, J., Wang, J.: Balancing accuracy and fun: designing camera based mobile games for implicit heart rate monitoring. In: Proceedings of the 33rd Annual ACM Conference on Human Factors in Computing Systems. ACM (2015)
5. Xiao, X., Wang, J.: Context and cognitive state triggered interventions for mobile MOOC learning. In: Proceedings of the 18th ACM on International Conference on Multimodal Interaction, pp. 378–385. ACM (2016)
6. Xiao, X., Wang, J.: Towards attentive, bi-directional MOOC learning on mobile devices. In: Proceedings of the 17th ACM on International Conference on Multimodal Interaction, pp. 163–170. ACM (2015)

Learning from Errors: Identifying Strategies in a Math Tutoring System

Jun Xie[1(⊠)], Keith Shubeck[1], Scotty D. Craig[2], and Xiangen Hu[1,3]

[1] The University of Memphis, Memphis, TN 38152, USA
jxie2@memphis.edu
[2] Arizona State University, Mesa, AZ 85287, USA
[3] Central China Normal University, Wuhan 430079, Hubei, China

Abstract. This study attempts to investigate how students gain knowledge by utilizing help and practice after making errors. We define three types of strategies used by students after errors: help-seeking (requesting two worked examples in the next attempts after an error), practice (solving the problems in the next two attempts after an error), and mixed (first requesting a worked example or first solving a problem in the next two attempts after an error). Our results indicate that the most frequently used strategies are help and mixed strategies. However, the practice strategy and mixed strategies facilitate immediate performance improvement. Additionally, the help strategy was found to interfere with delayed performance.

Keywords: Errors and learning · Help-seeking · Math · Intelligent tutoring systems

1 Introduction

Errors made during learning have gradually been considered to play an essential role in effective learning [1]. Current studies on how students learn from errors mainly focus on self-explanation, which is difficult to observe in a natural learning process [2]. Therefore, this study aims to investigate how students utilize help and practice to learn from errors instead of self-explanation within ALEKS (Assessment and LEarning in Knowledge Spaces). ALEKS is a self-paced online math tutoring system built on knowledge space theory (KST) [3]. KST imitates experts to assess online changes of a student's existing knowledge. Thus, ALEKS can provide material that students are most ready to learn at any time. Each topic in ALEKS has an enormous variety of instances to ensure that students never see the exact same problem twice. Students are required to provide the answers in the system (i.e., generating answers to fill in the blank, not multiple choice). Additionally, a worked example of a problem can be requested by a student to view all correct solution steps. A worked example for each unique instance can only be read once.

The existing literature suggests that both help and practice benefit learning [4, 5], but they should be embedded into learning cycles in lieu of separate learning sessions targeted on specific skills or knowledge [6]. This view of learning strategies is very similar to the learning phase theory [7]. The learning phase theory points out that

E. André et al. (Eds.): AIED 2017, LNAI 10331, pp. 590–593, 2017.
DOI: 10.1007/978-3-319-61425-0_71

during the early learning phase, students attempt to ask for more help and gain a basic understanding of the domain knowledge. During the intermediate phase, students pay more attention to learning how to solve the problems. Students in the late phase and focus on applying knowledge to solve problems in order to increase the speed and accuracy of their problem solving. Per the learning phase theory [7], students should exhibit three types of strategies after an error is made. That is, a help strategy, a practice strategy, and a "mixed" strategy involving help and practice. ALEKS matches topic difficulty with student prior knowledge, so students should begin their interactions with ALEKS inside the intermediate phase. For this reason, we assume that ALEKS is constructed in a way that best allows for students to adapt a "mixed" strategy.

Strategy changes over time is also an important feature to describe learning strategies in a self-regulated learning system. Disordered learning behaviors imply lower performance in learning [8]. We hypothesize that a disordered pattern of using strategy use will be correlated with low performance. Students with high prior knowledge tend to self-correct whereas those with low prior knowledge tend to overuse help [9]. Thus, they might be more likely to adopt the practice strategy to learn from errors.

2   Methods

Our data consists of ALEKS log files collected from an after-school math program [10]. This program aimed to improve sixth graders' mathematics performance ($N = 204$) especially students with low prior knowledge. The log file contained 118,995 erroneous attempts out of 336,842 attempts (35.3% error). A "attempt" in ALEKS describes a student action of either solving a problem or requesting a worked example.

The strategies of learning from errors are organized into four categories: help (only request worked examples in the next two attempts after an error); practice (only solve problems in the next two attempts after an error); and mixed (help_prac: request a worked example, and prac_help: solve a problem in the next two attempts after an error). D'Mello's likelihood metric formula [11] is used to measure the likelihood of strategies occurring after errors. Below, C represents the error, and X represents a strategy. A probability higher than zero indicates that the strategy occurs beyond its base rate. Otherwise the probability implies that strategy takes place below its base rate.

$$L[C \rightarrow X] = \frac{\frac{\Pr[X \cap C]}{\Pr[C]} - \Pr[X]}{1 - \Pr[X]} \tag{1}$$

Shannon entropy [12] was applied to capture dynamic changes of strategies used to learn from errors. A high entropy value indicates a disordered pattern of using strategies to learn from errors, whereas a low entropy implies ordered pattern. Below, x_i represents strategies to learn from errors.

$$H(X) = -\sum_{i=1}^{n} p(x_i) \log p(x_i) \qquad (2)$$

To capture prior knowledge, students' fifth-grade math scores on the Tennessee Comprehensive Assessment Program (TCAP) were collected. The students whose fifth-grade TCAP scores were higher than the median score (44) were clustered in a high prior knowledge group (M = 58.32, SD = 9.66). Other students were grouped as low prior knowledge (M = 29.72, SD = 12.86). Learning outcomes include immediate and delayed performance. Immediate performance was measured by the percentage of correctness in the next similar problem after a strategy. Delayed performance is measured by math score on the 6th grade TCAP, which was typically administered one month after the after-school math program ended.

3   Results

A one-way ANOVA revealed significant differences in likelihood of the four strategies' occurring after errors, $F(3,812) = 326.7$, $p < .000$, $\eta^2 = .55$. The multiple comparisons show that the likelihood of practice strategy (M = −1.70, SD = 1.40) was significantly lower than that of help strategy (M = .01, SD = .10) or prac_help (M = .05, SD = .05) or help_prac (M = .16, SD = .09). There was no difference among the likelihoods of help strategy and the two types of mixed strategies. The results imply that help strategy and the mixed strategies were most frequently used by students after making errors. Similarly, both students with low/high prior knowledge tend to use help strategy and mixed strategies more frequently than practice.

One-way ANOVA results revealed a significant difference on immediate performance between strategies, $F(3,797) = 34.83$, $p < .000$, $\eta^2 = .12$. Multiple comparisons revealed that students' immediate performance after implementing the practice strategy (M = .37, SD = .09), prac_help (M = .36, SD = .10), and help_prac (M = .38, SD = .10) was superior to students' immediate performance after using the help strategy (M = .26, SD = .15). Practice strategies and the mixed strategies were related to an increased likelihood to successfully solve the next problem. This relationship between strategies and immediate performance also appears in different levels of prior knowledge. The results of the linear mixed effects regression suggest that the likelihood of help strategy occurring after errors was negatively associated with delayed performance on 6th TCAP test. That is, students who are more likely to use help strategy after errors performed worse on the TCAP test than others who are less likely to use help strategy. Students were included as a random variable. Detailed results are provided in Table 1.

Table 1. Linear mixed-effect regressions of strategies on delayed performance

	Intercept	Help	Practice	Prac_help	Help_prac	Changes
Coefficient	51.98	−33.46	−.74	−30.84	3.41	−6.65
p		.03*	.02*	.40	.28	.84	.62

$^*p < .05.$ $^{**}p < .00.$

4 Conclusions

Our results suggest that in systems adaptive to students' prior knowledge, students tend to use a mixed strategy by combining worked example with practice to learn from errors. The positive effect of the practice strategy and mixed strategies on immediate performance indicates that students learn from errors by doing problems [4]. The finding that frequent help strategy use was detrimental to delayed performance is in line with previous research that found overuse of worked examples interfered with learning [5]. The practical implications of these results suggest that requesting worked examples consecutively may be a negative sign for learning in ALEKS. Students may need guidance on help-seeking from the system to avoid overusing worked examples. For example, integrating animated agents to help students read worked examples may be a way to prevent overuse of worked examples. Alternatively, ALEKS could suggest students to practice on problems when it detects their overuse of worked examples.

Acknowledgements. This research was supported by the Institute for Education Sciences (IES) Grant R305A090528 to Dr. Xiangen Hu, PI. Any opinions, findings, and conclusions or recommendations expressed in this material are those of the authors and do not necessarily reflect the views of IES.

References

1. Bjork, R.A., Dunlosky, J., Kornell, N.: Self-regulated learning: beliefs, techniques, and illusions. Annu. Rev. Psychol. **64**, 417–444 (2013)
2. Heemsoth, T., Heinze, A.: Secondary school students learning from reflections on the rationale behind self-made errors: a field experiment. J. Exp. Educ. **84**(1), 98–118 (2016)
3. Falmagne, J.C., Koppen, M., Villano, M., Doignon, J.P., Johannesen, L.: Introduction to knowledge spaces: how to build, test, and search them. Psychol. Rev. **97**(2), 201–224 (1990)
4. Christianson, K., Mestre, J.P., Luke, S.G.: Practice makes (nearly) perfect: solving 'students-and-professors'-type algebra word problems. Appl. Cogn. Psychol. **26**(5), 810–822 (2012)
5. Kalyuga, S., Chandler, P., Tuovinen, J., Sweller, J.: When problem solving is superior to studying worked examples. J. Educ. Psychol. **93**(3), 579–588 (2001)
6. Hattie, J.A., Donoghue, G.M.: Learning strategies: a synthesis and conceptual model. npj Sci. Learn. **1**, 1–13 (2016), Article No. 16013
7. VanLehn, K.: Cognitive skill acquisition. Annu. Rev. Psychol. **47**(1), 513–539 (1996)
8. Zimmerman, B.J., Pons, M.M.: Development of a structured interview for assessing student use of self-regulated learning strategies. Am. Educ. Res. J. **23**(4), 614–628 (1986)
9. Wood, H., Wood, D.: Help seeking, learning and contingent tutoring. Comput. Educ. **33**(2), 153–169 (1999)
10. Hu, X., et al.: The effects of a traditional and technology-based after-school program on 6th grade student's mathematics skills. J. Comput. Math. Sci. Teach. **31**(1), 17–38 (2012)
11. D'Mello, S., Graesser, A.: Dynamics of affective states during complex learning. Learn. Instr. **22**(2), 145–157 (2012)
12. Shannon, C.E.: Prediction and entropy of printed english. Bell Labs Tech. J. **30**(1), 50–64 (1951)

Can Short Answers to Open Response Questions Be Auto-Graded Without a Grading Rubric?

Xi Yang[1], Lishan Zhang[1,2], and Shengquan Yu[1,2(✉)]

[1] Beijing Advanced Innovation Center for Future Education,
Beijing Normal University, Beijing 100875, China
{xiyang85,lishan,yusq}@bnu.edu.cn
[2] Faculty of Education, Beijing Normal University, Beijing 100875, China

Abstract. Auto-grading short-answers seems to be sufficiently resolved. However, most auto-graders require comprehensive scoring rubrics, which were not always available. This paper used modern machine learning techniques to build auto-graders without expressly defining the rubrics. The result shows that the best auto-grading model is able to achieve a good inter-rater agreement (kappa = 0.625) with expert grading. The agreement can be further improved (kappa = 0.726) if the auto-grading model gave up scoring some of the answers.

Keywords: Auto-grading · SVM · LSTM · Short-answer

1 Introduction

Automated scoring of short-answer to open response questions has been extensively studied for a long time. C-rater [1] is probably the most well-known system. It performed very well even compared with recent auto-grading algorithms. Its accuracy was 84% on average. Other than auto-grading, short-answer evaluation technique has been also used in the intelligent tutoring systems like AutoTutor [2, 3], where adaptive feedback was selected based on a student's specific answer. The existing methods, including recent one [4], first analyzed student answers using statistical technologies, built scoring models, then the human made models were used for auto-scoring unseen answers. These methods required clear grading rubrics to facilitate auto-scoring. But not all the questions had such clear rubrics ready, especially for those complex ones. Making this kind of rubrics demands domain expertise as well as computing technologies.

With the development of machine learning techniques, we are wondering whether we can build auto-scoring models by only taking human graded answers into consideration and without rubrics. We took Chinese reading comprehension as the study domain, built auto-scoring models only with general syntactic features directly extracted from short answers and explored how many graded answers we need for the algorithms to figure out reliable scoring models. All the answers are divided into three levels of grades. So both accuracy and kappa were used to measure the scoring model.

© Springer International Publishing AG 2017
E. André et al. (Eds.): AIED 2017, LNAI 10331, pp. 594–597, 2017.
DOI: 10.1007/978-3-319-61425-0_72

The rest of the paper is structured as follow: first of all, we introduce the machine learning algorithms and data we used. Secondly, we describe how the algorithms were applied in auto-scoring. In the last, the results are presented and we conclude with remarks.

2   The Domain and Data

Our study domain is to auto-score 6th grade students' short answers to reading comprehension questions. We currently only conducted a pilot study for one question, but with 534 student answers. Each student answer can be labeled as one of the three different scores: 0, 1, 2, the higher the better. Two human raters were paid to grade all the questions manually. After clarifying grading criteria, they first graded 50 student answers individually and discussed to resolve all the conflicts. The kappa was 0.783. Then they graded the rest 484 students answers individually and discussed to resolve their conflicts. The overall kappa was 0.755.

3   Methodology

In this paper, we consider the auto-graded student answers problem as a text classification problem. Two classification algorithms are employed, i.e. support vector machine (SVM) and long short-term memory (LSTM) [5].

Long short-term memory (LSTM) is a type of artificial neural network architecture and has got a lot of successes recently in the field of natural language processing (NLP), facilitating many NLP tasks such as machine translation, speech recognition, etc. Like other artificial neural network algorithms, LSTM is consisted of many network units. The unit in LSTM can either remember long or short term duration of time. There are gate units in the network to control how long term units and short term units affect the final outputs.

Support vector machine (SVM) is a well-known classification algorithm. Basically, it managed to draw either linear or non-linear boundaries among the different groups of labeled data points. The boundaries then were used to classify unlabeled data points. The algorithm has been proved to be useful in many different applications.

Both of the two algorithms are supervised learning algorithms. It means that the algorithms need labeled data entries, which are essentially the answers with grades, to calibrate the models. Then, the trained model is used to auto-score the ungraded answers. We used slightly different types of features to train the two models based on their properties. We first built auto-grading models with LSTM and SVM separately, and then blended them together.

To preprocess the input for both algorithms, the answers were first tokenized by using a parser called "jieba" [6], which is a Python Chinese word segmentation module. Then based on the properties of the two algorithms, we adopted different feature engineering methods. Specifically, when SVM was used as the training model, tf-idf score of unigram and bigram was calculated. In a result, it made about 2700 features. While LSTM was used, frequency of each token was calculated to build the feature set. 78 features were used to train LSTM. To achieve a better performance, the two models were blended to form the third model. The average probability of LSTM and SVM for each possible grade was used while blending.

5–fold cross validation was applied to test the effectiveness of the three algorithms. All the answers were essentially classified into 3 categories, accuracy and kappa were used to evaluate the classifiers. To better understand how much data we need to achieve a satisfied accuracy, the size of training data was gradually increased, and the corresponding accuracy was depicted.

Furthermore, we also combined the two original grading models in an innovative way. For each answer, if the two models can make agreement on grading, the combined model output the grade. Otherwise, the combined model gives up.

4 Results and Discussion

LSTM performed slightly better than SVM. The accuracy of SVM model was 0.747 (kappa was 0.588) and the accuracy of LSTM model was 0.755 (kappa was 0.612). Running cross-validation for SVM model took less than 1 s, but running cross-validation for LSTM model took more 1000 s. When the two models were blended, the performance was slightly improved (accuracy was 0.766, kappa was 0.625). The accuracies were relatively low because we had three levels of grades. To further improve the grading accuracy, the two original models were combined in the way described earlier. The combined model graded 77.72% short-answers. Out of the graded answers, the accuracy was 0.836 and the kappa was 0.726.

In order to figure out how much data for each model to achieve a stable performance, the correlation between the size of training data and the accuracy of the classifier was illustrated in Fig. 1. The graphs implied that the trained model started to perform stably after half of the data had been used in training, which was about 267 graded short-answers.

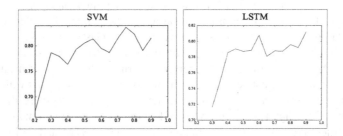

Fig. 1. The correlation between the size of training data and the accuracy

In general, both of SVM and LSTM performed well according to their kappa, and LSTM performed slightly better than SVM in this case. Given that LSTM used much less number of features, and the features were more straightforward, LSTM is probably a better choice in practice. Indeed, training LSTM model took much longer time, but techniques like Hadoop and GPU computing could potentially reduce its training time significantly. Despite of their performance, both of the algorithms need similar size of training data to achieve a stable performance. It means that for a grading task with three different levels, about 300 labeled training entries are need to have the auto-grading mechanism work. It provides an impression of when we should consider establishing auto-grading models. Clearly, it does not make any sense if an instructor only wants to grade answers for a single class. Indeed, more questions are needed to make the estimation of the size of training data more accurate and convincing. But our work perhaps can remind other researchers pay attention on this important aspect while applying machine learning algorithms in education.

When the two models were combined together, although the combined model failed to label 22.28% of the answers, the grading accuracy was improved significantly. In practice, we may have strict criteria on the reliability of grading, but full automation is not required. The innovative combining way then can be considered in this case.

5 Conclusion

With the help of NLP techniques and advanced machine learning algorithms, we managed to auto-grade short-answers without a rubric. By studying the correlations between classifier performance and the size of training data, we made a rough estimation on the size of training data for building stable auto-grading models. We also implemented a method that can significantly improve auto-grading algorithms by sacrificing some automation.

Acknowledgement. We are grateful to Prof. Ningning Zhao for her providing us the dataset.

References

1. Leacock, C., Chodorow, M.: C-rater: automated scoring of short-answer questions. Comput. Humanit. **37**(4), 389–405 (2003)
2. Graesser, A.C., Lu, S., Jackson, G.T., Mitchell, H.H., Ventura, M., Olney, A., Louwerse, M.M.: AutoTutor: a tutor with dialogue in natural language. Behav. Res. Methods **36**(2), 180–192 (2004)
3. Cai, Z., Gong, Y., Qiu, Q., Hu, X., Graesser, A.: Making autotutor agents smarter: autotutor answer clustering and iterative script authoring. In: Traum, D., Swartout, W., Khooshabeh, P., Kopp, S., Scherer, S., Leuski, A. (eds.) IVA 2016. LNCS, vol. 10011, pp. 438–441. Springer, Cham (2016). doi:10.1007/978-3-319-47665-0_50
4. Geigle, C., Zhai, C., Ferguson, D.C.: An exploration of automated grading of complex assignments. In: Proceedings of the Third ACM Conference on Learning@ Scale, pp. 351–360. ACM (2016)
5. Googfellow, I., Bengio, Y., Courville, A.: Deep Learning. MIT Press, Cambridge (2016)
6. Jieba GitHub page. https://github.com/fxsjy/jieba. Accessed 14 Mar 2017

Regional Cultural Differences in How Students Customize Their Avatars in Technology-Enhanced Learning

Evelyn Yarzebinski[1](✉), Cristina Dumdumaya[2],
Ma. Mercedes T. Rodrigo[2], Noboru Matsuda[3], and Amy Ogan[1]

[1] Human-Computer Interaction Institute,
Carnegie Mellon University, Pittsburgh, USA
{eey2,aeo}@cs.cmu.edu
[2] Department of Information Systems and Computer Science,
Ateneo de Manila University, Quezon City, Philippines
cedumdumaya@usep.edu.ph, mrodrigo@ateneo.edu
[3] College of Education and Human Development,
Texas A&M University, College Station, USA
noboru.matsuda@tamu.edu

Abstract. As AIED systems with agents and avatars are used by students in different world regions, we expect students to prefer ones that look like them according to the Similarity Attraction Hypothesis. We investigate this effect via a system with a customizable avatar deployed in 2 US regions and 2 Philippines regions. We find that US students do customize as expected, while students in the Philippines tend to select names and hairstyles from outside their culture. These results show the need for more nuanced system design to tailor options for regional-level preferences.

Keywords: Avatar · Personalized learning systems · Culture

1 Introduction and Related Work

Intelligent systems are now being distributed globally as classroom tools to support personalized learning. Many such systems now include an embedded pedagogical agent as part of the learning experience. Prior work has explored students' choices regarding these agents, in particular investigating the Similarity-Attraction Hypothesis (SAH), which states that people tend to be more attracted to those who match their personality and even physical characteristics [1]. For example, in a study of human tutoring, Hispanic students thought the most critical teacher quality was to "be Hispanic", indicating a desire for educators to be from the same background [2]. An investigation of the same principle with digital instructors found that minority students were much more likely to choose same-ethnicity agents than their Caucasian peers, yet those same students tended to have lower learning gains and ratings of the program than those who chose different-ethnicity agents [3]. However, the agents were preset rather than customized, and the ethnicities investigated were only within the US.

© Springer International Publishing AG 2017
E. André et al. (Eds.): AIED 2017, LNAI 10331, pp. 598–601, 2017.
DOI: 10.1007/978-3-319-61425-0_73

A related recent avatar study looked at how children in different cultures created their own avatar from scratch, but only evaluated the SAH with respect to gender; other results showed that e.g., Pakistani children drew more fantasy characters [4].

In this work we investigate how students customize an agent's appearance acrossregions in the US and Philippines. Students first customize the virtual partner they want to work with, including features like their peer's hairstyle and name. This system, SimStudent, has been successfully deployed in numerous studies in the US to teach math [5] and in contrast in the Philippines, where prior analysis of natural language system interactions revealed a very different population from typical US deployments [6]. Here we analyze students' hairstyle and name selections to answer: (1) Do students in different cultures customize their peer's avatar according to the SAH? (2) When given no constraints, do students select names in accordance with the SAH? We investigate the hypothesis that cross-cultural variation will be greater than within-culture variation, as a sub-hypothesis of the SAH. In this paper, we focus on *how* students customize avatars; future work should address related learning gains.

2 Methodology

We deployed SimStudent in five schools in two US states (3 in Pennsylvania [PA], 2 in Texas [TX]), and three schools in two Philippines states (2 in Luzon [LZ], 1 in Mindanao [MD]). These sites represent a range of student ethnicities, SES, and urban/rural areas. Based on the 2005 US census, ethnicities in TX were: 79.7% White and 12.5% Black/African American. Of these, 38.8% are Hispanic. In the same census, PA reported a 82.6% White and 11.7% Black/African American population. Of these, 6.8% are Hispanic. Philippines regional demographics are reported using different categories; we collapse across these categories to arrive at 96–100% Asian in LZ, with up to 4% as "Other", and 82–99% Asian in MD, with up to 18% "Other".

778 students ages 12 to 15 created avatars (TX = 104, PA = 428, LZ = 174, MD = 72). To understand the source of names that students used, we consulted lists of popular names in the US and the Philippines. Not all given names were included on these lists, so two team members (American and Filipina) coded the names, revising codes until they reached interrater reliability of $\kappa = 0.73$. Codes were: *Similar*: common names for children in my culture; *Dissimilar*: uncommon names for children in my culture; *Global*: names with distribution across cultures (including celebrity names); and *Nonsense*: not typically a name (i.e., wrestlinggod). We additionally coded for *Hispanic* to differentiate orthographically Hispanic names, since many of the deployment sites have heavy Hispanic influences. Finally, we grouped hairstyles by color to prune to 5 meaningful categories (Table 1).

Table 1. The 12 hair options, grouped by color.

3 Results

We ran hierarchical χ^2 tests, starting with All Sites, then moving to Country Level, with χ^2 tests for Philippines vs US, then moving to State Level, with separate χ^2 tests for Philippines states (LZ vs MD sites) and US states (PA vs TX sites). The χ^2 tests reveal significant differences in how students in each group customized their virtual peer's avatar. Most notably, the χ^2 test for **name selection** is significant at the top level (across all 8 sites) $\chi^2(28, N = 778) = 260.65$, $p < 0.001$, between the two countries $\chi^2(4, N = 778) = 219.3$, $p < 0.001$), and across US states $\chi^2(4, N = 532) = 13.8$, $p < 0.01$), but not across Philippines states $\chi^2(4, N = 246) = 9.0$, n.s.). There were no significant differences between sites in PA $\chi^2(8,N = 428) = 12.4$, n.s.) or in TX $\chi^2(4, N = 104) = 1.5$, n.s.), meaning that 3 distinct groups emerge for name source, confirmed with a final test $\chi^2(8, N = 778) = 233.53$, $p < 0.001$. Standardized residuals show observed values that are significantly different from the expected values if the residual is beyond ± 2 (see Table 2). These are calculated as: $(N_{observed} - N_{expected})/\sqrt{N_{expected}}$. Results show the significant categories in these locations are: Philippines sites (more Dissimilar + Global, fewer Similar), PA sites (more Similar, fewer Dissimilar + Global), and TX sites (more Hispanic, fewer Dissimilar + Global).

Similar patterns emerge for hairstyle. There are significant differences in students' **hairstyle selections** at the top level (all 8 sites), $\chi^2(28, N = 778) = 74.2$, $p < 0.001$; between the two countries, $\chi^2(4, N = 778) = 30.9$, $p < 0.001$; and across both Philippines states $\chi^2(4, N = 246) = 9.7$, $p < 0.05$) and both US states $\chi^2(4, N = 532) = 12.2$, $p < 0.05$. The significance again drops off after the state level, leaving 4 distinct groups for hairstyle choice, which were confirmed by a final test, $\chi^2(12, N = 778) = 53.1$, $p < 0.001$. Standardized residuals flag significant selections in: LZ (more hat, less blonde), MD (more black, less red), PA (more blonde + red), and TX (less hat). The reduction in significance after the state level implies that students in a state area are choosing similar hairstyles and types of names, yet in ways that are distinct from students in other states.

Table 2. Summary of χ^2 analyses for each site: Philippines sites MD and LZ, and US Sites PA and TX. Values listed are $N_{observed}/N_{expected}$; Standardized Residuals.

	χ^2 results: name selection				
Site	Similar	Dissimilar	Global	Hispanic	Nonsense
Philippines	93/166.3; −5.69*	68/25.6; 8.38*	55/22.4; 6.87*	9/10.8; −0.53	21/20.9; 0.03
PA	357/289.4; 3.98*	11/44.6; −5.03*	14/39.1; −4.01*	14/18.7; −1.09	32/36.3; −0.72
TX	76/70.3; 0.68	2/10.8; −2.68*	2/9.5; −2.43*	11/4.5; 3.03*	13/8.8; 1.41
	χ^2 results: hairstyle selection				
Site	Black	Brown	Blonde	Red	Hat
LZ	97/94.8; 0.22	33/28.2; 0.91	16/30; −2.55*	8/11; −0.89	20/10.1; 3.13*
MD	53/39.2; 2.20*	8/11.7; −1.07	7/12.4; −1.53	0/4.5; −2.13*	4/4.2; −0.08
PA	216/233.3; −1.13	62/69.3; −0.88	91/73.7; 2.01*	39/27; 2.32*	20/24.8; −0.96
TX	58/56.7; 0.18	23/16.8; 1.5	20/17.9; 0.49	2/6.6; -1.78	1/6.0; −2.04*

* = Standardized residuals significantly beyond the ± 2 threshold.

4 Conclusion

We found that students in different world regions customized and named their virtual peer's avatar in patterns similar to those in their own region, but different from those in other regions. Our findings confirm prior work that in the United States, students tended to select their peers' appearance according to the similarity-attraction hypothesis by state (including a higher proportion of Hispanic names in TX, a US region with a large Hispanic population, and blond hairstyles in PA, which has the highest percentage of Caucasian residents). However Filipino/a students instead drew names from other cultures. One possible explanation for why students at American sites used names from within their own culture but Filipino/a students did not may be due to historical effects of colonization in the Philippines, plus the broadening reach of American culture worldwide. This particular finding is inconsistent with other prior work and deserves further investigation. In fact, Moreno and Flowerday hypothesize that: "if the social cues represented in the same-ethnicity [agent] are not consistent with students' expectations, their perceptions about the program are hurt as well," leading to the lower learning gains seen in their study [3]. Therefore, future work will additionally consider the effects of customization on learning gains to reveal whether these effects hold at a regional level. One important implication of this work is that developers modifying personalized learning systems for use in other areas may need to consider regional-level nuances when providing options for agent customization.

Acknowledgements. We thank the Jacobs Foundation, NSF grant 1643185 and ALLS, DISCS, and ACED of the Ateneo de Manila University for their generous support of this research.

References

1. Byrne, D., Nelson, D.: Attraction as a linear function of proportion of positive reinforcements. J. Pers. Soc. Psychol. **1**(6), 659 (1965)
2. Espinoza-Herold, M.: Issues in latino education: Race, school culture, and the politics of academic success. Allyn & Bacon, Boston, MA (2003)
3. Moreno, R., Flowerday, T.: Students' choice of animated pedagogical agents in science learning: a test of the similarity-attraction hypothesis on gender and ethnicity. Contemp. Educ. Psychol. **31**(2), 186–207 (2006)
4. John, M.S., Arroyo, I., Zualkernan, I.A., Woolf, B.P.: Children creating pedagogical avatars: cross-cultural differences in drawings and language. In: AIED Workshop on Culturally-Aware Tutoring Systems (2013)
5. Matsuda, N., Yarzebinski, E., Keiser, V., Raizada, R., William, W.C., Stylianides, G.J., Koedinger, K.R.: Cognitive anatomy of tutor learning: lessons learned with SimStudent. J. Educ. Psychol. **105**(4), 1152–1163 (2013)
6. Yarzebinski, E., Ogan, A., Rodrigo, M.M.T., Matsuda, N.: Understanding students' use of code-switching in a learning by teaching technology. In: Conati, C., Heffernan, N., Mitrovic, A., Verdejo, M.F. (eds.) AIED 2015. LNCS, vol. 9112, pp. 504–513. Springer, Cham (2015). doi:10.1007/978-3-319-19773-9_50

Doctoral Consortium Papers

Teaching Informal Logical Fallacy Identification with a Cognitive Tutor

Nicholas Diana[✉], Michael Eagle, John Stamper, and Kenneth R. Koedinger

Human-Computer Interaction Institute, Carnegie Mellon University,
5000 Forbes Avenue, Pittsburgh, PA 15213, USA
{ndiana,koedinger}@cmu.edu, meagle@cs.cmu.edu, john@stamper.org

Abstract. In this age of fake news and alternative facts, the need for a citizenry capable of critical thinking has never been greater. While teaching critical thinking skills in the classroom remains an enduring challenge, research on an ill-defined domain like critical thinking in the educational technology space is even more scarce. We propose a difficulty factors assessment (DFA) to explore two factors that may make learning to identify fallacies more difficult: type of instruction and belief bias. This study will allow us to make two key contributions. First, we will better understand the relationship between sense-making and induction when learning to identify informal fallacies. Second, we will contribute to the limited work examining the impact of belief bias on informal (rather than formal) reasoning. The results of this DFA will also be used to improve the next iteration of our fallacy tutor, which may ultimately contribute to a computational model of informal fallacies.

Keywords: Cognitive tutors · Informal logical fallacies · Informal reasoning · Cognitive task analysis · Difficulty factors assessment

1 Introduction

Despite the recognized importance of critical thinking in traditional education, critical thinking is largely absent from the educational technology space (e.g., online courses/MOOCs, cognitive tutoring systems, etc.). Some of the recent work on critical thinking in educational technology has focused on comparing critical thinking in face-to-face and computer-mediated interactions. Researchers often use content-analysis to identify instances of critical thinking in online and face-to-face discussions [3,10]. In this work, critical thinking is not the primary focus of the course, but rather an epiphenomenon.

Other work, particularly in the domains of philosophy, writing and law, has addressed critical thinking more directly. For example, some recent work has demonstrated that argument diagramming using a graphical interface improved argumentative writing skills [6] as well as critical thinking skills more generally [5]. However, similar gains are seen using paper-and-pencil argument diagramming as well, suggesting the software may be more of a convenience than an necessary factor [4].

© Springer International Publishing AG 2017
E. André et al. (Eds.): AIED 2017, LNAI 10331, pp. 605–608, 2017.
DOI: 10.1007/978-3-319-61425-0_74

Despite the challenges of working in an ill-defined domain [8], another intersection of critical thinking and e-learning has been in intelligent tutoring systems (ITS). For example, Ashley and Aleven [1] built an ITS to teach law students to argue with cases more effectively. The study we propose extends this work on critical thinking in the ITS space to a more general population. We will build a cognitive tutor that teaches users to identify several common informal logical fallacies. We chose informal fallacies because they offer a degree of structure to the otherwise ill-defined domain of informal reasoning, making the content more amenable for use in a cognitive tutor. Using this tutor, we will conduct a difficulty factors assessment (a type of a cognitive task analysis) [7] to evaluate the impact of two factors on the user's ability to identify logical fallacies.

The first factor explored will be *type of instruction*. The Knowledge-Learning-Instruction (KLI) framework lists three types of learning processes, and suggests that the best instruction for teaching a specific skill depends on the type of process used to learn that skill. The purpose of the *type of instruction* manipulation is to better understand the learning processes that underpin the identification of logical fallacies. Specifically, we are interested in whether this skill is more efficiently learned using induction (e.g., showing many examples of the fallacy) or sense-making (e.g., providing detailed descriptions of the fallacy's mechanics). Textbooks used to teach logical fallacies often take both approaches, giving readers an explanation of a fallacy followed by some small number of examples. As this skill may consist of multiple, more fundamental skills (or knowledge components), the mixed approach used by textbooks may prove to be the most efficient. Nevertheless, the proportion of time to devote to each learning process remains an open question that this experiment may help answer.

The second factor that may negatively impact a student's ability to identify logical fallacies is *belief bias*, the tendency to judge arguments more favorably if we agree with the conclusion. Early work on belief bias explored its effect on formal reasoning using syllogisms [2,9], but there is some evidence that suggests that belief bias may operate differently in informal reasoning [11]. The proposed study builds on and contributes to this research by empirically testing the effect of belief bias on learning to identify informal fallacies.

2   Future Research Plans

2.1   Difficulty Factors Assessment

We will use a Difficulty Factors Assessment (DFA) to identify the factors (if any) that make it more or less difficult for students to learn how to identify logical fallacies. The proposed experiment will explore the impact of two primary factors as well as several secondary factors.

Type of Instruction. The proposed experiment will explore the impact of *type of instruction* by randomly assigning each participant to one of three conditions. In each condition, when the participant is given a problem and asked to identify the logical fallacy, they will be given a set of possible answers and the option to view more information about each of the answers. In the first condition, when participants ask for more information they will be shown a brief, but detailed description of the mechanics of each fallacy (sense-making). In the second condition, participants will be shown two examples of each fallacy (induction). In the third condition, participants will be shown a description and one example for each fallacy (mixed).

In addition to comparing the effect of increased examples between groups, we will be able to compare this effect within groups by treating completed problems as viewed examples. This analysis will help us pinpoint the average number of examples needed to be able to identify the fallacies used in the experiment, and compare that number to the average numbers seen in common textbooks.

Belief Bias. The proposed experiment will explore the impact of *belief bias* on a student's ability to identify logical fallacies by altering the political orientation of problem content and comparing performance on those problems with the participant's personal political orientation. Of the 36 problems presented, half will be apolitical (i.e., politically neutral) and half will be political. Of the political problems, half will have a conservative orientation, half a liberal orientation. The apolitical problems are also split into two categories (for and issue or against an issue) for balance. Problems can be broken down into three subcomponents: the prompt (either political or apolitical), the fallacy, and the conclusion (either for/against or conservative/liberal). Table 1 shows the breakdown of each problem.

Table 1. Breakdown of the problems used in the tutor. Note that *(F)*, *(A)*, *(C)*, and *(L)* correspond to *for, against, conservative* and *liberal*, respectively. For example, in the first cell of the table, we see an *apolitical* prompt, which *fallacy 1* is used to argue *for*.

	Apolitical	Political	Apolitical	Political	Apolitical	Political
Fallacy 1	(F)	(C)	(A)	(L)	(F)	(C)
Fallacy 2	(A)	(L)	(F)	(C)	(A)	(L)
Fallacy 3	(F)	(C)	(A)	(L)	(F)	(C)
Fallacy 4	(A)	(L)	(F)	(C)	(A)	(L)
Fallacy 5	(F)	(C)	(A)	(L)	(F)	(C)
Fallacy 6	(A)	(L)	(F)	(C)	(A)	(L)

Secondary Factors Explored. In addition to the main effects of *type of instruction* and *belief bias*, our design also allows us to explore several secondary factors. We can test whether *type of instruction* has a differential effect on specific fallacies. For example, sense-making may be more important for learning to identify a circular argument, while examples may be sufficient for learning to identify a Post Hoc fallacy. We can also test whether participants are more likely to identify a fallacy given the nature of the prompt (political vs. apolitical) or the valence of the conclusion (for/against or conservative/liberal).

Towards a Computational Model of Logical Fallacies. We hope that the results of this difficulty factors assessment will: (1) help us to better understand the factors that promote and hinder learning to identify informal logical fallacies, and (2) allow us to incorporate those findings into an improved iteration of our tutor. The ultimate goal is a cognitive tutor that can be used to train crowd-workers to classify a large number of examples of informal logical fallacies in the media. Those labeled examples can then be used to develop a computational model of informal logical fallacies.

References

1. Ashley, K.D., Aleven, V.: Toward an intelligent tutoring system for teaching law students to argue with cases. In: Proceedings of the 3rd International Conference on Artificial Intelligence and Law, pp. 42–52. ACM (1991)
2. Evans, J.S., Barston, J.L., Pollard, P.: On the conflict between logic and belief in syllogistic reasoning. Mem. Cogn. 11(3), 295–306 (1983)
3. Guiller, J., Durndell, A., Ross, A.: Peer interaction and critical thinking: face-to-face or online discussion? Learn. Instr. 18, 187–200 (2008)
4. Harrell, M.: No computer program required: even pencil-and-paper argument mapping improves critical-thinking skills. Teach. Philos. 31(4), 351–374 (2008)
5. Harrell, M.: Assessing the efficacy of argument diagramming to teach critical thinking skills in introduction to philosophy. Inq. Crit. Thinking Across Disciplines 27(2), 31–39 (2012)
6. Harrell, M., Wetzel, D.: Improving first-year writing using argument diagramming. In: Proceedings of the 35th Annual Conference of the Cognitive Science Society, pp. 2488–2493 (1987, 2013)
7. Koedinger, K.R., Terao, A.: A cognitive task analysis of using pictures to support pre-algebraic reasoning. In: Proceedings of the Twenty-Fourth Annual Conference of the Cognitive Science Society, pp. 542–547. Citeseer (2002)
8. Lynch, C., Ashley, K., Aleven, V., Pinkwart, N.: Defining ill-defined domains; a literature survey. In: Proceedings of the Workshop on Intelligent Tutoring Systems for Ill-Defined Domains at the 8th International Conference on Intelligent Tutoring Systems, pp. 1–10 (2006)
9. Morgan, J.J.B., Morton, J.T.: The distortion of syllogistic reasoning produced by personal convictions. J. Soc. Psychol. 20(1), 39–59 (1944)
10. Newman, D.R., Webb, B., Cochrane, C.: A content analysis method to measure critical thinking in face-to-face and computer supported group learning. Interpersonal Comput. Technol. 3, 56–77 (1993, 1995)
11. Thompson, V., Evans, J.S.B.T.: Belief bias in informal reasoning. Thinking Reasoning 18(3), 278–310 (2012)

Digital Learning Projection

Learning Performance Estimation from Multimodal Learning Experiences.

Daniele Di Mitri[✉]

Welten Institute, Research Centre for Learning, Teaching and Technology,
Open University of the Netherlands, Heerlen, The Netherlands
`Daniele.Dimitri@ou.nl`

Abstract. Multiple modalities of the learning process can now be captured on real-time through wearable and contextual sensors. By annotating these multimodal data (the input space) by expert assessments or self-reports (the output space), machine learning models can be trained to predict the learning performance. This can lead to continuous formative assessment and feedback generation, which can be used to personalise and contextualise content, improve awareness and support informed decisions about learning.

1 The Problem

Digital tools used for learning leave multiple data traces which can be scrutinised to derive meaningful insights that can improve teaching and learning [7]. This approach is at the basis of the learning analytics research. However, looking exclusively at the data available from one system risks to incur into the so-called "streetlight effect", i.e. searching for the lost key in the darkness only under the street lights, these being the only visible spots. The majority of learning management systems (LMSs) used for gathering educational data were not designed with analytics in mind: the digital traces that they record are poorly explanatory of the actual learning. In addition, modern learning is not limited to one single platform but is distributed across several media and resources [10]: there is a lot more happening "beyond the LMS" which needs to be taken into account [8]; for example the knowledge exchange happening in social media platforms [6]. Furthermore, learning is ubiquitous [2]: it happens everywhere, not only online in the "virtual world" (the digital space) but also offline, in the "real world" (the physical space) [3]. If we exclude from the domain of analysis moments like reading a book, having a face-to-face meeting and all the "offline" activities that do not leave immediate digital footprints as they are not mediated by digital devices, we end up jeopardising the digital representation of the learning process. Hence, new data must be generated by observing multiple modalities of learning; that will eventually lead us towards a more complex data representation which can be the basis for analysis and inference. The Internet of Things approach, can support this challenge. Several sensors and

E. André et al. (Eds.): AIED 2017, LNAI 10331, pp. 609–612, 2017.
DOI: 10.1007/978-3-319-61425-0_75

microprocessors can be used and applied also in education for capturing learning fragments and translating them into data [9]. Head movements, gaze, vital signals (heart rate, skin conductance, EEG), posture, gestures, handwriting, spoken words. All these "behavioural particles" have very low semantics if considered singularly [5], but if combined and integrated with information about the learning context and activity can become fine grained "digital projections" which can be mined and analysed with the aim to generate feedback and automatise formative assessment. This multimodal data collection has been conceptualised by Blikstein [1] with the name of *multimodal learning analytics*. Each modality requires an unique approach of collection, modelling and analysis. Some of these data streams are continuous and auto correlated (e.g. heart rate). Some other signals are occasional, voluntary human activities which should be seen as sequences of events happening randomly rather than continuous streams. The chronological order by which the different voluntary actions are performed can play a role in determining the success of learning performances. The actions are observed are executed in random order and have a sparse distribution. There is also an high inter-subject variance i.e. each learner executes a set of actions substantially different from their peers. To conclude time-dependent observations are useful to keep track of different learning moments of the learning journey as well as for discovering recurrent action-patterns.

2   Proposed Solution

The exposed background lead us to envision the Blueprint of Cognitive Inference through a multimodal digital projection. The core idea consists in inferring the intangible cognition and knowledge of the learners. The catch consists in back-tracking what is intangible, namely the human mind processes which underpin learning, by projecting in the digital space what is tangible, namely all the measurable modalities which surround learning. The approach is represented in Fig. 1 and consists of four phases. The first step is the *digital projection*, that happens when all the attributes of learning happening across physical and digital spaces are digitalised into data by mean of sensors and trackers. The second

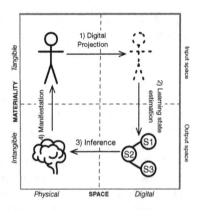

Fig. 1. Blueprint of Cognitive Inference

step corresponds to the exploitation of the collected data with data-intensive methods. It grounds its logic in the machine learning and autonomous agents theories. The idea is that by observing how people learn and how they perform in learning it is possible, with the help of machines to learn generalisation models, which based on history can estimate the current learning performance. This approach requires to clarify both the selected attributes (the input space) as well as the learning performance that is the output space of the model. The third step corresponds to the cognitive inference, which is the derivation of learner's affect and cognition, characterises in the learning process. This dimension is intangible and implicit as the processes take place in the human brain. Finally the last step refers to the link existing between cognitive states and the behaviour manifested in learning, the process through which being in a certain phase of the learning process influences physiological responses and behaviours.

2.1   Design and Methods

The research project lasts four years and consists in four main tasks: (1) a preliminary experiment, (2) a literature literature review, (3) a technology prototype and a (4) main experiment.

(1) Preliminary experiment – *"Learning Pulse: a machine learning approach for predicting performance in self-regulated learning using multimodal data"* [4], accepted as full paper at LAK17 combined data like heart rate, step count, weather condition and learning activity and looked whether they can be used to predict self-reported learning performance (stress, productivity and flow) in self-regulated learning settings. The insights got from this study grounded this research proposal.

(2) Framework – Planned literature review to search for similar multimodal data experiment and related learning performance used. This information should then be compiled into a framework that aim to establish of a new paradigm of investigation of learning: predictive applications using real-time multimodal data collection and machine learning methods. This framework will report on: techniques used to collect data, learning performance indicators used, data analysis approaches used and results.

(3) Technology prototype – Wearable Experience for Knowledge Intensive Training (WEKIT) is a European project (Horizon 2020, 2.7M Euro) whose aim is to develop and test a novel way of industrial training through smart wearable technology and augmented reality. The core of this project consists in developing an *Experience capturing API* by wiring the smart glasses (Microsoft Hololens) with different wearable sensors through a software architecture which will enable to capture, annotate, re-enact practical learning experiences.

(4) Main experiment – Planned experiment, doctor training using manikins: trainees are guided through this simulation program and need to fulfil some check-lists (e.g. checking heart rate, injecting medications). The multi-sensor scenario which these training labs provide is an ideal setup for using the WEKIT prototype. The aim is to track both the expert doctors and the trainees, checking movement, speed, precision and trying with machine learning techniques to predict their performance.

3   Main Contribution

This research can bring added value to education and learning, especially in work and practice based learning settings. While data-driven applications are proliferating, there is yet no integrated vision for using data to support processes like learning. With this research we show how to connect tangible and multimodal events to intangible cognitive abstractions which we name learning performance. If machine learning models are trained to estimate the learning performance accurately enough, that would allow to create personal cognitive tutors which can automatically assess the learner in a formative way by identifying where the learner stands in the process. This information can be used for personalisation, contextualisation or for just increasing awareness about the learning process.

4 Questions to Reviewers

Is the proposal sound and relevant for the AIED research community? In your knowledge were there similar research conducted? How to frame the proposal and the research questions in more clear boundaries? How to prevent the *garbage-in-garbage-out* effect when dealing with noisy sensors?

References

1. Blikstein, P.: Multimodal learning analytics. In: Proceedings of the Third International Conference on Learning Analytics and Knowledge - LAK 2013, p. 102 (2013). http://dl.acm.org.myaccess.library.utoronto.ca/citation.cfm?id=2460296.2460316
2. Bruce, B.C.: Ubiquitous learning, ubiquitous computing, and lived experience. In: International Conference of Networked Learning, pp. 583–590 (2007)
3. Delgado-Kloos, C., Hernández-Leo, D., Asensio-Pérez, J.I.: Technology for learning across physical and virtual spaces J. UCS Special Issue. J. Univ. Comput. Sci. **18**(15), 2093–2096 (2012)
4. Di Mitri, D., Scheffel, M., Drachsler, H., Börner, D., Ternier, S., Specht, M.: Learning Pulse: a machine learning approach for predicting performance in self-regulated learning using multimodal data. In: LAK 2017 Proceedings of the 7th International Conference on Learning Analytics and Knowledge (2017)
5. Dillenbourg, P.: The evolution of research on digital education. Int. J. Artif. Intell. Educ.**26**(2), 544–560 (2016). http://dx.doi.org/10.1007/s40593-016-0106-z
6. Ferguson, R., Shum, S.B.: Social learning analytics. In: Proceedings of the 2nd International Conference on Learning Analytics and Knowledge - LAK 2012, pp. 23–33 (2012). http://dl.acm.org/citation.cfm?doid=2330601.2330616
7. Greller, W., Drachsler, H.: Translating learning into numbers : a generic framework for learning analytics author contact details. Educ. Technol. Soc. **15**(3), 42–57 (2012)
8. Pardo, A., Kloos, C.D.: Stepping out of the box: towards analytics outside the learning management system. In: 1st International Conference on Learning Analytics and Knowledge (LAK11), pp. 163–167 (2011)
9. Schneider, J., Börner, D., van Rosmalen, P., Specht, M.: Augmenting the senses: a review on sensor-based learning support. Sensors **15**(2), 4097–4133 (2015)
10. Suthers, D., Rosen, D.: A unified framework for multi-level analysis of distributed learning. In: Proceedings of the 1st International Conference on Learning Analytics and Knowledge - LAK 2011, pp. 64–74. ACM (2011)

Learning with Engaging Activities via a Mobile Python Tutor

Geela Venise Firmalo Fabic$^{(\boxtimes)}$, Antonija Mitrovic,
and Kourosh Neshatian

Department of Computer Science and Software Engineering,
University of Canterbury, Christchurch, New Zealand
geela.fabic@pg.canterbury.ac.nz,
{tanja.mitrovic,kourosh.neshatian}@canterbury.ac.nz

Abstract. This paper presents work on a new mobile Python tutor – *PyKinetic*. The tutor is designed to be used by novices, as a complement to traditional labs and lectures. PyKinetic currently contains one type of activity – Parsons problems, which require learners to re-order lines of code to produce a desired output. We present results of studies conducted to evaluate the usability and effectiveness of PyKinetic for learning. The enthusiasm from the participants was encouraging. We have also evaluated menu-based self-explanation prompts in PyKinetic. Results revealed that participants significantly improved their scores from pre- to post-test. Furthermore, participants who self-explained learned more than those who did not. We aim to develop more activities for PyKinetic to support code reading and code writing skills. We also plan to improve the tutor by providing engaging features to maximise learning, and to provide adaptive pedagogical support. Evaluation studies will also be conducted for future versions of PyKinetic.

Keywords: Mobile python tutor · Parsons problems · Self-explanation

1 Introduction

It takes about ten years for one to become an expert programmer [1]. Novice learners find it difficult to grasp programming concepts, which may lower their motivation to learn more. Moreover, most novice programmers of this age are millennials, who usually have short attention spans [2]. It is essential for educators to explore more effective avenues in teaching programming catered to millennial novice programmers.

Python is a popular programming language, widely used nowadays to teach introductory programming, especially in the United States [3]. In New Zealand and Australia, a survey conducted in 2013 on 38 introductory programming courses revealed that majority of the courses are taught using Python [4]. This project aims to develop a mobile tutor hoping that it would appeal better to new generation of students, compared to desktop or Web-based educational tools. Apart from the booming popularity of smart phones, a mobile tutor could potentially be an effective vessel for engaging activities, which is one of the emphases of our project. The aim is not to focus on the strengths of a mobile device, but to use it effectively to the best of its advantages

© Springer International Publishing AG 2017
E. André et al. (Eds.): AIED 2017, LNAI 10331, pp. 613–616, 2017.
DOI: 10.1007/978-3-319-61425-0_76

for the tutor. The goals of our project are to: (R1) investigate the effectiveness of a mobile tutor with engaging activities to maximize learning, (R2) explore different activities for improving code reading, and code writing skills. Section 2 presents some background, while Sect. 3 describes PyKinetic and the studies we have performed.

2 Background

Parsons problems [5] are programming exercises which require a given set of randomized lines of code to be rearranged towards producing the expected output, usually by a drag and drop motion. Parsons problems are fitting for a mobile device and for novices since Lines Of Code (LOCs) only need to be rearranged to form the solution. Similarly, Ihantola et al. [7, 8] perceived the same insight and have developed Parsons problems for both mobile and web interfaces. Parsons problems have many variations, such as problems with and without scaffolding (curly braces and/or indentations), with and without distractors (extra lines of code) and limited editing of lines [6–9].

Self-explanation (SE), first introduced as open-ended questions, is an activity which requires the student to reason about the problem and generate justifications which are not directly presented by the material to promote deeper learning [10]. Self-explanation has been shown to improve learning outcomes in many domains, such as in database modeling [11], data normalization [12] and electrical circuits [13]. However, some studies like that of Johnson and Mayer [13] show that open-ended SE is not always suitable. They compared open-ended SE prompts to menu-based SE prompts using a computer application teaching electric circuits in a game-like environment. Participants were randomly assigned to an open-based SE group, menu-based SE group and without SE group. Their results revealed that menu-based SE group outperformed both the open-based SE group and without SE group [13].

3 PyKinetic

We have developed a mobile Python tutor, PyKinetic [14], which is designed to be a fun way for novices to learn Python while "on the go", and as a complement to lecture and lab-based courses. PyKinetic is developed using Android SDK and teaches Python 3.x. We have developed PyKinetic with three variants of Parsons problems: regular problems, problems with distractors, and with incomplete LOCs. The first prototype of PyKinetic contained 53 Parsons problems, with 0 up to a maximum of five distractors. The number of LOCs in problems ranges from 3 to 16.

We conducted a pilot study with students enrolled in an introductory programming course in Python and tutors involved in the same course. The pilot study had two goals: to evaluate the usability and the interface of the first prototype, and identify and compare strategies used by novices and experts. As expected, experts outperformed the novices in terms of speed and problem-solving strategies. Experts demonstrated having a mental model of the solution by moving LOCs in the correct order from top to bottom. On the other hand, novices displayed strategies showing lack of knowledge, such as trial and error, and moving lines based on indentations. Furthermore, enthusiasm from the participants was encouraging, with seven out of eight novices and two out of five experts interested to use the tutor again [15].

The current version of PyKinetic offers incomplete LOCs, and provides menu-based SE prompts after every correctly answered incomplete LOC [16]. An evaluation study was conducted in 2016. We recruited 83 volunteers: 13 high school students from Middleton Grange School and university students (47 from the University of Canterbury, and 23 from the Ateneo de Manila University). All participants were enrolled in an introductory programming course using Python and have had adequate knowledge for the study. Participants were randomly assigned into two groups, with the only difference between the control and experimental condition being that the latter received SE prompts. The study had two hypotheses: (H1) all participants will improve their Python skills by interacting with PyKinetic, and (H2) the experimental group will have higher learning gains than control group. Sessions were conducted in groups which lasted from 1.5–2 h and had a maximum of 13 participants. The study included a pre-test and post-test completed on paper. Both tests had eight questions: six conceptual questions composed of True/False and multiple choice, and two procedural questions (an output prediction question and a Parsons problem). All actions made during the study in PyKinetic were recorded.

We eliminated data collected from some participants due to unforeseen circumstances. We present results of the data collected from the remaining 76 participants. We used the Mann-Whitney U test to check for a significant difference between the prior knowledge of different populations, and between experimental and control groups. Results showed no difference on pre-test scores between populations and between groups. We used the Wilcoxon Signed Ranks test for measuring learning gains. The results revealed significant improvements for both groups from the pre- to post-test (experimental: $z = -3.315$, $p < .005$; control: $z = -2.45$, $p < .05$). Additionally, there was a significant improvement on conceptual questions ($z = -3.221$, $p < .005$; control: $z = -2.37$, $p < .05$), revealing that hypothesis H1 was supported. The experimental group had significantly higher post-test scores ($U = 529.5$, $p < .05$). Moreover, the normalized gain of the experimental group was also significantly higher ($U = 530$, $p < .05$). We have also calculated the Cohen's d effect size for both groups: experimental $d = .64$, control $d = .34$. Therefore, hypothesis H2 was also supported.

Towards achieving our research goals, other types of activities will be designed and developed, aimed at code reading and code writing skills. Erroneous examples and output prediction exercises are some examples of activities that we will implement in PyKinetic. For addressing our research goal R1, game elements will be introduced targeted to maximize engagement. An adaptive version of PyKinetic is also to be implemented to support enhanced learning experience with personalized problem selection and feedback. The contributions of this project include investigating the effectiveness of a mobile tutor in teaching Python and effective learning activities and pedagogical strategies within a mobile tutor. Several evaluation studies will be conducted with future versions of the tutor.

References

1. Winslow, L.E.: Programming pedagogy—a psychological overview. ACM SIGCSE Bull. **28**(3), 17–22 (1996)
2. Oblinger, D., Oblinger, J.L.: 2 is it age or IT: first steps toward understanding the net generation. In: Oblinger, D., Oblinger, J.L., Lippincott, J.K. (eds.) Educating the Next Generation, pp. 12–31. EDUCAUSE, Boulder, Colorado. (2005)
3. Guo, P.J.: Online python tutor: embeddable web-based program visualization for CS education. In: Proceedings of the 44th ACM Technical Symposium on Computer Science Education, pp. 579–584. ACM
4. Mason, R., Cooper, G.: Introductory programming courses in Australia and New Zealand in 2013-trends and reasons. In: Proceedings of the 16th Australasian Computing Education Conference, vol. 148, pp. 139–147. Australian Computer Society, Inc. (2014)
5. Parsons, D., Haden, P.: Parson's programming puzzles: a fun and effective learning tool for first programming courses. In: Proceedings of the 8th Australasian Conference Computing Education, pp. 157–163. Australian Computer Society (2006)
6. Denny, P., Luxton-Reilly, A., Simon, B.: Evaluating a new exam question: parsons problems. In: Proceedings of the 4th International Workshop on Computing Education Research, pp. 113–124 (2008)
7. Ihantola, P., Karavirta, V.: Two-dimensional parson's puzzles: the concept, tools, and first observations. Inform. Technol. Educ. **10**, IIP 119–IIP 132 (2011)
8. Karavirta, V., J. Helminen, Ihantola, P.: A mobile learning application for parsons problems with automatic feedback. In: Proceedings of the 12th Koli Calling International Conference Computing Education Research, pp. 11–18 (2012)
9. Ihantola, P., Helminen, J., Karavirta, V.: How to study programming on mobile touch devices: interactive python code exercises. In: Proceedings of the 13th Koli Calling International Conference Computing Education Research, pp. 51–58 (2013)
10. Chi, M.T., Bassok, M., Lewis, M.W., Reimann, P., Glaser, R.: Self-explanations: how students study and use examples in learning to solve problems. Cogn. Sci. **13**(2), 145–182 (1989)
11. Weerasinghe, A., Mitrovic, A.: Facilitating deep learning through self-explanation in an open-ended domain. Int. J. Knowl. Based Intell. Eng. Syst. (KES) **10**(1), 3–19 (2006). IOS Press
12. Mitrovic, A.: Scaffolding answer explanation in a data normalization tutor. Facta Univ. Ser. Elec. Energ. **18**(2), 151–163 (2005)
13. Johnson, C.I., Mayer, R.E.: Applying the self-explanation principle to multimedia learning in a computer-based game-like environment. Comput. Hum. Behav. **26**(6), 1246–1252 (2010)
14. Fabic, G., Mitrovic, A., Neshatian, K.: Towards a mobile python tutor: understanding differences in strategies used by novices and experts. In: Proceedings 13th International Conference Intelligent Tutoring Systems, vol. 9684, p. 447. Springer (2016)
15. Fabic, G., Mitrovic, A., Neshatian, K.: Investigating strategies used by novice and expert users to solve Parson's problem in a mobile Python tutor. In: Proceedings of the 9th Workshop on Technology Enhanced Learning by Posing/Solving Problems/Questions PQTEL 2016, pp. 434–444. APSCE (2016)
16. Fabic, G.V.F., Mitrovic, A., Neshatian, K.: Investigating the effectiveness of menu-based self-explanation prompts in a mobile Python Tutor. In: André, E., Baker, R., Hu, X., Rodrigo, M.M.T., du Boulay, B. (eds.) Proceedings of the AIED, vol. 10331, pp. 498–501. Springer, Cham (2017, in print)

Math Reading Comprehension: Comparing Effectiveness of Various Conversation Frameworks in an ITS

Keith T. Shubeck[1(✉)], Ying Fang[1], and Xiangen Hu[1,2]

[1] The University of Memphis, Memphis, TN 38152, USA
`kshubeck@memphis.edu`
[2] Central China Normal University, Wuhan 430079, Hubei, China

Abstract. Conversation based intelligent tutoring systems (ITSs) are highly effective at promoting learning across a wide range of domains. This is in part because these systems allow for the implementation of pedagogical strategies used by expert human tutors (e.g., self-reflection and deep-level reasoning questions). However, the various conversation frameworks used by these ITSs affect high domain knowledge students and low domain knowledge students differently. The experiment proposed in this paper will explore and test the added effectiveness of interactive dialogues and trialogues in learning Algebra I, utilized in a conversation based ITS. The experiment will compare learning across five conditions: (1) a static reading control condition, (2) a vicarious control dialogue condition with animated agents, (3) an interactive dialogue condition (i.e., human learner and tutor agent), (4) an interactive trialogue condition (i.e., human learner, tutor agent, and tutee agent) and (5) a vicarious monologue condition. This research will seek to answer questions concerning the effectiveness of dialogue and trialogue conversation environments in an Algebra 1 domain compared to vicarious learning, and whether trialogues provide an added benefit over dialogues within this domain.

Keywords: Intelligent tutoring systems · Math comprehension · Worked examples · Trialogue

1 Introduction

Over the years, intelligent tutoring systems (ITSs) have been utilized in a variety of ways to foster learning across a multitude of domains. ITSs have ranged from simpler worked-example systems to agent-enhanced and conversation-based systems. A common goal for the development and implementation of many ITSs is to provide effective and individualized learning experiences for both high and low domain knowledge students. The research described in this manuscript aims to garner a better understanding of the differing effects of various conversation frameworks on learners with different knowledge backgrounds. Specifically, the experiment described in this paper will compare learning across several agent-based conversation frameworks: static reading, vicarious monologue, vicarious dialogue, interactive dialogue, and interactive trialogue.

© Springer International Publishing AG 2017
E. André et al. (Eds.): AIED 2017, LNAI 10331, pp. 617–620, 2017.
DOI: 10.1007/978-3-319-61425-0_77

Human tutoring is often referred to as the gold standard of learning environments. The effectiveness of this learning environment is grounded in the constructivist learning theory, which put simply, suggests that learners benefit from being active participants in their learning process. Tutoring environments are also effective because the tutor can adjust to the individual needs of the learner. Students of expert tutors have shown learning gains of 2 sigma when compared to traditional classroom settings (i.e., monologues; Bloom, 1984). ITSs with animated pedagogical agents can be implemented in such a way that utilize the teaching strategies of expert human tutors [1–5]. Implementing these pedagogical strategies in conversation-based intelligent tutoring systems requires natural language processing (NLP), so the tutor-agent can respond appropriately to student input by matching the semantic meaning to a set of ideal answers, common misconceptions, etc.

While previous implementations of these pedagogical strategies in ITSs have seen a good deal of success (e.g., [6]) it should be noted, however, that the benefits of these systems can vary based on student domain knowledge. For example, in a vicarious implementation of agent-based dialogues and monologues, high-domain knowledge students did not appear to benefit as much as low-domain knowledge students in conditions with dialogues (e.g., conversation between a tutor agent and a tutee agent). In fact, the learning of high-domain knowledge students appeared to have been inhibited in the full "deep-level reasoning questions with explanations" condition [5]. High-domain knowledge students appear to suffer from an expertise reversal effect when presented with potentially extraneous information provided by conversations with tutor and/or tutee agents [7]. The additional information is likely placing a burden on these students' cognitive resources by forcing students to process and reaffirm familiar information into their existing knowledge structures. Alternatively, low-domain knowledge students benefit greatly from modeling the behaviors of virtual tutees who can illustrate effective learning behaviors in a tutoring environment (e.g., responding appropriately to deep-level reasoning questions, or providing self-reflections; [5, 8]).

These contrasting learning effects are not cause for alarm in the ITS community, and instead simply highlight the need for furthering our understanding of when to apply certain conversation frameworks over others. Students with high-domain knowledge may only require monologues to fine-tune their knowledge structures. Students with low-domain knowledge may need the help of virtual tutees, who can serve as learning peers in a daunting and new domain. Intermediate students may benefit from an increased engagement introduced by competition with a peer agent [9]. The current research seeks to contribute to a growing body of research concerning learning in conversation based ITSs, specifically those that involve math comprehension.

2 Proposed Methodology

In order to assess learning gains across a variety of conversation frameworks, a between subjects' pretest-posttest study design will be implemented. Participants will interact with AutoTutor Lite, a lightweight and online version of AutoTutor, in one of five conditions. AutoTutor Lite (ATL) utilizes a modular "shareable knowledge object" (SKO) framework that incorporates the AutoTutor-style conversation engine, which uses animated agents and NLP [9]. More than 60 unique SKOs (ATL modules) have been developed for the current experiment. Each SKO covers a specific Algebra 1 concept relating to one of five Algebra 1 problems. The five problems are from the ALEKS learning system (Assessment and LEarning in Knowledge Spaces), an online worked-examples based learning system [10]. The general AutoTutor conversation framework has typically been applied to domains that tend to be more verbal or conversational in nature. Latent semantic analysis, the NLP method utilized in ATL can struggle with interpreting differences between numbers and negation. With this in mind, our content focuses on math *reading comprehension*, that is, the underlying concepts behind each step of a worked example.

2.1 Conditions

In an effort to maintain content equivalency across conditions, careful considerations have been made during the script authoring process. Participants in the static reading condition (1) will read script of the vicarious monologue condition. Participants in the vicarious dialogue condition (2) will observe a simulated tutoring session between a tutor agent and tutee agent. Participants in the interactive dialogue condition (3) will be engaged in a one-on-one tutoring session with a tutor agent. Here, participants will occasionally be asked to respond to deep-level reasoning questions. Participant input will be assessed in real time, and the tutor agent will respond appropriately based on the expectation and misconception-tailored dialogue (EMT) featured in previous implementations of AutoTutor [11]. If students provide inaccurate responses to the questions, they will be provided hints by the tutor agent. If students do not respond correctly to the hints, they will be provided "prompts" (i.e., more specific hints). If students continue to provide incorrect responses, they will eventually be provided the correct answer by the tutor agent. Participants in the interactive trialogue condition (4) will interact with both a tutor and tutee agent. Here, questions from the tutor are occasionally directed to the tutee agent, who will either respond appropriately or will present a misconception. Finally, participants in the vicarious monologue condition (5) will essentially receive a lecture from the tutor agent.

High prior knowledge students may perform equally well across conditions, with a potential for performing slightly worse in the interactive conditions compared to the simpler conditions (i.e., static reading, vicarious monologue) given the expertise reversal effect. Low prior knowledge students are anticipated to perform best in conditions with a tutee agent present (i.e., vicarious dialogue, trialogue), which they can use for modeling effective learning behaviors. However, low domain students may still struggle in the interactive conditions given the findings of a meta-analysis on ITS effectiveness in K-12 mathematics, in which the authors suggest that low prior knowledge students may be less familiar with computers and lack self-regulation skills necessary to benefit from ITS [12].

3 Advice Sought

Perhaps the greatest challenge presented by the current experiment is the maintenance of content equivalency across the five conditions. Conditions requiring interaction (i.e., student input) will require more time to complete than the vicarious conditions. We are seeking advice regarding both script authoring strategies and analytical methods that can be utilized to reduce issues arising from the intrinsic time-on-task differences across the five conditions. Additionally, our experiment is currently poised to recruit participants from Amazon's Mechanical Turk (MTurk). Our experiment would also benefit greatly from advice regarding best-practices for using MTurk.

References

1. Chi, M.T., Roy, M., Hausmann, R.G.: Observing tutorial dialogues collaboratively: insights about human tutoring effectiveness from vicarious learning. Cogn. Sci. **32**(2), 301–341 (2008)
2. Graesser, A.C., Person, N.K., Magliano, J.P.: Collaborative dialogue patterns in naturalistic one-to-one tutoring. Appl. Cogn. Psychol. **9**(6), 495–522 (1995)
3. Olney, Andrew M., D'Mello, S., Person, N., Cade, W., Hays, P., Williams, C., Lehman, B., Graesser, A.: Guru: A Computer Tutor That Models Expert Human Tutors. In: Cerri, Stefano A., Clancey, William J., Papadourakis, G., Panourgia, K. (eds.) ITS 2012. LNCS, vol. 7315, pp. 256–261. Springer, Heidelberg (2012). doi:10.1007/978-3-642-30950-2_32
4. Craig, S.D., Sullins, J., Witherspoon, A., Gholson, B.: The deep-level-reasoning-question effect: the role of dialogue and deep-level-reasoning questions during vicarious learning. Cogn. Instr. **24**(4), 565–591 (2006)
5. Craig, S.D., Gholson, B., Brittingham, J.K., Williams, J.L., Shubeck, K.T.: Promoting vicarious learning of physics using deep questions with explanations. Comput. Educ. **58**(4), 1042–1048 (2012)
6. Graesser, A.C., Chipman, P., Haynes, B.C., Olney, A.: AutoTutor: an intelligent tutoring system with mixed-initiative dialogue. IEEE Trans. Educ. **48**(4), 612–618 (2005)
7. Kalyuga, S., Ayres, P., Chandler, P., Sweller, J.: The expertise reversal effect. Educ. Psychol. **38**(1), 23–31 (2003)
8. Graesser, A.C., Forsyth, C., Lehman, B.: Two heads are better than one: learning from agents in conversational trialogues. Teacher College Record (in press)
9. Hu, X., Nye, B.D., Gao, C., Huang, X., Xie, J., Shubeck, K.: Semantic representation analysis: a general framework for individualized, domain-specific and context-sensitive semantic processing. In: Schmorrow, D.D., Fidopiastis, C.M. (eds.) AC 2014. LNCS, vol. 8534, pp. 35–46. Springer, Cham (2014). doi:10.1007/978-3-319-07527-3_4
10. Craig, S.D., Hu, X., Graesser, A.C., Bargagliotti, A.E., Sterbinsky, A., Cheney, K.R., Okwumabua, T.: The impact of a technology-based mathematics after-school program using ALEKS on student's knowledge and behaviors. Comput. Educ. **68**, 495–504 (2013)
11. Graesser, A.C., D'Mello, S.K., Hu, X., Cai, Z., Olney, A., Morgan, B.: AutoTutor. In: McCarthy, P., Boonthum-Denecke, C. (eds.) Applied Natural Language Processing: Identification, Investigation, and Resolution, pp. 169–187. IGI Global, Hershey (2012)
12. Steenbergen-Hu, S., Cooper, H.: A meta-analysis of the effectiveness of Intelligent Tutoring Systems on K–12 students' mathematical learning. J. Educ. Psychol. (2013). doi:10.1037/a0032447

Industry Papers

4C: Continuous Cognitive Career Companions

Bhavna Agrawal[1(✉)], Rong Liu[1], Ravi Kokku[1], Yi-Min Chee[1],
Ashish Jagmohan[1], Satya Nitta[1], Michael Tan[2], and Sherry Sin[2]

[1] IBM T.J. Watson Research Center, Yorktown Heights, NY, USA
{bhavna,rliu,rkokku,ymchee,ashishja,svn}@us.ibm.com
[2] Deakin Digital, Melbourne, Australia
{michael.tan,sherry.sin}@deakindigital.com

Abstract. We explore the evolution of digital career advising companions for the rapidly growing knowledge economies to enable continuous evaluation and re-skilling of workforce in a wide range of domains. These companions deal with a variety of unstructured data sources to glean actionable insights. We present our experiences from building one such companion, and describe interesting natural language processing and machine learning challenges and open problems.

1 Introduction

Workforce re-skilling and life-long learning is taking center-stage today with the rapid growth of knowledge economies, fueled by technology-driven transformation of widely diverse domains (e.g. commerce, energy, telecom, etc.). Technology disruptions continuously increase automation level and change the work structure in these domains. Furthermore, the need for professional capabilities (such as leadership, critical thinking, problem solving etc.) that are harder to automate is gaining significant focus [5]. Consequently, there is an ever greater need for continuous career advising.

To this end, we explore the evolution of digital companions that continuously evaluate the changing interests and abilities of a person, suggest career choices, detect the gaps in her/his skills as the domain requirements evolve, and advise appropriate re-skilling opportunities. Interestingly, this problem turns out to be a natural language processing (NLP) and machine learning challenge due to the wide variety of unstructured data sources involved. Firstly, job profiles including resumes and social networking profiles (e.g. LinkedIn, Twitter, Blogs) are open-ended, descriptive, and unstructured. Secondly, open job postings and occupation profiles created by governments [1,9] are all specified again in unstructured or free form. Finally, descriptions of courses offered by universities and Massive Open Online Courses (MOOCs) platforms are specified in natural language too, and they are updated constantly as knowledge evolves.

Much of the previous work in matching careers to people has been done on generic personality profiling and keyword searches. The two most commonly used personality profiling methods are based on Holland's [6] categorization (RIASEC - Realistic, Investigative, Artistic, Social, Enterprising, Conventional)

© Springer International Publishing AG 2017
E. André et al. (Eds.): AIED 2017, LNAI 10331, pp. 623–629, 2017.
DOI: 10.1007/978-3-319-61425-0_78

and Briggs-Myer Type Indicator [8]. There are online tools based on these methods [2]. In addition, various tools (e.g. myNextmove.org, myfuture.edu.au, careerzone.ny.gov) have been developed to help people find careers from O*NET [9] using keyword/phrase search.

In this paper, we describe our experiences of exploring novel natural language processing (NLP) approach to matching core expertise (*e.g.* technical skills/expertise) and professional capabilities (or non-cognitive/soft-skills) required by evolving jobs and careers with interests and profiles of people. Specifically, we find that abstracting natural-language descriptions into a set of underlying concepts, and performing matching and recommendations at the concept level, makes the problem more tractable and helps realize continuous cognitive career companions. The exploration, however, highlights a number of remaining challenges including the lack of appropriate baselines for evaluating such companion solutions, and the need for significant amount of training data with annotated concepts and matched user-career/job pairs.

Next we describe the overall architecture and data sources in Sect. 2, followed by the cognitive recommendation engine and results in Sect. 3. Finally, Sect. 4 concludes this paper with challenges and future directions.

2   Architecture and Data Sources

Figure 1a gives the overall architecture of 4C tool. This architecture contains four primary data sources: (1) input users profile, (2) career data including occupation profiles and open job postings, (3) reference job professional capability profiles, and (4) course catalog. Each of these is described in details below.

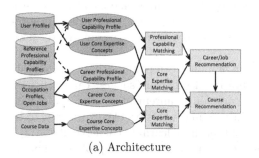
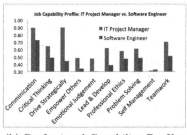

(a) Architecture   (b) Professional Capability Profiles

Fig. 1. Architecture of continuous cognitive career companions

User Profile: To generate personalized recommendations we ask for a user profile in a natural language format (e.g. similar to a LinkedIn profile, or a resume/cv). Specifically, this profile consists of current and ongoing academic qualifications/degrees, past experiences, additional certificates, and interests.

Career Data: We use two types of career data, both in natural language form: occupation profiles and open job postings. The occupation profiles (OP) are used for recommending a career/occupation direction to the user, and open jobs are used for recommending specific jobs. A typical OP (*e.g.* O*NET [9], Australian Government Job Outlook [1] etc.) contains information regarding duties and responsibilities, education and skill requirements, employment statistics etc., and may consist of many related job roles. For example, according to O*NET [9], occupation IT Project Managers contains of a family of job roles such as IT Manager, Program manager, Team Leader etc. We used [1] in our tool. In addition, we also collected open job postings for our experiment. A typical job posting contains attributes like title, company, location, and a large body of job description, which includes required core expertise, professional capabilities, and other qualifications.

Reference Professional Capability Profiles: For any occupation or job, professional capabilities are as equally as or even more important than core expertise [3]. Unfortunately, neither in user profiles nor in job postings, professional capability requirements are specified completely. One way to estimate professional capabilities of a user (or a job) is to interpret it based on reference job capability profiles, and the current job of the user (or the job posting).

We adopted a professional capability framework consisting of 10 professional capabilities, and trained a neural network model to identify professional capabilities from job posting description. We processed 100,000 open job postings using the trained model to discover their professional capabilities. Then reference job/occupation capability profiles can be created by aggregating capability requirements along multiple dimensions such as occupation, job role, profession, industry etc. Figures 1b shows reference professional capability profiles for two job roles: Software Engineer, and IT Project Manager. In this chart, each bar shows the percentage of jobs requesting a capability. For example, communication is required by about 90% of IT project manager jobs. As expected, an IT project manager job in general requires more professional capabilities than a software engineer job. Each capability profile can be represented as a vector *e.g.* for IT project manager it is [0.9, 0.64, 0.90, 0.49, 0.48, 0.62, 0.58, 0.61, 0.31, 0.71]. This vector measures the importance of each professional capability for an IT project manager job. This vector notation enables us to measure matching between two profiles by computing similarity between two vectors.

Course Data: In order to recommend relevant courses for a particular career, we use course catalogs from universities or MOOCs (e.g. edX, Coursera, Udacity). Each course usually consists of: course title, pre-requisites, and a description.

Next, we describe our recommendation engines which ingest these data sources to produce recommendations.

3   Cognitive Recommendation Engines

We now present recommendation engines for career pathways and corresponding course selections, as well as one for specific job recommendation based on user profile and available jobs.

3.1   Career and Course Recommendation

For each user profile, we extract core expertise concepts using Watson Concept Insights [4], a tool similar to DBPedia Spotlight [7]. The text for the profile shown in Fig. 2A can be annotated with concepts such as *Project Management, Management*, and *Information Technology* etc. Similarly, we can extract concepts from each career and course description. Each extracted concept is an entity defined in Wikipedia. Through the links among Wikipedia entities, we can estimate the relevancy among these entities. As a result, although two entities have different surface forms, they can still be matched based on their relevancy. For example, concepts Hadoop and Big Data can be matched because they have tight connection in the Wikipedia definitions.

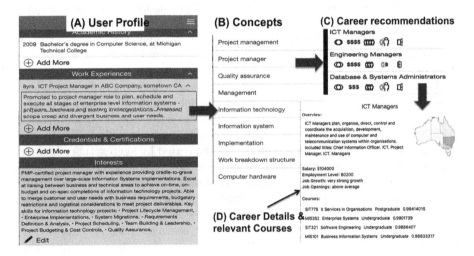

Fig. 2. Figure showing the flow of information from (A) User profile, to (B) concept extraction, to (C) career recommendation, to (D) course recommendation.

Besides concept matching, other information can be utilized to refine recommendation, for example, minimum years experience and academic degree requirements. With the annotated concepts shown in Fig. 2B, the most relevant careers are: ICT (Information & Communication Technology) managers, Engineering managers, ICT Business and System Analysts etc., as shown in Fig. 2C, which seem to be intuitively correct. In addition, with reference capability profiles available, professional capability matching can also be added to produce final matching.

Course recommendation is done in a very similar fashion as career recommendation - whereas concepts derived from the chosen career are matched with concepts derived from the course text. The results of course recommendations are also shown in Fig. 2D. Once again, the results make intuitive sense.

3.2   Open Jobs Recommendation

Job recommendation is based on both core expertise matching and professional capability profile matching. Similar to career recommendation, Wikipedia concepts are extracted from each open job and the user profile, and the relevancy between the two sets of concepts is computed as core expertise matching.

However, professional capabilities can not be extracted as Wikipedia concepts from the text because they are usually not *explicitly* stated. For example, the sentence "strong ability to present and articulate solutions to management team is a must" indicates *communication* and *leadership* capabilities although neither of these two capabilities is mentioned directly. Therefore, we use reference capability profiles described in Sect. 2 to map a user's professional capabilities based on the user's work experience, and current job. For example, for the user profile shown in Fig. 2, (current job title: IT Project Manager), we map it to the reference capability profile of an IT project manager, shown in Fig. 1b. Similarly, for each job posting, based on its title and description, it can be mapped to an appropriate reference capability profile. These mapped reference capability profiles can be further customized if specific capabilities can be firmly asserted from the user profile or the job posting text. With these mapped capability profiles, we can measure the matching between capability profiles of users and job postings as the similarity between the capability vectors.

Table 1. Ranked job recommendations based on two approaches: (1) based on professional skills and core expertise match, (2) based solely on core expertise match.

S.No	Professional capabilities + Core expertise	Core expertise only
1	Software Implementation Project Manager	Software Implementation Project Manager
2	Project Manager 2	Project Manager HR
3	Project Manager	Manager PMO - IT Program Development
4	Deputy Director - IT Services Competency Center	Project Manager 2
5	Advisor Program Management - CSPD	Deputy Director - IT Services Competency Center

The final matching score between a user profile and a job posting is the weighted sum of core expertise matching and professional capability matching, where weights are be chosen empirically or by cross validation. Job postings with top K final matching scores are selected as recommendations.

Table 1 shows ranked job recommendations for the user profile of Fig. 2A using two different strategies. One strategy considers matching of both professional capabilities and core expertise with equal weights, while the other only uses core expertise matching. The top recommendation by both strategies is the same because this job matches the user profile perfectly from both aspects. However, the other recommendations vary. When professional capabilities are considered, jobs in the categories similar to the user's can be ranked relatively high. On the other hand, when only core expertise is considered, jobs across different categories may be recommended. For example, "Project Manager - HR" is recommended because the job mentions all concepts shown in Fig. 2B. However, based on its description, this job is equivalent to HR manager instead of IT project manager.

4   Conclusion, Challenges, and Future Work

In this paper we describe our experience building a Continuous Cognitive Career Companion (4C) that recommends career paths, courses, and jobs to users based on matching of core expertise and professional capabilities using a variety of data sources involving natural language texts. Matching is done by extracting and comparing underlying semantic concepts from the texts. Several challenges remain to be addressed in future work, as we continue to leverage the advances in artificial intelligence techniques in the education domain. First, extracting the right Wikipedia concepts that can precisely capture core expertise for users or careers/jobs is a non-trivial problem. For instance, for the user profile shown in Fig. 2, a concept like "Project Management" is good, while the concept "computer hardware" is not informative. Second, professional capabilities play a critical role in career recommendations, but it takes significant effort to create right professional capability profiles for users, occupations and jobs. Often professional capabilities can only be inferred from job responsibilities, job titles, organization hierarchies, and company profiles; all this data is often accessible only internally to organizations and hence we lack sufficient datasets for accurate capability profiling. In addition, the evaluation of career/course recommendation is often subjective and hence need human validation in real settings over sustained periods of time. Finally, richer user profiles can be created with data from personal websites and social media data (*e.g.* Blogs, LinkedIn profiles, Tweets).

References

1. Australian government job outlook. http://joboutlook.gov.au/
2. CPP: strong interest inventory, strong. https://www.skillsone.com/contents/strong/Strong.aspx
3. Driving the skills agenda: preparing students for the future (2015). https://static.googleusercontent.com/media/www.google.com/en//edu/resources/global-education/files/skills-of-the-future-report.pdf
4. Franceschini, M.M., Soares, L.B., Lastras Montaño, L.A.: Watson concept insights: a conceptual association framework. In: Proceedings of the 25th International Conference Companion on World Wide Web, pp. 179–182 (2016)
5. Heckman, J.J., Kautz, T.: Hard evidence on soft skills. Labour Econ. **19**(4), 451–464 (2012)

6. Holland, J.L.: Making Vocational Choices: A Theory of Vocational Personalities and Work Environments. Psychological Assessment Resources, Odessa (1997)
7. Mendes, P.N., Jakob, M., Garcia-Silva, A., Bizer, C.: DBpedia spotlight: Shedding light on the web of documents. In: Proceedings of the 7th International Conference on Semantic Systems (I-Semantics) (2011)
8. Myers, I.B.: The Myers-Briggs Type Indicator. Consulting Psychologists Press, Palo Alto (1962)
9. O*net online. http://www.onetonline.org. Accessed 17 Nov 2016

Wizard's Apprentice: Cognitive Suggestion Support for Wizard-of-Oz Question Answering

Jae-wook Ahn[✉], Patrick Watson, Maria Chang, Sharad Sundararajan, Tengfei Ma, Nirmal Mukhi, and Srijith Prabhu

IBM T.J. Watson Research Center, 1101 Kitchawan Rd, Yorktown Heights, NY 10598, USA
{jaewook.ahn,pwatson,sharads,nmukhi,snprabhu}@us.ibm.com, {Maria.Chang,Tengfei.Ma1}@ibm.com

Abstract. Recent advances in artificial intelligence and natural language processing greatly enhance the capabilities of intelligent tutoring systems. However, gathering a subject-appropriate corpus of training data remains challenging. In order to address this issue, we present a system based on a hybrid Wizard-of-Oz technique, which enables cognitive systems to work in tandem with a human operator (the "wizard"), to enhance collection of dialog variants.

Keywords: Wizard-of-Oz · Intelligent tutoring systems · Hybrid user interface

1 Introduction

Intelligent tutoring systems [3] provide personalized feedback to learners, and provide a guide for complex topics and learning materials. Recent advances in artificial intelligence and natural language processing enhance the capabilities of intelligent tutoring systems by allowing cognitive agents to flexibly and adaptively respond to learner dialog actions. However, gathering a subject-appropriate corpus of training data remains challenging, particularly for deep and complex dialog trees that may involve large numbers of conversational moves between the student and the cognitive tutor.

In the current work we present a system designed to address this problem based on a classic UI development technique: the Wizard-of-Oz (WoZ) experiment [7,8]. In this technique, users dialog with what they believe to be a chatbot-style cognitive agent, but which is in fact a human user (the "Wizard"). WoZ has been used since the early 1980s. Gould [6] used the WoZ approach to simulate the use of a large-vocabulary "speech-driven" typewriter. Since then, it has been used in various problems: as a prototyping framework [11], dialog agent [10], intelligent tutors for teaching mathematics [4], multimodal mobile systems [12], Human-Robot Interaction [13], and to study and analyze chatbots [5,9].

The approach introduced in this paper integrates our best current dialog agent as a tool for the wizard, enabling them to update and edit the conversational tooling "online" as they converse with the user. In this way the system

© Springer International Publishing AG 2017
E. André et al. (Eds.): AIED 2017, LNAI 10331, pp. 630–635, 2017.
DOI: 10.1007/978-3-319-61425-0_79

collects user and Wizard dialog variations, and develops deep conversational structures based on a relatively small numbers of examples. The presence of the dialog agent prevents the wizard from getting sidetracked or stuck on an untrained example that happens to appear early in the dialog.

2 System Description – a Hybrid Wizard-of-Oz Supported by Cognitive Systems

Figure 1 shows the architecture of Wizard's Apprentice. It is composed of two modules: traditional WoZ (left) and Dialog Suggestion (right). The learner talks with the wizard through a chat interface (Fig. 2) to accomplish learning tasks. Like a traditional WoZ systems, the wizard is able to assist learning by asking questions of the learner, evaluating her answers, giving hints, and responding to learner questions. As in the traditional WoZ setup, wizards are also able to cope with unexpected learner responses (e.g., [5,9]), while collecting realistic examples of user input.

However, in tutoring domains, wizards may not have the same level of subject matter expertise that an instructor would possess. This limits wizards' ability to return appropriate answers. Furthermore, WoZ sessions often lead to deviations from the intended conversation topics, which generate noise in the collected answer corpus. This degrades efficiency especially when the collected data is meant to be used for the intelligent system training. Finally, in most WoZ systems, collected answer variants are labeled and scored post-hoc. This creates an additional source of training noise, since collected dialog moves lose contextual

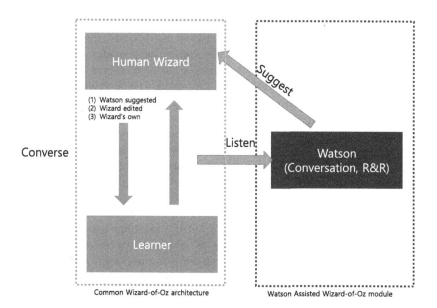

Fig. 1. Wizard's Apprentice diagram

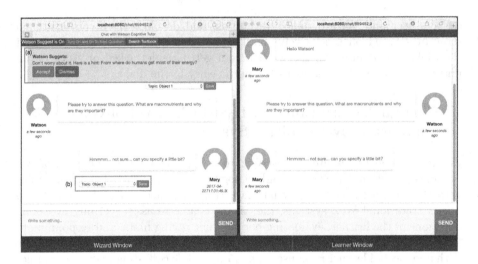

Fig. 2. Wizard's Apprentice user interface. A wizard and a user converse using their window (left and right respectively) while not seeing each other's screen.

information that could aid in assigning accurate labels to correct or incorrect responses.

To overcome these limitations, Wizard's Apprentice relays user responses to a back-end conversation tutor system that follows the dialog between the wizard and the learner as if the learner was interacting directly with the conversational tutor. This dialog system provides it's best cognitive conversation suggestion to the wizard. Figure 2(a) shows an example of the suggestions. The wizard is able to pass the apprentice's suggestions directly to the user, and to score and tag both the user's responses and apprentice's suggestions. Based on the users answer and feedback from the wizard, the apprentice provides a list of example responses (e.g., "That's correct!"), or show a list of hints for the learner. The wizard can "**Accept**" or "**Dismiss**" the apprentice's suggestion. Even when the wizard accepts the suggestion, she can still edit and improve the original response in the input box. When the wizard devices that the apprentice's suggestion is inappropriate due to the limitations of the back-end conversation engine, she may "**Dismiss**" the suggestion and type an appropriate answer. If the suggestion is dismissed, the back-end service is temporarily disabled to avoid deviation between the dialog flows. The wizard reactivates the apprentice when a new question begins.

In the prototype described here, the back-end was IBM's Watson Conversation service [1], supported with Watson's natural language classification service and Watson's Retrieve and Rank service [2] which allows the wizard to quickly search learning materials for related passages using user's queries. In addition, the prototype ingests transcripts (Fig. 4) between the wizard and the learner to a cloud-based database. These transcripts are timestamped and contain the wizard's tags and annotations as well as every conversation between the wizard and the user. The boxed line in Fig. 4 indicates the wizard's annotation on the

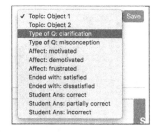

Fig. 3. Wizard's annotation on user response. Dropdown expanded when Fig. 2(b) is clicked.

```
"session": "Watson-Mary-659452",
    "chattext": "(2017-04-22T17:31:15.204Z) Watson: Hi, Mary. Welcome to the class!
(2017-04-22T17:31:22.626Z) Mary: Hello Watson!
(2017-04-22T17:31:36.359Z) Watson: Please try to answer this question.  What are macronutrients and why are they impo
(2017-04-22T17:31:49.308Z) Mary: Hmmmm... not sure... can you specify a little bit?
(2017-04-22T17:32:24.193Z) Annotation: Type of Q: clarification  on message: Hmmmm... not sure... can you specify a l
(2017-04-22T17:32:31.250Z) Watson: Don't worry about it.  Here is a hint: From where do humans get most of their ener
(2017-04-22T17:32:38.645Z) Mary: Humans get most of their energy from macronutrients
(2017-04-22T17:32:44.423Z) Watson: Correct!
```

Fig. 4. Transcript example. Boxed line is a wizard annotation saved during the session.

previous user response, using the Fig. 2(b) dropdown. By selecting an entry and clicking the "Save" button during the session (Fig. 3), the annotation and the corresponding user response is saved in the transcript.

3 Use Case Example and Preliminary User Feedback

We applied the Wizard's Apprentice technique to conversation-based intelligent tutoring systems (Figs. 1 and 2) to design the dialog flow. This conversational agent asks questions to students, classifies answers as correct, partially correct, or incorrect, and provides hints if the answers are partially correct. The prototype was tested by 20 researchers. Participants took turns acting as both the wizard or as a learner to produce 25 session transcripts. After the sessions the transcripts were analyzed in order to find the patterns of the interaction between the wizards and the users. Subjective feedback from the participants was also collected and analyzed.

Figure 5 shows the fraction of participant responses on five representative problems. The Wizard's Apprentice technique did identify usability issues in the front-end user interface (as in traditional WoZ), 61% of issues discovered by users during the Wizard's Apprentice procedure were related to the back-end conversation service (e.g., dialog flow, response classification, and dialog language), suggesting that user experience in tutoring is more easily improved by modification of the conversational service than the front-end. What's more, these dialog-based improvements could be rapidly integrated into the back-end conversation service via the ingested participants' conversation transcripts.

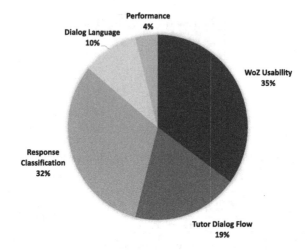

Fig. 5. Subjective user feedback on the Centaurus WoZ prototype

4   Conclusions

In this paper, we describe the "Wizard's Apprentice" system, a hybrid Wizard-of-Oz approach for intelligent tutoring systems. The Wizard's Apprentice system provides the wizard in a traditional WoZ system with an artificially intelligent conversational back-end system that observes wizard-user conversations and provides suggested dialog moves to the wizard. This system helps inexperienced wizards, minimizes deviation from the task topics, and collects user response variants to train the conversation system. Based on the preliminary user testing results, we were able to improve both the front-end UI and the back-end conversational agent (the "Apprentice").

We plan to develop this architecture as a pluggable service to enhance cognitive systems that employ the WoZ technique and incorporate more cognitive features such as related material suggestion, topic modeling, emotion analysis, and response analysis/recommendation. We also plan to conduct a comparative analysis with traditional WoZ based data in order to more clearly identify the advantages and characteristics of Wizard's Apprentice.

References

1. Watson Conversation (2016). https://www.ibm.com/watson/developercloud/doc/conversation/index.html
2. Watson Retrieve and Rank (2016). https://www.ibm.com/watson/developercloud/retrieve-rank.html
3. Anderson, J.R., Boyle, C.F., Reiser, B.J.: Intelligent tutoring systems. Science(Washington) **228**(4698), 456–462 (1985)

4. Benzmüller, C., Horacek, H., Kruijff-Korbayová, I., Lesourd, H., Schiller, M., Wolska, M.: DiaWOz-II – a tool for wizard-of-Oz experiments in mathematics. In: Freksa, C., Kohlhase, M., Schill, K. (eds.) KI 2006. LNCS, vol. 4314, pp. 159–173. Springer, Heidelberg (2007). doi:10.1007/978-3-540-69912-5_13

5. Fialho, P., Coheur, L.: ChatWoz: chatting through a Wizard of Oz. In: Proceedings of the 17th International ACM SIGACCESS Conference on Computers & Accessibility, ASSETS 2015. pp. 423–424. ACM, New York (2015). http://doi.acm.org/10.1145/2700648.2811334

6. Gould, J.D., Conti, J., Hovanyecz, T.: Composing letters with a simulated listening typewriter. Commun. ACM **26**(4), 295–308 (1983)

7. Green, P., Wei-Haas, L.: The rapid development of user interfaces: experience with the wizard of oz method. In: Proceedings of the Human Factors Society Annual Meeting, vol. 29(5), pp. 470–474 (1985). http://dx.doi.org/10.1177/154193128502900515

8. Kelley, J.F.: An empirical methodology for writing user-friendly natural language computer applications. In: Proceedings of the SIGCHI Conference on Human Factors in Computing Systems, CHI 1983, pp. 193–196. ACM, New York (1983). http://doi.acm.org/10.1145/800045.801609

9. Kerly, A., Bull, S.: The potential for chatbots in negotiated learner modelling: a Wizard-of-Oz study. In: Ikeda, M., Ashley, K.D., Chan, T.-W. (eds.) ITS 2006. LNCS, vol. 4053, pp. 443–452. Springer, Heidelberg (2006). doi:10.1007/11774303_44

10. Okamoto, M., Yang, Y., Ishida, T.: Wizard of Oz method for learning dialog agents. In: Klusch, M., Zambonelli, F. (eds.) CIA 2001. LNCS, vol. 2182, pp. 20–25. Springer, Heidelberg (2001). doi:10.1007/3-540-44799-7_3

11. Schlögl, S., Doherty, G., Karamanis, N., Luz, S.: Webwoz: a Wizard of Oz prototyping framework. In: Proceedings of the 2nd ACM SIGCHI Symposium on Engineering Interactive Computing Systems, EICS 2010, pp. 109–114. ACM, New York (2010). http://doi.acm.org/10.1145/1822018.1822035

12. Schlögl, S., Doherty, G., Luz, S.: Wizard of oz experimentation for language technology applications: challenges and tools. Interact. Comput. **27**(6), 592–615 (2015)

13. Steinfeld, A., Jenkins, O.C., Scassellati, B.: The Oz of Wizard: simulating the human for interaction research. In: Proceedings of the 4th ACM/IEEE International Conference on Human Robot Interaction, HRI 2009, pp. 101–108. ACM, New York (2009). http://doi.acm.org/10.1145/1514095.1514115

Interaction Analysis in Online Maths Human Tutoring: The Case of Third Space Learning

Mutlu Cukurova[1(✉)], Manolis Mavrikis[1], Rose Luckin[1],
James Clark[2], and Candida Crawford[2]

[1] UCL Knowledge Lab, University College London, London, UK
{m.cukurova, m.mavrikis, r.luckin}@ucl.ac.uk
[2] Third Space Learning, London, UK
{james.clark, candida.crawford}@thirdspacelearning.com

Abstract. This 'industry' paper reports on the combined effort of researchers and industrial designers and developers to ground the automatic quality assurance of online maths human-to-human tutoring on best practices. We focus on the first step towards this goal. Our aim is to understand the largely under-researched field of online tutoring, to identify success factors in this context and to model best practice in online teaching. We report our research into best practice in online maths teaching and describe and discuss our design and evaluation iterations towards annotation software that can mark up human-to-human online teaching interactions with successful teaching interaction signifiers.

Keywords: Online tutoring · Annotation software · Best practice modeling

1 Introduction

Improving the quality and quantity of the teacher workforce is one of the significant aims of educational research including the field of AIED. Recently, a report from the UNESCO Institute for Statistics stated that almost 69 million teachers need to be recruited globally by 2030 to ensure that international pledges on primary and secondary education are to be kept. The authors of the report argue that there are about 263 million children without a primary and secondary school to attend and there need to be major changes in teacher recruitment to overcome these massive shortages. These shortages are more significant in the subject areas of Science, Technology, Engineering, and Mathematics (STEM) and there is a need to improve the quality of existing teaching in all subject areas for the overwhelming majority of the globe. The concern with teacher quality is partly driven by a growing recognition, fueled by accumulating research evidence, of how critical teachers are to student learning [5, 10]. AIED technologies have great potential to tackle these challenges.

One potential solution to the lack of high-quality teaching at scale is online human teaching approaches. Online human teaching approaches can leverage digital technology to create a successful pedagogical model so that every child, irrespective of wealth or location, can access high-quality teaching. Third space learning (TSL) is a leading online teaching company focusing on primary Math education and the provision of an audio and shared working space platform for teacher to learner interactions.

© Springer International Publishing AG 2017
E. André et al. (Eds.): AIED 2017, LNAI 10331, pp. 636–643, 2017.
DOI: 10.1007/978-3-319-61425-0_80

A key challenge in this endeavor is the need to ensure that all online teaching sessions are high-quality. This quality assurance process requires many human evaluators who listen and watch a sample of each tutor's interactions every week. If there are any causes for concern, the teacher is evaluated more frequently and offered training.

The overarching goal of the research presented here is to automate this evaluation process through the careful design and implementation of AI. We report our early work as we progress towards this goal, in particular we present work towards annotation software to mark up TSL online teaching interactions with successful teaching interaction signifiers. Our aim is to understand the largely under-researched challenges and success factors in this context and to model best practice in online teaching. In this paper, we report our research into best practice in online Math teaching and we describe and discuss our early design and evaluation iterations towards the annotation tool described above.

2 Best Practice of Online Maths Tutoring

Best practice may be framed in different ways. Best practice measurements very often serve as proxies for effectiveness, hence they appear to be generally measured at the institutional level rather than the individual learner level. "Institution" in this case refers to a group of students, teachers and administrators who are together for a common purpose hence; it could be a school, a department of a school, or a programme in a department, for example.

At the individual tutor level, best practice of online tutoring is a combination of various verbal and non-verbal interactions that would lead to student learning. In this sense, best practice is an inseparable part of student leaning. Student learning is also a very broad term, which encompasses academic achievement; engagement in educationally purposeful activities, which lead to the development of certain intellectual attributes, such as the acquisition of desired content knowledge, and the development of skills, competencies and self-efficacy.

The list of dependent factors as proxies of student learning is extensive. However, three main themes emerge and must be taken into account in defining best practice:

1. The cognitive domain involves knowledge, understanding and skills about the studied content.
2. The metacognitive domain encompasses the acquisition of knowledge and skills related to one's own learning, in other words the learners' knowledge and understanding of their own learning.
3. The affective domain involves learners' capacities to deal with their emotions, such as attitudes, locus of control, self-efficacy and interest, for example.

2.1 The Cognitive Domain

The most important predictors of learner success are often related to the cognitive domain [11]. Cognitive attainment can be measured in many ways, but in most cases measurements are of what learners can achieve in terms of success at solving a maths problem, writing an essay, completing a multiple choice assessment or whatever form of assessment is in place. Few measurements of cognitive attainment consider the process through which learners achieve success, rather they evaluate success in this somewhat decomposed manner. AIED technology can and has considered the measurement of learners' progress towards attainment. For instance, The Andes Intelligent Tutoring System has rules that are based on a cognitive model of knowledge acquisition that has been developed by analysing protocols of physics students completing example problems. Similarly, Cognitive Tutors maintain a cognitive model instantiated as a system of if–then production rules that can generate the multiple possible correct or incorrect solution steps that a student might take.

2.2 The Metacognitive Domain

Metacognition can be broadly referred to as any knowledge or cognitive process that refers to, monitors, or controls any aspect of cognition. When confronted with an effortful cognitive task it is those with greater Metacognitive abilities who tend to be more successful. The Metacognitive domain encompasses actions such as effective goal setting, self-explanation of one's goals and cognitive processes, reflecting on ones' own learning activities and regulating them. It is argued that those students who have mastery goals [7]; skills clearly and concisely express their goals and thinking process [1], a growth mindset [3] a reflective practice [6] often outperform their peers.

2.3 The Emotional Domain

There is a rich literature on the relationships between emotions and learning [see review in 9]. One model previously used in the design of AIEd systems is the cognitive-motivational model [8]. This model describes how a student's learning is mediated by their motivation to learn, their learning strategies, and their cognitive resources. Emotions influence each of these constructs in different ways. For example, emotions direct attention and cognitive resources towards an object or a task, and they can trigger, sustains or reduce academic motivation. An emotional experience such as enjoyment of learning can, therefore, direct a student's full attention to the learning task, enhance a student's academic motivation, and enable the student to adopt flexible learning strategies such as elaboration or critical evaluation.

3 Annotating Best Practice in Online Teaching

The theoretical background from the three themes emerging form the literature provided an initial grounding for the first design iteration of the TSL annotation tool (illustrated in Fig. 1). Teacher and student interactions were coded in the three dimensions of cognitive, metacognitive and affective domains.

The top left corner in Fig. 1 presents the tutor's interface to the student. The top right corner has the emotional tags and the list of previously tagged actions. The bottom left corner identifies the observable student actions from the cognitive and the

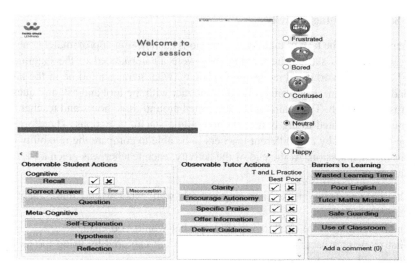

Fig. 1. Initial TSL annotation tool

meta-cognitive domains, the bottom center screen has the observable tutor actions, and the bottom right corner has the general barriers to learning items. The tool also has the feature of providing qualitative feedback to the tutor from the evaluator through the addition of a comment at the right bottom corner of the screen.

4 Prototype Evaluation

The overarching aim of this study was to identify observable features of online teaching in order to be able to use them to build a dynamic best practice model for the TSL AI system. The initial annotation tool was evaluated across 20 teaching sessions. These sessions were evaluated by 10 evaluators using the tagging tool. In this section, we analyse their feedback on the tool's potential to capture best practice online teaching according to two research questions:

(RQ1) What are the teachers' challenges tagging online tuition practice using the tool?

(RQ2) How can these challenges be addressed to improve the tagging tool's accuracy in capturing observable features of online tuition practice?

4.1 Participants

The participants were ten teachers aged between 24 to 41 years. Three of the teachers were recruited from the TSL's tutor evaluator's team, two of them were working as educational researchers and the remaining five were trained teachers enrolled in a masters course in Educational Technology at UCL Knowledge Lab.

4.2 Session Tagging Activity

Teachers were set the task of tagging two sessions each lasting approximately one hour. Before the teachers started the tagging they were all introduced to the tagging tool, trained on how it works and its design decisions (what items should be in the tagging tool and why). Then, they were allowed to interact with the tool and ask any questions that arose as a result. This training session lasted around three hours and teachers were subsequently allocated to tag two of the ten online teaching sessions. Therefore, each session was tagged by two different teachers to be able to compare the reliability of the tagging for each session. At the end of the activity, each teacher was given a form with four questions.

1. Which elements of the session tagger work well, what would make them even better?
2. Which elements were challenging to use, what would you change?
3. What relevant aspects of online teaching were not captured by using the tool?
4. How could we capture these?

Answers provided to these questions were accumulated in text and were qualitatively analysed using thematic coding.

5 Results

In this section, we present the analysis and results for research question 1: What are the challenges of teachers tagging online tuition practice using the TSL tool?

Two main themes emerged to the first open-ended question that relates to the positive features of the initial version of the session tagger.

- **The tagger was considered as a fast evaluation tool:** Eight teachers mentioned in their responses that the tagger had the potential to be a fast evaluation tool. It was a common feedback that the evaluation of a session might take up to three hours using traditional performance evaluation through open-ended questions. The tagging tool was therefore perceived as an efficient tool for evaluating teachers' performance.
- **The approach of real-time tagging was considered as potentially more accurate than post session evaluation of tuition quality:** Most teachers, six out of ten, thought that the tagging of real-time interactions could lead to more accurate evaluations of tutor performance compared to post-session evaluations of performances. Overall, post session evaluations were considered as more vulnerable to tutor evaluators' bias, compared to the tagging tool.

  Regarding the challenging features of the tagging tool five main themes emerged:
- **Too much to focus at the same time. Cognitive, metacognitive, and affective domains as well as barrier to learning aspects are hard to focus on simultaneously:** All of the participant teachers argued that it is not possible to focus on the items from all three domains at any given time. As a result, they appeared to be focussing on certain aspects for a while and then changing to another·aspect to tag after a while in a random manner.

- **It is hard to focus on student and tutor actions at the same time:** Again, all of the participants thought that it was confusing to focus on student actions and the tutor actions simultaneously. It appeared that the teachers were switching from tagging the tutor actions to student actions and vice versa in a random manner.
- **Hard to comprehend and identify some of the tags:** Seven out of ten teachers mentioned that they struggled to understand what exactly some of the tags meant (for instance specific praise, recall, misunderstanding) and what are the examples of these tags. Participants had all joined a training workshop about the annotation tool. Nevertheless, while completing the tagging, they needed some support to identify some of the tags of student and tutor actions.
- **The detection of the affective domain is challenging:** Half of the teachers argued that as the interface does not allow them to see the students while they are working, it was quite challenging to isolate certain nuances between the affective domain stages only from students voices. Although the happy and frustrated states can be identified relatively easily, the confused and bored stages were found challenging to identify.
- **Some user interface and technical challenges:** In addition to the points above some teachers commented on technical or user interface related challenges.

5.1   The Second Design Iteration of the TSL Annotation Tool

The results of this first iteration of the TSL annotation tool was the following changes:

(1) Separate the 'barriers to learning' section, which involves evaluation of some general teacher qualities, such as clarity of language. These features are less dynamic and can be judged post-session.
(2) Student and tutor actions should be coded separately in order to avoid confusion and increase the reliability of the tagging. This might be done through the selection of two equal length sections, one tagged from the student's perspective and the second from the tutor's perspective.
(3) Separate the evaluation of the affective domain from the cognitive and metacognitive domains, because of the intertwined nature of cognitive and metacognitive actions that makes them hard to isolate from each other.
(4) Provide evaluators with clear definitions and examples of all the tagging items.

Figures 2 and 3 present the revised versions of the annotation tool, with two different interfaces for tagging tutor actions and student actions separately. The tutor actions are categorised in three sections: Question, feedback, guidance and the student actions are categorised in four sections: Question, answer, reflection and self-explanation. These categories are based on the predominant pattern found in the online tuition dialogues of question-answer-feedback cycles where the tutor states a question, the student answers and the tutor follows up with appropriate feedback [2, 4]. Graesser et al. [4] elaborates on the one-to-one tutorial interactions by providing a five-step dialogue frame where (1) the tutor is asking a question; (2) the student is answering and explaining; (3) the tutor provides feedback on the answer; (4) the tutor

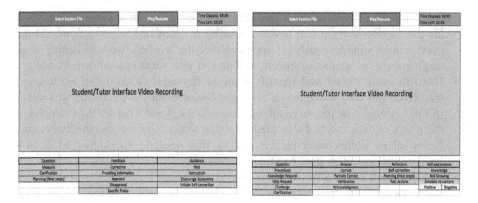

Fig. 2. Tutor actions tagging tool for primary Math teaching in online settings

Fig. 3. Student actions tagging tool for primary Math teaching in online settings

and the student are improving the quality of the answer by reflecting on it; (5) the tutor assesses student's understanding of the answer. Similar interactions were identified in more recent research studies [9]. We are now at the stage of evaluating these new prototype tools.

6 Conclusions

It is essential that industrial and academic partners work together at an early stage in the design of AIEd tools if the research they conduct is to optimally influence the design of the scaled technology. However, this early engagement also presents a dilemma, because, in the absence of an existing validated model of best practice on which to base the AI components, one has to build the model through design iterations with human participants playing the role eventually intended for automation by AI. Some of the problems faced by the human participants may not be an issue for an AI system. For example, the need to separate coding of teacher and learner interfaces. Other problems may be equally or more pertinent for AI systems. For example, the need for a precise definition of the meaning of each tag and the signifier it describes. The heart of the issue is that without this simplification for human evaluators to enable us to evaluate the tool prior to its automation we cannot build and validate our best practice model. A useful by-product of the human level evaluation process may be in its ability to inform the design of interface components for reporting back to teachers the results of the automated evaluation of their teaching sessions. For example, if the combination of teacher and student foci in the interface is confusing for evaluators when they are evaluating a teaching session, then it may well be difficult for teachers to understand when they are trying to use the interface to interpret the quality of their own teaching.

References

1. Chi, M.T.H., Wylie, R.: The ICAP framework: linking cognitive engagement to active learning outcomes. Educ. Psychol. **49**(4), 219–243 (2014)
2. Dillon, J.: The Practice of Questioning. International series on communication skills. Routledge, Owen Hargle (1990)
3. Dweck, C.S.: The perils and promises of praise. ASCD **65**(2), 34–39 (2007)
4. Graesser, A.C., Person, N.K., Magliano, J.P.: Collaborative dialogue patterns in naturalistic one-to-one tutoring. Appl. Cogn. Psychol. **9**(6), 495–522 (1995)
5. Hattie, J.: Visible learning for teachers: maximizing impact on learning, Routledge (2012)
6. King, P.M., Kitchener, K.S.: Developing Reflective Judgment: Understanding and Promoting Intellectual Growth and Critical Thinking in Adolescents and Adults. Jossey-Bass Higher and Adult Education Series and Jossey-Bass Social and Behavioral Science Series: ERIC (1994)
7. Locke, E.A., Latham, G.P.: New directions in goal-setting theory. Curr. Dir. Psychol. Sci. **15**(5), 265–268 (2006)
8. Pekrun, R., Goetz, T., Titz, W., Perry, R.P.: Academic emotions in students' self-regulated learning and achievement: a program of qualitative and quantitative research. Educ. Psychol. **37**(2), 91–105 (2002)
9. Porayska-Pomsta, K., Mavrikis, M., Pain, H.: Diagnosing and acting on student affect: the tutor's perspective. User Model. User-Adap. Inter. **18**(1–2), 125 (2008)
10. Sadler, P.M., Sonnert, G., Coyle, H.P., Cook-Smith, N., Miller, J.L.: The influence of teachers' knowledge on student learning in middle school physical science classrooms. Am. Educ. Res. J. **50**(5), 1020–1049 (2013)
11. Stankov, L.: Conservatism and cognitive ability. Intelligence **37**(3), 294–304 (2009)

Using a Model for Learning and Memory to Simulate Learner Response in Spaced Practice

Mark A. Riedesel[1](✉), Neil Zimmerman[1], Ryan Baker[2], Tom Titchener[1], and James Cooper[1]

[1] McGraw-Hill Education, 281 Summer Street, Boston, MA 02210, USA
{mark.riedesel,neil.zimmerman,tom.titchener,james.cooper}@mheducation.com
[2] University of Pennsylvania, 3700 Walnut Street, Philadelphia, PA 19104, USA
rybaker@upenn.edu

Abstract. McGraw-Hill Education's new adaptive flashcard application, StudyWise, implements spaced practice to help learners memorize collections of basic facts. For classroom use, subject matter experts needed a scheduling algorithm that could provide effective practice schedules to learn a pre-set number of facts over a specific interval of days. To test the pedagogical effectiveness of such schedules, we used the ACT-R model of memorization to simulate learner responses. Each schedule has one 30 min study session per day, with overall study intervals that ranged from one day for sets of less than 30 items to three weeks for sets of two hundred or more items. In each case, we succeeded in tuning our algorithm to give a high probability the simulated learner answered each item correctly by the end of the schedule. This use of artificial intelligence allowed us to optimize the algorithm before engaging large numbers of real users. As real user data becomes available for this application, the simulated user model can be further tested and refined.

Keywords: Spaced practice · LearnSmart · StudyWise · Adaptive flashcards · Mobile learning · iOS · Android

1 Introduction

For many subject areas, memorizing basic facts is an important first step in learning and mastering content. Examples include foreign language vocabulary, medical terms, and anatomy and physiology. Research over more than a century has shown that an effective way to memorize basic facts is through the use of spaced practice [2].

Applications designed for long-term memorization are often conceptually based on models for human memory that grew out of early work on how memories decay with time but can be reinforced by repetition spaced in time [3]. These include most existing commercial and open source adaptive flashcard applications. These are typically designed for learning large amounts of material (thousands of facts) over an extended period of time (weeks, months, or even years).

© Springer International Publishing AG 2017
E. André et al. (Eds.): AIED 2017, LNAI 10331, pp. 644–649, 2017.
DOI: 10.1007/978-3-319-61425-0_81

Such applications include SuperMemo, Anki, Duolingo, Brainscape, and Memorang [http://www.supermemo.com, http://ankisrs.net, http://www.duolingo.com, http://www.brainscape.com, http://www.memorangapp.com].

Significantly refined models for human memory developed over the past thirty years have been used to construct optimized schedules for spaced practice [5–7]. Research studies on this topic typically have two or three practice sessions separated by a day with one recall test at some specified time later, usually about a week [2,7]. The schedules created are designed to optimize the time between practice sessions as a function of the time between the last practice session and the recall test. These models have been tried in the classroom but are not yet in widespread use [4].

Based on the research done in the past fifteen years or so, it has also been found that a pattern of spaced practice designed to fit within the time constraints of an academic class can significantly enhance learning, even if the schedule is not optimally derived from a cognitive model [1]. In this case, the challenge is to find an algorithm to produce a schedule for spaced practice that will result in effective retention of the material by the learners while still fitting within the time constraints of the course schedule. Artificial Intelligence in the form of cognitive models can be used to design and test such schedules even if the equations that describe the models are not directly used to construct the schedules themselves.

2   StudyWise

The Higher Education division of McGraw-Hill Education (MHE) wanted to use MHE's new adaptive flashcard application, StudyWise, to facilitate memorization of existing educational content being used in college courses. To do this, StudyWise presents questions, known as probes, that come from MHE's existing LearnSmart [http://www.mheducation.com/highered/platforms/learnsmart.html] database of probes.

In LearnSmart, each probe is associated with a Learning Objective (LO). The LOs are organized by Topic, which in turn are related to a LearnSmart title's subject. There are currently about 1500 LearnSmart titles on a wide range of subjects. In a course that uses LearnSmart, the instructor creates a LearnSmart assignment for an instructor specified set of LOs. Students see only probes associated with the LOs for that assignment, which they do on-line.

StudyWise presents all of the LOs associated with a particular Topic and uses its spaced practice algorithm to present probes associated with those LOs to the learner. The algorithm is designed to allow the learner to master each LO by repeated practice. These LOs are associated with the individual topics in five existing MHE LearnSmart titles. These titles are Introductory Spanish, Anatomy and Physiology, Medical Assisting, Human Resources, and Medical Terminology. The app is an entirely mobile one and has IOS and Android versions.

2.1   Study Schedules for Sets of Learning Objectives

The number of LOs for each subject bundle (deck) and the desired time to cover this material was specified by the Subject Matter Experts (SMEs) for each area. They intend that learners use the app for a half an hour a day, four to five days a week. The desired schedules for covering the material were the following:

Table 1. Study schedule by deck size

Number of LOs in the deck	Total hours of study	Number of 30 min sessions (total study interval)
15–50	1–2 h	2–3 ($<$ 1 week)
51–100	2–3 h	4–6 ($\sim$ 1week)
100+	3+ h	7+ ($\sim$ 2 weeks)

2.2   Time per Probe from LearnSmart Data

For two of the LearnSmart titles from which the LOs were taken, we have data indicating how long students took to respond to each probe. This comes from college classes which have used these two LearnSmart titles. For these, we had data for 3,000,000 answers to about 1,500 different probes. This data indicated that a median response time of 15 s per probe was reasonable, giving a possible 120 probes in a 30-minute session.

2.3   StudyWise Spacing Algorithm

The challenge, then, was to find a spacing algorithm that could meet the following criteria: (1) distribute the appearance times for each LO within the targeted overall practice period for a given deck size, (2) have enough appearances for each LO that the learner will know it by the end of the practice interval, assuming no previous knowledge of the LO, and (3) not repeat a given LO more times than needed to learn it (i.e. don't waste students' time).

The starting point for the spacing algorithm used by StudyWise came from ALEKS QuickTables [http://www.aleks.com/k12/quicktables], which is used to teach elementary school children arithmetic tables for the numbers from 0 to 12. Hence it is optimized for a deck of $13 \times 13 = 169$ items or less. For StudyWise, we extended the QuickTables algorithm to allow the use of information on learner confidence for each probe and for the difficulty of each probe.

We needed to vary the parameters of the StudyWise algorithm to see if it was flexible enough to produce workable schedules for the range of deck sizes and the time constraints desired by the SMEs. To find viable schedules, we needed to simulate a learner who started with no initial knowledge of each LO but whose memory would improve with each repeat appearance. This would allow us to test a wide range of algorithm parameters and find the most effective algorithm parameters which might meet the SME's criteria.

3 Simulating Memorization Using the ACT-R Model

To model a learner memorizing new material, we chose the ACT-R-based memory model of Pavlik and Anderson [3,4]. This model can calculate the probability that a simulated learner would remember a given LO at each appearance of it in the learning sequence. The initial activation level (strength in memory) for each item is set at zero, so the simulation assumes no prior knowledge. With each appearance, the activation level increases but then immediately starts to decay in accord with the model. The memory strength decreases both because of interference between LOs within a learning session and the decay of memory with time between sessions. Parameters used for the ACT-R model were those given in Pavlik and Anderson [6].

With these assumptions the user always gets the answer wrong on an LO's first appearance, since they have no initial memory of it. On subsequent appearances, the probability of remembering the LO is calculated using the Pavlik and Anderson model. A random number weighted by that probability is then calculated to decide if the user actually remembered the LO at that time.

We varied the spacing algorithm's parameters to tailor the spacing and frequency of the appearance of each LO to try and fit the SME's desired learning windows. Random numbers are used in the algorithm's method of selecting an LO for presentation to the learner and within the simulation to decide if the learner has actually remembered an LO at a given appearance. We therefore did 100 runs for each LO to find the range of variation in the pattern of appearances for a set of LOs from a given deck size. If the simulated user was calculated to have not remembered an item, the StudyWise algorithm repeats that item at some time later until it is answered correctly, on a repeat schedule that is part of the algorithm. For an item to be considered finished it must be answered correctly on its last appearance.

The question, then, was this: Could we find, for each deck size, a parameterization for the algorithm for which the simulated user, over 100 trials, successfully completes the entire set of LOs within at least close to the specified practice interval? It was not obvious at the outset that this would be possible.

Happily, though, we were able to find algorithm parameters that fit the SME's specifications for time of study vs. deck size for all three cases in Table 1. This indicates that the SMEs intuition for how much a learner can memorize within a certain time interval agrees very well with how ACT-R models human learning and memorization. Simulation results for several deck sizes are given below.

3.1 Simulations for Decks of Varying Size

For a deck with 30 LOs, the tests indicated that all the LOs could be learned in less than two 30 min sessions. Figure 1 shows the appearance time for an LO on the x-axis and the LO number on the y-axis. If an item was answered incorrectly, as determined by the simulation, the point is plotted as a red dot. If answered correctly, the point is plotted in blue. All thirty LOs are blue at the end of practice and were completed within two sessions, as specified in Table 1.

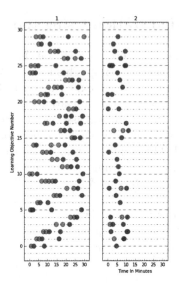

Fig. 1. LO number within a deck versus time of appearance for a deck of 30 items. A red dot indicates that the answer was incorrect, as calculated by the model, and a blue dots is for a correct answer. Each numbered block is a separate 30 min session. The start times of the sessions are separated by 24 h. (Color figure online)

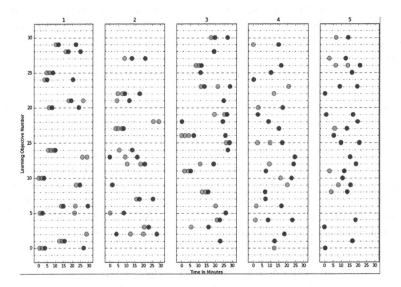

Fig. 2. Plots of the first 30 LOs from a 100 LO deck. Five 30 min sessions were needed to complete 100 LOs. Red dots indicate incorrect answers, as computed by the model, and blue dots are for correct answers. The start times for the sessions are separated by 24 h. (Color figure online)

For 100 LOs, five 30 min sessions were needed [Fig. 2]. All 100 of the LOs were answered correctly by the simulated user by the end of the last session. For 200 LOs eleven 30 min sessions were needed, just slightly in excess of the SME's target of two weeks.

4   Future Work: Comparison with User Data

The application is instrumented to anonymously record data about a user's session that is stored locally and then retrieved when the user has an internet connection. As this application is more widely deployed, we will be able to get direct feedback from the users and also to evaluate its effectiveness at helping users memorize the material and improve their performance in a class.

In sum, we have used artificial intelligence to develop an algorithm for MHE's adaptive flashcard applicaiton, StudyWise, which implements spaced practice to help learners memorize content connected to Learning Objectives in several existing MHE LearnSmart titles. Going forward, we can expand StudyWise for use with a wider range of subject areas and a more diverse set of content sources.

Acknowledgments. The target practice schedules were provided by Katie Ward and the MHE Higher Ed team of SMEs. The original QuickTables algorithm was developed by Jean-Claude Falmagne and Eric Cosyn.

References

1. Brown, P.C., Roediger, H.L., McDaniel, M.A.: Make It Stick: The Science of Successful Learning. Belknap Press: An Imprint of Harvard University Press, Cambridge (2014)
2. Cepeda, N.J., Vul, E., Rohrer, D., Wixted, J.T., Pashler, H.: Spacing effects in learning, a temporal ridgeline of optimal retention. Psychol. Sci. **19**(11), 1095–1102 (2008)
3. Ebbinghaus, H.: Memory, a contribution to experimental psychology, Dover, New York (1885)
4. Lindsey, R.V.: Probabilistic Models of Student Learning and Forgetting. Ph.D. dissertation, University of Colorado at Boulder (2014)
5. Mozer, M.C., Lindsey, R.V.: Predicting and improving memory retention: psychological theory matters in the big data era. In: Jones, M. (ed.) Big Data in Cognitive Science. Taylor & Francis (2016)
6. Pavlik, P.I., Anderson, J.R.: Practice and forgetting effects on vocabulary memory: an activation-based model of the spacing effect. Cogn. Sci. **29**, 559–586 (2005)
7. Pavlik, P.I., Anderson, J.R.: Using a model to compute the optimal schedule of practice. J. Exp. Psychol. Appl. **14**(2), 101–117 (2008)

Bridging the Gap Between High and Low Performing Pupils Through Performance Learning Online Analysis and Curricula

Tej Samani[1]([⊠]), Kaśka Porayska-Pomsta[2], and Rose Luckin[2]

[1] Performance Learning Education, 34 South Molton Street, London W1K 5RG, UK
tej@myperformancelearning.com
[2] UCL Knowledge Lab, UCL Institute of Education, University College London,
23-29 Emerald Street, London WC1N 3QS, UK

Abstract. Metacognition is a neglected area of investment in formal education and in teachers' professional development. This paper presents an approach and tools, created by a London-based company called Performance Learning Education (*PL*), for supporting front-line teachers and learners in developing metacognitive competencies. An iterative process adopted by PL in developing and validating its approach is presented, demonstrating its value to real educational practices, it's research potential in the area of metacognition, and its AI readiness, especially in relation to modelling learners' non-cognitive competencies.

1 Introduction

Metacognitive competencies are key to successful, life-long learning, especially in relation to the development of critical thinking, rationality, problem solving and identity [3,8,10]. Yet, metacognition is often a neglected area of investment in schools and in teachers' professional development [4,7]. This may be due to the lack of readily available definitions of metacognition that unify different disciplinary perspectives, as well as due to the complexity of, variety, and interdependency between key metacognitive domains, such as cognitive, emotional, attitudinal, and behavioural self-monitoring and regulation [10]. Despite best intentions, engaging with all of those domains in a systematic and routine way is likely beyond the capacities of many individual educators who tend to be forced into a pursuit of teaching to tests, and for whom an investment in their students' underlying metacognitive abilities may seem a luxury. Furthermore, frequently, many educators themselves lack sufficient appreciation of the relationship between learners' metacognitive abilities and learning outcomes, especially with respect to emotional and attitudinal dimensions. In turn, this may hinder some educators' sensitivity and ability to offer optimal support in this area [5,7,9].

This paper presents an approach adopted by a London-based company called Performance Learning Education (henceforth *PL*) in supporting learners'

E. André et al. (Eds.): AIED 2017, LNAI 10331, pp. 650–655, 2017.
DOI: 10.1007/978-3-319-61425-0_82

and front-line practitioners in developing metacognitive competencies and in demonstrating to them the key importance of such competencies to academic achievement.

2 About Performance Learning Education

PL was founded by a former struggling pupil turned professional tennis player who wanted to understand why some pupils perform better than others and how one could bridge the gap between successful and unsuccessful learners. The company dedicates special attention to disadvantaged students from low socio-economic backgrounds, students with English as an additional language and those with special educational needs. PL reached out to the grass roots of sports coaching to develop tools to help learners in mastering self-monitoring and self-regulation skills mainly in relation to non-cognitive aspects of their development. To date, PL worked with 35 schools across three countries (UK, United Arab Emirates and Germany), generating data from close to 7,000 students. It is estimated that PL will generate data from over 100,000 students in 2018, offering substantial potential for automating its approach, especially for computational modelling of the metacognitive competencies of interest.

3 Design of PL's Approach: Assessment and Coaching

PL's intervention starts at the UK primary level year 4 (ages 8–9) and continues through to secondary level year 13 (ages 17–18). The intervention is delivered either by Performance Learning Accredited Teachers employed by PL in schools or by delivering training to groups of teachers within the schools wanting to adopt it. PL's approach consists of two stages: (1) *assessment* (including both teachers' assessment of individual students and self-assessment by students), which aims to ascertain individual students' strengths and weaknesses along with the level of their needing an intensive intervention, and (2) *curriculum*, which coaches students in self-monitoring and self-reflection along key psycho-behavioural dimensions described in the following sections. The core focus of PL's assessment and curriculum is on coaching (i) students in how to attend to specific aspects of their lifestyles, attitudes, emotions and goal management and (ii) teachers in how to provide their students with relevant and informed support in a way that is systematic, targeted and sustained over time. To date, PL's approach and technology has gone through a three-stage iterative process of refinement, validation and technological implementation. We now briefly describe each stage taken and present key conclusions from each iteration.

3.1 Phase 0: Exploration and Scoping

Initially (Phase 0), PL partnered with Oxford Brookes University to understand the characteristics of academic high achievers. Sixty highest performing masters-level students participated in an interview aimed to gauge what may be respon-sible for their academic success. Here, academic success was defined in terms of the consistency of each student's results on tests (merit: 60–60% achievement on tests, or distinction: 70%+ level grades). The interview questions targeted specific dimensions such as the individual students': (i) foresight and clarity with respect to their own strengths and weaknesses, (ii) aspirations and evidence of being able to plan ahead, (iii) emotional balance, and (iv) ability to cope with anxiety and pressure. The interviews revealed that the higher performing pupils: (a) retain and recall the content of their modules and assignments with relative ease; (b) manage their time and have organisational skills such as ability to prioritise, plan, schedule and forecast; (c) schedule their social life around their academic ambitions and prioritise their academic work; (d) channel anxiety and cope with pressure in a positive manner, e.g. by increasing their effort to succeed.

Based on these results, PL developed its first intervention consisting of 28 subject-independent coaching lessons delivered on a one-to-one basis using paper-based training materials. The lessons were split into 3 categories: (i) "your lifestyle", focusing on sleep habits, energy patterns and emotions; (ii) "your classwork", focusing on self-understanding of strengths and weaknesses in basic literacy and numeracy, listening skills, memory and ability to complete homework; (iii) "your goals" relating to aspirations to overcome specific weaknesses such as poor memory, and desires such as building on and being noticed for particular strengths, e.g. effort in completing tasks. This first intervention was deployed in a pilot study over two and a half semesters at Oxford University, involving 14 students from an MSc programme in Marketing. The students' grades at the end of the first semester were compared with those at the end of the third semester to ascertain any improvements within the cohort. The descriptive analysis of the pilot data revealed an average increase of 7.74 points in the grades of the participating students, between the first and the third semester. These were further compared against the final grades of the students (N = 42) within the same masters programme who have not been exposed to PL's curriculum. The between-groups comparison shows that the PL students outperformed their non-PL peers, suggesting a possible advantage offered by PL's approach.

3.2   Phase 1: Refinement and Further Validation of the Approach

The results of Phase 0 led the company to trial its approach in primary and secondary schools in the UK. This next phase (Phase 1) consisted of a more systematic definition of the psychological and behavioural dimensions identified during Phase 0 and a refinement of PL's assessment procedures and methods. Through further research, 27 traits relating to grades, attitude to learning, behaviour, class attendance and participation were identified as common to pupils across the full range of academic abilities (lowest to highest performing). Performance Learning Online Analysis (PLOA) tools were developed to record and analyse students' self-assessments with respect to the 27 traits. These assessments informed PL's diagnosis of pupils in terms of five levels of risk assessment, ranging from level 1 (extremely high risk) to level 5 (no risk), where risk was defined as the degree to which a learner was believed to fail to reach a target or a predicted grade. The self-assessments also informed about possible barriers for pupil's learning, their response to different learning environments (e.g. home or school) and their general well being.

In this phase, the PL's assessment procedures were also refined, with the PLOA assessment being conducted at the start of a pupil's PL's curriculum, midway through and at the end, to establish any changes in pupils' self-assessments over-time. Twenty eight questions are used to elicit self-assessment from individual students at each point (beg, middle, end) in relation to the 27 psychobehavioural traits. The responses are scored within PLOA in terms of five risk levels and the results are placed in a report for the students and teachers, along with a set of improvement targets for each student to achieve over the course of PL's curriculum. For example, if a pupil selects responses that indicate a higher risk, as might be the case if they declare that they regularly go to sleep after 11pm and that during school time they feel overwhelmed and stressed, PLOA will diagnose them as a moderate risk category (level 2). Target PLOA scores for a subset of behavioural categories are proposed for that student, with the next lower risk level to that diagnosed being typically selected – here the target would be a level 1 risk category. For the intervention, the students are grouped according to their needs and risk levels derived based on PLOA assessments. Each group receives face-to-face sessions weekly and then fortnightly, with the view to gradually scaffold the learners into a habit of independent, critical and regular self-appraisal, goal-setting and action. The sessions are specific to the pupil reaching their target PLOA scores, with the teacher scoring the pupil within the system at the end of each lesson to record their progress.

113 pupils from two schools participated in PL's Phase 1 programme either fully (over 9 months) or partially (over 6 months): 37 pupils from one school and 76 pupils from a second school. Descriptive analysis was conducted on data from the two schools respectively to ascertain any changes in the grades obtained by the PL cohort following the PL curriculum as compared to those predicted for them prior to commencing the intervention. The final grades were also compared to the grades obtained by the students who did not participate in the programme (PL Nil; N = 299). Overall, PL students achieved higher grades than predicted across the core subjects (English, Math and Science), and in one of the schools also in Science as an additional subject. In both schools, the improvements in performance were particularly noticeable in English where the percentage of PL students achieved one or more grades higher than predicted and nearly double that of students in the PL Nil group, with the percentage of free-school-meal students who achieved one or more grade higher than predicted being four times above their PL Nil peers' grades for English, and around three times for math.

3.3   Phase 2: Towards Automating the PL's Approach

Presently PL's focus is on automating and further refinement of its approach to pupil assessment (Phase 2). PL sees a particular opportunity in mining of the data generated to (a) understand the behavioural patterns of relevance to self-reflection and self-regulation; (b) explore the relationship between routine self-monitoring and self-reporting and academic outcomes; (c) inform further development of its technology, especially focusing on real-time modelling of learners' behaviours and metacognitive competencies, and adaptive target setting for individual pupils.

During Phase 2, PL has made substantial enhancements to its: (i) method of assessment to allow the students to self-assess using non-discrete social, emotional and mental categories in a way that captures the nuance of their psychological states; (ii) personalisation of assessments with respect to the goals set for the individual students; (iii) delivery of lessons through online interactions with the system able to track and record data such as time on task, accuracy, completion attempts, quantity of usage; (iv) volume of data collected both from teachers' assessments and pupils' self-assessments, providing a unique opportunity for a systematic comparison between the two perspectives; (v) expanded set of psycho-behavioural traits and a scoring mechanism for qualifying students behaviours along a spectrum of their strengths and weaknesses.

In this phase, the assessment categories have been extended from the original 27 to 35 to provide a fine-grained basis for the pupils' reflections and to allow teachers to check their "gut feeling" assessments of their pupils' specific traits, strengths and areas for improvement. Of particular interest here are four mutually impacting psycho-behavioural domains: (i) sleep management, (ii) outcome oriented mind-set, (iii) memory, and (iv) emotion. For example, sleep deprivation is linked to impairments in cognitive performance and learning by affecting attentional control and working memory, and other prefrontal cortex-dependent cognitive functioning, including language, executive functions, divergent thinking and creativity [1,2]. The ability to pursue goals crucially involves key areas of executive control such as planning, prioritisation and effortful control, while emotions are known to substantially impact cognitive performance [6]. All of those areas form the basis for the next stage of PL's research and development.

4 Discussion and Future Work

This paper described the iterative process through which Performance Learning Education defined and developed its current product. The company is driven by a strong vision to provide affordable and effective support to individual learners in relation to metacognitive competencies as pre-requisites of academic achievement and life-long learning. It's approach is unique insofar as it caters for both learners' and teachers' perspectives, focusing chiefly on non-cognitive characteristics of the learners. PL's tools enable both learners and teachers to articulate their assessments of the pupils in an individualised way and in relation to factors that are fundamental to learning, including lifestyle changes, such as sleep and self management, to improve learner attitudes to learning and attainment. The goal is to instil a habit, both in teachers and learners, to regularly reflect on the key factors, as such reflection is known to lead to targeted planning and action and ultimately to better learning outcomes. The approach also provides a tangible basis for inspection, verification and discussion with real-time assessment of the pupil at the end of each lesson, and real time feedback for teachers on individualised pupils' mind-set, reactions and understanding of academic content.

When used in schools, PL's approach frequently comes as a revelation to teachers and learners who are often entrenched in a belief that academic success comes solely from content-specific drill and practice. Data generated by the company to date together with PL's continuous effort to improve its approach highlights the complexity of the area tackled by it. This is further supported by existing research demonstrating that metacognition is a multi-disciplinary and ill-defined construct which represents one of the more advanced human cognitive abilities. Although its component parts (self-monitoring and self-regulation) have been linked to people's healthy development, social functioning and learning, it is rarely an area of explicit and systematic investment in formal education.

The company increasingly seeks to ground its approach in interdisciplinary research and pedagogic best practices. Its partnership with UCL KL focuses on refinement of psycho-behavioural traits, preparation of data gathered for mining to inform the automation of the approach and to facilitate its delivery at scale, and conceptualisation of a strong foundation for the AI components. It is early days with respect to PL as an AIED company, but we can already see that the quality, granularity and quantity of data being collected, at the very least, provides a solid basis for mining behavioural patterns that may be indicative of metacognitive and self-regulated learning. The company aims to track how such patterns change over time and to cross-validate the learners' self assessment with teachers' assessments and with pupil's academic outcomes to develop informative Open Learner Models for everyday use in real world classrooms.

References

1. Alhola, P., Polo-Kontola, P.: Sleep deprivation: impact on cognitive performance. Neuropsychiatric Dis. Treat. **3**(5), 553–567 (2007)
2. Duckworth, A.L., Grant, H., Loew, B., Oettingen, G., Gollwitz, P.M.: Self-regulation strategies improve self-discipline in adolescents: benefits of mental contrasting and implementation intentions. Educ. Psychol. **31**(1), 17–26 (2011)
3. Flavell, J.: Metacognition and cognitive monitoring. a new area of cognitive-development inquiry. Am. Psychol. **34**(10), 906–911 (1979)
4. Hewitt, J., Pedretti, E., Bencze, L., Vaillaincourt, B.D., Yoon, S.: New applications for multimedia cases: promoting reflective practice in preservice teacher education. J. Technol. Teacher Educ. **11**, 483–500 (2003)
5. Horne, J.A.: Human sleep, sleep loss and behaviour. Implications for the prefrontal cortex and psychiatric disorder. Br. J. Psychiatry **162**, 413–509 (1993)
6. Immordino-Yang, H., Damasio, A.: We feel therefore we learn. Mind, Brain Educ. **1**(1), 2–10 (2007)
7. Lin, X., Schwartz, D.L., Hatano, G.: Toward teachers' adaptive metacognition. Educ. Psychol. **40**(4), 245–255 (2005)
8. Moshman, D.: Adolescent Rationality and Development: Cognition, Morality and Identity. Taylor Francis, Hoboken (2011)
9. Porayska-Pomsta, K.: AI as a methodology for supporting educational praxis and teacher metacognition. Int. J. Artif. Intell. Educ. **26**(2), 679–700 (2016)
10. Terricone, P.: The Taxonomy of Metacognition. Psychology Press, New York (2011)

Erratum to: Dusting Off the Messy Middle: Assessing Students' Inquiry Skills Through Doing and Writing

Haiying Li[(⊠)], Janice Gobert, and Rachel Dickler

Graduate School of Education, Rutgers University,
New Brunswick, NJ 08904, USA
{Haiying.li,Janice.Gobert,
Rachel.Dickler}@gse.rutgers.edu

Erratum to:
Chapter "Dusting Off the Messy Middle:
Assessing Students' Inquiry Skills Through Doing
and Writing" in: E. André et al. (Eds.), Artificial Intelligence
in Education, LNAI 10331,
https://doi.org/10.1007/978-3-319-61425-0_15

The original version of this chapter contained an error in the third author's name. The spelling of Rachel Dickler's name was incorrect in the header of the paper. The author name has been corrected.

The updated original online version of this chapter can be found at
https://doi.org/10.1007/978-3-319-61425-0_15

© Springer International Publishing AG 2017
E. André et al. (Eds.): AIED 2017, LNAI 10331, p. E1, 2017.
https://doi.org/10.1007/978-3-319-61425-0_83

Tutorials and Workshops

2nd International Workshop on Intelligent Mentoring Systems (IMS2017)

Vania Dimitrova[1](✉), Art Graesser[2], Andrew J. Hampton[2],
Lydia Lau[1], Antonija Mitrovic[3], David Williamson Shaffer[4],
and Amali Weerasinghe[5]

[1] University of Leeds, Leeds LS2 9JT, UK
[2] University of Memphis, Memphis, TN 38152, USA
[3] University of Canterbury, Christchurch 8041, New Zealand
[4] University of Wisconsin-Madison, Madison, WI 53706, USA
[5] University of Adelaide, Adelaide, SA 5005, Australia

Abstract. Mentoring constitutes an important aspect of professional development and lifelong learning, and Intelligent Mentoring Systems can expand the scope and accessibility by leveraging advances in digital learning environments and artificial intelligence. However, developing these systems requires deep understanding of complex issues such as learner modeling, technological capabilities, and contextual understanding, among many others. To foster this understanding, we invited the international community of AIED researchers to contribute to and shape the discussion of this stream of research in a collaborative workshop. We have proposed the themes of foundations, technology, and domains and contexts to focus our discussion.

Keywords: Intelligent mentors · Digital learning environments · Learner modeling · Pedagogical agents

1 Motivation

Mentoring is crucial for professional development and lifelong learning. It is seen by organisations as the most cost-effective and sustainable method for developing talent, for building transferable skills, for increasing motivation and confidence, for assisting with transitions across formal and informal education, for learning across workplace contexts, and for continuous career development. Studies show that investment in virtual mentors can help companies build the skills, productivity, engagement, and loyalty of their workforces.

The time is ripe for the emergence of a new breed of intelligent learning systems that provide mentor-like features. Crucial for intelligent mentors will be the ability to help learners connect their real-world experience with learning that is usually acquired through digital resources. Virtual mentors would be able to facilitate self-actualisation, helping learners realise their full potential. They would require a multi-faceted learner experience modelling mechanisms to get sufficient understanding of the learner, his/her current situation, and relevance to past experiences by the same learner (or by other people). Furthermore, they would embed new pedagogic strategies for promoting

© Springer International Publishing AG 2017
E. André et al. (Eds.): AIED 2017, LNAI 10331, pp. 659–661, 2017.
DOI: 10.1007/978-3-319-61425-0

reflection and self-awareness through interactive nudges, as well as new knowledge models formed by establishing connections and associations.

2 Themes

The main themes which will be discussed at IMS2017 have been derived from the discussion at the first workshop on Intelligent Mentoring Systems last year (IMS2016). These include the theoretical and practical foundations, issues surrounding the technologies employed, and a consideration of the domains and contexts in which these systems will be used.

2.1 Foundations

The discussion includes but is not limited to issues related to the foundations of Intelligent Mentoring Systems. These include main definitions in the field, such as mentoring, coaching, advising, etc. Also of importance are the main mentoring features, like contextual understanding, nudging, challenging, and motivating, that constitute an effective system. The scope of inquiry requires discussion, for example to differentiate between virtual mentors and virtual tutors. Methodologies for research design, ecological validity, and evaluation should factor prominently. Finally, we suggest a discussion of pedagogical models, including self-regulated learning, reflexive learning, social learning, vicarious learning, crossover learning, and transitions.

2.2 Technology

Any discussion of intelligent systems requires a thorough understanding of the technological affordances and constraints, as well as theoretical implications and models for optimizing utility. As such, we ask what computational models are required to realise mentor-like features; and what are the opportunities and challenges brought by these models? We offer examples of computational models that have contributed to and informed progress thus far, including social interaction spaces, situational simulations, open/interactive learner models, visualisations, interactive pedagogical agents, contextualised nudges, mobile assistants, cognitive computing, and wearable technology and sensors.

2.3 Domains and Contexts

Consideration of the environment and population in which and to whom these systems will apply constitutes a necessary aspect of planning and evaluation. To that end, we encourage discussion of what challenges are faced in traditional and emerging domains and contexts? Further, how can mentor-like features address these challenges? Domains and contexts that we note as worthy of consideration include, but are not limited to, peer mentoring, personalised assistants or buddies, social learning, flipped classrooms, workplace learning, career advisors, transferable skills, and tutor or mentor support.

3 IMS Workshop Series

Intelligent Mentoring Systems constitute an exciting and substantial line of research, requiring interdisciplinary support to help bring invaluable experience and learning to a wide array of students in disparate fields. We are excited to invite the international community of AIED researchers and educators to help discuss, evaluate, and plan the future of these systems. We have proposed three broad themes to focus our discussion – foundations, technology, and domains and contexts. The IMS workshop series aims to lay the foundations of this research stream, by forming an international research community and drawing a research roadmap. It will provide a forum to explore opportunities and challenges, identify relevant existing research, and point at new research avenues.

Workshop: Sharing and Reusing Data and Analytic Methods with LearnSphere

Kenneth Koedinger[1], John Stamper[1], Phil Pavlik[2], and Ran Liu[1(✉)]

[1] Carnegie Mellon University, Pittsburgh, PA, USA
{koedinger,ranliu}@cmu.edu, jstamper@cs.cmu.edu
[2] University of Memphis, Memphis, TN, USA
ppavlik@memphis.edu

Abstract. This workshop will explore LearnSphere, an NSF-funded, community-based repository that facilitates sharing of educational data and analytic methods. The workshop organizers will discuss the unique research benefits that LearnSphere affords. In particular, we will focus on Tigris, a workflow tool within LearnSphere that helps researchers share analytic methods and computational models. Authors of accepted workshop papers will integrate their analytic methods or models into LearnSphere's Tigris in advance of the workshop, and these methods will be made accessible to all workshop attendees. We will learn about these different analytic methods during the workshop and spend hands-on time applying them to a variety of educational datasets available in LearnSphere's DataShop. Finally, we will discuss the bottlenecks that remain, and brainstorm potential solutions, in openly sharing analytic methods through a central infrastructure like LearnSphere. Our ultimate goal is to create the building blocks to allow groups of researchers to integrate their data with other researchers in order to advance the learning sciences as harnessing and sharing big data has done for other fields.

Keywords: Intelligent tutoring system · Collaborative learning · Usage logs · Multimodal data · Multimodal analytics

1 Introduction

Due to a confluence of a boom of interest both in educational technology and in the use of data to improve student learning, student learning activities and progress are increasingly being tracked and stored. There is a large variety in the kinds, density, and volume of such data and to the analytic and adaptive learning methods that take advantage of it. Data can range from simple (e.g., clicks on menu items or structured symbolic expressions) to complex and harder-to-interpret (e.g., free-form essays, discussion board dialogues, or affect sensor information). Another dimension of variation is the time scale in which observations of student behavior occur: click actions are observed within seconds in fluency-oriented math games or in vocabulary practice, problem-solving steps are observed every 20 s or so in modeling tool interfaces (e.g., spreadsheets, graphers, computer algebra) in intelligent tutoring systems for math and science, answers to comprehension-monitoring questions are given and learning

© Springer International Publishing AG 2017
E. André et al. (Eds.): AIED 2017, LNAI 10331, pp. 662–664, 2017.
DOI: 10.1007/978-3-319-61425-0

resource choices are made every 15 min or so in massive open online courses (MOOCs), lesson completion is observed across days in learning management systems, chapter/unit test results are collected after weeks, end-of-course completion and exam scores are collected after many months, degree completion occurs across years, and long-term human goals like landing a job and achieving a good income occur across lifetimes. Different paradigms of data-driven education research differ both in the types of data they tend to use and in the time scale in which that data is collected. In fact, relative isolation within disciplinary silos is arguably fostered and fed by differences in the types and time scale of data used (cf., Koedinger et al. 2012; Newell 1990).

Thus, there is a broad need for an overarching data infrastructure to not only support sharing and use within the student data (e.g., clickstream, MOOC, discourse, affect) but to also support investigations that bridge across them. This will enable the research community to understand how and when long-term learning outcomes emerge as a causal consequence of real-time student interactions within the complex set of instructional options available (cf., Koedinger et al. 2013). Such an infrastructure will support novel, transformative, and multidisciplinary approaches to the use of data to create actionable knowledge to improve learning environments for STEM and other areas in the medium term and will revolutionize learning in the longer term.

LearnSphere transforms scientific discovery and innovation in education through a scalable data infrastructure designed to enable educators, learning scientists, and researchers to easily collaborate over shared data using the latest tools and technologies. LearnSphere.org provides a hub that integrates across existing data silos implemented at different universities, including educational technology "click stream" data in CMU's DataShop, massive online course data in Stanford's DataStage and analytics in MIT's MOOCdb, and educational language and discourse data in CMU's new DiscourseDB. LearnSphere integrates these DIBBs in two key ways: (1) with a web-based portal that points to these and other learning analytic resources and (2) with a web-based workflow authoring and sharing tool called Tigris. A major goal is to make it easier for researchers, course developers, and instructors to engage in learning analytics and educational data mining without programming skills.

2 Workshop Objectives

Broadly, this workshop offers those in the AIED community an exposure to LearnSphere as a community-based infrastructure for educational data and analysis tools. In opening lectures, the organizers will discuss the way LearnSphere connects data silos across universities and its unique capabilities for sharing data, models, analysis workflows, and visualizations while maintaining confidentiality.

More specifically, we propose to focus on attracting, integrating, and discussing researcher contributions to Tigris, the web-based workflow authoring and sharing tool. Workshop submissions will involve a brief description of an analysis pipeline relevant to modeling educational data as well as accompanying code. Prior to the workshop itself, the organizers will coordinate with authors of accepted submissions to integrate their code into Tigris. A significant portion of the workshop will be dedicated to hands-on exploration of custom workflows and workflow modules within Tigris.

Authors of accepted submissions will present their analysis pipelines, and everyone attending the workshop will be able to access those analysis pipelines within Tigris to a variety of freely available educational datasets available from LearnSphere. The goal is to generate – for each workflow component contribution in the workshop – a publishable workshop paper that describes the outcomes of openly sharing the analysis with the research community.

Finally, workshop attendees will discuss bottlenecks that remain toward our goal of a unified repository. We will also brainstorm possible solutions. Our goal is to create the building blocks to allow groups of researchers to integrate their data with other researchers we can advance the learning sciences as harnessing and sharing big data has done for other fields.

References

Corbett, A.T., Anderson, J.R.: Knowledge tracing: modeling the acquisition of procedural knowledge. User Model. User-Adap. Inter. **4**, 253–278 (1995)

Koedinger, K.R., Booth, J.L., Klahr, D.: Instructional complexity and the science to constrain it. Science **342**(6161), 935–937 (2013)

Koedinger, K.R., Kim, J., Jia, J.Z., McLaughlin, E.A., Bier, N.L.: Learning is not a spectator sport: doing is better than watching for learning from a MOOC. In: Proceedings of the 2nd ACM Conference on Learning@ Scale, pp. 111–120 (2015)

Koedinger, K.R., Corbett, A.T., Perfetti, C.: The Knowledge-Learning-Instruction framework: bridging the science-practice chasm to enhance robust student learning. Cogn. Sci. **36**(5), 757–798 (2012)

Newell, A.: Unified Theories of Cognition. Harvard University Press, Cambridge (1990)

Pavlik, P.I., Cen, H., Koedinger, K.R.: Performance factors analysis – a new alternative to knowledge tracing. In: Proceedings of the 14th International Conference on AIED, pp. 531–538 (2009)

How Do We Unleash AIEd at Scale to Benefit All Teachers and Learners?

Rose Luckin[1]([⊠]), Manolis Mavrikis[1], Mutlu Cukurova[1],
Kaska Porayska-Pomsta[1], Wayne Holmes[2], Bart Rienties[2],
Daniel Spikol[3], Vincent Aleven[4], and Laurie Forcier[5]

[1] University College London, London, UK
r.luckin@ucl.ac.uk
[2] The Open University, Milton Keynes, UK
[3] Malmö University, Malmö, Sweden
[4] Carnegie Mellon University, Pittsburgh, USA
[5] Pearson, London, UK

Abstract. The application of artificial intelligence to education (AIEd) has been the subject of academic research for more than 30 years, a period during which much technical progress has been made, but few in-roads into mainstream education have been achieved. With the upsurge of interest in AI in general and increasingly in AI for education in particular, what role could and should the AIED research community play?

Keywords: Mainstream · Scale

1 Introduction

In this workshop we will explore 'how we get to next' when it comes to AI for education (a phrase borrowed from https://howwegettonext.com). We will discuss the challenges and opportunities and propose some possible ways forward.

The workshop proposers have a wealth of experience and expertise in the field of AIEd and each will present their perspectives on the opportunities, challenges and recommendations for scaling up. In addition, we invite papers from others who are motivated to engage in this agenda. The workshop will be a full day session with short presentations in the morning, followed by an activity to collate all the ideas presented. The afternoon session will consist of a moderated discussion and a collaborative writing session to produce a set of recommendations that can be taken forward by workshop participants in their individual countries and institutions.

2 The Opportunities of AIED

As a community, AIEd researchers have already demonstrated that we can:

- Assess and tutor one to one accurately and effectively;
- Build dynamic models of learner cognitive development and non-cognitive development e.g. metacognition, motivation to enable personal scaffolding;

E. André et al. (Eds.): AIED 2017, LNAI 10331, pp. 665–667, 2017.
DOI: 10.1007/978-3-319-61425-0

- Open up the 'black box' of learning for students and teachers;
- Support collaborative learning through facilitating group formation, facilitating the process of collaboration, provide virtual collaborators, provide intelligent moderation
- Provide cultural modeling;
- Build intelligent VR and AR for authentic learning environments;
- Support the development of 21 century skills.

In addition to the current state of the art, we also know that AIEd has the potential to be scaled up and to radically change education. In particular, AIEd might reinvent assessment; support social mobility and address the achievement gap. There is also enormous potential to support learners holistically and in a context sensitive way; and we could address the chronic and acute teacher shortages across the globe, by helping teachers to be both more efficient with their time and more effective in their teaching.

In the publication 'Intelligence Unleashed' [1] we outlined some of these key areas where we believe that AI can drive a revolution in education. For example, AIEd can:

- Help learners gain 21st century skills: AIEd has the tools and techniques to conduct the fine-grained analysis that allows us to collect evidence from an increasing range of data capture devices – such as biological data, voice recognition, and eye tracking. This evidence collation and analysis can drive tracking of each learner's development of multiple skills, capabilities and subject knowledge as they interact and learn over time. Tracking of individual learners can then be collated and interpreted as required to provide knowledge about progress at the school, district, and country level. And the collection of mass data will enable us to track learner progress against different teaching approaches, to develop a dynamic catalogue of the best teaching practices suited to different learner needs, in particular 21st century skills, across a range of environments.
- Support a Renaissance in Assessment: AIEd will provide just-in-time assessments to shape learning. The boom in 'big data' and learning analytics enables us to recognise data patterns of potential educational interest. The addition of AI will provide just-in-time information about learner performance, behaviour, emotions and needs that can then be used to shape the learning experience itself. For example, to identify changes in learner confidence and motivation while learning a foreign language or a tricky equation.
- Embody new insights from the learning sciences: AIEd will continue to leverage new insights in disciplines such as psychology and educational neuroscience to better understand the learning process, and so build more accurate models that are better able to predict – and enhance – a learner's progress, motivation, and perseverance.

All this means that AIEd can help us to address some of the large and unsolved issues in education, such as achievement gaps, and teacher development, retention and shortages. For example, well designed AIEd means that students who need extra help can be offered one-to-one tutoring from adaptive AIEd tutors, both at school and at home, to improve their levels of success. For teachers, AIEd could help them find and share the best teaching resources and intelligent support for teachers could also help address the issue of teacher retention where we see many skilled professionals leaving the profession due to 'burn-out' [2].

3 The Opportunities of AIED

So how do we unleash AIEd to the benefit of all teachers and learners? Suggestions to date include:

1. Learning from the approach that jump-started driverless cars. In 2005, the US Defense Advanced Research Projects Agency (DARPA) offered $2 M for the team that developed a self-driving car that could navigate a 142-mile route. Five vehicles completed the course. The winning team was led by Stanford University's Sebastian Thrun, who went on to lead Google's autonomous vehicles team and, when there, began 'hoovering up' the best engineers from the DARPA challenges. Could well-funded, global challenge prizes that pose complex learning problems, and then reward those who provide the most exciting and effective AIEd solutions?
2. Create centres of independent interdisciplinary expertise in AIEd, funded long term and focused on delivering real-world capabilities. What could we achieve if the improvement of our schools, universities, and community colleges was supported with properly researched and comprehensively evaluated AIEd?
3. System change: AIEd will need to function effectively in blended learning spaces where digital technologies and traditional classroom activities complement each other. This means addressing the 'messiness' of real classrooms, universities, or workplace-learning environments, and involving teachers and learners in a co-design process. What more could we achieve if we focused on designing and describing how AIEd concretely fits within the lived experience of real learners and educators

References

1. Luckin, R., Holmes, W., Griffiths, M., Forcier, L.B.: Intelligence Unleashed. An argument for AI in Education. Pearson, London (2016)
2. House of Commons Library. Teachers: Social Indicators. SN/SG/2626 (2015)

Turn Theories into Products: Implementation of Artificial Intelligence in Education

Ryan Baker[1], Xiangen Hu[2], Jeff Wang[3], and Will Ma[3(✉)]

[1] University of Pennsylvania,
3700 Walnut Street, Philadelphia, PA 19104, USA
rybaker@upenn.edu
[2] University of Memphis,
400 Innovation Drive, Memphis, TN 38152, USA
xhu@memphis.edu
[3] Learnta Inc., 135 Yanping Rd, Jing'an District, Shanghai 2000042, China
{jeff,will}@learnta.com

Artificial intelligence is transforming one field after another. Education, a field with long and rich history, is faced with grand challenges and opportunities with the advances of artificial intelligence. Over the last decades, adaptive learning, intelligent tutoring, learning analytics, and educational data mining have attracted the enthusiasm of numerous talented researchers and significant progress have been achieved. A portion of these research outputs has been translated into learning systems proven to be effective by rigorous efficacy studies: ALEKS, ASSISTments, Cognitive Tutor, Learnta… just to name a few.

While some progress is being made to bring artificial intelligence to the education field as described above, these efforts pale in comparison to advances in the non-education field. Why is education lagging behind? Despite advances in research, successful implementation of artificial intelligence in education requires more.

The workshop aims to shed light on crucial ingredients of the implementation of artificial intelligence in education. How can the community – academic, industry, governmental – turn research results and innovations into effective products that directly benefit millions of students?

This will be a full-day workshop, consisting of presentations, panel discussion and moderated open forum. The participants will review the evolution of artificial intelligence in education. The participants will share their experience in developing learning system, assessing the effectiveness of the system, and improving the system. The participants will discuss the models of transfer of research and innovation to products. The participants will also debate on the key factors of making an effective learning product.

© Springer International Publishing AG 2017
E. André et al. (Eds.): AIED 2017, LNAI 10331, p. 668, 2017.
DOI: 10.1007/978-3-319-61425-0

AutoTutor Tutorial: Authoring Conversational Intelligent Systems

Zhiqiang Cai[1(✉)], Xiangen Hu[1,2], Keith Shubeck[1], Kai-Chih Bai[3],
Art Graesser[1], Bor-Chen Kuo[3], and Chen-Huei Liao[3]

[1] University of Memphis, Memphis, USA
zcai@memphis.edu
[2] Central China Normal University, Wuhan, China
[3] National Taichung University of Education, Taichung City, Taiwan

There have been decades of efforts on research and development of intelligent tutoring systems (ITS). Many tutoring systems provide rich media content and allow students interact with content in many different ways, such as multiple choice answer selection, drag and drop objects, rearranging objects, assembling objects, and so on. Intelligent systems assess students' performance from the data collected from the interactions and then adaptively select knowledge objects and pedagogical strategies during the tutoring process to maximize learning effect and minimize learning cost. Delivering content with conversation is always attractive to content authors and students. For example, when a piece of knowledge is delivered through a text, wouldn't it be more interesting to have a conversation between a "tutor", human or machine, and a student to talk about what is in the text? Research has shown that delivering content through conversation is much more effective than a text. Unfortunately, creating conversational content is difficult. First, in order to have a natural language conversation with a student, the machine has to be able to "understand" the student's natural language input. This involves a research field called "natural language understanding." There isn't a perfect natural language algorithm that can really understand user's free language. Second, preparing tutoring speeches for conversations is hard. The essential difficulty is that an author needs to consider enough many (if not infinitely many) responses to all possible student inputs. The third, it is hard to create and test conversation rules. Conversation rules decide the condition under which a prepared speech is spoken. Since the tutoring conversations often go with other displayed content, such as text, image, video, etc., conversation rules need to take into account all things happen in an learning environment, in addition to the natural language inputs from students. The rule system varies because different environment may have different things to happen. Creating and testing the rules is time consuming. Other difficulties involve talking head techniques (speech synthesizing, lip synchronization, emotion, gesture), speech recognition, emotion detection, and so on.

The AutoTutor team at the Institute for Intelligent systems (IIS) at the University of Memphis has been working in this direction since 1990s and has been providing solutions to overcome the difficulties in conversational ITSs. About a dozen of conversational ITSs have been successfully developed in IIS, including computer literacy tutor, conceptual physics tutor, critical thinking tutor (OperationARIES!), adult literacy

© Springer International Publishing AG 2017
E. André et al. (Eds.): AIED 2017, LNAI 10331, pp. 669–670, 2017.
DOI: 10.1007/978-3-319-61425-0

tutor (CSAL), electronics tutor (ElectornixTutor), etc. A team at National Taichung University of Education has developed a Chinese language tutor.

AutoTutor helps students learn by holding deep reasoning conversations. An AutoTutor conversation often starts with a main question about a certain topic. The goal of the conversation is to help students' construct an acceptable answer to the main question. Instead of telling the students the answers, AutoTutor asks a sequence of questions (hints, prompts) that target specific concepts involved in the ideal answer to the main question. AutoTutor systems respond to students' natural language input, as well as other interactions, such as making a choice, arranging some objects in the learning environment, etc. This tutorial focuses on the authoring process of AutoTutor lessons, including discourse strategies in AutoTutor dialogues and trialogues, conversation elements, media elements, conversation rules and template based authoring.

Participants need to bring Windows laptops. A Windows authoring tool will be released on site. An example AutoTutor lesson will be provided to participants. Participants will create one's own AutoTutor lesson by modifying the example lesson.

1   Tutorial Format

Session 1: Introduction to AutoTutor.
9:00–9:15 Introduction – Introdcution of presenters and participants
9:15–10:30 Overview and Demo of AutoTutor Systems
Coffee Break.
Session 2: AutoTutor Script Authoring Tool.
11:00–12:30 A step by step guidance to creating an AutoTutor lesson
Lunch Break.
Session 3: Team practicing.
14:00–15:30 Each teams (2–3 people) produce an AutoTutor lesson by modifying provided example.
Session 4: Team report and discussions.
16:00–17:00 Team report
17:00–17:30 Conclusion

Matching Techniques: Hands-on Approach to Measuring and Modeling Educational Data (Tutorial)

Vivekanandan Kumar$^{(\boxtimes)}$, David Boulanger, and Shawn N. Fraser

Athabasca University, Athabasca, Canada
vivek@athabascau.ca

Abstract. This tutorial will introduce three matching techniques (Coarsened Exact Matching, Mahalanobis Distance Matching, and Propensity Score Matching) and three data imbalance metrics (L1 vector norm, Average Mahalanobis Imbalance, and Difference in Means) to assess the level of data imbalance within matched sample datasets in an interactive setting. It explains key traits of observational studies that are relevant for AIED, considering comparable traits of fully randomized experiments. Using randomized and non-randomized data, participants will conduct an observational study by approximating blocked randomized experiments. The hands-on session specifically targets skills that will enable participants to run observational studies using R packages such as MatchingFrontier, CEM, and MatchIt through an interactive Shiny web application and programmatically by writing an R script. A discussion on a matching-based observational study design for a learning analytics application that uses large, fine-grained, and self-similar datasets concludes the tutorial.

Keywords: Matching · Propensity score matching · Randomized experiment · Interactive analysis · Observational study · Learning analytics · Data imbalance · Causality

1 Objectives

This tutorial introduces observational study; explains matching techniques like Propensity Score Matching [1], Coarsened Exact Matching [2], and Mahalanobis Distance Matching [3] along with their corresponding imbalance metrics, that is, L1 vector norm, Average Mahalanobis Imbalance, and Difference in Means; offers a hands-on observational study with randomized and non-randomized data [4–6] using R libraries (MatchingFrontier [7], CEM, and MatchIt) and the web application framework for R called Shiny; and discusses ways to measure impact of learning analytics applications.

© Springer International Publishing AG 2017
E. André et al. (Eds.): AIED 2017, LNAI 10331, pp. 671–674, 2017.
DOI: 10.1007/978-3-319-61425-0

2 Audience

The tutorial targets AIED researchers, data scientists, and teachers. Some background in statistics (e.g. descriptive statistics, probability, analysis of variance) and research methods (e.g. randomized designs, observational studies) is an asset.

3 Outcomes

- Describing experimental methods and studies in education/learning analytics
- Proposing a valid observational study design using matching
- Comparing different matching techniques: Coarsened Exact Matching, Mahalanobis Distance Matching, and Propensity Score Matching
- Demonstrating the suboptimality of Propensity Score Matching, the most popular matching technique in observational studies [8]
- Measuring the accuracy (in terms of data imbalance) of the proposed design against a randomized experiment
- Performing interactive observational studies using Shiny/R
- Discussing why it is important to have valid designs of observational studies; whether machine learning deals mainly with observational data; what is the real impact of handling properly observational data on learning analytics

4 Observational Studies

Given the discriminatory nature of completely randomized experiments and the ethical issues that they raise in educational settings, observational studies are being investigated in educational research to supplement and possibly replace randomized experiments. The research community at large refers to the randomized experiment as the gold standard [9–13] and many view observational studies as "having less validity because they reportedly overestimate treatment effects" [10]. The results of observational studies are disputed since they may contain undetected confounding bias. On the other hand, one should not oversimplify the benefits of randomized experiments [11]. Silverman [12] indicates that observational studies can complement findings in randomized experiments by using a larger and more diverse population over longer follow-up periods.

This tutorial pursues a design of observational study using matching techniques as prescribed by King [8], where new sensors are increasingly available to better observe/record teaching and learning experiences at real time. It will demonstrate the embedding of observational sensors as part of learning analytics processes and will advance blocked randomized experiments as measurements of impact of analytics. It strives to empower teachers themselves to step into the roles of analytics researchers using Shiny's interactive analyses.

5   Tutorial Interaction

The tutorial is designed to be 1/3 presentation, 1/3 hands-on, and 1/3 discussion. Participants, in small groups, will discuss key traits of matching methods, imbalance metrics, and key differences between observational studies and randomized experiments. They will have an opportunity to work, individually or in small groups, with hands-on data, tools, and models to perform an observational study [14] using Coarsened Exact Matching, Mahalanobis Distance Matching, or Propensity Score Matching. For those who desire, they will also interact in small groups to respond to different types of research questions using an interactive Shiny web application. Different levels of participation will be offered: (1) listening to the presentation (every step will be shown on slides), (2) a web application will be available for non-programmer participants to run their analyses without any coding activity, and (3) an R script will be available for those who are interested in programming directly some portions of the analyses. For more information, please visit the tutorial's website at http://learninganalytics.ca/research/psa-tutorial/.

References

1. Olmos, A., Govindasamy, P.: Propensity scores: a practical introduction using R. J. MultiDiscip. Eval. **11**(25), 68–88 (2015)
2. Iacus, S.M., King, G., Porro, G., Katz, J.N.: Causal inference without balance checking: coarsened exact matching. Polit. Anal. 1–24 (2012)
3. King, G., Nielsen, R., Coberley, C., Pope, J.E.: Comparative effectiveness of matching methods for causal inference. Unpubl. Manuscr. **15**, 1–26 (2011). http://doi.org/10.1.1.230.3451
4. LaLonde, R.J.: Evaluating the econometric evaluations of training programs with experimental data. Am. Econ. Rev. 604–620 (1986)
5. Dehejia, R.H., Wahba, S.: Causal effects in nonexperimental studies: reevaluating the evaluation of training programs. J. Am. Stat. Assoc. **94**(448), 1053–1062 (1999)
6. Dehejia, R.H., Wahba, S.: Propensity score-matching methods for nonexperimental causal studies. Rev. Econ. Stat. **84**(1), 151–161 (2002)
7. King, G., Lucas, C., Nielsen, R.: The balance-sample size frontier in matching methods for causal inference. Am. J. Polit. Sci. (2014)
8. King, G., Nielsen, R.: Why propensity score should not be used for matching (617) (2016)
9. Hannan, E.L.: Randomized clinical trials and observational studies: guidelines for assessing respective strengths and limitations. JACC: Cardiovasc. Interv. **1**(3), 211–217 (2008). http://dx.doi.org/10.1016/j.jcin.2008.01.008
10. Concato, J., Shah, N., Horwitz, R.I.: Randomized, controlled trials, observational studies, and the hierarchy of research designs. New Engl. J. Med. **342**(25), 1887–1892 (2000)
11. Medical Publishing Internet, Kent W. The advantages and disadvantages of observational and randomised controlled trials in evaluating new interventions in medicine. Educational article [Internet]. Version 1. Clinical Sciences. Accessed 9 Jun 2011. https://clinicalsciences.wordpress.com/article/the-advantages-and-disadvantages-of-1blm6ty1i8a7z-8/

12. Silverman, S.L.: From Randomized controlled trials to observational studies. Am. J. Med. **122**(2), 114–120 (2009). http://dx.doi.org/10.1016/j.amjmed.2008.09.030
13. At Work, Issue 83, Winter 2016: Institute for Work & Health, Toronto
14. Sullivan, G.M.: Getting off the "gold standard": randomized controlled trials and education research. J. Graduate Med. Educ. **3**(3), 285–289 (2011). http://doi.org/10.4300/JGME-D-11-00147.1

Author Index

Adams, Deanne 540
Adderton, Elliot 553
Agrawal, Bhavna 623
Ahn, Jae-wook 630
Albacete, Patricia 137
Aleven, Vincent 3, 582, 665
Allen, Laura K. 485
Allessio, Danielle 28
Almiyad, Mohammed A. 450
Al-Shanfari, Lamiya 15, 445
Alvin, Chris 455
Alyuz, Nese 250
Andres, Juan Miguel 238
Arroyo, Ivon 28
Arslan Esme, Asli 250
Aslan, Sinem 250
Auerbach, Daniel 544
Ayedoun, Emmanuel 459
Azevedo, Roger 149, 335

Baber, Chris 15, 445
Bai, Kai-Chih 669
Baker, Ryan S. 40, 274
Baker, Ryan 238, 494, 644, 668
Banawan, Michelle 548
Barnes, Tiffany 311
Basu, Satabdi 490
Beck, Joseph E. 371
Bienkowski, Marie 490
Billinghurst, Mark 450
Biswas, Gautam 430
Bonn, Doug 287
Bosch, Nigel 359
Botelho, Anthony F. 40
Boulanger, David 671
Bourrier, Yannick 463
Boyer, Kristy Elizabeth 212, 299
Bratko, Ivan 162
Brawner, Keith 238
Bremgartner, Vitor 467
Brisson, Janie 381
Broisin, Julien 570
Bulgarov, Florin 472

Burleson, Winslow 28
Butler, Deborah 287

Cai, Zhiqiang 506, 669
Chang, Maria 630
Chase, Catherine 3
Chee, Yi-Min 623
Chen, Huili 359
Chen, Xingliang 476
Chi, Min 536
Chung, Zachary T. 480
Clark, James 636
Conati, Cristina 149
Connolly, Helena 3
Cooper, James 644
Corbett, Albert 494
Core, Mark G. 544
Cortez, Joanna Feliz 574
Craig, Scotty D. 590
Crawford, Candida 636
Crossley, Scott A. 523
Cui, Xia 553
Cukurova, Mutlu 665

D'Mello, Sidney 359
Dai, Jianmin 485, 557
Dascalu, Mihai 52, 485
Dawson, Luke 553
de Magalhães Netto, José 467
De Roock, Roberto 548
DeFalco, Jeanine 238
Demmans Epp, Carrie 15, 445
Di Eugenio, Barbara 519
Di Mitri, Daniele 609
Diana, Nicholas 490, 605
Dickler, Rachel 175
Dillenbourg, Pierre 570
Dimitrova, Vania 224, 659
Dong, Yi 430
Donnelly, Patrick 359
Dorn, Brian 565
Dumdumaya, Cristina 548, 598

Eagle, Michael 490, 494, 605

Fabic, Geela Venise Firmalo   498, 613
Fang, Ying   617
Farzan, Rosta   540
Fialko, Sarah   578
Forcier, Laurie   665
Forlizzi, Jodi   540
Forsyth, Carol M.   502, 506
Fossati, Davide   519
Frankosky, Megan H.   212, 299
Fraser, Shawn N.   671
Furtado, Pedro   510

Gal, Ya'akov (Kobi)   64
Garbay, Catherine   463
Genc, Utku   250
Georgila, Kallirroi   544
Georgoulas, Vasiliki   238
Glenberg, Arthur M.   578
Gobert, Janice   175
Grace, Lindsay   502
Graesser, Art   188, 506, 659, 669
Grawemeyer, Beate   514
Green, Nick   519
Grover, Shuchi   490
Guerrero, Tricia A.   125, 201, 485, 557
Gulwani, Sumit   455

Hampton, Andrew J.   659
Hansen, Alice   514
Harsley, Rachel   519
Hayashi, Yuki   459
Hayashi, Yusuke   90, 418, 510
Hebert, Del   502
Heeren, Bastiaan   77
Heffernan, Neil T.   40
Hindi, Shaked   64
Hirashima, Tsukasa   90, 418, 510
Holmes, Wayne   665
Horiguchi, Tomoya   90
Hu, Xiangen   590, 617, 668, 669

Inglese, Pat   502
Ishii, Takatoshi   102
Ishola, Oluwabukola Mayowa   113
Ives, Joss   287

Jackson, David   553
Jackson, Tanner   502
Jacovina, Matthew E.   201, 485

Jagmohan, Ashish   623
Jambon, Francis   463
Jeuring, Johan   77
Jimmieson, Phil   553
Johnson, Amy M.   125, 523, 557
Jones, John Christopher   553
Jordan, Pamela   137

Karumbaiah, Shamya   544
Katz, Sandra   137
Kennedy, Keith   553
Koedinger, Kenneth   662
Koedinger, Kenneth R.   605
Kokku, Ravi   623
Kopp, Kristopher J.   523
Kumar, Amruth N.   528
Kumar, Vivekanandan   671
Kuo, Bor-Chen   669
Kurvers, Hub   52

Lallé, Sébastien   149
Lamnina, Marianna   3
Lau, Lydia   224, 659
Lazar, Timotej   162
Lehman, Blair   502
Lentini, Jennifer   506
Lester, James C.   212, 238, 299, 323, 335
Li, Haiying   175, 188
Liao, Chen-Huei   669
Liew, Chun W.   532
Lin, Chen   536
Lind, Mats   347
Liu, Ran   662
Liu, Rong   623
Livni, Adva   64
Luckin, Rose   636, 650, 665
Luengo, Vanda   463

Ma, Tengfei   630
Ma, Will   668
Maass, Jaclyn K.   262
MacLaren, Benjamin   494
Majumdar, Rupak   455
Marks, Jenna   3
Martinez, Joshua   574
Mason, Ben   553
Massey-Allard, Jonathan   287
Mathews, Moffat   224, 476
Matsuda, Noboru   598

Mavrikis, Manolis   514, 636, 665
Mayer, Richard   540
Mazziotti, Claudia   514
McCalla, Gordon   113
McCarthy, Kathryn S.   201, 557
McLaren, Bruce M.   494, 540, 582
McNamara, Danielle S.   125, 201, 485, 523, 557
Menezes, Crediné   467
Min, Wookhee   212, 299
Mitchell, Aaron   494
Mitrovic, Antonija   224, 476, 498, 613, 659
Mott, Bradford W.   212, 238, 299
Možina, Martin   162
Mudrick, Nicholas V.   149
Mukhi, Nirmal   630
Mukhopadhyay, Supratik   455
Muldner, Kasia   28

Neshatian, Kourosh   498, 613
Nguyen, Huy   532
Nielsen, Rodney   472
Nitta, Satya   623
Nkambou, Roger   381
Norton, Darren J.   532
Nye, Benjamin   544

Oakden-Rayner, Luke   450
Ocumpaugh, Jaclyn   238
Ogan, Amy   548, 598
Okur, Eda   250
Oliehoek, Frans A.   553
Olney, Andrew M.   262

Pailai, Jaruwat   418
Palatnic, Alik   64
Paquette, Luc   238, 274
Paredes, Yancy Vance   574
Pavlik, Phil   662
Pavlik Jr., Philip I.   262
Perez, Sarah   287
Perret, Cecile A.   557
Peters, Stephanie   506
Pezzullo, Lydia G.   299
Pham, Phuong   561, 586
Plumbley, Adam   553
Popescu, Octav   3
Porayska-Pomsta, Kaśka   650, 665
Prabhu, Srijith   630

Price, Thomas W.   311
Prusak, Naomi   64

Restrepo, M. Adelaida   578
Riedesel, Mark A.   644
Rienties, Bart   665
Robert, Serge   381
Rodrigo, Ma. Mercedes T.   371, 480, 548, 574, 598
Roll, Ido   287
Rowe, Jonathan   238, 323, 335
Rummel, Nikol   514
Ruseti, Stefan   52

Samaco, Japheth Duane   574
Samani, Tej   650
Savani, Rahul   553
Sawyer, Robert   323, 335
Schwarz, Baruch   64
Segal, Avi   64
Seta, Kazuhisa   459
Shaffer, David Williamson   659
Sharma, Kshitij   570
Shinohara, Tomoya   90
Shubeck, Keith   590, 617, 669
Silvervarg, Annika   347
Sin, Sherry   623
Sjödén, Björn   347
Smith, Andy   335
Snow, Erica L.   201
Soto, Christian M.   485
Sottilare, Robert   238
Spikol, Daniel   665
Stamper, John   490, 494, 605, 662
Stepanek, Nicholas R.   565
Stewart, Angela   359
Stratou, Giota   544
Sundararajan, Sharad   630
Swidan, Osama   64

Talandron, May Marie P.   371
Tan, Michael   623
Tanriover, Cagri   250
Tato, Ange   381
Taub, Michelle   149
Thien, Nguyen Duc   393
Tighe, Elizabeth L.   125
Titchener, Tom   644

Tokel, S. Tugba   544
Trausan-Matu, Stefan   52

Ueno, Maomi   102, 393
Uto, Masaki   393
Utsuro, Takehito   480

van Leeuwen, Anouschka   514
Venant, Rémi   570
Vidal, Philippe   570
Villamor, Maureen   574

Wagner, Angela   494
Walker, Erin   406, 578
Wang, Jeff   668
Wang, Jingtao   561, 586
Wang, Shang   406
Watson, Patrick   630
Weerasinghe, Amali   224, 450, 659
Westera, Wim   52
Wiebe, Eric N.   212, 299
Wiggins, Joseph B.   299

Wixon, Naomi   28
Wong, Audrey   578
Woolf, Beverly   28
Wunnasri, Warunya   418
Wylie, Ruth   406

Xhakaj, Françeska   582
Xiao, Xiang   586
Xie, Jun   590

Yamada, Atsushi   90
Yang, Xi   594
Yarzebinski, Evelyn   548, 598
Yee, Nikki   287
Yu, Shengquan   594

Zapata-Rivera, Diego   506
Zhang, Lishan   594
Zhang, Ningyu   430
Zhi, Rui   311
Zimmerman, Neil   644

Printed in the United States
By Bookmasters